The Blackwell Guide to Research Me
Bilingualism and Multilingualism

The Blackwell Guide to Research Methods in Bilingualism and Multilingualism

Edited by Li Wei and Melissa G. Moyer

Blackwell Publishing

© 2008 by Blackwell Publishing Ltd

BLACKWELL PUBLISHING
350 Main Street, Malden, MA 02148-5020, USA
9600 Garsington Road, Oxford OX4 2DQ, UK
550 Swanston Street, Carlton, Victoria 3053, Australia

The right of Li Wei and Melissa G. Moyer to be identified as the authors of the editorial material in this work has been asserted in accordance with the UK Copyright, Designs, and Patents Act 1988.

First published 2008 by Blackwell Publishing Ltd

2   2008

Library of Congress Cataloging-in-Publication Data

The Blackwell guide to research methods in bilingualism and multilingualism / edited by Li Wei and Melissa Moyer.
   p. cm.
  Includes bibliographical references and index.
  ISBN 978-1-4051-2607-6 (hardcover : alk. paper) – ISBN 978-1-4051-7900-3 (pbk. : alk. paper)
1. Bilingualism–Research–Methodology. 2. Multilingualism–Research–Methodology. I. Wei, Li, 1961– II. Moyer, Melissa G., 1956–
  P115.B575 2008
  404′.2072–dc22

2007038438

A catalogue record for this title is available from the British Library.

Set in 10/13pt Sabon
by Graphicraft Limited, Hong Kong
Printed and bound in Singapore
by C.O.S Printers Pte Ltd

The publisher's policy is to use permanent paper from mills that operate a sustainable forestry policy, and which has been manufactured from pulp processed using acid-free and elementary chlorine-free practices. Furthermore, the publisher ensures that the text paper and cover board used have met acceptable environmental accreditation standards.

For further information on
Blackwell Publishing, visit our website at
www.blackwellpublishing.com

Contents

List of Figures

List of Tables

Notes on Contributors

Jubin Abutalebi, MD (abutalebi.jubin@hsr.it), is a cognitive neurologist and Assistant Professor of Neuropsychology at the Faculty of Psychology, University Vita Salute San Raffaele, Milan, Italy. His main research activities focus on the cerebral architecture underlying bilingualism which he studies by employing functional neuroimaging techniques. He is author of many journal articles and co-editor of two forthcoming books: *Neuropsychological Research: A Review* (Psychology Press) and *Cognitive Neurology* (Oxford University Press).

Ad Backus, PhD (A.M.Backus@uvt.nl), is Associate Professor in the Department of Language and Culture at Tilburg University, The Netherlands, and a member of the Babylon research group, which specializes in the study of multiculturalism and multilingualism. His empirical work has mostly been on Turkish-Dutch code-switching and contact-induced language change in the immigrant variety of Turkish. Most analyses are done within a cognitive-linguistic theoretical framework. He publishes widely in journals such as *Linguistics*, the *International Journal of Bilingualism*, and *Bilingualism: Language and Cognition*.

Adrian Blackledge, PhD (A.J.Blackledge@bham.ac.uk), is Professor of Bilingualism at the School of Education, University of Birmingham, UK. His main areas of research are multilingualism and social justice in linguistic minority settings, and discourse and power in multilingual contexts. His publications include *Teaching Bilingual Children* (Trentham Books, 1994), *Literacy, Power, and Social Justice* (Trentham Books, 2000), and *Discourse and Power in a Multilingual World* (John Benjamins, 2005). He has also co-edited two volumes: *Multilingualism, Second Language Learning, and Gender* (with Aneta Pavlenko, Ingrid Piller, and Marya Teutsch-Dwyer, Mouton De Gruyter, 2001) and *Negotiation of Identities in Multilingual Contexts* (with Aneta Pavlenko, Multilingual Matters, 2004).

Holly Cashman, PhD (holly.cashman@asu.edu), is Assistant Professor of Spanish Linguistics in the School of International Letters and Cultures at Arizona State University, USA. Her main research interests include code-switching, bilingual conversation, identity in interaction, and variation in Spanish in southwestern USA. She is currently co-editing (with Ashley Williams) a special issue of *Multilingua* on the emergence of bilingual identity in interaction, and she has authored articles in several journals including the *Journal of Pragmatics*, the *Journal of Multilingual and Multicultural Development*, and the *Journal of Politeness Research*.

Ignasi Clemente, PhD (iclemente@mednet.ucla.edu), is a postdoctoral research fellow in the Department of Pediatrics, D. Geffen School of Medicine at the University of California Los Angeles, USA, and an international trainee in the Canadian Institutes of Health Research Strategic Training Program on Pain in Child Health. His main research interests include the sociocultural and communicative aspects of pain and suffering, health communication and shared decision-making in pediatric care, and embodied communication in multilingual settings. In his PhD dissertation, he examined how Spanish- and Catalan-speaking patients, parents, and doctors negotiated the limits of uncertainty and non-disclosure throughout unpredictable cancer trajectories at a hospital in Barcelona, Catalonia (Spain).

Eva Codó, PhD (eva.codo@uab.es), is Lecturer in English and Linguistics at both the Faculty of Education and the Faculty of Arts of the Universitat Autònoma de Barcelona, Spain. Her main research interests include multilingualism in institutional settings, language, immigration and processes of social exclusion, and the sociolinguistics of English as a contact language in Spain. She is author of the book *Immigration and Bureaucratic Control: Language Practices in the Public Administration* (Mouton de Gruyter, in press).

Annabelle David, PhD (annabelle.david@ncl.ac.uk), is a Research Associate at Newcastle University, UK. Her main research interests include second and bilingual language acquisition, especially of vocabulary. She also has an interest in the use of digital technologies to facilitate L2 research. She has recently finished her doctoral thesis and published in the *International Journal of Bilingualism and Bilingual Education*.

Pasquale Anthony Della Rosa (dellarosa.pasquale@hsr.it) is a PhD student at the Department of Psycholinguistics of the University of Geneva, Switzerland and holds a junior research fellowship at the University Vita Salute San Raffaele, Milan, Italy. He is actively working in the field of functional neuroimaging and masters all technical knowledge for acquiring, analyzing, and interpreting functional brain data.

Paola Dussias, PhD (pdussias@psu.edu), is Associate Professor of Spanish, Linguistics and Psychology at Penn State University, USA. Her main research interests include sentence comprehension processes in bilingual speakers and second language learners, and the use of experimental techniques to study psycholinguistic processes involving code-switched utterances. Her work has appeared in *Bilingualism: Language and Cognition*, *Studies in Second Language Acquisition*, the *International Journal of Bilingualism*, and *Handbook of Bilingualism*.

Penelope Gardner-Chloros, PhD (p.gardner-chloros@bbk.ac.uk), is Lecturer in the School of Languages, Linguistics and Culture at Birkbeck, University of London,

UK. Her main research interests include code-switching, language contact, and terms of address in European languages. She is the author of *Code-switching* (Cambridge University Press, 2008), *Language Selection and Switching in Strasbourg* (Oxford University Press, 1991), co-editor of *Vernacular Literacy: A Re-evaluation* (Oxford University Press, 1997), and a founding member of the LIPPS Group, which has set up a database of bilingual texts for researchers (see Special Issue, *International Journal of Bilingualism*, 4(2) June 2000).

Chip Gerfen, PhD (cgerfen@gmail.com), is Associate Professor of Linguistics and Spanish Linguistics at Penn State University, USA. His main research interests include phonology, experimental linguistics, psycholinguistics, and bilingualism. He is the author of *Phonology and Phonetics in Coatzospan Mixtec* (Kluwer, 1999) and has published in journals such as *Bilingualism: Language and Cognition*, and the *Journal of Phonetics*.

Monica Heller, PhD (mheller@oise.utoronto.ca), is Professor at the Ontario Institute for Studies in Education, University of Toronto, Canada. Her main research interests concern bilingualism, ethnography, globalization, and linguistic minorities, with a focus on francophone Canada. Her most recent publications include (as editor) *Bilingualism: A Social Approach* (Palgrave, 2007) and (co-edited with A. Duchêne) *Discourses of Endangerment: Ideology and Interest in the Defense of Languages* (Continuum, 2007). She has published articles in such journals as the *Journal of Sociolinguistics*, *Langage et Société*, and *Language in Society*.

Judith Kroll, PhD (jfk7@psu.edu), is Distinguished Professor of Psychology, Linguistics, and Women's Studies and Co-Director of the Center for Language Science at Pennsylvania State University, USA. The research that she and her students pursue concerns the acquisition, comprehension, and production of words in two languages during second language learning and in proficient bilingual performance. She served as a co-editor of *Bilingualism: Language and Cognition* from its founding in 1997 until 2001 and as its coordinating editor from 2001 to 2002. Together with Annette de Groot she co-edited *Tutorials in Bilingualism: Psycholinguistic Perspectives* (Erlbaum, 1997) and the *Handbook of Bilingualism: Psycholinguistic Approaches* (Oxford University Press, 2005). She is a member of the editorial boards of the *International Journal of Bilingualism*, the *Journal of Memory and Language*, the *Journal of Experimental Psychology: Learning, Memory, and Cognition*, and *Psychological Science*.

Elizabeth Lanza, PhD (elizabeth.lanza@iln.uio.no), is Professor of Applied Linguistics at the Department of Linguistics and Scandinavian Studies, University of Oslo, Norway. Her main research interests are in sociolinguistic approaches to the study of multilingualism, including discourse/conversation analysis, social network analysis, language ideology, and identity in language socialization. She is author of *Language Mixing in Infant Bilingualism: A Sociolinguistic Perspective* (Oxford University Press, 1997/2004) and numerous book chapters and articles in journals such as the *International Journal of Bilingualism* and the *Journal of Child Language*.

Li Wei, PhD (li.wei@bbk.ac.uk), is Professor of Applied Linguistics at the School of Languages, Linguistics and Culture, Birkbeck, University of London, UK. His main research interests are in BAMFLA (bilingual and multilingual first language acquisition), code-switching, language choice and language shift, and cross-cultural pragmatics. He is author of *Three Generations, Two Languages, One Family* (Multilingual Matters, 1994) and editor of the bestselling volume *The Bilingualism Reader* (Routledge, 2000/2007). He has also co-edited *Handbook of Multilingualism and Multilingual Communication* (Mouton de Gruyter, 2007), *Language Learning and Teaching as Social Inter-Action* (Palgrave Macmillan, 2007), *Bilingualism: Beyond Basic Principles* (Multilingual Matters, 2003), and *Opportunities and Challenges of Bilingualism* (Mouton de Gruyter, 2002). He has been the Principal Editor of the *International Journal of Bilingualism* since 1997.

Melissa G. Moyer, PhD (melissa.moyer@uab.es), is Associate Professor of English Linguistics at the Universitat Autònoma de Barcelona, Spain. Her research interests include multilingualism and migration in institutional contexts, sociolinguistics, and language contact. She has published numerous articles and book chapters on these topics. She is author of the award-winning book *La cárcel de las palabras: Ensayo sobre el lenguaje y la desigualdad social* (1988, with J. M. de Miguel). Her most recent work, in collaboration with Luisa Martin Rojo, is "Language, Migration and Citizenship: New Challenges in the Regulation of Bilingualism," in M. Heller (ed.) *Bilingualism: A Social Approach* (Palgrave, 2007).

Jacomine Nortier, PhD (Jacomine.Nortier@let.uu.nl), is Associate Professor at the Department of Dutch Language and Culture and the Research Institute of Linguistics UiL-OTS, Utrecht University, The Netherlands. Her main areas of research interest are multilingualism, code-switching, and sociolinguistics. Her publications include *Dutch-Moroccan Arabic Code Switching among Moroccans in the Netherlands* (Foris, 1990), and *Murks en Straattaal. Vriendschap en taalgebruik onder jongeren* (Prometheus, 2001).

Aneta Pavlenko, PhD (apavlenk@temple.edu), is Associate Professor at the College of Education, Temple University, Philadelphia, USA. Her research focuses on the relationship between language, emotions, and cognition in bilingualism and second language acquisition. She is the author of *Emotions and Multilingualism* (Cambridge University Press, 2005), winner of the 2006 BAAL Book Prize; the editor of *Bilingual Minds: Emotional Experience, Expression, and Representation* (Multilingual Matters, 2006), and co-editor with A. Blackledge, I. Piller and M. Teutsch Dwyer of *Multilingualism, Second Language Learning, and Gender* (Mouton De Gruyter, 2001), with B. Norton of *Gender and English Language Learners* (TESOL, 2004), and with A. Blackledge of *Negotiation of Identities in Multilingual Contexts* (Multilingual Matters, 2004). Her work has also appeared in edited volumes and numerous scientific journals.

Tony Purvis, PhD (tony.purvis@ncl.ac.uk), is Lecturer in Media and Cultural Studies, in the School of Education, Communication and Language Sciences at Newcastle University, UK. His main research interests include media analysis, cultural theory, and psychoanalytic criticism. He is author of *Media and Cultural Studies* (Edinburgh University Press, 2006) and co-author of *Television Drama: Theories and Identities* (Palgrave, 2006), and has published articles in scholarly and professional publications.

Natasha Tokowicz, PhD (tokowicz@pitt.edu), is Assistant Professor of Psychology and Linguistics, and Research Scientist at the Learning Research and Development Center, University of Pittsburgh, USA. Her research focuses on how ambiguity, working memory, and cross-language similarity affect second language learning and cross-language processing. She is the author of articles in journals such as *Bilingualism: Language and Cognition*, *Language and Cognitive Processes*, and *Studies in Second Language Acquisition*.

Maria Teresa Turell, PhD, is Professor of English Linguistics at the Universitat Pompeu Fabra in Barcelona (Spain). Her research interests include language variation, forensic linguistics, multilingualism, and language contact. She has published extensively on English, Catalan, and Spanish sociolinguistics and applied linguistics. Her most recent publications are *Multilingualism in Spain* and *Lingüística Forense, Lengua y Derecho*. She is currently working on a volume on forensic linguistics with John Gibbons.

Wang Xiaomei (guoguo101@hotmail.com) is a PhD candidate in the Department of Chinese, Translation and Linguistics at City University of Hong Kong, China. Her main research interests include language spread, language maintenance and shift. She has published articles in books and journals such as the *Journal of Chinese Sociolinguistics*.

Tessa Warren, PhD (tessa@pitt.edu), is Assistant Professor of Psychology and Linguistics, and Research Scientist at the Learning Research and Development Center, University of Pittsburgh, USA. Her research focuses on the way cognition constrains the computation of syntax and semantics during language comprehension. She is the author of articles in journals such as *Cognition*, *Language and Cognitive Processes* and *Psychonomic Bulletin and Review*.

Xu Daming, PhD (xudaming@nju.edu.cn), is Professor of Linguistics in the Department of Chinese Language and Literature at Nanjing University, China. His main research interests include sociolinguistics and bilingualism. He is author of *A Survey of Language Use and Language Attitudes in the Singapore Chinese Community* (NJU Press, 2005) and many articles in journals such as the *Journal of Asian Pacific Communication*.

Zhu Hua, PhD (zhu.hua@bbk.ac.uk), is Senior Lecturer in Applied Linguistics in the School of Languages, Linguistics and Culture at Birkbeck, University of London, UK. Her main research interests include cross-linguistic studies of speech and language development and disorder in young children, and cross-cultural communication. She is author of *Phonological Development in Specific Contexts* (Multilingual

Matters, 2002) and *PAC: Phonological Assessment of Chinese (Mandarin)* (Speechmark, 2008), co-author of *DEAP: Diagnostic Evaluation of Articulation and Phonology* (Psychological Corporation, 2002), and co-editor of *Phonological Development and Disorder: A Multilingual Perspective* (Multilingual Matters, 2006) and *Language Learning and Teaching as Social Inter-Action* (Palgrave Macmillan, 2007). She has published in journals such as the *Journal of Child Language*, *Clinical Linguistics and Phonetics*, the *International Journal of Language and Communication Disorder*, and the *Journal of Pragmatics* and *Multilingua*.

Acknowledgments

We are grateful to the vast number of students and researchers with whom we have worked in various contexts over the years, who gave us the idea and initial impetus for doing a volume of this kind. Needless to say, the volume would not have been possible without the contributions of a truly outstanding team of international researchers. They responded to our various queries in a very positive way and showed tremendous professionalism and collegiality during the whole process.

Steve Smith and Philip Carpenter at Wiley-Blackwell gave the project their crucial backing from day one. The past and current editorial team members, Ada Brunstein, Sarah Coleman, Haze Humbert, and Danielle Descoteaux, have been very patient and professional. Louise Cooper of the marketing department has been very helpful.

Piers Gardner gave us valuable advice and support at a time when we most needed it.

Many of the contributors read each other's draft chapters and made valuable comments. We are also very grateful to the readers Blackwell commissioned for their constructive comments. Much of this work was done while Li Wei was at Newcastle. He is most grateful for the support the University, especially the School of Education, Communication and Language Sciences, gave him during the project. Thanks are also due to the Department of Filologia Anglesa at the Universitat Autònoma de Barcelona, the Spanish Ministerio de Educación y Ciencia for grant BF2001-2576, and the Centre de recherche en éducation franco-ontarienne (Créfo) at the University of Toronto, for supporting Melissa G. Moyer during the project.

Preface

The *Blackwell Guide to Research Methods in Bilingualism and Multilingualism* was inspired by our belief that there is an urgent need for a "know-how" book that enables students and researchers to carry out a research project by themselves. The number of "know-what" publications on bilingualism and multilingualism is overwhelming for both the novice and the experienced. Yet, there is almost nothing that specifically deals with methodology in a comprehensive and systematic way. Nor is there anything that addresses the links between theory, method, and data for student use. A student of bilingualism and multilingualism is expected to "pick up" much in the way of knowledge and skills: the most effective way to collect data, how best to analyze and interpret them, what variables to consider in designing an experiment or case study, and what are workable or unworkable topics for a research project.

This essential guide to research methods in bilingualism and multilingualism is aimed at advanced undergraduates and postgraduate students as well as new researchers in a variety of disciplines, especially in linguistics, psychology, speech and language pathology, sociology, anthropology, and education. It guides the reader through a wide range of research topics, key concepts and approaches, methods and tools for collecting and analyzing data. It also contains valuable information about research resources, conference presentation, and journal publication. The chapters are written by an international team of established and young researchers with first-hand experience in bilingualism and multilingualism research.

The Guide consists of three parts. Part I contains two chapters. The first contextualizes the field of bilingualism and multilingualism by reviewing the major theoretical strands and the questions and hypotheses that researchers are currently investigating. The second chapter introduces bilingualism and multilingualism research as practice, offering practical advice on the process of doing research and the way theory, methods, and data are connected.

Part II is the main part of the Guide; it contains 17 chapters that cover various procedures, methods, and tools for data collection and analysis. The sequence of the chapters broadly follows the process of a research project, starting with decisions on the source of data and where to find it, continuing with design options of the study, and concluding with various ways of analyzing the data.

We have deliberately avoided grouping these chapters under the traditional "sociolinguistic" or "psycholinguistic" labels for two main reasons. First, we do not believe that these labels accurately describe the complex nature of bilingualism and multilingualism research, which has always been highly multidisciplinary. Second, we wish to offer the reader an opportunity to read beyond their immediate discipline of interest and to learn about other perspectives. While readers with specific interests and experience can dip in and out of specific chapters as they require, it would be highly desirable, time permitting, to read all the chapters in this part of the Guide.

The amount of detail and practical advice given in the different chapters in Part II varies. This is intentional, as some methods can be learned and applied fairly easily by the student while others require elaborate facilities and support. Even in the latter case, however, we believe that reading the chapters in this part (e.g. imaging technologies) will enable the student to better understand and appreciate the published studies on bilingualism and multilingualism. In some chapters, the term bilingualism is used as a convenient label to cover multilingualism as well.

Part III contains information and advice on project ideas, disseminating research results, and research resources. The aim of illustrative project ideas is to help new researchers to think creatively and make links between their personal research interests and broad themes of wider concern.

The Guide is intended to complement, rather than replace, existing textbooks and readers on bilingualism and multilingualism. We have tried to make the Guide as practical as possible. As this type of publication is still rare, we would be glad to hear any comments and suggestions for revision.

Li Wei, London
Melissa Moyer, Barcelona

Part I Researching Bilingualism and Multilingualism

1 Research Perspectives on Bilingualism and Multilingualism

Li Wei

1.1 Introduction

For many people, bilingualism and multilingualism are a fact of life and not a problem. Contact between people speaking different languages has been a common phenomenon since ancient times. Increased international travel and modern information and communication technologies provide even more opportunities for people of different tongues to get to know each other. Even if one was born and brought up as a monolingual, the opportunity to learn other languages is no longer a luxury for the elite. Nevertheless, some regard bilingualism and multilingualism as an issue of concern, and raise questions such as: Can learning more than one language at a time affect children's intellectual development? Do bilingual and multilingual children present special educational needs? Can bilingualism and multilingualism result in schizophrenia, split or confused identity, or mental illness? Do bilingualism and multilingualism lead to social disorder between communities? These are legitimate questions, the answers to which depend on one's experience, knowledge of the phenomenon, and point of view. They are also worthwhile research questions that need to be addressed scientifically. Findings from scientific research on bilingualism and multilingualism can provide strong evidence for answering these questions.

1.2 Societal and Individual Bilingualism and Multilingualism

Fishman (1980) made a useful distinction between bilingualism or multilingualism as an individual phenomenon and as a societal phenomenon. A quick look at the statistics will tell us that most of the countries in the world are multilingual – there are 193 countries and over 6,000 different languages. This does not mean, however, that the individual citizens of multilingual countries are necessarily multilingual themselves. In fact, countries which are officially multilingual, such as Belgium and Switzerland, may have many monolinguals in their population, while officially monolingual countries, such as France and Germany, have sizeable multilingual populations. Several questions arise here: Why are some countries officially multilingual whereas others are officially monolingual? What rights do different languages have, in government, in education, or in social interaction? What are the effects of the language policies of a country on its citizens? What are the effects of bilingualism and multilingualism on the country's economic and social development?

A multilingual individual is anyone who can communicate in more than one language, be it active (through speaking and writing) or passive (through listening and reading). Multilingual individuals may have become what they are through very different experiences: some may have acquired and maintained one language during childhood, the so-called first language (L1), and learned other languages later in life, while others have acquired two or more first languages since birth. What is the relationship between the languages in the process of language acquisition? Are early and late bilinguals and multilinguals different kinds of language users? Are some languages more easily learned and maintained than others? These are some of the questions that could be researched with regard to bilingualism and multilingualism as an individual phenomenon.

Whenever two people meet, they need to decide whether they want to interact with each other and in what way. When bilingual and multilingual speakers meet, an issue for consideration and negotiation is which language should be used. Most bilingual and multilingual speakers seem to know which language is the most appropriate for a given situation, but how do they know it? Most bilingual and multilingual speakers switch from one language to another in the middle of a conversation, but why do they do it? Bilingual and multilingual interaction can also take place without the speakers switching languages. In certain areas, it is not uncommon for speakers to consistently each use a different language. This phenomenon is found, for example, in Scandinavia, where speakers of Swedish and Norwegian can easily communicate by each speaking their own language. To what extent are these speakers aware of the differences between their languages?

Individual and societal bilingualism and multilingualism are by no means entirely separate. Multilingual speakers in officially monolingual countries often find themselves constrained by official policies and unable to utilize their full linguistic repertoire, just as monolinguals in officially multilingual countries find it difficult to cross linguistic boundaries to make full use of the opportunities and resources available. Can these kinds of tensions be resolved through legislation? What would be the long-term effect of tensions of this kind?

1.3   Research Perspectives

Research on bilingualism and multilingualism has a very long history. Detailed documentation of societal language contacts in Europe, for example, dates back to the seventeenth century; Whitney's analysis of the grammatical structure of bilingual speech was published in 1881; and Cattell's experiments, which compared word associations and reaction times of bilingual and monolingual individuals, were published in 1887. Nevertheless, bilingualism and multilingualism became a major focus of scientific research only in the last century, especially from the 1970s. Three broad research perspectives can be identified: linguistic, psycholinguistic, and sociolinguistic. Each of these perspectives has its distinct themes and research methodologies.

1.3.1   *Linguistic perspective*

Research on bilingualism and multilingualism is central to the contemporary linguistics agenda. Chomsky (1986) defined three basic questions for linguistics:

1   What constitutes knowledge of language?
2   How is knowledge of language acquired?
3   How is knowledge of language put to use?

For bilingualism and multilingualism research, these questions can be rephrased to take into account knowledge of more than one language (see Cook, 1993):

1   What is the nature of language or grammar in a bi- or multilingual person's mind, and how do different systems of language knowledge coexist and interact?
2   How is more than one grammatical system acquired, either simultaneously or sequentially? In what respects does bi- or multilingual acquisition differ from monolingual acquisition?
3   How is the knowledge of two or more languages used by the same speaker in bilingual interaction?

With regard to the first question (the nature of multilingual knowledge), a key issue is whether and how the different languages in the multilingual person's mind interact with one another. One important characteristic of the multilingual is their ability to move between different languages: they can speak one language at a time, behaving more or less like a monolingual; or mix languages in the same sentence, clause, or even word, resulting in a linguistic phenomenon known as code-switching. There is a very large body of literature describing the structural patterns of bilingual code-switching. It is clear that code switches take place at specific points in an utterance; they are structurally well formed and seem to con-form to the grammatical constraints of the languages involved. Muysken (2000), for example, offers a typology of code-switching: "insertion" of material (lexical items or entire constituents) from one language into a structure from the other language; "alternation" between structures from languages; and "congruent lexicalization" of material from different lexical inventories into a shared grammatical structure. Linguists have developed various models specifying the grammatical constraints of these processes. For instance, models of the insertional type of code-switching view the constraints in terms of the structural properties of some base or matrix language, e.g. the Matrix Language frame model of Myers-Scotton (1997), while models departing from alternation see the constraints on code-switching in terms of the compatibility or equivalence of the languages involved at the switch point, e.g. Poplack (1980).

As is often the case in linguistics, counter-examples are reported as soon as a new model or constraint is proposed. More recent linguistic studies of code-switching question the theoretical value of the various grammatical constraints, arguing instead for the application of the basic principles already afforded by Universal Grammar. MacSwan (2004: 298), for example, goes as far as to say that "Nothing constrains code switching apart from the requirements of the mixed grammars." Put differently, the generative-universalist position is that all of the facts of bilingual code-switching may be explained in terms of principles and requirements of the specific grammars used in each specific utterance. MacSwan also questions the status and explanatory power of the matrix language, a concept that is widely believed to exist by code-switching researchers and is central to models such as the one proposed by Myers-Scotton. While it is generally accepted that the two languages involved in code-switching tend to play different roles – one providing the morphosyntactic frame while the other provides specific items, usually open-class content morphemes – the concept of matrix language is not theoretically motivated and probably not needed for explaining the structural patterns or constraints.

The second major area of linguistic studies of bilingualism and multilingualism concerns the acquisition of linguistic knowledge. Earlier studies of bilingual acquisition attempted to chart the developmental paths and stages of the bilingual child. Volterra and Taeschner (1978) suggested that bilingual acquisition went through three key stages:

Stage I: the child has one lexical system comprised of words from both languages;
Stage II: the child distinguishes two different lexicons, but applies the same syntactic rules to both languages;
Stage III: the child speaks two languages differentiated both in lexicon and syntax, but each language is associated with the person who uses that language.

Although some studies both before and after Volterra and Taeschner's had evidence supporting the model, there has been much criticism particularly of the claims made regarding the first two stages. This is generally known as the "one-system-or-two" debate; i.e., do bilingual children begin with a fused linguistic system and gradually differentiate the two languages, or do they start with a differentiated system? Part of that debate centers around the question: What counts as evidence for differentiation or fusion? Volterra and Taeschner (1978) and Taeschner (1983), for instance, based their decision on whether the child made appropriate sociolinguistic choices, i.e., whether the child spoke the "right" language to the "right" person. It was argued that awareness of the two languages as distinct plays a crucial role in deciding the issue of differentiation, and a child's ability to make appropriate language choices reflects that awareness. However, as McLaughlin (1984) points out, the argument that bilingual children separate the languages when they are aware there are two systems is circular unless some criterion is provided for assessing what is meant by awareness other than that children separate the languages. In any case, we need to bear in mind that a child's apparent (in)ability to choose the right language for the right addressee is a rather different issue from whether the child has one or two linguistic systems. Part of the problem is the familiar one of what we can infer about competence from performance.

In a longitudinal study of a girl named Kate who was acquiring Dutch and English simultaneously, De Houwer (1990) provided strong evidence for the separate-development argument. De Houwer reported that Kate used only Dutch with monolingual Dutch speakers, but would occasionally switch to English when interacting with Dutch-English bilinguals. Thus, the child seemed aware of the linguistic abilities of the interlocutors. De Houwer further suggested that Kate used English and Dutch in the same manner as do children monolingual in one of her languages. She was, according to De Houwer, already fully bilingual by the age of 2;7. Although lexical mixing was not a focus of De Houwer's analysis, the phenomenon was discussed. In the majority of Kate's mixed utterances, a single-word item, most often a noun from one language, was inserted into an utterance that was otherwise completely in the other language. These mixed utterances were well formed, that is structurally grammatical. De Houwer used this as evidence for the child's separate rule systems of the two languages.

Meisel (1989) also took issue with Volterra and Taeschner (1978), criticizing their stage of syntactic mixing for being too vaguely defined; he pointed out that the evidence given by Volterra and Taeschner was not sufficient to support the hypothesis that bilingual children must undergo an initial stage of syntactic mixing, a situation which would need to be explained by the child's processing both languages as a single system. Meisel argued that one could only consider those aspects of grammar where the two adult systems differed as valid empirical evidence for instances of syntactic mixing or of differentiation between systems. In addition, one should try to find evidence for or against a non-differentiated syntax in structural areas where the language production of monolingual children in each language differed. Meisel further suggested that if it could be shown that young bilingual children used linguistic structures in which the two adult target systems differed, this would constitute evidence against the one-system hypothesis. There now exists a large body of literature rebutting the "fused" system hypothesis, arguing instead that bilinguals have two distinct but interdependent systems from the very start (e.g. Genesee, 1989; Meisel, 1989; De Houwer, 1990; Döpke, 1992; Lanza, 1997; Deuchar & Quay, 2000).

While the one-versus-two-systems debate continues to attract new empirical studies, a more interesting question has emerged regarding the acquisition of bilingual and multilingual knowledge. More specifically, is bilingual and multilingual acquisition the same as monolingual acquisition? Theoretically, separate development is possible without there being any similarity with monolingual acquisition. Most researchers argue that multilingual children's language development is by and large the same as that of monolingual children. Nevertheless, as Genesee (2002) points out, one needs to be careful about the kinds of conclusions one draws from such evidence. Similarities between bilingual and monolingual acquisition do not mean that (1) the two languages a bilingual child is acquiring develop in the same way or at the same speed, or that (2) the two languages a bilingual child is acquiring do not influence and interact with each other (see e.g. Paradis & Genesee, 1996; Döpke, 2000).

There is one area in which multilingual children clearly differ from monolingual children, namely, code mixing. Studies show that multilingual children mix elements from different languages in the same utterance as soon as they can produce two-word utterances (e.g. De Houwer, 1990; Lanza, 1997; Deuchar & Quay, 2000; and David, 2004). Like adult code-switching, multilingual children's language mixing is highly structured. The operation of constraints based on surface features of grammar, such as word order, is evident from the two-word/-morpheme stage onward, and the operation of constraints based on abstract notions of grammatical knowledge is most evident in multilingual children once they demonstrate such knowledge overtly (e.g. verb tense and agreement markings), usually around 2;6 years of age and older (see further Meisel, 1994; Koppe & Meisel, 1995). As Genesee (2002) points out, these findings suggest that, in addition to the linguistic competence to formulate correct monolingual strings, multilingual children have the added capacity to coordinate their two languages on-line in accordance with the grammatical constraints of specific languages during mixing. While these studies provide further evidence for the separate-development (or two-systems) argument, they also suggest that there are both quantitative and qualitative differences between multilingual and monolingual acquisition.

Although much of the language acquisition research focuses on children, learning languages can be a lifelong experience. The field of second language acquisition (SLA) addresses some of the fundamental issues of how learners who may have begun their lives as monolinguals acquire additional languages at a later time. For example, what effect does the timing of additional language acquisition have on the later-learned languages as well as earlier-acquired ones? Clearly one of the key objectives of second language acquisition is to become bilingual. But why do some learners appear to be able to achieve a much higher level of proficiency in the later-learned languages, and at a much faster rate than other learners? Can the attainment level in the later-learned languages be maintained when the speakers reach an advanced age? What aspects of their multilingual knowledge may be subject to attrition and loss? While many of these issues are typically addressed in SLA, which is generally considered to be different from bilingualism and multilingualism research, second language learners and other later-acquired language users are regarded as an important and distinctive group of bilinguals and multilinguals.

The third major area of linguistic research on bilingualism and multilingualism concerns how bilinguals put their knowledge of two or more languages to use. Earlier studies of multiple language use focused on language choice in different contexts and for different purposes. Fishman's domain analysis (2000 [1965]), for example, outlined the ways in which speakers make their language choices according to topic, setting, and participant. Gumperz (1982a) identified a range of discourse functions of bilingual code-switching, including quotation, addressee specification, interjections, reiteration, message qualification, and personalization versus object-ivization. Such descriptive accounts laid the foundation for later, still developing research on the pragmatics of multilingual speech.

Invoking the notion of "contextualization" – the processes by which speakers construe the local and global contexts which are necessary for the interpretation of their linguistic and non-linguistic activities – Auer (1984, 1995) argued that multilinguals alternate their languages in conversation to build a frame of reference for the interpretation of each other's intentions. According to Auer, the interpreta-tion of function(s) or meaning(s) of code-switching is influenced by the sequential patterns of language choice. He proposed a distinction between discourse-related and participant-related code-switching. Discourse-related code-switching contributes to the organization of the ongoing interaction, while participant-related code-switching permits assessment by participants of the speaker's preference for and competence in one language or the other.

From the speaker's point of view, language choice allows them to calculate the relative costs and rewards of speaking one language rather than another. This is the premise on which Carol Myers-Scotton builds her "rational choice model." Under such a model, what makes choices "rational" is the premise that the speaker makes cognitive calculations that take account of how the speaker views available evidence that indicates likely outcomes of choices, but the speaker also considers his or her own values and beliefs. So rational choices are subjective, with the emphasis on mental calculations about getting the best outcome (Myers-Scotton & Bolonyai, 2001).

1.3.2 Psycholinguistic perspective

Psycholinguists working on bilingualism and multilingualism are interested in essen-tially the same three key issues – multilingual knowledge, multilingual acquisition and multilingual use. Yet the research methodologies are quite different from those of theoretical and descriptive linguistics. Psycholinguistic research tends to use experimental and laboratory methods to investigate multilingual behavior. They are less concerned with describing and explaining structures of multilingual speech, but more so with the cognitive processes involved in receiving and producing multilingual speech.

Psycholinguistic research on the cognitive organization and representation of bilingual and multilingual knowledge is inspired and influenced by the work of Weinreich. Focusing on the relationship between the linguistic sign (or *signifier*) and the semantic content (*signified*), Weinreich (1953) distinguished three types of bilinguals. In Type A, the individual combines a signifier from each language with a separate unit of signified. Weinreich called them "coordinative" (later often called "coordinate") bilinguals. In Type B, the individual identifies two signifiers but regards them as a single compound, or composite, unit of signified; hence "compound" bilinguals. Type C relates to people who learn a new language with the help of a previously acquired one. They are called "subordinative" (or "subordinate") bilinguals. His examples were from English and Russian:

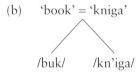

Weinreich's distinctions are often misinterpreted in the literature as referring to differences in the degree of proficiency in the languages. But in fact the relationship between language proficiency and cognitive organization of the bilingual individual, as conceptualized in Weinreich's model, is far from clear. Some "subordinate" bilinguals demonstrate a very high level of proficiency in processing both languages, as evidenced in grammaticality and fluency of speech, while some "coordinative" bilinguals show difficulties in processing two languages simultaneously (e.g. in code-switching or in "foreign" words identification tasks). It must also be stressed that in Weinreich's distinctions, bilingual individuals are distributed along a continuum from a subordinate or compound end to a coordinate end, and can at the same time be more subordinate or compound for certain concepts and more coordinate for others, depending on, among other things, the age and context of acquisition.

Weinreich's work influenced much of the psycholinguistic modeling of the bilingual lexicon. Potter, So, Von Echardt, and Feldman (1984) presented a reformulation of the manner in which bilingual lexical knowledge could be represented in the mind in terms of two competing models: the Concept Mediation Model and the Lexical Association Model. In the Concept Mediation Model, words of both L1 and L2 are linked to modal conceptual representations. In the Lexical Association Model, on the other hand, words in a second language are understood through L1 lexical representations. As can be seen in figure 1.1, the models are structurally equivalent

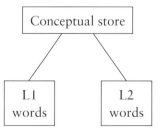

Figure 1.1: Concept Mediation Model

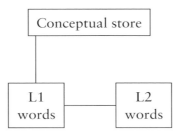

Figure 1.2: Lexical Association Model

to Weinreich's distinction between coordinative and subordinative bilingualism. At the same time, several researchers (e.g. Kolers & Gonzalez, 1980, and Hummel, 1986) presented evidence for the so-called dual-store model, as represented in figure 1.2. This latter model has also generated considerable research on the existence of the putative "bilingual language switch" which has been postulated to account for the bilingual's ability to switch between languages on the basis of environmental demands (e.g. MacNamara, 1967; MacNamara & Kushnir, 1971).

Subsequent studies found conflicting evidence in favor of different models. Some of the conflicting evidence could be explained by the fact that different types of bilingual speakers were used in the experiments in terms of proficiency level, and age and context of acquisition. It is possible that lexical mediation is associated with low levels of proficiency and concept mediation with higher levels, especially for those who have become bilingual in later childhood or adulthood. Some researchers called for a developmental dimension in the modeling of bilingual knowledge. Indeed, although the various psycholinguistic models were initially proposed without reference to bilingual acquisition, they clearly have important implications for acquisitional research and need to be validated with acquisition data. Kroll and Stewart (1994), for example, proposed the Revised Hierarchical Model which represents concept mediation and word association not as different models but as alternative routes within the same model (see figure 1.3).

As well as developing new models of bilingual mental lexicon, psycholinguists have used the latest functional neuroimaging technologies to investigate the cognitive organization of languages in the bilingual brain (see Abutalebi, Cappa, & Perani, 2005, for a summary). The key research question here is the relationship between the pre-wired neurobiological substrate for multiple languages and environmental, time-locked influences such as age of acquisition, exposure, and proficiency.

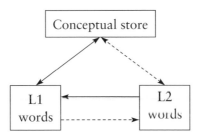

Figure 1.3: Revised Hierarchical Model

It has been found that while the patterns of brain activation associated with tasks that engage specific aspects of linguistic processing are remarkably consistent across different languages and different speakers, factors such as proficiency seem to have a major modulating effect on brain activity: more extensive cerebral activations are associated with production in the less proficient language, and smaller activations with comprehending the less proficient language.

Psycholinguistic studies of bilingual and multilingual use centers around two issues: activation level of the contributing languages and selective access to the lexicon. As discussed earlier, an important distinctive feature of being multilingual is to be able to make appropriate language choices. Multilingual speakers choose to use their different languages according to a variety of factors, including the type of person addressed (e.g. members of the family, school-mates, colleagues, superiors, friends, shopkeepers, officials, transport personnel, neighbors), the subject matter of the conversation (e.g. family concerns, schoolwork, politics, entertainment), location or social setting (e.g. at home, in the street, in church, in the office, having lunch, attending a lecture, negotiating business deals), and relationship with the addressee (e.g. kin, neighbor, colleague, superior–inferior, stranger). However, even more complex are the many cases where a multilingual talks to another multilingual with the same linguistic background and changes from one language to another in the course of conversation. On the basis of such observations, Grosjean (1998) proposed a situational continuum that induces different language modes. At one end of the continuum, bilinguals are in a totally monolingual language mode, in that they are interacting with monolinguals of one – or the other – of the languages they know. At the other end of the continuum, bilinguals find themselves in a bilingual language mode, in that they are communicating with bilinguals who share their two (or more) languages and with whom they normally mix languages (i.e., code-switch and borrow). These are endpoints, but bilinguals also find themselves at intermediary points. Figure 1.4 is a visual representation of the continuum. The base languages (A and B) are located in the top and bottom parts of the figure, and the continuum is in the middle. Additional dimensions can be introduced when more than two languages are involved. At the monolingual end of the continuum,

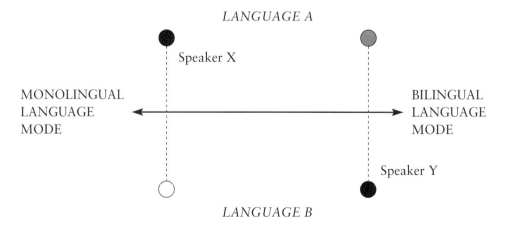

Figure 1.4: Language mode

bilinguals adopt the language of the monolingual interlocutor(s) and deactivate their other language(s) as far as possible.

When a bilingual is in bilingual mode, he or she will access or select words from two languages to produce sentences. How words are accessed or selected in speech production has been a central issue in psycholinguistics. In psycholinguistic research on bilingualism, the question becomes that of how different lexical items in different languages may be accessed or selected differently. Following earlier psycholinguistics models of speech production and more recent work by Clahsen (1999), Pinker (1999), and Jackendoff (2002), Myers-Scotton (2005) proposes a Differential Access Hypothesis for bilingual production. The hypothesis assumes what is known as the 4-M model, which differentiates four types of morphemes: content morphemes, and three types of system morphemes – early system morphemes, bridge late morphemes and outsider late system morphemes. It is suggested that the different types of morpheme under the 4-M model are differentially accessed in the abstract levels of the production process. Specifically, content morphemes and early system morphemes are accessed at the level of the mental lexicon, but late system morphemes do not become salient until the level of the formulator as in Levelt's Speaking model (1989). The hypothesis has received considerable attention in the literature and is being tested with a range of language contact phenomena.

1.3.3   Sociolinguistic perspective

The sociolinguistic perspective differs from the linguistic and psycholinguistic perspectives outlined above in terms of both its research methodologies and its fundamental concerns. Sociolinguists see bilingualism and multilingualism as a socially constructed phenomenon and the bilingual or multilingual person as a social actor. For the multilingual speaker, language choice is not only an effective means of communication but also an act of identity (Le Page & Tabouret-Keller, 1985). Every time we say something in one language when we might just as easily have said it in another, we are reconnecting with people, situations, and power configurations from our history of past interactions and imprinting on that history our attitudes towards the people and languages concerned. Through language choice, we maintain and change ethnic group boundaries and personal relationships, and construct and define "self" and "other" within a broader political economy and historical context. So, the issue of language use that linguists and psycholinguists are concerned with becomes an issue of identity and identification for the sociolinguist.

The notion of identity has gone through considerable changes in sociolinguistics. In the earlier variationist sociolinguistic work, as exemplified by the work of Labov (1972b), identity was taken to mean the speaker's social economic class, gender, age, or place of origin. It is assumed that speakers express, rather than negotiate, identities through their language use. Several scholars, such as Cameron (1990) and Johnstone (1996), later criticized such assumptions and argued instead that identities are negotiated through social interaction. Linguistic forms and strategies have multiple functions and cannot be directly linked to particular identities outside of interactional contexts. Work by Rampton (1995, 1999) and Lo (1999), for example, demonstrated that identities are locally constructed. More recent work by Pavlenko and Blackledge (e.g. Blackledge & Pavlenko, 2001; Pavlenko & Blackledge, 2004a) emphasizes the negotiation of identities.

The idea that identity is negotiable can be traced back to the work of social psychologists who were interested in group processes and inter-group relations (e.g. Tajfel, 1974, 1981). Identity, from this particular perspective, is reflective self-image, constructed, experienced, and communicated by the individual within a group. Negotiation is seen as a transactional process, in which individuals attempt to evoke, assert, define, modify, challenge, and/or support their own and others' desired self-images (Ting-Toomey, 1999: 40). Identity domains such as ethnic, gendered, relational, facework, are seen as crucial for everyday interaction. Speakers feel a sense of identity security in a culturally familiar environment, but insecurity in a culturally unfamiliar environment. Satisfactory identity negotiation outcomes would include the feelings of being understood, valued, supported, and respected.

There are two major problems with the inter-group social-psychological approach to identity and identity negotiation. First, the categories used in the analysis are often rigid and ill-defined and have a monolingual and unicultural bias. The world is often seen as consisting of "them" and "us," "in-group" and "out-group," or "we code" and "they code." The so-called negotiation, in this particular perspective, is unidirectional – the native speaker abandoning (or at least modifying) his or her first language and culture in order to learn the language of the host culture. This process is often known as "convergence" or "acculturation." The second major problem concerns the approach's static and homogeneous view of culture and society. It does not take into account the historical, ideological, and economic processes that led to the present social grouping or stratification.

Adopting a poststructuralist approach to the notion of identity, Pavlenko and Blackledge (e.g. Blackledge & Pavelenko, 2001; Pavlenko & Blackledge, 2004a) argue that the relationship between language and identity is mutually constitutive and that identities are multiple, dynamic, and subject to change. For them, negotiation of identities is the interplay between reflective positioning (after Davies & Harré, 1990), that is, self-representation, and interactive positioning, whereby others attempt to reposition particular individuals or groups. Their analyses of multilingualism and identities in a variety of social contexts demonstrate that languages are appropriated to legitimize, challenge, and negotiate particular identities, and to open new identity options. Identity options are constructed, validated, and performed through discourses available to individuals at particular times and places – that is, certain linguistic resources may be available to certain groups of speakers, while others may not (Tabouret-Keller, 1997).

Parallel to the work on multilingualism and negotiation of identities, sociolinguists critically examine some of the concepts and notions commonly used by other researchers in the field of bilingualism and multilingualism. For example, the very idea of code-switching raises questions as to what a language is. Instead of thinking of languages as discrete systems, sociolinguists tend to see multilingual speakers as actors of social life who draw on complex sets of communicative resources which are unevenly distributed and unevenly valued. The linguistic systematicity therefore appears to be a function at least as much of historically rooted ideologies (of nationality and ethnicity) and of the ordering practices of social life as of language *per se* (Gal & Irvine, 1995). This perspective goes beyond a focus on mental representation of linguistic knowledge and opens up the possibility of looking at bilingualism and multilingualism as a matter of ideology, communicative practice, and social process.

This particular sociolinguistic perspective has important implications for the way researchers collect, analyze, and interpret data. Informed by developments in anthropology, sociology, and cultural studies, sociolinguists have examined communicative practices within and across sites that can be ethnographically demonstrated to be linked. Working with the ideas of *trajectories* (of speakers, linguistic resources, discourses, institutions) across time and space and of *discursive spaces* which allow for, and also constrain, the production and circulation of discourses, Heller (e.g. 1995b, 2006) has examined multilingual practices in a number of communities and argued that such practices contribute to the construction of social boundaries and of the resources those boundaries regulate. They therefore also raise the question of the social and historical conditions that allow for the development of particular regimes of language, for their reproduction, their contestation and, eventually, their modification or transformation.

A further, closely related, area in which sociolinguists have extended the work of linguists and psycholinguists on bilingualism and multilingualism is that of the acquisition of linguistic knowledge. Building on earlier research on language socialization, which focused on young children acquiring their first language in culturally specific ways, scholars such as Kulick (1992), Crago, Annahatak, and Ningiuruvik (1993), Zentella (1997), and Schecter and Bayley (2002) examine bilingual and multilingual children's developing competence in various speech and literacy events. Particular attention is given to the range of linguistic resources available, or not, in bilingual and multilingual communities and the ways in which children, as well as adolescents and adults, learn to choose among these resources for their symbolic value. The researchers emphasized language socialization as an interactive process, in which those being socialized also act as agents rather than as mere passive initiates. This line of inquiry also demonstrates how domains of knowledge are constructed through language and cultural practices, and how the individual's positioning affects the process of knowledge acquisition and construction (see further Bayley & Schecter, 2003).

1.4 The Transdisciplinary Future

There is no doubt that a much more nuanced picture of the human language faculty, and indeed of the human mind, has emerged as a result of extensive research on bilingualism and multilingualism over many decades. We understand more about the human capacity for language through such research than the monolingual perspective can ever offer. Theories of human language and mind have become informed in new and essential ways by research on bilingualism and multilingualism. New research questions have been asked, hypotheses formulated and paradigms constructed. The multidisciplinary nature of bilingualism and multi-lingualism research as evidenced in the above discussion of the various research perspectives has been a clear strength of the field. Nevertheless, the future of the field requires a more comprehensive framework that transcends the narrow scope of disciplinary research. So, what are the main challenges to bilingualism and multilingualism research as it moves forward to a transdisciplinary future?

First, there is the issue of language. Each discipline develops its own jargon. Communication across disciplines may prove to be difficult since it requires the use of technical terms that are not well understood by colleagues in the other relevant disciplines. Even when the same terms are used, the intended meanings and connotations may be misinterpreted due to lack of a common background. For example, the very term "language" may suggest a fairly discrete linguistic system to a psychologist, but may be very problematic to define for a linguist. Similarly, how is a "bilingual" person defined? Researchers from different disciplinary back-grounds may come up with very different answers. Some may insist on having no monolingual experience at all; others are happy to include adult second or foreign language learners as bilinguals. Still others may argue that language proficiency and dominance are determining factors.

Second, research methods. Disciplines are often devoted to their own methods of investigation. This may lead to misunderstanding of and opposition to the research findings. It is important to remember that research methods are chosen for a purpose and have to be appropriate for the research questions. Yet the research questions are not at all value-free. They are often posed with particular disciplinary, even ideological, biases. Even apparently neutral, scientific terms, such as "accom-modation" and "variation," can be used to serve particular biases, and require *in situ* explanations. Certain research questions favor certain research methods. Con-sequently, evidence from studies that employ different methods may be brushed aside as irrelevant.

Third, there is a confusion of "multi-/interdisciplinarity" and "innovation." A com-prehensive understanding of any complex social phenomenon such as bilingualism and multilingualism requires contributions from a variety of disciplines. The multidisciplinary and interdisciplinary approach has definitely generated research outcomes that challenge the received wisdom about the human mind and society. But being multidisciplinary or interdisciplinary does not in itself entail innovation. Innovation requires thinking creatively, breaking new ground, adding value, and making a difference. Innovation often results in the constitution of a new approach or discipline.

Fourth, the tension between "basic" research and "applied" research. At a time when research funding and resources are limited, applied research that has more direct and immediate impact on policy and practice receives more attention and support than studies that address basic research questions. There is also a tendency to misapprehend applied research as naturally interdisciplinary and basic research as narrow. Yet without advances in basic research, there would be no firm basis for knowledge transfer, which is the key to applied research. Basic research can address social concerns. In fact, it can be argued that the majority of the research questions in the bilingualism and multilingualism field come from the concerns of individuals and their communities. They can be, and have been, turned into basic research questions.

The increased amount of bilingualism and multilingualism at both the individual and societal levels offers the research community new opportunities to evaluate their knowledge base and develop their theories and models of language and communication. Society's interest in bilingualism and multilingualism is also growing. A challenge to the research community is to make what may be viewed as scientific research socially relevant as well. Academic researchers working in the field of bilingualism and multilingualism feel rightly proud of the fact that they not only have a lot to say about the linguistic and psychological theories and models, but also make significant contributions to sociopolitical debates about the world we are living in today. Researchers should look forward to moving away from narrow focuses on individual disciplines, learn from each other's perspectives, and create new ideas. It is the responsibility of researchers to lay the irrational fears of bilingualism and multilingualism to rest through good science. It is equally important that bilingual and multilingual researchers address sociopolitical issues head-on.

2 Research as Practice: Linking Theory, Method, and Data

Melissa G. Moyer

2.1 Introduction

Research is an activity that requires analytical and critical thinking at all stages. The present chapter discusses the process of doing research bearing in mind the various frameworks currently being practiced. Furthermore, it presents current thinking about research on bi/multilingualism and the manner in which theory, methods, and data can be addressed in the ongoing process of generating new knowledge. The study of bi/multilingualism covers various disciplinary approaches and methodological traditions that assume quite distinct views of the world, and of the very nature of the research enterprise. Research methods for investigating bilingualism and multilingualism need not be different from methods already available to us in related disciplines. The choice of methods, however, is central to a study and will depend on theoretical ideas concerning the phenomena we are asking questions about. Good research practice – no matter what the approach – requires a clear understanding of where one's research fits into the overall picture of explaining bilingualism. It also involves an ability to critically analyze a research design and to understand the purpose and underlying assumptions that go with selecting a particular topic. Reflexivity throughout the research process is necessary in order to be able to evaluate and choose the most appropriate methods and tools to answer the research questions set out. Despite different disciplinary perspectives or epistemological standpoints, researchers share a concern for producing knowledge and furthering understanding about bi/multilingualism. They also agree about the need to carry out rigorous investigation following principled research procedures and techniques.

The present chapter also provides a starting point for reflecting on the various approaches and techniques used to formulate and answer questions that are relevant to the field. Section 2.2 situates the study of bilingualism, taking into account the ontology (or the nature) of bilingual data and the various epistemologies (or theories of knowledge) that can be addressed. A discussion follows in section 2.3, with a set of questions that seek to promote reflection about research from a critical and analytical stance. Next, in section 2.4, a discussion is presented of the basic elements and activities involved in the process of doing research and of the manner in which questions, theory, method, and data are related. A summary of ideas about research as a dynamic and ongoing process is presented last.

2.2 Data and Knowledge on Bilingualism and Multilingualism

Bi/multilingualism as an area of inquiry raises certain challenges for a linguistics that has centered on monolingual speakers in a linguistically homogeneous speech community. Highly competent bilingual speakers have two language systems, which they can decide to combine or keep apart. The manner in which the language systems interact in the mind, and the extent to which a person can intentionally or consciously keep the two systems apart depends on factors related to the acquisition process (age, context, type of exposure to each language) and universal biological features of the human brain. In the skin of a bilingual from real life, this means that a person not only has at least two ways of saying the same thing but also that they have the ability to combine two languages in a conversation, a sentence, or a word. This is a language competence not accounted for by traditional monolingual linguistic explanations. Other linguistic disciplines such as pragmatics or sociolinguistics are better equipped with theoretical frameworks and methods to deal with the new meanings and the social relations of conflict and control connected to language that can be found in bi/multilingual individuals and communities.

In order to situate a particular research question in the wider context of the study of bilingualism, it is helpful to have an understanding of the *epistemologies*, or what constitutes the object of knowledge and the *ontologies*, or what has traditionally counted as data in the field. The various types of knowledge that dominate the field at the present time are construed on the basis of different philosophical conceptions of language that dictate what gets counted as data. Four perspectives on language taken up in current research on bilingualism, described below, can be characterized as: language as form and structure; language as competence and tacit knowledge; language as production and perception; and language as social action and practice.

2.2.1 Language as form and structure

Language as form or structure can be observed in everyday language use. Language structure is empirically and observationally based because it can be traced back to a physical speech event in the real world that was produced at a particular time in a particular context. It is a speech event that can be audio- or video-recorded and reproduced over and over at any time (see Clemente, chapter 10 in this volume). A linguistic form constitutes a datum that becomes the object of linguistic analysis. The classification into types or categories and the manner in which structural forms are represented will depend on the particular theoretical paradigm and the way it defines what counts as data (Lehmann, 2004; Mereu, 2004). In the field of bilingualism, structures can be represented by traditional linguistic units of analysis such as clauses, nouns, verbs, and so on. Bilingual language forms can also be classified according to whether they are instances of *embedded constituents*, *convergence*, or *nonce borrowings*. The complexity of bilingual language contact phenomena as opposed to monolingual data led Muysken (2000) to organize bilingual data in categories (*insertion*, *alternation*, and *congruent lexicalization*) that suggest different cognitive processes that have an empirical reality in actual bilingual language use (see Nortier and Gardner-Chloros, chapters 3 and 4 in this volume, for a definition of these terms).

Linguistic structures, once identified, can be analyzed in a variety of ways. Quantification is needed in order to establish which forms are representative for a group of speakers and should therefore constitute a reliable object/input for further theoretical elaboration in fields such as sociolinguistics, formal linguistics, or functional linguistics. It is also a method that is useful for responding to questions that have to do with degree or level of acquisition, or with language shift, change, and convergence (Klavans & Resnick, 1996; Bod, Hay, & Jannedy, 2003). For example, sociolinguistics is a perspective that is fundamentally concerned with explaining variation of structure (phonological and morphological) within the system. Rigorous methodological tools and principles were set out by Labov (1982b) for collecting the appropriate linguistic data to capture the regularities of variation according to a set of social variables (social class, gender, age, and ethnicity). The quality of data in this approach is primordial for constructing reliable theories of language change, which is one of its key objectives.

2.2.2 *Language as competence*

Language as competence uses judgments and intuitions as primary data in formal and theoretical approaches to language within a generative grammar tradition. Language within this paradigmatic approach is understood as a person's tacit knowledge of grammar. This knowledge tells us how to form and interpret words, phrases, and sentences in a language. It is viewed as a highly organized system of signs where grammar is central. Language structure obtained through judgments should fulfill observational and descriptive adequacy in relation to the ideal speaker-hearer. Formal, theoretical, and generative approaches to language have been concerned with cognition and the relation of language to mind. This has led to an emphasis on theory and the development of categories, along with operational notions and constraints proposed to account for the syntactic phenomena of language. What gets counted as data in this tradition, though, is narrowly delimited and, as some linguists point out (Abney, 1996; Schütze, 1996), it requires more careful methodological procedures.

The study of bilingualism represents a certain challenge to the Chomskyan conception of language as the competence or innate knowledge of the monolingual speaker-hearer in a homogeneous speech community. Bilingual language phenomena such as *code-mixing*, *convergence*, *attrition*, and *second language acquisition* are well-established areas of research for which obtaining judgments and intuitions is simply not a reliable method – on its own – for finding out about a bilingual's competence. Judgments about bilingual structures can be rejected because mixing two languages is often considered unacceptable or ungrammatical. This conception of data as intuitions is also problematical when researching children acquiring two languages as they are also unable to express grammatical judgments, especially if they are very young. The use of performance data and statistics (frequencies) obtained from corpora of data is a good method to assure reliable grammatical theorizing (see Tokowicz & Warren, chapter 12 in this volume).

2.2.3 Language as production and perception

Experimental research traditionally carried out in the field of psycholinguistics takes *language as a form of production* or as an *object of perception*. One of the goals of examining language in strictly controlled laboratory settings is to discover how two language systems are activated and how they interact in the brain. The results of experimental studies are universally applicable to all human beings who share a similar language background to the subjects in the experiments. Psycholinguistics, neurolinguistics, and the study of language acquisition are the disciplines that have traditionally adopted experimental methods to discover the nature of bilingual cognition and the principles that constrain or permit interactions across cognitive systems (see Kroll, Gerfen, & Dussias, and Abutalebi & Della Rosa, chapters 7 and 8 in this volume). Experimental research follows a step-by-step procedure. For example, a hypothesis about the effect of proficiency and age in the way bilinguals process, produce, and understand words, sentences, and phonemes from different languages will be formulated within the framework of a particular theory. The experimental design must ensure that the *dependent variables* (items affected by experimental treatment) are measured, while the effects of selected *independent variables* (items systematically altered by the experiment) are controlled for. Experiments are artificial situations that enable the researcher to control and manipulate given variables. Usually, statistical tests establishing the significance of experimental results are used to confirm or counter a proposed hypothesis (Hatch & Farhady, 1982). The interaction of different factors concerning the acquisition of each one of the languages, such as age, context, and level of formal instruction, and the effect this may have on lexical or phonological access in a given situation, are examples of questions addressed in experimental research.

2.2.4 Language as social action and practice

An ethnographic approach to the study of bilingualism takes *language use as a form of social action* that has consequences for interlocutors as well as for ourselves as researchers. Language is a practice that is used to enact social roles as well as relations of power and control (Cameron, Frazer, Harvey, Rampton, & Richardson, 1992; Sarangi, 2001). It is through language that social structure and the organization of society are constructed and reproduced. Speakers are social actors who use language as a resource to interact and establish social relations with others. From this perspective, linguistic signs are taken as representations of the world, and these connections to the world are never neutral. Language as action can help us to understand linguistic activities as cultural practices. A social approach to language makes a whole different set of assumptions about what counts as data and what methods are appropriate for collecting those data. One can take different perspectives on the relation between language and society. One approach places language within a social, cultural, and political matrix of human relations (Silverman, 1993). Linguistic forms (deictics, agentive expressions), or "language" as an ideal construction concealing complexities across so-called linguistic boundaries, are elements or systems that are used by speakers (and can be retrieved by analysts) to discover agency and processes of social and cultural meaning for a particular human group.

Another approach understands language more directly as a form of social action that sheds light on the ideological stances that get reproduced through linguistic practices. The researcher in this approach is continually present in the object being studied and throughout the descriptive account, but also, and more importantly, she or he is present in the explanation and the proposed analysis. Vital to this perspective is an awareness of one's position as a researcher as well as a good amount of reflection about one's own role throughout the research process. While language data are central to this approach, they are often complemented by non-linguistic data such as documentary, observational, and even statistical data that supplement ethnographic evidence.

2.3   Questions for Critical Thinking

Research is a skilled activity that involves a set of conventions that can be formally learned. It requires a systematic approach to finding answers to a set of questions or testing hypotheses, and it is best understood as an ongoing process that calls for critical and creative thinking at all stages (Blaxter, Hughes, & Tight, 1996). Rather than offering a blueprint or a set of fixed instructions to follow, this section seeks to help researchers question the automatic application of research protocols and to make them more aware of the decisions they take at each stage and of the reasons they are taking them. Research design is more than deciding upon the most appropriate methods or data sources for investigating a particular intellectual puzzle; it requires an understanding of the implications of the research questions and how they are related to certain methods. In the process of determining how your research questions are connected to your methodology (which includes a specific set of tools and techniques) it will be necessary to establish (1) the nature of the bi-/multilingual phenomena to be investigated, (2) what constitutes knowledge for the bilingual phenomena being investigated, (3) what is the best way to engage in the questions, (4) the most appropriate ways of generating and assembling such knowledge, and (5) the evidence you need to support your claims. It is also possible to work backwards from an assessment of the data sources or methods which are available towards the set of research questions.

There are several analytical questions researchers should attempt to answer when planning their research design. The intellectual considerations presented below are prerequisites to any investigative process; if the researcher manages to make these points explicit, or provide at least an initial answer to them, she or he will be better situated for successfully undertaking research. The basic queries for any researcher setting out to investigate bi/multilingualism are covered below.

2.3.1   *What is the broad nature of the bi/multilingual phenomena you wish to study?*

The nature of the bi/multilingual phenomena to be investigated must be clear in a researcher's mind from the start. There are various ways to think about this first question, and more often than not it is a matter of personal choice or preference. For example, one may wish to collect and analyze qualitative data or, rather, carry out an investigation that involves analyzing quantitative data. Another way of thinking about the nature of bilingual phenomena is to identify an interest in the bilingual mind, or in power and multilingual language practices in a given context, or even in some aspect related to the acquisition of a third language. These are all very broad themes that entail particular perspectives, which usually have an established history in the field. Recognizing alternative ontological perspectives that tell different stories about bilingual individuals or communities makes a researcher more aware of their own views and concerns.

2.3.2   *What represents knowledge for a particular type of bilingual phenomenon?*

The second question to be addressed is: What represents knowledge for a broad theme or area of interest? Suppose that one is interested in investigating language, social inequality, and power in a bilingual context. The first thing to decide is what would constitute knowledge about this theme in the social world. The researcher could also ask what kind of evidence is needed to support claims or knowledge about this theme. Asking these questions forces a researcher to work out whether her or his interest is more closely connected to ethnographic or qualitative research methods, in which knowledge is that which is observed and recorded by the researcher. Evidence for deciding this comes from various sorts of data, and the methods used to collect them (oral and written language practices, interviews, documents, and observations). It is important for the researcher to be able to relate questions about what sort of bilingual phenomena they prefer (ontology) to a clear idea of what sort of knowledge is important or relevant to investigate, and to what one will need to do in the research process to demonstrate that knowledge. Inconsistencies between what constitutes knowledge about a certain theme and what sort of evidence is needed should be dealt with at an early stage. A person's understanding of knowledge about a theme goes with the realization that there are other approaches to studying bilingualism.

2.3.3 *What is the specific topic and intellectual puzzle?*

A third question requires the researcher to narrow down a broad theme of research to a specific topic, and to think about how their research is going to contribute new knowledge. As Mason (1996/2002: 14) stresses, researchers must discover the *intellectual puzzle* that will motivate them to seek an answer. At this point in the research process, one must be familiar with what has been written in the particular area of inquiry in order to establish how the question or puzzle formulated will make a theoretical or empirical contribution to knowledge. For example, Kroll, Gerfen, & Dussias (chapter 7 in this volume) are concerned with several disciplinary puzzles that require different sorts of explanations. Some examples of the research puzzles they pose are: How is speech produced with or without a foreign accent? How are sentences produced and comprehended when the grammar of the two languages is similar in some ways but different in others? What can bilinguals tell us about cognition? These puzzles are associated with a broader theme, namely, how bilinguals manage the presence and the interaction of two languages in the brain. More specific research questions that stem from this interest are: (1) How do bilinguals recognize words when they are spoken or read in each language? (2) How are the sounds of each of the bilingual's two languages processed when they are heard or spoken? and (3) How are the grammatical structures and preferences associated with each of the bilingual's languages affected by the presence of both languages? The ultimate goal of these researchers is to explain the way two languages coexist in our mind, and what the consequences are for the way the mind is organized and for bilingual language production and comprehension.

2.3.4 *What is the purpose of undertaking this research project?*

The fourth question asks about the purpose of the research you choose to do. The main reason people usually give for undertaking a research project is to make a contribution to our knowledge about a given topic. In other cases research has an applied and practical outcome. It is important to know how what you are doing advances knowledge on a particular topic. One must also recognize the sociopolitical context, and whose professional and academic interests are being served by one's research. There may be more mundane reasons for doing a particular sort of research, such as an institutional research call for developing a specific theme. Therefore, it may be necessary to relate one's project to a specific topic, which has been given priority by a funding body. Whatever the case, the motives for doing research are closely connected to the results and consequences they have for society and the participants involved.

2.3.5   *What ethical considerations should be taken into account?*

Ethics is the last but not the least important consideration to take into account. Research on bi/multilingualism is concerned with collecting data from people and this inevitably raises questions about how researchers should treat their subjects, respondents, participants, and interviewees (Oliver, 2003). There are also ethical requirements concerning research with institutions or other sites that are studied and which may wish to maintain a certain anonymity. Most professional associations have a code of ethics for their members. Ethics committees from universities and other research institutions are responsible for granting approval and advising members of the research community on how to comply with the ethical standards of their institution. Anyone who undertakes research, however, should be committed to an ethical protocol that guarantees that their research will not harm their participants in any way. Confidentiality, and respect for an informant's privacy, must be maintained at all times. Unless a participant has formally waived the right to anonymity, all information that can be used to identify that person must be omitted. Participants should be volunteers who have been explicitly informed beforehand about the study. Informed consent from subjects or participants is a basic research requirement, and researchers should disclose their identity and affiliations as well as the source of their funding. It should be made clear at the start of the project that a participant is free to withdraw at any point.

2.4   Linking Research Questions, Theory, Method, and Data

It is helpful to view research as an ongoing and dynamic process that involves a series of activities that do not necessarily have to follow a step-by-step order. From the start of a project, a researcher should be constantly evaluating the link between the theoretical framework, the research questions, the methods for data collection, the analysis as well as the best way to present and argue for the results. Implicit in the choice of a bilingual language phenomenon to investigate is a given research tradition that relies on an established understanding of what constitutes knowledge, along with the research tools and the forms of data that can be used as evidence. Familiarity with these traditions and how research is conducted within them is part of the way to understand the link that exists between questions, theory, methods, and data. Another way this connection is made is in the actual practice of doing research. Figure 2.1 shows the central activities present in all research. Each element in the figure is related to a different task or activity that is further discussed below. The process of doing research can sometimes be ridden with difficulties related to data collection, to finding a representative sample of participants, or just to understanding certain puzzling results. These issues are normal but they require flexibility

Melissa G. Moyer

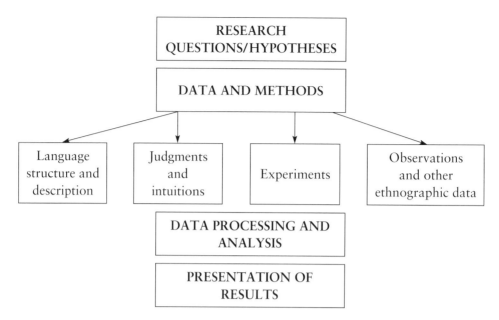

Figure 2.1: Basic research tasks

throughout the duration of the research activity. Moving back and forth to different research activities is a desirable practice and it should not surprise anyone that if, for example, a certain sample of subjects could not be found, one will need to reevaluate the initial premises of the project or even reformulate a hypothesis or a research question.

2.4.1 Choosing a topic

Research on multilingualism can focus on the individual or the group. There are many interesting topics in which the individual is the object of study; generalizations about bi/multilingual human beings can be made on the basis of the study of a single person. Experimental research to learn about how the human brain stores the words from two languages or how a bilingual produces or perceives the sounds, words, and sentences of different languages requires few subjects. Studies of grammatical constraints on the mixing of two languages in a sentence can also be carried out with data produced by a few individuals. The search for universal properties of the human brain or a person's bilingual linguistic competence can be explored with a single representative (see Kroll, Gerfen, & Dussias, chapter 7 in this volume). From a different theoretical stance, it is possible to study individual life narratives in order to gain an understanding of the way bilingual and bicultural people make sense of and construct their experience of two societies with different language, cultural, and thought patterns (see Pavlenko, chapter 18 in this volume). The individual in this type of research provides knowledge about the culture patterns of a society at large.

Topics that center on groups of people often seek to characterize a particular bi/multilingual community, a given site such as a school or other public institution, or a network of bilingual speakers (see Xu, Wang, & Li, chapter 15 in this volume). A given activity or community of practice focuses on the way bilingualism is practiced when a specific activity is performed. Studies of groups and communities can be undertaken with a quantitative or qualitative research design (see Hua & David, chapter 6 in this volume). The methodological conventions and the data to be collected are different in each case, but they can be complementary. Quantitative research is concerned with the collection and analysis of data in numeric form. This may seem more objective or empirical but, although the classification of persons or objects into a fixed set of categories is a useful way to understand reality, at the same time it is a subjective process carried out by the researcher. Quantitative studies also generally rely on large-scale representative samples of data that are processed statistically. This approach to research generally requires that the dependent and independent variables of the study be defined.[1]

Quantitative research can also be used in laboratory experiments and approaches where the individual is the object of inquiry. Studies carried out with this technique are concerned with determining cause and effect. The statistical tests applied seek to establish the cause–effect relationship between the independent variable (the one the researcher manipulates under controlled conditions) and the dependent variables (the ones that are measured for changes).

Qualitative research is concerned with gathering and analyzing all sorts of data that are informative. Observational data, documents, interviews, language interactions, and even numerical data are typical data types. (For further information on different approaches that use a qualitative frame see chapters 13, 17, and 20 in this volume.) In this perspective nothing is taken as predefined. Context is central to qualitative work, and experience is treated as a whole rather than as a set of separate variables. The aim of this approach is not only to understand experience from the point of view of the members of the group, but also to adopt a theoretical framework that provides an explanation of localized practices in a wider societal context. A qualitative approach assumes fieldwork, and a preference for ongoing language choice practices and naturally occurring data.

Your preference for investigating either individual bilingual language production or group multilingual linguistic practices, along with the resources available to you or the skills you have acquired, will undoubtedly influence in a broad sense your topic of research. If you are shy and do not like talking to people, you should consider whether qualitative research involving fieldwork is a good choice. The area of research you choose should take into account your interests as well as your skills. It is helpful to think about additional research topics beforehand in case, when you start investigating, your initial ideas turn out to be impracticable. Furthermore, you should be flexible and prepared to change direction or reassess your research at any point.

---

[1] A variable can be defined as an attribute of a person or a category, which varies from person to person or from category to category. For example, in a study of language choice in relation to topic of conversation, language choice would be the dependent variable, which is affected by the causal or independent variable, that is, the topic.

2.4.2   Questions and hypotheses

A hypothesis or a set of research questions arises from the earlier choice of a topic or an area of interest to pursue for a project. There are many ways to ask questions, and many systematic ways of answering them. Familiarity with the different method options will enable you to choose the best and the shortest way to find answers. One of the guarantees of success when beginning to design research is to narrow down the topic to a few discrete questions. It is alright to start out by asking who? what? when? where? and why? in relation to your research topic. Such basic questions direct you in the critical reading of the literature related to your topic and also help you to identify what questions have not yet been adequately answered in the field. The role of reading is crucial at all points of your research but at different stages you will be asking different questions about what you are reading. Reading and guidance from an experienced investigator – especially when embarking on research for the first time – are basic for deciding what questions are interesting and which ones will make a new and original contribution to the field. Research questions in qualitative approaches are not always generated at the beginning of a research project but sometimes after fieldwork experience and the collection of some preliminary data. Once a general research question has been identified – at whatever point in the first stages of the research process – you must narrow it down.

2.4.3   Theory and methods

The methods described in the present volume for gathering bilingual data belong to different epistemological perspectives regarding what constitutes knowledge in the field. Each research method or technique is presented separately as if its single application were sufficient for investigating a particular research topic (Wray, Trott, & Bloomer, 1998). In fact, in the field of bilingualism, a combination of methods may be most appropriate, because a bilingual system is not so neatly defined as the language system of monolingual speakers. The use of statistics to determine which structures should be selected for undertaking further linguistic analysis makes grammatical theorizing more reliable than the linguistic judgments of a sole speaker.

   Theory may be a starting point for generating a set of hypotheses or research questions in formal and experimental approaches to bilingualism. The intent of a researcher working from this perspective is to test a theory and to discard it if it is not supported by the results of an experiment or by intuitions and judgments. This is a *hypothetico-deductive* way of working, where a hypothesis that is intended to explain a particular bilingual phenomenon is either supported or discarded. From a hypothesis, a sufficient number of explicit predictions of further phenomena can be deduced, and they should be observable as a consequence of the hypothesis. A researcher always has a theoretical stance or orientation to their work, whether or not they are conscious of it at the start. Preconceived theoretical positions are made more or less explicit at the start, but the point is to understand what they are. In spite of this prior positioning, there is another way of incorporating theory into research, which is known as *theory building*. The conclusions of qualitative research can become the basis for formulating a set of hypotheses that is used to develop theory (Sarangi, 2001; Sarangi & Candlin, 2001). This way of proceeding from a limited set of observations and facts to a general law or principle is known as the *inductive method*. It is a process of reasoning in which the premises of an argument support a conclusion, but do not ensure it. No matter whether you choose to do experiments in a laboratory or ethnographic work in the field, a theory is needed in order to make sense of the findings and to give a coherent account of what has been observed. A model or theory is often implicit in the choice of research topic; it must be taken into account when narrowing the research question down or setting up the hypotheses. Sometimes when deciding on a topic you are not aware of the fact that you are already choosing (to a greater or lesser extent) a theory. This is why it is important to have guidance from someone who is familiar with the field of bilingualism.

2.4.4 Data

Data are the predicted outcome of applying a research method or technique that was carefully selected at the research design stage. Data generated in the study of bilingualism are not limited to the representation of two or more languages. Quantification (a person's performance results in an experiment), images (neural imaging, gaze, and gestures), and written texts (describing observations of linguistic practices) are other forms of data that represent additional ways of expressing relevant information about bilinguals. Before the data can be analyzed, they need to be processed and organized in such a way that patterns of regularity can be observed, measured, and represented. A further consideration about bilingual language data is their spatio-temporal context. All language is produced at a given time and in a given context and recognition of these dimensions is relevant for language contact and change and for bilingual language acquisition. A linguistic structure that is identified in a bilingual corpus can represent different levels of abstraction. It can be a datum that serves to make claims about the interaction of two languages in the mind or it may simply be an observable descriptive fact. A researcher should decide early on whether to concentrate on one or on several specific aspects of the language (phonetics/phonology, morphology, syntax, conversation, semantics, pragmatics) she or he wishes to study.

Data collection should be carefully planned. A key consideration in this activity is the selection and sampling of the participants or of the data sources – documents, settings, or different contexts. Careful thought needs to be given to choosing data sources that are representative of the wider universe one is investigating. The process of answering a question in a systematic and rigorous way requires that certain conventions be followed, with the aim of reaching an answer or obtaining results that are generalizable, reliable, and valid. These three measures relate to the quality of an investigation. They should be explicitly dealt with at the beginning of the research enterprise, because they could influence decisions taken during the research process.

Whether you carry out an ethnographic study or a laboratory experiment, your findings need to be applicable beyond the immediate focus of the study. It is important to know whether the site, the group, or the individual you study has relevance for other individuals, institutions, groups, or social processes in the world. In other words, it is important to establish whether your sample is representative of or *generalizable* for all members of the group under study.

For the results or findings to be *reliable*, it is necessary to have followed the appropriate research conventions of the linguistic perspective you have chosen to follow. The interpretation of the results may differ according to the theoretical framework used, but the findings should be the same if the study is replicated in the same setting or under the same experimental conditions.

The *validity* of a study refers to the correct application of research conventions (i.e., methods, approaches, and techniques) to address the questions or issues you set out to study. For research to be valid, it must observe, identify, and measure what it claims to. *Validation* is a process of gathering evidence and constructing theoretical arguments to support the results and their interpretation. It is related to the operationalization of concepts, and a researcher must establish how well a particular method and data shed light on the concepts selected.

2.4.5   *Processing data and analysis*

Once data are obtained they need to be *organized* and *processed* in some fashion before an analysis can be undertaken. Processing data for analysis is a good way to become familiar with what you have. It is always good for the analyst to take part in the collection, transcription, coding, and identification of the bilingual phenomena to be studied. In cases where data come from several sources (interviews, documents, field notes, audio and video recordings) it is helpful to have an easy and systematic way to access this information. A thoughtful classification may involve a system of coding, such as that used for analyzing a specific structure that appears in a given context in a bilingual corpus (see Backus, chapter 13 in this volume). If data are documents, field notes, or written descriptions it will help to select those pieces of text that provide evidence for your claims and to highlight them with a color scheme. A detailed discussion of transcription is presented by Turell and Moyer (chapter 11 in this volume). Organizing data is not a neutral process rather it involves the task of categorizing and assigning meaning. It is crucial for a researcher to be aware of the criteria used for classifying and labeling their data, since this organization is the basis upon which analytical claims and evidence for a claim are made (Sarangi, 1987). Quantification using statistical tests is another way to process data from experimental and variationist paradigms and organize the results. Analysis can proceed once the data have been organized. This stage in the research process is concerned with searching for an explanation. An analysis brings in the theoretical framework and concepts that have guided the project to account for the findings. This is the point at which the uniqueness of one's data can be highlighted. It is also the point at which both theoretical and conceptual innovations can be brought in to explain the results and formulate new research questions.

2.4.6   *Presentation of results*

The manner in which the *results* of an investigation are *presented* will depend on the researcher's purpose for undertaking a research project in the first place. Research that is meant to fulfill academic requirements for a degree will require much more detail about methods and literature review, for example, than a presentation for a professional conference or a peer-reviewed journal. In the latter case, the researcher will need to be able to extract the key points of their theoretical assumptions, the methods adopted, and the results and their interpretation. This requires the analytical skills discussed throughout the chapter. Research is a contribution to knowledge and it is the responsibility of researchers and funding institutions to make their contribution known. See chapters 20 and 21 in this volume for further information on resources and advice on how to present research results.

2.5   A Summary of Research as an Ongoing Process

Research is an activity in which the researcher is positioned in a specific disciplinary and methodological tradition by the very nature of the topic and the research questions posed. It is important to be aware of the position one holds and how it is different from other ways of approaching the study of bi/multilingualism. All research implies taking a critical and analytical stance that involves engaging in an activity of reflection and evaluation of your research as you proceed through each task.

An understanding of the various kinds of knowledge (epistemology) about bilingualism and what counts as data or evidence to support a particular field of knowledge (ontology) is a first step towards situating the research one does in the appropriate context. Different types of knowledge about bilingualism rely on different conceptions of language, discussed at length in section 2.2. Critical and analytical thinking is a skill that can be learned by trying to respond to a set of key questions that relate to both the object and the content of a project. While full answers to these questions may not become clear until a project has been completed, reflection and an initial attempt to answer them are still valuable. Section 2.3, on the *ins and outs* of research, includes a discussion of some of the basic considerations and tasks that are involved in the research endeavor. Certain elements are present in all research projects, and in a sense these must follow a particular order, but other research activities such as formulating research questions, hypotheses, making the appropriate methodological choices, writing, data processing, and data collection can be developed and worked on throughout the process of doing research. The consistency of a research project refers to how well the research questions are linked to the theoretical framework, the methods, and what gets counted as data or evidence. The theory, the method, and the data are not disconnected choices; rather, they are related to the topic and the research questions established from the start of a project. It is for this reason that familiarity with the research traditions in bilingualism is of key importance.

Part II Procedures, Methods, and Tools

3   Types and Sources of Bilingual Data

Jacomine Nortier

3.1   Introduction

This chapter would not have been written if the situation were as follows:

> In an English-speaking country, two students of bilingualism, native speakers of English, want to collect English-Arabic code-switching data, so they go out on the streets, one carrying a tape recorder and the other having a questionnaire. They randomly ask passers-by whether they are English-Arabic bilinguals; if they are, they ask them whether they want to say a few things using bilingual sentences. Satisfied, the students return home after a few hours of hard work, with tapes stuffed with useful material waiting to be analyzed.

Unfortunately, the situation described above does not exist. Collecting bilingual data is not an easy task. People might not switch codes in front of a microphone, or in front of a stranger. Careful preparation is needed before code-switching data can be recorded. It takes much work, but it can be done (see Clemente, chapter 10 in this volume). The following sections present information about collecting bilingual language data. By the end, any serious student of bilingualism should be able to collect code-switching data (see Gardner-Chloros, chapter 4 in this volume).

The key question in this chapter is: What research or theoretical questions can be addressed with which type of data? This question already implies that there are different types of data which can be used for different purposes. It will become clear that each type of data collection has its advantages and its disadvantages. Therefore, students of bilingualism need to decide before they start what questions they want to answer and what type of data will be most helpful for their purposes (see Moyer, chapter 2 in this volume). This chapter may help in making such choices.

In general, there is not one single best way of collecting data. A combination of two or more data collection methods will give the finest results. The pros and cons of each method have to be weighed carefully.

The following sections discuss a series of frequently used methods of data collection. In the first stage of a study on bilingualism it is necessary to get a clear picture of the people and situations involved in bilingual behavior. Therefore, the next three sections concentrate on three ways of developing such a picture: censuses and sample surveys on the macro-level (3.2), questionnaires on the meso-level (3.3), and observations on the micro-level (3.4). An additional method used to find out about speakers' attitudes is the matched-guise test, discussed in 3.5. The following sections are dedicated to the collection of linguistic data. This can be done through the analysis of spontaneous or semi-spontaneous conversations (3.6) or through elicited data obtained in experimental settings (3.7). Finally, we will take a look at written sources (3.8).

The types of sources described in this chapter are by no means discrete. On the contrary, it will become clear that there is quite some overlap. They are not mutually exclusive, but supplementary in relation to each other. The best results are obtained by combining different methods.

3.2   Census and Sample Surveys

A census is an enumeration of all the members of a specific population, as for example in Wales, where all inhabitants of the country were questioned about a range of topics, varying from age, education, and health to linguistic proficiency and housing.[1] Another census is carried out yearly by the Department of Education of the state of California, of all students with non-English-speaking backgrounds.[2] They are questioned about matters such as their mother tongue and their proficiency in English.

While a census includes the whole population, a sample survey is a study carried out on a part of the population. This part is supposed to be representative of the whole. In the social sciences, a survey is more or less equivalent to a study, but in practice the term survey is used to describe a large-scale study with quantitative measurements (see Lanza, chapter 5 in this volume).

In many instances, a census is not taken only for the purpose of finding linguistic information, but serves a much broader purpose. Questions relevant to language can be extracted from the total set. If you want to study bilingual behavior, census data will certainly be helpful in making a first selection between possible informants. When people are asked what languages[3] they speak, they can be divided into groups of bilinguals, and you can concentrate your study on a particular group.

In a census or a large-sample survey, data from a large group of informants are collected, usually with the help of standardized written questionnaires. Of course, when you want to study aspects of the behavior of thousands of people, it is not practical to use individual answers to open questions; you need to let the computer do the reading work. This means multiple-choice questions, yes/no questions, or five- or seven-point scales. It would be great if people could be asked about their

---

[1]   www.statistics.gov.uk/census2001/default.asp.
[2]   www.cde.ca.gov/ds/sd/lc/.
[3]   Whenever the word *language* is used, *dialect* is meant as well.

bilingual behavior in a census or a sample survey, but probably the answers would reflect their attitudes rather than their behavior. When the prevailing attitude towards certain behavior is negative, people tend to underreport that type of behavior. When the attitude is positive, respondents will overreport. For example, in a survey study carried out in a multilingual neighborhood in the city of Utrecht (The Netherlands), a woman born in Morocco was asked (in Dutch) what language she spoke at home. She answered that she would never use any Moroccan (Arabic or Berber) at home, only Dutch. At that particular moment her daughter came in and the woman started to talk Arabic to her immediately, without realizing that she had just stated she would never talk that way at home with her children. The difference between reported and observed linguistic behavior, as illustrated in this example, shows that the norm is Dutch (at least in front of the interviewer), in her eyes the prestigious language.

The same mechanism is true for code-switching behavior. Attitudes towards code-switching are not always positive or neutral: the general opinion is that code-switching is a sign of a poor command of the languages involved, of disrespect towards languages, and of linguistic nonchalance. When bilinguals report that they never switch codes, the researcher should be aware of the possibility of a confusion of attitudes and actual behavior, in other words, between reported and observed linguistic behavior.

Apart from how many languages the informants have command of, more detailed information can be asked in a survey, e.g., with respect to the aspects of language (reading, writing, speaking, and listening). For code-switching research, the most important parts of language are speaking and listening. Reading and writing skills are less relevant, and sometimes completely irrelevant, since many languages and dialects, like Berber, do not have a (standard) written form.

Questions about the degree to which a language is mastered can be asked in a survey. Although standardized grammatical tests would give a more precise and trustworthy indication of linguistic proficiency, there are aspects that are not measured in such tests, such as familiarity with and experience of language use. Besides, speakers can be quite proficient without knowing and applying all grammatical rules perfectly. Poplack, Sankoff, and Miller (1988) used self-report as the main method of determining the linguistic proficiency of their informants. A question like "How proficient are you in Language X?" can safely be asked and used in an analysis. Usually, however, this method is combined with other methods of determining linguistic proficiency. Poplack (1980) and Berk-Seligson (1986) both determined linguistic proficiency on the basis of a combination of self-report and analysis of their speakers' sociolinguistic background. Nortier (1990) used both methods, and as a third method native speakers in the informants' original countries were asked to judge tape-recorded fragments. The results of these different methods showed high correlations.

According to some researchers (e.g., Poplack, 1980), bilinguals have to be balanced and highly proficient in both languages in order to switch effectively. For others, like Myers-Scotton (1993b), proficiency in L2 need not be very high and there is no clear level of proficiency in each language that a speaker must have in order to code-switch effectively. If we take a look at bilingualism worldwide, we see that in most bilingual communities there is an unequal division between the languages involved. Perfect balanced bilingualism is an exception to the rule of unbalanced bilingualism, both on the individual and on the societal level. If we believe Myers-Scotton, this means that, even if one were able to determine bilingual proficiency on the basis of a sample survey, it would not predict the (non-)occurrence of code-switching.

It should be clear that the methods discussed in this section show quite some overlap: in both censuses and sample surveys large numbers of informants may be involved, and both are analyzed quantitatively. In many studies, it is not necessary to carry out both a census and a sample survey. Findings from other studies may serve as a starting point. Usually, national and local governments have statistical resources that can be very useful. For example, when we began our earlier-mentioned project on the mixing of languages and cultures in a multilingual and multicultural neighborhood in Utrecht, we knew from the local statistics that one particular area called Lombok met the conditions we had set, which made the choice easier.

In summary, surveys can give information about the scale on which certain languages are spoken, and to a certain degree about proficiency in the languages involved, on the condition that it is combined with other methods of determining linguistic proficiency. Surveys are not very reliable as a means of detecting code-switching behavior, but they can be very useful on the preparatory level.

Section summary: Censuses and sample surveys

- Some overlap
- Census: whole population
- Sample survey: representative part of the population
- Helpful in the selection of informants
- Quantitative analyses
- May help to determine linguistic proficiency
- Not for measuring attitudes

3.3   Questionnaires

The previous section focused on censuses and surveys, i.e., the groups questioned, and also on questions to be asked in such studies. In this section the focus will be exclusively on the questions (see Codó, chapter 9 in this volume).

A sociolinguistic profile of the informants, based on a questionnaire, is necessary to predict bilingual behavior, or to exclude certain informants from participation. But a sociolinguistic profile is also helpful in explaining bilingual language behavior post hoc. One of the most important reasons for asking questions about the sociolinguistic background is to find out how proficient bilinguals are in both languages, whether one of the languages is dominant, and what the language preferences are. To find out about this, four types of questions can be asked.

1 *Language history*: for example, how and at what age the languages were acquired or learned. Speakers are likely to have a very good command of languages acquired in early childhood and used ever after. When a language was learned at a later age, by formal instruction, the command may be much lower.
2 *Language choice*: questions concerned with language choice, associated with interlocutor, topic, physical environment, or formality. For example, speakers may choose to speak one language with their parents and older siblings, and another with friends, colleagues, and younger siblings. Within a school or work environment speakers may choose to use a language that is different from the one they use at home or in a family environment. This is related to formality: in court or in a church or mosque, the preferred languages may be different from the languages used in a pub or a swimming pool.
3 *Language dominance*: questions concerning what language they are most proficient in. Speakers are very reliable when they are asked this, but in case the researcher wants an extra check, control questions can be asked. Examples are: What language do you use when you write in your diary? What language do you use when you write shopping lists? What language do you use when you talk to your pet rabbit/cat/dog/horse? What language do you use for swearing, cursing, other emotional outbursts? And you can ask your informant to calculate a complicated addition in his or her head, something like 586 + 961. He or she will probably mumble the numbers before giving you the final answer (1,547). The language that is used in all the answers (including the mumbling) will probably be the dominant language.
4 *Language attitudes*: questions concerning the values speakers attach to various languages. It was illustrated in the previous section that reported and observed behaviors are not necessarily the same. In a questionnaire, of course, only reported behavior can be investigated. Speakers can be asked about what language they prefer to speak, and what language they consider (not) to be beautiful or useful. Questions about attitudes, and whether languages are associated with friendship and solidarity on the one hand, or power and distance on the other hand, should not be asked only in a direct way ("What is your attitude towards . . . ?"), since there is a fair chance that answers will not be reliable. Rather, a matched-guise test should be used as well, or instead. Further discussions are found in section 3.5.

The four categories of questions can be asked and answered in both written and oral form. The advantage of oral questionnaires is that possible reading and writing difficulties do not interfere with what the respondents want to say. When the answer deviates from the type of thing the researcher was expecting, he or she can ask for clarification. The advantage of written questionnaires, on the other hand, is their relative anonymity, particularly with respect to the fourth category. Informants may feel more free when they are not talking in front of an interviewer who they may want to please with socially desirable answers.

The language of the questionnaire should be one that informants are very familiar with. But since languages may not have a written form, this is not always a realistic option. In practice, it is not possible to prescribe in what language the questions should be asked, and answered. Sometimes the use of both languages will be more convenient. In the research that Treffers-Daller (1991) reported on in her PhD thesis on code-switching between French and Brussels Flemish, the informants could choose a French or a Dutch version of the questionnaire. In E-Rramdani (2003) an oral questionnaire was presented to bilingual Moroccans in the Netherlands. The informants could choose between Berber, Moroccan Arabic, and Dutch.

Section summary: Questionnaires

- To make sociolinguistic profiles
- To explain and sometimes also to predict bilingual behavior
- Four types of questions: history, choice, dominance, attitudes
- Oral and written

3.4   Observations

It sounds so simple: look at what people do and how they behave; observe them and you will see how they function as individuals, or in a group. But of course, it is more complex than that. Imagine a stranger watching and taking notes while you and your best friends are chatting during a coffee break. With an outsider present, your chat would not be natural anymore. You would avoid topics that you usually would discuss, and if you knew the observer was a linguist you might speak with great care and mind your language. (Observations are a main feature in ethnographic fieldwork: see Heller, chapter 14 in this volume.)

It would be different if you knew the observer and, even better, if she or he was a member of your peer group at that particular moment. And that is exactly what observers try to do if they want to avoid the so-called observers' paradox. Instead of looking into a group from the outside, an observer should try to look from the inside, as a group member. This is called participant observation. The advantage is clear: the people who are observed behave more naturally if the observant is an insider. At the same time, the disadvantage is clear too: it takes precious time and energy to become a participant observer. Besides, it is not always possible to become a participant observer. In my study on code-switching between Dutch and Moroccan Arabic among young Moroccans in the Netherlands I knew that I, as a Dutch female, would never be able to become an insider in a group of young Moroccan men. Fortunately, we were able to recruit a Moroccan man to take over the task of observing and collecting data. It turned out that he was accepted as a participant observer (see Nortier, 1990).

The study on which Joshua Fishman and his colleagues based their famous book *Bilingualism in the Barrio* was also carried out by using participant observation techniques. The researchers studying bilingualism in a Puerto Rican- and English-speaking community became (temporary) members of the neighborhood they were studying. They went to weddings and funerals, sat outside on the streets with the people, and looked after their children, and thus had a perfect opportunity to study the community and its linguistic behavior from the inside (Fishman, Cooper, Ma, et al., 1971).

Observations can help in selecting and understanding the context in which bilingual behavior is taking place. By observing, you can decide whether a particular group and situation are suitable for your purposes. As long as it is not possible to predict exactly in what situations code-switching will occur, it will be necessary to make careful observations. A group of second-generation Moroccan school kids in a Dutch playground will probably use more Dutch than a group of first-generation Moroccan men gathering in the mosque before their weekly prayers on Friday. But their choice for code-switching will depend on other factors that cannot easily be controlled.

Not only whether or not bilinguals will switch codes, but also the type of code-switching that can be expected, depends on factors that cannot easily be manipulated. What types of code-switching can be distinguished? Code-switching may be intra-, inter-, or extrasentential. According to Poplack (1980), switching within sentences (intrasentential code-switching) will occur primarily in the speech of balanced bilinguals, since a high command of both languages is required in order to mix the two lexicons and grammars involved (cf. section 3.2). An example of intrasentential code-switching between Swahili and English is given in (1), taken from Myers-Scotton (1993b; Swahili in italics):

(1) . . . *Ni-ka-maliza* all the clothing.
    ". . . And I've finished [washing] all the clothing."

Backus (1996), however, found that the balanced bilinguals in his corpus of Dutch/Turkish material prefer to switch intersententially (between sentences). The paradoxical findings from Poplack and Backus show that it is impossible to predict the type of code-switching that will occur. Other factors like societal dominance patterns and conventionalization of code-switching habits within a speech community may play important roles (Nortier, 1995). Again, all factors being equal, one group may use predominantly intrasentential code-switching, while the other group switches intersententially. An example of intersentential code-switching is given in (2). The languages involved are Spanish and French (Ramat, 1995; Spanish in italics)

(2) *Yo mañana empiezo, me levanto a las siete de la mañana.* Je suis malade rien que de le savoir.
    "Tomorrow, I start work, I've got to get up at 7 o'clock. I feel sick just thinking about it."

Extrasentential switching, the third type of code-switching, occurs in all sorts of bilingual conversation and is not restricted to speakers with high or low bilingual proficiency. Unbalanced bilinguals with only a very poor command of one of the languages are able to switch extrasententially.

This type of switching takes place outside the grammatical scope of the sentence, as illustrated in (3), taken from Nortier (1990, on code-switching between Dutch and Moroccan Arabic; Moroccan Arabic in italics):

(3)   Maar de tijd die gaat toch voorbij, *fhemti*?
      "But the time goes by, you understand?"

A special type of observation is the language diary. With this method, informants are asked to keep a diary with respect to the languages they use. Questions that can be answered with the help of these diaries are: In what circumstances is what language used? With what speech partners? About what topics? How frequently and for how long? Language diaries are, of course, highly subjective, and there is little possibility for the researcher to check the information. Besides, they put quite a strain on the informants, who have to be alert. Those who are interested can read more about language diaries in Romaine (1983). Zekhnini, who studied Moroccans' acquisition of Dutch outside the classroom, used "language contact charts" in which informants filled in data about their language use in daily life during a period of five days. Each informant had to fill in three different charts: one for oral interactions in Dutch, one for audiovisual encounters with Dutch, and one for use of the written form of Dutch (Zekhnini, 2001).

Large-sample quantitative surveys and questionnaires are helpful in selecting informants who will provide bilingual data. On a smaller and much more detailed scale, observations may help to select the right informants in a qualitative way.

Section summary: Observations

- Participant observation
- Observers' paradox
- Selection of informants
- Types of code-switching

3.5   Matched-Guise Tests

Researchers who want to know more about attitudes towards two varieties in relation to each other can make use of so-called matched-guise tests.

In such tests speech samples in two (or more) varieties from one and the same speaker are taped, so that all person-related variation is excluded. Informants have to judge the samples. When a distracter is used between the samples, the fact that one person is responsible for both samples is not recognized. One of the earliest and best-known uses of this method was conducted by Lambert (1967). In his matched-guise test he collected information about the informants' attitudes by asking questions about the speakers' integrity, attractiveness, intelligence, kindness, sense of humor, dependability, ambition, leadership qualities, and sincerity. Usually informants have to give their reactions on a five-point scale to statements like "This person is friendly." Scores would vary from 1 (totally agree) to 5 (totally disagree). Although personal comments in replies to open questions would be very useful, the problem with open questions is that the answers are hard to quantify.

Lambert found through this matched-guise test that French-speaking Canadians (in 1967) had a poor impression of themselves as compared to English-speaking Canadians, and men even more than women.

The matched-guise test shows how important it is for a bilingual to choose the appropriate code. People have different judgments about various codes, accents, languages, or dialects, ranging from "beautiful" to "ugly" or even "unacceptable." An illustration is provided by a 17-year-old Moroccan woman living in the Netherlands, explaining why some Dutch, Moroccan, and Turkish youngsters would prefer a Moroccan accent in their Dutch:

(4) Het is algemeen bekend dat Marokkanen een beetje leuk, ja, een beetje leuk accent hebben.
     "It is generally known that Moroccans have a rather charming, yes, a rather charming accent."

Examples of studies in which matched-guise tests have been used are Doeleman (1998) and Ryan (1979), which distinguished status and solidarity factors. More about matched-guise tests, including criticisms, can be found at http://www6.gencat. net/llengcat/noves/hm02estiu/metodologia/a_solis2_5.htm.

Now the question of what exactly you want to study is important: if you want to know in what contexts code-switching occurs, (participant) observation is a powerful instrument. Are you interested in linguistic data? In that case, observations cannot provide you with what you are looking for. But observations will help you to find the context data that you need as a starting point for your data collection.

Section summary: Matched-guise tests

- One person: two varieties (guises)
- Informants give scores on questions about the varieties
- Languages/varieties/accents are judged in different ways

3.6 Spontaneous and Semi-Spontaneous Conversations

The great majority of code-switching studies are based on the analysis of language use in spontaneous conversations, and for very good reasons: code-switching is a phenomenon occurring in natural circumstances and the most natural linguistic circumstance is the conversation. The more participants concentrate on the content instead of on the form of what they are saying, the more informal their conversation will be. To achieve this, people have to be at ease, and should be familiar with each other and with each other's linguistic behavior. Recorded conversations provide information about individual code-switching behavior, and the ways participants react to each other's language use and choice.

The presence of a researcher during such conversations can make the situation less spontaneous, if she or he is an outsider. This can be avoided by asking one of the participants to take care of the recordings. Usually this is a very reliable method. Although people might focus on the tape recorder in the beginning, most linguists studying code-switching find that after the first 10–20 minutes, the presence of the tape recorder is not a disturbing factor anymore, since people get used to it.

The advantages of recording spontaneous conversations without a researcher present are obvious. It is the most natural type of language use one can think of, not biased by the informants' beliefs about what the researcher wants. But there are disadvantages as well: the recording, transcription, and analysis of natural conversations are time-consuming. Not every student of bilingualism has so much time. But if the time is available, it is the best way of getting acquainted with a dataset through and through. Working with one's own data takes a lot of time, but it is more fun than working with data collected by someone else. Research without personal involvement is poor research!

Another problem might be that usually the informants are not aware that it is bilingual language use the researcher is looking for. There is a risk that no code-switching will occur at all. With a researcher present, there is a possibility of directing the conversation to topics that trigger code-switching, but then of course the conversations are not completely spontaneous anymore. But I do not see how that might affect the outcome negatively. On the basis of former observations, the researcher should know what conversational topics trigger most switching. In my own study on Dutch-Moroccan Arabic code-switching among Moroccans in the Netherlands, the recordings were made in the mid-1980s, by a Moroccan research assistant. He knew that if he let the participants talk about topics like discrimination, sports, or holiday trips to Morocco, they would be carried away by the topic and the form of their language use would be less important to them.

Earlier, a study on the mixing of languages and cultures in a multicultural neighborhood was mentioned. This was carried out in the city of Utrecht between 1998 and 2001. In this study, spontaneous conversations in several groups of speakers, varying from young Turkish and Moroccan children to elderly Dutch people, were triggered with the help of a book with pictures. The subjects of the pictures varied from famous football players to Saint Nicholas (Santa Claus) and a Christmas tree. The purpose of these conversations was not always to collect code-switching data. Topics like language shift and loss were also studied, along with various cultural topics. The main purpose of the picture book was to avoid long silences, and it turned out to be a very helpful instrument which any student of bilingualism can easily adapt to his or her own purposes.

Another solution to the problem of long silences is to confront the informants with provocative statements. The content of the statements would depend on the informants, their backgrounds, and their interests. The more the informants are involved in the topic, the more strongly they will react and the more attention they will pay to the content rather than the form of their language.

Yet another way to make people talk informally is to ask them to watch television programmes together and give comments while watching. Again, one has to be sure that the informants are bilingual.

It is generally accepted by linguists studying code-switching that the informants should not be aware that it is code-switching the researcher is looking for. The idea behind this is that people who think about their language behavior and who switch languages deliberately, in order to please the researcher, might produce other types of code-switching than those who are fully unaware of the purpose of the study. I am not sure whether I agree with this point of view. In my experience, informants who are aware of the purpose of the study (i.e., collecting code-switching data) pay attention to the form of their language during the first 10–20 minutes of the conversation, but as they get carried away with the topics, they pay more attention to the content and stop checking the form of their utterances all the time.

This discussion is connected with an ethical question. Participating in a linguistic study takes time. Sometimes informants are paid, but it is always the researcher who asks informants to do them a favor, to cooperate. Therefore, informants have to be treated with respect. Is it ethically wise and sensible not to tell the informants in advance what the purpose of the study is? A solution often chosen is to tell the informants that the study is about certain attitudes (towards football, Islam, poverty, education, or whatever), which may indeed play a role on the sidelines. When informants are aware that language is involved, they may want to perform well. It is difficult to convince informants that they will not be judged, but that only their behavior will be studied. There are no strict rules about how to behave as a researcher. But whatever you do, respect the integrity of your informants!

To summarize, spontaneous and semi-spontaneous conversations are the best sources for code-switching research. Before recording a conversation, some preparatory work has to be done, for example by using the results of a survey study to select informants with the right linguistic background, and observations to select the right situations and conversational topics. Conversations can be recorded with or without a researcher present, and both forms have their own advantages and disadvantages.

A problem with spontaneous data not already mentioned is that not all possible kinds of code-switching will occur in the data. If you want to know, for example, whether code-switching occurs between subject and finite verb, and you cannot find any instances in the data, you will never know whether the informants avoid that type of switching on purpose or by accident. If they avoid such constructions on purpose, it may be the consequence of a grammatical constraint: code-switching between subject and finite verb is not allowed according to rule or constraint X. But if such a rule does not exist, the absence of the switch under consideration will be an accidental gap. The longer the recorded conversations are, the more chance there is that all possible constructions will eventually occur. But then the burden of making long, time-consuming transcriptions and analyses increases as well. There is no reasonable way to solve this problem when you collect data through spontaneous data exclusively. Therefore, complementary data are needed in the form of elicited data.

Section summary: Spontaneous and semi-spontaneous conversations

- Self-recording
- The more spontaneous, the more realistic, but the more time-consuming
- Ways to manipulate conversations: show pictures, introduce certain topics, watch TV together
- Informants' awareness of code-switching: does not always have to be avoided
- Non-occurrence of certain switches: on purpose or by accident?

3.7   Elicited Information in Experimental Settings

At first glance, elicited data seems to be the opposite of spontaneous data. But in fact they are at the extremes of a continuum. It has been shown that data obtained in spontaneous conversations are the most natural. The further one is from spontaneous data, the less natural the data will be, but the more time will be gained. Opting for the advantages at one end of the continuum means conceding some of the advantages at the other end. Figure 3.1 is a schematic representation of

Continuum for Data Collection

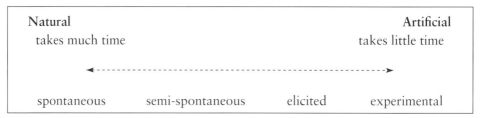

Figure 3.1: Continuum for data collection

the continuum. If it takes too long for certain constructions to occur, the researcher may want to turn to semi-spontaneous data by influencing or directing the topics of conversation. If the researcher wants to ensure that certain constructions occur, she or he can elicit them from the informants in an experimental setting, i.e., a setting in which relevant parts of reality are imitated. Experiments, of course, make the data even less spontaneous.

There are several ways to elicit monolingual data. One possibility is to ask informants to describe pictures, or to tell a story. For bilingual data this method is not necessarily successful, unless the informants are instructed to react bilingually. This, again, has its drawbacks, as was mentioned before.

Another method, which is more likely to be successful, is to ask informants to perform a sentence repetition task. In those sentences, the researcher may have hidden some code-switches that are supposed to occur in natural speech, but also switches that will not occur according to constraints that are tested. If, for example, the earlier-mentioned switch between a subject and a finite verb is not allowed according to constraint X, the expectation is that informants will find it difficult to produce that particular code-switch, even when repeating a sentence. The thought behind it is that speakers will not repeat what they hear parrot-fashion, but adapt the sentence to their own internal grammatical rules. In Lijmbach (1995), the researcher confronted Portuguese/Dutch bilingual children with bilingual sentences in which a code-switch between subject and final verb occurred (Portuguese in italics):

(5)   Het meisje *leva*   het boek *que é velho*.
     The girl   carries the book that is old

For the purpose of the current discussion, only the first code-switch in (5) is relevant.

Seven children (aged between 7 and 13) repeated the sentence. Three children switched from Dutch to Portuguese after the subject, as in the example. The other four children each chose to realize subject and finite verb in the same language, either Dutch (three times: 'Het meisje draagt . . .') or Portuguese (once: 'A menina leva . . .').

Repetition tasks are only useful when a lot of work has been done before: it must be clear what theory, hypothesis, or grammatical constraints are to be tested. And of course, the informants have to be familiar with bilingual language use, in order to have an internalized set of bilingual rules.

It should be clear from this chapter so far that the collection of bilingual data in experimental settings has major advantages, primarily the low cost in terms of time. Besides, researchers are less dependent on the informants' production and they are able to manipulate the data. Therefore, linguists have tried to create experimental settings where spontaneity is preserved as far as possible. In terms of the continuum in figure 3.1, attempts have been made to combine the advantages of both ends of the continuum.

In 2004, Ivana Brasileiro Reis Pereira, a PhD student at Utrecht University carried out a project in which the success of experiments designed to elicit code-switching was tested. This project was conducted at the Max Planck Institute in Nijmegen (Brasileiro Reis Pereira, 2004).

Although the experiment was the heart of the project, it was impossible to leave out other ways of data collection. First, Dutch/Papiamentu bilingual informants were selected on the basis of a sociolinguistic questionnaire. In the next stage, a more or less spontaneous conversation between four informants took place, about topics of their own choice. The last part of the project was a standardized L2 (Dutch) test. In between, there were three experimental tasks, of which the most important was the so-called Party-game, developed by Pieter Muysken. In this game, two teams of two persons each played against each other. The input informants got was both written and pictorial, and they had to finish the written sentences with the help of the pictures as quickly as they could. The written input consisted of monolingual or bilingual sentences, made up of an NP, a PP, and a verb. The pictorial input consisted of a drawing that served as direct object to a written verb. Examples of input stimuli were (Papiamentu in italics):

(6a) Het kind op het feest   *ta rementa*   [picture of a red balloon]
(6b) *E mucha na e fiesta*   knalt   [picture of a red balloon]
     the child at the party   bursts   [a/the red balloon]

(7a) De vrouw aan tafel   *ta dobla*   [picture of a green spoon]
(7b) *E mohe na mesa*   buigt   [picture of a green spoon]
     the woman at (the) table   twists   [a/the green spoon]

Because the experiment was presented as a game, informants enjoyed participating and did not concentrate on their language choice, which made the experiment quite natural. Due to time pressure conscious choices of one or the other language were avoided.

The purpose of the experiment was to elicit code-switching. In this project, no particular hypotheses were tested. The main aim was to find out whether it was possible to elicit code-switching data in experimental settings. The elicited code-switches were compared to the switches found in the spontaneous conversations and two other tasks. Even though the results of the project were promising, it is clear that experiments alone cannot provide the necessary data. Additional tests and spontaneous data remain necessary.

Section summary: Elicited information in experimental settings

- Continuum between elicited (artificial) and spontaneous (natural) data
- Ways to elicit data: sentence repetition tasks; experimental tasks

3.8   Written Sources: Books, Song Lyrics, and the Internet

All the types of data that have been discussed so far were collected with the purpose of making analyses of bilingual language use. There are other data that were produced earlier, and with different purposes. A famous example is Tolstoy's novel *War and Peace* in which the main characters frequently switch between French and Russian. Timm published an article in which those switches were analyzed (Timm, 1978). An example of the bilingual material found in *War and Peace* is (Russian in italics):

(8)   Les femmes et le vin   *ne ponimayu*
      women and wine   I don't understand

Not only books but song lyrics can be bilingual as well. The Algerian rai-singer Cheb Khaled is very popular among young people all over the world. He sings in French and Arabic. The beautiful song Aicha is his most famous song and parts of it are bilingual, as can be seen in the fragment below. The text is taken from http://lyricsplaza.nl/teksten.php?id=856 with minor adjustments. The English translation is provided by me (Arabic in italics).

> Comme si j'n'existais pas
> Elle est passée à côté de moi
> Sans un regard, Reine de Saba
> J'ai dit, Aicha, prends, tout est pour toi
>
> *Nbrik Aicha ou nmout allik*
> *'Hhadi kisat hayaty oua habbi*
> *Inti omri oua inti hayati*
> *Tmanit niich maake ghir inti*
>
> [As if I did not exist
> She just passed me by
> Without a glance, Queen of Sheba
> I said, Aicha, take it, it's all for you
>
> I want you, Aicha, and I die for you
> This is the story of my life and my love
> You are my breath and my life
> I want to live with you and only with you.]

There are many artists who sing in two or more languages. Nowadays, texts can easily be found on the Internet.

Other written sources can be found in newspapers and advertisements written for a bilingual audience in bilingual areas such as Corsica, India, Belgium, and numerous other parts of the world.

The final source I would like to draw attention to here is the forum sites of
bilingual groups on the Internet. I found a lot of sites from minority groups in the
Netherlands and other countries where participants write bilingually. Here are
some random examples of bilingual contributions to several forum discussions;
translations are provided in brackets [. . .].

(9a)   Eiric on www.scotland.com/forums/ (English–Gaelic; Gaelic in italics):
       "I larnt me first *Gàidhlig* [Gaelic] from me grannys mother, whom, sadly
       died when I was 6 years old . . . (I'm only 17$^{1}/_{2}$ years old now . . . Some of
       you seems to think I'm much older, no I'm just sooo intelligent ☺)
       Tiridh an tràth-seo!" [Goodbye for now][4]

(9b)   Clark on www.antimoon.com/forum/ (English–Yiddish; Yiddish in italics):
       "Thanks. *Bischt du en Yid? Ich bin net en Yid awwer ich mag die yidde*
       Kultur."
       [Are you a Yid? I am not a Yid but I like the Yiddish culture.]

(9c)   Abrid on www.amazigh.nl (Dutch–Berber; Berber in italics):
       "Voor degenen die het niet weten *tasertit* betekent politiek *s dmazighth*."
       [For those who don't know it *tasertit* means politics in Berber]

(9d)   Dogan on www.lokum.nl (Dutch–Turkish; Turkish in italics):
       "pfffff, *senin baban benim kafadan, senimi dinliyecek benimi, hem seni*
       dinlese bende babama soylerim mijn vader is groter als jou vader mijn vader
       is 1.88 (. . .)"
       [pffff, your father thinks about it just like me, you think he will listen to you
       or to me, if he would listen to you, I would tell my daddy my dad is bigger
       than your dad my dad is 1.88 . . .]

The advantage of forum sites as compared to the very popular chatrooms is that
you do not always need a password to take a look, and you do not need to
participate in the discussions yourself. The material on the forum sites is more
informal than in other written sources, which is clear from the large number of
writing errors. Everyone who can use the Internet has access to a huge number
of bilingual discussion sites with an incredible amount of bilingual data waiting
to be analyzed linguistically . . . This possibility has not been explored much, but
I am sure it can compete with the other types and sources of data discussed in
this chapter. A lot of time can be saved if these sources are used. But there are
drawbacks: there is no background or sociolinguistic information about the participants except what can be read from the texts. As shown in the discussion about
surveys (section 3.2), the sociolinguistic background of speakers is very important
in determining how bilingually proficient they are. Berber has no standard way
of writing, but that does not seem to be a problem, as shown in the example above.
This is more evidence of the informality of language use in forum discussions,
and an argument in favour of the usefulness of such data for researching code-
switching – and other aspects of bilingualism. More about bilingual Internet

---

[4]   I am grateful to Karen Corrigan for her help in translating the Gaelic fragment.

sites can be found in, among others, Androutsopoulos (2003) and Danet and Herring (2003).

Finally, narratives can be a rich source of bilingual data (cf. chapter 15 in this volume).

Section summary: Written sources: books, song lyrics, and the Internet

- Data not produced for the purpose of studying bilingualism
- Examples in bilingual books, song lyrics, and bilingual Internet sites

---

3.9   Conclusion

This chapter has discussed some of the most frequently used sources of bilingual data and types of collection. This list is not exhaustive, but it will be useful for students of bilingualism.

The first step in collecting data is fact finding. If the researcher has no picture at all of the group that is to be studied, she or he can analyze (parts of) a survey or census, on a macro-level. On the meso-level, it is possible to use a questionnaire about particular topics, in order to obtain more detailed profiles based on questions about language, sociolinguistic, and bilingual behavior. Questionnaires will give more specific information than surveys and censuses. But the best way to find out about people's linguistic behavior towards each other is to observe real-life situations. This can be done by observing either from outside or from inside, by participant observation. Once both the speakers and the situations in which bilingual behavior occur are clearly defined, data collection can start. There are several methods. New data can be obtained from sources ranging from recordings of (semi-)spontaneous conversations to more or less experimental settings. Another type of data is found in a special kind of spontaneous language, like songs, texts, and discussion sites on the Internet. The functions of those texts are diverse, from expressive to purely referential.

Finally, there is the possibility of using bilingual data collected by others in the past, and that are brought together in large databases. This chapter has said nothing about such data; they are the subject of chapter 8 in this volume (Abutalebi & Della Rosa).

None of the methods discussed in this chapter can be considered best or preferable to others. Much depends on the research questions you ask. For example, if you want to study code-switching among Turks in Berlin, and you are familiar with a group of Berlin Turks, you do not need to carry out a large-scale quantitative study in order to find informants. Depending on the degree of familiarity, you can choose to use a questionnaire, to observe from inside as a participant observer, or both. If you want to find information about the attitudes of the target group, or about the attitudes of others towards the target group and its language use, a matched-guise test can be carried out.

Further reading and resources

An example of a language contact study based on a very large corpus is Shana Poplack, David Sankoff, and C. Miller (1988), The social correlates and linguistic processes of lexical borrowing and assimilation, *Linguistics* 26, 47–104. A discussion on methods used to determine bilingual proficiency is given in chapter 6 (pp. 95–119) of Jacomine Nortier, *Dutch-Moroccan Arabic Code-switching among Moroccans in the Netherlands*, Dordrecht: Foris, 1990.

Yahya E-Rramdani describes how a questionnaire was used for his study on Berber-speaking children who could choose between Dutch, Moroccan Arabic, and Berber: *Acquiring Tarifit-Berber by Children in the Netherlands and Morocco*, Studies in Multilingualism, Amsterdam: Aksant, 2003.

One of the earliest and most famous studies on participant observation in an English/Spanish bilingual context in New York is Joshua Fishman, Robert Cooper, Roxana Ma, et al., *Bilingualism in the Barrio*, Language Science Monographs, 7, Bloomington: Indiana University, 1971.

A discussion of the matched-guise test can be found at http://www6.gencat.net/llengcat/noves/hm02estiu/metodologia/a_solis2_5.htm.

At the Max Planck Institute in Nijmegen, the Netherlands, experimental ways of collecting code-switching data are investigated. Since this is work in progress, a reference to the website is given: www.onderzoekinformatie.nl/nl/oi/socialewetenschap/psychologiep/OND1313239/.

A recent publication on code-switching on the Internet is Lars Hinrichs, *CS on the Web: English and Jamaican Creole in E-mail Communication*, Amsterdam: John Benjamins, 2006.

4 Bilingual Speech Data: Criteria for Classification

Penelope Gardner-Chloros

4.1 Introduction

In this chapter we will first consider what is meant by "bilingual data" and the different types of linguistic performance and behavior which are covered by this heading. We will then look at the different levels at which bilingual data can be analyzed, at the types of data which are found, from the transfer of individual words to complex code-switching, and finally at the way in which different subdisciplines within linguistics approach the task of classification and analysis (see Li Wei, chapter 1 in this volume).

4.2 What is "Bilingual Data"?

The term "bilingual data" presupposes that there is a clear distinction between monolingual and bi/plurilingual speech. In fact, this is not as straightforward as it seems. First, even within monolingual data there are often changes of dialect, accent, or register. Such changes may be more or less "conscious" on the part of speakers, and more or less deliberate – exactly like changes from one *language* to another among bilingual speakers. "I can do *ought* when you're with me, I can do anything," said a male speaker in his sixties in a recent radio interview, talking to his wife in an aside – *ought* being Sheffield dialect, which he then repeats in Standard English as 'anything.'

Secondly, bilingual data may include talk between bilinguals who share the same varieties, or between a bilingual and a monolingual, or even two monolinguals who speak different languages but nevertheless understand one another. We will look here mainly at data of the first type – though of course the speakers may still be of uneven competence in each language.

Thirdly, the use of the term "data" assumes that we are adopting the point of view of an analyst, rather than that of the speaker. But as we will see, the analyst's

view of when two languages are being used may not coincide with the speakers'
or the listeners' view. The analyst, faced with a recording or a transcription, may
identify different varieties where there are no significant differences between them
for the speaker. Conversely, an outsider may fail to notice that a speaker is drawing
on two or more different varieties, even though this alternation may be relevant
for the meaning which is being put across. Since it is impossible for analysts
working on bilingual data to be personally acquainted with the linguistic repertoire
of each of their subjects, we need to be as sure as we can that bilingual data is
properly categorized.

   We will look below at the criteria which can be used to classify bilingual data
when they take the form of recordings and transcriptions of natural conversations
(i.e. not produced solely for the purposes of research). This type of data is used by
sociolinguists and conversation analysts, though it can be used for other types of
study as well. Different types of data are gathered – and different criteria are
applied – when bilingual speech is studied from the standpoints of: psycholinguistics
(Green, 1986; Grosjean, 2000, 2001); grammar (Muysken, 2000; Myers-Scotton,
1997); first language acquisition (De Houwer, 1995; Lanza, 1997); second language
acquisition (Poulisse & Bongaerts, 1994; Dewaele, 2007a, 2007b); bilingual education (Martin-Jones, 1995, 2000); social psychology of language (Sachdev & Bourhis,
2001; Sachdev & Giles, 2004). The type of categorization employed in each of
these disciplines will be discussed briefly, but for a fuller view readers are referred
to the works just cited for each of these subfields or to a comprehensive volume on
bilingualism (e.g. Hamers & Blanc, 2000; Bhatia & Ritchie, 2004).

4.2.1 Two examples

The first example is from a recording of "spontaneous speech," i.e. speech which is
affected as little as possible by the fact that it is being studied. The speaker is a man
in his twenties, bilingual in French and Alsatian, a variety of German spoken in the
northeastern region of France, Alsace, which borders on Germany. He can speak
monolingual French without any difficulty, but when speaking to his peer group,
and trying to convey the thrills of one of his favorite video games, he alternates
fluently between the two varieties, thus both adding to the pace and excitement of
his description and ensuring that his friends feel they are part of an in-group where
such alternation is understood and considered appropriate.

(1) Wenn d'mit drüewwer witt, *alors il cogne, alors la moto se renverse, puis il
     faut la remettre sur pied. Moi, je suis arrivé à 80.* S'isch e *truc,* wenn's e
     paarmol gemacht hesch, hesch's hüsse, *après il y a des difficultés,* kannsch e
     programme deux mache, noh muesch, *pour pouvoir traverser,* isch dann
     d'*distance entre le début et la fin de l'obstacle,* un vorhär hesch e so grosser
     Platz g'hett, *disons.*

     If you want to get across with it, *then he knocks, and then the motor-
     bike turns over and you have to right it again. I got up to 80. Thingie is,*

when you've done it a couple of times, you've cracked it, *then there are difficulties,* then you can put on *programme 2,* then you must, *in order to cross,* there's the *distance between the beginning and the end of the obstacle,* and before that you've had, say, this much space, *let's say.*

(Gardner-Chloros, 1991: 153)

As this shows, bilingual data is not always made up of *standard* varieties. The speaker here is bilingual in Standard French plus a *dialect* of German: it is the combination of these which defines his "code" in this context. We will return below to the question of whether it is appropriate to say that this speaker is using two separate "languages."

In (1), there was no problem of communication. The speaker's friends were also "double native speakers" and employed a similar mixture of French and Alsatian. At the other end of the scale, there are many out-group encounters between speakers of different languages where problems of communication *do* arise.

(2)   At an airport snack-bar in England, a French speaker was trying to order a beer in English. Although the French for beer, *bière,* is quite close to the English, and the Frenchman was attempting to pronounce the word *in* English, his pronunciation was such that the waitress, even after several repetitions, did not grasp what he wanted. His desperate attempt to resolve the problem by asking instead for a *blonde* (in French a light beer), needless to say, did not help matters.

These two examples give an idea of the range of phenomena which the term "bilingual data" can encompass. The categorization which follows is intended to be as broad as possible, so as to provide a simple toolkit for handling bilingual data of various types.

4.3   Levels of Analysis within Bilingual Data

Like monolingual data, bilingual data can be considered at different levels.

4.3.1   *The lexical level*

In the early days of research on bilingualism, it was generally thought that lexical transfers – by which people often meant *nouns* – were the commonest type of bilingual data. Weinreich, for example, wrote about the "transfer of words" from one language to another by bilinguals, dismissing this as a "mere oversight" (1953: 73–4) – syntactic or phonological transfers were also dismissed as *interference.* A major question is whether all nouns transferred from one language into another should be classed as *loans.* This question is addressed in greater detail below.

In second language acquisition, speakers often transfer words, consciously or unconsciously, from their mother tongue when they do not know the word in their target language. This is sometimes provoked by the fact that the source and target language have similar-sounding words, though these may have quite different meanings in each of the languages (*false friends*). An example is English *eventually* and French *éventuellement* (which means *perhaps*, *under some circumstances*).

4.3.2   *The syntactic level*

Speakers manipulate the syntax of the relevant languages in various ways, especially when they are using two varieties that are structurally close to one another, like the speaker in (1). Where a bilingual speaker's two languages share a common syntactic structure, the speaker will tend to use that common structure rather than any alternative ones which fulfill the same function but do not exist in both languages (Pfaff, 1979; Boeschoten, 1998). Their speech may appear unremarkable from a monolingual standpoint. Depending on their competence, they may also directly transpose a syntactic structure from one language to another. For example, French-English bilingual children who have acquired the French question marker *est-ce que* may use this structure to ask questions in English, as in "*Est-ce que* you sleep here?" (Hamers & Blanc, 2000: 59). Alternatively, a whole expression may be translated literally, a phenomenon known as a *calque*. At the lexical level, this gives rise to terms like *Wolkenkratzer* in German and *gratte-ciel* in French, literal translations of 'skyscraper.' An example of a syntactic calque – incorrect by monolingual standards – is the use, by French people speaking English, of the conditional mode to report unconfirmed news when speaking English, as occurs in French, as in "Tony Blair would have had a secret meeting with President Bush," meaning "It *appears that* Tony Blair has had a secret meeting . . ."

4.3.3   *The phonological level*

In L2 learners' productions, phonological transfer is called a foreign accent, but it occurs also in other types of bilingual data. In Alsace, for example, dialect-speakers often stress the first syllable of each word, in accordance with the dialect/German model, even when speaking monolingual French. This even occurs in Alsatians who do not speak the dialect at all.

One-off phonological transfer, due to the use of two languages in close proximity to one another, as in code-switching, may also occur, the first word or words after the switch generally being the ones most affected. Psycholinguists conclude from the fact that bilinguals sometimes accidentally pronounce a word in one language with the phonological characteristics of another that phonological and other characteristics of words are separately "stored" in the brain.

4.3.4   *The morphological level*

There are three possibilities for individual words which are transferred from one variety to another.

They are sometimes transferred into the recipient language with their original morphology intact, as in *the paparazzi*, which keeps the Italian *-i* plural ending.

They may be integrated morphologically with the recipient language, as in the Luxemburgish participle *gepuisert*, from the French *épuisé* (exhausted), with a German prefix and ending.

They may be taken over as *bare forms*, as in (3): the verb 'suspect' is neither inflected in accordance with English, which would require an -s, nor adapted to Greek verbal inflections.

(3)   **kseri   ime kipreos   tSe nomizo oti** *suspect you*
       he knows I am a Cypriot and I think that (he) *suspect(s) you*
       an men tu miliso ellinika
       if I don't speak Greek to him.

Bilinguals are often inconsistent as to which of these strategies they adopt and the same speaker may do all three at different times. The more integrated the word is with the recipient language, the more this is likely to be indicative of language change at work.

Section summary

- Borrowing, transfer, and interference can all be studied at the lexical, syntactic, phonological, morphological, and semantic levels.
- Most research has been done at the lexical level, since the process of borrowing individual words, especially nouns, has long been recognized.
- Syntactic transfer is also common, as speakers tend to adopt various techniques to minimize the difference between their languages.
- Phonological transfer is tied up with the question of accent, and is often difficult to distinguish from it.
- Morphological integration of transferred words may be indicative of the first stage in a process of language change.
- Semantic transfer also occurs when a notion from one language is taken over into another without the formal properties of the original term or structure being retained.

4.4   Types of Bilingual Data

The type of material available to researchers varies depending on the bilingual speakers who are studied (see Lanza, chapter 5 in this volume): their competence in the two varieties, the type of community in which they live (e.g. *autochthonous* vs. *migrant*) and the nature of the language contact. In a *diglossic* situation, where the different languages are used in different domains, speakers switch languages according to topic, setting, etc., but not so much *within* utterances (Myers-Scotton, 1986). In regional minorities, the minority language tends to draw in words and structures from the dominant, majority language, rather than the other way round (Thomason & Kaufman, 1988). In an immigrant minority, again the influence is mainly from the majority language to the immigrant one. But on top of this, there are likely to be marked *intergenerational* differences: over two or three generations, there tends to be a shift in competence towards the host language, whereas older speakers are dominant in the language of origin (Li Wei, 1994).

Different approaches to the analysis of bilingual data demand different types of material to work on.

In *psycholinguistic* studies, subjects are often confronted with a controlled experimental task, such as pressing a button whenever they detect a change of language in a recorded text (Kroll & Dussias, 2004). Such studies do not so much inform us about natural bilingual behavior as advance our knowledge of language processing in the brain, how bilinguals separate their languages, and how they connect them. Most of the tasks presented to subjects involve *lexical* decisions, and many psycholinguists think in terms of individual words carrying "language tags" in the brain (see Kroll, Gerfen, & Dussias, chapter 7 in this volume).

Social psychologists of language, for example, are interested in how people's *attitudes* to different varieties affect their *choice* to speak those varieties under different circumstances. They define the varieties as clearly distinguishable entities, then measure the relevant population's attitudes to those varieties, and then observe, or experimentally induce, the choices made by that population in controlled circumstances. In Lawson and Sachdev (2000), people were asked directions on a Moroccan street in order to observe their choice of Moroccan or French depending on several variables (e.g. the language in which they were addressed).

In studies of *child bilingualism*, researchers must be aware of what sort of input the child has received from their entourage, both quantitatively and qualitatively, in each of the languages. Child language is less explicit than adult language, so a knowledge of the context (physical context, addressee, topic) is crucial to understanding the choices the child makes. Consequently, many studies of child bilingualism consist of detailed observations of parent–child interaction over a period of months or even years (De Houwer, 1990; Lanza, 1997). A child's early mixing of two varieties may simply be a reflection of what they have learnt to say in each language. Alternatively, it may reflect difficulties associated with particular aspects of the languages themselves. In a study of two Japanese-English bilingual children, Morita (2003) found that the children avoided the complex Japanese forms of address – or substituted the single-form English *you*, until they felt more confident with the Japanese system. Some studies, however, have claimed that even young children's switching is predominantly related to the preferences of their interlocutor, which they grasp from an early age.

Studies of *second language acquisition* focus primarily on data produced by learners in the target language (see Hua & David, chapter 6 in this volume). However, it is now understood that learners' errors and hypotheses about the language they are learning are largely dictated by aspects of their mother tongue. So their L2 productions – though they appear to be in one language – are themselves a type of bilingual data and can be analyzed accordingly (Mitchell & Miles, 2004).

Grammatical studies of bilingual speech involve studying the structure of sentences produced by bilinguals in order to build up a (predictive) theory. Recordings and transcriptions can provide relevant material. Two problems intervene, however. On the one hand, natural speech does not usually consist of full grammatical sentences, so much of the data is of no use. Secondly, the sentences produced by bilinguals often show grammatical inconsistencies or innovations compared with the monolingual norms, so these too are often rejected. Grammars of bilingual speech, like monolingual grammars, therefore represent an idealization compared to the actual productions of speakers.

Section summary

- A range of subdisciplines in linguistics are concerned with bilingual data, and each makes use of different types of material.
- Psycholinguists seek to control as many aspects of the decoding and the production process as they can.
- Sociolinguists and conversation analysts, at the other end of the scale, strive to obtain data which is as uncontrived as possible.
- A variety of methodological approaches are adopted. These range from large-scale quantitative studies, which allow different populations to be compared in terms of the amount and type of transfer which occurs, to the micro-study of conversational interaction (Muysken, 2000).

4.5   From Borrowing to Code-Switching

In this section, we will look at the more complex outcomes which can be found in the speech of bilinguals, especially code-switching, which has only been mentioned briefly so far.

In recent years, code-switching (CS) has increasingly been a focus of bilingual research. The term is used here as a broad label for cases where it appears that two different varieties are being used in alternation. Bilingual behavior itself is often fluid and varied, with bilinguals combining their languages in a variety of ways at different times or even within the same stretch of discourse. The terminology employed by researchers, on the other hand, is part of an attempt to draw clear lines between different phenomena. One of the most widely discussed distinctions is that between code-switching and borrowing, which we look at next.

4.5.1   Code-switching and borrowing

Are all instances of single words transferred across languages loans? Certainly, virtually all languages contain well-established loans (e.g. *coup de grâce* or *curry* in English). These are the outcome of a historical process, and are used by monolinguals as well as bilinguals. Their presence in an utterance tells us little about the speaker's bilinguality. Poplack (2000), however, distinguishes between the *processes* involved in borrowing and in code-switching. She claims that whereas in borrowing the languages show signs of convergence, in CS they retain their separate identity. Thus, if a word is integrated with the surrounding language at a morphological or phonological level, she claims it must be a loan, even if it occurs only once (*nonce loan*). This claim is tied up with a grammatical hypothesis regarding *constraints* on code-switching (see below).

Although it is sometimes thought that borrowing applies to single words or expressions, whereas CS is broader, it has proved difficult to draw a line between the two on this basis (Myers-Scotton, 1992; Romaine, 1995). In many datasets, single-word CS is a very productive process, one reason being that importing a noun theoretically does not carry too many grammatical implications for the rest of the sentence (Aitchison, 1994: 62). Other criteria which have been used to distinguish CS from loans are that:

1   Loans fill a "lexical gap" in the borrowing language, whereas code-switches do not. In fact, code-switching may also arise for such reasons (cf. *mot juste* switching, Poplack, 1988: 28).
2   Loan words tend to be phonologically – and morphologically – integrated with the surrounding language, whereas code-switches retain their "monolingual" identity. But loans can also retain their original phonology or their morphology – we say *phenomena* not *phenomenons*. Conversely, one-off, spur-of-the-moment code-switches may be adapted; for example, Halmari (1997) and Eliasson (1989) give examples of verbs as well as nouns being morphologically adapted between typologically very different languages.

It is reasonable to conclude that loans start off as code-switches and then become generalized in the borrowing language, until they are recognized and used even by monolinguals.

We cannot tell a loan from a code-switch by its linguistic form alone. It is the nature of the sociolinguistic contact which prevails at the time when an element is switched or borrowed which determines in what manner it is adapted or altered.

Even within the same language pair, when words are borrowed in different historical periods, they may go through different processes of integration and end up looking different in the receiving language. Heath (1989), for example, has shown how some French verbs, borrowed in the early French colonial period, were adopted in Moroccan Arabic without inflectable verb frames. Others, borrowed more recently, have been instantly provided with Moroccan Arabic inflectional frames. Their phonemes have also been imported wholesale, and show signs of stabilizing as such (Heath, 1989: 203).

4.5.2 *Cultural and core loans: Semantic transfers*

Cultural loans are sometimes opposed to *core loans*. They are motivated by the need to express a notion in one language which has no close equivalent in the other, so they often concern culinary (*paella* taken over by English from Spanish), technological (*Komputer* taken over by German from English), or other culturally determined domains. *Core loans* are loans which have no specific cultural *raison d'être* and which could be expressed by a native term. A recent example is the use of the verb *crasher* in French from the English *crash*. *Semantic loans* are found when, instead of taking over the relevant expressions in their original form, bilinguals use a translation equivalent (as in the *skyscraper* example above).

4.5.3 *Code-switching and the notion of "mixed code"*

Regardless of the differences between them, languages may be blended into a *code* in which the individual switch points are not significant. Gafaranga (2005) has shown how many Rwandese use an alternated Kinyarwanda-French variety exactly as monolinguals use a single language. "The notion of code and that of language are not necessarily equivalent . . . in bilingual conversation, the code that has been switched from need not consist of one language in the grammatical sense. It can also be bilingual" (Gafaranga & Torras, 2002: 18). In (4), French and Kinyarwanda together are "the medium." The underlined sentence is in Swahili (2002b: 8–9).

(4) A: ubu rero ab (.) [C helping him to wine] buretse (.) abazayuruwa bagiye
         gutangira ngo (.) <u>fukuza munyarwanda</u>
     B: //**avec raison puisque** turi imbwa
     A: //xxx (laughter) ariko
     C: **avec raison** ( ) none se none wanzanira ibibazo iwanjye
     A, B, C: (laughter)

     A: *now Zairians Zair (.) [C helping him to wine] wait minute (.) Zairians are*
         going to start saying **kick out Rwandese**
     B: // *rightly so as we do not deserve any respect*
     A: // xxx (laughter) *but*
     C: *rightly so* ( ) *if you brought problems to my door*
     A, B, C: (laughter)

Further examples of such "mixed codes" in various settings are discussed in Alvarez-Caccamo (1998). He calls such codes "alloys" and warns against the assumption that bilingual speech is made up of two clearly defined "languages."

4.5.4   *Code-switching and code-mixing*

Various terms have been used to designate the *range* of results of language contact. CS is one of them, though some have reserved it for subcategories within it. Muysken (2000), for example, uses *code-mixing* to cover the three main outcomes of bilingual speech. His subdivisions are (1) *code-switching*, which he also calls *alternation*; in this type of combination, the languages are said to retain their individual identity, (2) *insertion*, in which only short elements from language A are inserted into language B, and again the structure of B is not altered, and (3) *congruent lexicalization*, in which there is a largely shared structure, lexicalized by elements from either language.

(5)   *Weet jij [waar] Jenny is?*
      Do you know where Jenny is? (Dutch: waar Jenny is)
                    (Crama and van Gelderen, 1984, quoted in Muysken, 2000: 5)

As Muysken points out, *where* is close to Dutch *waar*, and the name Jenny is shared by both languages, so *where Jenny is* could be either English or Dutch.

McCormick (2002: 89), on the other hand, specifies: "I refer to language varieties and to switching between them as 'codes' and 'code-switching' only where the varieties and the switching between them seems to have some significance for the members of the speech community. Where switching is not significant, I refer to it as 'language switching.' I use 'switching' to refer to the alternation of phrases or longer chunks in one code or language with those in another, whereas 'mixing' is used to refer to the incorporation of single lexical items from one language into phrases in the other."

What McCormick calls "language switching" would be called a mixed "medium" by Gafaranga (see above), and what she calls mixing would be called "borrowing" or "nonce loans" by, for example, Poplack (1980).

Section summary

- Researchers working on bilingual data attempt to classify more complex stretches of bilingual data in a range of ways. They often distinguish code-switching from *borrowing*, though we have argued here that these two are opposite ends of a continuum.
- Where the varieties concerned are linguistically close, the notion of *compromise forms* may be useful to explain the fluid sliding between varieties which is observed. Even when varieties are very different, researchers need

to be alert to the emergence of *mixed codes*, in which the individual switch-points, though noticeable to an outsider, are of no particular significance to the speakers.

- Muysken classifies of bilingual data into *code-switching/alternation, insertion* and *congruent lexicalization*, his umbrella term for the three types of occurrence being *code-mixing*.
- McCormack shows that the terminological question is very complex, and each author tends to use the available labels in a different way. Good discussions of this issue are to be found in Milroy and Muysken (1995) and Li Wei (2000).

4.6   Classifying and Analyzing Bilingual Speech

Code-switching, or -mixing, depending on the terminology used, is one of the commonest outcomes when bilinguals talk to one another. We will proceed from a simple classification based on the size and type of unit which is switched to a consideration of three important approaches to the analysis of such speech: the grammatical, the sociolinguistic, and the conversational/pragmatic (see Turell & Moyer, chapter 11 in this volume).

4.6.1   *Single-word CS, multi-word CS, and turn-switching*

CS is often divided into single-word switching vs. multi-word switching, and switching within the sentence ("intrasentential") vs. switching between sentences ("intersentential"). Switching *within* the word – adapting a word at the phonological or the morphological level – is also common in some contexts (see the discussion of borrowing in section 4.5). Switching between conversational turns or between speakers is also significant, particularly in the context of a pragmatic analysis.

Even these simple distinctions are often problematic to apply. For example, how are we to treat single-word switches which occur immediately before an interruption or self-interruption? We do not know in which language the speaker would have continued the utterance if uninterrupted. The term *triggering* (Clyne, 1967) refers to the use of a switched word or expression, which triggers a longer switch to the language of that word.

4.6.2   *Word classes in single-word CS*

As we have seen, it is commonly thought that nouns are the type of word which is switched most frequently, although verbs are often switched as well. Like nouns, they can occur as *bare forms* or be morphologically integrated, but bilingual creativity extends still further: a noun, verb, adjective, or adverb from one language may be combined with an "operator" from another, usually the verb for "make" or "do." Such structures occur in a wide range of language combinations, from Greek-English (e.g. '*kano* stretching,' lit. 'I *do* stretching,' meaning 'I stretch') to Punjabi-English (e.g. '*ple* kerna,' lit. 'play *I do*') (Edwards & Gardner-Chloros, 2007).

Switching of other word classes is less frequent, but still common in some contexts. For example, in one study of Punjabi-English, conjunctions such as 'or,' 'but,' or 'because' were frequently the only switched word in the sentence.

(6)   "It's nice when you've got a er good job and good money coming in **par jidthor** (*but when*) you haven't got a nice job and much money coming in then trying to make a living on one of you is very hard isn't it?"

(Gardner-Chloros, Charles, & Cheshire, 2000: 1331)

The switched conjunction highlights the break between the two parts of the sentence, drawing attention to the contrast which underlies the sentence.

Another category commonly found in studies of CS is *tag-switching*. For example, in Alsace, the question tags *gel?* and *nitt?* ('isn't that so?') are frequently attached to remarks in French. Such switching is available even to non-fluent speakers and allows them to show symbolic belonging to the ethnic group whose language is represented by the tag.

Crossing, another form of symbolic switching, arises when speakers adopt elements of speech from a community with which they have no ethnic or family ties, in order to align themselves with the relevant ethnicity at a symbolic level, for example English white teenagers using elements of Creole speech in London (Rampton, 1995).

4.6.3   *Intrasentential and intersentential switching*

Just as it is often difficult to decide whether a single-word switch is a one-off insertion or part of an – interrupted – planned longer code-switched segment, so the distinction between *intrasentential* and *intersentential* switching is complicated by the difficulty of cutting up informal, spoken language into sentences.[1] Auer (2000) illustrates the problem with this example of German-Italian CS:

(7)   **zum beispiel** due sbaglie cinquanta **an'anschläge abziehe**
      for instance two mistakes fifty   *tou- touches subtract*
      "For instance (if you make) two mistakes, they will subtract 50 points"

[1]   A distinction is rarely made between CS within the *clause* and within the *sentence*, although CS within the clause would seem to be 'deeper' than between the clauses which make up a sentence.

This can be segmented in at least three different ways:

1 /**zum beispiel** /due sbaglie /cinquanta **an'anschläge abziehe**/
2 /**zum beispiel** due sbaglie /cinquanta **an'anschläge abziehe**/
3 /**zum beispiel** due sbaglie cinquanta **an'anschläge abziehe**/

None of the suggested analyses segments the utterance in terms of conventional grammatical units. A different unit, the *utterance*, based on a combination of grammatical and *tone unit* criteria, provides a more appropriate unit for analyzing spontaneous speech (LIPPS Group, 2000).

4.6.4 Turn-switching

Analysts interested in pragmatic and conversational aspects of CS often concentrate on switches between speaker turns. Such switching can be due to the fact that one speaker is more competent in one language and the other speaker in the other. This often occurs, for example, between grandparents and grandchildren in bilingual communities. But it is also often indicative of degrees of cooperativeness between speakers. For example, Valdes-Fallis (1977) found that women switched more often than men to match the language of the previous speaker, a finding which fits in with other evidence about gender differences in cooperative behavior.

Section summary

Although the basic categories within CS seem obvious – single-word, multi-word, inter- and intrasentential – it is often difficult to make these distinctions in practice. The categories are useful in making a rough characterization of a dataset – to say, for example, that it contains very little *within-turn* switching, but plentiful switching between speakers. They can also highlight broad differences between comparable sets of data (Poplack, 1988; Cheshire & Gardner-Chloros, 1998).

4.7   Grammatical Approaches to Analyzing CS

Like "language," "grammar" is a term used in different senses (Gardner-Chloros & Edwards, 2007). The main types of grammar which have been applied to CS are listed below. Problems for the grammatical description of CS include

1 *variability* in CS, within communities and even within the speech of a single individual.

2 the fact that CS is found in spontaneous, natural speech, which is rarely made up of full, "correct" sentences like those on which grammatical descriptions are traditionally based. Switches occur between sentences, between turns, and frequently in *paratactic* positions, e.g. 'La cassette, wie lang as se geht?' 'The cassette, how long does it run?' (Gardner-Chloros, 1991).

4.7.1 Constraints

Various researchers (Lipski, 1978; Pfaff, 1979; Poplack, 1980; Woolford, 1983) formulated constraints on where CS could occur in the sentence, relating to surface word order. Most in effect stated that CS cannot occur at points in the sentence where the surface structures of the two languages differ. For example, the equivalence constraint (Poplack, 1980) stated that a switch could only occur where the two languages had the same syntactic order. Unfortunately, as more data were collected, it became apparent that the proposed constraints did not generalize to other datasets. In (8), the adjective placement rules of Greek and English conflict:

(8) 'irthe **daskala** private'
     came **teacher** private
     (A private teacher came)

                                   (Gardner-Chloros, unpublished example)

   The constraints, however, were still defended, on the basis that the weight of *quantitative* evidence was in their favor, and in Poplack's case on the basis that violations of the constraints were instances of *borrowing* and not of CS – an argument which many considered circular.

4.7.2 Government

Attempts to explain CS in terms of Government relations typically contend that there can be no switching between a governor and the governed element. However, counter-evidence is provided by many common switches, such as those between subject NP and main verb ("La plupart des canadiens **scrivono** 'c'" *Most Canadians write 'c'*; Di Sciullo, Muysken, and Singh, 1986: 15). The proposals were later modified and restricted to lexical government by non-function words, but this prediction was also falsified by counter-evidence, in particular in the Dutch-Moroccan Arabic data of Nortier (1990), e.g. "Wellit **huisman**" *I-became houseman* (Nortier, 1990: 131; see the discussion in Muysken, 2000: 23–4).

4.7.3 Generative frameworks

Mahootian (1993) and Chan (1999), with some differences in theoretical orientation, both proposed "null" theories of CS grammar, meaning that CS can be described in terms of the grammatical principles that apply to the relevant monolingual grammars, without CS-specific devices or constraints. According to Mahootian, this implies, for example, that where a verb is selected from Farsi, an SOV language, the structure projected from Farsi verbs determines that an object will precede the verb, regardless of the language of the object. This proposal is also called into question by counterexamples (e.g. Eppler, 1999). MacSwan (2004) has concentrated on integrating the facts of CS with Minimalism, itself a constantly developing set of theories.

4.7.4 *The Matrix Language Frame*

Myers-Scotton's "Matrix Language Frame" (1997, 2002), a grammar devised specifically for CS data, is based on the idea that all utterances have a dominant underlying language or *matrix*. This ties in with the psycholinguistic notion of one language being more "activated" in the brain, and with the notion of the socially "unmarked language" developed in Myers-Scotton's Markedness model (1993). Others (Joshi, 1985; Klavans, 1985) had already posited a "frame" into which elements of the other language could be embedded, but Myers-Scotton's model goes further. It stipulates that in code-switched sentences, only the matrix language (ML) can supply the closed-class (i.e. grammatical) words, except where there are embedded language (EL) "islands" (i.e. inserted EL chunks).

The ML is primarily defined as the language that provides the greater number of morphemes. One problem is that this produces a different outcome depending on the amount of data one chooses to analyze (Moyer, 1998). On this basis, many bilingual conversations would change ML several times (Bentahila & Davies, 1998: 31).

In response to criticisms, the theory has been repeatedly revised, and arguably watered down (Myers-Scotton & Jake, 2000; Jake, Myers-Scotton, & Gross, 2002). It now allows for the ML to change over the course of a conversation, and even for a "composite ML": the ML is no longer identified as a specific language, but may be, as it were, "pre-mixed."

Section summary

- Grammatical approaches to the description of CS have had difficulty in coping with the *variability* which such data present and with bilingual speakers' creative strategies and disregard for conventional sentence patterns.
- The Matrix Language Frame is an evolving, comprehensive, ad hoc attempt to describe the grammatical facts of CS, but it has proved difficult to maintain its basic tenet, that there is a single underlying grammar to all CS productions.

4.8   Sociolinguistic and Pragmatic Approaches

Sociolinguistic approaches deal with the circumstances in which, and the reasons why, bilinguals code-switch. For example, do women code-switch more than men in a given setting? Does CS arise in language-death situations? What is the significance of a switch from a national language to a local dialect? Pragmatic approaches deal with the significance of CS *within* conversations: what factors dictate that a speaker switches at the particular moment when they do? What effects does this have within the conversation? The two approaches share many aims and can be seen as the macro- and the micro-ends of the same field of enquiry (see Cashman, chapter 16 in this volume).

4.8.1   *The sociolinguistic study of CS*

Gumperz and Hernandez (1969: 2) wrote that CS is found "each time minority language groups come into contact with majority language groups under conditions of rapid social change." Unlike pidgins and creoles, which arise as lingua francas, CS arises in groups where most speakers are bilingual (Thomason, 1997). It can have a subversive edge, representing a rebellion against the state-sanctioned language. As we saw, the language of the socially dominant group is adopted by the minority rather than vice versa. Language change often occurs when a minority group becomes bilingual and adopts features of the L2 in the L1, as in the case of Asia Minor Greeks adopting features of Turkish (Thomason, 2001).

4.8.2   *Domains and diglossia*

Language use in multilingual settings can be broken down in terms of *domains* of use (Fishman, 2000 [1965]). These are major areas within the social arena, such as education, religion, the family, etc. If each of these areas is strictly associated with a particular language, as in strict diglossia (Ferguson, 2000 [1959]), then, by definition, no CS can occur. However, the various features which make up a domain are rarely present as a complete package – diglossia is often "leaky," which allows for CS to arise.

4.8.3   *Markedness*

Where a socially unexpected language choice is made, this can be described as a "marked" choice (Myers-Scotton, 1983, 1993; Myers-Scotton & Bolonyai, 2001): in any given social circumstances, a particular variety is the expected or "unmarked" one. For example, switching to the local vernacular when talking about home/family is "unmarked" CS, whereas doing the same in the middle of a public speech is "marked." In stable bilingual settings, CS itself may be the only truly "unmarked" choice. This is the case, for example, in Alsace, where, in informal situations, using either French or the Alsatian dialect on its own is a marked, almost political statement.

Speakers who do not participate in a wide variety of domain activities – for example women who interact exclusively in a domestic sphere – may have no occasion to use anything *but* a CS mode (Romaine, 1986). In other cases, CS constitutes a "compromise" mode. Thus "ethnic" radio and TV channels often use CS as a way of reaching as wide an audience as possible.

4.8.3   We-code/they-code: Conversational vs. situational

Blom and Gumperz (1972) claimed that CS often results from alternation between a *we-code* and a *they-code*. The former is usually the informal dialect or vernacular used at home and among friends; the *they-code* is generally the national or official language. In a study of a Norwegian village, they showed how two villagers used Standard Norwegian (*they-code*) to discuss business, and switched to the local dialect (*we-code*) to discuss family matters. Such CS, in an unchanged setting, is termed *conversational* CS, as opposed to *situational* CS, which coincides with a change in setting or participants.

Example (9) is an instance of conversational CS, with *metaphorical* function. A Punjabi-English bilingual talks about the loss of Punjabi culture in Britain. The loss is poignantly embodied in the switch half way through the sentence, and by the use of the English word "culture."

(9)   **Culture** tha   aapna......rena tha   hayni **we know it, we know it, we know it's coming**
      (culture [stress] our.........stay [stress] is-not)
      *Our **culture** is not going to last, **we know it, we know it, we know it's coming***

                                        (Gardner-Chloros, Charles, & Cheshire, 2000: 1322)

4.8.5   CS and Network Theory

Li Wei, Milroy, and Pong (2000) propose Social Network Theory as a suitable means of relating CS and language choices by individuals to broader social, economic, and political contexts. Whether or not a second- or third-generation member of the Chinese community on Tyneside can converse fluently in Chinese determines the extent to which they can take part in conversations with the oldest members of the community, who are often monolingual Chinese speakers. Their social networking with people their own age is also governed by their linguistic abilities. Their associations with English or Chinese speakers in turn reinforce their preferences and abilities in those languages (Milroy & Li Wei, 1995; Li Wei, 1998; Xu, Wang, and Li, chapter 15 in this volume).

4.9   The Pragmatic Study of CS

CS has a dual function of indexing the values or associations of the two varieties as described above, but also of creating contrasts and transitions which help to structure the meaning of an exchange. It is a form of "footing" (Goffmann, 1979), or a "contextualization cue," which Gumperz glosses as "verbal or non-verbal cue that provides an interpretive framework for the referential content of a message" (1982a: 131).

4.9.1   *Verbal action and preference organization*

Auer (1998) considers CS to be part of "verbal action." As a conversation analyst, he looks for meaning in units going beyond the sentence, and argues that the only way the analyst can prove that a given set of co-occurring linguistic features is perceived by participants as a distinct code is "by showing that switching between this set and another is employed in a meaningful way in bilingual conversation" (1998: 13). So if, for example, an interlocutor fails to respond to a question until the first speaker repeats the question in the other language, we may assume that the language choice is significant.

(10)   A is an 8-year-old girl, and C is A's 15-year-old brother. B is their mother who is in her forties.

     A: Cut it out for me (.) please
     B: (2.5)
     A: Cut it out for me (.) mum.
     C: [Give us a look
     B: [**Mut-ye?**
        (***What?***)
     A: Cut this out.
     B: **Mut-ye?**
        (***What?***)
     C: Give us a look.
        (2.0)
     B: **Nay m ying wa lei?**
        (***You don't answer me?***)
     A: (To C) Get me a pen.

(Li Wei, 1998: 171–2)

The failure of A to switch to her mother's preferred language, Cantonese, in spite of the latter's repeated attempts to encourage her, is indicative of a lack of cooperation. This type of conversational "game" is known as *preference organization*.

4.9.2 CS compared with monolingual conversational moves

In other cases the *contrast*, rather than which language is chosen for what, is the significant factor. For example, it is common in CS to switch languages in order to quote someone in the language which they actually spoke, but there are also instances of switching to mark off a quote, to a language which the original speaker would *not* have used.

CS allows speakers to indicate to whom a remark is directed, to mark an aside, repetition, or reinforcement, or to personalize or objectify a remark (Gumperz, 1982a; Zentella, 1997). All these functions are accomplished in monolingual conversation as well: the use of CS simply provides an additional way to mark their significance (Gardner-Chloros, Charles, & Cheshire, 2000).

Section summary

- *Code-switching* covers a variety of bilingual data which occurs in very different sociolinguistic contexts. Researchers have tried to correlate the linguistic outcomes with aspects of the societies where it is found. A society where different domains require different language choices will dictate a more rigid and predictable alternation than one with more fluid internal boundaries. Even in the latter, however, language choices may be used in a "marked" or unexpected way to draw attention to particular associations or identities.
- Often, however, within the same community and language combination, *different* patterns can be found, according to the speakers' age, education, social background, context, topic, and above all social network (Li Wei, 1998).
- At a pragmatic level, CS can provide a means of structuring bilingual conversations by exploiting the contrast between the varieties. In conversational contexts, the speakers' knowledge of their interlocutors' linguistic preferences is often brought to bear, indicating cooperativeness or the lack of it.

4.10 Conclusion

Bilingual data may issue from a whole community, from a particular group, or from individuals. The type of data produced is affected by the type of bilinguality involved – whether the speaker's competence is balanced or unbalanced, whether both languages are "native" in their community or whether they are just learning one of them, whether the speaker's attitudes to both are positive or negative, whether they are bicultural as well as bilingual, and numerous other factors (Hamers & Blanc, 2000). The analysis of bilingual speech needs to take account of these factors, and involves different types of emphasis in different cases. All or some of the following analytical steps may be appropriate:

1   Describing/classifying the speech produced by bilinguals and its patterning from a linguistic perspective.
2   Relating it to the context in which it occurs, context being construed in the widest possible sense to include the characteristics of the community, the languages' respective status, the presence or likelihood of language change, and the occurrence of borrowing or code-switching.
3   Relating the mixed productions to the speakers' competence and attitudes, and to the characteristics of the conversation. Within a given community, the varieties present may be used and combined in a variety of ways by different (or even the same) speakers.

Owing to the many factors which are relevant to it, research on bilingual speech would gain by being as interdisciplinary as possible. For example, even though one might be interested principally in grammatical aspects of bilingual speech, sociolinguistic factors must be considered, as they influence the type and extent of language contact.

Like monolinguals, bilinguals have access to a *repertoire* which may include different dialects or registers as well as different languages – singly or in combination. In order to examine and compare these various *codes* effectively, it is helpful to refer to comparable data. Increasingly, computerized databases are providing the best means to examine larger bodies of data (Gardner-Chloros, Moyer, & Sebba, 2007). Steps towards achieving this in the bilingual field have been taken by the LIPPS/LIDES system, described elsewhere in this volume.

Further reading and resources

Substantial chapters or sections have been devoted to bilingual speech in the principal volumes on bilingualism and language contact, e.g. Romaine, 1995; Coulmas, 1997; Hamers and Blanc, 2000; Li Wei, 2000; Thomason, 2001; Clyne, 2003; Winford, 2003; Bhatia and Ritchie, 2004. Edited collections and special issues of journals devoted to different aspects of bilingual speech include Heller, 1988; Eastman, 1992; Milroy and Muysken, 1995; Auer, 1998; Jacobson, 1998, 2001; Dolitsky, 2000; Li Wei, 2005c.

Monographic case-studies of bilingual situations include Bentahila, 1983; Agnihotri, 1987; Gibbons, 1987; Heath, 1989; Nortier, 1990; Gardner-Chloros, 1991; Backus, 1992; Treffers-Daller, 1994; Haust, 1995; Halmari, 1997; Zentella, 1997; Nivens, 2002; McCormick, 2002.

Two books have been devoted to the grammatical aspects of CS (Myers-Scotton, 1997; Muysken, 2000). Myers-Scotton has written a book on the Markedness Model (1993) and a further one in which she develops her grammatical theory in the broader context of language contact (2002). An interdisciplinary approach to CS is described in Gardner-Chloros (forthcoming 2008). CS is regularly the subject of papers in the two main journals on bilingualism, the *International Journal of Bilingualism* and *Bilingualism: Language and Cognition*.

5 Selecting Individuals, Groups, and Sites

Elizabeth Lanza

5.1 Introduction

This chapter focuses on the process of selecting the speakers or participants who will provide the data on linguistic structure and/or language use that are to be analyzed in a research project involving bilingualism. These individuals may belong to a group that is defined by, for example, language, e.g. Chinese in England (Li Wei, 1994), geography, e.g. Cape Town's District Six (McCormick, 2002), or linguistic disability. And within these larger groups, we may find other groups to which individuals belong by virtue of such variables as age, gender, socioeconomic status, language ideology, and so forth (see Heller, chapter 14 in this volume). Furthermore, the selection of the site for data collection from a particular group, for example, home or school, will have an impact on the study. Once the research question has been formulated (see Moyer, chapter 2 in this volume), the selection of the individuals, groups, and sites that will be the source of the relevant data will be decisive for the success of the study. Why is it so important to consider carefully the selection of individuals, groups, and sites? This chapter addresses the complexity of the issue.

The premise in this chapter is that bilingualism is socially embedded and that whether the focus of the study is on individuals, as in psycholinguistically oriented studies, or on groups, the study of bilingualism must take into account relevant sociolinguistic parameters. Cameron, Frazer, Harvey, Rampton, and Richardson (1992) go so far as to state that if we do research on language, we are social scientists. An important consideration in the social sciences, and more specifically the sociolinguistic study of language, is how the researcher affects the research process (cf. Milroy & Gordon, 2003). Data are not collected in a social vacuum. A focus on the bilingual's language use does not preclude interest in the actual languages involved, as in the investigation of the more formal aspects of code-switching. In this regard, the researcher's competence in these languages will play a part in the research design. And finally, many studies of bilingualism involve immigrants and although ethical considerations are relevant for all research, immigrant populations are particularly vulnerable.

In what follows, I discuss the various considerations and implications involved in selecting individuals, groups, and sites for a study on bilingualism. I first highlight the importance of the selection process. Then I elaborate upon the issue of researcher identity and how that may bear directly on the research process, and particularly the selection process. Subsequently, I focus on the selection of individual participants in a research study focusing on individual bilingualism. Thereafter, I will discuss the selection of groups or communities of speakers as the point of departure for selecting individual participants. Even within a particular community or site, there is a need to consider variation, and the selection process has to take this into account. Finally, I bring up ethical considerations that are particularly relevant in bilingual research.

5.2   The Importance of the Selection Process

The selection of the participants and the site for a study is closely linked to the research design of the study (see Hua & David, chapter 6 in this volume). Every study will be motivated by a research question or hypothesis, the research design being the overall plan for addressing the issue in focus. The research design will have a theoretical motivation that includes a plan for the collection of the data to be used as the basis for investigating the research questions, for the operationalization of variables so that they can be measured, and for the analysis of the results. The research design will also provide information about who will comprise the study population, how they will be identified and contacted, and how informed consent will be sought (cf. Kumar, 1999). Paramount in this is that the procedures followed are adequate to obtain valid and reliable answers to the research questions. The research design is coherent in that theory, method, and data are all interconnected in a properly designed research study (see Moyer, chapter 2 in this volume).

The selection process is motivated by the study's objectives. For example, the starting point of a research question may be: What are the language choice patterns of non-Western second-generation immigrants in a Western society? Further specification of the research question will need to be made in order to help us in the selection process. Hence we may ask: What are the language choice patterns of children of Turkish immigrants in Denmark? But once again we will need to delimit the research question in order to restrict the selection process. This may be done by further specifying whether the Turkish immigrants have a Turkish or a Kurdish background, the age of the children, whether their language use patterns concern the home, school, or community club setting, whether gender is an issue, whether the children live in a larger metropolitan area or in a rural area, and so forth. A theoretical perspective that accentuates the importance of mapping variation will incorporate different types of speakers and different types of data used by the same speaker. In other words, the research question will assist us in planning the selection of individuals, groups, and sites from which to secure the necessary data.

The extent to which we can generalize the findings from our research will depend to a significant degree on our selection process. If the individuals from whom we collect linguistic data are representative of larger groups to which they belong, we may be able to generalize our findings concerning the individuals to the larger group. This involves the issue of *representativeness* and a process called *sampling*. Sampling will be discussed in more detail in section 5.4. Suffice it to say here that the selection process is clearly related to, and a vital component of, the research design. And even when the focus is on individual bilingualism, the speakers will need to be selected according to carefully delineated profiles of bilingual competence, language use, and sociological variables.

The selection of participants for the study may affect other aspects of the research design, for example, the type of data that *can* be collected. If the population is an immigrant one involving older individuals who may not be literate, then for example an oral interview will be preferred to a written questionnaire, even though someone may be able to assist the individual in recording the responses (cf. Kroll, Gerfen, & Dussias, chapter 7 in this volume). This intervention could endanger the validity and reliability of the data. Awareness of these issues is important in our selection of research participants and data collection methods.

In the research question put forward above, Turkish immigrants in Denmark were proposed as examples of the broader category of non-Western immigrants in a Western society. However, one could have easily chosen Moroccan Arabic speakers in the Netherlands, or Filipinos in Norway. The particular selection process of a research study will invariably be related to the researcher's identity. This is the topic of the next section.

Section summary: Why is the selection of speakers and sites so important?

- It is an integral part of the research design of the study.
- It will affect the degree to which we can generalize our findings.
- It may affect other aspects of the research design, for example, the type of data that can be collected.

5.3 The Researcher's Identity in the Selection Process

The researcher's own identity, including his or her own particular interests, will greatly influence the research agenda. This identity is usually implicit in studies of bilingualism; however, as Li Wei (2000: 476) points out, we need to be aware of issues such as the researcher's linguistic competence, ethnicity, gender, age group, education level, disciplinary background, and attitude towards bilingualism. Indeed, one's gender identity may be decisive in, for example, a Muslim community where only women have access to Muslim women and their families. The researcher's identity, as an insider or outsider to a community, may facilitate or complicate any attempts to overcome the "observer's paradox" (Labov, 1972c) – the problem that arises when the people being observed change their behavior in response to the observer's very presence. Some examples will illustrate how a researcher's identity can influence the research process, including the selection of participants and the site for research (see ideas on ethnography in Heller, chapter 14 in this volume).

Lanza (2004a) is a longitudinal study of the bilingual first language acquisition of two children in families in which the mother was American and the father Norwegian. As a bilingual speaker of English and Norwegian, I had the competence to analyze the language development of the children. Moreover, given the insight I had gained as the mother of bilingual children and my extensive network of bilingual families, the selection of this language and culture combination as the locus for my research was clear. I had a positive attitude towards bilingualism and I was personally motivated to learn more about how children acquire two languages simultaneously in a situation often referred to as "elitist" bilingualism (Harding-Esch & Riley, 2003). As an insider, I could observe how parents actually talked to their bilingual youngsters. A clear disadvantage of being an insider is that members of the group or community may not take seriously your questions and probes about the issue in focus for the research. Moreover, as I was undertaking research for my doctorate, my role as a researcher was hard to conceal despite my genuine interest in the mothers' attitudes and experiences. I was expected to have the answers for how to "successfully" bring up a child bilingually.

Zentella (1997), in her work on a New York Puerto Rican community, points out various dilemmas in being an insider to the community under investigation, especially when the group is a stigmatized one "which some readers wish to see vindicated and others hope to see chastised or rehabilitated" (p. 8). She states that, although there are definite advantages, "The closer the researcher is to the group, however, the more myopic the researcher may become about the significance of everyday acts that group members take for granted" (p. 7). Moreover, issues of power and solidarity may be at play. There are advantages and disadvantages to being an insider to a community. Hence identity as an insider is not decisive for the success of a study. Moyer (1998, 2000) investigated bilingual conversational data in Gibraltar, and was not an insider. However, not only was the researcher a bilingual speaker of English and Spanish, she was also familiar with language use patterns for communication in the community, as well as the social meanings associated with each language.

Some researchers are not insiders to the community selected and may in fact lack the necessary linguistic knowledge to engage in the project without assistance from within the group. Such studies are more often than not motivated by a need to gain more research-based knowledge about a particular community in order to provide better social or educational support for these individuals. Hence a need motivates the selection of a group, rather than the researcher's actual identity as an insider, or his or her competence in the minority language. Involving insiders in the research process can resolve the problem of the researcher's lack of linguistic competence; however, certain safeguards need to be taken. An example can illustrate this.

In Norway the largest group of minority language students come from Pakistan and have an Urdu/Panjabi background. Due to the lack of bilingual linguists with the necessary language competence, there has been an absence of studies of the language development and use of these children, who reportedly do poorly academically. The situation necessitates resorting to other methods in order to compensate for this lack, as demonstrated in Aarsæther (2004). He investigated negotiation skills among 10-year-old bilingual children of Pakistani origin in an Oslo school where the children used both Norwegian and Urdu/Panjabi effectively in their communication. Although the researcher was not competent in the minority language, he had had extensive experience in teaching children with that particular background, which enabled him to witness their language alternation in a school environment. In order to compensate for his lack of relevant linguistic skills, Aarsæther engaged the children's mother tongue instructor in the transcription and interpretation of the data. These interpretations were further cross-checked with other native speakers of Urdu/Panjabi to ensure validity and reliability. Hence the relationship in such a case between the researcher and the researched involved what Cameron, Frazer, Harvey, Rampton, and Richardson (1992) call "empowerment," in that individuals from the group under study are actually involved in the research process and in the interpretation of the results (cf. section 5.5).

The following example illustrates more explicitly how the selection process may be influenced by the researcher's identity and linguistic competence, all the while taking into account the theoretical motivations of the research design. Hvenekilde and Lanza (2001) is a study on language choice and social networks among Filipinos in Oslo. The actual choice of the city of Oslo was based on the fact that my colleague and I were residents of Oslo, and hence data collection would be easier to manage and accomplish. Moreover, we knew the city well. There was also a theoretical justification for this choice. Norway has become increasingly multilingual and multicultural despite images of Scandinavian homogeneity. And Oslo, with the greatest concentration of immigrants, fit the multilingual and multicultural profile sought after (see also Lanza & Svendsen, 2007).

The selection of the particular community of immigrants, the Filipinos, was not random. Many research manuals stress the importance of objectivity in research methods and that this requires a certain distance from the object of study. In recent years, however, there has been more social involvement in language-related issues among linguists as they attempt to address issues of social inequality related to language (cf. Wodak & Meyer, 2001; Fairclough, 2003a). What is important is that the researcher be aware of her or his ideological influences on the aims and objectives of the research. As Li Wei (2000: 479) states, ". . . bilingualism research can never be truly 'value-free.'" My colleague and I both had favorable attitudes towards bilingualism. I myself was an immigrant to Norway, having come as an adult, although as noted in Lanza (2004a: 74), the term *innvandrer* ('immigrant') has become reserved for those whose culture and language differ markedly from the Norwegian. Hence although I did not share the same ethnicity as members of the community in focus, I did share some common identity. My colleague and I were also both concerned about the negative media coverage that immigrants in Norway were receiving, focusing on the problems that certain immigrant groups had. Through our research we hoped to highlight some positive sides to immigration by focusing on a group that at the time had received little, if any, attention in the media. Although several groups could have been selected, we chose the Filipinos. The selection of the Filipinos was also motivated by another aspect of my identity, as I had contact with this group through my participation in Oslo's Catholic cathedral parish where the Filipinos are the largest immigrant group.

The Filipinos also fulfilled the criteria that we had set up for selection. They maintained very close networks (Macdonald & Pesigan, 2000) and so provided an interesting case for testing theoretical claims concerning the impact of social networks on language maintenance (cf. Li Wei, 1994; see Xu, Wang, & Li Wei, chapter 15 in this volume). Our theoretical motivation was to investigate the relationship between ethnicity in social networks and language choice, particularly in the home with children, with an eye towards linguistic and cultural maintenance. Filipinos are multilingual before they arrive in Norway and thus have an extensive linguistic repertoire. Neither my colleague nor I had competence in any Filipino language; however, English is an official language in the Philippines and most Filipinos are competent in it. Moreover, these Filipino immigrants were competent in Norwegian to various degrees. To gain insider access to the community and to help us compensate for our lack of linguistic competence in Filipino languages, we employed the "friend-of-a-friend" fieldwork procedure (cf. Bossevain, 1974; Milroy & Gordon, 2003). My colleague knew a Filipino former student who had an extensive social network, and she became our field assistant. In section 5.4 below, I will return to this study and discuss how we actually selected the individual participants that we interviewed within the community, also addressing the issue of representativeness.

Section summary: The researcher's identity in the selection process

- The researcher's identity is an integral aspect of the research process, including the selection of individuals, groups, and sites.
- This identity includes the researcher's linguistic competence, ethnicity, gender, age group, education level, disciplinary background, and attitude towards bilingualism, as well as whether or not the researcher is an insider to the community.
- There are advantages and disadvantages to being an insider to the community you are studying.
- It is important that we are aware of our ideological influences on the aims and objectives of our research.

5.4   A Focus on Individual Bilingualism

Many studies in bilingual research focus on the bilingual individual and his or her competence in, or use of, two languages. In such cases, representativeness is not an issue as we are looking at human traits that are assumed to be universal. Laboratory designs take the individual into account (see Kroll, Gerfen, & Dussias, and Abutalebi & Della Rosa, chapters 7 and 8 in this volume). The number of speakers is not as important as the criteria for selection. If we are focusing on variation in one particular aspect of bilingualism, and want to compare bilinguals, then we will need to match these bilinguals in respect of the other individual differences. As Grosjean (1998: 132) points out, although some research questions, for example those dealing with a bilingual's grammar, may be able to abstract away individual differences, most will not be able to do so. Hence these differences must be taken into account in our selection of speakers. Grosjean provides the most comprehensive list of basic individual differences that need to be accounted for when choosing bilingual speakers. These include the individual's language (acquisition) history and language use patterns, and the typological differences between the bilingual's languages. Other issues are how stable the languages are, and whether the bilingual is in the process of acquiring one or more languages, or losing them. To what extent is the bilingual proficient in each of his or her languages in each of the four skills: speaking, listening, writing, reading? Another issue concerns the bilingual's language modes. How often is the individual in a context that triggers a monolingual mode of language processing, or a bilingual mode? When in a bilingual mode, how often does code-switching take place? And finally, what are the traditional sociological variables represented by the bilingual, for example, age, gender, socioeconomic status, education, and so forth?

A crucial variable in the selection of bilingual children, which is also an important variable for the selection of adult participants in a study (cf. Hernandez, Bates, & Avila, 1994; Guion, Harada, & Clark, 2004), is the age at which the child acquired the two (or more) languages. The distinction is between bilingual first language acquisition and second language acquisition, otherwise referred to as simultaneous or infant bilingualism and consecutive or sequential bilingualism (cf. De Houwer, 1995). The study of each type of bilingualism poses different research questions. A traditional cutoff point between these two types has been three years, an age at which the child was considered essentially to have acquired his or her first language (McLaughlin, 1984). Bilingual first language acquisition research, however, has become increasingly stringent in its definition of the field: the child is expected to receive input from both languages from early on, indeed from birth (De Houwer, 1990). Input may come from interlocutors from outside of the family already from birth; nevertheless, the family has figured as the prominent source of input in available studies (cf. Lanza, 2004a, 2004b). Romaine (1995) set up a typology of six basic types of language use patterns in the home as a framework for selecting children for bilingual acquisition studies. These types varied according to the native language of the parents, the language(s) of the community, and the strategy the parents employ with the child. Some types render situations of simultaneous acquisition of two or even more languages (cf. Quay, 2001), others sequential acquisition. When selecting young bilingual children, the researcher needs to pay attention to the age at which the second language was introduced and to variation in the input.

Studies of young bilingual children are often case studies. Studies of bilingual aphasics and other brain-damaged individuals have also been case studies of individual patients, multiple case studies, or group studies (e.g. Gil & Goral, 2004, and the contributions in Paradis, 1995). In order to determine how many patients we will select for a study and what the selection criteria should be, we have to ask what the goal of the study is. For example, is the goal of the study to create a profile for patients with a particular injury, or to find appropriate measures for therapy? If the goal of the study is, say, to discover a linguistic structure typical for patients with Broca's aphasia, then a group study is necessary. A problem with a group study, however, is the lack of homogeneity among individual brain-damaged patients. In other words, in order to make a generalization about the group that is defined according to a particular syndrome, we must assume that the variation is trivial. Nonetheless, such variation has proven to be theoretically interesting. Furthermore, the border between the various syndromes may be vague, and the extreme cases are masked by any generalization. If the research question concerns a general phenomenon such as recovery patterns in bilingual aphasics (cf. Paradis, 2004: ch. 3), language proficiency and age of acquisition of each language can be important criteria for separating the participants. Individual and multiple case studies are common in bilingual language pathology; in fact, groups in such studies are often quite small. Individuals with brain damage are indeed an exceptional population and hence practical considerations will often be decisive in the selection of participants as we may not always be able to get exactly the type of speaker we wish for a study.

Whether dealing with bilingual brain-damaged patients or other bilingual speakers, our research design will determine whether or not we will need to select a control group of speakers. In a cause and effect research design we are measuring the impact that the independent variable has on the dependent variable (see Moyer, chapter 2 in this volume). However, we know that there are other extraneous variables that may be working in synergy with, or at odds with, the independent variable. In order to minimize the effect of these variables so that we may with greater confidence attribute the change in the dependent variable to the independent variable, we will need to select and set up a control group. For example, the study of the development of form and function in bilingual children has greatly profited from the use of the "frog story" (cf. Verhoeven & Strömqvist, 2001). The task itself, of letting the child browse through the pictures and then recount the story, may be a challenge to lexical retrieval and trigger hesitation. In order to measure the impact of these effects, we can establish a control group of monolingual children in each of the bilingual children's languages who will perform the same task. In this way the groups will be matched by the same social variables, with the marked variable separating them being that of bilingualism.

Section summary: A focus on individual bilingualism

- When focusing on the individual, the number of speakers is not as important as the criteria for selection.
- Some basic individual differences that must be accounted for when selecting speakers are the following:
  - speaker's language (acquisition) history,

- language use patterns,
- the typological differences between the languages,
- whether the individual is in the process of language acquisition or attrition,
- the individual's proficiency in each of the four skills,
- the degree to which the individual is in a monolingual or bilingual mode of language processing,
- and finally, traditional sociological variables such as age, sex, socio-economic status, education, etc.
- Our research design will determine whether or not we need to select a control group of speakers in order to measure the effect of extraneous variables.

5.5   A Focus on the Group or Community

In a discussion on regional and immigrant minority languages, Extra and Gorter (2001) discuss the advantages and disadvantages of certain criteria that can be used to define and identify population groups in a multicultural society: nationality, birth country, self-categorization, and home language (see also Xu, Wang, & Li Wei, chapter 15 in this volume). In a study focusing on a particular bilingual population, once we have chosen the group or community for our research we are left with the selection of the individual participants from that group or community. Once the individuals are selected, the selection of the actual site for data collection is also important, as language used in different sites may represent society in different ways than correlations between individual and social variables such as age and gender.

In order to be able to say something about a community that is indeed *representative* for the community, we would ideally study the entire population. However, it is quite clear that such an endeavor would be a drain of human and financial resources. We need to resort to a sample, or subgroup, of the larger population that is our object of study. *Sampling* is the process of selecting a limited number of individuals from a group in order to estimate or predict aspects of the group. We may say that sampling is a compromise between accuracy and resources. If the sample is used as a basis for making statements about the entire community or population, the criteria for selecting the sample are paramount if we are to feel confident in the validity of our findings. Two factors may influence the degree of certainty about the inferences drawn from a sample: the size of the sample and the extent of variation in the sampling population – the greater the variation, the larger the sample needs to be. However, it is clear that practical considerations will also play a role in sample size. In order to avoid bias in the selection of the sample, we may resort to two types of sampling procedures: random/probability sampling designs and non-random/non-probability sampling designs.

A sampling design is a *random* or *probability sample* when each individual in the population has an equal and independent chance of inclusion in the sample (see Zhu & David, chapter 6 in this volume). If there are important social dimensions of variation such as age, gender, socioeconomic status, education, then a so-called *stratified* sample is needed which reflects these variables in the community. There are various methods in the social sciences for drawing a random sample, such as the fishbowl draw, computer programs, tables of random numbers, and picking, say, every tenth person. Ngom (2003) investigated lexical borrowing in the multilingual community on the island of St. Louis in Senegal where Arabic, French, and English each carry different prestige. All of the participants had Wolof as their native language. Two hundred participants were divided into two distinct age groups, each age group consisting of 50 males and 50 females. Ngom (p. 355) states, "Subjects were sampled randomly from houses on each of the major 20 streets and meeting places (where people from all over the island meet to spend time together) . . ." Thus age and gender were variables used to stratify the random sample. Why these variables were chosen was the researcher's judgment that they were relevant variables for the community under investigation (see below).

Large-scale variation studies may resort to random sampling. However, such methods assume that the universe from which the sample is drawn is known. There may be difficulty in achieving a random sample when dealing with bilingual minority communities as no relevant sampling frames or lists may exist that identify all of the individuals in the population. It would not be valid to use a telephone catalogue and pick out all persons that have, say, a Russian or a Chinese family name. Census information may try to document the number of people with a certain immigrant background but this is not always reliable. In immigrant communities, some members may be clandestine and wish to avoid public acknowledgment. Trying to map out bilingualism in a geographical area such as a larger city or a region may involve contacting all of the relevant sites and finally resorting only to the ones that actually respond. Because of the lack of census data on multilingualism due to political sensitivity, De Houwer (2004) reports on contacting principals of Dutch-medium primary schools throughout Flanders to ask them to cooperate on a large-scale survey of language use in the home. Those who were willing to participate had all of the children in the school fill out the questionnaires, totaling 18,046. Although the sample may not be representative, in that some school principals did refrain from participating for whatever reason, the study was able to reveal empirically "some idea of the incidence of multilingualism and of the languages involved" (p. 120). Deprez (1999) used a similar approach to reveal the bilingualism in the schools in Paris. Once the bilinguals are identified, follow-up work can be done.

Another type of sampling involves a *non-random* or *non-probability sampling* design. This does not follow the theory of probability in the choice of individuals from the sampling population. Such a sampling design is used when the number of people in a population is either unknown or cannot be identified. Hence it is quite suitable for bilingual research. A potential disadvantage of such a design is that it is not based on probability, and thus one cannot in principle generalize the results to the entire sampling population. However, as Milroy and Gordon (2003) point out with regard to many large-scale sociolinguistic variation studies that have employed stratified random sampling, the number of individuals in each subgroup may be so small that generalizability becomes questionable. And more often than not, such sampling ends up being judgmental, a type of non-probability sampling.

In judgmental or purposive sampling, the individuals selected from a group or community are judged suitable by the researcher, usually on the basis of participation – observation of the group or community (see Codó, chapter 9 in this volume). Most studies of bilingual communities employ this method of selection. Judgmental sampling can also be used to study unique cases that are especially informative. Quota sampling may be used as an added dimension to judgmental sampling. The researcher identifies certain types of speakers, representing such social variables as age and gender, and then selects a certain quota of speakers who fit the profile.

Judgmental sampling is employed not only in studies in which the focus is on the language user but also in those that focus on the languages themselves in grammatical studies of code-switching. In her grammatical analysis of Turkish–Norwegian code-switching, Türker (2000) used data from eight bilingual speakers, three women and five men, all between the ages of 16 and 24 at the time of the recordings, who were born in Turkey and brought to Norway by their parents at various ages, and hence were of the intermediate generation judged to be representative of active code-switchers. In addition to being a judgmental sample, the sample may also contain a quota of individuals representing relevant social variables. Eze (1998) based his language contact study on data from 20 adult speakers in Nigeria fluent in Igbo and English. He states (p. 185), "The informants (9 women and 11 men) represent a variety of occupational groupings, including teachers, traders, and students, among others, and range in age from 18 to 45. All were born in Nigeria, and are highly educated, and learned Igbo as their first language and English at school age." The object was to get as representative a sample as possible. The participants in these two studies had the same native language. Proficiency in one of the languages may have an impact on the grammatical structure of the utterances exhibiting language contact. The selection of participants in both studies was guided by the theory the researchers used. Türker's theoretical framework was the Matrix Language Frame Model (Myers-Scotton, 1997, 2002) and her interest was in how Turkish as the matrix language would accommodate Norwegian as an embedded language, so she selected participants who were more proficient in Turkish. Eze's study is in the quantitative paradigm in variation theory (Poplack, 1993; Poplack & Meechan, 1998) applied to bilingual corpora (see Backus, chapter 13 in the present volume, on data banks and corpora) with an interest in loan words incorporated into Igbo speech.

Another type of non-random/non-probability sampling is referred to as *snowball sampling* (Scott, 2000). The sampling techniques discussed thus far took as a starting point the individual as a representative of a certain social variable. Snowball sampling is used as a sampling technique in examining social networks and hence takes a pre-existing group as the point of departure. This technique can be illustrated with the Filipino study (Hvenekilde & Lanza, 2001; Lanza & Svendsen, 2007) mentioned above. With the help of our field assistant, we contacted a few individuals, who were interviewed. After each interview, the participant was asked to nominate others for the study. These individuals were then interviewed and asked to nominate further participants for the study. This procedure continued, building up the selection of participants like a snowball. There are advantages and disadvantages in selecting participants through this technique. Participants are easily located and as they are recommended by someone they know, access is easier for the researcher. Moreover, in studies of social networks, information gleaned from the interviews can be used to check and cross-check the structure of the participants' reported networks. On the other hand, the composition of the entire sample rests upon the choice of individuals at the first stage. If these individuals belong to a particular faction or have strong biases, the study may be biased. Moreover, it is difficult to use this technique when the sample becomes fairly large. In the Filipino study, although many participants were contacted through this procedure, the sample was supplemented by judgmental sampling in order to gain a more diversified sample.

Once we have selected the individuals from a community or group that we wish to study, we will need to consider possible factors contributing to variation in language use and form among the bilingual speakers. Will, for example, the family be the site for data collection or the school, or any other institution? Jørgensen (1998) studied bilingual Turkish–Danish children's code-switching for wielding power in a school context. He states (p. 242), "The further away from the children's everyday world, the more we find hostility towards the minority tongue, the less it is considered useful or even appropriate." Yet at the interactional level in a school setting, there were only occasional attempts to allude to the superior position of Danish (see Cashman, chapter 16 in this volume). Svennevig (2003) investigated a certain conversational structure in native/non-native interaction in consultations at public offices. Although the structure is not uncommon, the linguistic asymmetry that occurs in such an institutional setting renders the structure particularly salient. Hence, the selection of the site for data can have theoretical importance. It can reveal various aspects of the bilingual's competence and represent society in a different way than traditional correlations between linguistic and social variables such as socioeconomic status, gender, age, and so forth.

When studying a bilingual community, the researcher may wish to select a particular site for investigating language contact, acquisition, or use, merely as a point of departure. McCormick (2002) initially selected a nursery school for her study of District Six, an inner-city neighborhood in Cape Town, characterized by code-switching between English and Afrikaans. She was interested in children's code-switching ability but soon realized that she would need a more thorough grasp of language attitudes and practices in the neighborhood in order to fully understand the children's use of language. Hence, an initial sample may be extended or even modified as the research progresses and we ask further questions. Indeed, the study of one bilingual community can reveal interesting dimensions in another bilingual community, sharing, for example, the same language. Lane (1999) investigated language contact in a bilingual Finnish community in Norway while Lane (2006) investigates code-switching patterns in a bilingual Finnish community in Canada in order to understand the roles of typology and social factors in language contact patterns.

The focus in this section has been on selecting individuals in a group or community that will be representative, in order to assure the generalizability of the findings. However, we may wish to restrict our attention to a case study of a particularly interesting group, or community of practice, even though that group is not necessarily representative for all similar groups. For example, language use in a particular bilingual youth community club may be an interesting and legitimate object of inquiry even though that club may differ from other bilingual youth community clubs (cf. Kallmeyer & Keim, 2003). In this case, generalizability is not an issue.

Section summary: A focus on the group or community

- *Sampling* is the process of selecting a few individuals from a larger group in order to estimate or predict aspects of the larger group.
- A sampling design may be a *random or probability* sample, or a *non-random or non-probability* sample such as judgmental or snowball. In principle, one can generalize from the former type, but not from the latter. Because of the difficulty of defining the universe from which a sample is drawn in bilingual studies, a non-random or non-probability sample is suitable for bilingual research.
- Samples can be *stratified* to reflect various social variables such as age, sex, socioeconomic status, etc.
- In *judgmental* samples, the individuals selected are judged suitable by the researcher.
- *Snowball sampling* is used in studies involving social networks.
- In a case study of a particular group, generalizability is not necessarily an issue.

5.6 Ethical Considerations

As researchers we must be aware of ethical issues involving how we treat those whom we have selected, how we collect our data, and what we do with our results. This involves all research; however, as noted above, minority groups are particularly vulnerable as our research may be used to reinforce pre-existing stereotypes, or may be misused politically or culturally (cf. Zentella, 1997; Li Wei, 2000). Svendsen (2004) reports that the parents of some of the children in her study were at first skeptical due to previous participation in a project that had negative consequences for their work situation.

Many countries will have legal safeguards for participation in research projects. These involve informed consent by the participant, often in written form (see the consent form taken from Lanza, 2004a, in the appendix at the end of this chapter). Surreptitious recording is usually illegal. The participants should clearly understand the purpose and relevance of the study. They must, furthermore, be guaranteed anonymity and must have access to the recordings made of them. Moreover, they may have the right to withdraw from a project at any time and demand that the data be destroyed.

Some populations, for a number of reasons, may not feel at ease with a particular method of data collection (such as an interview), or comfortable about expressing opinions in a questionnaire. A population can in fact be tired of always being the object of study, especially if the members feel they do not get any feedback concerning the results of the study, or feel that such results may be used to their disadvantage. Sensitivity to such issues is the researcher's responsibility. Indeed the researcher's responsibility to the community has become a burning issue, particularly in sociolinguistic research. Cameron, Frazer, Harvey, Rampton, and Richardson (1992) point out that research in the social sciences is often about power relationships, and discuss the potential for developing a research process through which both the researcher and the researched can benefit. What they advocate is the "empowering approach," which gives greater power to the researched by rendering the process one of "research *on*, *for* and *with* social subjects." Every researcher of bilingualism will have to think consciously about how the researched may be involved in the research process. The ethical issues raised here should be an integral part of any work on bilingualism.

Further reading

There are many good introductory books to research methods in the social sciences, particularly aimed at graduate students and containing a chapter on sampling such as Kumar (1999) and Neuman (2003). Milroy and Gordon (2003), Chapter 2, on "Locating and Selecting Subjects," relates specifically to sociolinguistic methods. Johnstone (2000), Chapter 4, discusses "Some Legal and Ethical Issues" in sociolinguistic research. Concerning bilingualism more specifically, see Grosjean (1998) for an excellent overview of methodological and conceptual issues in studying bilinguals, including the selection of individuals, particularly from a psycholinguistic perspective. Li Wei (2000) provides a reflected discussion of methodology particularly from a sociolinguistic perspective. Chapter 3 of Lanza (2004a) presents a detailed discussion on the search for, and selection of, bilingual children and families for case studies of bilingual first language acquisition. Zentella (1997) is a comprehensive study of a bilingual community; Chapter 1 provides an interesting discussion concerning the issue of researcher identity in studying bilingualism in the community context. Fabbro (1999) and Paradis (2004) cover some methodological considerations in neurolinguistic studies of bilinguals.

Appendix: Consent form
(from Lanza, 2004a: 349)

We agree to participate in, and to permit our child to participate in, a study of bilingual language development, conducted by Elizabeth Lanza (a Ph.D. Candidate in linguistics from Georgetown University, Washington, D.C., and NAVF fellow here in Norway) with the understanding that:

(1) The purpose of the study is to observe and describe how young children from bilingual families learn and use language under ordinary circumstances. The intent is <u>not</u> to change our behavior or our child's behavior;

(2) Our child will be audio-taped by E. Lanza in our home for about one hour every month for several months. After this taping session, we will record up to 90 minutes of the child interacting with family members (and/or friends). These tapes will record the child's speech and activities as she/he interacts routinely with family (and/or friends). Scheduling of taping sessions will be made at our convenience;

(3) A diary of our child's language development will be kept by us during the study. At the end of the project, the diary will be our possession; (cf. (7) below)

(4) All tapes will be listened to and analyzed only by E. Lanza, and a limited number of associates, and only for educational and scientific research purposes. The same applies to the material in the diary. At all times our identity will be kept confidential;

(5) Neither we nor any member of our family shall be identified by our actual names in any use made of the tapes or the entries in the diary;

(6) We shall have the right to listen to all audio tapes and to erase any of them or part of them;

(7) At the end of the project, E. Lanza is allowed to keep these tapes and a copy of the diary for future educational and scientific research purposes.

The collection of data of the type in this study is subject to authorization by *Datatilsynet* (cf. *Personregisterlovens* § 9). The conditions stated above in this consent form fulfill the guidelines provided by *Datatilsynet* and the Norwegian Social Science Data Service (NSD).

Signature of parents:

_____

_____

Signature of investigator:

_____

6 Study Design: Cross-sectional, Longitudinal, Case, and Group

Zhu Hua and Annabelle David

6.1 Introduction

This chapter deals with study design from the perspective of experimental psychology. Its emphasis is therefore different from that of chapter 5 and closely related to that of chapter 7. In bilingualism research, as in any research on individuals and their behaviors, study design is an important consideration. A number of factors determine what kind of study design may be appropriate. The most important of all is the nature of research questions. Trochim (2000) identifies three basic types of research questions:

- *Descriptive* studies are designed primarily to describe what is going on or what exists;
- *Relational* studies are intended to look at the relationships between two or more variables;
- *Causal* studies aim to determine whether there is a cause-and-effect relationship between variables.

These three types of research questions are not exclusive of each other. For example, a relational study will usually need to describe the variables first before looking at the relationship, and a causal study assumes that the variables are related to each other.

Once the nature of the inquiry has been determined, two other issues need to be considered: the duration of the study and the number of subjects to be included. This chapter considers study design on these two dimensions. Specifically, we consider cross-sectional and longitudinal, case and group studies. We illustrate the kind of research questions each of these study designs can address, and the advantages and disadvantages of each design. It should be pointed out that these study designs are used in a wide variety of research, not just bilingualism and multilingualism research. However, we use published studies of bilingualism and multilingualism as examples where possible.

6.2   Overview

The four study designs we consider here differ on two dimensions: the duration of the study and the number of subjects to be studied. A study can be a snapshot of a particular moment in time or cover a considerable period of time; it can include one subject or a group of subjects. The two dimensions also interact: a single-case study and a group study can both be carried out at particular points in time or over a period of time. Which study design is used depends on what research questions are to be addressed. For example, if a study is to profile the typical language behavior of English/Spanish speakers of different age groups, socioeconomic backgrounds, and educational levels, a cross-sectional study which can be completed within a short period of time is appropriate. If the study is to track changes in behavior over time or to evaluate the effect of educational and clinical intervention, a longitudinal study is required.

Study design may affect the type of data to be collected and ultimately analyzed, and the research instrument one can use. For instance, single-case longitudinal studies tend to produce large quantities of recorded conversations (see chapter 10) and observations, while cross-sectional group studies often involve interviews, questionnaires (chapter 9), laboratory experiments, and tests in controlled conditions (chapter 7). It is worth noting that study design of the kind we are considering in this chapter is most often discussed in psycholinguistic and clinical research. It appears to be of a lesser concern in ethnographic research or conversation and interactional analysis (see chapter 16). This is partly because the very nature of the research paradigm and approach has predetermined the length of study and the number of subjects to be studied. For example, conversation analysis (chapter 16) tends to examine data from a fairly small number of individuals, and ethnographic studies (chapter 14) are often conducted over an extended period of time.

6.3   Cross-Sectional Design

In a cross-sectional study, data is usually collected at one point in time, either from the entire relevant population or from a subset which is selected according to carefully defined criteria. In bilingualism research, cross-sectional studies usually involve a few groups which differ either in age or in other variables such as exposure to a second language, language proficiency, etc. Cross-sectional studies are used for a number of purposes. First, they can explore the relationship between variables and generate hypotheses for future research. In studies of this type, subjects are often grouped according to different variables and their performance or behavior is sampled. The differences or similarities in their performance or behavior will be used to interpret the role of the variables in the particular behavior. For example, to examine the impact of acquiring two languages on the phonological system, Study 1 uses language background (monolingual vs. bilingual and French vs. English) as a variable, and children's speech production as another.

Study 1

J. Paradis (2001) Do bilingual two-year-olds have separate phonological systems? *International Journal of Bilingualism*, 5(1), 19–38.

Research questions: Do bilingual two-year-olds have separate phonological systems? If so, are there cross-linguistic influences between them?

Subjects: 18 English-speaking monolingual, 18 French-speaking monolingual, and 17 French-English bilingual children (mean age = 30 months).

Data collection: children's speech (in particular, four-syllable target words) was collected in a nonsense-word repetition task.

Results: Bilingual two-year-olds have separate but non-autonomous phonological systems and there is restricted cross-linguistic effect.

Second, in studies of language acquisition, cross-sectional design is often used to arrive at normative data by profiling the language behavior of participants in different age groups. The norms may then be used either for cross-linguistic comparison or for identifying children with speech and language difficulties. In a typical cross-sectional normative study, a number of subjects are selected from different age bands and a large amount of data is collected from them on the assumption that if sufficient data are collected, a typical developmental pattern will appear. In essence, age is treated as a variable in this type of cross-sectional study. Oller and Eilers (2002) have carried out several cross-sectional studies in order to evaluate the linguistic and academic effects of bilingualism in school children. One of their research questions and the corresponding research design are summarized below.

Study 2

D. K. Oller and R. E. Eilers (eds.) (2002) *Language and Literacy in Bilingual Children*. Clevedon: Multilingual Matters.

Research question: What is the comparative performance of monolingual English and bilingual children on English standardized tests?

Subjects: 952 elementary students in the Dade County public school system.

Data collection: a battery of standardized tests of oral language and academic performance.

Results: Monolinguals outperformed bilinguals in English, although the gap between monolinguals and bilinguals in both types of educational programs did tend to narrow across grade.

Third, cross-sectional studies can estimate prevalence figures for disorder (i.e. the number of cases of a disorder that exists in a defined population at a specified point in time). For example, Dodd, Holm, Zhu Hua, Crosbie, and Broomfield's study (2006) suggests that prevalence of speech impairment is 6.4 percent.

The advantages of cross-sectional studies are many:

- Economy in time and cost. Cross-sectional designs can collect a large number of data over a shorter period of time. They can be very short in study duration and are quicker to carry out than longitudinal studies.
- Increased statistical robustness. As the amount of data increases, it is possible to make statistically robust generalizations and claims.
- Multiple variables and multiple subjects who might be located at different places.
- Replicability. This is an advantage that cannot be overlooked in the field of multilingualism research, in which similarities and differences in developmental patterns of children speaking different languages or language pairs are an important issue. One way of mapping similarities and differences in such a context is to compare the normative data collected through cross-sectional studies carried out with comparable criteria. Alternatively, language background can serve as a variable, and the effect of different language backgrounds on developmental patterns is examined, as illustrated in Study 1.

There are a number of pitfalls associated with cross-sectional studies.

- Inability to measure sequential developmental patterns and change. Although the norms derived by means of a cross-sectional design describe what is typical of different age groups, cross-sectional studies are unable to trace a sequential developmental pattern of a particular subject or change over time.
- Inability to assess individual differences. Since cross-sectional studies are usually concerned with typical patterns associated with a particular bilingual or multilingual group, individual differences are often overlooked in the process of generalization.
- Weaker evidence of causality. Cross-sectional studies can explore the interrelationships between variables, but they cannot prove the causal nature of the relationship.
- Increased chances of error with more subjects.
- Increased cost with more subjects.
- High demand on inter- and intra-researcher consistency in the data collection.
- Limited availability of bilingual samples. The heterogeneity of the bilingual population is one of the problems specific to large-scale bilingual studies. In order to reach a generalization, a researcher sometimes has to recruit a certain number of bilingual speakers as subjects. However, bilingual populations tend to differ in the age of acquisition of another language, language proficiency, etc.

In order to run a cross-sectional study, the researcher needs to carry out the following stages:

1 Determine and define the research questions

Cross-sectional studies usually answer one or several questions such as what and when.

2   Select samples and determine data gathering and analysis techniques

The size of the sample is crucial in cross-sectional studies. A balance must be struck between the improved representativeness of the findings and the increased cost and chances of error incurred by a larger study. Ideally, the greater the size, the more representative the findings will be in statistical terms and the more likely it is that a typical pattern minimizing individual differences can be generalized. However, there are two restraining factors. One is the heterogeneity of the bilingual population (the bilingual population varies in sequence of acquisition, language proficiency levels in the two languages, age of exposure to the second language, etc.). The other is problems associated with large-scale studies: a tremendous amount of time and effort is needed to contact subjects and collect data from them.

Cross-sectional studies allow a number of data collection techniques such as surveys, observation, tests, or instruments.

3   Collect data in the field

Given the fact that cross-sectional studies usually involve large samples, intra- and inter-researcher consistency in the data collection needs to be monitored carefully.

4   Evaluate and analyze the data

A critical interpretation of the findings in a cross-sectional study is essential. The most important issue in this type of study is differentiating a causal relationship from simple association. As noted earlier, cross-sectional studies are able to explore the interrelationships between variables, but not cause-and-effect relationships. For example, a cross-sectional study may find an association between a low socioeconomic status (SES) family background and the occurrence of speech and language disorders. There are a number of plausible explanations for this: children from families with low SES may have input of poor quality, which in turn results in disorder in language and speech development.

Another problem in cross-sectional normative studies is "regression." The process of language acquisition and learning is not linear, but can involve regression; that is, a child may fail to produce sounds, words, or features which she or he has used correctly on previous occasions. This phenomenon occurs not only at an individual level, but also at a group level, though other factors such as statistical probability and the representativeness of the sample complicate the situation more when it comes to a group trend, especially in the context of a normative study. For example, it may be found that more than 90 percent of one age group can produce a language feature correctly, while only 80 percent of an older age group can do so. When this happens, a minimal number of consecutive age groups which have satisfied the acquisition criteria, say, three age bands, need to be set up to maintain consistency across different features.

5   Prepare the report

One way to report data collected from a cross-sectional study is first to describe the typical patterns of each group and then to compare data on different groups in data analysis and discussion. Alternatively, a comparison can be made first and then examples from each group given.

A good cross-sectional study report is transparent about the limitations of the study due to problems inherent in the design or as the result of the specific research context.

Section summary

Cross-sectional studies collect data from groups of people at a single point in time. The advantages are:

- Economy in time and cost
- Statistical robustness
- Multiple variables and multiple subjects
- Replicability

The pitfalls are:

- Inability to measure sequential developmental patterns and change
- Inability to assess individual differences
- Weaker evidence of causality
- Increased chances of error
- Increased cost with multiple subjects
- High demand on inter- and intra-researcher consistency
- Limited availability of bilingual samples

6.4 Longitudinal Design

In a typical longitudinal study, a small number of subjects are observed over a considerable period of time or repeatedly sampled at predetermined intervals within a period. Longitudinal studies examine one or more groups of participants at several points in time. They usually deal with a fairly small number of subjects because of the demanding nature of the data collection process. The timescale varies enormously, from a few weeks to a few years depending on the research question.

Longitudinal study research can address issues and support data collection methods in ways that are not possible with cross-sectional design (see section 6.5 for differences between cross-sectional and longitudinal studies). In particular, longitudinal studies are valuable for answering the following research questions:

1 Changes over a period of time. For example, changes in linguistic performance.
2 Age-related bilingual language development and change. Study 3 addresses the same question as Study 1, but adopts a different design.

3   Incidence of disorder (i.e., the number of new cases that develop during a specified time interval).
4   Cause-and-effect relationships between variables; participant variability is controlled by the fact that the participants can be compared with themselves.
5   Evaluating the effectiveness of treatment in the clinical context.
6   Evaluating the effectiveness of a particular teaching method or program in a bilingual educational context.

Study 3

M. H. Kesharvarz and D. Ingram (2002) The early phonological development of a Farsi-English bilingual child. *International Journal of Bilingualism*, 6(3), 255–69.

Research question: Do bilingual children begin phonological acquisition with one phonological system or two?

Subject: a Farsi/English bilingual child, aged from 8 months to 20 months

Data collection: the child's speech sampled over a year through regular diary observation, periodic audio recording, and occasional informal experiments on comprehension and production.

Results: The child has acquired two separate phonologies with mutual influence in that he makes occasional use of phonological features of Farsi in English words and vice versa.

Within longitudinal studies, there are many variations in the design with regard to how participants are sampled and how many times they are studied. Two classification systems are given below to demonstrate the boundaries of longitudinal studies.

First, longitudinal studies can be classified as either trend, panel, or cohort studies, according to whether the same participants are studied at different times and how.

A *trend* study samples different groups of people from the same population at different points in time. An example is the opinion poll. It provides information about changes at an aggregate level, but it cannot tell how many people changed their position and how many stayed with their original choice.

A *panel* study measures the same sample of respondents at different points in time. Panel studies can provide data suitable for comparison and are particularly useful for predicting long-term or cumulative effects. Among the best-known panel studies are the US Panel Study of Income Dynamics (PSID), the British Household Panel Study (BHPS), and the German Socio-Economic Panel (SOEP).

A *cohort* study examines the same groups of people over time. Each group comprises people who share a certain condition or receive a particular treatment. The group is followed over time and compared with another group whose members do not share the condition or receive the treatment under investigation. Three birth cohort studies, the National Child Development Study (1958 cohort), the 1970 British Cohort Study, and the Millennium Cohort Study, all carried out by the Centre for Longitudinal Studies, Institute of Education, UK, are good examples. This study design is usually used to evaluate the effect of a treatment or teaching method.

Another aspect of the different kinds of longitudinal studies is the number of times data are collected from the participants. Studies in which data are collected twice or a few times are *repeated measures*. Those in which data are collected many times are *time series*.

The advantages of longitudinal study design include:

- Capability of capturing sequential developmental patterns and changes. Since longitudinal studies track changes over time, they can examine the sequential developmental patterns of a particular bilingual population or the long-term effects of treatment.
- Capability of examining individual differences. Since longitudinal studies usually include a small number of subjects, they are very sensitive to individual differences.
- Increased comprehensiveness and representativeness of the data. Longitudinal studies allow for a large amount of data to be collected from every single individual over time. This provides a more comprehensive and representative picture of the variables under investigation.
- Multiple data sources. Longitudinal studies can utilize quantitative vs. qualitative data or primary data vs. secondary data. Primary data can be gathered by various data collection methods such as interviews, observation, surveys, diaries, tests, and instruments. Secondary datasets, such as government censuses and statistics, are usually designed and collected by a third party.

Longitudinal design also has its pitfalls:

- A long study span. Longitudinal studies are very time-consuming and slow as the data need to be collected several times over a period.
- Cost. The fact that longitudinal studies are slow and time-consuming makes them expensive to run. Maintaining contact with the participants can be very costly in terms of time, research personnel, and money.
- Participant attrition. A small number of samples and a long study duration mean that longitudinal studies are vulnerable to attrition: subjects may drop out for a variety of reasons such as lack of interest or of the ability to perform the test, or unforeseeable events such as illness or death.
- Practice effect. When subjects have been tested several times, their improvement in performance may be due to their getting used to the test or to the additional practice the test has given them.
- Lack of statistical robustness. The small number of participants makes statistical analyses less reliable or even infeasible. Significant differences between participants limit the generalizability of the research findings.
- Vulnerability to missing data or chance error. In a small-scale study, any missing data or data entry errors can jeopardize the generalizability of research findings.
- High demand on consistency. When participants have to be tested a number of times over a long period of time, the consistency in the data collection method needs to be monitored over time.

Apart from being aware of the advantages and pitfalls inherent in a longitudinal study, a researcher needs to carry out the following stages during a research cycle.

1   Determine and define the research questions
A longitudinal study usually answers questions such as whether there are changes over time and how these changes happen.

2 Select samples and determine data gathering and analysis techniques
Depending on the research question, decisions need to be made on:

- whether samples should be selected randomly or according to certain criteria;
- whether or not to group subjects with the same background or condition together;
- how many samples to include, bearing the balance between generalizability of findings and the potential cost incurred by using more samples;
- whether or not to include extreme or rare samples in the study.

Longitudinal studies that examine social, language, and cognitive development usually use a small number of subjects. They are sometimes referred to as longitudinal case studies or group studies.

Longitudinal studies provide opportunities to examine multiple variables and use multiple data sources.

3   Collect data in the field
Although it is important to maximize consistency between each data collection, data collection methods in longitudinal studies may change for a number of reasons:

- more effective measures may be developed as the study progresses;
- additional research questions emerge during the data collection;
- changes in resources: resources which were formerly available are now unavailable, or vice versa.
- strategies are developed to cope with participant attrition and "practice effect."

Special efforts and long-term commitment are needed to maintain contact with the participants during the course of longitudinal studies.

4   Evaluate and analyze the data
The longitudinal study design provides researchers with opportunities to trace change and development over time by comparing data collected at different times. For example, if other variables are stable over time (gender, SES, etc.), researchers on language acquisition can put the collected data on one subject together, comparing each observation with some earlier or later one. If there are changes, researchers can make reliable estimates of the interrelationship between age factor and changes.

5   Prepare the report
When presenting data collected in longitudinal studies, researchers need to achieve a balance between information and conciseness. Generally, there are two ways to present data. In the first, data collections from different times are first presented in chronological order and then compared. In the second, a comparison or a summary account is presented first, and a detailed account of the patterns emerging out of the data collected at different times follows.

In comparisons of data in longitudinal studies, graphs or charts delineating patterns at different times are a useful tool.

Section summary

A longitudinal study collects data from a small number of subjects a few times over a period. This has the following advantages:

- Ability to track sequential developmental patterns and change
- Individual differences
- Comprehensive data
- Multiple data sources

But there are pitfalls too:

- Long study span
- Cost
- Participant attrition
- Practice effect
- Lack of statistical robustness
- Vulnerability to missing data or chance error
- High demand on consistency

6.5 A Comparison of Cross-sectional and Longitudinal Study Designs

There are two essential differences between cross-sectional study and longitudinal studies. First, cross-sectional studies describe how populations differ according to age by comparing groups of individuals of different ages at one point in time, while longitudinal studies focus on changes over time. Secondly, cross-sectional studies are useful for identifying correlations between variables, while longitudinal studies can go one step further and examine causal relationships between variables.

These differences can be highlighted by comparing two empirical studies which explore the same research question but use different designs. Study 1 uses a cross-sectional study and a nonsense-word repetition task to collect speech data; Study 2 adopts a longitudinal case study and a variety of methods (observation, diaries, etc.) to collect speech data. They reach almost the same conclusion, namely that the bilingual child or children they studied have separate phonological systems which are subject to mutual influence from two languages, but, as our current interest is in study design, we give a critical interpretation of their findings to show the strengths and weaknesses of the two studies.

First of all, which population does the conclusion apply to in the two studies? Since Study 1 recruited a number of bilingual children (17), it seems to be more generalized than Study 2, which only examines one child. As the authors of the second study suggested, "other children may show a different pattern, depending on their exposure to the two languages and the role of language dominance." In effect, the finding in Study 2 is very tentative.

Second, which aspects of phonological systems are examined in the studies? Study 2 explores multiple sources of data and covers more aspects of phonological systems than Study 1: it examines stress, consonant inventory, and substitute patterns of some sounds in the subject's phonological system, while Study 1 focuses only on the phenomenon of word truncation (i.e. deletion of syllables that are not stressed) in the speech produced under experimental condition.

Third, how reliable are the conclusions in the two studies? Study 1 strengthens its conclusion by using the control group and statistical analysis of the quantitative data. In contrast, Study 2 compares the size of bilinguals' consonant inventories with those of monolingual children of the same age reported in other studies. It does not exploit the benefit of longitudinal study by looking into the sequential development of the child.

In summary, using a cross-sectional study design, Study 1 seems to achieve more reliability in its conclusion by including a control group and more generalizability in terms of population by examining groups of children. However, it only looks at one particular aspect of phonology (i.e. weak syllable deletion). It remains to be seen whether other aspects of bilingual phonology are operating the same way. The longitudinal case study in Study 2 uses multiple sources of data, and hence its findings apply generally to various aspects of phonology. However, the fact that only one bilingual child was included in the study jeopardizes the generalizability of the findings.

6.6   Case Studies

Studies of bilingualism, especially of bilingual acquisition, are often based on single cases. One of the most well-known and earliest case studies is Leopold's of the speech development of his daughter who was brought up bilingually (Leopold, 1970). A more recent case is Deuchar and Quay's (2000) study of the first author's daughter.

Case studies are in-depth investigations of a single participant or a small group of participants. They are associated with the following characteristics:

- The number of cases in case studies is usually very small, though in theory they can include multiple cases. Some authors use *single*, *double*, or *multiple* case studies to differentiate studies that include a single subject and those that include data from two or more subjects.
- Case studies are usually concerned with the individual, not with the general patterns of a population.
- Case studies often use qualitative methods of data analysis that stress the interpretation of the data, rather than quantitative or statistical methods.

- Case studies generally use naturalistic data, though single-participant experiments which involve manipulation of variables by the researcher are commonly used in clinical settings to trace the natural course of a disorder or in psychology to test treatments.
- Case studies can be done over any length of time.

Case studies can be used for the following types of research activities:

1 To describe cognitive, social, language, or conversational behavior of a particular member of or group within a bilingual population.
2 To describe the natural course of a disorder or the effect of treatment.
3 To refute a generalization. The findings of a case study, if they contradict the predictions of a well-established theory, can be used as counter-evidence to refute a generalization. For example, in studies on language acquisition, Jakobson (1941/1968) claimed that the order of acquisition of phonemes was related to the frequency of the phonemes in the world's languages. However, a number of subsequent case studies find that this claim cannot account for the fact that bilingual children often have different sequences of acquisition of the sounds shared by the two languages (for a review, see Zhu Hua & Dodd, 2006).
4 To show what is possible and to propose new hypotheses for further research. Such studies can open up new areas of study and offer new questions or variables for further research. Study 4 is a good example of the use of case studies to explore new approaches.
5 In extreme or unique cases where the phenomenon being studied is acutely visible, to draw inferences which can subsequently be generalized to less extreme cases.

Study 4

D. Friedland and N. Miller (1999) Language mixing in bilingual speakers with Alzheimer's dementia: A conversation analysis approach. *Aphasiology*, 13, 427–44.

Research question: How successfully can conversation analysis explain and describe language-mixing problems?

Subjects: four bilingual women with Alzheimer's dementia.

Data collection: spontaneous speech data and formal language and neuropsychological tests.

Results: The conversation analysis approach provides more insight than quantitative approaches in the analysis of code-switching.

The case study design has a number of advantages. A key strength is that it allows *multiple sources and techniques* in the data-gathering process. Data can be both qualitative and quantitative and can come from primary research as well as from secondary sources such as government publication, novels, etc. Tools for collecting data can include surveys, tests, instruments, interviews, and observation.

By allowing multiple sources of data and recognizing the uniqueness of each individual, a case study is able to provide *rich and in-depth data* on the behavior of an individual or small group.

Case studies can afford *intensive study* of a particular case or group, especially those rare, unique, or *extreme cases* that are usually overlooked in cross-sectional study or group study.

There are of course drawbacks to the case study design. They include:

- Limitations in the generalizability of the conclusion. In the past, case studies have been considered as lacking in scientific value, since they do not allow generalization. Findings from a case study are in most cases tentative and subject to individual variations.
- Susceptibility to bias. Case studies are more subject to research bias than any other method, for many reasons. For example, during an intensive study, the researcher will need to be in constant contact with the person being studied. It can be difficult to remain detached about the data collection and interpretation. The data might be influenced by the practice effect.
- Unsuitability for statistical analysis. While some data can be reduced to quantitative forms such as totals and averages in most cast studies, most of the data cannot be analyzed in statistical forms.
- The need for repeated access to subjects.
- The need for skills in many techniques. Multiple sources of data require a researcher to be adept in a variety of data-collection techniques.

While a case study has a similar research cycle to cross-sectional studies and longitudinal studies, there are considerations that researchers need to be aware of during the stages of a case study. These are listed below; for a more comprehensive review, see Stake (1995) and Yin (2003a, 2000b).

1   Determine and define the research questions
Case studies generally answer questions which begin with "how" and "why."

2   Select cases and determine data-gathering and analysis techniques
Depending on the research questions, a researcher needs to decide the following issues:

- whether to study cases which are unique in some way or cases which are considered typical;
- whether to select a single case or multiple cases;
- what data-collection method(s) to use and how they will help the researcher to avoid losing sight of the original research purpose.

3   Collect data in the field
Since case studies are susceptible to researcher's bias, it is important to document how data are collected, stored, and analyzed with rigor (i.e. comprehensively and systematically, in formats that can be referenced and sorted) to ensure readers' confidence in the data.

4   Evaluate and analyze the data
Depending on the number of cases included in studies, there are two broad types of analysis: within-case and cross-case analysis. With within-case analysis, a researcher

studies all the relevant data about each case to identify unique patterns within the data for the single case. With cross-case analysis, a researcher examines, for example, similar pairs of cases for differences, or dissimilar pairs for similarities.

5 Prepare the report

A case study report will benefit from a clear rationale at the beginning. Since case studies have been regarded as less capable of making generalizations, researchers need to justify the use of a case study to explore the issues they are interested in. A good case study report is transparent about the limitations of the study in terms of methodological pitfalls and the constraints the context places on the data collected. It will also put forward questions for further research and bring in a wider theoretical context.

The data in case studies should be presented in accessible ways, such as:

- describing each case in a separate and parallel section or chapter before comparing cases;
- providing a detailed chronological account of each case (sometimes in the form of story);
- presenting particular factors or aspects of the case in graphs or charts;
- including the "raw data," or part of it, in an appendix where applicable.

These techniques serve three purposes: to increase confidence in the findings by offering readers opportunities to reach their own conclusions; to allow comparison with data from similar case studies which may not be analyzed or presented in the same way as the current one; to uncover patterns that are considered not relevant to the current research questions but may become relevant later, or patterns that are not central to the current research questions but relevant to other researchers with different perspectives.

Section summary

A case study collects data from a single or several cases. Its advantages are:

- Multiple sources of data
- Richness and depth of data
- Intensive study and possibility of considering extreme cases

The pitfalls are:

- Limitations in generalizability
- Susceptibility to bias
- Unsuitability for statistical analysis
- Need for repeated access to subjects
- Need for skills in many techniques

6.7   Group Studies

Unlike case studies, group studies have only recently developed into a separate research design, though boundaries between group studies and case studies are not always clear-cut. Group studies are intensive studies of a group of subjects who are examined in parallel with each other. Since the number of participants in case studies can be one, two, or a few, group studies can be seen as a special category of case studies. However, there are differences between multiple-case studies and group studies. For example, when multiple cases are used, each case is treated as a single case. Each case's conclusions can then be used as information contributing to the whole study, but each case remains a single case. In contrast, group studies are more interested in the group trend.

The main differences between group studies and cohort studies (a subtype of longitudinal study, see section 6.4) are that:

- group studies examine only one group; cohort studies often include several groups;
- group studies are aimed at comparing individuals *within* the group; cohort studies are concerned with similarities and differences *between* groups;
- group studies can be a snapshot or span a period; cohort studies are, by definition, carried out over a period.

The main differences between group studies and cross-sectional studies are that:

- group studies examine only one group; cross-sectional studies, by definition, include several groups;
- group studies try to depict a group trend without overlooking individual variations; cross-sectional studies focus on generalizations.

6.7.1   *Specific types of research questions*

Group studies are mainly used to establish trends within a population. If the group is small, it may be possible for a group study to highlight individual variations. David (2004) carried out a group study to examine differences in development of lexical categories.

Study 5
A. David (2004) The developing bilingual lexicon. PhD thesis, Newcastle University, UK.
Research question: What is the distribution of lexical categories in the first 500 words of young bilingual children?
Subjects: 13 French/English-speaking bilingual children.
Data collection: repeated quantitative (vocabulary checklists) and qualitative (speech samples, socio-demographic questionnaires) data collection between 1 and 3 years old.

Research findings: Bilinguals' lexical categories follow the same pattern as those of monolinguals, despite cross-linguistic influences.

As the result of an increased number of subjects and a shift in the focus, group studies have the following strengths compared with single-case studies:

- They are suitable for statistical analysis. With more subjects, statistical analysis of quantitative data becomes feasible.
- They are less subject to participant attrition than group studies, and missing data will not jeopardize the research findings.
- They use a balanced sample. With careful control of variables, group studies are less likely to be influenced by extreme cases.

Group studies also have a number of inherent problems:

- They give less priority to individual differences. Individual differences sometimes have to be overlooked, either not to lose sight of group trends or due to the pressure on limited resources imposed by a larger number of subjects.
- Group studies can be very time-consuming and costly.
- It is difficult to measure multiple variables because of limited resources. Group studies tend not to report on single individual results.
- Consistency between data collections needs to be monitored.

To run a group study, the following cycle is to be followed:

1 Determine and define the research questions
Group studies usually focus on group trends and answer questions that begin with "what."

2 Select samples and determine data-gathering and analysis techniques
A researcher needs to decide on the number of subjects to be included in a study, taking into account that the more subjects are included,

- the more generalizable and reliable the group trend will be,
- the less attention will be given to each individual, and the more likely it is that individual variations will have to be overlooked, and
- the more time-consuming and costly the study will be.

3 Collect data in the field
Consistency between successive rounds of data collection needs to be monitored when those data are collected repeatedly from the same subject or from different subjects.

4 Evaluate and analyze the data
Group studies tend to use quantitative measures and statistical analysis. Similarities and differences between subjects need to be examined in the context of research questions.

5   Prepare the report

There are two ways to present the data:

- present the group trend first before going into some level of detail about each individual; or
- present each individual as a case study first before comparing the whole group and teasing out the group trend.

Graphs or charts can show the reader the distribution of the whole group according to various variables.

A good group study report often acknowledges the research dilemma facing larger-scale research, namely the subtle yet crucial balance between group trend and individual differences, generalizability and practicality.

Section summary

Group studies collect data, usually repeatedly, from a group of subjects who are examined in parallel. The advantages are:

- Suitability for statistical analysis
- Less vulnerability to participant attrition
- Balanced sample

The pitfalls are:

- Less priority to individual differences
- Cost in time and money
- Difficulty of measuring multiple variables
- High demand on consistency in data collection

6.8   Combination of Designs

The four study designs reviewed above are not exclusive of each other. Some of them can be combined in one project. For example, in the studies cited and summarized in previous sections, Study 2 combines longitudinal and case studies, and Study 5 combines longitudinal and group studies. Table 6.1 shows possible combinations of these studies.

It is also possible to have a repeated cross-sectional study: cross-sectional data are repeated over time and the time dimension is incorporated into the design. Studies 6 and 7 are an example of how a cross-sectional study is combined with a

Table 6.1 Possible combinations of four research study designs

	Cross-sectional	*Longitudinal*	*Case*	*Group*
Cross-sectional		Possible (repeated cross-sectional study)	Never Very often	Possible Possible
Longitudinal	Possible (repeated cross-sectional study)			
Case	Never	Very often		Subtype
Group	Possible	Possible	Subtype	

time dimension. In Study 6, a cross-sectional approach was used to investigate developmental changes in basic-level lexical production and cognitive processing in early sequential bilinguals, exploring the effects of age and years of experience during single-language and mixed-language picture naming. Study 7 reports on the performance of a subgroup of the original study participants on the same experimental task.

Study 6

K. Kohnert, E. Bates, and A. E. Hernandez (1999) Balancing bilinguals: Lexical-semantic production and cognitive processing in children learning Spanish and English. *Journal of Speech, Language, and Hearing Research*, 42(6), 1400–13.

Research questions: What are the profiles of the developmental changes in lexical production skills, and highlighting the effects of age, years of experience, and basic-level cognitive processing (e.g. resistance to interference) on lexical performance?

Subjects: a total of 100 sequential bilinguals, 20 at each of five age levels (5–7, 8–10, 11–13, 14–16, and young adults). All had acquired Spanish from birth at home and been formally exposed to English from age 5.

Data collection: timed picture-naming task.

Results: Spanish dominance in early childhood developed into English dominance in early adulthood and, despite slower responses in mixed-language condition, evidence was found of ability to resist cognitive interference.

Study 7

K. Kohnert (2002) Picture naming in early sequential bilinguals: A 1-year follow up. *Journal of Speech, Language and Hearing Research*. 45(4), 759–71.

Research question: What are the effects of age and years of experience during single-language and mixed-language picture-naming?

Subjects: time 1 testing: 28 Spanish-English bilingual children, mean age = 9.2 years; time 2 testing: the same children, mean age = 10.2 years.

Results: L2 seems to be developing faster than L1 with age and years of language experience, as a result of cognitive development in the control of the dual-language system.

6.9   Conclusion

This chapter reviews the key characteristics of four study designs: cross-sectional, longitudinal, case, and group. Each has its advantages and disadvantages. They serve to address different types of research questions. It is important to emphasize therefore that it is the research question that determines what study design a project should follow. All research projects should follow the research cycle outlined in the chapter. A combination of different designs often helps to fill the gaps that a single design may leave.

Further reading

Introduction to all the designs

Bryman, A. (1988) *Quantity and Quality in Social Research*. London and New York: Routledge.

Cross-sectional studies

Baltes, P. B., H. W. Reese, and J. R. Nesselroade (1988) *Life-Span Developmental Psychology: An Introduction to Research Methods*. Hillsdale, NJ: Lawrence Erlbaum Associates.
Creswell, J. W. (1998) *Qualitative Inquiry and Research Design: Choosing among Five Traditions*. Thousand Oaks, CA: Sage Publications.
Davies, R. B. (1994) From cross-sectional to longitudinal analysis. In A. Dale and R. B. Davies (eds.), *Analysing Social and Political Change: A Case Book of Methods*. London: Sage Publishers.

Longitudinal studies

Menrad, S. (1991) *Longitudinal Research*. Newbury Park: Sage Publications.
Ruspini, E. (1999) Longitudinal research and the analysis of social change. In E. Ruspini (ed.), Longitudinal analysis: A bridge between quantitative and qualitative social research. Special issue of *Quality and Quantity*, 33(3), 219–27.

Case studies and group studies

Gomm, R., M. Hammersley, and R. Foster (eds.) (2000) *Case Study Method: Key Issues, Key Texts*. Thousand Oaks, CA: Sage.
Stake, R. E. (1995) *The Art of Case Study Research*. Thousand Oaks, CA: Sage.
Yin, R. K. (2003a) *Applications of Case Study Research*. Thousand Oaks, CA: Sage.
Yin, R. K. (2003b) *Case Study Research: Design and Methods*. Thousand Oaks, CA: Sage.

Appendix: An overview of cross-sectional, longitudinal, case, and group studies

Study type	Study duration	Number of subjects	Types of research question	Strengths	Weaknesses
Cross-sectional	Usually snapshot	A few groups	Descriptive Relational	Economy in time and cost Statistical robustness Multiple variables and multiple subjects Replicability	Inability to measure sequential developmental patterns and change Inability to assess individual differences Weaker evidence of causality Increased chances of error Increased cost with multiple subjects High demand on inter- and intra-researcher consistency Limited availability of bilingual samples
Longitudinal	A period of time	Usually a small number	Descriptive Relational Causal	Ability to capture sequential developmental patterns and change Ability to capture individual differences Comprehensive data	Long study span Cost Participant attrition Practice effects Lack of statistical robustness Vulnerability to missing data High demand on consistency
Case	Varies	One or several subjects	Descriptive Relational Causal	Multiple data sources Multiple sources of data Richness and depth of data Allowing intensive study and consideration of extreme cases	Limitations in generalizability Susceptibility to bias Unsuitability for statistical analysis Need for direct or repeated access to subjects Need for skills in many techniques
Group	Varies	Usually a single group of a large number of subjects	Descriptive Relational	Suitability for statistical analysis Less vulnerability to participant attrition Balanced sample	Less priority to individual differences Cost in time and money Difficulty of measuring multiple variables High demand on consistency

7 Laboratory Designs and Paradigms: Words, Sounds, and Sentences

Judith F. Kroll, Chip Gerfen, and Paola E. Dussias

7.1 Introduction

In the past 10 to 15 years there has been a notable increase in the number of studies that take a psycholinguistic or cognitive approach to bilingualism. Although there is a long history of research on issues such as whether there is a critical period[1] for second language acquisition (see Birdsong, 1999a, for a review), it is only recently that cognitive scientists have begun to see that bilingualism is the norm for most of the world's population. Because cognitive science seeks to identify universal properties of thought, the bilingual has become a model subject of study rather than a marked case. Researchers have come to see that studies of bilingual cognition provide critical evidence regarding the principles that constrain or permit interactions across cognitive systems. At the same time, the development of a set of laboratory tools to investigate language performance and its neurocognitive basis has enabled a new experimental approach to bilingualism that is informed by studies of cognitive processing and brain function, in addition to the linguistic approaches that have traditionally characterized bilingual research.

What do bilinguals tell us about cognition? And what can cognitive approaches tell us about bilingualism? In the sections that follow we introduce readers to some of the laboratory designs and paradigms that are commonly used in experimental studies of bilingualism. The methods that we describe have been used to ask how a bilingual manages the presence of two languages in a single mind. If the two languages were entirely independent of one another, then the question might not be as pressing. However, as we will see in the discussion that follows, there is a great deal of evidence that suggests that the bilingual is not two monolinguals in one

---

[1] The term 'critical period' refers to a time in early childhood, typically assumed to be prior to the onset of puberty, when individuals are hypothesized to be sensitive to the input of the languages to which they are exposed in a manner that allows native-like acquisition. Although there is agreement that early exposure results in superior language acquisition, there is little agreement about its basis.

(Grosjean, 1989). Instead, the recent experimental research demonstrates that the bilingual's two languages interact closely. These interactions influence the way in which bilinguals understand words spoken and read in each language, how speech is produced with or without a foreign accent, and how sentences are comprehended and produced when the grammar of the two languages is similar in some ways and distinct in others. What is remarkable is that the observed interactions are not restricted to the second language, but affect the native language as well. The methods that have been developed to examine language processing in bilinguals have been used to explore the scope of these interactions and the constraints that are imposed by the structure of the specific languages themselves. Although it might seem that a language system that has to cope with two sets of competing alternatives might suffer in some respects, the recent evidence suggests that bilingualism confers benefits to cognition by virtue of forcing the development of cognitive skills to negotiate the activity of the two languages (e.g., Bialystok, 2005) and that there may even be structural consequences for brain organization (e.g., Mechelli, Crinion, Noppeney, et al., 2004).

In this chapter we review three major areas of research activity in experimental psycholinguistics. Section 7.2 examines the way in which bilinguals recognize words when they are spoken or read in each language and when they produce words in the language in which they intend to speak. Section 7.3 addresses speech to ask how the sounds of each of the bilingual's two languages are processed when they are heard or spoken. Section 7.4 examines sentences to ask how the grammatical structures and preferences associated with each of the bilingual's languages are affected by the presence of both languages. Within each of these topics our review will necessarily be brief, but we hope to illustrate the logic of the experimental approach in a way that will provide a useful guide to the primary literature.

7.2   Words

When a bilingual hears, reads, or speaks a word in one of his or her two languages, is the other language also active? A great many studies of visual and auditory word recognition have investigated the question of whether the bilingual lexicon is an integrated representation across the word forms of both languages or whether words in each language access independent representations, one for each language. A full discussion of the theoretical alternatives associated with this debate is beyond the scope of the present chapter, but there are a number of summaries of this work available in recent articles and chapters (e.g., Dijkstra & Van Heuven, 2002; Kroll & Dussias, 2004; Costa, 2005). In brief, most of the evidence suggests that lexical access is non-selective, in that alternatives in both languages appear to be activated in parallel when words are processed in one language alone.

How can we draw the conclusion that lexical access occurs in parallel across the bilingual's two languages? Here we describe three paradigms that will serve to illustrate the logic of research on the bilingual lexicon: (1) visual lexical decision,

(2) eye tracking, and (3) the picture-word Stroop task. These paradigms have been used, respectively, to examine visual word recognition, spoken word recognition, and spoken word production.

7.2.1 *Visual lexical decision*

In lexical decision, a string of letters is presented on a computer screen and the participant must decide whether it forms a real word or not. Typically the participant presses a "yes" button when the letter string is a real word and a "no" button when it is not, and the speed and accuracy of his or her decision is recorded. When the letter string is a real word, the word can be common and familiar (e.g., cat) or a word that is only infrequently seen (e.g., obtuse). It can be a word whose spelling resembles many other words (e.g., cat looks like hat, mat, rat, etc.) or few, or a word that is concrete and easy to visualize (e.g., cat) or abstract and hard to visualize (e.g., obtuse). When the letter string does not form a real word, it is typically a possible word in that is pronounceable and follows the spelling rules of the language (e.g., blart). Using non-words that are possible words in the language ensures that the participant cannot use spelling or phonology alone to make the lexical decision; the mental lexicon itself must be accessed to determine whether the word is known. The task has been used extensively in psycholinguistic research within a single language to examine lexical access (e.g., Balota, 1994).

For bilinguals, lexical decision provides a context in which a set of factors can be manipulated to determine whether only one or both languages are active when a string of letters is presented. The logic in many of the bilingual studies is to exploit similarities that exist across languages in orthography or phonology. For example, in languages such as Dutch and English there are a significant number of translation equivalents that are identical or very similar in their spelling patterns. These translations are called cognates and provide a clever means to determine whether bilinguals are able to function monolingually in performing a task such as lexical decision. In Dutch and English the words 'bed' and 'hotel' are cognates because they have the same spelling in both languages. Other cognates, such as 'tomaat' in Dutch and 'tomato' in English are similar, but not identical, in the two languages. If a bilingual can access a word in one language without contacting the other, then lexical decision performance for cognates should be no different than lexical decision for words that are unambiguous. Thus, a Dutch-English bilingual performing lexical decision exclusively in English (i.e., are these strings of letters words in English or not?) should not be influenced by the fact that cognates have representations that are similar in Dutch (see figure 7.1 for an illustration of the task). The results of many experiments (e.g., van Hell & Dijkstra, 2002) show that bilinguals are in fact faster to decide that a string of letters is a real word in one language alone when it is a cognate.

A related type of experiment uses interlingual homographs, or words that have similar orthography and/or phonology in two languages, but different meanings. For example, in Dutch, the word 'room' means cream, as in cream for your coffee. If a Dutch-English bilingual can effectively switch off his or her Dutch when

English lexical decision: Is the string of letters a real word in English?

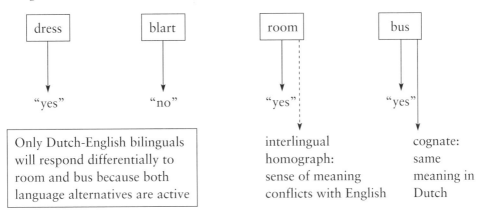

Figure 7.1: An illustration of a lexical decision task performed in English exclusively but including words that are ambiguous with respect to language membership. For a Dutch-English bilingual, the word *room* is an interlingual homograph, meaning room or cream. The word *bus* is a cognate, with the same meaning in Dutch and in English.

reading in English, then a word like 'room' should be processed no differently than any other English word that does not have this special relation to Dutch. The alternative sense of the word 'room' should not intrude. However, many experiments have shown that the unintended language does affect lexical decision performance (e.g., Von Studnitz & Green, 2002). When lexical decision is performed in the second language (L2), there is interference from the unintended sense of the word in the first language (L1). However, Dijkstra, Van Jaarsveld, and Ten Brinke (1998) have shown that when the lexical decision task is altered slightly to be a language-general task (what they call generalized lexical decision), there is facilitation for interlingual homographs because under these conditions any activated sense of the word is sufficient to make a "yes" response that the string of letters is a word.

A criticism of the logic of these word recognition studies is that both languages are necessarily active by virtue of the participant's knowledge that the experiment is about their bilingualism. Grosjean (2001) has argued that when bilinguals are in "bilingual mode" with both languages active to some degree, there will necessarily be evidence for cross-language interactions of the sort that have been reported. A number of recent studies have attempted to address this criticism and to evaluate the effect of the participant's expectations by keeping participants in a strictly "monolingual mode" in one language alone. For example, van Hell and Dijkstra (2002) recruited Dutch university students to participate in an experiment in Dutch exclusively. Unbeknownst to the participants, some of the items in the experiments were cognates in Dutch and English or in Dutch and French. They showed that there was facilitation in recognizing cognates related to controls even when English and French words were not present in the experiment and there was no explicit instruction regarding any language other than Dutch, their L1. The result is striking because Dutch was the native and dominant language of these bilinguals and one might expect that they would be able to function independently in their L1, yet the L2 and L3 affected their performance in the task.

7.2.2 Eye tracking

Monitoring the movements of the eye while a person reads visually presented text is a task that has often been used to infer the processes that underlie skilled reading (see section 7.4 below on processing sentences). Recent studies of spoken word recognition have also used eye movements to track the pattern of eye fixations when a listener hears a word while looking at a display of objects whose names bear some similarity to the phonology of the spoken word. This paradigm, developed initially in the domain of spoken word recognition in the native language to test the seriality of lexical selection mechanisms (e.g., Allopenna, Magnuson, & Tanenhaus, 1998), has been extended to investigate the parallel activation of words in both of the bilingual's languages when they hear a word in one language alone (e.g., Marian & Spivey, 2003; Ju & Luce, 2004).

In this task, the participant, wearing a head-mounted eye tracker, is seated in front of a display that contains four objects (either real objects or pictures on a computer display). The person is instructed to fixate on a central point on the screen until he or she hears a spoken target word. In the computerized version of the task, the participant clicks on the picture that corresponds to the spoken word. The critical manipulation in these studies is the presence of objects whose names sound like the spoken word either in the language presented or in the bilingual's other language. To illustrate, we use the materials in Spanish and English from the Ju and Luce (2004) study (see figure 7.2). Here, the spoken target word is *playa* (meaning beach in Spanish). The correct response is to click on the picture of the beach. However, one of the distractor pictures shows a pair of pliers (in Spanish the word for pliers is *alicate*). If a bilingual can perform this task in one language exclusively, then the presence of the pliers should have no effect on performance because the Spanish word *alicate* bears no resemblance to the word *playa*. However, if both language alternatives are activated in parallel, then the English word *pliers*, which is phonologically similar to *playa*, should intrude momentarily and the pattern of eye fixations should reveal that participants are more likely to glance at the picture with a phonologically similar name than at other control pictures. A series of experiments by Marian and colleagues (e.g., Marian & Spivey, 2003) has shown that Russian-English bilinguals appear to activate both language alternatives. However, Ju and Luce modified this claim to show that whether evidence for parallel activation was obtained depended on the acoustic properties of the spoken word. If the word was spoken with Spanish-appropriate voice onset times, bilinguals were less likely to fixate pictures with names that were phonologically similar in English. For present purposes, the main point of this illustration is to demonstrate the sensitivity of the cognitive system to processes that reveal themselves over time and across modalities. Here, the pattern of eye fixations corresponds to the nature of the lexical information that is activated when a spoken word is heard. The process of perceiving spoken language can of course be studied within the auditory

Eye tracking: Click on the picture of "playa" (beach in Spanish)

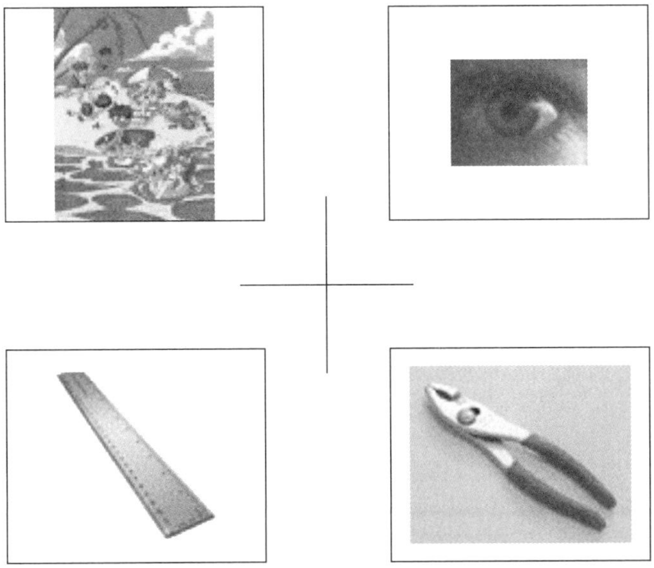

Figure 7.2: An illustration of the eye-tracking paradigm used to study cross-language activation in spoken word recognition. The materials are adapted from Ju & Luce (2004). Here a Spanish-English bilingual hears the word *playa* and must click on the appropriate picture of a beach scene. The question is whether the bilingual glances briefly at the picture of the pliers which is an English word that is phonologically similar to the Spanish word *playa*.

domain alone (see section 7.3 below on phonology and Grosjean & Frauenfelder, 1997, for a review).

7.2.3 Picture-word Stroop

The final example we describe to illustrate how lexical processing has been studied in bilinguals focuses on the way in which bilinguals plan spoken utterances to produce a single word in only one of their two languages. Language production has been far less studied than comprehension, in part because it is difficult to devise tasks that encourage speakers to produce uniform utterances. As a consequence, most of the early research on language production relied on patterns that could be inferred from large corpora of speech errors (see Poulisse, 1999, for an example of a speech error analysis for L2 learners). Although errors are informative with respect to the constraints that guide speech planning, they do not provide a sensitive means to examine the planning process as it unfolds over time when speech is produced accurately. A solution to this problem has been to invent tasks that simultaneously constrain spoken utterances and provide a method for asking what sort of information is available to the planning process at different points in time prior to articulation.

The picture-word Stroop task has been used extensively in recent studies of monolingual and bilingual language production to examine the time course of planning and to evaluate alternative models of the planning process (e.g., Levelt, Roelofs, & Meyer, 1999). The task is a variant of the color-word naming task first described by Stroop (1935). In the original Stroop task, participants named the color of the ink in which printed words appeared. The Stroop effect is the interference that is induced when a color word appears in an incongruent color (e.g., the word *blue* printed in red ink). In the picture-word task, a picture is presented and the participant is asked to speak its name aloud as quickly as possible. At some point just prior to or following the presentation of the picture, a word distractor is presented either auditorily or visually. The participant is told to ignore the word and name the picture. By manipulating the relation of the distractor word to the picture's name and the timing of its presentation, it has been possible to map out the time course of speech planning. Generally, there is interference for semantically related distractors when they are presented early in the planning process and facilitation for phonologically related distractors when they are presented late in the planning process.

The overall pattern of distractor effects in picture-word interference suggests that the phonology of the spoken utterance can only be encoded once the meaning of the intended utterance is specified. A debate in this area of research is whether the sequencing that allows speech planning to proceed from meaning to phonology is a strictly serial and encapsulated process or one that reflects interactions across different levels of information (e.g., Dell & O'Seaghdha, 1991; Levelt, Roelofs, & Meyer, 1999). Although a full discussion of the theoretical background is beyond the scope of the present chapter, for the purpose of extending the methods used into the bilingual domain, we consider briefly the focal issue towards which the research has been designed.[2]

Like research on bilingual word recognition, the question in bilingual word production has been whether alternatives in the non-target language (i.e., the language not spoken) are active during the planning of an utterance (see Costa, 2005, for a review of this literature). Unlike word recognition, production is a process that is initiated by a conceptual event (e.g., a picture to be named, a word to be translated, an abstract idea to be spoken), so it might seem that in the course of conceptualizing the intended utterance only the language to be produced would be active. Although there is debate in the literature about the selectivity of language production (e.g., Costa, 2005), a great deal of evidence suggests that words in both of the bilingual's languages are active at least to the level of abstract lexical representations and perhaps to the point of actually specifying the phonology associated with the translation.

How can the picture-word Stroop paradigm be used to inform the debate about whether alternatives in the bilingual's other language are active when they intend to speak in one language only? A number of studies have varied the language of the

[2] The issue of whether processes are encapsulated refers to a longstanding debate in psycholinguistics concerning the modularity of language (e.g., Fodor, 1983). The basic question is whether certain language functions (e.g., parsing a sentence into its grammatical components or retrieving the meaning of a word) are separate from other cognitive representations and goals, or are guided by them.

Picture-word Stroop task: name the picture, ignore the distractor

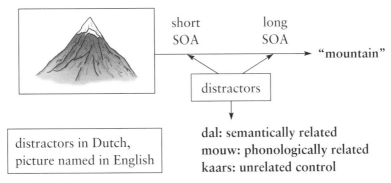

Figure 7.3: An illustration of the cross-language picture-word Stroop task. The materials are adapted from Hermans, Bongaerts, De Bot, & Schreuder (1998). Here a Dutch-English bilingual names a picture in English and attempts to ignore distractor words presented in Dutch.

distractor and the language in which the picture is to be named to investigate this issue (e.g., Hermans, Bongaerts, De Bot, & Schreuder, 1998; Costa, Miozzo, & Caramazza, 1999). An illustration of the paradigm adapted from Hermans et al. (1998) is shown in figure 7.3. Here a Dutch-English bilingual is asked to name a picture of a mountain as the word *mountain* in English. The distractor is presented at the same time as the picture, at a brief delay following the picture, or after a longer delay. The interval between the presentation of the picture and the onset of the distractor is known as the stimulus onset asynchrony, or SOA. In this example, the distractor is the word *dal* in Dutch which means valley in English and is therefore semantically related to the word to be spoken but presented in the non-target language. By comparing the time it takes bilinguals to name the picture when it is accompanied by a semantically related word, like *dal*, a phonologically related word like *mouw*, which sounds like the first syllable of 'mountain' in English but means sleeve, or an unrelated control word, like *kaars*, which means candle in English, it is possible to estimate what sort of information is active at any given moment in time before the word 'mountain' is actually spoken. Hermans et al. found a similar pattern of results in picture naming in the L2 regardless of whether the language of the distractor was L1 or L2. Semantically related distractors produced interference relative to unrelated controls and the semantic interference was greatest early in the time course of speech planning. Phonologically related distractors produced facilitation relative to unrelated controls, and the facilitation was greatest late in the time course of speech planning. Costa, Miozzo, and Caramazza (1999) reported similar results for Catalan-Spanish bilinguals. The finding that distractors in the non-target language also produce interference and facilitation in picture naming suggests that, as seems to be the case for bilingual word recognition, lexical access in bilingual speech production is initially language-non-selective, with alternatives activated in both languages in parallel. Other production paradigms have produced evidence that converges with these general conclusions. These include speaking the translation of individual words (De Groot,

1992; Kroll & Stewart, 1994) and monitoring the phonemes in the names of pictures (Colomé, 2001).

7.3   Sounds

A longstanding issue in the study of bilingual phonology is the question of how L2 phonetic categories are both produced and perceived. Much of the research focuses on late bilinguals, i.e., bilinguals who have learned their second language near or past puberty and who, in many cases, have lived for extended periods of time in the L2 environment. As is well known, late L2 speakers often differ in their production and perception of phonetic categories from native speaker norms. From the perspective of the researcher, the phonology and phonetics of bilingualism provide a fertile testing ground for exploring hypotheses about the critical period for language acquisition, for examining issues of neural plasticity throughout the development of L2 proficiency, for probing how L2 learning is constrained in comparison to L1 learning and/or by the phonological system of the L1 (see Flege, 2003, for a review), and for understanding the generally complex issue of accentedness in L2 speech production and perception (see Piske, MacKay, & Flege, 2001, for a review). While a lengthy discussion of the various theoretical alternatives associated with the issues noted here is beyond the scope of this chapter, in the rest of this section we will examine a number of particular studies that both exemplify a range of techniques employed and inform the theoretical questions noted above.

7.3.1   *Production*

Production tasks are commonly employed as a means of assessing bilingual speech for numerous theoretical goals. These can differ in terms of both elicitation technique and size of the speech sample elicited. In most cases, the task involves having participants read aloud either target phrases (e.g., Flege, 1987; Moyer, 1999), single words (e.g., Flege & Eefting, 1987; Moyer, 1999), or larger chunks such as paragraphs (e.g., Moyer, 1999), and recording their speech production for subsequent analysis. Some studies have also employed repetition techniques in which participants listen to and then repeat experimental items produced by a native speaker either immediately (e.g., Markham, 1997) or after a delay designed to minimize the chances of direct imitation from sensory memory (e.g., Piske, MacKay, & Flege, 2001). Finally, other studies have employed less controlled techniques designed to elicit speech tokens under increasingly natural conditions, such as asking participants to talk about events in their lives (e.g., Moyer, 1999). In broad strokes, the recorded data are subjected to two kinds of analyses, depending on the goals of the research. The first involves carrying out acoustic analyses of the bilingual production data and comparing the results with measurements of native speaker controls. The second involves using native speakers to rate the L2 productions of the participants, an approach used extensively in studies assessing L2 accentedness (see Piske et al., 2001, for an overview of rating techniques).

Flege (1987) provides a useful example of a typical production study and illustrates how acoustic measurement techniques can be used to address questions of neural plasticity and the critical period hypothesis, i.e., the hypothesis that language learning (or, in our case, speech learning) is rigidly constrained by a critical period in maturation ending around puberty (see DeKeyser, 2000, for a review). Flege examined the L1 and L2 productions of English/French and French/English bilinguals for the French and English alveolar stop /t/ and for the /i/ and /u/ vowels in English and the /y/ and /u/ vowels in French. For reasons of space, we focus here on the production results for /t/.

Both French and English have the voiceless stop /t/ in their phoneme inventories. In English, the category /t/ (like other voiceless stops) is realized phonetically as a long lag or aspirated stop [tʰ] when initial in a stressed syllable (such as /tu/ *two*). In French, however, /t/ is produced as a short lag or unaspirated stop [t] in the same position (as in *tous* /tu/ 'all'). The term *lag* refers to voice onset time (VOT), i.e., to the interval of time between the moment when the closure of the stop consonant is released and the onset of voicing in the following vowel. VOT can be measured with great precision from a display of the acoustic waveform, as can be seen in figure 7.4, made with the Praat acoustic analysis software (Boersma & Weenink, 2005).

Flege (1987) measured the VOTs of the stop /t/ for three groups of late English/French bilinguals whose experience with French varied (US students 3–6 months removed from a 9-month abroad program in France; French professors whose L1 was English and who were living in an English-language context; and L1 English speakers living in Paris for an average of 11.7 years) and for a group of late French/English bilinguals living in an English context (French women living in Chicago for an average of 12.2 years). Their data were compared to production data from monolingual English and French speakers collected under the same experimental conditions. As is standard in such phonetic studies, multiple repetitions of the critical phonetic context were produced by each speaker to allow for the calculation of a reliable mean VOT value for each participant. Data were elicited in two conditions. In Condition 1, participants read seven phrases in isolation. All phrases were matched for the initial phoneme sequence /tu/ by employing the same

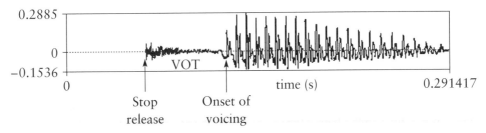

Figure 7.4: An illustration of how VOT is measured as the time interval between the release of the stop (as indicated by the arrow to the left) and the onset of voicing in the vowel following the stop. This is the acoustic wave for a token of the English CV syllable [pʰo].

initial word. The English phrases began with the word *two* (e.g., <u>two</u> little boys), while the French phrases began with the word *tous* (e.g., *tous les soldats* 'all the soldiers'). In Condition 2, participants were prompted to use each of the phrases in an original sentence while being cued by the written phrases from Condition 1. VOT was measured for each instance of initial /t/ in each condition, and a mean was calculated for each speaker by condition. After Speaking Condition was found to be non-significant for VOT duration, a mean of the two means was calculated for each speaker and used in the analysis.

Of particular interest here are the results for two of the groups, the Americans living in Paris and the French women living in the United States. Specifically, Flege's results show that for the bilingual L1-English/L2-French speakers, VOT durations in English are significantly shorter than those of monolingual English controls. Likewise, the bilingual L1-French/L2-English group produces the French stops with significantly longer VOTs than do the French monolingual controls. That is, in these bilinguals, the VOT targets for /t/ in their L2s (longer in English and shorter in French) are reshaping the realization of their respective /t/ categories in their L1s. Here we can see how bilingualism again provides a fundamental tool for testing theories of language learning. The logic of the argument in this case is that a strong critical-period hypothesis incorrectly predicts that late learning of an L2 should not reshape the phonetic space of an L1. By contrast, theories which do not assume that the neural plasticity necessary for speech/language acquisition declines precipitously after a critical period predict that sufficient experience in an L2 (such as longtime residency in an L2 context and constant use of the L2) may affect even aspects of the phonetic system of the L1.

7.3.2 Perception

As with production, the perception of phonetic categories in an L2, particularly by late L2 learners, often diverges from the perception of the same categories by native speakers. Though theoretical models differ in the specifics of their approaches to the problem, there is a general consensus that L2 perception is filtered by knowledge of the L1 phonological system (see, e.g., the Perceptual Assimilation Model, Best, 1995, and the Speech Learning Model, Flege, 1988, 2002). Much research indicates that one particular way that L1 learning shapes the perception of L2 categories is that L1 acquisition involves perceptual tuning to the phonetic properties necessary for producing and perceiving phonological distinctions in the L1. Over the course of maturation, this tuning leads to a warping of the acoustic space through which subsequent L2 learning is filtered (e.g., the Native Language Magnet, Kuhl, 2000).

A number of experimental paradigms have been deployed to examine questions of both how and how well L2 phonetic categories are perceived. For example, Iverson, Kuhl, Akahane-Yamada, et al. (2003) utilize three different tasks in examining how language experience with the L1 shapes the perception of non-native categories. Specifically, they examine how Japanese listeners differ from native English listeners in their perception of the English /l/ vs. /r/ contrast. For their stimuli, Iverson et al. created a set of 18 CV syllables, synthesizing a continuum from /ra/ to /la/ in English by systematically varying two spectral properties, the frequencies of the second (F2) and third (F3) formants of the initial liquid consonant. They tested their participants in three ways: via the collection of identification and goodness ratings, via similarity scaling, and via a discrimination task.

The identification and goodness tasks involved having participants listen to a stimulus item – items were presented twice in this experiment in two randomized blocks – and identify it with a phonetic category in their native language. Upon identification, participants were also asked to rate each token on a scale of 1 (bad) to 7 (good) as an exemplar of that category. In similarity-scaling tasks, participants are also asked to provide ratings. In this case, however, participants were presented aurally with pairs of stimuli and asked to rate their similarity on a scale of 1 (dissimilar) to 7 (similar). Stimuli were presented in a single randomized experimental block of 306 trials, with every pair of the 18 stimuli items presented in both possible orders. Finally, AX discrimination tasks consist of asking participants to listen to a pair of stimuli and make a determination as to whether they have heard the same or different items. In this experiment, stimuli were presented in a single randomized block of 480 trials, consisting of 48 same-pair and 48 different-pair trials for each pair of stimulus items. The different condition pairs differed in this task only along the dimension of the third formant (F3).

For Iverson et al. (2003) the similarity-scaling and discrimination tasks yielded converging results. Japanese listeners are, erroneously, well tuned to changes along the F2 dimension, while American listeners are finely tuned to changes along the F3 dimension that signal the phonetic category boundary between English /r/ and /l/. Iverson et al. argue that the identification and goodness ratings are relevant in that they provide a means of explaining why Japanese listeners differentially tune to spectral components of the stimuli. Specifically, as F2 falls Japanese listeners begin to identify stimuli as belonging to the Japanese /w/ category instead of as belonging to /r/. That is, their experience with Japanese has shaped their acoustic space in such a way as to lead them to attend to cues such as the F2 difference signaling the contrast between /r/ and /w/. By contrast, the F3 changes to which English speakers are highly tuned fall within a single Japanese category, /r/, and Japanese listeners thus show a reduced sensitivity to change along this dimension.

If L2 perception is constrained by the filter of L1, the question then arises of how malleable the system is over the course of L2 learning. Escudero and Boersma (2004), tested Spanish speakers' perception of the English /i/ ~ /ɪ/ contrast using a synthetic /i/ ~ /ɪ/ continuum which varied both the frequency of F1 and the duration of the synthetic vowel in an experimental design similar to that of Iverson et al. (2003). This contrast is notoriously difficult for Spanish learners of English (cf. Bradlow, 1995; Fox, Flege, & Munro, 1995). Interestingly, Escudero and Boersma tested two groups of L1 Spanish speakers living in the L2 environment: a group living in a Scottish English environment where the /i/ ~ /ɪ/ distinction is realized primarily by differences in the frequency of the first formant (F1) of the vowel – a property inversely related to vowel height – and a group living in southern England, where the dialect primarily uses duration differences in realizing the difference between the categories. In the Escudero and Boersma study, participants listened to each stimulus token in isolation and performed a forced-choice task, selecting between a picture of a *sheep* (indicating the /i/ category) and a picture of a *ship* (indicating the percept of the /ɪ/) category. The task is different from the Iverson et al. (2003) identification task in that participants in this study were forced to choose between L2 categories (indirectly in the form of pictures) rather than identifying the stimulus item with an L1 category. Importantly, the results indicate that although they did not exhibit native-like perception with respect to the L1 English speaker controls, more advanced L2 learners adopted strategies that involved tuning to the properties of the dialect in which they were immersed, thus exhibiting a good degree of plasticity in their developing sensitivity to dialect-particular acoustic cues.

A striking contrast with the cases of L2 plasticity that we have noted in both production and perception can be found in the research conducted on the /e/ ~ /ɛ/ contrast in Spanish/Catalan bilinguals – a phonemic distinction present in Catalan but lacking in Spanish. In a series of experiments (Sebastián-Gallés & Soto-Faraco, 1999; Bosch, Costa, & Sebastián-Gallés, 2000; Pallier, Colomé, & Sebastián-Gallés, 2001) researchers have employed a range of techniques and found that highly proficient yet Spanish-dominant early Spanish/Catalan bilinguals perform in a non-native fashion in tasks involving the processing of the Catalan /e/ ~ /ɛ/ distinction, in comparison with the superior performance of Catalan-dominant early Catalan/Spanish bilinguals. Two of these studies are particularly useful in that they allow us to review additional experimental approaches found in the bilingual perception literature.

Sebastián-Gallés and Soto-Faraco (1999) employ a modified version of the gating technique (Grosjean, 1980, 1988) to probe for differences in the way that highly proficient Spanish-dominant, i.e. Spanish/Catalan, bilinguals process the Catalan /e/ ~ /ɛ/ distinction (among other contrasts) in comparison with the performance of highly proficient Catalan-dominant, i.e. Catalan/Spanish, bilinguals. In a gating experiment, an aurally presented stimulus, usually a word, is played for participants in successively larger increments. In this sense, the participant's exposure to the stimulus is gated. At each gate, participants must make a forced choice between possible forms and then rate the confidence with which they have made their choice. In the Sebastián-Gallés and Soto-Faraco study, gated stimuli consisting of one of two minimally distinct non-words in Catalan were presented while written pairs of the non-words were shown on a computer screen. During each gating trial, participants chose one of the displayed forms and rated the confidence of their choices on a 1 to 9 scale. The authors analyzed their results in terms of two key points: (1) the *isolation point*, the gate at which participants correctly identified a target word with no further change in their subsequent choices upon hearing larger chunks of the gated form; and (2) the *recognition point*, the gate after which participants expressed a confidence rating of 8 or higher in their choice. The results indicate that despite the fact that the Spanish/Catalan bilinguals are all highly proficient Catalan speakers who had acquired Catalan in their early childhood, these speakers are less efficient, i.e., they need significantly more acoustic information than did the Catalandominant bilinguals to successfully complete the gating task. Arguably, then, the gating task provides a fine-grained way of distinguishing in a fairly precise manner between even highly proficient bilingual groups. In a larger sense,

Sebastián-Gallés and Soto-Faraco claim that their results demonstrate that the tuning effect of L1 categories (in this case, driven by the lack of an /e/ ~ /ɛ/ distinction in the L1 Spanish) may persist deeply into L2 acquisition, even when an individual's L2 is learned early, involves intensive exposure, and is used extensively.

With the exception of the gating task (the status of which is ambiguous; see, e.g., Grosjean, 1996), the techniques most often used in bilingual phonetic perception studies involve off-line tasks. Pallier, Colomé, and Sebastián-Gallés (2001) provide a useful example of how on-line tasks can also be used to address the issue of how the phonological system of L1 filters the perception of L2 phonetic categories. In continuing to examine the difficulty that highly proficient Spanish/Catalan bilinguals have in perceiving the Catalan /e/ ~ /ɛ/ distinction, Pallier et al. employ a medium-term auditory repetition priming technique. The auditory repetition priming technique is a variation on an auditory lexical decision task. Specifically, it involves presenting participants with both spoken words and non-words and asking them to make a decision as quickly as possible regarding whether the presented stimulus is a word or not. The task is called an auditory repetition priming technique, because some of the words and non-words in the stimuli list are presented twice. A general finding of this task is that real words are responded to more rapidly when seen for a second time (i.e., they are primed), while response times for non-words are not faster when presented a second time. Pallier et al. capitalize on this effect by including minimal pairs of Catalan words such as [pere] 'Peter' and [perɛ] 'pear.' The logic of their experimental design is that if listeners process such minimal pairs as acoustically different and thus distinct lexical items, no priming effects should be found for them. On the other hand, if listeners hear such forms as homophones by failing to perceive the difference in their final vowels, priming effects are expected. Their results are consistent with the other studies in which Spanish-dominant Spanish/Catalan bilinguals do not perform in the same fashion as Catalan-dominant bilinguals. Specifically, the Spanish-dominant group differs significantly from the Catalan-dominant group in that the former exhibit a facilitation effect for minimal pairs of Catalan forms that is of the same magnitude as the facilitation effect found for real repetitions of identical forms. This indicates that Spanish-dominant participants are not appropriately tuned to the spectral differences cueing contrasts such as /e/ vs. /ɛ/. At the same time, the overall reaction-time data corroborate the authors' claim that they are testing highly proficient bilinguals, given that the Spanish-dominant group did not differ significantly from the Catalan-dominant group in either their response times or their error rates in the lexical decision task for Catalan words. Methodologically, these results are interesting for our purposes in that they show how converging results can be obtained with a variety of tasks involving both behavioral, on-line techniques, gating, and off-line tasks such as discrimination and identification.

7.3.3   Imaging

Recent advances in imaging techniques have also been brought to bear on many of the questions addressed above. Though a thorough review is beyond the scope of this chapter (for further discussion see chapter 8 in this volume), we will discuss here Winkler, Kujala, Tiitinen, et al.'s (1999) event-related potentials (ERP) study of phonetic category perception in native, naive non-native, and proficient L2 speakers of Finnish (see Handy, 2004, for an overview of ERP experimental designs, approaches, and applications). Broadly speaking, ERP is a functional brain-scanning technique that allows for the non-invasive measuring of brain activity during cognitive processing. Electrodes are attached to the scalp in order to measure ongoing electrical activity as an electroencephalogram (EEG). Event-related potentials are calculated as averages of electrical activity in the brain that are time-locked to the presentation or to the response of particular stimuli. The experimental approach taken in Winkler et al. employs a design in which a "standard" binaurally presented stimulus (a synthesized Finnish /e/ vowel) is played repeatedly to participants (82.5 percent of the time) and occasionally interrupted by one of two "deviant" stimuli (either the Finnish vowel /æ/ or the Finnish vowel /y/, also both synthesized). The experiment tests for the elicitation of what is known as a mismatch negativity event-related potential (MMN) during the processing of the deviant stimuli. Research has shown the MMN potential to be associated with bottom-up, preattentional phonetic processing (see Näätänen, 2001, for an extensive review). Of most relevance here is that elicitation of the MMN reflects the perception of change along a particular phonetic dimension, in this case as a function of change from the repeated "standard" to the "deviant" stimulus.

Winkler et al. (1999) tested the perception by Hungarians of a Finnish vowel contrast /e/ ~ /æ/ that falls in the acoustic space of a single vowel category in Hungarian. Given the preattentional nature of MMN elicitation, they reasoned that an ERP study of the perception of non-native contrasts would provide a useful mechanism for exploring the issue of brain plasticity in the late learning of a second language. Specifically, they hypothesized that if Hungarian speakers are unable to perceive the vowel contrast, they should also fail to elicit MMN potentials on deviant trials. By contrast, the elicitation of MMN potentials on deviant trials would indicate a deep, low-level sensitivity to the acoustic difference between the two vowel categories in Finnish. Importantly, they found that MMNs were not elicited for the naive Hungarian speakers when exposed to the Finnish vowel contrast, i.e. in response to the presentation of the deviant stimuli /æ/ vowels. In keeping with the performance of a different group of naive speakers on an off-line discrimination task, the ERP data indicated that these naive speakers were simply not perceiving the difference between the Finnish vowels but rather were perceiving both /e/ and /æ/ as tokens of a single vowel category. By contrast, the relatively proficient Hungarian L2 speakers of Finnish displayed a clear MMN response to the presentation of the deviant tokens – a response pattern, in fact, that did not differ significantly from that of native Finnish-speaking control participants. These results are a bit of a conundrum when compared to the apparent non-plasticity characterizing the early and highly proficient Spanish/Catalan bilinguals' performances on an array of tasks as described above. For the late L2 Hungarian speakers, the results, when taken together with the non-elicitation of MMN responses in the naive group, strongly suggest that late L2 learning is characterized by continued brain plasticity at the very lowest levels of phonetic perception. Finally, from a methodological perspective, imaging studies are interesting in that they show how non-behavioral tasks can add to our arsenal of experimental paradigms for testing questions of bilingual phonetic processing.

7.4   Sentences

When we try to comprehend sentences in our second language (and, for that matter, in our first), we face many uncertainties about how the people or objects referred to are connected to one another. This is so because when our eyes move along the printed text in a left-to-right fashion, the information needed to establish correct dependencies between word strings is not yet available. In other words, we need to wait.

So what does the L2 reader do under these conditions of uncertainty? Given that L2 speakers approach the task of sentence processing with a fully developed processing system from their L1, one may ask what representations are created while speakers process written text in their L2, what types of information are used in constructing them, and when these representations are formed. It is reasonable to imagine that during the earlier stages of L2 learning, L2 speakers rely, at least partially, on sources of information from their first language (e.g., lexical information encoded in verbs, such as verb argument structure) to construct a licit syntactic construction (i.e., *parse)* in the L2. And one would expect that as language proficiency increases, sentence processing in the L2 should approximate that of monolingual speakers of the target language.

Experimental work in L2 sentence comprehension has investigated these questions using an array of psycholinguistic techniques, ranging from the very simple to the more highly sophisticated and powerful (Juffs & Harrington, 1996; Weber-Fox & Neville, 1996; Frenck-Mestre & Pynte, 1997; Hahne & Friederici, 2001; Dussias, 2003; Felser, Roberts, Gross, & Marinis, 2003; Fernández, 2003). This rapidly growing body of work suggests that, when the L2 learner parses sentences in the L2, his or her performance is sometimes strikingly close to that of native speakers, but other times it is not. The most compelling type of evidence in support of the first claim comes from studies that have used event-related brain potentials (ERPs) while speakers are exposed to sentences that vary systematically with respect to particular semantic characteristics. Monolingual English speakers and L2 speakers of English faced with the sentence *The scientist criticized Max's event of the theorem* will be, by and large, equally sensitive to the semantic anomaly contained within it (Weber-Fox & Neville, 1996). At the same time, apparent discrepancies between L1 and L2 speakers have been obtained in the ambit of syntactic processing, providing support for the second claim.

Methodological advances in psycholinguistics have provided the community of researchers interested in L2 sentence comprehension with valuable information about the experimental techniques commonly used to advance our understanding of the psychological processes underlying sentence comprehension, as well as with rich and remarkably detailed evaluations of what each technique can and cannot reveal about comprehension processes. In this section, we consider the methods that have been most commonly used to investigate L2 sentence comprehension. Because researchers are most often interested in tracking L2 sentence processing as it unfolds in real time, we will limit our discussion to a family of techniques that have come to be known as *on-line* methods.

7.4.1 Self-paced reading

Without a doubt, self-paced reading has been the on-line method most widely used in L2 sentence comprehension research. In this task, a stimulus sentence is presented on a computer screen, segmented into words or phrases commonly referred to as *displays*, which are presented one at a time. Typically, the participant initiates the experiment by pressing a *trigger* (e.g., a pedal, or a key on a button box or a computer keyboard). This action brings up the first display. Participants read the display, press the trigger to request the next display, and continue performing the same routine until they reach the end of the experiment. In this task, the measure of interest is the time that participants spend reading a critical display (i.e., the time that has elapsed between successive trigger presses), compared to a control condition.

Self-paced reading tasks have been extensively used in the L2 parsing literature to investigate how the L2 parser proceeds in the absence of lexical constraints, as is the case of adjunct phrases or modifier phrases. In one such study, Dussias (2003; see also Felser, Roberts, Gross, & Marinis, 2003; Fernández, 2003; Papadopoulou & Clahsen, 2003) employed the task with Spanish-English and English-Spanish bilinguals to investigate their attachment preferences for structures of the type NP1-of-NP2-RC (e.g., *El perro mordió al cuñado de la maestra/ que vivió en Chile/ con su esposo/* 'The dog bit the brother-in-law of the teacher (fem.) who lived in Chile with her husband'). All sentences were segmented into three displays – as indicated by the forward slashes in the example above. When the first sentence was requested, the first display of an item appeared centered on the screen and the clock started. The participants read this display and then pressed a key to request the second display. The time that elapsed between the onset of the first display and the request for the second display was recorded. Additionally, the first display was replaced by the second display, and the clock started again. This sequence of events repeated itself until the end of the sentence was reached. The critical comparison in this study was the reading time for the last display; however, reading times for displays 1 and 2 were also compared to ensure that there were not significant differences between them. The findings revealed that the control groups (Spanish and English monolinguals) showed the conventional bias for high attachment and low attachment (respectively) reported in the literature. The English-Spanish bilinguals did not exhibit any preference for high or low attachment when processing the ambiguous sentences, but, remarkably, the Spanish-English speakers showed a consistent preference for low attachment when reading sentences in their first and second languages, suggesting that the parsing routines used to process the L2 had an impact on the processing of the L1, and that the methodology did not distort the cognitive processes that are linked with the detection of the syntactic ambiguity being studied. Like the studies reviewed earlier on recognizing words and speech sounds, these results suggest a high degree of plasticity and interaction across the bilingual's two languages.

In one variation of the self-paced reading task, dubbed the *moving-window programme* (Just, Carpenter, & Woolley, 1982), the display moves from left to right with each trigger press to allow the words of the sentence to occupy the same position in the screen that would surface if the sentence had been displayed as a whole. All letters, apart from the letters of the word in current view, are replaced with dashes (or equivalent markers). In the reading moving window paradigm, the text can be presented in a *non-cumulative* fashion (i.e., as each successive word in the sentence is prompted, the previous one disappears) or *cumulatively* (previously read words remain on the screen as new ones are added). Because the cumulative version has the disadvantage that participants may press the trigger to display all the words in a sentence, and only later initiate the actual reading task, researchers typically favor non-cumulative displays over cumulative ones.

One advantage of the moving window task is that it allows for the collection of word-level reading times, thereby allowing the experimenter to identify the specific loci of processing difficulty. To illustrate, Juffs and Harrington (1996) compared a full-sentence presentation task with a non-cumulative moving window task to examine how Chinese learners of English processed sentences such as *Who did Ann believe ____ likes her friend?* and *Who did Ann believe her friends like ____?* The sentences differed in that the first one is assumed to require extraction of the *wh* element from a subject site (indicated by ____), whereas the second requires extraction from an object site. Juffs and Harrington predicted that subject extraction sentences ought to present more difficulty for the parser than object extraction sentences, because the former would force the parser to reanalyze the *wh*-gap several times before finally arriving at a complete analysis of the sentence. Although the overall findings supported the claim that extraction from a subject site was more difficult than extraction from an object site, the different techniques produced somewhat different results. For example, no significant differences were found between subject and object extractions from finite clauses in the full-sentence condition, whereas these effects emerged in the moving window condition. Moreover, the Chinese learners had proportionally more difficulty than the monolingual English group in judging ungrammatical sentences in the moving window condition than in the full-sentence condition, suggesting that the increased processing demands of the moving window task placed a greater burden on the participants' available cognitive resources.

One of the criticisms leveled against self-paced reading in all its forms is the likelihood that syntactic parsing may be influenced by the type of segmentation employed by the experimenter (Gilboy & Sopena, 1996; but see Mitchell, 2004, for a counter-argument). Gilboy and Sopena (1996) found that relative clause ambiguity resolution was affected by whether the sentences were broken into large segments (e.g., *El perro mordió al cuñado de la maestra/ que vivió en Chile/ con su esposo/*) or smaller segments (e.g., *El perro mordió/ al cuñado/ de la maestra/ que vivió en Chile con su esposo*). A second objection raised against the task is that it relies on a secondary task (a button, a key, or a pedal press) to produce the dependent measure. These and other factors (see, e.g., Mitchell, 2004) have led researchers to favor methods that provide a richer body of data than the single latency that results from self-paced reading. In the next section, we discuss a few of the measures that have allowed researchers to determine with more precision the existence, locus, and time course of processing difficulty.

7.4.2   Eye movements

Eye-movement records have become a very popular technique in the study of sentence comprehension because they provide an on-line measure of processing difficulty with high temporal resolution, and do not require additional tasks (e.g., button or pedal presses) to yield the dependent measure. An additional advantage of eye-movement records is their high ecological validity. For example, eye movements are a normal characteristic of reading, the reader is free to move back and forth along the printed lines of text, and the text under examination need not be segmented into unnatural displays.

The existence of a large body of literature in experimental psychology that studies eye movements to answer questions about language processing has helped us to better understand the cognitive processes involved in reading. For example, we know that readers extract useful information from a restricted area of the text, usually spanning about 4 characters to the left of a fixation and about 15 characters to the right of the fixation (McConkie & Rayner, 1975). This maximum region from which information is extracted is referred to as the *perceptual span*. We also know that our eyes do not move smoothly along a line of printed text, but rather advance in short jumps called *saccades*. The average English reader makes about three to four saccadic movements in a second, each lasting between 20 and 40 ms. When a word is brought into fovea by a saccade, it is fixated for an average of about 225 ms, though a reader's fixation patterns over a text vary greatly depending on the linguistic characteristics of the words (Pollatsek & Rayner, 1990; Carreiras & Clifton, 2004). For instance, a word's lexical frequency affects its first fixation duration and gaze duration even when length is controlled (Just & Carpenter, 1980; Rayner & Duffy, 1986). Also, the predictability of a word from prior context influences the first fixation duration and the gaze duration on that word (Balota, Pollatsek, & Rayner, 1985), as well as the time it takes to incorporate it into the representation that the reader is constructing for a particular sentence.

What dependent variables are available to the investigator when collecting eye-movement records? For any critical region or regions of interest, a number of measurements can be distinguished. The earliest measure is *first fixation*, defined as the first time the eyes land on a region (whether a single word or a string of words). This measure appears to be sensitive to word frequency. The next measure is *first-pass time*, and refers to the sum of all fixations in a region, from first entering it until the eyes exit to the left or right of the region. On regions with only one word, first-pass time equals *gaze duration* (e.g., Rayner & Duffy, 1986). First-pass time has been found to be most informative in revealing detections of syntactic anomalies.

A. First-pass fixations

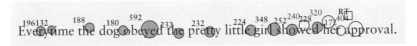

B. Re-fixations on the critical region

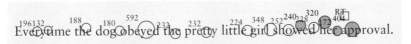

Figure 7.5: An illustration of eye-movement records while Spanish-English speakers are reading a structurally ambiguous sentence. The materials are adapted from Frenck-Mestre & Pynte (1997).

We note here that for both gaze duration and first-pass time, most researchers exclude trials in which the region is initially skipped. Another commonly used measure is *second-pass time*, which refers to the time spent reading a region after leaving the region (in other words, excluding first-pass time or after an initial skip of the region). Finally, *total time* is the sum of all fixations in a region (effectively, the sum of first-pass time and second-pass time). In addition to the measurement of time, another useful dependent measure is the *probability of a regression*, defined as the percentage of regressive eye movements (leftward movements in a language like English) out of a region. This index is usually restricted to first-pass regressions.

Figure 7.5 provides an illustration of an actual eye-movement record of a highly proficient Spanish-English bilingual reading a structurally ambiguous sentence (see Frenck-Mestre & Pynte, 1997, for a discussion of how French-English and English-French bilinguals process this ambiguity). Arrows indicating the trajectory of the eye have been omitted to simplify the image (fixation duration values appear to the left of the fixation). The ambiguity in this construction arises because the noun phrase 'the pretty little girl' can be interpreted either as a complement of the verb 'obeyed,' or as the subject of the ensuing clause. A reader who commits to the first interpretation will be forced to revise the attachment decision once the eyes reach the disambiguating region 'showed.' We observe for the first word in the sentence (i.e., 'every') a fixation on the letter *r*, with a duration of 196 ms. Given that no other fixations occurred on this word, first fixation and gaze duration equal 196 ms. The reading proceeds fairly smoothly, until the participant reaches the disambiguating region (i.e., 'showed'). First fixation on this region occurs on the letter *s*, at a duration of 348 ms. The two subsequent left-to-right fixations fall on the letter *o* and the letter *d*. These are sequenced fixations, with duration values of 252 ms and 228 ms respectively. Because all three fixations occurred before the eye was launched to another region in the sentence, gaze duration for this region equals the sum of the three fixations (828 ms). The next fixation occurs at the word *her*, and lasts 320 ms. The participant then launches a regressive movement back to the disambiguating region, which lands on the letter *e* and lasts 228 ms. In this case, then, second regression time equals 228 ms, and the total time spent reading the region is 1156 ms. It is worth noting at this point that processing difficulty at the disambiguating region occurred during early stages of cognitive processing as indexed by first-pass reading times. This finding could easily have been missed if the data had been collected with self-paced reading, because initial analysis and reanalysis cannot readily be distinguished. Returning now to our example, we note that the last word of the sentence is fixated twice, for 404 ms and 172 ms (576 ms). Generally, the last word in a sentence will show elevated fixation durations because it is the point in the construction where the sentence can be comprehended as a whole (Just & Carpenter, 1980). Therefore, it is standard practice not to place the region of interest at sentence-final position. Likewise, the first-word position of the sentence is a poor region for analysis as this region is skipped more frequently than other regions of the sentence.

In spite of the richness of information that can be obtained from eye-movement data, eye-movement records have been used less extensively in the study of L2 sentence parsing for a number of reasons (a notable exception is the work by Frenck-Mestre and colleagues). For one, eye-tracking equipment is very costly to purchase and to maintain, and can be technically demanding. In contrast, self-paced reading studies are easy to implement and relatively inexpensive. Virtually any experiment can be set up on a standard desktop or laptop computer, and experiment-generated software is available for different platforms at a modest cost. In addition, many of the signature results found with eye-tracking measures have been obtained using self-paced reading (Mitchell, 2004).

7.4.3   *Event-related potentials (ERPs)*

As noted previously, ERPs are small voltage changes measured at the surface of the scalp, which reflect brain activity that is triggered by sensory stimuli or cognitive processes. An ERP consists of positive and negative voltage peaks, referred to as *components*. In ERP studies, participants listen to or read text while electro-encephalographic recordings are taken from different positions on the scalp. With this methodology, changes in ambient conditions such as lighting are kept at a minimum, and blinks are discouraged as the resulting waveforms can obscure the time course of linguistic processing. By varying information-processing requirements through the use of different tasks, qualitatively different ERP patterns have been found to correlate with particular aspects of language processing. For instance, Kutas and Hillyard (1980) demonstrated that sentences ending in a word that could not be semantically integrated into the prior sentence context ("He spread the warm bread with socks") elicited a negative-going waveform peaking at around 400 ms after the onset of the presentation of the critical word; therefore difficulty with semantic integration is associated with an *N400*-component. A second component, the *P600*, is a positive waveform with an onset at about 500 ms, which has been correlated with syntactic anomalies of various types (Osterhout & Holcomb, 1993).

One particular strength of ERP methodology over other techniques that are based exclusively on reading is that it allows a natural way of studying how linguistic material is processed when it is presented in an auditory modality (Mitchell, 2004). In this respect, ERP measures have been used successfully in L2 sentence-processing studies to determine whether the specific semantic and syntactic subprocesses engaged during L2 language comprehension are different for second language speakers as compared to native speakers. For example, Hahne (2001) compared semantic and syntactic processing in proficient second language learners of German who are native Russian speakers. ERP responses to auditory stimuli containing semantic and syntactic anomalies were recorded. Similarly to previous findings (Weber-Fox & Neville, 1996), the differences in processing semantic incongruities between native and L2 speakers were only quantitative, but there were qualitative differences with regard to syntactic processing between the two groups, suggesting that the L2 learners did not process or integrate syntactic information into the existing phrase structure in the same way as native listeners. In contrast to the reading studies described above, which show that structural processing of sentences in one language are affected by the presence of the other language, the ERP evidence suggests constraints in the degree to which the syntax of the L2 can be processed in a native-like manner (see MacWhinney, 1997, for another view of cross-language interactions in sentence processing, and Tokowicz & MacWhinney, 2005, for evidence that the ERP record may provide a sensitive means to detect the formation of syntactic representations in the L2 during early stages of acquisition).

7.5   Summary

In this chapter we introduced a subset of the laboratory methods that have been used to investigate the way in which bilinguals and second language learners recognize words, understand and produce speech, and process sentences in each of their languages. As noted earlier, our review is hardly exhaustive, but we have attempted to illustrate the methods that are representative of experimental approaches to bilingualism. In the process of doing so, we hope to have shown how these tools can be used to infer the nature of the cognitive processes that bilinguals bring to the tasks of comprehension and production in their two languages. We have also tried to provide a glimpse into the theoretical debates that guide this research. A list of laboratory designs without the theoretical foundation would be misleading, because it is these questions about how the mind accommodates the presence of two languages that lead us to the methods that we use. We invite the reader to sample the primary literature on experimental approaches to bilingualism. We also append below a section on resources that may provide useful information for laboratory investigations of bilingualism. We believe that this approach will inform not only theories of the bilingual mind but also cognitive and language science more generally.

Acknowledgments

The writing of this chapter was supported in part by NSF Grant BCS-0418071 and NIH Grant MH62479 to Judith F. Kroll and by NIH Grant HD50629 to Paola E. Dussias. We thank Natasha Tokowicz for helpful comments on an earlier version of the chapter.

Further reading and resources

There are a wealth of tools available to students new to experimental laboratory research. We list below a number of programs that are commonly used by psycholinguists to implement the sorts of experimental paradigms we have reviewed in this chapter. We also provide information on databases that may be useful in generating experimental materials. Students interested in pursuing laboratory research are well advised to take courses in experimental design and statistics. There are many introductory texts on each of these topics. The resources listed below are intended to supplement a basic introduction to research design and statistical methods. Although some of the techniques reviewed in the chapter (e.g., eye tracking and acoustic analysis) require additional training that cannot be easily accomplished without immersion in a laboratory setting, others (e.g., lexical decision and picture naming) can be sampled in web-based experiment programs that are readily available.

Programs for experimentation and analysis

Boersma, P. and D. Weenink (2005) Praat: Doing phonetics by computer (Version 4.3.22) (computer program). www.praat.org/.
Cohen, J. D., B. MacWhinney, M. Flatt, and J. Provost (1993) PsyScope: A new graphic interactive environment for designing psychology experiments. *Behavioral Research Methods, Instruments, and Computers*, 25, 257–71.
Forster, K. I. and J. C. Forster (1999) *DMDX* (computer software). Tucson: University of Arizona.
PST (Psychology Software Tools, Inc.). *E-prime*. www/pstnet.com/.

Websites for on-line experimentation

There are a number of websites where you can participate in actual experiments or try out demonstrations of psycholinguistic phenomena. Here are a few of those sites:

psych.hanover.edu/research/exponnet.html
psychexps.olemiss.edu/
www.york.ac.uk/res/prg/

Useful databases for psycholinguistic research

Note: The Psychonomic Society has recently established an archive that contains many useful databases: psychonomic.org/archive/; and the Max Planck Institute for Psycholinguistics in the Netherlands maintains a database of relevant corpora: www.mpi.nl/world/corpus/index.html/.
Balota, D. A., M. J. Cortese, K. A. Hutchinson, et al. (2002) The English lexicon project: A web-based repository of descriptive and behavioral measures for 40,481 English words and non-words. Available at elexicon.wustl.edu/.
Buchanan, L. and C. Westbury (2000) Wordmine Database: Probabilistic values for all four to seven letter words in the English language. Available at www.wordmine.org/.

Davis, C. J. and M. Perea (2005). BuscaPalabras: A program for deriving orthographic and phonological neighborhood statistics and other psycholinguistic indices in Spanish. *Behavior Research Methods, Instruments, and Computers*, 37, 665–71.

Prado, M. (1993) *Spanish False Cognates*. Chicago, IL: NTC Publishing Group.

Sebastián-Gallés, N., M. Martí Antonín, and F. Cuetos Vega (2000) *Léxico informatizado del Español*. Barcelona: Edicions de la Universitat de Barcelona.

Snodgrass, J. G. and M. Vanderwart (1980) A standardized set of 260 pictures: Norms for name agreement, image agreement, familiarity, and visual complexity. *Journal of Experimental Psychology: Human Learning and Memory*, 6, 174–215.

Tokowicz, N., J. F. Kroll, A. M. B. De Groot, and J. G. Van Hell (2002) Number-of-translation norms for Dutch-English translation pairs: A new tool for examining language production. *Behavior Research Methods, Instruments, and Computers*, 34, 435–51.

A guide to writing experimental reports

Publication Manual of the American Psychological Association (2001). 5th edn. Washington, DC: American Psychological Association.

8 Imaging Technologies

Jubin Abutalebi and Pasquale Anthony Della Rosa

8.1 Introduction

Investigations into the neural basis of language focus on how the brain processes language. For achieving this, it must be underlined that language is a most complex function, one that encompasses numerous subprocesses, including the recognition and articulation of speech sounds, the comprehension and production of words and sentences (see also chapter 7 in this volume), and the use of language in pragmatically appropriate ways. Underlying and interacting with these are also the functions of memory and attention. All contribute in more or less combined ways to our ability to process language, and the human brain may in fact handle each differently.

Early studies of brain and language relationships relied on a precise neurological examination as the basis for hypothesizing the site of brain damage that was responsible for a given language deficit. The advent of structural brain imaging, first with computed tomography (CT) and later with magnetic resonance imaging (MRI), opened the avenue for more precise anatomical localization of language deficits that are manifest after brain injury. In recent years, functional neuroimaging, broadly defined as techniques that provide measures of brain activity, has further increased our ability to study the neural basis of language. Indeed, functional neuroimaging techniques make it more feasible to address crucial questions related to the cerebral organization of languages. With these techniques we can focus on healthy bilingual subjects with well-defined language backgrounds, and by using well-designed paradigms we can attempt to characterize the neural architecture of the bilingual brain. These techniques roughly fall into two classes: the "electromagnetic" approach measures brain activity directly by recording the electromagnetic fields generated by certain neuronal populations. On the other hand, the "hemodynamic" approach estimates brain activity by detecting changes in vascular variables that are indirectly coupled with modifications in the neural activity. Importantly these methods differ in a number of aspects, above all the prerequisites for detecting a signal, the homogeneity with which neural activity is sampled from different parts of the brain, and the relative accuracy in determining *when* versus *where* neural activity takes place. These two approaches, therefore, provide complementary views of neural activity (see table 8.1 on p. 156 for a summary of techniques). The explosion of information about brain function in the last decade has resulted in large part from these two techniques.

In the present chapter, we will illustrate the essentials of both types of approaches and how they may be employed in the study of the neural basis of bilingualism. Before that a brief historical overview of how the brain and language relationship emerged as a research topic is in order.

8.2   The Brain and Language Relationship

Since the mid-eighteenth century, brain scientists have proposed that several different parts of the brain are involved with language. In the nineteenth century there was a rapid expansion of knowledge, because of the systematic investigation of the effects of localized brain damage on language processing. Indeed, brain scientists began to understand that damage to certain cerebral areas could generate peculiar language deficits. The latter type of investigation is also known as the "anatomo-clinical" method for which a particular cognitive deficit such as aphasia (i.e., loss of language which may be complete or not) is correlated to an anatomical location in the brain. The rationale for this kind of correlation was the following: if a certain brain area is damaged and the patient has become aphasic, then the evidence was sufficient to state that the damaged brain area was responsible for language processing. For example, on the basis of anatomical-pathological observations in a patient suffering from a severe aphasia (he was only able to utter "tan-tan" and became famous as "patient tan-tan"), the French surgeon Paul Broca (1861) suggested the importance of the third left frontal convolution in spoken language (which was damaged in his patient). A similar observation was made ten years later by the German neuropsychiatrist, Carl Wernicke, who observed that a lesion in the left superior temporal gyrus generated severe disorders in language understanding without provoking any speech disorder (Wernicke, 1874). Broca's and Wernicke's observations proved that the ability of human beings to speak and understand language depends on two distinct areas of the left hemisphere of the brain. These studies formed the foundations of neuro-psychology. Within the next dozen or so years, many different cerebral centers for various functions were defined, comprising centers for writing, reading, calculating, and so on. In general, these implicated the left side of the brain (henceforth called the "dominant" hemisphere). Moreover, these discoveries gave scientists the first glimpses of the distributed nature of language function in the brain. The brain seemed to have no single location where language is created or stored. Instead, it looked as if different parts of the brain controlled different aspects of speech and language.

Interest in aphasia in bilinguals developed concurrently with the discovery of these various language centers, and reflected the numerous controversies about the representation of language in the brain. In particular, it was observed that, if a bilingual subject was affected by an aphasia-producing left hemispheric lesion, the two languages were not always affected to the same degree. Moreover, the recovery of language, which could follow, was not always equal for both languages. Many different language recovery patterns have been described (for a classification, see Paradis, 1983). In order to account for patterns of recovery of languages in bilingual aphasia, neurologists have invoked differential cerebral localization for each language. For example, Scoresby-Jackson (1867) postulated that the foot of the third frontal convolution (Broca's area) should be a sort of language organ only for native languages, whereas the remaining part of the convolution might be responsible for a second language (L2). He gave this explanation to account for an aphasic patient who selectively lost the use of his L2 after brain damage.

Pitres (1895), who was the first to perform a multiple single case study of bilingual aphasia, strongly argued against this view of different cerebral localization for different languages. From then on, the debate of a hypothetical differential localization of multiple languages in the same brain has invigorated discussion (for review, see Paradis, 1998; and Fabbro, 1999). Some authors argued against an anatomical segregation for multiple languages within the language areas (Penfield, 1965), whereas the majority of researchers were inclined to consider various kinds of differential representation, including distinct neuroanatomical localization. Segalowitz (1983) argued that it would be surprising if bilingualism had no effect on brain organization, and that there are numerous reasons to believe that cerebral representation of language is not entirely the same in polyglots as in monolinguals. Others have proposed that bilinguals are somewhat less lateralized than monolingual speakers, with the right hemisphere prevalently subserving one of the languages of the bilingual (Albert & Obler, 1978). In contrast, Michel Paradis, one of the most influential researchers in this field, argued (1987, 1998) against an anatomical segregation for multiple languages within the language areas and, to date, Paradis's assumptions seem to prevail.

As to the methodology, it should be mentioned that the traditional anatomo-clinical approach was clearly flawed, since it is based not on an anatomical-functional organization but on the observation of vascular-cerebral lesions (infarctions or cerebral hemorrhages), which are usually extensive and can damage several cerebral areas depending on the distribution of arteries. A further limitation is the fact that in the case of a restricted cerebral lesion, following which patients can fortunately survive for years, anatomist-pathologists are not in a position to detect it on a timely basis (i.e., the exact anatomical location of the lesion that caused the language deficit may only be known on the autopsy table). This limit has been overcome thanks to structural imaging techniques, computerized tomography (CT) and magnetic resonance (MR), all of which have been widely used since the early 1970s and 1980s. Structural or "morphological" neuroimaging techniques have significantly contributed to the advancement of our neuroanatomical knowledge based on the anatomo-clinical study model mentioned above, but with the enormous advantage of being able to describe from disease onset the lesion site in the brain (Press, Amaral, & Squire, 1989; Damasio, 1992).

However, there are limitations to the generalizability of aphasia data to neurologically healthy individuals. Concerns about the anatomo-clinical approach as well as the structural neuroimaging approach include the inability to determine whether specific language deficits are the result of damage to a specialized brain component at the lesion site, or the damaged area is simply part of a larger neural network that mediates a given component of language (Abutalebi, Cappa, & Perani, 2001, 2005; Green & Price, 2001; Vaid & Hull, 2002). It is evident that complex mental operations such as language processing cannot entirely depend on restricted areas of the brain, but rather are controlled by distributed neural systems (Mesulam, 1990). Understanding how these systems work is a prerequisite and a top priority for neuroscientific research.

The use of functional imaging with PET and fMRI techniques and electrophysiological techniques such as the ERPs – the techniques we are dealing with in the present chapter – may assist in the investigation of the neural networks that underlie language functions.

Section summary

The aphasia data were the first to point to the brain and language relationship and have provided a rich source of evidence on the range of language disorders and language recovery patterns in bilinguals. However, there are limitations to the generalizability of such data to neurologically healthy individuals. Nevertheless, studying the effects of brain damage on linguistic function in bilinguals has led to a number of interesting observations about the nature and course of language impairment and recovery, which in turn have stimulated researchers to apply functional neuroimaging techniques to the investigation of bilingual language processing.

8.3 The "Electromagnetic" Approach

8.3.1 *Time-locked EEG recording (ERPs)*

Over the past 30 years recordings of event-related potentials (ERPs) from normal individuals have played an increasingly important role in our understanding of human cognition. In particular, we will consider what has been learned and what might be learned about bilingualism by measuring the electrical activity of the brain.

The ERP technique is relatively straightforward. Electrodes placed on the scalp measure the voltage fluctuations that are produced by large populations of brain cells (neurons). When neurons are activated, local electrical current flows are produced and the electrodes placed on the scalp surface measure these electrical currents. Only large populations of active neurons can generate electrical activity recordable on the head surface. The measurement of these electrical currents is known as the electroencephalogram (EEG), which reflects the spontaneous electrical activity of the brain across time (also called the baseline activity). ERPs, on the other hand, do not represent the baseline electrical activity of the brain but rather the electrical activity related to specific stimuli (i.e., experimental conditions). For instance, listening to a sentence that contains a semantic anomaly is a proper stimulus to elicit a specific electrical potential in posterior brain areas (the so-called N400; see below).

8.3.2   How to extract ERPs

Since the ERP signal is weak (5–10 microvolts) and embedded in the stronger but noisy EEG signal (50–100mv) it is necessary to extract the former from the latter. To this end, averaging techniques are employed to extract the "signal" (the stimulus-locked ERP) from the "noise" (the background or baseline EEG). This involves recording a sufficient number of ERPs, each being time-locked to the repetition of the same type of event or stimulus. The ERPs for each time-point in the background EEG are then averaged to yield a single value representing the average activity related to the stimulus. This is the average event-related potential. Through such analysis techniques, the baseline or background EEG activity is basically eliminated and the activity resulting from the processing of the stimulus remains. As more stimuli are included in the analysis, the ERP signal becomes cleaner (in terms of the ERP waveform).

The resulting averaged ERP waveform consists of several positive and negative deflections that are called "peaks," and "components," and are simply named with a "P" or an "N" to indicate a positive or a negative deflection. Moreover, when a positive deflection occurs with, for instance, a latency of 600 milliseconds after the stimulus onset, it is referred to as "P600." A further parameter that may be important is the amplitude of the average ERP waveform (in microvolts) implicitly linked to the amount of electrical brain activity elicited by a particular stimulus. Hence, the polarity (positive or negative), the latency (in milliseconds), and the amplitude are the three main characteristics of the ERP waveform.

8.3.3   ERP "Components"

After extracting the signal, researchers generally focus on some specific feature of the resulting ERP waveform (for example, a peak or trough), and this particular feature then becomes the component of interest. For instance, the abovementioned N400 is an ERP component specific to language processing. According to Donchin, Ritter, and McCallum (1978), a "component" is a part of the ERP waveform with a circumscribed scalp distribution (alluding to the neurons that generated the ERP) and a circumscribed relationship to experimental variables (alluding to the cognitive function served by the activity of this population of neurons).

It is worth stressing that the electrical activity generated by a specific neural population may be propagated through the brain tissue and be also detectable at other brain locations (where other electrodes may be placed). For instance, the single voltage measured at a particular electrode (placed over a certain brain area) and at a particular time may well be attributable to the activity of a variety of different neurons from different spatial locations. This may give rise to an overlap of components. Component overlap refers to the fact that the ERP waveform we observe by measuring the voltage at the scalp results from the summation of electrical activity that may be generated by several different sources in the brain. For example, an ERP peak with a latency of 200 ms might reflect not the activity of a single neural population maximally active at that time, but the combined activity of two (or more) populations, maximally active before and after 200 ms, but with electrical activity that summates to a maximum at that time. To overcome this apparent ambiguity, some researchers prefer defining components in terms of the underlying neural function such as a particular cognitive function. This is also called the "functional approach" to components (see Donchin, 1979), with reference to the functions of the neurons whose activity is recorded at the scalp.

What can we gain from the concept of an ERP component? Despite the difficulties surrounding their definition and measurement, components serve at least three purposes. First, they provide a language that allows communication across experiments, paradigms, and scientific fields. Second, they can provide a basis for integrating ERP data with other measures of brain activity. Third, components can serve as physiological markers for specific cognitive processes such as the N400.

8.3.4 ERPs and language

With specific reference to language processing, several ERP components with different temporal and spatial characteristics have been identified, indicating that distinct mechanisms may mediate at least semantic and syntactic processes (Hagoort, Brown, & Osterhout, 2000).

ERP language research began with the seminal study by Kutas and Hillyard (1980) on the semantic processing of written sentences. These authors examined the ERPs produced when their subjects read sentences that ended with either a semantically congruent or incongruent word. They observed a component that peaked about 400 ms after the onset of the incongruent word. This so-called N400 component is a broad, posteriorly distributed negative wave.

Several factors seem to affect the amplitude of this component, including: the critical word's cloze probability – less predictable lexical items have a larger N400 amplitude than more predictable ones (Kutas & Hillyard, 1984); word frequency – high-frequency words have a larger N400 amplitude than low-frequency words (Rugg, 1990; Van Petten & Kutas, 1990); word concreteness – abstract words have a larger N400 than concrete words (Paller, Kutas, Shimamura, & Squire, 1987); word class – content words have a larger N400 component than function words (Besson, Kutas, & Van Petten, 1992); semantic relation between words – unprimed words have a larger N400 than primed words (Bentin, McCarthy, & Wood, 1985); and word repetition – the first presentation has a larger N400 than the second one (Besson, Kutas, & Van Petten, 1992).

Moreover, this component has been observed under a wide range of conditions: in different languages including English, Dutch, German, French, and Italian, in different modalities including visual, auditory, and even sign language; and with different experimental procedures (Kutas & Van Petten, 1994). Thus, it seems that the amplitude of the N400 component provides a proper measure of the difficulty encountered by the reader in integrating the lexical element with the preceding context.

Interestingly, the presentation of syntactic violations such as verb subcategorization violations (Osterhout & Swinney, 1989; Osterhout & Holcomb, 1990) did not produce an N400 component, but rather an increase in the positivity with a biparietal distribution (the centro-posterior areas of the brain), several hundred milliseconds later. This effect has been called P600 (Osterhout & Holcomb, 1992) or late positive syntactic shift (Hagoort, Brown, & Groothusen, 1993).

Some researchers have claimed that the P600 component is not specifically linguistic, but belongs to the family of P300 effects, often observed after the repetition of any unexpected stimuli. Still others (Osterhout, Holcomb, & Swinney, 1994) have claimed that the amplitude of the late positive peak may be related only to the "cost of processing." Experiments have subsequently compared more varied types of syntactic violations, and a P600 has generally been recorded for all types of syntactic violations presented. It is interesting to note that certain studies have obtained also an earlier component, which is violation-specific. In particular, some researchers (Friederici, Pfeiffer, & Hahne, 1993) have observed an early component with an "early left-hemispheric anterior negativity" (ELAN) between 200 and 400 ms after the onset of the word that violates the basic phrase structure of the language. This ERP component was observed for both visual (Osterhout & Holcomb, 1992) and auditory (Friederici, Pfeiffer, & Hahne, 1993) modes of presentation. It appears thus that the processing of the syntactic category information of a word precedes the processing of its lexical syntactic information (N400), which is a striking finding.

In conclusion, three ERP components, the N400, the P600, and the ELAN, have been observed during the processing of linguistic stimuli. The N400 is elicited whenever a semantic anomaly occurs, the P600 is associated with syntactical reanalysis and repair of incongruencies, and the ELAN appears to reflect a first-pass parsing stage responsible for the building of local phrase structure.

8.3.5   How to build an ERPs experiment

ERPs must be recorded reliably, analyzed properly, and interpreted creatively. These general principles of science applied within the specific arena of ERPs raise an important issue concerning how experiments should be designed. In order to relate ERP waveforms to language processing and bilingualism, the ERPs should be recorded with an adequate experimental paradigm.

8.3.5.1   Experimental paradigms

Historically, the most frequently used ERP paradigm is the "oddball" paradigm, which involves the detection of an improper target stimulus (such as a number) in a train of standard stimuli (such as letters). Hence, the number within the letters is the improper stimulus that has to be detected. This paradigm elicits large ERP components, and provides useful information about how the brain discriminates stimuli. However, even though it can be adapted to the study of many cognitive processes, including language and bilingualism, it is often better to create paradigms more specific to language processing, such as verbal categorization tasks (see below).

Once the experimental paradigm has been set and the experimental conditions derived according to the rationale for the study, the set-up of experimental conditions must be controlled. Different experimental conditions can occur in separate blocks of trials or can be combined within blocks of trials. For example, bilingualism can be studied by having subjects listen to sentences in one language in one block of trials and sentences in another language in a separate block of trials (block design), or by having subjects attend to both types of sentences in the same block of trials (mixed design). In both cases, the amount of time required for each block of trials and the sequence in which the blocks are delivered must be controlled. For instance, many aspects of behavior and many components of the ERP change over time, and such changes should not be confounded with the experimental manipulations. It is therefore advisable to balance experimental conditions over time either within each subject or across subjects. Time is only one of many factors that must be controlled, because cognitive behavior is very flexible and heavily influenced by context. In addition, the rules by which the stimulus sequences are generated should be specified, i.e. whether they will occur in a completely random order or according to set probabilities, because subjects may be capable of picking up regularities and rules of stimulus sequences and subtle changes in these can lead to ERP effects.

When complex stimuli such as words or sentences in two different languages are used, they should be selected with an awareness of which of their properties might affect their processing. Factors such as familiarity, word frequency, and meaning are of crucial importance when studying words, for instance. If not manipulated in the experiment, these factors should be controlled rigidly and kept constant across conditions and comparable among languages. The stimulus duration and the intervals between the stimuli should also be controlled.

8.3.5.2 *Measurement of ERP waveforms*

Once the ERPs have been recorded, they must be measured in order to define the components. As mentioned above, the simplest approach is to consider the ERP waveform as a set of deflections, to define the peaks and troughs, and to measure the amplitude and latency at these deflections. Averaging is then required to render the measurements distinguishable from noise. This averaging process is locked to a triggering mechanism that ensures that the ERPs are reliably time-locked to the events to which they are related. When ERP waveforms are averaged important questions may arise, chief among them whether or not an ERP is at least present. This question is important when defining the significance threshold of the ERP for detecting a stimulus or discriminating a difference between stimuli.

A second issue is whether ERPs recorded under different conditions are significantly different (such as under a semantic and a syntax incongruency condition). A simple way to examine ERP differences between the conditions is to subtract the recorded waveform in one condition from that recorded in the other. The resultant "difference waveform" is assumed to represent physiological processes that are different between the two conditions. The weakness of this approach is that physiological processes are usually not additive; consequently, the interpretation of the difference waveform is not straightforward. The difference waveform represents only additional activity caused by the physiological processes present in one condition and not in the other. However, it does not rule out that the same physiological processes may be involved in both conditions. This last issue leads to the conclusion that, when using difference waveforms, it is essential to take into account various factors, including the cognitive manner of information processing between the two conditions, or more physiological ones such as changes in the latency of one or more components in the unsubtracted ERPs. All of the variables mentioned above might affect the subtraction by differentially affecting the two conditions from which the difference is calculated.

These issues concerning "cognitive subtractions" are not unique to ERP research; they arise with other techniques, such as PET or fMRI, that will also be discussed at length in the present chapter.

8.3.5.3   Source analysis

As already mentioned, ERPs are signals recorded over both time and space. There are two main ways to display these data. The first is as a change in voltage over time (the ERP waveform described above). The second is as a change in voltage over space, the ERP topography scalp distribution map (see figure 8.1 for the scalp distribution of the N400 effect during a semantic incongruency task).

Changes in ERP waveforms across the scalp (as derived from the distribution of the electrodes over the head) provide important evidence about the number and topographies of the underlying components, and are crucial for comparing experimental effects across subjects. This information may also be employed to distinguish ERPs from extracranial artifacts that may arise from eye movements (such as blinking) or muscle activity (such as wrinkling the forehead). Moreover, comparing the structure of waveforms at different brain sites is very useful for determining whether more than one component is contributing to a voltage measure at a particular time point. Indeed, as mentioned above, different components may correspond to the processing of a specific type of information by a particular population of neurons. Thus, a topographic map allows the researcher to visualize the distribution of the electric field generated by the ensemble of neurons (i.e., two different surface topographies are most likely produced by different sets of neural populations; Fender, 1987). If we accept that a cognitive function can be defined by specific neuronal activity, one can conclude that ERPs deriving from distinct neural populations reflect different psychological processes. The study of the topography of the components hence makes it possible to define neural populations activated during a specific cognitive task.

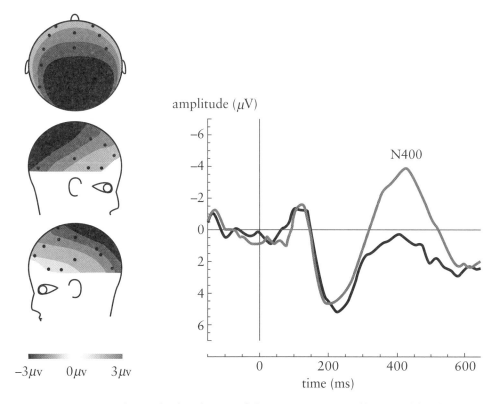

Figure 8.1: Topographic scalp distribution of the semantic N400-effect. Modified from Hagoort et al., 2004.

8.3.5.4 Statistical analysis

In designing statistical analyses for ERP data, investigators are not restricted to one specific or commonly used statistical method. Although parametric statistics have advantages that give them pride of place, there are many other approaches to statistical inference. In many situations, techniques such as non-parametric statistics, permutational statistics (Blair & Karniski, 1993), and bootstrapping (Wasserman & Bockenholt, 1989) may be more appropriate, because they make no assumptions about the distribution of the data. These techniques may be particularly helpful in the analysis of multichannel scalp distributions (Fabiani, Gratton, Corballis, Cheng, & Friedman, 1998). As Tukey (1978) pointed out, statistical analysis can be used as a tool for either decision making or data exploration. Hence, investigators do not view statistical analysis as a ritual designed to obtain the blessing of a "level of significance" but as a way to interact with the data.

Moreover, the number of subjects in an experiment must be sufficient to allow statistical tests to demonstrate the experimental effects. The sample must also be large enough to represent the population over which the results are to be generalized. Because ERP data can vary considerably from one subject to the next, it is often advisable (for instance, when using small numbers of subjects) to sample from a population as homogeneous as possible in terms of age, gender, educational level, and handedness.

8.3.6   *Important issues: Subject's behavior and ERPs' limits*

When using ERPs to evaluate cognitive processes, it is useful to monitor behavioral responses concurrently with the recorded electrophysiological responses. In many perceptual tasks, a simple motor response (such as the button press of the response box) to a detected target may provide a behavioral measure of the speed and accuracy of performance. In general, the more behavioral data are available, the more readily the psychophysiological measures can be evaluated within the context of an information-processing model. The type of behavioral data collected will depend on the type of correlations that may be hypothesized. Nevertheless, in some experiments ERPs are used as a relatively unobtrusive monitor of cerebral processes without the need for recording behavioral responses. A classic example is measuring the ERPs to unattended stimuli. This measurement can indicate how these stimuli are processed without the need to ask for overt responses to the unattended stimuli, which could clearly disrupt the focus of attention. However, in language-related experiments it may be advantageous if subjects' performance is also behaviorally monitored. Most authors agree that whenever concurrent monitoring is not possible for technical reasons, an additional session aimed at recording only behavioral responses can be helpful in determining the timing and performance of the cognitive process of the study. However, in some language studies the concurrent recording of behavioral responses may even be counterproductive (Kutas & Van Petten, 1994; Kutas, 1997). Consider, for instance, a lexical-decision task. This kind of task may elicit a decision-related P300, which may obscure other ERP components such as the N400 deflection. In order to compare ERP results with a behavioral counterpart using tasks such as lexical decision and naming, which are incompatible with ERP recording due to artifacts caused by tongue movements and muscle activity, a useful strategy has been to conduct a behavioral study first, followed by an ERP study with the same stimuli. In other cases, it has been of some interest to compare ERP data obtained under general "read" or "listen" instructions with those obtained from an overt task that forces attention onto some aspect of the stimuli. Such comparisons can reveal which aspects of stimuli are processed automatically versus those that are optional. For instance, these comparisons have shown that sentence semantic congruity effects occur independently of the assigned task (Connolly, Stewart, & Phillips, 1990), but that rhyming effects for visually presented word pairs occur only when rhyme monitoring is the assigned task (Rugg & Barrett, 1987).

Regarding the limits of the ERPs approach, it must be underlined that ERPs generally provide poor information about the spatial localization of neural activity generated by a specific cognitive process. Moreover, there is not a transparent relationship between an electrical field observed on the scalp and the brain regions giving rise to that field. For example, if an ERP effect is maximal over frontal scalp sites, this does not necessarily mean that the activity that gives rise to this effect is in the frontal cortex. Clearly, it would be of considerable value to be able to discern the sources of ERP data that lie within the brain. Such knowledge would enhance the functional and neural interpretations of the data, and greatly facilitate their integration with findings from studies using other methods such as fMRI. At the moment, any statistically significant difference in scalp distribution could be considered as evidence for potential functional differences. However, the spatial resolution with which ERP scalp fields are sampled is continuously increasing, and along with it the power to detect subtle differences in scalp distribution.

8.3.8 ERPs studies in bilinguals

Very few investigators have utilized ERP recording techniques in bilingual populations but all data point to both quantitative and qualitative differences between L1 and L2 processing. Kutas and Kluender (1991), for instance, found that the N400 component in response to semantic anomaly was delayed and showed lower amplitude in the bilingual's less fluent language. Likewise, Webber-Fox and Neville (1996) found the N400 present in all groups of Chinese-English bilinguals though it was more delayed in those who had learned the L2 after the age of 11–13 years. More critically, in contrast to monolinguals, there was a distinct pattern of response to phrase-structure violations in bilinguals. Only individuals acquiring L2 before the age of 4 showed no difference from native learners of L2. Hahne and Friederici (2001) examined the effects of phrase structure violations and semantic anomaly in native Japanese speakers who acquired their L2 (German) relatively late in life. The authors confirmed a delayed N400 effect in response to semantic anomaly, but also found a right anterior central negativity in L2. Unlike in native German speakers there was no early anterior negativity in response to syntactic violation. Hahne and Friederici (2001) concluded that late learners identify lexical content independently of morphological form and construct a representation directly based on conceptual information.

Section summary

ERPs reflect the electrical neural activity related to specific stimuli (i.e., experimental conditions) and are extracted from a baseline EEG recorded on the scalp. Three ERP components, the N400, the P600, and the ELAN, have been observed during the processing of linguistic stimuli. The N400 is elicited whenever a semantic anomaly occurs, the P600 is associated with syntactical reanalysis and repair of incongruencies, and the ELAN appears to reflect a first-pass parsing stage responsible for the building of local phrase structure.

ERPs have been successfully employed to study bilinguals, and most evidence points to qualitative differences in waveforms (i.e., absence of ELAN) and quantitative differences in latencies (i.e., delayed N400) for bilinguals with later ages of L2 acquisition.

8.4   The "Hemodynamic" Approach

The quest for an understanding of the functional organization of the normal human brain, using techniques to assess changes in brain circulation, has occupied mankind for more than a century. One has only to consult William James's monumental two-volume text *Principles of Psychology* (1890, vol. 1: 97) to find reference to changes in brain blood flow during mental activities. He refers primarily to the work of the Italian physiologist Angelo Mosso (1881), who recorded the pulsation of the human cortex in patients with skull defects following neurosurgical procedures. Mosso showed that these pulsations increased regionally during mental activity and concluded that brain circulation changes selectively with neuronal activity. Despite a promising beginning, interest in this research virtually ceased during the first quarter of the twentieth century and it was the advent of structural brain imaging in the 1970s, first with computed tomography (CT) and later with magnetic resonance imaging (MRI), that opened the avenue. The modern era of functional brain imaging was introduced with the use of positron emission tomography (PET) and in more recent years functional magnetic resonance imaging (fMRI) has rapidly emerged as an extremely powerful technique with many advantages over PET for studying cognition.

Consider that there are many ways to visualize the human brain *in vivo*. One of these is by using radioactivity to measure cerebral metabolism, cerebral blood flow, or neuroreceptors–neurotransmitters by means of PET. fMRI does not require radioactivity and can give very high-spatial-resolution images reflecting neuronal activation. These techniques allow neuronal activity to be explored. It is well known that a large part of the metabolic needs of the brain (and therefore of glucose consumption) is to maintain synaptic activity. Given that the brain does not have the ability to store oxygen and glucose, the intake of these energy resources through the cerebral blood flow is crucial to a constant neural activity. It has been proven that under normal conditions, there is a high level of coupling between energy metabolism and regional cerebral flow (rCBF) (Sokoloff, 1975); a number of experiments have proven that the increase in rCBF exceeds the local energy demand (Fox & Raichle, 1986). This observation is important because it proves that changes in regional blood flow can provide more meaningful parameters than direct measurements of cerebral metabolism.

8.4.1   PET

8.4.1.1   Basic principles

PET is a technology that creates pictures of the distribution of radiation within the central opening of a doughnut shaped PET scanner. To obtain measurements of functional parameters, such as regional cerebral flow (rCBF) and glucose consumption, PET scanning requires the combination of three fundamental elements: a positron emission tomograph, a cyclotron (an accelerator of particles that produce positron-emitting radiotracers), and a method of data analysis. Radioactive substances, called tracers, are employed to "image" different physiological processes, such as brain blood flow or metabolism (i.e., glucose consumption). Indeed, PET shows the 3D brain distribution of positron-emitting radiotracers attached to molecules such as fluorine-deoxyglucose when the measurements refer to glucose consumption, or to water molecules when the measurements refer to rCBF. In the latter case, areas of higher blood flow will have a larger amount of radioactive tracer, and thus emit a stronger signal. As noted before, blood flow is an indirect measure of local synaptic activity.

Regarding the study of cognitive functions, most commonly studies investigating increases in rCBF (cerebral activation) linked to the performance of cognitive tasks (e.g. language, memory, attention) have been employed. These studies used labeled oxygen ($^{15}O_2$) as the radiotracer, i.e. oxygen which has had an electron removed from its atom to create an unstable compound capable of emitting positrons. The $^{15}O_2$ is used in the form of water ($H_2^{15}O$), which is administered intravenously. The advantage of this tracer is that it decays in a short time (approximately two minutes). This means that it is possible to make several scans (up to about 16) during a single session, thus enabling researchers to study different conditions while patients carry out different tasks. At the beginning of each PET scan, a small amount of labeled water is injected into a subject's vein, while her or his head is placed inside the PET scanner. After about 30 seconds, the tracer starts appearing in the brain and the next 30 seconds constitute the critical window when radiation reaches its peak in the brain. Images of rCBF are obtained during this critical window. Using data analysis methods, a 3D representation of the brain is obtained in the form of a mapping of radioactivity distribution, which indicates cerebral activity linked to the cognitive task.

8.4.2 fMRI

8.4.2.1 Basic principles

The fMRI technique is based upon the magnetic properties of hydrogen atoms (a component of water, the most abundant substance in the body) and hemoglobin (the blood's oxygen carrier) (Howseman & Bowtell, 1999). The main signal is created by applying a magnetic field to artificially align the hydrogen atoms along a main pole, and then transient pulses of radio frequency energy are used to tip the magnetization of the atoms away from the main pole. The energy released as the atoms relax back to the main pole is measured by a radio-wave source (the detection device) sited within an enclosed tunnel where the subject is placed. This equipment sends its signals to a connected computer to create images of the distribution of the magnetic signal within the whole brain.

8.4.2.2 The BOLD effect

The generation of images that are related to blood flow takes advantage of an additional property of the system: hemoglobin has different magnetic properties when it is not carrying oxygen (deoxyhemoglobin) than when it is carrying oxygen (oxyhemoglobin, or simply hemoglobin). Functional MRI using the blood oxygen level-dependent method (BOLD) is sensitive to changes in blood volume and the concentration of deoxygenated hemoglobin across the vessels of the brain. The rationale is that more deoxygenated blood in an area causes a decrease in BOLD signal, and neural activity is accompanied by increased blood flow, which dilutes the concentration of deoxygenated hemoglobin and produces a relative increase in signal (Ogawa, Lee, Kay, & Tank, 1990; Hoge, Atkinson, Gill, et al., 1999). When the rCBF to a particular brain area is increased, the number of oxygen-carrying hemoglobin molecules is also increased. In fact, the tissue use of oxygen does not keep pace with the increase in hemoglobin, so as a result areas that are functionally active experience a decrease in the percentage of deoxyhemoglobin. The magnetic properties of deoxyhemoglobin disrupt the strength of the local signal produced by the hydrogen atoms, and so, as the amount of deoxyhemoglobin decreases, the local signal created by the hydrogen atoms in the nearby tissue increases. Altogether then, the method permits images of changes in blood flow to be measured indirectly through the effects of changing percentages of deoxyhemoglobin (Howseman & Bowtell, 1999).

Unlike with PET, images of the changes in blood flow are created in seconds; thus a single two-hour imaging session may generate more than 1,000 images of the brain (as compared to 10 for PET). However, the signal-to-noise ratio in an individual image is very low, so it is necessary to average many images together to generate an image that shows changes reliably.

8.4.3   Potential limitations of PET and fMRI

8.4.3.1   Spatial limitations

There are limitations that restrict what both PET and fMRI can measure. The spatial resolution of PET precludes experiments testing for neural activity in focused areas of the brain (e.g., mapping receptive fields of cells in the visual cortex). fMRI has a much greater spatial resolution but this technique also often cause distortions of the images in areas that are close to interfaces between tissue and air. For instance, crucial structures of the brain (in particular, orbito-frontal and inferior temporal regions and the temporal pole) may not be visualized because the air enclosed in adjacent structures (the middle ear and the mastoid bone) creates serious interference with the magnetic field, resulting in a loss of their visualization.

Artifacts. Artifactual activations (i.e., patterns that appear to be activations but that arise from non-neural sources) may arise from a number of sources and can affect both PET and fMRI activations. Functional MRI also contains more sources of signal variation due to noise than does PET, including changes in the signal due to physiological processes accompanying heart rate and respiration. Moreover, i.e. due to the excellent spatial resolution (< 1mm) of fMRI, even minimal movements made by the patient introduce features that can alter functional results (the recent introduction of image co-recording algorithms seems to reduce this problem).

8.4.3.2 *Temporal resolution and trial structure*

Another important limitation of scanning with PET and fMRI is the temporal resolution of data acquisition. PET and fMRI measure very different things, over different timescales. Because PET computes the amount of radioactivity emitted from a brain region, at least 30 seconds of scanning must pass before a sufficient sample of radioactive counts is collected. This limits the temporal resolution to blocks of time of at least 30 seconds, far longer than the temporal resolution of most cognitive processes. fMRI has its own temporal limitation due largely to the latency and duration of the hemodynamic response to a neural event. Typically, changes in blood flow do not reach their peak until several seconds after a neural event, so the locking of neural events to the vascular response is not very tight.

8.4.3.3 *Duty cycle*

A final limitation of both PET and fMRI concerns what is often called the duty cycle of a task. In order for a neural event to create a measurable hemodynamic response, the neural event must take up a substantial proportion of the time taken in any measurement period. For example, if only a small number of nerve cells fire for some process or if the duration of firing is small with respect to the temporal resolution of the measurement technique, then the signal-to-noise ratio for that event is low and it may be difficult to detect.

8.4.3.4 *Repeatability*

Since fMRI does not require radiation and is a non-invasive technique, the patient can be examined more than once and the cognitive test repeated many times. This is obviously not the case for PET imaging. Moreover, PET imaging is also expensive because of the radiotracers employed.

Section summary

Both PET and fMRI are powerful tools in the measurement of brain activity. They achieve this in an indirect manner since both measure more properly the regional cerebral blood flow (rCBF). However, changes in rCBF indicate that a certain brain area is working; hence, these techniques allow neuronal activity to be explored. PET imaging employs radioactivity to achieve this while fMRI takes advantage of the paramagnetic properties of hemoglobin. Apart from being non-invasive, fMRI provides very high-spatial-resolution images as compared to PET.

8.5   How to Build a Neuroimaging Experiment

The most obvious rationale for conducting functional neuroimaging experiments is to correlate structure with function. Consider that complex psychological processes are best described in terms of combinations of constituent elementary operations. These elementary processes may not be localized in single locations in the brain; they are often the result of networks of neurons acting together. The assumptions of neuroimaging lead us naturally to search the brain activations that accompany elementary psychological processes and analyze what combinations of elementary processes are involved in a cognitive task (Hernandez, Wager, & Jonides, 2002).

Consider also that cognition is a distributed process and hence cognitive functions, such as language, may not be localizable to a single brain region (Berns, 1999). Most evidence points towards networks of regions functioning with a particular choreography that gives rise to a cognitive function. Therefore, to study the neural basis of cognition, one needs a technique that can measure neural function simultaneously in the entire brain. Although it may never be possible to measure the state of every neuron in the brain, PET and fMRI provide enough spatial and temporal resolution to make meaningful conclusions about the roles specific brain regions play during cognition. In the following, we will illustrate how to construct, carry out, analyze, and interpret a functional neuroimaging experiment. It is clear that before starting a neuroimaging experiment, several important issues must be taken into consideration. First, a specific hypothesis must be chosen. Second, appropriate methods must be selected and, third, the experiment must be appropriately conducted, analyzed, and interpreted. These choices will be constrained by the nature of the task chosen, the available imaging technology and its limitations, and the types of inference one wishes to draw from the study.

8.5.1   Task design

The design of a task limits the ultimate interpretability of the data. Tasks must be chosen that yield theoretical insight into the neural and psychological processes under investigation, and they must avoid the influence of nuisance variables. Nuisance variables may be neural processes unrelated to the question of interest, either prescribed by the task or unrelated to it. They may be technological artifacts or physiological artifacts due to processes such as heart rate, respiration, and eye movements, that may interfere with the rCBF. To the extent that nuisance variables influence the brain activations in a task, they will mitigate the uniqueness of an interpretation that one may place on the data. Constructing adequate tasks can be quite challenging, and it may not be possible in some situations.

Once an adequate task is chosen, important decisions need to be made concerning the right frame to fit around the task, i.e., the experimental paradigm. This decision is also constrained by the technique we decide to employ and it is related to the advantages and limitations linked to the physical properties underlying the detection of a specific signal.

A final caveat with regard to certain cognitive paradigms is that the brain systems involved do not necessarily remain constant through many repetitions of the task. Rather, when a task is novel major changes can occur in the systems fired by the task. Such changes have both practical and theoretical implications when it comes to the design and interpretation of cognitive activation experiments.

The predominant paradigms for analyzing task-related changes using PET or fMRI are so-called "blocked" paradigms and "event-related" designs.

8.5.1.1 Blocked designs

A blocked design is the standard experimental design used in PET activations studies because long intervals of time (30 seconds or more) are required to collect sufficient data to yield a good image. In a blocked design, different conditions in the experiment are presented as separate blocks of trials (e.g., naming in L1 in one block and naming in L2 in a different block), with each block representing one scan during an experiment. The activations of interest in a PET experiment are ones that accumulate over the entire recording interval of a scan. If one is interested in observing the neural effect of some briefly occurring psychological process (e.g., the activation due to a briefly flashed light stimulus), in a PET experiment one would have to iterate the event repeatedly during a block of trials so that activations due to it accumulate over the recording interval of a scan. One could then compare the activations in this scan with an appropriate baseline control scan in which the event did not occur. However, given its temporal limitation PET is not well suited to examining the fine time course of brain activity that may change within seconds or fractions of a second. The blocked structure of PET designs is a major factor in the interpretability of results, and most commonly activations related to slowly changing factors such as different tasks that alternate themselves within the paradigm (for example, naming a picture or repeating a word) are captured within this type of design.

Many studies using fMRI also have made good use of blocked designs. Again, in these blocked paradigms, subjects alternate between active (e.g., naming in L2) and control tasks (i.e., a rest condition) for short time periods (e.g., 30 seconds), and then the images acquired during the active task blocks are statistically compared with the images acquired during the control task block. One advantage of using a blocked design with fMRI is that it offers more statistical power to detect a change.

8.5.1.2 Event-related designs

To take advantage of the rapid data-acquisition capabilities of fMRI, the event-related fMRI technique has been developed to create images of the neural activity related to specific stimuli or cognitive events within a trial. The technique involves spacing stimuli far enough apart in time for the hemodynamic response to a single stimulus or cognitive event to return to baseline before the onset of the next stimulus or event. Most researchers consider 14–16 seconds enough time for this to occur (Dale & Buckner, 1997; Aguirre, Zarahn, & D'Esposito, 1998). Using this technique, signals from individual trials of the same task (e.g., reading single words in L1) can be averaged together, and the time course of the hemodynamic response within a trial can be determined. This technique permits the randomization of trials from different conditions (e.g., presenting L1 and L2 stimuli intermingled), which is essential for certain tasks. It also allows researchers to analyze only selected types of trials in a mixed trial block, enabling the study of a number of processes that occur only on some trials.

The limiting factor of this type of design lies in the temporal resolution of fMRI: not the speed of data acquisition, but the speed of the underlying hemodynamic response to a neural event, which peaks 5–8 seconds after that neural activity has peaked. However, the recent advent of "rapid event-related fMRI techniques" has allowed us to perform experiments in which successive stimuli or cognitive events can be presented with as little as 750 ms intervening (Dale & Buckner, 1997). Importantly, the potential effects of fatigue, boredom, and systematic patterns of thought unrelated to the task during long intervals between trials are minimized with such designs. When "rapid event-related fMRI techniques" are employed the inter-trial interval must be varied from trial to trial. Without jittering of the inter-trial interval, the neural events would occur too rapidly to be sampled effectively.

8.5.2   Data analysis

Once a task is designed and data are collected, analysis of those data is composed of two important substages: preprocessing of the images and statistical analysis of the resulting activations. Preprocessing refers to image processing in which the various images in a set of data must be aligned to correct for head motion that may have occurred from one image acquisition to the next. Following alignment, images are often normalized to a standard brain template (often implemented in the data-analyzing software) so that results from several subjects can be combined into averages and plotted in standard 3D brain coordinates for comparison with other studies. Many researchers also smooth images, in order to give the noise in the images a more Gaussian distribution. This smoothing of images effectively produces a weighted average of the signal across neighboring voxels (three-dimensional pixels). Although smoothing decreases the spatial resolution of the images, giving the smoothed images a blurry appearance, it helps to estimate and control for statistical noise.

It is useful to know that data in neuroimaging experiments are in the form of a matrix of signal-intensity values in each region of the brain expressed in voxels (the smallest distinguishable box-shaped parts of a three-dimensional image). Following these preprocessing stages, statistical tests are performed on the data.

8.5.3   How to contrast experimental conditions

The problem with making inferences about cognitive processes from neuroimaging data is that nearly any task performed alone produces changes in most of the brain.

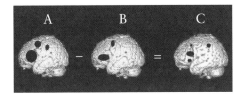

Figure 8.2: The subtraction method in functional neuroimaging experiments.
Modified from Perani et al., 2003.

To associate changes in brain activation with a particular cognitive process (e.g. word fluency in L2) requires that we isolate changes related to that process from changes related to other processes (e.g., word fluency in L1). At its simplest, the fMRI experiment can be considered a "subtraction experiment" in which we acquire images during each of two conditions (e.g., L1 and L2) and subtract them to identify "differences" (e.g., L1 versus L2). However, as will be discussed at length below, a number of considerations may limit such a simplistic study design.

The logic of subtraction is the following: if one tests two experimental conditions that differ by only one process, then a subtraction of the activations of one condition from those of the other should reveal the brain regions associated with the target process (for an example see figure 8.2).

At first sight the simplest experimental condition is between a stimulus applied or task performed during "block A" and a "rest block" in which no stimulus is applied and no task is performed. This is often referred to as the "A vs. Rest" design. While conceptually simple (the hypothesis is that there is "some" activity during block A and "no" activity during the rest block), it may be difficult to ensure that there is no confounding brain activity during the rest block (simply instructing the subject "not to think of anything" may not suffice to ensure no neural activity). An alternative approach is to set up a condition during the "rest block" to distract the subject from confounding memory, imagination, or continued activity. In fact, the "block A" vs. "block rest" design can be considered a special case of the more general "block A" vs. "block B" design (e.g., L1 naming in block A and L2 naming in block B) in which different activity is expected between blocks A and B and the purpose of the analysis is simply to identify those differences. Clearly, this places a considerable burden on the choice of an appropriate "block B" to complement "block A" without (unintentionally) obscuring or canceling out activation that might be common to both.

Once the experimental conditions are built in order to adequately highlight the activations elicited by different cognitive processes, the subtraction is accomplished one voxel at a time. Together, the results of the voxel-wise subtractions yield a three dimensional matrix of the difference in activation between the two conditions throughout the scanned regions of the brain.

8.5.4 Statistical approaches to fMRI data

Given the block design acquisition discussed above, with multiple images acquired during either "Rest" or "Condition A" blocks, a number of analysis strategies are available. In principle, the mean signal intensity of images acquired during "Condition A" and those acquired during "Rest" (or "Condition B," etc.) can be compared on a voxel-wise basis. The significance of any observed difference can then be tested using a simple Student's t-test.

A more elegant extension of this is to compute the correlation coefficient of each voxel's signal-intensity time course against a reference "box-car" function defined as −1 during rest and +1 during condition A. The magnitude (r) and significance level (p-value) can then be described on a voxel-wise basis and used as a basis for constructing color overlay maps, in which "activated pixels" are identified in color overlaid on grayscale source images.

On the other hand, the choice of a correlation coefficient threshold to delineate "significant" activation from "spurious" noise introduces a somewhat uncomfortable arbitrariness in analysis. The interpretation of significance is clouded by consideration of the many multiple comparisons being made in the simplified approach described above. Consider an image matrix of 128 × 128 pixels (>10,000 pixels). Assuming that a significance level of $p < 0.05$ is considered "significant," it is clear that we might expect >500 pixels to pass this threshold "by random chance." But a single pixel's signal-intensity behavior is neither truly independent nor exactly dependent on other pixel responses. It is reasonable, therefore, to entertain the notion that "neighboring" pixels might have similar underlying neuroanatomy and thus similar physiologic responses, but how neighboring and how similar? These two questions clearly invite some form of correction to the simple t-statistic.

The simplest approach is the Bonferroni correction method, which approximates the actual probability of N comparisons as N times the p-value at any one voxel. The uncorrected (or voxelwise) p-values indicate the *proportion* of voxels in the image that will light up by chance, while the corrected (or mapwise) p-values indicate the *probability* of false positive voxels occurring anywhere in the image. These represent two rather extreme viewpoints, whereas what really matters is the proportion of voxels *that have been declared active* which are likely to be false positives. This corresponds to the so-called false discovery rate, which has been recently incorporated into several of the standard analysis packages although it has not yet become the standard reporting method in the literature.

Section summary

Creating a functional neuroimaging experiment may be challenging. In general lines, it is of advantage to have a specific experimental hypothesis. The choice of the experimental paradigm will be constrained by the nature of the task chosen, the available imaging technology and its limitations, and the types of inference one wishes to draw from the study. Several statistical methods are available for the analysis of the data set. The most used is the "subtraction method," in which brain activity related to one experimental condition is subtracted from that related to a different experimental condition, and vice versa.

8.6   An fMRI Study on Bilingualism

Before providing a short summary on what has so far been achieved in the field of bilingualism, we give an illustrative example of the implementation of neuroimaging techniques within research on bilingualism. We consider the recent experiment carried out by Wartenburger, Heekeren, Abutalebi, Cappa, Villringer, and Perani (2003). These authors desired to study at the neural level whether the age of L2 acquisition or the degree of L2 proficiency is more important for the representation of L2. Psycholinguistic evidence surrounding this issue is controversial. Theories range from the postulation of biologically based "critical periods" for some aspects of language such as grammatical processing, to differences between infant and adult learning contexts (Lenneberg, 1967; Johnson & Newport, 1989; Birdsong, 1999b). Likewise, some authors argue that at least for lexical-semantic aspects the level of language proficiency would be more important for the mental representation of an L2 (Kroll & Stewart, 1994). Hence, Wartenburger and colleagues tried to enrich this discussion by providing neurobiological evidence on how the brain handles L2 representations. fMRI was used to investigate the effects of age of acquisition (AOA) and level of proficiency (PL) on the neural correlates of grammatical and semantic processing in Italian-German bilinguals who learned the second language at different ages and showed different proficiency levels.

8.6.1   Subjects

To assess the effects of AOA and PL, three groups of Italian-German bilinguals were considered for the experiment. They were:

- EAHP (early acquisition and high proficiency) group: subjects who acquired L2 from birth and showed a high proficiency in both languages
- LAHP (late acquisition and high proficiency) group: subjects who acquired L2 late but showed a proficiency level comparable with group 1
- LALP (late acquisition and low proficiency) group: subjects who learned L2 late and showed a low L2 proficiency at the time of the experiment.

When using neuroimaging techniques to make some inferences on a process of interest it is important to use an appropriate number of subjects in order to give enough statistical power to the experimental design. This will allow us to extend our findings to an entire population of individuals. In this experiment the groups were made up of ten subjects on average. Language proficiency and language exposure investigations were carried out. This should be a prerequisite of all imaging studies focusing on bilinguals (see for discussion Abutalebi, Cappa, & Perani, 2001, 2005) because information regarding these variables is important for the interpretation of findings.

8.6.2   Stimuli

The stimulus material consisted of 180 short sentences, 90 in German and 90 in Italian. Forty-four of the German and Italian sentences were semantically and grammatically correct. In both languages the remaining 46 sentences contained either semantic (23 sentences) or grammatical (23 sentences) violations. Thus there were four conditions. German grammatical judgment, Italian grammatical judgment, German semantic judgment, and Italian semantic judgment. A large number of stimuli within each experimental condition is necessary in order to elicit the desired effect on the cognitive process under investigation.

8.6.3   Experimental paradigm and task

The sentences were divided into 12 blocks (i.e., a block design was used), lasting 128 seconds, resulting in 3 blocks for each of the 4 conditions. After an initial resting period (60 seconds) the blocks of sentences were presented in a random order. Between each block a fixation cross appeared for 32 seconds indicating a rest period. Each block was made of 15 pseudo-randomized correct and incorrect sentences and was preceded by an instruction sentence (e.g., grammatical judgment German). After each sentence was presented, a fixation cross was displayed for 4 seconds. Subjects under the scanner were asked to judge if sentences in both L1 and L2 were semantically or grammatically correct and were asked to indicate by right-hand button press when they identified a correct sentence.

8.6.4   Data acquisition and analysis

fMRI measurements were performed on a 1.5 Tesla scanner and subsequently scans were realigned, normalized, and spatially smoothed in order to create contrast images for each condition. Images were also created for the differences between each condition across L1 and L2 for each subject. Contrast images for each condition and for differences between the respective conditions in L2 and L1 were computed for each subject. Moreover, group effects were computed using these contrast images by a random-effects analysis so that the observed effects could be generalized to the population (Friston, Holmes, Price, Buchel, & Worsley, 1999). Within-group analyses were performed using one-sample t-tests separately for each group in order to identify regions within the groups that show greater activation in L2 than in L1 (i.e., L1 serves as baseline condition in within-group comparisons); a statistical threshold of $p < 0.005$ was employed. Two-sample t tests were performed between groups to identify regions that were significantly more activated by one group than the other ($p < 0.005$). That way one may compare the EAHP and LAHP group (effect of AOA) and the LAHP and LALP group (effect of PL) in each grammatical and semantic judgment condition.

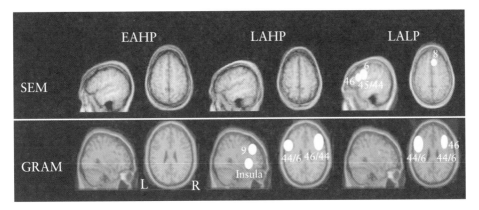

Figure 8.3: Brain activity patterns during grammatical processing (GRAM, bottom row) and semantic processing (SEM, top row) as displayed on brain templates in three different groups of bilinguals. Modified from Wartenburger et al., 2003.

8.6.5 Results

While the pattern of brain activity for semantic judgment was largely dependent on PL, AOA mainly affected the cortical representation of grammatical processes (see figure 8.3). In detail, in the case of grammar, a comparable performance/ proficiency on L1 and L2 was not associated with the same pattern of neural representation. These findings may support the hypothesis that parameters for grammar are set in a critical period within the very first years of life, and that this fixation is associated with a distinct pattern of brain activity, which is highly specific and cannot be attained, even in the case of a highly proficient acquisition, later in life. The same did not apply to semantic processing, for which the only difference in the pattern of brain activity appeared to depend on the level of attained proficiency. Thus, these findings support the notion of the existence of a critical period of language acquisition and indicate that grammatical processing, given its dependence on age of acquisition, is based on a competence which is neurologically "wired in." This experiment is a good example of how neurobiological evidence through functional neuroimaging may enrich linguistic and psycholinguistic debates. Functional imaging techniques may thus contribute significantly to theories of language representation and language processing.

8.7 Final Remarks

Extensive reviews focusing on the bilingual brain as studied with functional neuroimaging are available in the literature to which the reader is referred (Abutalebi, Cappa, & Perani, 2001; Vaid & Hull, 2001; Abutalebi, Cappa, & Perani, 2005;

Table 8.1: Summary of brain-imaging techniques
This table summarizes the advantages and disadvantages of the tools for measuring brain activity that we reviewed in this chapter. We have added two techniques that are not discussed in this chapter (MEG and TMS), but the reader may find studies on bilinguals that use these techniques. Each of the techniques presented in the table has some unique features that make it suitable for certain types of experiments.

Properties	ERPs	PET	fMRI	MEG	TMS
Physiological signal	Measured electrical brain activity	Oxygen or glucose metabolism in brain tissue	Oxygen in brain tissue	Magnetic counterpart of ERPS	None (interference technique)
Accuracy of spatial localization of the signal source	10–15 mm	4 mm	1.0–1.5 mm	5 mm	2–3 mm
Temporal resolution	Very high <1 ms	Low 45 secs	Low 3–5 secs	Very high <1 ms	High 5–200 ms
Experimental methods	Very well developed with experimental psychology designs	Block designs	Block designs and event-related designs	As well developed as ERPs but with limitations of application	Well developed but requires prior knowledge and many precautions
Application	Not invasive	Invasive: injection of radioactive tracer	Not invasive	Not invasive	Invasive
Costs	Low	High	Medium	High	Low

Perani & Abutalebi, 2005; but see also Paradis, 2004, for a critical viewpoint). In broad outlines, functional neuroimaging has shed new light on the neural basis of L2 processing, and on its relationship to native language (L1). First of all, the long-held assumption that L1 and L2 are necessarily represented in different brain regions or even in different hemispheres in bilinguals (Albert & Obler, 1978) has not been confirmed. On the contrary, functional neuroimaging has elegantly outlined that L1 and L2 are processed by the same neural devices. Indeed, the patterns of brain activation associated with tasks that engage specific aspects of linguistic processing are remarkably consistent across different languages, which share the same brain language system. These relatively fixed brain patterns, however, are modulated by a number of factors. Proficiency, age of acquisition, and exposure can affect the cerebral representations of each language, interacting in a complex way with the modalities of language performance. Consider as an example the complex process of L2 acquisition. This process may be considered as a dynamic process, requiring additional neural resources in the early stages. These additional neural resources are mostly found within the left prefrontal cortex (more anteriorly to the classical language areas) and seem to be associated with the greater control demand when processing a "weaker" L2 (i.e., for preventing unwanted L1 inter-ferences when processing L2) (Abutalebi & Green, 2007). However, once the L2 learner gains sufficient L2 proficiency, the neural representation of L2 converges to that of L1 (see Green, 2003 for theoretical claims about the neural basis of neural convergence). At this stage one may suppose that L2 is processed in the same fashion as L1, as psycholinguistic evidence indicates (Kroll & Stewart, 1994). This latter point is an important one because many functional neuroimaging studies did not take into consideration linguistic and psycholinguistic evidence (Paradis, 2004). Yet, evidence from neuroimaging should be integrated with the psycholinguistic findings (see for discussion Grosjean, Li, Munte, & Rodriguez, 2003) to the mutual advantage of both research traditions. Integrating these findings with the psycho-linguistic theory may allow us to demonstrate the biological consistency of different models, organize and consolidate existing findings, and generate novel insights into the nature of the cerebral organization of bilingualism.

Further reading

Abutalebi, J., S. F. Cappa, and D. Perani (2001) The bilingual brain as revealed by functional neuroimaging. *Bilingualism: Language and Cognition*, 4, 179–90.

Abutalebi, J. and D. W. Green (2007) Bilingual language production: The neurocognition of language representation and control. *Journal of Neurolinguistics*, 20, 242–75.

Green, D. W. (1998) Mental control of the bilingual lexico-semantic system. *Bilingualism: Language and Cognition*, 1, 67–81.

Kroll, J. F. K. and A. M. B. De Groot (2005) *Handbook of Bilingualism: Psycholinguistic Approaches*. Oxford University Press.

Mechelli, A., J. T. Crinion, U. Noppeney, J. O'Doherty, J. Ashburner, R. S. Frackowiack, and C. J. Price (2004) Structural plasticity in the bilingual brain. *Nature*, 431, 757.

Paradis, M. (1998) Language and communication in multilinguals. In B. Stemmer and H. Whitaker (eds.), *Handbook of Neurolinguistics*. San Diego, CA: Academic Press, pp. 417–30.

Paradis, M. (2004) *A Neurolinguistic Theory of Bilingualism*. Amsterdam/Philadelphia: John Benjamins.

Perani, D. and J. Abutalebi (2005) Neural basis of first and second language processing. *Current Opinion in Neurobiology*, 15, 202–6.

Price, C. J. (2000) The anatomy of language: Contributions from functional neuroimaging. *Journal of Anatomy*, 197, 335–59.

9 Interviews and Questionnaires

Eva Codó

9.1 Introduction

This chapter considers in detail the use of interviews and questionnaires as data-collection techniques for studies on multilingualism and language contact. The suitability of one or the other instrument will depend on the specific goals of our research project.

Questionnaires are useful for collecting biographical information on speakers, and quantifiable data on language abilities, practices, and attitudes. Survey research can thus provide an overview of the language situation of a given population. In community studies, for example, questionnaires are helpful to get an idea of who, when and where the different languages are spoken and of attitudes towards them. In migrant group contexts, they may be used to investigate the extent to which family languages are maintained. If, by contrast, researchers want to acquire in-depth knowledge of particular bilingual contexts or speakers and they seek to answer complex questions, such as what it means to be bilingual in a given setting, they will need to use interviews.

Interviews produce extended accounts from informants. Although interview data can also be subject to quantification (one can count, for example, how many times a speaker switches from one language to another), the interview is not as efficient a technique as the questionnaire for collecting discrete pieces of information; besides, it is much more costly and time-consuming. But the interview does not only enable researchers to collect declarative data on language use. As a verbal event, the interview is also an authentic communicative situation in which naturally occurring talk is exchanged. Interviews may thus be studied as forms of social interaction and as sources of real language data. This is a specific use of the interview in linguistics which has no parallel in the social sciences.

This chapter is organized in two main parts. In section 9.2, I focus on the interview as a research tool (see also Nortier, chapter 3 in this volume). This section examines the two main ways in which interviews can be used, i.e. as sources of information and as instances of real language use. A number of issues connected with the conduct of interviews are discussed, more specifically, the planning stage, the phrasing and organization of questions, and the practicalities of interviewing. In the second part of the chapter I focus on survey research. Different types of questionnaires and modes of administration are described. In addition, a list of themes about which a questionnaire designed to gather information on a multilingual situation can enquire is provided. By way of conclusion, a final comparison of the two methods is presented. The chapter ends with a resource section which contains further bibliographical references on the use of interviews and questionnaires as data-gathering procedures.

9.2   Interviews as Sources of Data on Language Contact

The interview is a fairly versatile technique for gathering data on multilingualism. It can be employed to obtain both linguistic productions from bi-/multilingual speakers and content data. In this second case, researchers aim to gather biographical and other relevant contextualizing information from language users together with their views, values, and attitudes towards their own and others' linguistic practices. As will be discussed later, self-report data, that is, data in which speakers assess and comment on their own language practices is a type of linguistic data, which should, however, not be used as a substitute for naturally occurring speech. Self-report data can yield interesting insights, especially into multilingual language use, but researchers should be aware of the multiple conditionings shaping speakers' expressed opinions and of their contextually situated nature. The analysis of speakers' real verbal productions may show them to be rather different from what actors reported them to be.

It must be highlighted that the two types of data that may be elicited from interviews, i.e. content and language use data, are not mutually exclusive. Interviews primarily designed for gathering speech samples are often also used to obtain contextualizing biographical and language-related information from respondents. The opposite case is less likely but also plausible. Pujolar (2001), for example, uses the talk produced in group discussions to analyze the code-switching practices of working-class youngsters living in Barcelona.

9.2.1   Interviews for linguistic and conversational analysis

The advantages offered by the interview as a method for gathering samples of spoken data are two. First, it is generally easier to set up an interview with selected informants than to get permission to record naturally occurring talk; secondly, the interview offers a more controlled environment for researchers looking for specific language forms (e.g. instances of past simple use by Spanish-English bilinguals) than naturally occurring social interaction. However, the semi-spontaneous nature of interviews may also limit the appearance of certain forms of bilingual speech, especially in communities where they are highly stigmatized. A possible solution is to conduct group interviews. In some contexts, peer group interaction may facilitate the appearance of language alternation phenomena. However, it is also true that in some other contexts, and depending on the social composition of the groups, the production of bilingual speech forms may be inhibited. That means that it is very important for researchers to get to know the social context they intend to investigate and to be aware of the connections between power issues and socially appropriate forms of language use.

The technique for using sociolinguistic interviews to collect natural speech data was developed by Labov and his associates (for further details see e.g. Wolfram & Fasold, 1974; Wolfson, 1976; and Labov, 1984). A basic requirement of this type of interview is that the data obtained must be as similar as possible to spontaneous talk. It is important to build a rapport with informants so that they feel comfortable talking to the researcher and become less self-conscious about their speech. Otherwise, respondents may not switch between languages, or they may not use socially stigmatized linguistic varieties or forms. The code employed by the researcher, or even just the kind of person the researcher is taken to be, can also constrain the degree of linguistic alternation in informants' speech. In that case, the choice of a community member interviewer may solve the problem.

Language alternation can also be facilitated by choosing topics that connect with the use of a specific language spoken by the interviewee, like memories of a previous life in a foreign country, the description of a past way of life, or stories from one's childhood (for further details on how to alleviate the tension created by the interview situation see sections 9.2.2 and 9.2.3.1). If, after conducting an interview, researchers feel that informants got more relaxed as time went by, one possibility is to discard the data recorded during the initial stages and concentrate on the most spontaneous parts. Alternatively, more conscious and less conscious modes of talk may be used for comparison purposes. To encourage informants to talk extensively, interviews must be designed in ways that facilitate the elicitation of longish pieces of discourse, such as narratives, descriptions, or accounts of some kind.

Researchers working on the lexical and syntactic aspects of language mixing (see Treffers-Daller, 1994; Backus, 1996; Eppler, 2004; Gardner-Chloros, chapter 4 in this volume) have traditionally employed the interview situation to collect samples of bilingual speech for analysis. Likewise, interview data has been used by variationist researchers studying the borrowing/code-switching distinction (cf. the papers in the special issue of the *International Journal of Bilingualism* edited by Poplack & Meechan, 1998).

Apart from formal linguistic traditions, interactivist schools have also been interested in the study of the interview as a speech event. Interviews of various kinds where the interviewer acts as a *gatekeeper*, that is, controls access to important socioeconomic resources, have been the favorite object of study of many interpretive sociolinguistic works (Roberts & Sayers, 1987; Sarangi, 1996; Kerekes, 2006). This research has focused both on global aspects of interview management, like schemata and role relationships, and on specific details of talk, like conversational inference, contextualization cues, register, and style. From strict conversational perspectives, the interview has also been a fruitful interactional space to investigate processes of identity construction and group affiliation (Widdicombe, 1998).

Section summary: Interviews for linguistic and conversational analysis

- Group interviews may facilitate the production of bilingual speech forms in contexts where they are stigmatized, but they may also inhibit certain language alternation practices. It is essential for researchers to have a deep understanding of the social context they want to investigate.
- Interviewers should avoid informants becoming too self-conscious about their speech. It is essential that a rapport is built so that interviewees feel comfortable talking to the person conducting the interview.
- A community member interviewer and the choice of certain topics may facilitate the production of bilingual speech forms.
- The types of questions asked should facilitate the production of longish pieces of discourse.
- Interviews as sources of real language data have been studied from structural, variationist, and interactivist perspectives.

9.2.2   *Interviews for content analysis*

This is the most common purpose of interviews in bilingualism studies. Interviews are employed either to obtain information which may otherwise be very difficult to gather (like certain biographical details, which may not become available even after long and intensive involvement in the field) or to explore issues that can only be accessed indirectly if interactional data is considered (such as language attitudes and ideologies). For examples of how content analysis can be used, see Blackledge, chapter 17 and Pavlenko, chapter 18, in this volume. In fact, the interview is a very efficient research tool in that it allows investigators to gather fairly large bodies of data in relatively little time.

There are two types of content information researchers may obtain from interviews. One is factual details, like age, years of schooling, and employment situation; the other is what Hammersley and Atkinson (1983) refer to as "perspective" information, that is, subjects' understandings of the value and meanings of their bilingual speech practices. In both cases, the type of data gathered is declarative. The interview format can, additionally, be employed to discuss extracts of interactional data with informants.

It must be pointed out that, although useful in its own terms, declarative data can never be employed as a substitute for data on speakers' actual linguistic behavior. Self- or other-reports of bilingual language practice may not match observed conduct, since many phenomena related to performance, like code-switching, operate on a subconscious level. Mismatches can also have a language-ideological component. Speakers of varieties with low social prestige may want to claim that they do not use them, though in fact they do. In any case, these are very interesting sites of analysis (Pujolar, 2001) because they point towards the many conflicts and contradictions that inform linguistic practices in contexts of multilingualism.

In qualitative studies, the data obtained in interviews are often employed for triangulation purposes (see Heller, 2006). The opinions expressed by speakers are put side by side with other types of data, such as participant observation and electronically recorded interactions, to throw new light on the bilingual phenomena observed. The beliefs and attitudes expressed by interviewees are essential to researchers' interpretive processes, whether to change their understanding of the meaning and value of speakers' bilingual productions, or to validate their interpretations. Finally, interview data may also be conceptualized as a means to open up research to the researched and give them a voice. Influenced by critical ethnography, the current tendency is towards devising ways of allowing interviewees to have more control over the interpretation process and to retain authorship over the final text (see Pavlenko & Blackledge, 2004a).

One of the difficulties often mentioned in connection with the use of interview data for content analysis is the issue of "truth." Researchers often fear that informants' responses may differ from their "actual" opinions on certain themes, because they either want to please the researcher, feel constrained by the interview situation from expressing their views, or aim to project a given image for themselves and their community. Subjects' "untrue" responses, it is claimed, may lead researchers to draw inaccurate conclusions about the bilingual context or speakers investigated. Although, as we shall see later, there are ways in which interviewers can try to make interviewees feel comfortable so that they voice their opinions freely, researchers should be aware that there is no external "truth" to be sought, and that people's knowledge and opinions are always constructed in the course of situated communicative events.

One important weakness of interviews is that there may be limits to the amount and kinds of details the researcher is able to gather. This can be due to a number of reasons. To start with, using direct questioning to find out information is standard practice in Western societies but may not be so in other cultures (see Eades, 1982; Briggs, 1986). Thus, researchers should not take the usefulness of direct interviewing for granted, as information gathering may be more efficiently carried out through other means (e.g. through engaging in pedagogical discourse with community elders, as exemplified by Briggs, 1986). Familiarizing oneself with alternative practices for collecting information, however, requires intensive fieldwork in order to acquire a basic understanding of the communicative norms and patterns of the society investigated; this is very time-consuming. Secondly, asking questions can be considered inappropriate in certain contexts, or perceived as threatening by some informants. In the fieldwork I undertook at an immigration office, a very sensitive institutional context, I realized state officials were reluctant to provide "insider" institutional information if asked directly. Especially at the beginning, they were unsure about my presence in the office, and so direct questioning was felt to threaten my position as a fieldworker (for further details see Codó, 2003). Thirdly, the types of aspects researchers on bilingualism seek details on, like values, attitudes, beliefs, and motivations, tend to be difficult to verbalize. Besides, rarely do speakers reflect on these issues in an explicit manner unless awareness of language is heightened (Heller, 1988). As regards the nature of what is said, the format of the interview may limit the amount and types of details provided (Briggs,

1986). The question–answer turn structure imposes important relevance constraints on informants' talk.

9.2.2.1   Overcoming difficulties

There are different ways to overcome some of the drawbacks discussed above. Undertaking fieldwork in the setting investigated and spending time with the researched will work to overcome their initial reluctance to open up and will probably make them stop worrying about the image of themselves and their communities they are trying to project. Researchers' practical knowledge of the context investigated will also help them to search for alternative, less intrusive means of information gathering, which may be more efficient than the interview.

If it is not possible to meet informants beforehand, interviewers should make every effort to create a relaxed and friendly atmosphere at the outset of the interview and build a rapport with informants. As is well known, there is a range of factors that contribute to enhancing solidarity among speakers, such as speech variety and tone, and conversational and interviewing style, but also age, ethnicity, dressing style, and general demeanor. Some of these factors can be modified, like interviewing style, while others cannot, like gender and ethnicity. If the latter are perceived to have an obvious negative influence, it is better to ask somebody else to do the interview for us.

Another technique mentioned earlier which may help alleviate the tension generated by the one-to-one interview is group interviews. Interviewees may feel freer and be more forthcoming among peers. Group interaction may facilitate the appearance of bilingual forms, indigenous speech activities, or key themes of which the researcher was not aware. Additionally, speakers' divergent opinions on certain issues (like speakers' motivations for language choice) may encourage participation and force interactants to refine arguments. By contrast, the problems associated with group discussions are poor quality of recordings, difficulty in identifying speakers and/or languages, the dominance of certain interactants, and the lack of participation of others. Group discussions and face-to-face interviews need not be mutually exclusive. It is possible to integrate both in a single piece of research (see Pujolar, 2001).

Although the above recommendations may help facilitate the exchange of ideas, researchers should not be deluded into thinking, as we mentioned above, that they can get to respondents' "real" thoughts. This claim, typical of positivist approaches, rests on two erroneous assumptions. First, it is often assumed that knowledge exists independently of its expression. This may be true of factual information but certainly not of other kinds of knowledge, typically investigated in bilingualism research, like ideologies, beliefs, and attitudes. These are often constructed in the course of their verbalization and are shaped by the associations of ideas and thoughts generated as the interview unfolds. The second false assumption concerns the issue of reactivity, that is, the idea that it is possible to elicit talk that does not in some way or other react to the presence of the researcher. This is not feasible. The interview is a co-constructed event between interviewer and interviewee. Silverman (1993) refers to interview data as "situated narratives"; Briggs (1986) claims that interview discourse is highly "indexical" of the social and sequential context in which it is produced. Interview talk is always produced for a particular audience and shaped in ways that are considered appropriate by speakers according to their definition of the situation. What researchers can do is try to modify interviewees' perception of the event as more or less formal and of the relationship with their interlocutor, but they cannot elicit talk which is acontextual. The most honest position to take is to acknowledge the ways in which the conditions of production of the interview may have shaped the data and interpret them accordingly.

Evident influences on the talk need not be conceptualized as a disturbance. They may prove a very interesting locus of research. For example, the use in the interview of a particular language or speech variety by the researcher may lead the interviewee to understand the event as related to a specific social domain (for example, the school), where this language is dominant or preferred. Switches from and into this language in the construction of the interview will index the social functions and values associated with each of the languages of the bilingual community researched (see Cots & Nussbaum, 2003).

Section summary: Interviews for content analysis

- Interviews can be employed to obtain factual and/or perspective information, and to discuss data extracts with informants.
- Interview data are best employed in combination with other types of data (triangulation).
- Researchers should aim to get as close as possible to informants' "true" responses, though they should be aware of the constructed and situated nature of knowledge.
- The interview situation imposes constraints on the information provided.
- Face-to-face interviews may be combined with group discussions to facilitate the exchange of ideas.
- Contextual influences on informants' responses may constitute an engaging locus of research.

9.2.3 *Planning the interview*

The first thing researchers need to do in the planning stage is reflect on the need, usefulness, and feasibility of collecting interview data. For technical details see Clemente (chapter 10 in this volume). Logically, it is necessary to have first-hand knowledge of the multilingual speakers or community investigated to get an accurate picture of how suitable and/or feasible collecting interview data might be. Researchers may even want to conduct a few preliminary interviews before making a final decision (Redmond, 2000). When doing research on societies other than one's own, it is necessary to take into account that asking questions may not be considered appropriate in certain social situations, that it may be better not to enquire about certain topics, that there might be restrictions as to who can have access to information, and that only "knowledgeable speakers" may be able to provide certain types of information (Eades, 1982; Briggs, 1986). These are all things researchers need to consider in the planning stages.

Another aspect that merits some thought is the type of interview researchers plan to administer and the format they want to give to their questions. This will of course depend on the goals of the research, the intended target group, and the analytic treatment they want to give to their data.

Interview formats may range from unstructured, non-directive questioning to fairly directive modes. Any one interview can contain both format types. It may start by being fairly directive (by asking, for example, specific questions about language use) and progressively become transformed into a less structured event, or vice versa.

Researchers need to bear in mind that the more interviewees participate in defining the content and pace of the interview, the more varied and numerous will be the details provided. In fact, unstructured interview formats are preferred in ethnographically oriented language research. The problem is that the data obtained from different interviews may not be easily comparable. For this reason, even if questions are not formulated in a standard manner, it is always advisable to have a list of topics to cover so that at least some points of comparison can be established. If responses are to be quantified, then standardization is absolutely necessary. In that case, the multiple-choice format might be the most appropriate one (see subsection 9.3.2 for details).

Closely connected with unstructured interview formats are life histories and stories. They are special kinds of interviews centered on the self (see Pavlenko, chapter 18 in this volume). Their advantage over interviews is that tellers are allowed more freedom to organize the "stories that shape their lives" (Linde, 1993) thematically and chronologically, to identify significant life stages, and to pin down crucial events (the turning points, or "epiphanies" as Denzin (1989b) calls them). Life narratives are used to investigate who informants are, how they have come to be the people they are, and what events and experiences have shaped their lives. As language plays a fundamental role in self and other-construction, biographical narratives are a good technique for exploring the experiences of bilinguals in contexts of migration and displacement (see, for example, Hoffman, 1989; Dorfman, 1998; Pavlenko, 2004).

When deciding on a format, researchers must also take into account their relationship with interviewees. With strangers, for example, it is easier to conduct directive than non-directive interviews, as open formats may cause bewilderment. The sociocultural expectations associated with the interview as a speech event are that interviewers ask questions about the topic(s) they are interested in and that interviewees respond. The role of the interviewers is thus expected to be fairly directive. As Wolfson (1976) notes, if they relinquish this cultural prerogative without a previous explanation, informants may feel puzzled or annoyed, produce hesitant talk, or, in the worst-case scenario, start wondering about the researcher's hidden intentions. This is why it is essential to discuss the format and goals of the interview with informants before starting.

In assessing the suitability of a given format it is important to consider the familiarity of the interviewee with the interview as a speech event. For instance, migrant school children are regularly asked to engage in semi-formal interviews, as assessments of linguistic and academic competence are often made on the basis of their performance in interviews (Cots & Nussbaum, 2003). It is surely easier for them to participate in these events than for other population groups. This is something researchers need to bear in mind during the planning process.

The third issue to be thought about is at which stage in the research project researchers will want to administer the interview. As with format, this depends on the type of research that they are carrying out. If they intend to answer a quantitative research question using interview data, and plan to interrogate a fairly large population sample, a few introductory sentences explaining the nature and goals of their research may be enough. Interviews can be carried out straight away bearing in mind the recommendations outlined in subsection 9.2.4. If, by way of contrast, researchers intend to integrate the use of interviews with the analysis of real-life interactional data and ethnographic observations, the administration of interviews should be delayed until later stages. In those cases, interviews are often used to explore themes that emerge from the analysis of the talk and to check preliminary interpretations of sociolinguistic behavior with informants. It is thus best for researchers to first analyze small samples of interactional data so that they have a clearer idea of what it might be relevant to focus on. In addition, if formal interviewing is postponed until the researcher has conducted ethnographic observations and is fairly familiar with the setting and the social actors investigated, she or he can make more informed decisions as to which participants must be interviewed and what sorts of questions need to be asked.

This leads to the fourth aspect researchers need to consider, namely the type and number of informants they will need. Informant selection is a fundamental issue. If interviewees are not carefully selected, the data may be misleading. For a detailed discussion of informant selection see Lanza, chapter 5 in this volume. A final aspect concerns decisions on the organization and formulation of questions. These will be considered in detail in the following section.

9.2.3.1 *Phrasing and organizing questions*

The first obvious thing researchers on multilingualism need to think about is the language(s) in which the questions will be formulated. Language is a key factor, because it sends messages about the interviewer's ethnolinguistic affiliation and educational background, and the formality of the speech event, among other things. These aspects will define the interviewee's understanding of the context of the interview and shape responses in multiple ways. If researchers want interviewees to speak unconstrained, it is often best to let them choose the language of the interaction. In migrant contexts, this may entail enlisting the help of a community member, both to carry out the interview, and to transcribe and translate the responses provided. This complicates the process of data collection and analysis but certainly enhances the value and depth of the responses provided.

As was mentioned earlier, direct interviewing may not be effective or even advisable in certain social contexts. Likewise, standard question formats may elicit little information. In the Aboriginal societies studied by Eades (1982) in Australia, for example, explanations or stories are best elicited through "triggering," which consists in the information-seeker stating something known about the desired topic and then pausing for the knowledgeable speaker to start talking about the topic. A similar function is accomplished by interjections and repetitions of preceding talk. Briggs (1986) attested comparable behavior in his study of *Mexicano* society, where information on traditional knowledge may be elicited by taking up parts of elders' talk and using final rising intonation. These two examples show how important it is for researchers to acquire knowledge of native ways of information seeking first and not just take the Western-based question–answer format for granted.

Another relevant aspect for researchers to consider is that the way questions are worded directs respondents' thoughts. This is something that they will presumably want to avoid. In Erill, Marcos, and Farràs (1992) informants are asked to answer a question on the status of Catalan which is phrased in the following terms (my translation): "Just as Spanish is the only official language of Spanish-speaking territories, do you believe that it would similarly be natural for Catalan to be the only official language of Catalan-speaking territories?" By framing the question against the backdrop of the situation of Spanish, respondents are more inclined to answer "yes" than if the question were phrased in more neutral terms, like "Do you think that Catalan should be the only official language of Catalonia?"

Varying the type and format of questions makes the interview less monotonous and serves to maintain the interest of informants. As a general rule, yes–no questions should be avoided, as we want interviewees to provide extended accounts. Another aspect to consider is that questions should be short and easy to understand (taking into account the target population is essential here too). Special attention must be paid to avoiding double meanings, vagueness, and ambiguity. This is particularly important if researchers and/or respondents are second or foreign language speakers of the linguistic code employed. The goal is to establish a "common referential frame" (Briggs, 1986) in which interviewer and interviewee agree on the type of information being sought.

A method of easing comprehension is to try to bring questions close to interviewees' real-life worlds. This can be done in two ways. First, the researcher can use a linguistic style, variety, or code to which respondents can quickly relate, and avoid jargon. This makes comprehension easier and enhances rapport. Secondly, the researcher can show interviewees pictures and/or texts, and ask them to discuss specific events, actions, or speakers rather than hypothetical ones. So, instead of the question "What language would you speak to a stranger?" it is preferable to ask "What language do you speak to strangers?" Another interesting example is provided in Treffers-Daller (1994). She asked her Brussels informants to think of six individuals to whom they talked regularly and specify their names. Obviously, the names were of no interest to the researcher but the question helped interviewees to focus on real-life individuals rather than groups of people like friends or neighbors.

A relevant aspect linked to the wording of questions is how to formulate sensitive questions. The basic rule is that they should never be asked right away. It is fundamental that an atmosphere of trust is created before sensitive issues are introduced. It is also better not to leave these questions to the final stages of the interview. The best place is towards the middle of the interaction. This way, if the interviewer perceives that sensitive questions have strained his or her relationship with the interviewee, he or she can repair the damage as they move along. One technique for phrasing sensitive questions is to allow the interviewee to distance him- or herself from the themes discussed. Using formulae like "There are people who say/think that . . . ," "Do you know of anyone who . . . ?" may be useful. Finally, the researcher must not forget to make explicit at the outset of the interview that the interviewee may opt out of any of the questions if she or he does not feel comfortable with them.

There are different ways of organizing questions in interviews depending on the type of interview, the research goals, and the relationship between participants. As a general rule, questions should be grouped by themes. The first ones within each theme should be relatively easy to answer. They are meant to pave the way for subsequent queries which the researcher might actually be more interested in.

The second aspect to be taken into consideration is the breadth of questions, that is, whether they ask for specific information or are relatively open. There are two types of organization. In the first type, the interviewer moves from the general to the specific, whereas in the second type it is the opposite. When researchers use the first mode, they seek specific information but want to avoid influencing respondents' opinions. If they use the second type, they are more interested in subjects' reflections, accounts, and understandings of the world. The way questions are ordered may vary at different stages in the interview depending on the theme tackled.

Section summary: Planning the interview

- Before starting, researchers need to assess the feasibility and suitability of conducting interviews in a particular multilingual context.
- They should be aware of culture-specific restrictions on who, what, and when to ask.
- The less directive an interview, the more prone respondents will be to provide details.
- The language(s) of the interview frames the event in significant ways. It is best to allow interviewees to choose what language(s) to speak.
- Interviewers should avoid asking yes–no questions or channeling informants' responses.
- Varying the format and type of questions makes the interview less monotonous.
- Questions should be short, easy to understand, and unambiguous.
- Sensitive questions should be not formulated right away and researchers should allow interviewees to distance themselves from the themes discussed.

9.2.4   *Conducting the interview*

Before conducting the interview, it is essential to pilot it. The more feedback researchers get the better. It may be the case that the interview is too long, that questions are ambiguously worded, or that they do not focus interviewees' responses on the desired themes.

A time and location for the interview must be chosen. Usually, it is left up to informants to decide. They may prefer the safe environment of their homes, or they may choose a less private location, such as a public park, a cafeteria, or a room in a library. If a public place is chosen, it might be a good idea to visit it beforehand, especially if researchers are planning to record the interview (it may be too tiny or too noisy, or have no sockets to plug their recording equipment into).

Once the day comes, researchers should think about how they are going to dress. They need to remember that interviewees should feel comfortable in their presence. So, they should choose a way of dressing which harmonizes with their informants' but does not conflict with the image they want to project. For instance, wearing very informal clothes can, in some contexts, raise doubts as to their seriousness as researchers and the extent to which they are to be trusted. This may shape responses in undesired ways.

One key issue to consider before conducting the interview is ethics. This refers not only to the need to gain informed consent from informants, but also to questions that have to do with the researcher's moral conduct during the interview. That is, apart from ensuring that participants' anonymity is guaranteed, we need to ensure that we deploy ethical interviewing practices. That means avoiding damaging informants in any conscious way, but also being aware of the potential for distress that some of our questions may have.

The initial words exchanged in an interview are important in terms of the definition of the communicative event and its general tone. Researchers should take advantage of the opening turns to start building rapport. But most importantly, they must make all efforts to explain how the event will unfold and what kinds of answers they expect. Logically, they should avoid determining respondents' behavior, though some influence is unavoidable, due to, as we said, the contextually situated nature of spoken data.

Researchers' demeanor is also important throughout. They must show that they are attentive to the talk exchanged, as significant themes may arise that were not expected. Researchers need to pick up on informants' cues if they want to pursue them. Researchers' responsiveness is also important for interviewees. The latter may want to know whether they are being understood and whether what they are saying seems to be relevant for the researcher.

One way of displaying interest is by taking notes. Yet note-taking may work to direct respondents' talk towards certain themes if they infer that these are what researchers are after. If the interview is being recorded, note-taking can take place afterwards. Making notes on the interview is always recommended, especially if the interview is not video-recorded. But even if it is, researchers can use notes to write down interesting topics they may want to pursue later on in the interview, or any ideas that come to mind during the interaction and that may become relevant during the process of analysis. It is also advisable for researchers to note down impressions about the interviewee and the way the interaction unfolded. Listening to – and if possible transcribing – the interview right afterwards helps the recall process. If content recordings are not possible, note-taking is facilitated by having a form with preallocated spaces for the pieces of information researchers want to gather.

9.2.5   Analyzing the data

The interpretation of data elicited in interviews must take into account its deeply contextual nature, that is, the fact that it is produced in the framework of a particular speech event and that it stands in a sequential relationship with preceding talk (see Heller, chapter 14 in this volume). Interview talk is also situated temporally, spatially, experientially, and socioculturally, that is, it is produced at a particular time and place by specific speakers, who have specific background experiences, and who operate within particular sociocultural systems. This is especially significant in terms of the researcher's assessment and understanding of the information provided (Briggs, 1986).

With regard to the presentation of data, researchers may opt to gloss over respondents' talk, or they may decide to furnish longish quotes. The first option makes it difficult for readers to assess the accuracy of researchers' interpretations. The second option enables readers to "hear" speakers' voices (for an example see Mills, 2004), which is particularly interesting when, for example, code alternation is employed. Yet this entails a risk, namely, that researchers shy away from interpretation, the assumption being that the data speaks for itself. This is erroneous, as interview data – like any data – is not transparent to the observer, but requires careful and informed interpretation.

Section summary: Conducting the interview and analyzing the data

- Piloting is essential to detect possible flaws in the design of the interview.
- Researchers must think about their dress style and the image they want to project.
- Researchers must be attentive to the talk exchanged and engage with interviewees.
- The data must be interpreted in its context of production.
- Providing extracts from interviewees' responses enables readers to check on the accuracy of interpretations and gives the researched a voice.

9.3 Questionnaires

Questionnaires are an efficient tool for gathering quantifiable information on bilingual speakers or communities rapidly and systematically. Like interviews, questionnaires are useful for collecting declarative data but not data on performance; besides, the directive mode of questioning and the close-ended nature of the answers constrains severely the depth of the knowledge to be acquired. If contextually rich accounts of bilingual phenomena are desired, questionnaires are best employed in combination with other types of data, such as participant observation, recordings of social interaction, ethnographic notes, and interviews.

Survey research procedures are the most appropriate ones if the goal of the project is to obtain quantifiable data on languages and speakers from a large population sample. An interesting example is the Multilingual Cities Project (Extra & Yagmur, 2004), conducted in six European cities, whose objective is to gather data on the linguistic profiles of ethnic minorities in Europe in order to determine the degree of vitality of native languages and make cross-national comparisons.

The knowledge gained through a questionnaire survey can be put to different uses. It may be employed to obtain a general picture of language use in a given community to plan further research; it may serve as contextualizing information on the social actors investigated (cf. Boix, 1993; Treffers-Daller, 1994); it may be used to identify target subjects from a large population sample (e.g. multilingual school children). In the latter case, the information gathered constitutes the first step in data collection. The information obtained enables researchers to identify target informants. Instances of this type of research are provided in Deprez (1999) and Vilardell (1998). When the number of questionnaires to be processed is high, it is useful to have a *screening question* to discriminate between informants.

Most of the considerations regarding the phrasing, organization, and piloting of questions that were discussed in relation to interviews apply equally to questionnaires and will not be discussed in the sections that follow.

9.3.1 *Planning the use of questionnaires*

The first thing researchers need to decide on is sampling and data collection mode. Sampling is crucial as it will condition the types of claims they will be able to base on the data (see chapter 5 in this volume for a detailed explanation of sampling procedures). Sampling will also affect administration mode. For instance, if random-digit dialing is employed, the survey will be most easily carried out by phone. Different modes of data gathering offer different advantages and disadvantages (for further details see Fowler, 1984), but they all have an influence on the format and number of questions to be asked.

Questionnaires can be self- or interviewer-administered. Self-administered questionnaires are filled in by informants in writing; they can be completed in a group or individually, and can be returned immediately after completion or mailed to the researcher. Because they place a lot of emphasis on reading and writing, self-administered questionnaires are not a suitable procedure when the population investigated may have literacy difficulties (e.g. migrant community members who are not literate in their own language(s) and/or the language(s) of the host country). Another major difficulty concerns the official status of some written questionnaires (like those designed to gather census information). This may make informants reluctant to cooperate. An additional difficulty with self-administered question- naires that are not filled in "on site" is that researchers have no way of knowing who completes them, which may bias the results. Finally, in multilingual contexts it is necessary to have questionnaires translated into the different languages spoken, even if these are dialects or varieties different from the standard. This will enhance closeness with informants and encourage participation.

As regards positive aspects, self-administered questionnaires are less costly than interviewer-administered ones, and may be more efficient for enquiring about sensitive issues, since interviewees may be less reluctant to admit to negatively evaluated behaviors than in the presence of an interviewer. Yet there is no general agreement on this (Fowler, 1984). If they are to be useful, it is essential for self-administered questionnaires to be user-friendly and short. Enclosing a cover letter explaining the objectives of the research and the instructions for filling in and returning the questionnaire is important to increase motivation and response rates. If mailed, follow-up procedures must be established to ensure that questionnaires are returned. High response rates are best obtained by administering questionnaires "on site," usually in groups (at a school or factory, for example).

As mentioned previously, questionnaires can be administered verbally by an interviewer. The event can be conducted face to face or over the phone. Phone surveys can be carried out to identify target informants, with whom a more in-depth interview can later be arranged. In interviewer-administered survey procedures, the event resembles an interview but questions tend to be closed and interviewers must follow standardized interviewing procedures to avoid biasing the results. The advantage of having interviewers is that they can clarify questions for informants and may increase motivation. It is also possible to combine the use of an inter-viewer with some self-administered parts. The feasibility of using interviewers will depend on sampling procedures and available funds.

9.3.2   *Format of questions and answers*

An important thing to bear in mind is that the questionnaire must not be too long (four pages maximum) and should not take more than 30 minutes to complete (Dörnyei, 2003). Otherwise, our informants will get tired and start answering randomly, which reduces the reliability of the instrument. Another fundamental consideration has to do with the way questions are phrased. Generally speaking, it is advisable that they are short and easy to understand, but the most important thing is that they are adequate for the population group we intend to survey.

Because of the analytical treatment given to questionnaire data, it is essential for questions to be close-ended. Yet including some open-ended questions is also advised, as they may provide insights into unexpected significant themes and categories. To facilitate quantification, the multiple-choice format is advised. Researchers must be careful to offer a choice of categories which is in tune with respondents' reality. For example, when asking whether bilingual speakers would employ language A or B in a particular situation or to talk to specific interlocutors, possible answers might be "a mixture of languages A and B" or "neither A nor B but C." So, those categories have to be offered in the questionnaire. Researchers must also be aware of local ways of referring to certain language varieties and refer to them in the same way in their questionnaires. One possibility is to conduct pilot research with open questions and then use the information collected to created closed questions.

A variation on the multiple-choice format is the ranked scale, where the response requested is a matter of degree. The five-point scale covers a broad enough range of answers. For example, to the question "How good is your understanding of informal conversations in language A?" the response options could be "very good – quite good – good – quite poor – poor." Bear in mind that, if numbers are employed, it is essential to indicate what each number stands for (5 = very good, 4 = quite good, 3 = good, 2 = quite poor, 1 = poor). Another thing that must be made clear at the outset is how many responses will be accepted per question, that is, in the case of multiple-choice answers, whether it is possible to tick two boxes at the same time.

Nowadays it is possible to use commercial software packages to handle the data obtained in automatic ways (see Extra & Yagmur, 2004, for details). This facilitates the researcher's task enormously. The design of the questionnaire must take into account the technical requirements of the programs to be employed.

The items on a questionnaire can be formulated in three different ways: as interrogative sentences ("Which kind of school did you attend as a child?"), as directives ("Indicate three radio stations you listen to") and as declaratives ("Speaking Basque helps people get a better job"). Varying the format of questions makes the questionnaire less monotonous. The first two types of formats are meant to gather factual information, while the third one requires respondents to state their degree of identification with the statement. It is geared towards investigating the beliefs, values, and attitudes of speakers, as these are better asked about indirectly. Another way of investigating language attitudes is by providing verbal stimuli to the re- searched. A well-known method is the matched-guise technique, devised in French Canada and employed, for example, by Woolard (1989) in Catalonia. Bilingual speakers are recorded reading the same text in the two languages. The idea is to investigate linguistic attitudes by keeping all variables constant (gender, age, ethnicity, tone and quality of voice, and text) and modifying only the language in which the text is read.

The types of questions that might be pertinent for a study on bilingualism will depend on the nature and goals of the project. Table 9.1 shows a list of possible themes, which is of course not meant to be exhaustive.

Table 9.1: Possible themes for a questionnaire on bilingualism

Themes	Subthemes
Biographical information (on informants but also parents, partner, and children)	age place of birth place of residence (current/previous) schooling (how many years, type of school(s), language(s) of instruction, level attained) occupation (current/previous) leisure activities (membership of clubs, associations, etc.)
Language use and choice	languages spoken to different interlocutors (father, mother, partner, children, friends, workmates, neighbors, government officials, strangers) languages spoken by other people to the interviewee languages spoken by different groups of people among themselves language spoken in particular social situations/social domains reasons for language choice newspapers habitually read favorite radio station(s)/TV channel(s) favorite TV programs use of foreign languages
Language proficiency	declared competence (written and oral comprehension, written and oral production, specific genres) knowledge of foreign languages
Language dominance	languages spoken/read/understood/written best reasons for dominance
Language acquisition/ learning	time and mode of acquisition/learning motivations reactions in social environment reasons for and types of acquisition/learning difficulties factors facilitating/hindering learning
Language attitudes/ preferences	attitude towards: speakers of a given language; norms of linguistic conduct; promotion of languages; types of linguistic attitudes; use of languages in specific social domains degrees of identification with languages and cultures preferred languages (for speaking, reading, listening to, writing in).
Social status and value of languages	languages with low/high social prestige negative/positive individual consequences of language choice measures to promote knowledge/use of languages

9.3.3 *Administering the questionnaire*

Before conducting a large-scale survey it is essential to pilot the questionnaire to see how effectively it meets the researcher's objectives. The piloting stage will provide crucial information on what needs to be improved.

When handing out the questionnaire, it is very important to explain clearly to informants what kinds of responses are expected from them and to give them a chance to ask any questions they may have. If questionnaires are not completed "on site" it is essential to have clear instructions at the beginning on how to fill it in and procedures for returning it. Thanking respondents for their help is also recommended (Sebba, 1993).

Section summary: Questionnaires

- Questionnaire surveys are useful for collecting information on a large number of speakers.
- The depth of the knowledge obtained through questionnaire survey is limited.
- Careful planning of sampling and delivery mode is necessary.
- Questionnaires should be short.
- The way questions are phrased should take into account the target group. As a general rule, they should be clear and easy to understand.
- Response options in multiple-choice formats must match existing categories in bilinguals' real contexts.
- Precise instructions for filling in questionnaires must be provided.

9.4 Comparing and Contrasting Interviews and Questionnaires

This chapter has presented the main characteristics of interviews and questionnaires and the ways in which they can efficiently be employed in bilingualism research. Interviews and questionnaires have a common core goal, which is to obtain information about bilingual individuals and/or communities, including self- or other-report data on language use. They differ in the type and depth of the information collected and the ways in which this information is most appropriately handled (quantitatively in the case of questionnaires, qualitatively in the case of interviews). Questionnaires can be administered in writing or orally. In the latter case, they are actually directive interviews involving interaction between interviewer and respondent. What we have referred to as interviews in this chapter are less structured events that tend to elicit fairly extended responses from informants.

The "extended" interview event is also a naturally occurring interactional situation which can be used to gather samples of real-life bilingual speech.

Acknowledgments

I would like to thank the editors, Melissa Moyer and Li Wei, for their insightful comments on the various drafts of this chapter. Any remaining shortcomings are, of course, my own. The course "Research Methods in Sociolinguistics" taught by Joan Pujolar at the Universitat Autònoma de Barcelona provided inspiration for many of the ideas in this chapter.

Further reading and resources

On the interview as a research technique

Briggs, C. L. (1986) *Learning How to Ask: A Sociolinguistic Appraisal of the Role of the Interview in Social Science Research*. Cambridge: Cambridge University Press.

Gubrium, J. and J. Holstein (eds.) (2002) *Handbook of Interview Research: Context and Method*. Thousand Oaks, CA: Sage.

Labov, W. (1984) Field methods of the project of linguistic change and variation. In J. Baugh and J. Sherzer (eds.), *Language in Use: Readings in Sociolinguistics*. Englewood Cliffs, NJ: Prentice Hall, pp. 28–54.

Redmond, M. V. (2000) *Communication: Theories and Applications*. Boston/New York: Houghton Mifflin, chs. 8 and 9.

On biographical narratives and bilingual identities

Pavlenko, A. and A. Blackledge (eds.) (2004) *Negotiation of Identities in Multilingual Contexts*. Clevedon: Multilingual Matters.

On the questionnaire as a technique

Dörnyei, Z. (2003) *Questionnaires in Second Language Research: Construction, Administration and Processing*. Mahwah, NJ: Lawrence Erlbaum.

An interesting example of a recent large-scale language survey using questionnaires

Extra, G. and K. Yagmur (2004) *Urban Multilingualism in Europe*. Clevedon: Multilingual Matters.

10   Recording Audio and Video

Ignasi Clemente

10.1   Introduction

This chapter begins with a description of the advantages that audio and video recording offer researchers working in the field of bilingualism. Section 10.2 reviews some important considerations when planning to record data for research purposes. Section 10.3 provides information on purchasing equipment and other preparatory tasks. Section 10.4 covers the practical mechanics of recording. Finally, section 10.5 offers suggestions for managing post-recording activities and includes a discussion of the hardware and software requirements for preparing recorded data for analysis.

10.2   Why Record?

Recording talk has been an essential method of data collection in the study of bilingualism (Myers-Scotton, 2006), particularly in sociolinguistic, sociological, and anthropological approaches (Heller, 1995a). For instance, despite theoretical differences over phenomena such as code-switching, mixing, and convergence, both grammatical and interactional analyses have relied on recordings (Myers-Scotton, 1993a; Li Wei, 1994; Auer, 1998; Moyer, 2000). Even macroanalytic research on the relationship between social categories and linguistic forms, particularly ethnic identity (Gumperz & Hymes, 1972; Gumperz, 1982b), language ideology (Schieffelin, Woolard, & Kroskrity, 1998), language shift (Hill & Hill, 1986; Kulick, 1992), and multilingual socialization (Slobin, Gerhardt, Kyratzis, & Guo, 1996; Zentella, 1997; Garret & Baquedano-López, 2002) has combined recordings of elicited oral texts, interviews, and naturally occurring talk, with other forms of data collection for their analyses.

Thus, researchers interested in bilingualism, across theoretical orientations and interests, converge on the value of using recorded data. Multiple reasons explain such a broad use. First of all, recording allows other researchers to review the actual data used and to draw independent conclusions. Recordings are intrinsically

selective, and thus, no "unmotivated" recorded data exist. However, unlike ethnographic field notes, recordings give other researchers the opportunity to observe the
data somewhat independently. Second, recording makes possible the creation of audio
and video databases, which can then be used for detailed comparative analysis of
bilingual phenomena. Third, recording allows for repeated and deferred observation,
and for the data to be made available to support analytic claims. This is necessary
in qualitative microanalysis, where the complexity and validity of the analysis rely
on the detailed transcription of verbal and non-verbal behavior. Finally, recordings
capture the immediate context of the bilingual phenomenon which is the focus of
analysis, such as accompanying linguistic, paralinguistic, and non-verbal behaviors
that may be essential to understanding its meaning and function. This is especially
important for researchers interested in naturally occurring bilingual phenomena,
where, unlike in laboratory or experimental research, the setting of the unique
instances of talk being analyzed cannot be artificially reproduced.

10.2.1 Audio versus video: What is the research purpose?

The research purpose is the most important guide for making decisions about
recording. The technical, logistic, financial, human, and ethical aspects of conducting research can only be worked out once a clear rationale has been established.
To decide between audio or video recording, it is necessary to have a clear idea of
both the phenomena to be studied and the types of data needed to support research
findings. For instance, if the behaviors of speakers and respondents are of equal
analytical relevance, then the simultaneity of behaviors makes the use of video
indispensable. Video is also necessary if the phenomenon is multimodal, such as
the coordination of verbal and non-verbal communication, or the synchronization
of communication and the manipulation of objects. However, audio recording
alone may be sufficient if non-verbal data are unnecessary, as for experimental
studies that focus on the production of talk, studies in which the interviewee's
verbal behavior is the only phenomenon of analytic interest (e.g., for term elicitation,
taxonomies, and content and contrastive analyses), or for narrowly delimited types
of quantitative analyses focused on verbal behavior. Audio recording has the further
advantages of being cheaper and simpler than video recording. If only a general
visual sense of the setting is needed, segmented visual information (e.g., still photography) can be used instead of video. In sum, audio recording alone can be a good
choice if it is certain that active non-verbal data will not be analyzed.

Second, in the past, researchers sometimes chose to make only audio recordings
because it was considered to be less intrusive than video. This is no longer the case.
Video cameras have become so small that they do not distract research participants
any more than audio recorders would. Further comfort may be found in the fact
that participants generally become accustomed to the presence of any kind of
recording device (Duranti, 1997: 345). Participants may at times modify their
conduct because of the presence of the camera and the researcher, but as Duranti
and other scholars have underscored, "people usually do not invent social behavior,
language included, out of the blue" (Duranti, 1997: 118). Participants (as well as

researchers) may still be apprehensive about video recording. However, as my own video recording of interactions with children with cancer and their families attests (Clemente, 2005), participants' ease with the presence of the camcorder depends more on the researcher's own behavior than on whether it is audio or video.

A different matter is whether research participants feel the need to protect their identities. Honoring research participants' wishes is not only an ethical obligation, but also a sign of good research. If participants decline to have their images recorded, audio recording alone may be an option. However, if non-verbal data are needed, research participants should be excluded from the study. In addition, although researchers have at times made audio recordings without the knowledge or consent of those being taped, using only audio recordings does not exempt one from the obligation to obtain consent from research participants. The advent of human protection research and ethical committees (particularly in American universities) has made research that depends upon covert recordings subject to the same approval processes and regulatory oversight as all other types of data collection.

10.2.2 *Analogue versus digital: Financial and logistic considerations*

The last consideration involves finances and logistics. Prices of recorders vary greatly. The choices are, from cheapest to most expensive, audio analogue, video analogue, audio digital, video digital. Quality follows price, with commercial amateur analogue audio recorders rendering the lowest sound quality, and professional digital recordings rendering the highest. Two new digital recorders have recently emerged: the high definition (HDV) video recorder and the compact flash card (or CFC) audio recorder; they both double the recording quality of earlier technologies. As will be discussed below, researchers are unlikely to need the latest and most expensive HDV video or CFC 96 kHz audio recorders. Researchers with low budgets may be able to meet their recording needs with equipment from university digital laboratories. With so many options available, researchers should be able to reach a compromise between affordability and quality.

Regardless of whether audio or video is chosen, digital recording has many advantages. It is affordable, user-friendly, and of high quality. Not only does it allow for easy data transfer and reproduction, it retains the quality of the original when files are copied or uploaded. Analogue recordings, on the other hand, lose quality each time a dub or a copy is made. Moreover, as digital replaces analogue technology, it will probably become difficult to find analogue tapes, playback devices, and repair services. Because of this, digital recording is recommended over analogue.

Researchers with the financial and staffing resources may consider using stand-alone audio, in addition to video, as an inexpensive security back-up for video recordings. For instance, an audio back-up can be helpful when the activity being recorded outlasts the duration of a single video tape. Since video and audio tapes or memory cards have different recording times, if both are used no activity will go unrecorded if the researcher has to change tapes. There is, however, a logistic disadvantage: the more equipment one uses, the more difficult it is to run it all.

Thus, it is important to consider, when making equipment purchasing decisions, (1) the number of field researchers who will be working on any given recording, (2) the length of the event to be recorded, and (3) whether the benefits of having an audio back-up outweigh the logistic challenges.

Section summary

Repeated and deferred observation of naturally occurring bilingual phenomena is the main advantage of recording. Three important criteria to be taken into account when deciding whether to use audio, video, or a combination of the two are: (1) Why are the data being collected? (2) How will the presence of the researcher and the recorder impact the activities being studied? and (3) What are the financial and logistic constraints?

10.3   Preparing to Record

Most of the work involved in recording is preliminary to the recording itself. As introduced above, this includes purchasing equipment, determining equipment compatibility (e.g., whether a specific microphone will work with one's video camera, or whether recorded data are transferable to one's computer), deciding how data will be manipulated (e.g., coded, transcribed), and obtaining legal permissions from university institutional review boards and research participants. The following subsection focuses on purchasing equipment.

10.3.1   Purchasing equipment

It is difficult to make specific equipment recommendations because technology becomes outdated quickly, and manufacturers continually make better equipment available at lower costs. For these reasons, it is wise for researchers to conduct their own research into the equipment available at the time of purchase. Some ways to research recording equipment are (1) the Internet, including users' and manufacturers' sites, (2) consulting with audiovisual technicians and salespeople, and (3) seeking recommendations from colleagues whose research is similar to the type for which you plan to use the equipment.

10.3.1.1   Video recorders

Since the quality of the recorder determines the quality of the sound and images with which you will work, consider making a high-quality recorder a budget priority. Once a recording has been made, it is difficult to improve the quality, and the amount of improvement is limited. For most research purposes, the higher range of non-professional digital camcorders is more than adequate. However, if a professional camcorder is affordable, it is money well spent.

What is the highest recording quality? In general, digital video recording quality is described in terms of the number of pixels that are scanned per horizontal and vertical line. The higher the resolution (i.e., the greater number of pixels scanned), the sharper the image. For instance, a standard resolution for most NTSC MiniDV camcorders is 720×480, that is, 720 pixels per horizontal line by 480 vertical scan lines. PAL MiniDV is 720×576. High-definition digital resolution begins at 1280×720. In addition to resolution, the recording format also influences the quality. The main recording formats are digital8, MiniDV (small compact tapes, about half the size of a digital8 tape), DVD (mini or full), and hard disk (Microdrive, Compact Flash, or built-in hard drive). Digital8, a hybrid that uses Hi-8 tapes but records digitally, makes the lowest-quality recordings. The other recording formats offer approximately the same quality of recording. High-definition digital recording uses the same MiniDV tapes used for normal digital video. Hard disk and DVD camcorders do not use tapes at all.

The downsides of currently available hard-disk camcorders are storage limitations, since the higher the recording quality, the less one can record, and the fact that files must be downloaded to make room for new recordings. DVD camcorders also have downsides. Files are compressed, that is, made smaller in order to take up less memory, thereby reducing the quality of the original recording. Also, they often use MPEG-2 as their default formatting. In this formatting, the audio and the video are recorded as two separate files. Sometimes they can be merged together into one single file later on, but often not. Finally, the downside of high-definition video MiniDV camcorders is the high price. In view of these limitations, standard MiniDV camcorders offer excellent quality at an affordable price, without excessive compression or storage limitations, and taped video data that can be captured easily into a computer file.

In addition to the recording format, digital camcorders vary in their features. The minimal requirements to look for are:

- resolution of at least the MiniDV standard, that is, 720×480 scan lines for NTSC and 720×576 for PAL
- optical zoom of at least 10X–16X, an optical zoom being better than a digital one
- image stabilization, optical being better than digital
- a liquid crystal display of at least 2.5 inches (65 cm)
- low-light operation, to reduce blurring
- a 3-CCD imaging system, for excellent resolution and color reproduction for still photography and for extracting still image frame grabs from movies
- FireWire connectivity, also known as IEEE 1394a or I-link compatible DV IN/OUT, for miniDV camcorders, or USB 2.0 connectivity for DVD and hard-disk camcorders, to allow the real-time transfer of video data to a computer
- long-lasting batteries (at least 4–5 hours of continuous recording time)
- attachments for external microphones and a wide-angle lens.

To ensure adequate battery life, it is best to purchase long-lasting lithium batteries. Despite advertising claims, the battery that comes with the camcorder will not hold a charge long enough for many research purposes. Battery operation for video recorders is necessary, since there may not be access to a power outlet during recordings. Camcorders purchased in the US come with 100–240 volt AC power adaptors. For researchers working in different parts of the world, this eliminates the need for a transformer, but outlet jack adaptors may still be required.

10.3.1.2   *Audio recorders*

Audio recorders can be used alone or in combination with camcorders. In order to obtain the highest quality of audio recording for duplication and archival storage, there are three considerations to bear in mind: the physical recording medium, the recording quality, and the formatting possibilities for subsequent transfer to other formats.

Three main physical media are used for audio recordings: tape (analogue or digital), disk (MiniDisk and CD), and computer-based media (computer disks and hard-drives). Analogue tapes are the traditional magnetic cassette tapes that come in standard and mini formats. Digital tapes, similar to mini cassettes, are small and are known as DAT (digital audio tape). Choose the audio-recording medium according to the type of planned data analysis: spectrograms, phonetics, and prosody require maximum quality, while for content analysis lower quality is fine.

In theory, analogue and digital equipment can produce recordings of equal quality, but this is rarely the case in practice for non-professional users. Despite the fact that analogue recordings capture true sound while digital recordings capture sound by sampling it at specific rates, most non-professional analogue recordings are of lower audio quality than digital ones. Among digital audio recorders, there are many choices to be made: mono or stereo; sampling rate (32 kHz or 44.1 kHz used in CD, and 48 kHz used in DAT); and data recording size (12 and 16 bit). The higher the sampling rate (i.e. 48 is higher than 32 kHz) and the larger the size of the data sample and its range (16 is higher than 12 bit), the better the sound quality and the larger the overall size of the audio file. For most researchers 48 kHz, 16-bit stereo will be sufficient. Avoid compression, which reduces the quality of the sound and may prevent data transfer and reformatting.

For high-quality audio, DAT recorders have been the top choice for some years, but the sound quality of newer CD and MP3 recorders is creating competition in this area. CFC devices record sound at 24-bit and 96 kHz, doubling the recording quality of DAT recorders. They record compressed and uncompressed data, and instead of tapes they use files which are downloaded via a USB 2.0 port or a CFC. However, they are still not as small as other devices and they cost more. Nonetheless, the combination of superb audio quality, large storage capability, ability to work with uncompressed files, easy tapeless file transfer, and falling computer memory prices, makes CFC recorders highly desirable for research. Tapeless MP3 and MiniDisk recorders are also alternatives for researchers who need neither high sound quality nor uncompressed files. Finally, digital voice recorders, particularly models with high sampling frequencies (e.g. 44.1 kHz and above), and noise and voice filters, hold much promise.

A final word of advice: *never* use original recordings for data analysis. The original recording should be played once in order to create a working back-up copy. After being copied, originals should be stored safely away. Repeated play-back can then be conducted with the copies or computer files.

10.3.1.3   *Microphones*

Microphones can be internal (i.e. built in), external wired and wireless, and directional or omnidirectional. The two top brands for all high-quality microphones are Sennheiser and Audio-Technica. Note that external microphones may not work well with all recorders. To guarantee the sound quality you want, it is important to confirm compatibility and to test it out. Contact the manufacturers or read the online model specifications to confirm that the microphone you are considering is designed to work with the recorder that you will be using. After purchase, test the microphone with the recorder, and return it if there are any problems.

For researchers working away from their home institutions, it is imperative to run recording tests before leaving for the field. The tests should simulate the research activity as closely as possible. If possible, create a model of the research environment, and test the equipment under a range of conditions, such as a varying number of participants, and their movements and activities. Pay attention to external noise and to what happens when participants face or turn away from the microphone. Experiment also to find the best location for the recorder. Finally, listen to the test recordings on the type of equipment (e.g., computer) that will be used for analysis. These steps will help to ensure that the field recording produces the desired results.

A rule of thumb when choosing an external microphone is that the closer the microphone is to the subjects, the higher will be the quality of the sound. Thus, if the recorder can be kept close to the speakers at all times, the built-in microphone may be sufficient. When the microphone cannot be kept close to subjects, external microphones are recommended. One common problem is ambient noise. Solutions to this problem include directional wired microphones (e.g., shotgun) and two-piece (transmitter and receiver) omnidirectional wireless lavalier lapel microphones. Advantages of the latter are enhanced-quality recording of the target speaker who is wearing it, freedom of movement, increased safety (by avoiding accidents with cords), and assurance that the microphone will be close to the subject at all times. Disadvantages are poorer recording of speakers who are neither wearing mikes nor standing close to the targeted speaker, interference with other electronic devices and magnetic fields, transmission loss because the transmitter and receiver are too far apart, and problems associated with the speaker wearing the microphone (e.g., noise of fabric rustling or from the speaker touching the microphone). Although most of these problems are solvable – for instance, by relocating the receiver, modifying the direction of the antenna, or trying out different frequencies – it is best to work out as many of these details as possible before the actual recording.

For these reasons, if the budget allows, purchasing two external microphones, a directional wired shotgun and an omnidirectional wireless lavalier, is the safest option. However, if two external microphones are not an option, a wireless lavalier may work best for research activities involving abundant speaker movement, distance between the recorder and the participants, and ambient noise. In other situations, a wired directional shotgun will work best. Since the choice of a microphone will depend on the research activity, it is essential that you become as familiar as possible with the acoustic conditions of the activities you will be recording.

Finally, external microphones require upkeep and monitoring. Batteries eventually die, so it is wise to change them regularly. Some researchers place fresh batteries in microphones for each recording session. Microphones also need to be monitored during recording, using headphones, to ensure that they are working properly.

10.3.1.4 *Tapes*

Tapes are a cheap budget item, and buying in bulk will reduce the cost even further. Use the Internet, friends, and colleagues to find suppliers who sell in bulk. When deciding how many to buy, consider whether they will be needed at more than one stage of the research, such as for archiving/backing up or making working copies.

10.3.1.5 *Additional equipment*

It is useful to have instruction manuals and a good bag for storage and transportation. Instruction manuals can be lifesavers when something goes wrong. Carry them with you, and review them frequently. If manuals are lost, they can be downloaded from the manufacturers' websites. An equipment bag makes it easy to find things quickly and helps ensure that essential and expensive pieces of equipment are not left behind at home or at the field site. A small luggage cart can be used to protect researchers from carrying excessive weight.

Second, researchers must have a set of headphones to monitor the quality of the sound of audio and video recordings. Additionally, for video recordings in small settings, such as doctors' offices or conference rooms, a wide-angle lens may be needed to include everyone in the room in the frame.

A third group of additional equipment consists of camera-mounting devices, such as tripods, magic arms, and auto poles. Use a tripod for video recording whenever possible, since hand-held videotaping is challenging. New camcorders come with a steady shot function. However, steady shot does not provide the stability of a tripod. Slight oscillations of the image may be fine for casual home recordings, but they may become annoying to researchers during the repeated playback required for detailed transcription and analysis. There may be situations in which a tripod is not practical, such as when participants move substantial distances or there is physically no place to put it. In these cases, assessing whether recording will be mostly static or dynamic will determine the solution.

Dynamic hand-held recording is more challenging than static recording. Researchers will have to experiment to find suitable solutions to the specific problems presented by the activities to be recorded. Smaller stands or tripods may provide a compromise between stability and mobility. They come with one or three small legs, require less space to stand, are light, and can be picked up and moved around easily. If there is no room for a tripod but the recording is mostly static, a magic arm should be considered. A magic arm is a mounting system with ball joints to which the camcorder (up to 5 lb/2.25 kg) is attached. Combined with another part called a super clamp, the magic arm allows camcorders to be hung from a supporting structure, such as a door or a TV stand. Magic arms make it possible to mount cameras in hard-to-reach locations, but they make it difficult to stand behind the camera. Consequently, this mounting system requires that the angle of the camera and the measurements of a shot be established at the time of set-up, prior to actual taping.

Finally, the auto pole is a lightweight (about 5 lb/2.25 kg), adjustable metal pole (extending up to 145.7 inches/3.7 m), usually used for lighting purposes, which works well with the magic arm. It comes with a lever-operated locking system that allows the pole to be mounted either vertically or horizontally in a room by exerting pressure that wedges the rubber suction cups on each end of the pole securely between the floor and ceiling or wall to wall. Auto poles can be used when there is no structure onto which to clamp the magic arm. These three pieces of equipment, magic arm, super clamp, and auto pole, are especially useful for static recording in small and cramped spaces.

10.3.1.6 *Computer digital laboratories*

Personal computers serve as researchers' primary digital laboratories for manipulation of recorded data. Connectivity, computer memory, and processing power need to be considered when purchasing equipment. First, a computer needs to be thought about as a hub for transferring data to and from peripherals, including recorders, external hard drives, printers, scanners, and digital still cameras. Connectivity is a particularly important consideration for researchers traveling abroad who will need to be self-reliant in terms of their equipment. To ensure connectivity, it is necessary to have at least one iLink IEEE port (also known as 400MB FireWire, IEE1394a, or IEE1394) and at least two or three USB 2.0 ports in a laptop computer. A desktop computer should have at least two FireWire and four-to-six UBS 2.0 ports. An iLink FireWire is necessary to transfer files from the camcorder to the computer. A second iLink FireWire port is recommended for laptop and desktop computers, to avoid sharing the same port with other equipment. iLink ports, with data transfer at a speed of up to 400 MB per second, come in two configurations: the 4-pin and the 6-pin. A 4-pin or 6-pin FireWire cable connects a DV camcorder or a Video Walkman digital video cassette recorder to the computer. A 6-pin to 6-pin FireWire cable connects other devices to the computer, such as an external hard drive. There also exists a faster 800-MB 9-pin to 9-pin IEE1394b FireWire, which is used to connect hard drives. There are two types of USB ports: USB 1.1, with a rate of transfer of 12 MB per second, and USB 2.0, with a transfer rate of 480 MB per second. Digital audio recorders come with USB ports and not with FireWire. This is not a problem since a USB 2.0 is slightly faster than a 400 MB FireWire. For this reason, make sure that both your computer and your digital audio recorder are equipped with USB 2.0 ports. Finally, be aware that Apple computers come with FireWire ports but PCs may not have them unless specifically requested, and that external hard drives often come with both Firewire and USB 2.0 ports.

Computer memory and processing power become major concerns when working with video data. Without the necessary memory and processing power, certain tasks will take an exceedingly long time. Researchers working in a collaborative project may consider purchasing a server for storage of large amounts of data and easy access from multiple computers.

10.3.2 Obtaining informed consent

In research carried out in the US or by a representative of a US institution, recording can only proceed once the required institutional permissions and the consent of participating subjects have been obtained. In the US and countries with similar requirements, it is important to start the approval process early, since the process can be slow. Good places to begin are University Institutional Review Boards' websites, which usually have sample consent forms that can be used as models (see, for example, UCLA's www.oprs.ucla.edu/). Additionally, ask colleagues who have completed successful IRB applications to share copies of their applications and forms. In other countries, there may not be formal institutional legal requirements, but it is good research practice to ensure that informed consent is obtained from participants. Field researchers are recommended to take the time to introduce themselves to participants, to explain what they are asking of them, and to encourage them to spend as much time as they need going over the consent forms and asking questions.

Section summary

When purchasing equipment, (1) consider the advantages of digital technology, (2) reach a balance between quality and affordability, and (3) check connectivity between the different equipment components. Before recording, obtain informed consent and always treat research participants with respect.

10.4   Recording in the Field

The best way to avoid recording problems is to ensure that the field researchers doing the recording are well prepared. Since the technical skills needed to operate recorders are minimal, the more important preparation involves developing the observational skills to attend to the activities of the people being studied and to develop familiarity with the physical and social environments. Comprehensive lists of ways to improve the quality of recordings are available in Duranti (1997) and Goodwin (1993), so only a brief list of practical guidelines is included here.

On the day of the recording: have a checklist of tasks and equipment and actually remember to check it; remove the plastic wrappings of the blank tapes you plan to use, and make sure there are extra blank tapes in your equipment bag; insert a tape into each recorder and record for about 30 seconds at the beginning of the tape (this is done because the beginnings and ends are the parts of the tape most vulnerable to deterioration); and plan your travel so that you arrive early at the research site, giving yourself more time than you need for equipment set-up. At the research site, set up the recorder in as unintrusive a place as possible. If you can, close doors and windows to minimize surrounding noise; reduce overly strong sources of light; use headphones to check sound quality; coach participants to speak into their microphones; and, if necessary, attach a wide-angle lens in order to include all the participants in the frame, adjusting the zoom as needed.

Start recording a few minutes before the target activity begins; avoid excessive movement of the camera; use the zoom sparingly; use only the smaller viewfinder and close the LCD screen (this extends battery life). Take field notes when not attending to the equipment. Writing field notes is one of the best ways to develop observational skills, which in turn can improve recording quality. Continue recording for a few additional minutes after the activity ends. Then, take your time packing things away, and use this time to continue to observe participants' behavior. As soon as possible, protect your data from being erased by snapping the safety tabs in cassette tapes or sliding the red tab on the bottom of other types of tapes. In addition, label and code as per study protocol. I recommend charging batteries, backing up tapes and reviewing them at the end of each day of recording. This allows mistakes to be detected so they can be avoided the next time one records. Finally, store tapes in a dark, dry, and protected place.

Section summary

To avoid problems, start preparing early on the day of recording. Arrive early at the recording site to have time to set up and to solve any problems that may arise during set-up. At the end of the day, watch the recordings as you back them up in order to catch problems and to ensure that the recorded data match your analytic objectives, as they may evolve during data collection.

10.5   Post-Recording Data Manipulation

Backing up is probably the most important among the post-recording maintenance tasks. Back-up copies of data should be of the highest quality possible. Researchers may consider making one back-up copy for safety storage and another as a working copy for repeated playback during analysis. Copies can easily be made with two camcorders or two audio recorders. An increasingly affordable alternative is to transfer the data onto a computer or external hard drive without compression. However, computer and external hard drives can fail, so it is always advisable to back up onto tapes. Researchers who plan to back up onto CDs or DVDs should remember that these involve compression and quality loss.

Creating a content log for each recording is also recommended (Goodwin, 1993; Duranti, 1997). By content-indexing, researchers can easily locate a specific activity in the corpus of collected data.

Finally, when conducting research at their home institution, researchers can make use of digital laboratories if they are available. Even when the project has its own equipment, researchers can benefit from the support of digital-media computer lab technicians. Researchers working abroad should consider the following. They should check that the recorder's warranty is good for the country where the research will be conducted. Unfortunately, the NTSC/PAL/SECAM divide has been carried over to digital video. Researchers will be able to view their recordings on their camcorder LCD screen, laptop computer, or DVCR Video Walkman, but not on local TV monitors. The NTSC/PAL split also complicates backing up, since researchers may not be able to rely on equipment at institutions in the host country. Thus, researchers working abroad should be self-reliant in terms of equipment and back up their data using two camcorders or burning their own DVDs while in the field. Backing up copies before traveling, particularly at times when transportation security regulations are tight, is an additional way of protecting research data (and researchers' nerves).

It is beyond the scope of this chapter to review in detail the editing tasks involved in preparing the data for analysis. Before concluding this section, I will briefly introduce the main tasks, which are: capturing audio/video; segmenting; playback; annotating and highlighting of data segments; adding subtitles for presentations; and converting and compressing data for storage on hard drives, CDs, and DVDs. No highly advanced software is necessary to carry out these tasks, and there is no single software application that will do all of them.

Free software applications that do these tasks are available for download on university websites, such as *Praat* at the University of Amsterdam (spectrograms/ pitch tracks), *VoiceWalker* and *SoundWriter* from the University of California, Santa Barbara (transcription and alignment of sound and transcripts), *Elan* from the Max Planck Institute for Psycholinguistics in the Netherlands, and *Transana* at the University of Wisconsin-Madison (with a US$50 licensing fee). Editing software applications for professionals or high-end technical consumers are expensive. Researchers may be able to purchase them at a discount from university websites and computer stores. This is the case for *Adobe Premiere* and *Avid Xpress Pro* and for Apple and PC users. Apple users can also use *Final Cut Pro* (with its cheaper version *Final Cut Express*). Other applications that may be used for research purposes are *Pitchworks*, *Soundforge*, BIAS *Peak* and *InqScribe*. Free preinstalled operating system software, such as Windows Movie Maker or iMovie, or inexpensive applications such as QuickTime Pro, can also be used to do most of these editing tasks. Finally, new transcription software often has the feature of a USB 2.0 port pedal. This allows researchers to play, stop, and rewind without moving their hands from the computer keyboard. An example of this is *Express Scribe*, which can be downloaded for free, so the only expense is purchasing a pedal.

10.5.1 *Preparing for transcription*

Preparatory work is part of the analysis itself, since it involves selecting specific parts of the data and not others. Transcription is an iterative process. There is neither a need nor an analytic reason to transcribe all the recorded data. In qualitative work, one's ongoing analysis guides transcribing decisions.

Nonetheless, how, and how much, to transcribe remain important decisions that researchers must make. The following guidelines may be of help. First, use analytic goals to determine whether to transcribe verbal or non-verbal communication, or both at the same time. Application software can then be chosen accordingly. Next, transcribe in modality layers. Both audio and video recording machines gather enormous amounts of data indiscriminately. Thus, it may be best to start with one aspect of communication and then add others (e.g., one participant's talk, then overlapping talk, gaze, hand gestures, bodily posture, vocal non-verbal behavior, and so on) as they become relevant. A transcript is an analytic tool (Ochs, 1979) and therefore is never finished: the researcher is the one who decides analytically when to stop enriching the transcription of a specific segment. The presentation of sequential verbal and simultaneous non-verbal data in writing has been the object of much discussion (Edwards & Lampert, 1993; Duranti, 1997; Bucholtz, 2000; Poyatos, 2002). These problems are solved by inserting representations of the data into the transcript itself in the forms of frame grabs (which can be extracted from a video clip with most editing applications), pitch plots, photographs of material objects, charts, and diagrams. An excellent example of this use can be seen in Charles Goodwin's work, for instance in his article on time in action (Goodwin, 2002). Another option is to have transcripts available on-line. In such a case, additional consent should be obtained from the research participants whose images will be included.

Section summary

- There are a number of routine tasks to be carried out after recording. Among them, backing up your data is particular important, and creating a content log for each tape is recommended.
- The logistic problems and solutions that researchers face when editing will vary depending on whether they are working at their home institution or abroad.
- Researchers may need to combine different software applications, since a single application may not do everything they need.
- Researchers should consider the preparatory work as part of the analysis itself, particularly when choosing what aspect of communication to start with and how to integrate multimodality in a transcript.

10.6   Conclusion

This chapter has presented some advantages that recording offers researchers studying bilingual phenomena. Producing and using recorded data is complex. It requires a commitment of time and resources, including purchasing equipment, deciding when and how to record, and manipulating data for analysis. The best way to approach all the tasks involved in recording is as a learning process, where one does not learn everything at once, but rather improves one's understanding over time by trial and error. Charles Goodwin states:

> I view taping as an iterative, progressive process. The first time you tape in a setting, and then work with the materials you've collected, you find both wonderful things and problems in what you've done. What I like to do at this point is go back and try to get the stuff I missed the first time. (Goodwin, 1993: 194)

Recording, despite its challenges, is a research effort worth pursuing. With clear theoretical goals in place, technology makes possible the collection of new forms of data, which can in turn be used to inform and expand our current understanding of bilingual phenomena.

Acknowledgments

I would like to express my gratitude to the editors, M. Moyer and Li Wei, and to M. H. Goodwin, C. Goodwin, A. Duranti, C. Álvarez Cáccamo, and A. Maestrejuan for their helpful advice. I am grateful to J. Heritage, J. D. Robinson, and T. Stivers for introducing me to the use of magic arms and auto poles. I am also grateful to P. Connor, digital laboratory director at the UCLA Sloan Center on Everyday Life of Families, who patiently answered each and every one of my questions. Finally, I am especially indebted to M. Katz for her careful editing. All mistakes that remain are my own.

Further reading and resources

On the ethical, methodological, technical, and analytic implications of using audio and video recording devices to study communication in general, readers are encouraged to consult the following: (1) on the impact of recording devices on the phenomena to be studied, see chapter 4, "Ethnographic methods," in Duranti (1997), a debate on this topic by Speer and Hutchby (2003a, 2003b), and Hammersley (2003); (2) on transcription as a part of the analytic process, see Ochs (1979), Edwards and Lampert (1993), Bucholtz (2000), and chapter 5, "Transcription: from writing to digitized images," in Duranti (1997); (3) for specific instructions on how to record, see Jackson (1987), Goodwin (1993), and "Appendix: practical tips on recording interaction" in Duranti (1997); finally (4), on the transcription of non-verbal communication, see Goodwin (2002), Payrató (2002), and Poyatos (2002)).

The Internet is the ultimate resource for computers, audiovisual technology, and digital electronics: books tend to become outdated quickly. To name just a few, websites such as crutchfieldadvisor, ehow, and camcorderinfo, and online magazines such as videomaker, pcworld, and macworld, will help the reader stay abreast of current information: they often contain introductory webpages with essential information for non-professional audiences, as well as reviews, comparisons, and ratings of the latest recording devices and technologies so that researchers can make informed purchases.

11　Transcription

Maria Teresa Turell and Melissa G. Moyer

11.1　Introduction

Transcription is one step in the analysis of bilingual and multilingual spoken data which is fundamentally a methodological choice, but which has often been neglected and taken for granted in studies of bilingualism. The present chapter introduces key considerations for transcription along with specific proposals to deal with issues that arise when transcribing multilingual data. There is not a single, unique, correct method of transcription, but rather a variety of options that are related to choices taken at the decision and the realization stages of research (see figure 11.1). The identification and transcription of a particular kind of data will depend on the research question and hypotheses set out at the beginning of a project (see Moyer, chapter 2 in this volume). In other words, whatever methodology and theoretical perspective is used, a researcher will ultimately depend on the research design devised at an earlier realization stage, that is, when corpus and sample size have already been decided, and the instruments of data collection have been selected.

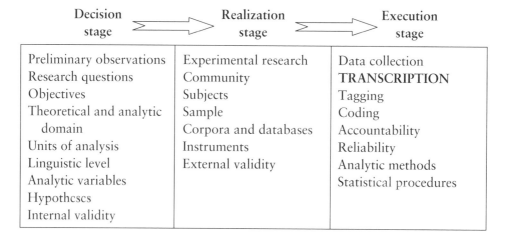

Decision stage	Realization stage	Execution stage
Preliminary observations	Experimental research	Data collection
Research questions	Community	**TRANSCRIPTION**
Objectives	Subjects	Tagging
Theoretical and analytic domain	Sample	Coding
Units of analysis	Corpora and databases	Accountability
Linguistic level	Instruments	Reliability
Analytic variables	External validity	Analytic methods
Hypotheses		Statistical procedures
Internal validity		

Figure 11.1: The location of transcription in the research process

The activities at the realization stage shown in figure 11.1 are directly linked to the research questions and the theoretical approach and to the objectives and hypotheses formulated at the decision stage. This research framework is summarized in the figure. The location of transcription in the research process is indicated in bold uppercase letters.

Several proposals related to transcription, tagging, and encoding of oral language data have been proposed (Edwards & Lampert, 1993; Leech, Myers, & Thomas, 1995), with very few references to the idiosyncratic aspects of transcribing and coding bilingual data, which involve language interaction phenomena such as code-switching and borrowing, and syntactic and semantic calquing. The aim of this chapter is to provide the novice researcher with the background needed to transcribe and tackle the analysis of data in this field. Before taking up the transcription of multilingual data it is necessary to familiarize oneself with (1) the sorts of transcription methods available, (2) the transcription choices and decisions involved, and (3) the most suitable transcription and coding conventions for answering a particular research question. A researcher may develop or adapt a system of transcription to comply with the requirements of a particular type of data or a new research context. It is important not to lose sight of reliability requirements in transcription in order to ensure the internal and external validity of the research results.

Section 11.2 deals with the issues that come up when rendering speech into writing. The notion of transcription as an interpretive and analytical tool is presented along with questions related to amount, detail, and approach to transcription techniques. Section 11.3 discusses some practical information to bear in mind when undertaking transcriptions, such as the use of digital recording equipment, options for storing data and various software programs helpful for the task of tagging. Section 11.4 introduces basic information on the LIDES system for transcribing, coding, and analyzing bilingual data. Section 11.5 presents examples and practical considerations for structuring and coding different types of analytical units (parts of speech, utterances, turns). Section 11.6 goes into ways plurilingual data can be tagged when using the LIDES system: this system enables the marking of the languages in a transcription as well as other audio or visual elements that a researcher considers necessary for representing speech. Section 11.7 deals with coding and the ways research-specific coding can be done. Finally, section 11.8 discusses questions of reliability in transcription.

11.2   From Speech to Writing

Transcription is the process of representing oral language with orthographic conventions. The outcome of rendering oral language into written form is not a neutral process of representation. Writing is a standardized form of language in which lexical, phonetic, and syntactic deviations can be represented. Considerations such as accents, overlaps between speakers, pauses, hesitations, emphasis, gaze, and paralinguistic phenomena are just some of the additional elements that contribute to the meaning and the structure of utterances. Other traits typical of oral interaction, such as the expression of intimacy, secrecy, or hostility, do not usually have verbal counterparts. It is similar with vocal gestures, expressed by paralinguistic phenomena but which may be relevant.

Before setting out to do a transcription, a researcher will need to have a clear idea about what additional linguistic information will need to be represented in addition to the words uttered. In the case of bilingual data or language-acquisition data, decisions about the status of an item as a borrowing or a code-switch will need to take into account criteria such as their phonetic realization (Poplack & Meechan, 1995) or their frequency of occurrence. A decision to standardize oral language, by eliminating hesitations or by using standard orthographic spelling when a word might have been pronounced as a rough approximation, must be based on a conscious and informed choice. So, transcription involves many decisions about which a researcher needs to be aware in order to guarantee the validity of their research results.

Transcription is already a first step in interpretation and analysis. As Roberts (1997: 168) points out, the challenge facing the transcriber is to produce transcriptions that are accurate and readable, but that are also reflexive in how they make explicit to the analyst the constructed nature of written talk. Decisions about what to transcribe and how much detail to include involve interpretation that can influence the analysis of those data by readers and, more importantly, subsequent analyses by other researchers. A more detailed account of interpretive and representational issues that arise in the transcription of oral language are discussed in depth by Ochs (1979) and Bucholtz (2000).

The approach one takes to the transcription of oral language is as important as the amount of detail. Both will ultimately depend on choices made at the decision and realization stages of research (see figure 11.1). As to transcription detail, one very simple approach is to just transcribe, that is, render into writing, the words uttered, without introducing any conventions to signal linguistic information, pauses, and other elements that co-occur in speech production. All kinds of linguistic information may be represented: phonetic, morphological, syntactic, semantic, or discourse structures. Further information on annotation can be found at www.ldc.upenn.edu/annotation/. It is possible at this address to find information on very specific areas of linguistic annotation such as *phonological aligners*, related to automatic speech recognition (ASR) and involving automatic phonemic transcription (Kvale, 1993; Black & Campbell, 1995; Kohler, 1995; Rapp, 1995), *morphological aligners* (Schmid, 1995), and *lexical aligners* (Kohler, 1994; Baayen, Piepenbrock, & Gulikers, 1995).

In the case of bilingual data transcription involves a motivated approach to plurilingual talk in that the transcription system requires the identification of (1) the languages involved in the interaction, (2) the types of language interaction phenomena (borrowings, calques, bivalent forms), and (3) the structural and functional contexts in which these phenomena occur. See Gardner-Chloros (chapter 4 in this volume) for further information on the options available for classifying bilingual data.

Bilingual speech usually reflects speakers' language, sociolinguistic, and stylistic competence. Additional information on dialect, sociolect, and agelect, and the appropriateness of register (frozen, formal, consultive, informal, or intimate) following Joos (1967) can also be identified and transcribed. A typical dilemma that arises when transcribing for the first time is a natural tendency to turn the oral into standard written language. It is important to bear in mind that talking is qualitatively distinct from writing sentences. The structure of an utterance often does not coincide with fully structured written sentences. People do not finish what they start to say or they start over and reformulate their initial words. The transcription works with different structural units. Pauses, intonation, and paralinguistic factors are often key criteria for distinguishing where one utterance ends and another starts. In cases where the transcription of bilingual/multilingual speech involves two closely related languages with similar or identical orthography, phonetic realization may be the only way of distinguishing to which language the given token belongs. Researchers often choose their own way of transcribing their data but there are advantages to using a system compatible with data analysis programs that allow you to get basic statistics and correlations, and also to choosing a transcription system that allows computerized comparisons with other datasets.

Section summary

- Standard writing is not an objective representation of speech
- Transcription is already a first step in interpretation and analysis
- Transcription of bilingual data requires distinguishing (1) the languages in the interaction, (2) the type of bilingual phenomena, (3) the structural context, and (4) the functional or contextual meaning

---

11.3   Transcription: Practical Tips

As researchers who have been involved in transcription know, transcribing is intensive and time-consuming work. In order to optimize this activity and meet quality requirements, scholars should consider aspects of transcription which are often taken for granted, such as the equipment used, the physical environment or context, the procedure, and the time needed.

As a general rule, it is advisable to digitize data. Storing audio or video data on a computer (hard-disk or CD-ROM) makes accessing particular sections of the interaction, or frames, easier and more straightforward. Several research institutions have developed computer-assisted audio and video analyses, which involve digitization as well. One very powerful tool is the Max Planck Institute for Psycholinguistics CAVA, which includes a transcription and a tagger unit for the analysis of recordings. The TED (Transcription Editor) creates text transcription files with references to the number on the video time counter, and the MediaTagger – Mac-based video transcription – creates multimedia documents and closely links transcription text to digital audio and digital video. Digital video movies are stored using an HSM (Hierarchical Storage Mechanism) system on a UNIX server. The MediaTagger can combine these movies with the relevant transcription and coding data from the database, and a query generator lets the user create complex time-related queries in an intuitive, graphically oriented way. See www.mpi.nl/world/tg/CAVA/CAVA.html for additional information.

Bilingual data is usually produced in natural-language interactions, that is, in spontaneous situations involving several speakers at a time, in which it is not possible to ask participants to come to a laboratory and have the recording meet technical standards that would optimize the transcription. So, digital transcription begins with the use of digital voice recorders, which are often much easier to use and much more technologically advanced than analogue ones (see Clemente, chapter 10 in this volume). There is no completely automated system for transcribing and tagging bilingual data, so in order to analyze bilingual data it is necessary to use a written text, which is transcribed by means of a more traditional method by a transcriber. The best equipment for transcribing is usually one that allows for slow-motioned reproduction of audio or video data. You will need a headset, and a control pedal that can be connected either to computer, transcriber, or recording device.

Before starting a transcription, it is necessary to decide what form it will take. In other words, the information to be transcribed from an audio or video recording has to be organized in a legible and coherent form, so that when it is consulted and analyzed by researchers, either in paper or computer form, they can find the information they need easily. All transcriptions should begin with a heading section that includes information on the participants in the interaction and on the linguistic situation involved, along with the additional elements shown in figure 11.2.

Participants	Gender
	Age
	Educational level
	Occupation
Situation	
Languages involved	
Notes	
Date of recording	
Researchers	
Date of transcription	
Transcribers	

Figure 11.2: Required information to be included with transcription

One thing is to actually use a transcriber in order to render a recording into text, and another very different thing is to decide on the transcription conventions that are to be used and the format that the transcription needs to have in order for databases to be created which can be used to compare bilingual data from different contexts and to encourage coordinated approaches to bilingualism. The idea is that, depending on the transcription format used, an individual transcription of bilingual data can remain an isolated piece of data or become part of a machine-readable corpus, which can be better exploited by individual researchers or by teams of researchers having the same or different research aims. The theoretical, methodological, and practical difficulties encountered in the transcription of monolingual data are even more evident when the transcription involves bilingual or multilingual data.

Section summary

- The equipment needed to do a transcription is a digital recorder, a transcribing machine, computer software, a headset, and a pedal
- The quality of recording, storing, and accessing material is best if it is digitized
- The physical conditions of the recording and timing are important
- Key information is required for labeling transcription files

---

11.4   The LIDES System

LIDES stands for the Language Interaction Data Exchange System; it provides a system for transcribing and coding plurilingual speech along with a set of tools for analysis. The system is adapted from CHILDES (Child Language Data Exchange System) created by MacWhinney and Snow (1990) and MacWhinney (1995) to forward the study and exchange of adult–child language data. LIDES addresses specific issues that arise in the transcription and analysis of plurilingual data. More importantly, it is the first coordinated effort in the field of bilingualism to provide a system whereby researchers can share their data. Until now, individual researchers have used their own transcription conventions when carrying out studies of bilingualism. However, current research in bilingualism asks certain questions that can only be answered by means of comparisons between data sets and plurilingual language structures; if common coding and transcription criteria are not adopted such studies cannot be carried out reliably. The purpose of this section is to provide an overview of the main features of LIDES. Practical information on how to use the system can be obtained from Barnett, Codó, Eppler, et al. (2000), henceforth referred to as the *LIDES Coding Manual*, and from MacWhinney (1995) (the CHILDES manual). The adoption of LIDES allows researchers of bilingual and multilingual data to use a *standard format* for transcribing and coding plurilingual data that offers the following features:

- Transcriptions in a format that is not word-processor dependent. The LIDES format for transcribing and coding data (CHAT) is very flexible and allows the researchers to reflect many types of linguistic facts and phenomena that occur in natural bilingual speech datasets;
- Transcriptions and coding conventions that include many types of information that will help researchers achieve their analytical goals. It is a system that involves a "motivated" approach that is flexible enough to allow different analytical perspectives;
- A transcription system that allows researchers to optionally activate different features and coding specifications that may be relevant to their research questions at different stages of their research.

Another point in favor of the CHILDES system is the formal way in which the system is set up. One development that was incorporated in 2003 is an interface between CHAT and XML formats. XML is a markup metalanguage of the World Wide Web with powerful tools for analyzing data on the Web. It is a standard way of marking up texts (both spoken and written), which is independent of any word processor or computer system. A program for converting CHAT files to XML can be downloaded from the CHILDES web page (http://childes.psy.cmu.edu/). Another recent addition to CHILDES that has been incorporated by LIDES is the Unicode encoding system. The set of computerized language analysis programs (called CLAN) developed in the CHILDES project recognizes this new system. Unicode is important for research on multilingual data because it allows language interaction researchers to use their computer keyboard to represent different writing systems and character sets, such as Arabic, Chinese, or the International Phonetic Alphabet (IPA). A further advantage to using Unicode is that it permits researchers working in the field of discourse and conversation analysis (CA) to use the conversation analysis programs of CLAN (CACLAN) to analyze utterances, turns, overlaps, and other conversation phenomena used in the transcription conventions put forward by Atkinson and Heritage (1984). A far-reaching expansion that has also been developed in recent years is the linking of original digitized audio and audio–video recordings to transcribed files. Linking can be done at the same time as one carries out the transcription. New avenues for spoken language analysis and possibilities for checking and revising transcriptions can easily be carried out. More detailed information on linking is provided with the CHILDES programs. A computer program called Praat, with which it is possible to analyze, synthesize, and manipulate speech, has been developed by Paul Boersma and David Weenik (2001). This program is especially useful for splicing short audio files into a single large file. The CHILDES project is currently developing further CLAN support for this program (Gardner Chloros, Moyer, & Sebba, 2007: 95).

It is more than obvious that not everything can be transcribed when rendering speech to writing. Decisions involved in choosing what to transcribe, how to do the actual transcription, and how to store the transcription results will depend on the research aims established in a particular study involving bilingual data. The reason why the LIDES system is recommended for bilingual data is that it ensures optimality of efforts, in the sense that it allows inclusion of all the information needed for data analyses, and accessibility for other researchers working from similar or different perspectives. When using LIDES it is useful to distinguish (1) *transcription choices*, in terms of the organization that the transcribed text of bilingual data has to adopt and the marking up of the text in terms of speech production, (2) *tagging choices*, that is, marks in the transcribed text that identify the languages involved in the interaction, different language-interaction phenomena observed, the possible specification of different descriptive linguistic features that may be of interest to include on the main transcription line (called in the CHILDES and LIDES systems the main tier), instead of coding them on separate dependent tiers (those lines connected to the transcription found on the main tier), and finally, (3) *coding choices*, that is, the specification of codes directly related to research objectives and hypotheses, usually presented in dependent tiers.

For transcribing in LIDES it is advisable to use the existing CHAT transcribing and coding conventions. CHAT is very flexible and allows researchers to reflect many kinds of phenomena that occur in natural speech data. CHAT also allows the researcher to add any type of code that is needed as long as it is used consistently and defined in the proper way. A CHAT data file must fulfill certain requirements that are specified in the *LIDES Coding Manual*. The CLAN tools apply to transcriptions in a CHAT format; they provide many possibilities for automatic analysis, although they are not a substitute for the researcher's efforts to analyze and interpret the data. More detailed information about how CHAT and CLAN can be used with plurilingual data can be found in the *LIDES Coding Manual*.

In order to check for errors and compare the files created with the prescribed format, the CHILDES system adopted in LIDES provides a special CHECK program which runs twice over the files; on the first pass, it checks for errors regarding the general requirements of file headers and the main and dependent tiers; on the second pass, it checks whether the transcription symbols and codes have been declared in the *depfile* or, more specifically, the *depfile.cut* file, and the *depadd* file or *00depadd.cut* file. These files verify the syntax and structure of the data, listing the legitimate headers and dependent tiers as well as the strings allowed within the main tier and the various dependent tiers. *Depfile.cut* is a standard file that is delivered with the CLAN programs, whereas *00depadd.cut* is a file that can be created by researchers themselves in order for the CLAN and CHECK programs to run with the new symbols, new headers, and any new coding symbol that may be relevant to the purposes of bilingual data analysis.

All transcribed datasets that use LIDES should incorporate a *readme* file (00readme.doc), which provides general information about the datasets and includes details of acknowledgments, researchers, community, sample, hours of recording, transcription hours, special transcription and coding parameters, interaction types, definitions of language interaction phenomena, instruments, and changes made in the depadd file (*LIDES Coding Manual*: 162).

Section summary

- LIDES provides facilities for the transcription of bilingual data
- These include tools from CHILDES for the analysis of language (CHAT and CLAN)
- Transcription and coding are shown on main and dependent tiers
- Tagging and coding decisions can be annotated
- The CHECK program looks for errors in the transcription files
- LIDES requires depfile, depadd, and readme files

11.5 Organization, Structure, and Analytic Units in Transcription

The CHAT transcription format is organized around basic linguistic units such as morphemes, words, and utterances, but researchers may define other units, such as turns, according to the needs of their analysis, as will be explained in this section.

11.5.1 Morphemes

Since there are certain representational issues involved in the transcription of morphemes and words, this section takes up some of the issues that arise in the segmentation of these units. The first is how to represent units smaller than words, that is, morphemes, in the transcription of the main tier. The CHAT format of CHILDES uses five symbols for coding morphemes of different types (MacWhinney, 1995): + for compounds (mountain+bike); - for suffixes (like-ed); & for fusion (sing&ed); # for prefixes (un#tie), and ~ for clitics in Spanish for example (da~me~lo, or da ~me ~lo, if clitics have to count as separate words). With apostrophes, as in French for example, the recommendation is to use a space after the apostrophe, e.g. *l'avocat* → *l' avocat*; dashes should be replaced with a space, except with compounds where the compound marker + should be used; finally, with contractions, two representations are suggested: *was-'nt* or *wasn't [was-'nt]*; in the latter case the CLAN programs will substitute the text in front of the brackets by the text in the brackets. The actual representation of morphemes in transcription is better observed when tagging for language at the same time. Morpheme representation for prefixes is illustrated in example (1):

(1) Mandinka/English: Haust and Ditmar (1998: 88), adapted to CHAT
     @Languages: Mandinka (1), English (2)
     *S09:   ì@1 ka@1 ì#@1 rectify@2 .
     %glo: they usually you- rectify
     %tra: they usually rectify you

                                               (*LIDES Coding Manual*: 170)

11.5.2 Utterances

CHAT requires speech to be split up into utterances. There is no fixed way to define where an utterance begins or ends. It is open to the researcher to suggest the criteria to be used in order to define such a unit with respect to their data. The most natural way of defining utterances would be through the tone unit, but many researchers still prefer syntactic criteria. A proposal for defining and transcribing utterances on the main transcription tier is INTROS (INformant's TRanscriptiOn String). Utterances are defined as units, which may consist of single words, single phrases, or single and complex units that may not coincide with a sentence unit. INTROS establishes the utterance as the basic transcription unit on the main tier in order to present speech data in a more accessible way for further analysis. An illustration of an INTROS unit involving a complex sentence (Utterance [clause constituent]) is shown in boldface in (2):

(2) Catalan/Spanish: Pujadas, Pujol Berché, and Turell (1988–92), adapted to CHAT
    *INF: **diu@1 no@2 lo@2 conociamos@2 esto@2 .**
    %tra: she says: we didn't know you're up to this
                                                    (*LIDES Coding Manual*: 174–5)

As observed in the previous sections, the choice of one transcription unit or another will very much depend on the research needs involved in a particular analysis of spoken bilingual data. The units which are usually taken as transcription units of bilingual data are the morpheme, the word, and the utterance, although it is also possible to identify and segment tone units. The CLAN programs cannot make analyses of data transcribed in CHAT and organized in terms of turns, but a solution must be found because some language-interaction research may need to consider the turn as a unit of analysis. If the solution involves representing the turn on the main tier, the transcription will read as in (3):

(3) Catalan/Spanish/English: Turell and Forcadell (1992), adapted to CHAT
    @Begin

@Filename:	prgaed6.asa
@Participants:	BRO Brown Adult, SMI Smith Adult, FER Ferrer Adult
@Languages:	Catalan (1), Spanish (2), English (3)
@Date:	30/06/92
@Date of coding:	14/05/95
@Coder:	Turell, Forcadell
*SMI:	England@3 is@3 very@3 simple@3
*BRO:	mechanisms@3 # a@3 sort@3 of@3 # discourse@3 # not@3 at@3 the@3 technological@3 level@3 ## that@3 's@3 one@3 problem@3 !
*SMI:	like@3 the@3 fenomenos@2 tormentosos@2 ["] # what@3 have@3 you@3 instead@3 of@3 a@3 tormenta@2 ## fenomenos@2 tormentosos@2 y@2

	viento@2 con@2 componente@2 norte@2 ["] or@3
	something@3
*BRO:	and@3 just@3 call@3 it@3 north@3 wind@3
*SMI:	north@3 wind@3
@End	

In this example the second turn of speaker *SMI is represented by a main tier that extends over four lines.

11.5.3 Turns

Another solution is to split up utterances by using the GEM header @G and the turn number to signal turn beginning and turn end; then the GEM program in the CLAN programs, to be run before any other program, will analyze the part of the transcription between the GEM headers as a unit. This transcription solution is shown in (4):

(4) Catalan/Spanish/English: Turell and Forcadell (1992), adapted to CHAT

@Begin

@Filename:	prgaed6.asa
@Participants:	BRO Brown Adult, SMI Smith Adult, FER Ferrer Adult
@Languages:	Catalan (1), Spanish (2), English (3)
@Date:	30/06/92
@Date of coding:	14/05/95
@Coder:	Turell, Forcadell

*SMI:	England@3 is@3 very@3 simple@3 .
@G:	001
*BRO:	mechanisms@3 # a@3 sort@3 of@3 # discourse@3 .
*BRO:	not@3 at@3 the@3 technological@3 level@3 .
*BRO:	that@3 's@3 one@3 problem@3 !
@G:	002
*SMI:	like@3 the@3 fenomenos@2 tormentosos@2 .
*SMI:	["] what@3 have@3 you@3 instead@3 of@3 a@3
	tormenta@2 ## fenomenos@2 tormentosos@2 y@2
	viento@2 con@2 componente@2 norte@2 ["] or@3
	something@3 .
@G:	003
*BRO:	and@3 just@3 call@3 it@3 north@3 wind@3 .
@G:	004
*SMI:	north@3 wind@3 .
@G:	005
@End	

This coding system is useful if you wish to mark the turns that contain particular phenomena you wish to study.

11.5.4 Using a gloss-dependent tier

The %glo tier provides a word-for-word gloss of the transcription on the main tier. Transcribers of bilingual data must bear in mind that there may not always be a straightforward correspondence between the number of units in the transcribed language and the language used in the %glo tier, assuming in this case that that language is English. This lack of correspondence may involve two types of context. One is the context in which one word in the language of the transcribed text on the main tier corresponds to two words in the language of the %glo tier; the other context involves the reverse situation, that is, when two units in the language of the transcribed text on the main tier correspond to one unit in the language of the %glo tier.

One such case is the Spanish contraction *al* (preposition + determiner), corresponding to *to the* in English, which is illustrated in (5); the correspondence is maintained by joining the words on the dependent tier with an underscore: 'to_the.'

(5) Spanish/English: Moyer (1992: 307)
     @Languages: Spanish (1), English (2)

    *TEA: porque@1 como@1 no@1 les@1 cuesta@1 nada@1 tampoco@1 al@1
                  employer@2 .
    %glo: because as not them cost nothing neither to_the employer
    %tra: because it doesn't cost them anything, nor the employer
                               (*LIDES Coding Manual*: 159)

Infinitives expressed in one word in specific languages are indicated with an underscore: **to_inf**, as in example (6):

(6) Catalan/Spanish: Pujadas, Pujol Berché, and Turell (1988–92), adapted to CHAT
    *INF: hacemos@2 cosas@2 yo@2 ## estoy@2 en@2 un@2 grupo@2 #
                  para@2 **hacer@2** cosas@2 del@2 pueblo@2 .
    %trn: 852
    %glo: we_do things I am in a group for **to_do** matters of_the village
    %tra: we do things I'm in a group to take care of village matters

Diminutive nouns are expressed by means of adjective_noun, as illustrated in (7):

(7) Catalan/Spanish: Pujadas, Pujol Berché, and Turell (1988–92), adapted to CHAT
    "INF: vull@1 dir@ teniem@1 un@1 **banquet@1** .
    %trn: 134
    %glo: I_want to_say we_had a **little_bench**

In terms of syntactic functions, the subject of the utterance is not explicitly marked on the %glo tier when the verb is already marked for person, as in (8):

(8) Catalan/Spanish: Pujadas, Pujol Berché, and Turell (1988–92), adapted to CHAT
     *INF: que@1 no@1 **soc@1** tan@1 jove@1 com@1 aixo@1 .
     %trn: 109
     %glo: that not **am** so young as this

However, it is marked in all other cases, that is, when the verb form in the language used in the %glo tier is not marked for person, as in (9):

(9) Catalan/Spanish: Pujadas, Pujol Berché, and Turell (1988–92), adapted to CHAT
     *INF: mhm@1 home@1 com@1 **vols@1** dir@1 .
     %trn: 138
     %glo: mhm man how **you_want** to_say

The %glo tier doesn't incorporate the English preposition 'to' to express objects, as illustrated in example (10):

(10) Catalan/Spanish: Pujadas, Pujol Berché, and Turell (1988–92), adapted to CHAT
      *INF: ahora@2 **le@2** hablo@2 en@2 catalan@2 ## ahora@2 .
      %trn: 100
      %glo: now **her** I_speak in Catalan now

Also, when one word in the transcribed language corresponds to two words in the language of the gloss, a dash is used to keep the correspondence, as in (11):

(11) Spanish/English: Moyer (1992)
      *ELI: ahora@2 verás@2 .
      %glo: now will-see

                                        (*LIDES Coding Manual*: 159)

In other cases, particularly with agglutinative languages such as Turkish, the correspondence between the morphemes on the main tier and those on the %glo tier is one to one, as illustrated in (12):

(12) Turkish: Backus (1996)
      *III: saat@1 onikide@1 yatarsak@1 ne@1 olacak@1 .
      %glo: hour twelve-at go-to-bed-if-we what be-will
      %tra: if we go to bed at twelve o'clock then what's gonna happen

The second context illustrates a non-correspondence involving two units in the language of the transcribed text on the main tier which correspond to one unit in the language used on the %glo tier, for example, Spanish *hay que* (*must* in English). One way of showing that the value is attributed to one of the units on the transcription line or main tier would be to join these two units by means of *: "must*that," when providing the gloss on the %glo dependent tier.

Section summary

- Conventions for coding morphemes
- Transcribing utterances in CHAT
- Turn scope with @GEM
- Issues in glossing transcriptions with %glo

11.6   Tagging Choices

Transcription also involves tagging and coding, although the difference between the two is not always clear-cut. The tagging and coding of the bilingual text can be included either on the main tier or on a dependent tier. Usually on the main tier you find (1) tags regarding language and the different language-interaction phenomena observed, that is the dependent analytical variables, and (2) symbols regarding the physical production of speech, which researchers may not wish to code on a separate dependent tier. The marking up and coding of the transcribed text can also be done on separate dependent tiers that include the microlinguistic analysis of these language-interaction phenomena.

Language tagging involves the use of the tag @ after every word or morpheme, followed by the numbers chosen to refer to the languages of the transcribed bilingual text. The language tag can be used with more numbers to assign a tag to mixed words, and it can be made more explicit by using a tag for mixed words with language 1 or language 2 in any language set. However, this solution could be more problematic for language pairs involving agglutinative and non-agglutinative languages, and it would require a specific LIDES coding system to be developed for this purpose. The language tag can also be used to code single-word borrowings, calques, and all other language-interaction phenomena, instead of using some of the other conventions described below. This will depend on the research goals of the investigator.

Finally, it is also possible to expand the language tag to a two- (or more) digit system, the "turbo language tag," as referred to in the *LIDES Coding Manual*, where the first digit could denote the language of the word and the second the word class. This procedure, however, involves incorporating redundant information that can also be elicited from the %glo dependent tier, which is precisely proposed to favor contrastive analysis between different databases. All these points are illustrated with examples in the *LIDES Coding Manual* (pp. 166–8).

11.6.1   Language-interaction tag

With some bilingual datasets it is not possible to account for the scope of a certain language-interaction phenomenon because the phenomenon involves a unit larger than a single word.

(13)   Sardinian/Italian: Rindler-Schjerve (1998: 243), adapted to CHAT
       @Languages: Sardinian (1), Italian (2), syntactic calque of Italian in Sardinian (3)
       *GUI: ca@1 sa@1 veridade@1 happo@1 accontentadu@3 su@3 cliente@3 .
       %glo: because the truth I_have satisfied the client
       %tra: the truth is I satisfied the customer
       %com: Italian: accontentato il cliente; "satisfied the client";
                 Sardinian: accontentadu a su cliente, "satisfied 'to' the client."
                                                       (*LIDES Coding Manual*: 181)

In example (13), it is not possible to identify whether *accontentadu@3 su@3 cliente@3* is three consecutive syntactic calques, or one syntactic calque consisting of three words, unless one reads the %com dependent tier. In order to solve this problem, it is proposed that researchers use the Language Interaction Code (*LIDES Coding Manual*: 181), which implies marking up the text by using two sets of symbols: (1) angle brackets < > to indicate a scope phenomenon when the phenomenon in question involves strings of more than one word, and (2) square brackets [ ] containing the $ symbol plus a code specifying the type of phenomenon, following a single word or the text within the angled brackets, <text>. The *LIDES Coding Manual* specifies four basic language-interaction phenomena: *code-switch*, coded = c; *borrowing*, coded = b; *syntactic calque*, coded = y, and *semantic calque*, coded = e. These codes must be declared in the *depadd* file, and explained in the *readme* document.

Other interesting conventions for tagging and coding included in CHAT (found also in MacWhinney, 1995), and later adapted by LIDES (*LIDES Coding Manual*: Appendix 1), refer to more or less familiarity with identifying and representing orthographic symbols related to the speaker's performance in terms of (1) repeating and restating, such as false starts and unfinished utterances, (2) the speaker–hearer interaction, with the eventual monitoring between speaker and hearer, and (3) the need to measure the length of pauses.

A specific tagging proposal is made here to represent the non-correspondence between the existing formal word categories (verbs, adjectives, and others) in a language and their expression in the %glo tier expressed in English. With parts of speech such as verbs, example (14) shows the specific tag [auxpast], used to express in the %glo tier the periphrastic perfect in Catalan (anar + a + INF) and avoid the use of 'to go,' which would be the corresponding translated unit, thus missing the exact verbal meaning of **vam@1**:

(14)   Catalan/Spanish: Pujadas, Pujol Berché, and Turell (1988–92), adapted to CHAT
       *INF: mira@1 **vam@1** buscar@1 aixo@ .
       %trn: 009
       %glo: looks **we_[auxpast]** to_search it

With pronouns, example (15) proposes the tag [courtesypro] to represent the use of the deference pronoun, both implicitly and explicitly, in several languages: *Vosté* in Catalan, *Usted* in Spanish, *Socé* in Portuguese:

(15)   Catalan/Spanish: Pujadas, Pujol Berché, and Turell (1988–92), adapted to CHAT
       *EN4:   quan@1 [/] quan@1 # **voste@1** va@1 arribar@1 aquí@1 .
       %trn: 010
       %glo: when when **[courtesypro]** [auxpast] to_come here

Example (16) shows how syntactic functions can be coded. The tag [impers] is used in the %glo tier when the impersonal character of the clause subject has to be indicated:

(16)   Catalan/Spanish: Pujadas, Pujol Berché, and Turell (1988–92), adapted to CHAT
       *INF: hi@1 havia@1 una@1 casa@1 al@1 costat@1 de@1 l'@1 Orfeo@1
               ##que@1 encara@1 hi@1ha@1 un@1 magatzem@1 alli@1 que@1
               es@1on@1 **es@1** va@1 fer@1 aquella@1 vetllada@1 tambe@1 .
       %trn: 041
       %glo: there was a house at_the side of the Choral_Society that already
               there is a warehouse there that is where **[impers]** [auxpast] to_do
               that evening party also

The tag [idiom] is used, as in example (17), to account for idiomatic expressions, which are transcribed word by word.

(17)   Catalan/Spanish: Pujadas, Pujol Berché, and Turell (1988–92), adapted to CHAT
       *INF: llegaron@2 ya@2 rumores@2 de@2 que@2 yo@2 chivataba@2 #
               a@2 las@2 [/] a@2 las@2 madres@2 de@2 [/] de@2 ellos@2 de@2
               que@2 # algunas@2 veces@2 **hacian@2 manitas@2** con@2 las@2
               chicas@2 que@2 se@2 veian@2 .
       %trn: 592
       %glo: (. . .) arrived already rumours of that I told XXXxxx to the
               mothers of of them of that sometimes **[idiom] they_did little_hands**
               with the with the girls that [pronominal] they_saw

---

Section summary

- Criteria for tagging on either the main or the dependent tier
- Coding for larger-scope phenomena
- Non-correspondences between main tier and dependent tiers

11.7   Coding

In order to make transcriptions natural and readable, the main tier should be kept as simple as possible, leaving the dependent tiers for more extensive coding, that is, tagging related to the microlinguistic analysis of the language-interaction phenomena under observation. Another advantage of coding on the dependent tier is that it makes the transcription on the main tier easier to read. Whenever possible the already existing CHAT dependent tiers should be used to facilitate parallel contrastive analysis between different bilingual datasets. New dependent tiers can be created to serve the researchers' specific interests. Again, all new dependent tiers and codes within these tiers must be declared in the *depadd* file and explained in the *readme* document.

For comparative purposes the coding information specified on the dependent tiers should be kept as separate as possible. Researchers may decide which analytical procedures should be merged in view of the nature of their analysis. The decision to include many dependent tiers can also be a disadvantage. A reasonable alternative would be to include all relevant coding on one dependent tier. Dependent tiers can be word-related, utterance-related, or turn-related. Examples are given in the following subsections.

11.7.1   Word-related dependent tiers

The word-related dependent tier *par excellence* is the %glo tier, whose nature and characteristics in relation to segmentation problems were considered earlier. The use of the %glo tier allows researchers to show a one-to-one relation between this tier and the main tier, with considerable use of hyphens and underscores when one word on the main tier is glossed with two or more words on the %glo tier, or when two or more words on the main tier correspond to one word on the %glo tier. Example (18) illustrates morphological coding on the %mor dependent tier:

(18)   Wolof/French: Poplack and Meechan (1995: 215), adapted to CHAT
       @Languages: Wolof (1), French (2)
       *S02:   fexeel@1 ba@1 nekk@1 ci| tête@2 de@2 liste@2 bi@1 rek@1 .
       %mor: V|try&IMP   CONJ|until   V|be&INF   PREP|at   N|head
                 PREP|of   N|list   DET|the&DEF   ADV|only
       %tra: Try to be only at the head of the list
                                                   (*LIDES Coding Manual*: 184)

       Key to symbols and codes:
       Format of the %mor tier:
       part-of-speech| syntactic category: subcategory
                                         stem in the original language
       & fusion code
       # prefix code
       – suffix code (MacWhinney, 1995)

When the information to be coded on the dependent tier refers to only one part of the main tier, all the slots corresponding to the other words on the main tier which are not coded on the dependent tier should be filled in on the %mor tier by a suggested marker ";", as illustrated in example (19), in order to maintain the one-to-one relation:

(19) Wolof/French: Poplack and Meechan (1995: 215), adapted to CHAT
    @Languages: Wolof (1), French (2)
    *S02:   fexeel@1 ba@1 nekk@1 ci| tête@2 de@2 liste@2 bi@1 rek|@1 .
    %mor: ; ; ; ; N|head PREP|of N|list ; ;
    %tra: Try to be only at the head of the list

(LIDES Coding Manual: 184)

The utterance-related dependent tier *par excellence* is the %tra tier, which renders the idiomatic or expressive meaning of the main tier. Another useful utterance-related tier is the %add (addressee) tier, which may mention the directionality of the interaction or the native/non-native language knowledge of the interlocutors; it can also be used in combination with GEM headers as a turn-related tier, and is very useful for indicating information at the utterance level, as example (20) shows:

(20) Italian/Italian_dialect: Ramat (1995: 50), adapted to CHAT
    @Begin
    @Participants: MMM shop_owner's wife, DDD customer, CHI
                  child_with_DDD
    @Languages: Italian (1), Italian_dialect (2)
    *MMM: oh@1 che@1 bel@1 bimbo@1 !
    %add: DDD
    %tra: oh, what a nice little baby
    *DDD: l' @2 è@2 'l @2 bagaj@2 d' @2 la@2 Lice@2 .
    %add: DDD
    %tra: it's Lice's child
    *MMM: ah@2 sì@2 ?
    %add: DDD
    %tra: Oh really?
    *MMM: ma@2 l' @2 è@2 zamò@2 gnit@2 grand@2 .
    %add: DDD
    %tra: but he has grown up so much
    *MMM: l' @2 è@2 tyt@2 la@2 facia@2 d' @2 so@2 maar@2 .
    %add: DDD
    %tra: he looks like his mother
    *MMM: prendi@1 pure@1 lepatatine@1 caro@1 .
    %add: CHI
    *tra: take the crisps, dear
    *MMM: te@1 lo@1 regalo@1 io@1 quelle@1 .

```
%add:        CHI
%tra:        I'm giving them to you
*DDD:        sù@1 rigrazia@1 la@1 signora@1 .
%add:        CHI
%tra:        come on, say thank you to the lady
@End
```

(LIDES Coding Manual: 185–6)

Coding intonation patterns can also be incorporated on a %pho dependent tier, as shown in (21):

(21)   Intonation patterns: Selting et al. (1998: 14), adapted to CHAT
```
       *A:        // hier fängt der transkriptext / an .
       %pho:      {TF \                    \}
       %glo:      here starts the transcription_text
       %tra:      the text of the transcription starts here
```
(LIDES Coding Manual: 180)

Key to symbols:
```
 //    primary stress
 /     secondary stress
 T     global tone height
 F     falling
 { }   scope
 \     falling intonation
```

Another useful utterance-related dependent tier is the %syn tier, which allows the coding of syntactic groupings (clauses and phrases) and also syntactic functions. The CHAT format is as follows:

%syn: <functions of words < roles [XP] > [XP]>

This can be realized as <subject, predicate < [NP] > <[VP] > >.

For other proposals on syntactic coding, see the *LIDES Coding Manual* (188–93). A final dependent tier worth mentioning is the %spa tier, where some pragmatic information is shown. This tier is described in MacWhinney, 1995: 101–3 and is illustrated in (22), where the %add tier is also specified:

(22)   Cantonese/English: Example from Milroy and Li Wei (1995: 149), adapted to CHAT
```
       @Begin
       @Participants:   MOT Mother, DAU daughter, SON son
       @Languages:      Cantonese (1), English (2), undetermined (0)
       @Age of DAU:   9
       @Age of SON:   11

       *MOT:   who@1 want@2 some@2 ?
       %add:   DAU, SON
```

```
*MOT:    <crispy@2 a@1> [>] .
%spa:    $i:yq
*DAU:    <yes@2> [<] .
%spa:    $i:aa
*MOT:    yiu@1 me@1 ?
%spa:    $i:yq
%glo:    want some
*DAU:    hai@1 a@1 .
%spa:    $i:aa
%glo:    yes
( . . . )
@End
```

(LIDES Coding Manual: 147)

Key to symbols:
$i: illocutionary force code follows
yq   yes/no question
aa   answer in the affirmative to yes/no question
an   answer in the negative to yes/no question
cl   all attention to hearer by name or by substitute exclamation

In a transcription done via the CHAT format in CHILDES, dependent tiers can be added at the level of the turns taking place in an interaction. Turns can be expressed by means of, and included within the scope of, the GEM headers. However, a special turn tier, %trn, can be created, which could include information about the languages used in the turn, or whether a language-interaction phenomenon occurred at the turn boundary or across the turn boundary.

If researchers prefer to code all aspects of a language-interaction phenomenon on one tier, they can use a %cod tier, described as the general-purpose tier. There are many ways of doing this: one can use coding schemes via letter codes, which are easy to understand, or more abstract codes for which you need to have coding information available when interpreting the results generated by the execution of the CLAN programs in CHILDES. Other dependent tiers that can be used in a transcription done via CHAT refer to non-linguistic activities. For example, the %act tier can hold comments on the particular activities in which speakers are engaged, and the %gpx tier can used to express facial gesture, body language, and proxemic information.

Section summary

- Coding word-related information
- Coding utterance-related information
- Coding intonation and phonetic features
- Coding syntactic categories and speech acts

11.8   Conclusions: Reliability and Transcription

As a general principle, to make a reliable transcription of bi-/multilingual texts, transcribers must have sufficient knowledge of the languages. It is also very important that the transcribers are clearly instructed in the transcription conventions so that the transcribed texts are consistent.

The consistency of a transcription of bilingual data can be measured using statistical procedures, but a *sine qua non* is that variation of transcribing practices should be kept to a minimum, within the work of each transcriber and across different transcribers. As has been mentioned, clear formulations of transcription conventions help to reduce variation, but individual factors, such as individual learning rate or fatigue may have an effect on transcription reliability. In order to attain reliability and check the consistency of a transcription, it is necessary to double-score the transcribed material. When only one transcriber is involved, inter-rater agreement can be measured by having the transcriber transcribe the material for a second time at a time interval long enough for the original transcription to have been forgotten. When another transcriber can participate, this person should retranscribe the material following the same conventions.

The amount of material which needs to be transcribed a second time depends on the total amount of data available. Rietveld and van Hout (1993) suggest 10 percent and that the material should be selected randomly to avoid any bias. There are also different methods for calculating the agreement between two transcripts (Rietveld & van Hout, 1993) for specific aspects such as glosses, segmentation, tagging, and coding. Agreement of approximately 80 percent is considered quite acceptable, although the ideal is between 95 and 100 percent. With lower scores it is necessary to analyze the source of the errors and evaluate the best way to correct them. Sometimes it is a question of improving the clarity of the transcription conventions; at other times the problem may be related to specific problems with the glossing, or the coding, because of related research and analytical issues.

Another principle that should be taken into account when addressing transcription of bilingual texts for the first time has to do with accountability, that is, the fact that, in linguistics in general but in language contact analysis in particular, it is as important to be able to identify when a specific variable under analysis occurs – in this case, when language-interaction phenomena occur – and the context in which they occur, as it is to identify when those variables or phenomena do not occur. The isolation of the occurrence of non-salient, non-overt phenomena, in this case in language interaction, is often a challenge for both qualitative and quantitative analysis of bilingual oral data, and one that has not yet found a solution in automated approaches to language and language behavior.

Further reading

For more detailed information on coding and transcribing bilingual data, see: P. Gardner-Chloros, M. Moyer, and M. Sebba, Coding and analyzing multilingual data: The LIDES Project, in Joan C. Beal et al. (eds.), *Creating and Digitizing Language Corpora: Volume 1, Synchronic Databases*, London: Palgrave, 2007; the publication by the LIPPS Group "The LIDES Coding Manual: A Document for Preparing and Analyzing Language Interaction Data," special issue of the *International Journal of Bilingualism* 4 (2): 139 pp., 2000. The LIDES project is based on the CHILDES system designed and developed by Brian MacWhinney. The CHILDES manual provides a complete inventory of the transcription conventions and analytical tools upon which the LIDES project is based. Further information on CHILDES and the manual can be obtained at http://childes.psy.cmu.edu/.

Additional ways of annotating a transcription can be found at www.ldc.upenn.edu/ annotation/. It is possible to look up at this address very specific areas of linguistic annotation, such as *phonological aligners*, related to automatic speech recognition (ASR) and involving automatic phonemic transcription (Kvale, 1993; Black & Campbell, 1995; Kohler, 1995; Rapp, 1995), *morphological aligners* (Schmid, 1995), and *lexical aligners* (Kohler, 1994; Baayen, Piepenbrock, & Gulikers, 1995).

12 Quantification and Statistics

Natasha Tokowicz and Tessa Warren

12.1 Introduction

The variety of questions that has been asked about bilingualism is made richer by the range of methods that different disciplines bring to the study of the topic. Increasingly, questions about bilingualism are studied from multiple perspectives. In this chapter, we wish to provide a broader view of the diversity of questions about bilingualism that are studied using quantification and statistics. This is not intended to be an exhaustive list, but rather to demonstrate the variety of questions on bilingualism to which quantification and statistics are applied.

Researchers who are interested in understanding the consequences and under-pinnings of bilingualism face several challenges. One of the largest is variability in linguistic behavior and other phenomena of interest. Many factors impact linguistic behavior, including reading skill, motivation, social status, and social situation. Bilinguals vary in all of these factors, and also vary in their language-learning history and cultural history. Differences across bilingual groups in language pairings may also increase variability in behavior. Although this variability can itself be the subject of study (for example, some investigations focus on individual differences), it can also make it difficult to identify true differences and commonalities among bilinguals.

To deal with these challenges, researchers investigate the effects of different factors on performance or behavior and then use statistics to determine whether their findings generalize across individuals (e.g., early vs. late bilinguals) and/or linguistic items (e.g., words, sentences). In this chapter, we review some of the benefits of using a statistical hypothesis-testing approach and give an overview of the statistical tools that are particularly relevant to the study of bilingualism. We first review a formal experimental approach (see also chapters 6 and 7) and contrast this with a corpus analysis approach (chapter 13). Throughout this chapter, we use actual data collected with bilingual samples to exemplify statistical techniques.[1] We also refer the reader to relevant examples in the literature.

[1] The research referred to in the examples was conducted from a psycholinguistic perspective on bilingualism. Therefore, although the term "bilingual" sometimes refers only to individuals who learned two languages during childhood, the example data come from a study in which the term bilingual was applied more broadly to individuals who have achieved proficiency in two languages.

12.2   Experimental Approach

12.2.1   Designing experiments

Before designing an experiment, researchers identify a question and learn as much as possible about previous research related to that question. The literature review is critical in developing questions that are appropriate for study, and for choosing an appropriate method for addressing a particular question. In section 12.5 we address some pitfalls associated with choosing an appropriate question for study. Once a question has been identified, researchers draw a hypothesis about the way they expect a particular manipulation to affect behavior, and from this hypothesis establish predictions about data patterns. One way to test these predictions is to design an experiment. Formal experiments are the only type of investigations that allow the researcher to draw strong cause-and-effect conclusions.[2] Therefore, formal experimentation, though not without its limitations, is preferred over other research methods when the goal is to draw a strong cause-and-effect conclusion. A first step in any investigation is to determine which variables are to be examined.

12.2.2   Types of variables

A *variable* is anything that has a value that can vary, such as the number of years of second language (L2) study, or native language. Variables differ in their types. Some are *continuous*, in that they have values that vary along a continuum, like the number of years of L2 study. Others are *categorical*, in that the options constitute different categories, like native language or part of speech. The types of variables that are studied determine the statistical tools that should be used to analyze the data.

12.2.3   Descriptive statistics

There are several statistics that can be used to describe measures on a population. The most commonly reported descriptive statistics are the *mean*, or average across all individuals on a measure, and the *median*, which is the middle score of a group of scores. The *standard deviation* (SD) indicates how much each score deviates from the mean, on average, and the *range* indicates the range of observed values (minimum to maximum observed score). Typically, means or medians are compared across the conditions of an experiment to determine whether a manipulation has had an effect on performance, but variability (e.g., standard deviation) must be taken into account when deciding whether any observed differences are due to the manipulation or just to chance.

---

[2]   This is predicated on the assumption that certain conditions will be met (see section 12.2.10 on experimental control).

12.2.4   Correlation coefficient

An additional statistic is the *correlation coefficient*, which represents the relationship between two variables. The correlation coefficient ranges from −1 to 1; a correlation coefficient of 0 indicates no relationship and coefficients with larger *absolute values* (numerical values disregarding the sign of plus or minus) represent stronger relationships. Generally speaking, coefficients with absolute values above 0.70 represent strong relationships, those between 0.30 and 0.70 represent moderate relationships, and those lower than 0.30 represent weak relationships; however, a table that takes into account the number of observations on which a correlation is based should be used to determine whether a particular correlation coefficient is *statistically significant*, i.e. unlikely to be due to chance alone. The *sign* (positive or negative) of the correlation coefficient indicates the direction of the relationship; a positive correlation coefficient indicates either that as scores increase on one measure, they also increase on the other, or that as scores decrease on one measure, they also decrease on the other. By contrast, a negative correlation coefficient indicates that as scores decrease on one measure, they increase on the other.

In a study that will form the basis of several examples in this chapter, participants named pictures in their L2, translated words from their first language (L1) to L2 and vice versa, and completed a language history questionnaire (Tokowicz, 1997). In this study, a total of 38 English-Spanish and Spanish-English bilinguals (native English speakers proficient in Spanish, and vice versa) translated single words presented on a computer screen, out loud, as quickly and accurately as possible. We used accuracy on a separate L2 picture-naming task as an objective measure of proficiency. On the *language history questionnaire* (see Tokowicz, Michael, & Kroll, 2004, for a copy), each participant indicated how long she had studied her L2. We examined the relationship between the number of years of L2 study and L2 proficiency. We found a moderate correlation of 0.50, which represents a statistically significant positive relationship, such that as the number of years of L2 study increases, so does L2 proficiency. Note that studies using a correlational approach only describe relationships among variables, and cannot be used to determine cause-and-effect relationships. For this reason, researchers often use formal experimentation in conjunction with or instead of correlational studies.

12.2.5   Identifying variables

In formal experiments, researchers manipulate variables to determine their effects on data patterns. *Independent variables* are those that are manipulated or chosen to vary in a particular way by the experimenter. *Participant variables* are also selected to vary but are specific to individuals. The *dependent variable* is what is measured during the experiment. In a formal experiment, the independent and participant variables are often referred to as *factors*. For categorical variables, the *levels* of each variable can be identified.

For example, in the study mentioned above (Tokowicz, 1997), we examined how accurately bilinguals with varying levels of L2 proficiency translated words from their L1 to their L2. Thus, L2 proficiency was a participant variable, with two levels: less and more. For the purposes of this example, we are assuming that our proficiency measure identified two distinct groups of individuals (less proficient and more proficient). However, if we could not identify two distinct groups of individuals using our measure, we would not consider this to be a factor with two distinct levels; instead we would treat it as a continuous variable that varies along a continuum (see subsection 12.2.9 for more information regarding this issue).

Our independent variable was *cognate status*, which is the degree to which translations (words that mean roughly the same thing across languages) share lexical form, including spelling and sound (see Friel & Kennison, 2001, for a review of how cognate status has been defined in past research). For example, the English-Spanish translation pair color–color would be considered *cognates*, because they share both meaning and spelling/sound. By contrast, the English-Spanish translation pair bed–cama would be considered *noncognates*, because they share meaning but not spelling/sound. The particular questions of interest in this experiment were: (1) whether cognates are translated more accurately than noncognates (the "cognate advantage"), and (2) whether the magnitude of this cognate advantage changes with increased proficiency in the L2.

From these questions and models of bilingual language processing (De Groot, 1992; Kroll & Stewart, 1994), we developed the following predictions. We predicted that cognates would be translated more accurately than noncognates (e.g., De Groot & Nas, 1991). We also predicted that more proficient bilinguals would generally translate words more accurately than less proficient bilinguals. Finally, we predicted that cognate status would have a greater impact on the performance of less proficient bilinguals than on that of more proficient bilinguals, such that the less proficient bilinguals would have a much higher accuracy on cognates than noncognates (a large cognate advantage), whereas more proficient bilinguals would show a smaller cognate advantage.

Experiments with *factorial designs* examine all possible combinations of each level of every independent variable. In our example study, more and less proficient participants translated both cognates and noncognates. Therefore this study had a 2 (relative L2 proficiency: less vs. more) × 2 (cognate status: cognate vs. noncognate) factorial design, crossing L2 proficiency with cognate status, resulting in four different conditions (see table 12.1).

It is important to consider that any given set of variables can be studied using a variety of paradigms. As an illustration, to study how cognates are processed by bilinguals, one could conduct a study using the translation production paradigm, as in our example study, or using the visual lexical decision paradigm in which individuals indicate whether visually presented letter strings are real words in a given language (e.g., Dijkstra, Grainger, & van Heuven, 1999). See Kroll, Gerfen, and Dussias (chapter 7 in this volume) for a review of laboratory paradigms relevant to the study of bilingualism from a psycholinguistic perspective.

Often, convergence from several paradigms is ideal in that it can help to provide a more complete picture of language processing. A classic example of the importance of converging evidence comes from the literature on bilingual memory representation,

Table 12.1: Factorial design crossing L2 proficiency and cognate status

Cognate status	Relative L2 proficiency	
	Less	*More*
Cognates	Less proficient individuals translated cognates	More proficient individuals translated cognates
Noncognates	Less proficient individuals translated noncognates	More proficient individuals translated noncognates

in which experiments that focused on lexical-level tasks suggested that the bilingual's two languages were represented separately in memory (e.g., Gerard & Scarborough, 1989), whereas research that focused on meaning-level tasks suggested that the bilingual's two languages were represented in a shared memory store (e.g., Chen & Ng, 1989). Subsequent research concluded that the two languages were functionally separate at the lexical level but mostly shared at the meaning level (e.g., Snodgrass, 1984). Without converging evidence from different tasks, we would not have as complete an understanding of how the two languages are represented in bilingual memory.

Section summary

- Formal experiments are the only types of investigations that allow the researcher to draw strong cause-and-effect conclusions.
- The *correlation coefficient* represents the relationship between two variables. A correlational research approach can only describe relationships among variables, and cannot be used to determine cause-and-effect relationships.
- Experiments with *factorial designs* examine all possible combinations of each level of every independent variable.
- Convergence from several paradigms is preferable to examining an issue using only one paradigm because it can help to provide a more complete picture of language processing.

12.2.6   Statistical tools

Researchers use statistical tools to test the probability that differences in their data are driven by differences in the values of their independent variables, rather than just by chance. Think of running an experiment as an attempt to gather a sample (or subset) of data from all of the possible data from all possible participants and items over which the researcher intends to generalize. If a manipulation has a true effect on behavior, it will change the observed effects associated with the different levels of the manipulation. So, for example, the *distributions* (collections of values) of accuracy scores may be different for more versus less proficient bilinguals. This would indicate that more and less proficient bilinguals would have different mean accuracies. However, it is possible to find differences between means or medians that were not drawn from different underlying distributions. For example, let us assume that cognate status has no effect on the language processing of more proficient bilinguals. In any given experiment, more proficient bilinguals could show a higher mean accuracy for cognates than for noncognates, even if the true accuracy distributions for cognates and noncognates were the same. This is because when data are collected, researchers randomly sample from an underlying distribution, and just by chance the sample may include more data points from one part of the distribution than another. One way to minimize the chance that this will happen is to make the sample as large as possible, by including a large number of participants and items.

Statistical tests provide a measure of the probability that two samples are from the same or different underlying distributions. The default assumption (the *null hypothesis*) is that the samples are from the same distribution, which indicates that the different levels of the experimental factor did not affect the data patterns. Researchers are justified in rejecting the null hypothesis, or in concluding that their manipulation had a true effect on the data pattern, if a statistical test indicates that there is a very low probability that the samples came from the same distribution.

There are two kinds of errors that can be made when determining whether to reject the null hypothesis. A *Type I error* is the possibility that the null hypothesis is correct, but the researcher rejects it, incorrectly concluding that there is a difference in means, for example. By contrast, a *Type II error* is the possibility that the null hypothesis is not correct, but the researcher accepts it, incorrectly concluding that there is no difference between means. The probability of a Type I error is referred to as the *significance level*, and is set by the experimenter. The convention in psychology is to interpret differences between samples that have less than a 5 percent chance of being drawn from the same distribution as reflecting true differences; this corresponds to a statistical significance level of 5 percent.

When only two means are being compared, a t-test can be used. The two means can come from two measures on the same group of individuals (based on two conditions of an experiment), measures based on two different groups of individuals (based on a participant variable), or one observed measure and another measure to which it is compared (e.g., a hypothesized population mean). Although a researcher may wish to compare several pairs of means, it is inappropriate to use multiple t-tests to compare several pairs of means collected in a single experiment; because each t-test carries with it the chance of making a Type I error, conducting multiple t-tests would inflate the total experiment-wide error rate to above an acceptable level. To compute the experiment-wide error rate, multiply 5 percent by the number of statistical tests. Note that after ten t-tests, you would have a 50–50 chance of making a Type I error!

Because of the restriction on the number of means that can be compared using the t statistic, perhaps the most frequently used analysis technique is the Analysis

Table 12.2: Accuracy data (%) for the sample experiment crossing L2 proficiency and cognate status

	Noncognates (%)	Cognates (%)	
Less proficient	52	72	Cognate effect for less proficient: 20%
More proficient	62	82	Cognate effect for more proficient: 20%
	Proficiency effect for noncognates: 10%	Proficiency effect for cognates: 10%	

of Variance (ANOVA), which does not have this restriction. This technique allows the researcher to investigate the effects of categorical variables (such as cognate status) on data patterns. When a categorical variable influences the dependent measure independent of any effect of any other variable, it is said that there is a *main effect*. When an ANOVA is computed, the resulting statistics, *F* statistics, are used to determine whether the effects are statistically significant.

As an example, in our sample experiment we used an ANOVA to determine the effects of cognate status and relative proficiency on translation accuracy. We found that cognates were translated more accurately than noncognates (see table 12.2), regardless of L2 proficiency. Therefore, there was a main effect of cognate status in our study. We also found a main effect of L2 proficiency, such that more proficient participants translated both cognates and noncognates more accurately than less proficient participants.

ANOVAs are often used because they allow for exploration of potential *interactions* among variables. Interactions come in several forms and occur when the effect of one variable depends on the level of another variable. Sometimes there is a larger effect of one variable at one level of another variable, as would be the case if the cognate advantage were larger for less proficient than for more proficient bilinguals. Other times there is a complete reversal of the effect for the two levels of another variable, as would be the case if less proficient bilinguals more accurately translated cognates, but more proficient bilinguals more accurately translated noncognates. Finally, sometimes there is only an effect of one variable at one level of the other. This would be the case if, for example, less proficient bilinguals showed a cognate advantage, but the more proficient bilinguals showed no difference in their translation of cognates and noncognates. Thus, ANOVAs are useful when interactions among factors may occur. In our study, there were no statistically significant interactions.

12.2.7   Item effects

A common practice in research that uses linguistic items is to calculate the findings in a way that can determine whether the effects generalize across items as well as across participants. In such analyses, the F statistics for both are reported; the analysis by participants is referred to as F_1 and the analysis by items is referred to as F_2 (or they are combined into one measure, *min F'*; Clark, 1973). If the researcher finds a significant effect across participants but not across items, it would indicate that some subset of the items do not show the effect. This information can then be used to determine what item characteristics may be responsible for the variability. In our study, there was no discrepancy between the analyses by participants and by items. There is disagreement among researchers regarding the necessity of computing F_1 and F_2 or *min F'*. The interested reader is referred to a recent review of this issue by Raaijmakers (2003; see also Raaijmakers, Schrijnemakers, & Gremmen, 1999).

12.2.8 *ANOVA design and power*

Researchers who use factorial designs should be careful to keep their designs simple. Consider a researcher who wants to compare the effects of L1 on identifying a grammatical violation in L2. It might seem that the best approach would be to choose many different L1s and many different types of violations in L2, and compare them all. After all, including as many languages and violations as possible will mean that any results will generalize over all of those different kinds of languages and violations. However, including more factors and levels of factors increases the variability in the data, decreasing the power of the experiment to find statistically significant patterns. An experiment testing five different L1s and six different kinds of L2 violations would have to use a 5 × 6 ANOVA to interpret the results, and would require many participants and items to find reliable effects. A better approach would be to narrow the predictions and run multiple individual experiments. For example, the researcher might decide to compare two L1s (e.g., Fender, 2003) and three kinds of L2 variations to test a specific hypothesis about how differences in L1 might affect violation detection. This experiment would have more sensitivity to find a statistically significant effect of a given size. If different results were predicted for different L1 pairs, the researcher could carry out more experiments. An additional advantage of breaking a single experiment testing many levels of a factor into smaller experiments testing fewer levels of those factors is that smaller, simpler experiments are more likely to generate simple and easily interpretable findings.

There are multiple methods that researchers can use to be sure that an experiment has sufficient power or is sufficiently sensitive to detect an effect of a given size. Ideally, a researcher would conduct a power analysis before carrying out an experiment, to determine how many items and participants will be necessary to detect an effect of a specific size given their research design. However, this type of calculation requires that certain information on effect sizes and variability be available before the experiment is run. If it is not possible to base power analyses on information from previous experiments, it may be possible to carry out tests using observed power or effect sizes from an experiment after it is run to verify that sufficient power was attained. For a full treatment of this issue, see Cohen (1988).

12.2.8   Regression

ANOVAs are not appropriate in situations in which the independent variables
under investigation are continuous. An exception to this guideline occurs when the
continuous variable is *bimodally distributed*, or is distributed so that there are two
distinct or qualitatively different groups (i.e., there are two "bumps" in the distribution). Note that some variables can be defined appropriately either in a categorical
or in a continuous way. One such variable is cognate status, which can be defined
in terms of translations with complete spelling overlap versus incomplete overlap
(cognates versus noncognates), or in terms of the relative degree of overlap, as
rated by bilingual speakers (e.g., De Groot & Nas, 1991; Tokowicz, Kroll, De
Groot, & van Hell, 2002). Therefore, in our example experiment involving L2
proficiency, it would have been more appropriate to use a regression analysis
than an ANOVA unless the distribution of L2 proficiency scores were bimodal.
Dichotomizing or categorizing continuous variables can lead either to spurious statistical significance or to failure to find significant effects. Although the probabilities of
these outcomes increase when more than one continuous variable is dichotomized,
the general practice is considered statistically inadvisable (Cohen, 1983; Bissonnette,
Ickes, Bernstein, & Knowles, 1990a, 1990b; Maxwell & Delaney, 1993). Therefore,
for investigations involving continuous variables such as number of years of L2
study, the regression approach should be used because it allows for the investigation of continuous and categorical variables simultaneously (consider also analysis
of covariance).

   Regression analyses allow researchers to predict scores on one measure using
information from one or more other measures. Like correlation coefficients, regression equations express a relationship among variables. De Groot, Dannenburg, and
van Hell (1994) used a regression analysis to determine how much of the variance
in reaction times during translation could be accounted for when a variety of item-
based factors (such as word length, frequency, and concreteness) were taken into
account. An advantage of this approach is that a more representative set of items
can be used, which avoids the need to find groups of words that match each other
on critical dimensions. Further, hierarchical regression analyses can be used to
statistically account for *confounding variables*, which are factors that vary along
with your independent variable but are not of interest in your study (see Cohen &
Cohen, 1988, for a description of this method; see Tokowicz, Kroll, De Groot, &
van Hell, 2002; Tokowicz, Michael, & Kroll, 2004, for examples of this method
applied to research on bilingualism). Confounding variables will be discussed further
in the section on experimental control below (12.2.11).

12.2.10   Data trimming

Outliers are scores that deviate from the distribution of observed scores by virtue
of being either excessively high or excessively low. These scores are of concern to
researchers because they may not reflect the processes that the researcher intends to

investigate. Extremely fast scores may reflect anticipatory processes, whereas extremely slow scores may result from lapses of attention. Additionally, models of language performance (e.g., the Bilingual Interactive Activation Model of visual word recognition, Dijkstra & van Heuven, 1998) normally make predictions about *typical* scores rather than *extreme* scores. Therefore, samples that include extreme scores may not be fair tests of such models. Ratcliff (1993: 511) suggests that "the goal for our models and empirical research should be to account for the middle 85–95% of the observations in our reaction time distributions; these are the data that are most likely to come from the real processes under consideration and also most likely to be critical in testing hypotheses and models." Because outliers increase variance, they also reduce *statistical power*, which is the likelihood that an existing difference will be detected.

Furthermore, scores that lie far from the center of the distribution, even if valid, will have a strong influence on certain statistics such as the mean. For example, imagine that it takes a relatively proficient bilingual speaker one second, on average, to translate a word from her L1 to her L2. On one occasion, however, it takes this bilingual nine seconds to translate a word. One could assume that this extreme observation is due to a lapse of attention, but in reality, she simply could not remember the correct translation for nine seconds. One could argue that this score should remain in the analysis because it reflects the amount of time it *can* take a person to translate a word. Others may argue that even though this score reflects true translation time, it should be removed because it does not reflect *typical* translation time, which is the object of the investigator's interest. Thus, researchers' goals will determine the criteria they should use for identifying outliers.

In general, it would be ideal to remove as many outliers as possible from a dataset while maintaining as many valid scores as possible. This is not easy, especially for observations at the extremes of the distributions, which may be either outliers or valid scores. The problem of deviant observations has been of concern to researchers for more than 150 years (Pierce, 1852). Despite the many years of interest in this problem, there is no consensus on any one method for identifying and removing or replacing outliers. The appropriate choices depend on the researcher's goals and often on convention in the field.

One method that can be used to minimize the effect of outliers on data analysis is to use the median score in analyses rather than the mean score, because the median is less sensitive to extreme values. However, it may not be appropriate to use the median with measures for which there are more likely to be extreme scores in one direction than in the other. For example, although it may sometimes take a bilingual an unusually long amount of time to think of the translation of a word, it is unlikely that the same bilingual will take an extremely short amount of time to translate a word. This is because certain processes necessarily precede the successful translation of a word (reading the to-be-translated word, identifying the translation, etc.).

Another common method for identifying outliers in research on bilingualism involves calculating a "restricted mean." This is accomplished by calculating the mean and SD for a sample, then considering any score that falls more than a set number of SDs away from the mean in either direction an outlier. Researchers typically use values from 2 to 3 SDs to identify outliers using this method. Therefore, if a bilingual typically translates words in 2 seconds, and the standard deviation is 0.5 second, then, using a cutoff of 2 SDs, we would remove scores for any translations that took longer than 3 seconds, or shorter than 1 second (2 ± 1 second). An alternative but related procedure is to replace outliers with the mean or a less extreme observation (e.g., the mean ± 2 SD).[3]

12.2.11   *Experimental control*

When attempting to answer a research question with data, it is vital that researchers consider everything that may contribute to the data pattern. In experiments, researchers generally manipulate one or two independent variables, to determine their effects on the experiment's dependent measure. However, if other properties of the stimuli vary in the same way as the independent variables, these confounding variables may cause differences in the dependent measure. For example, a researcher setting up an experiment to test whether bilinguals are faster at translating cognates than noncognates should make sure that he or she tests cognate and noncognate words that have the same printed word frequency and length. This is important because shorter and more frequent words are processed more quickly than longer and less frequent words (e.g., De Groot, Dannenburg, & van Hell, 1994). If all of the cognate translations were shorter or more frequent than the noncognate translations, then faster performance on cognates might be due to their cognate status, or possibly to the fact that they were processed more quickly as a result of their higher frequency or shorter length.

The best way to make sure data patterns reflect only the intended manipulations in an experiment is to change as little as possible between experimental conditions. In some bilingualism experiments that investigate the influence of previous context or syntactic structure on comprehension, it is possible to take the dependent measure across exactly the same words. For example, consider a study examining whether the L1 of a speaker of English as an L2 determines the amount of difficulty he or she will have in understanding a particular construction in English. One way to test this would be to compare participants' reading times across two English constructions, one that is similar in L1 and L2, and one that is different in L1 and L2. It would be ideal to use constructions that allow the researchers to measure reading times across exactly the same words, because then differences between words could not cause unintended effects in the data. For example, the researcher could measure reading times across the same verb in different constructions.

---

[3]   Although not specific to research on bilingualism, Ulrich and Miller (1994) surveyed articles published in the *Journal of Experimental Psychology: Human Perception and Performance*; they found that of all the papers in the 1992 volume that reported reaction times, the median was used to compensate for outliers 15% of the time, a restricted mean was used another 15% of the time, setting upper and lower criteria ("truncation") was used 26% of the time, and all other methods were used 9% of the time. Somewhat surprisingly, in 37% of the articles, no mention was made of extreme observations at all.

Sometimes it is not possible to design an experiment so that most properties of the stimuli are exactly the same. For example, in our cognate experiment, a particular translation pair can be either a cognate pair or a noncognate pair, but not both. This means that it is necessary to compare two different translation pairs. In this case, researchers use one of two approaches. One approach is to try to match the different stimuli on all dimensions that might affect the dependent measure. As mentioned above, in the cognate experiment, it would be necessary to choose cognate and noncognate stimuli that were equated for frequency and length. A very careful researcher would also equate the stimuli for concreteness (see De Groot, 1992; De Groot, Dannenburg, & van Hell, 1994; Tokowicz & Kroll, 2007) and for the age at which the words were acquired in both L1 and L2 (Bird, Franklin, & Howard, 2001; Hirsh, Morrison, Gaset, & Carnicer, 2003; Izura & Ellis, 2004), because these factors also influence how quickly a word is processed. This approach requires researchers to identify all of the potential factors that might affect their data and control as many of them as possible.

There are situations in which it is not possible to control all potentially confounding variables. For example, studies investigating beginning L2 learners may only have a very small set of L2 vocabulary available to test. There may be so few words that it is not possible to find enough pairs of stimuli that differ along one dimension but are balanced along all others. In situations like these, researchers generally use regression analyses to account for the contributions of multiple factors to a dependent measure. In this case, a researcher would gather measures of the frequency and length of each stimulus, and then enter those and other relevant measures into a regression equation with the experimentally manipulated factor. This equation would indicate whether the manipulated factor has an effect on the data pattern over and above the effects of frequency, length, and the other potentially confounding variables.

When designing a well-controlled experiment, it is important not only to control for or statistically partial out the effects of potentially confounding factors in the stimuli, but also to take into account potentially confounding differences across individuals. Most researchers interested in bilingualism use a Language History Questionnaire to learn as much about their participants' language background as possible (e.g., Li, Sepanski, & Zhao, 2006, with associated online version at http://cogsci.richmond.edu/questionnaire/L2_questionnaire.html). These questionnaires ask participants how many and which languages they know, when they learned them, in what settings they use them, how well they know them, and many other questions related to language experience. Data from these questionnaires can be used to divide participants into groups if language experience is a manipulated variable in the experiment. Or, data from these questionnaires can be used to account for attributes of the participants that could potentially influence the data. For example, L2 proficiency may affect translation performance. To determine whether cognate status affects translation performance even after the effects of proficiency are accounted for, a researcher could do a regression analysis and enter both L2 proficiency and cognate status as predictors of the data patterns.

Although formal experimentation may be the best way to answer many questions about bilingualism, there are other kinds of questions relevant to bilingualism that cannot be answered through experimentation. For example, experimentation would not help a researcher who was interested in subtle characteristics of the social or linguistic environment that might cause a bilingual to switch from one language to another. One reason experimentation would likely fail in this case is that participants in an experiment are rarely fully comfortable and consequently do not act naturally. The kinds of questions posed by an experimenter, or even the social context created by participating in an experiment, may affect the linguistic behavior of the participants. Investigations based on a carefully gathered sample of natural linguistic behavior can avoid these pitfalls. Therefore, some researchers may find that a corpus analysis approach fits their needs better than the experimental approach.

Section summary

- Researchers use statistical tools to test the probability that differences in their data are driven by differences in the values of their independent variables, rather than just by chance.
- T-tests are used to explore differences between two means. Multiple t-tests should not be used to examine many pairs of means because it inflates the experiment-wide error rate. Analyses of variance can be used to explore multiple means, and also potential interactions among variables.
- A common practice in research that uses linguistic items is to calculate the findings in a way that can determine whether the effects generalize across items as well as across participants.
- Dichotomizing or categorizing continuous variables can lead either to spurious statistical significance or to failure to find significant effects.
- *Confounding variables* are factors that vary along with your independent variable but are not of interest in your study. Care should be taken to control for as many potential confounding variables as possible, either experimentally or statistically.
- *Outliers* are scores that deviate from the distribution of observed scores by virtue of being either excessively high or excessively low. Outliers may not reflect the processes that the researcher intends to investigate. A researcher's goals will determine the criteria to use for identifying outliers.

12.3   Corpus Analysis Approach

12.3.1   *Corpora*

Researchers who are interested in studying fully natural linguistic behavior generally use a corpus analysis approach. In this approach, researchers gather large samples of natural-language use with the goal of developing a corpus that is as representative as possible of the language variety that is being investigated. Many corpora are available to researchers free or at low cost. When deciding whether to use an existing corpus as data to address a research question, it is important to consider how, when, and where the corpus was gathered, as these factors will influence its suitability.

Some corpora are comprised of written materials. For example, a corpus of contemporary novels and short stories including Spanish-English code-switching served as the data for Callahan's (2002) study of grammatical constraints on code-switching. Others are gathered by recording (with permission) and transcribing natural interactions between members of a language community. Many of the corpora used to investigate language contact, transfer, and variation have been gathered from carefully conducted interviews. Because many language-contact phenomena are most likely to occur in informal interactions with in-group members who also exhibit the phenomena in question, it is important that interviewers be part of the language community under investigation (Poplack, 1993).

12.3.2   *Child Language Data and Exchange System (CHILDES)*

One of the most important corpora for language researchers is the Child Language Data and Exchange System (CHILDES) corpus, directed by Brian MacWhinney (MacWhinney, 2000) and available on the Internet at http://childes.psy.cmu.edu/. CHILDES has been developed specifically to aid researchers studying language acquisition, and includes transcripts of conversational interactions in languages from English to Portuguese to Tamil. These conversational interactions include ones with normally developing mono- and bilingual children, L2 learners, and children and adults with language disorders. Most of the transcripts in CHILDES are coded in such a way that it is possible to use specialized software (called CLAN) to search for particular words or syntactic structures, or even semantic environments. Certain commands (available within the command window of CLAN) can be used to export summary statistics, including total number of utterances and mean length of utterance (MLU). More sophisticated options allow for analysis of overlap between two utterances, such as those between a parent and a child (Sokolov & MacWhinney, 1990).

One example of a research question that has been tested with CHILDES is how exposure to two languages influences a bilingual child's tendency to use a particular kind of syntactic structure. Paradis and Navarro (2003) used CHILDES to investigate whether a Spanish-English bilingual child's use of null subjects in Spanish might reflect properties of the parents' null subject utterances rather than or in addition to interference between the child's English and Spanish grammars. These researchers searched through transcripts of the linguistic interactions between a Spanish-English bilingual child and her parents, and noted pragmatic/discourse properties of the contexts in which the parents and child did and did not overtly express sentential subjects in Spanish. They found a relationship between parental input and the child's behavior. Because this was a correlational study, the researchers were not able to conclude that particular properties of the parents' input *caused* the child's pattern of null subject use. However, the existence of a relationship suggests that linguistic input should be considered as a potential influence on a child's linguistic patterns. CHILDES is particularly useful for investigating questions about the kind of linguistic input a learner receives, as it provides large samples of actual input. This frees researchers from relying on potentially unreliable estimates from parents or observers.

12.3.3   The importance of quantification in the variationist paradigm

Research on language variation relies crucially on corpus data. Researchers following the variationist paradigm (e.g., Poplack, 1993) *quantify* or investigate the frequencies of use of different forms of the same linguistic construction during normal language use (e.g., *ne ... pas* vs. *Ø ... pas* in French). Such quantification is important because language use can vary not only in type (e.g., a word is used in one dialect but not another), but also in quantity, so that a particular word or construction is used more often by members of certain groups. These preferences for one variation over another can be a source of evidence for language contact and/or transfer (Silva-Corvalán, 1994). For example, Silva-Corvalán (1986) showed that Spanish/English bilinguals in Los Angeles who acquired English earlier and/or were less proficient in Spanish were more likely to use the verb *estar* in some environments in which modern standard Spanish either only allows or strongly prefers the verb *ser* (both verbs are translated as 'to be' in English). The data supporting this finding were frequencies of non-standard usages of *estar* in 40 hours of interviews with 27 Spanish/English bilinguals from a Los Angeles community. Silva-Corvalán hypothesized that this finding could reflect an influence of early exposure to English on language change in the Spanish spoken in this community, but remained agnostic as to whether the influence might have been due to specific properties of English or to more general processes of language evolution. She pointed out that the fact that English has only one word to express a concept like 'to be' could induce a tendency to move towards using a single word in languages with two words for that concept. Alternatively, languages may have a general tendency to evolve towards using a single word to express a concept, and being exposed to more languages earlier might speed this natural evolution.

The statistics applied to corpus data are similar to those used to evaluate experimental data. Because corpus studies often measure frequency, and frequency is a continuous variable, many corpus studies are analyzed using regressions. Studies that categorize utterances and compare whether reliably more utterances fall into one category than another generally are analyzed with either ANOVAs or chi-square "goodness-of-fit" tests. ANOVAs are only appropriate to use when the distribution of data is normal (i.e., follows a bell-shaped distribution), the population variance is homogeneous, and the measurement scale is interval or ratio. Chi-square tests are used whenever any of these criteria is not met. For example, a researcher might investigate the hypothesis that social context affects bilinguals' language choice and predict that in certain kinds of situations bilinguals will never use a more marginalized language. A chi-square test would be appropriate for testing the frequencies of usage of this marginalized language in different contexts, because a prediction of zero occurrences assumes the data are not normally distributed.

12.4 Individual Differences

One of the most interesting questions in bilingualism/L2 learning relates to the issue of variability across individuals. Why are some people better than others at learning an L2? What aspects of the individual influence their ability to learn or use a second or third or fourth language (DeKeyser, 1991; Tokowicz, Michael, & Kroll, 2004)? One of the possible ways to study such variability while still taking a group approach is to form groups of individuals who vary on a particular dimension. Some of the dimensions that have been used to study individual differences are cognitive skill measures such as working-memory span (e.g., Michael, 1998; Tokowicz, Michael, & Kroll, 2004; see Michael & Gollan, 2005, for a review of research on this topic). It is also possible to use a more case-based approach to examine the variability across individuals (e.g., DeKeyser, 1991).

12.5 Pitfalls in Selecting Research Questions

Statistics are only as good as the research questions and data to which they are applied. For example, in the study of cognate status, a careful review of the literature would lead an interested researcher to the conclusion that there are many ways in which cognate status has been defined in past research (Friel & Kennison, 2001). For example, some researchers consider only identically spelled translations to be cognates. However, a researcher who is interested in how language processing is speeded by overlap of translations may not get a complete view of this issue if she uses this restricted definition of cognate status. For example, there are some regular ending changes that occur between Spanish and English (e.g., -dad to -ty). If this information is taken into account, translation pairs such as universidad–university would be considered cognates; whether these types of translations are considered to be cognates will impact the conclusions that are ultimately drawn from the investigation. Although this is just one example, it demonstrates the importance of taking the researcher's goals into account when *operationalizing* variables, or devising explicit definitions applied to variables in research.

In addition to issues of operationalization, statistics can be applied to data that are not able to address the questions of interest for a variety of reasons. One example would be looking at the total number of deaths that occur in two different towns. You could conduct a t-test to examine whether there is a statistically significant difference between the two, but it would not be meaningful unless you took into account how many people lived in each town. An example more relevant to the study of bilingualism would be the use of code-switched speech in two communities. It would be possible to use a corpus to quantify the number of code-switches that occur during interlocutions between community members in each of the two communities, and then conduct a t-test to examine whether more code-switches occur in one of the two communities. However, without knowing whether the two communities are bilingual (or the extent to which the community members are proficient in the two languages), this would not be a meaningful question to ask.

The most important source of information in developing a good research question is a thorough literature review. Only by surveying the research that has already been conducted on a topic can a researcher identify the majority of potential confounding variables in research and most clearly articulate a research question that can be operationalized and addressed using the quantitative and statistical methods outlined here.

Section summary

- Researchers who are interested in studying fully natural linguistic behavior generally use a corpus analysis approach. In this approach, researchers gather large samples of natural language use with the goal of developing a corpus that is as representative as possible of the language variety that is being investigated.
- Many corpora are available to researchers free or at low cost, including the CHILDES database, which includes conversational interactions in many languages and which can be searched for particular words or syntactic structures.
- Research on language variation relies crucially on corpus data; in this paradigm, researchers quantify or investigate the frequencies of use of different forms of linguistic construction during normal language use.

12.6   Conclusions

In sum, a wide range of experimental and statistical methods are available to researchers interested in studying bilingualism. The most appropriate combination of methods to answer a particular research question will depend on the nature of both the data and any potential confounds. In this chapter, we have provided a general overview of some of the most common statistical methods that are used in the study of bilingualism; however, we have not covered all of the constraints that datasets must meet to satisfy the assumptions of different statistical tests. Therefore, we refer the reader to more advanced statistics texts to learn more about the most appropriate methods to ask and answer research questions in bilingualism.

Further reading

Specific to this chapter

Cohen, J. (1988) *Statistical Power Analysis for the Behavioral Sciences*. Hillsdale, NJ: Erlbaum.

Cohen, J. H. and P. Cohen (1988) *Applied Multiple Regression/Correlation Analysis for the Behavioral Sciences*. 2nd edn. Hillsdale, NJ: Lawrence Erlbaum.

MacWhinney, B. (2000) *The CHILDES Project: Tools for Analyzing Talk*. 3rd edn. *Vol. 2: The Database*. Mahwah, NJ: Lawrence Erlbaum Associates.

General reference books

Ritchie, W. C. and T. K. Bhatia (eds.) (1996) *Handbook of Second Language Acquisition*. San Diego, CA: Academic Press.

Doughty, C. J. and M. H. Long (eds.) (2003) *The Handbook of Second Language Acquisition*. Malden, MA: Blackwell.

Fabbro, F. (1999) *The Neurolinguistics of Bilingualism: An Introduction*. Hove, Sussex: Psychology Press.

Kroll, J. F. and A. M. B. De Groot (eds.) (2005) *Handbook of Bilingualism: Psycholinguistics Approaches*. New York: Oxford University Press, pp. 389–407.

13 Data Banks and Corpora

Ad Backus

13.1 Introduction

This chapter is about the corpus-based study of bilingualism. It is therefore concerned with those aspects of bilingualism that can be studied by looking at actual language use, since the nexus between bilingualism and corpus-based research naturally limits our interest to precisely those aspects. The field thus defined roughly corresponds to what is known as contact linguistics: the study of what happens to a language when it is in contact with another language. This excludes many other useful and worthwhile research considerations, such as the societal and educational issues that surround bilingualism, the study of socio-psychological attitudes of and towards bilinguals, and the question what determines when bilinguals use which language. Such topics are generally analyzed on the basis of other types of data, such as questionnaires, document analysis, or interviews. Instead, this chapter relates to what can be investigated through the study of how people actually talk in everyday conversation. For further information on approaches to bilingualism from a conversational perspective see Cashman (chapter 16 in this volume). This includes first and foremost the phenomena of code-switching and interference.

I will first explain why these are the bilingual phenomena that are preferably studied by making use of corpora. In the process, I will introduce some of the strong points of corpus linguistics, which is a field of study in itself, but may be best thought of as a supporting discipline for contact linguistics. Section 13.3 goes into the methodological requirements for corpora, and discusses in very practical terms some of the things you need to be aware of before you start building one, and how you go about it. Finally, section 13.4 will illustrate the use of corpora through some brief sample analyses from my own study of contact-induced change, using a corpus of Turkish as spoken by the immigrant Turkish community in the Netherlands.

13.2   Bilingual Phenomena that can be Investigated in a Corpus

Most studies of speech-based research questions in the field of bilingualism, i.e. questions that are answered by looking at people's actual language use rather than, for instance, their answers to questionnaires, are based on some sort of corpus. However, virtually all of these corpora are fairly rudimentary, in the sense that they were collected for one specific research project, with one specific research question in mind, and usually with limited funding. They tend to be small, hard for other researchers to get access to, and without much annotation, all characteristics that are generally held to be the opposite of what a good corpus has to offer. For instance, my own corpus of bilingual Turkish-Dutch speech, which I used for my dissertation (Backus, 1996), is hard to use for other people, not because I refuse to give them access to my data, but because the pressure to finish my dissertation on time kept me from adding such basics as translations, let alone glosses. In addition, since my research questions (basically "What is the structure of Turkish-Dutch code-switching?") didn't require much in the way of quantitative analysis, I didn't bother putting the transcripts in a standard format (such as CHAT) but developed my own tailor-made transcription and annotation system, just right for what I needed to get out of the data, but hard to use for outsiders. I'm sure this account will sound familiar to many readers.

   The point is, organizing your data as a corpus has two big advantages: it improves the possibilities for your own research, and it is beneficial to your colleagues. The crucial question you should first ask yourself is: to what extent does corpus organization help me do my analyses? This question cannot be answered in a straightforward way, because it depends on what you want to know. I will get back to it in section 13.4, where I will argue that corpus tools improve your quantitative analysis and facilitate your qualitative analysis.

   The second advantage is relevant for the whole of your field. Ideally, your corpus is fully transcribed, fully annotated, and linked to corpus software that allows easy searches and statistical computations of all kinds of features. However, this situation won't present itself, primarily because you don't have the time to do all that. Many corpora in the field of bilingualism are built up as part of doctoral work. They contain the data that are needed to answer a very specific research question. The individual researcher does not have the time, or the expertise usually, to get the corpus into such a state that it can be released to the wider academic community. If your supervisor and your career opportunities require you to prioritize, and first get a good dissertation out into the world, you would be wasting your time if you annotated your data for aspects you are not interested in. Initial transcription of one hour of speech takes about ten hours, and much more if you add careful phonetic or pragmatic detail. Annotation will take another big chunk of your time. If your time is limited, you may just want to transcribe those portions of the data that are most useful for you.

However, what you can and should do is observe a few guidelines that allow those other researchers to later build on your work and adapt the corpus to suit their needs as well as yours. While researchers come and go, and the compiler of an original corpus may move on to bigger and better things, the data are often very well suited to other analyses, but if they are unavailable, new researchers will have to collect new data. And although every linguist should get some training in fieldwork, it seems foolish to let all those data that already have been collected go to waste. The long-term solution to this problem would be that people in the field join forces and link various separate data collections into a bigger database. This may be feasible in the long run for some of the well-studied contact situations, such as Spanish in the US, Punjabi or Bengali in the UK, Turkish in northwestern Europe, or Arabic-French contact. However, it would require quite a bit of coordination: totally unrelated researchers will have to be convinced to follow the same guidelines, to adhere to certain standards that ensure that those data remain accessible. At the same time, these shouldn't put too much of an extra burden on the poor soul who gets the corpus started. Extra fieldwork to collect additional data will often be necessary anyway, and each addition makes the corpus a better one. Eventually, we might end up with a corpus that has been of use to many people and, because of all the adaptations that have been made to it in the process, will be of even more use to yet other researchers. Minimum standards are the focus of section 13.3. In the remainder of this section I will introduce some of the questions that a corpus can help analyze.

The features in which bilingual speech differs from monolingual speech are: (1) the use of lexical material from two or more languages (code-switching) and (2) the use of structural (e.g. grammatical, phonological, semantic) features not found in or typical of the speech of monolingual speakers of the languages, and perhaps taken from the other language (interference).

Code-switching and interference are generally studied in total separation from each other. The researchers involved tend to be different ones, and they use different datasets and different methods and theories. Yet, there are good reasons to synthesize research, since all the phenomena mentioned are instances of the same phenomenon, contact-induced language change (Backus, 2005). Code-switching brings in new words (while pushing others out of use) and is thus responsible for lexical changes. Interference patterns can become conventional and in the process become the new grammatical norm. At that point, the interference has of course ceased to be interference: the language has simply changed its structure. In addition, there is the empirical point that code-switching and interference usually co-occur in conversational data from bilingual speakers. Any given corpus of bilingual data is likely to include all of the following:

- a certain amount of code-switching between sentences (alternation)
- mixing of the two languages within a single clause (insertion)
- other patterns of mixing/switching
- deviant word-order patterns
- words used with deviant meanings

- unconventional word combinations
- increased preference for certain ways of combining clauses (and decreased preference for other ways).

The last four are instances of structural interference, and the examples can be multiplied at will.

Be that as it may, most of the time our interest is limited to just one or two of these phenomena, and usually to one language pair. Typical leading research questions could be any of the following (and the list can be extended indefinitely; these have all been taken from the vast literature on language contact):

On code-switching:

- What is the structure of Malay-English code-switching?
- How are French nouns incorporated into the nominal structure of Moroccan Arabic?
- How are Dutch verbs incorporated into Turkish?
- How are Russian discourse markers used in Uzbek?
- What Spanish elements are used in everyday Otemi speech?

On structural borrowing:

- What Chinese structural elements do we find recreated in Colloquial Singaporean English?
- Have Tiwi structural elements found their way into the English spoken by Tiwi people?
- To what extent has Basque word order been influenced by Romance languages?
- Do Spanish speakers in the US use more overt subject pronouns than monolingual speakers in Mexico or Puerto Rico?

Absent from this list is another set of questions often asked of bilingual data: why do people code-switch? For more detailed discussions of bilingual data see Nortier and Gardner-Chloros (chapters 3 and 4 in this volume). Though such questions are also investigated on the basis of a corpus of bilingual speech, I will leave this subfield out of consideration, on the grounds that analyses generally focus on the detailed transcription of isolated key portions of the corpus. They don't focus on quantitative overviews of the entire dataset, and for good reasons: it would be a gigantic task to annotate an entire corpus for pragmatic functions of utterances *and* do detailed conversational analyses on the mass of data that results. Obviously that doesn't mean it shouldn't be a point of attention for the future but, for the moment, corpus tools are most suitable for the structural and lexical issues in bilingualism research.

Section summary

For various reasons it would be good if bilingualism researchers would pay more attention than has been customary to organizing their data in the form of corpora. There is always a somewhat uneasy discrepancy, however, between the requirements of a good corpus and available time. Luckily, it is not too time-consuming to stick to a few basic rules. Bilingualism phenomena that lend themselves well to corpus-based research are code-switching and structural interference.

13.3   Building a Corpus

In an ideal world, we would be able to think up a research question and then download a freely available corpus on which we can perform the analysis we need to do to answer that question. Such a situation, unfortunately, will almost never exist if the research question has anything to do with bilingualism. This section will tell you what you can do to improve this situation.

First, however, it is perhaps useful to look for the reasons this situation is the way it is. The commercial value of bilingualism is limited; there are no dictionaries or grammars of bilingual speech, so it is not in the interests of big publishers to fund the same type of projects for bilingual speech that they fund for, for example, spoken English. The study of bilingualism is firmly rooted in the sociolinguistic tradition of concern with victimized and marginalized groups. Funding for this type of research comes almost exclusively from public money, which is usually not in the magnitude required for building a large corpus. As a result, large corpora of bilingual speech don't exist.

Of the available corpora, most are useless for bilingualism research. There are many monolingual corpora available, either free or for a fee, mostly downloadable from the Internet or available on CD-ROM (see the various introductory textbooks to corpus linguistics for an overview, e.g. Kennedy, 1998). Most of them have been set up with the intention of allowing academic users around the world to access them and perform all kinds of useful analyses. This means the compilers will have been aware of the minimum requirements to make the corpus easy to use. If you want to build your own corpus of bilingual speech, it's a good idea to visit the websites of a few existing monolingual corpora and see for yourself how the data are presented. Your time and funding probably won't allow you to replicate what you see, but you will certainly get some good ideas. Table 13.1 summarizes the main differences between monolingual and bilingual corpora.

There is at least one exception to the rule that monolingual corpora are not useful for students of bilingualism. In the International Corpus of English, subcorpora of Englishes as spoken in East Africa, India, Singapore, and other places are

Table 13.1: Differences between monolingual and bilingual corpora

Monolingual corpora	Bilingual corpora
large	small
easy to get access to	hard to get access to
annotated	usually not annotated
suited for general use	suited for specific use only

included, giving the student of bilingualism an excellent opportunity to study the effects of one major kind of contact-induced language change: the changes that occur as a result of language shift (Thomason, 2001). When people start using the former second language as their primary language (or eventually often as their only language), the result may be different from the majority variety of that language, or the original target of second language acquisition. In immigration contexts we then speak of ethnolects, in postcolonial contexts of new varieties (e.g. the Outer Circle Englishes, cf. Schneider, 2004).

The only two sets of corpora I'm aware of that contain the type of bilingual speech that researchers of code-switching and structural borrowing work with are the various corpora collected by Shana Poplack and associates, most notably the Ottawa-Hull corpus of French-English bilingual speech (see Poplack, Sankoff, & Miller, 1988), and the collection of samples contained in the LIDES database, set up by a group of researchers worried about the lack of accessibility of the wealth of bilingual corpora that are out there, languishing in researchers' desks and bookcases (cf. LIPPS Group, 2000, which contains a whole manual); references to the relevant websites are given in the Further Reading section at the end of this chapter. Particularly, Shana Poplack must be singled out as a figure of influence, since she was clearly ahead of the times in her emphasis on accountability: whatever one says about bilingual speech must be based on a corpus of data that is open to inspection by others and that allows the researcher to establish patterns of usage rather than just a collection of interesting examples. Another initiative that was launched in the Netherlands recently (by Pieter Muysken) is the Dutch Bilingual Database, which will contain the digitized sound files and transcripts of all kinds of bilingual data from many different language pairs collected since the early 1980s. It's likely that similar initiatives are being undertaken in other parts of the world. Finally, the CHILDES data-base, on which LIDES is based, is a data bank of child language acquisition data, and it includes data from children growing up with two languages simultaneously (MacWhinney, 1995).

The rest of this section describes the process of corpus building, highlighting the things you should pay attention to in the planning and execution stages. Most of the information can also be found in handbooks of corpus linguistics, but I will focus on the limitations imposed on most of the readers of this book, who are interested in bilingualism and thus cannot make use of an existing corpus, and who are not part of a big team or consortium and thus don't have a big budget or much time.

13.3.1 Basic requirements

Bilingualism studies normally deal with spoken data. For obvious reasons, it is much more difficult to compile a spoken corpus than a written one: spoken language needs to be transcribed, while written data can generally simply be copied from some electronic source to the corpus (see Turell & Moyer, chapter 11 in this volume).

When contemplating the building of a corpus, you need to make a few decisions beforehand. You need to decide, first, on the kind of data you want to use and, second, on the kinds of analyses these data should allow. Thinking these things through minimizes regret later, and maximizes accessibility of the corpus for later work by you or by other researchers. The most important question to answer is: what do I want to do with this corpus? That is, even if you take the goal of comparability and longevity seriously, you still are likely to have an immediate goal in mind for compiling it. That goal is the answering of your research question. The corpus should be compiled in such a way that it allows you to do that. Having said that, there are certain universal guidelines you should follow.

13.3.1.1 Representativeness

Though representativeness is a serious and tricky concern for the huge monolingual corpora that are used to base dictionaries on, it is a lesser one for corpora set up to deal with bilingual speech. This is because we want to know the characteristics of a phenomenon rather than to find out how an entire speech community talks. Guidelines regarding informant selection are given in Lanza, chapter 5 in this volume, but it should be obvious that, if you are doing a study on code-switching, you may want to create circumstances in data collection that are especially conducive to producing bilingual speech, even though your informants may also have many encounters in everyday life in which they stay in one language. None of this is a problem, as long as there is a general introduction to the corpus in which the initial goals and the circumstances of data collection are clearly explained.

A concern for representativeness can nevertheless be built into the corpus plan by creating the right circumstances for later elaboration of the corpus, by you or others. Slowly but surely, by filling in the gaps in informant selection, the corpus can become more and more representative of the community of whose speech it is a sample. Obviously, as with any other form of research making use of informants, as many background characteristics of the informants as possible should be noted down and made available along with the data.

13.3.1.2 Size

The spoken part of the British National Corpus contains 10 million words, and that's only 10 percent of the total. It's obvious that this is an unattainable figure for the lone investigator of bilingual speech in a given bilingual community who attempts to set up a corpus sampling that speech. Luckily, it isn't necessary either, at least not for most of the research questions we tend to ask. Large corpora are especially useful for practices that need access to the usage of individual content words, such as lexicography. Individual content words don't occur frequently, so a corpus needs to be large to maximize the chances of encountering these words a good number of times. Bilingual lexicography, as far as I know, does not exist, except in the guise of isolated observations of "odd" usage of particular words by bilinguals (cf. Otheguy, 1992, on Spanish *atras* 'back' in US varieties of Spanish).

The design of your corpus should be guided by two factors: some minimum of general corpus-building guidelines, and your research questions. The first set of factors functions as a non-negotiable baseline; letting your research questions guide you in what you actually incorporate in the way of transcripts and annotations protects you from doing things that you don't have time for and that have no direct use for you. These principles have consequences for the size of your corpus. For instance, if you are researching phenomena that occur in virtually every sentence, such as word order, determiners and other functional elements, or phonological features, your corpus doesn't have to be all that large. If your research question is about the way foreign verbs are embedded, on the other hand, you may want to collect a lot of data to ensure that enough relevant cases occur, but decide to only transcribe those portions of the data in which the foreign verbs occur.

13.3.1.3   Storage and maintenance

There are few things as frustrating as losing your original data, or the sinking feeling that you have just overwritten the latest version of a transcript with an old one, losing all that annotation work you've been doing the last hour. It is important to take steps that minimize these dangers. In the case of spoken language, the originals are generally minidisks, cassette tapes, etc. Make sure you store these "masters" safely somewhere, digitize them as soon as possible, work only from the copies, and develop a system that keeps track of where everything is. When making a transcript, for instance, it is safest to work from a digitized sound file (e.g. in "wav" format) rather than directly from your minidisk or cassette tape. Sound files take up a lot of disk space, though, so they are best stored on a server if you have access to space on one, and/or on separate CD-ROMs. Apart from the sound files, your corpus is unlikely to be too big for your personal computer, so storage shouldn't be a problem. Even then, though, it's important to have backups stored elsewhere. See Clemente, chapter 10 in this volume, for further technical advice on recording.

It is also advisable to use a standardized system that documents what your corpus consists of and what the relevant features are of the individual recordings and transcripts. There are many ways of doing this, but it is best to use software specially made for this task by professionals. The software I use myself is the IMDI Metadata system developed at the Max Planck Institute in Nijmegen (www.mpi.nl/tools). Keeping track of master tapes, originals, and copies, and the last versions worked on, can be a real challenge, so taking some time to learn a system such as IMDI will be worth the effort. It is one more thing future users of your corpus will be grateful to you for. Systems such as IMDI work with predefined fields and pull-down menus, making it less likely that you forget to record essential information about a given recording, such as how old the participants are or what particular language competences they have.

Metadata software organizes your data for you in some sort of hierarchical structure. IMDI, for instance, offers the following features: each recording session gets a unique name; there are standard formats for (1) descriptions of the interaction (including which languages are used and roughly how often), (2) details about the recording and the transcription (for instance how accurate the transcript is and what kind of annotation is available), and (3) descriptions of the informants (including pull-down menus for all kinds of background factors); and the IMDI file can be linked to the corresponding sound file and to the transcript. In the case of IMDI, it is also possible to use a browser that searches the IMDI files, so that it becomes very easy to extract all recordings or transcripts that include, for example, informants who are second-generation immigrants.

13.3.1.4 *Transcription*

Linguistic analysis of conversational data usually requires the raw data to first pass through the filter of transcription. Transcripts – written-out verbatim reports of what is said during the recordings – are the main work documents for analysts. Transcription is, therefore, very important, and is discussed separately (see Turell and Moyer, chapter 11 in this volume). Luckily, fully developed systems are available (e.g. CHAT or ELAN) that take many tricky decisions out of your hands and make it easier for others to work with your transcripts. The LIDES manual mentioned earlier has added some conventions to CHAT that make it more useful for bilingual conversations between adults, though the improvements are limited to the possibility of adding a language tag to every word. These make it possible for the associated statistical software (CLAN) to compute the relative contributions of the two languages to the conversations.

An important point to keep in mind is that the informants' privacy has to be respected. This is certainly an issue once transcripts are published or made available on-line, and the problem looms especially large when sound files are to be made available. It is advisable to ask informants to sign a written form of permission and allow them to veto any fragments that should then be taken out of at least the publicly available portion of the corpus. However, even if only transcripts are going to be made available, you should get into the habit of immediately anonymizing (i.e. substituting false names for) the people who appear on the tapes, both those speaking and those spoken about.

13.3.1.5 *Annotation*

Just as important as transcription is annotation. This is really the first step in analysis, since it aids you in extracting those portions of the data that are relevant to your research question. The big monolingual corpora tend to have two kinds of annotation: morphological coding (often called "tagging") and syntactic coding (often called "parsing"). Tags identify all words in the transcript as belonging to a particular part-of-speech class (e.g. "noun," "discourse marker," "tense marker"), while syntactic annotation identifies subjects, direct objects, etc. For many languages, automatic tagging and parsing is possible, with the help of specially designed software that can attach the correct codes in most cases (a correct score of over 95 percent is usually what is aimed for). These codes are useful for all kinds of basic analyses, such as frequency counts of different parts of speech, different word orders and constructions, and many other things, but these tend not to be so prominent among the research questions students of bilingualism are interested in. Still, some familiar research questions do call for tagging and/or parsing: say you want to know at what sentential positions foreign words occur in code-switching, then it is a big help if your corpus allows you to extract all foreign words in subject position, in direct object position, etc. Similarly, if you have a tagged and parsed corpus of Wolof speech that includes a lot of French nouns, you can easily have the software compute the proportion in which French nouns co-occur with various Wolof functional elements (e.g. articles, plural markers), and compare it to the proportion in which Wolof nouns co-occur with these elements.

There is software that allows automatic tagging and parsing for various languages. Such software uses pre-compiled vocabulary lists in which words (including inflected forms) are identified as nouns, verbs, etc., and attaches the appropriate label to the words in the corpus. Handy as this may be, it is only worthwhile if the accuracy rate is over 95 percent or so, since otherwise there will be so many errors that have to be corrected by hand that it doesn't really save much time. Automatic taggers exist for many languages, though mainly for the most widely used ones. Since one of these languages is generally at least one of those involved in code-switching corpora (normally the embedded language), the use of such taggers should always be contemplated. It goes without saying that it is important that the corpus has few spelling errors, as misspelled words will not be recognized by the tagging program. Proofreading 1,000 words takes about 45 minutes to an hour for a native speaker, so for most individual corpora this should not be a big problem.

Don't expect too much from software beyond these common coding tasks, though. Interesting research questions are those that have not been investigated before; almost by definition that means there are no ready-made annotation tools available for semi-automatic analysis. You'll have to develop these yourself. If your research question is something like "How many Turkish clauses in my Turkish-Dutch corpus preserve Turkish SOV word order and how many of the Dutch ones preserve Dutch verb-second word order?," then you probably want to annotate your data for word order. There are still good reasons for morphological tagging and morphosyntactic parsing, certainly if software is available: they allow for better quantitative and qualitative analysis. Quantitative analysis is made easier to do and more accurate, and extraction of all relevant cases that you may want to look at more closely for qualitative analysis is made possible.

Below are lists of aspects of bilingual data you could annotate if you were interested in the sorts of questions listed in section 13.2. They can also be gleaned from such basic works on language contact as Myers-Scotton (1997) and Muysken (2000) on code-switching, and Thomason (2001) and Johanson (2002) on contact-induced change. For code-switching (the combination of material from two or more languages), you might want to annotate:

- type of code-switching: insertion or alternation
- type of insertion: single word or larger chunk
- type of inserted word: noun, verb, discourse marker, etc.
- type of inserted chunk
- presence or absence of morphosyntactic integration
- matrix language for the insertion at hand
- type of alternation: at sentence boundary, at clause boundary, etc.
- pragmatic function of the alternation.

For contact-induced change (the combination of structural features from two or more languages), the list might read as follows:

- word order
- unconventional constructions, lexical choices, word combinations, etc.
- pronunciation and intonation characteristics
- presence or absence of overt subject pronouns
- and many more.

While the coding categories for code-switching phenomena are relatively easy to enumerate, there are probably hundreds of structural phenomena one may wish to annotate. Realistically, it's best to deduce carefully from your research questions what aspects of the data you need to single out for further investigation. Those are the ones you need to annotate. Then you select a random portion of your data for a pilot phase, in which you try out an initial version of your annotation instrument. The hard part is to arrive at the right level of detail: your annotation needs to provide useful information, but should not be so detailed that you get bogged down in difficult decisions all the time.

Categories can always be further subdivided. For example, researchers interested in alternational code-switching will not limit themselves to noting those instances in the data where some form of alternation is going on: they will want to investigate what kinds of alternations there are, when they occur, what their characteristics are, etc. A good rule of thumb is that if you find yourself thinking hard about how to code many of the instances that you are looking at, you're probably working at too detailed a level. In such cases, devising an annotation scheme and annotating your data amounts to doing the actual linguistic analysis: by the time you're finished you have no doubt accumulated all the knowledge you set out to gather. Chances are, however, that you will realize halfway through that the coding categories you've been using are not quite the right ones, which would mean you'd have to go back to the beginning and start all over again. When you find yourself in the position of having to start annotating for a certain category from scratch, it's best to follow the following steps (these will be illustrated briefly in section 13.4.2):

- Work out a rough coding scheme.
- Select a small portion of the data for a pilot phase.
- Annotate this portion and adjust the coding scheme as you go.
- Evaluate your work and settle on a coding scheme that is relatively easy to use (a useful guiding principle is that a student assistant should be able to use the coding scheme without too much instruction; otherwise, the scheme is too difficult and, therefore, the category you're working on is not amenable yet to annotation).
- Write down the coding scheme, which then becomes a real annotation manual.

13.3.1.6 Release

An annotated corpus is ready for analysis, as will be shown in the next section. An important principle of corpus linguistics is that if the corpus is ready for analysis by you it must also be ready for analysis by others. This is made possible by releasing the corpus. Normally, you do this after your initial study (e.g. your dissertation) has been completed.

Time limitations aside, there are some basic requirements that you should adhere to when presenting your corpus to the outside world. Ideally, the following will be available:

- information on the structure of the corpus
- metadata (basic information about the informants, recordings, etc.)
- transcripts
- sound files
- translations in a major language (e.g. English)
- glosses
- language tagging
- morphological tagging
- annotation.

The first three are absolutely necessary; inclusion of the others would be nice. Inclusion of sound files makes it possible for others to transcribe as yet untranscribed conversations or to improve on the existing transcripts (e.g. by adding phonetic detail). Glosses – the morpheme-by-morpheme translation of every element in the original – are needed for many types of analysis, and are a necessary part of the corpus if it is to be used by non-specialists in the language. Language tags, morphological (parts of speech) tags and morphosyntactic annotation were discussed earlier in this section. It must be emphasized that only the first three categories are necessary: even a corpus containing just these elements is very useful, since others can fill in the missing elements at a later point in time. In fact, even corpora containing all the mentioned elements can always be improved by further annotation.

> **Section summary**
>
> Big corpora of bilingual speech hardly exist, in contrast to the ready avail-
> ability of huge monolingual corpora of many languages, quite often based on
> written language. You will often have to build your own corpus, and for this,
> it is useful to adhere to some basic requirements. Be sure that background
> characteristics of the informants are retrievable, store the data in such a way
> that future colleagues can add to the work (new data, new transcriptions,
> new annotations, corrections), and be clear about what transcripts and
> annotations are available. It is not necessary to transcribe and annotate
> everything: just do what you need to do to get your work done and create
> the opportunities for others to further improve the corpus at a later date.

13.4   Possibilities for Analysis

The initial step in analysis will likely be to search for relevant passages, relevant,
that is, to the research question you are interested in. Retrieval software is needed
for this task, since it would be too time-consuming to read through the entire
corpus first and manually extract everything that is relevant. The promise of
automatic retrieval was the main motivation for annotation in the first place.
Most programs of course include a simple search function, and in some cases that
might work perfectly well, but in many cases possibilities are greatly improved if
software can be used that can not only search, but also provide you with, for
instance, concordances, frequencies, and preferably also some easy display options
(e.g. if you want to quickly extract a sentence for use as an example in your paper,
complete with glosses and translation, but without any of the annotation and other
markup features).

There follow two examples of corpus-based bilingualism research, one on code-
switching and one on interference, both taken from my own work.

13.4.1   Example 1: Code-switching between Turkish and Dutch

The code-switching corpus is from the early nineties and consists of the transcripts
of seven recordings made on a tape-recorder (cf. Backus, 1996). The recordings
featured seven different social networks in three different cities in the Netherlands.

The transcripts were not written into a pre-structured transcription format (e.g.
CHAT). There were various reasons for this, ranging from the prosaic circumstance that I didn't know much about what was available, to the practical problem
that existing formats were either not very easy to use with the sorts of data I had
(bilingual unstructured conversations with more than two participants – the LIDES

initiative had not yet been launched) and so required all kinds of adjustments, or they required the entry of many details that I wasn't interested in, given my research question. This mode of working fit me fine for the task at hand, but made it very hard to use the data afterwards for other analyses, either by me or by somebody else. There were no glosses, just rough translations. There was no formal indication of what was Turkish and what Dutch, just indications of where the language switched. There were annotations, though, coding all kinds of aspects of code-switching. Along with a coding key, they allowed me to search for these aspects. However, since they were entered into WordPerfect (later converted to Word), not much more than searching could be done with them. I could not, for instance, extract all relevant examples of a certain phenomenon to a separate file, and any count of tokens had to be done manually.

The transcripts were also not formally organized into a larger structure, a database. This was, again, fine for my purposes, since I pretty much knew my data by heart, and the size seemed manageable anyway, but, obviously, it makes them inaccessible, or at least hard to access, to outside researchers.

Despite this litany of shortcomings, there were, of course, things that could and can be done with this corpus. With the ordinary Search function that any word processor makes available, I could look for instances of particular types of annotation.

Some of the categories I could search for are given in table 13.2, along with an indication of why one would want to search for them.

The nice thing about annotation is that it can always be extended as new research questions are brought to bear on the same set of data. At later stages, for instance, I have added codes for whether or not a switch that contains more than a word consists of a lexical chunk, i.e. a unit that happens to consist of more

Table 13.2: Annotating code-switching

Searchable annotation	*Useful for determining, among other things*
monolingual Turkish turns	relative contribution of the languages
monolingual Dutch turns	relative contribution of the languages
bilingual turns	relative contribution of the languages
instances of code-switching	frequency of code-switching
code-switching at turn boundaries	speakers' behavior at turn boundaries
code-switching at the start of a sentence	degree to which code-switching takes place at particular junctures
switches to Dutch	properties of switches to Dutch
switches to Turkish	properties of switches to Turkish
intrasentential code-switching	dominant type of code-switching
extrasentential code-switching	degree to which code-switching is done outside sentence structure
insertion of nouns, verbs, adjectives, etc.	properties of noun insertion, verb insertion, etc.

than one word (e.g. a collocation, an idiom), and for the pragmatic functions an utterance has.

It is important to remind oneself that corpus techniques are a research tool: they don't take the place of interpretation and explanation. Having the computer give you all insertions of foreign nouns, and perhaps also give you the total breakdown of how often these appear in what syntactic positions, does not mean your job is finished. You will want to know something about those inserted nouns: how frequent are they in relation to all nouns that are used in the corpus, what semantic features do they have, are they syntactically integrated in particular ways, why are they found in particular positions, and what do these and other things tell us about code-switching? Many of these issues can be investigated using still more refined corpus tools (mainly by adding new annotation), but the final question can only be answered by taking a long hard look at your results, comparing them to what you know about code-switching from other people's work, and evaluating them. That work has to be done by your brain, not by your computer.

13.4.2   Example 2: Dutch interference in immigrant Turkish

In my more recent work my colleagues and I have been putting together a corpus of spoken Turkish that, I think, will be fairly typical of the second generation of language-contact corpora. These corpora will be limited in size, like the earlier ones, but will take cognizance of the idea that data should be shared and exchanged, and should thus be stored and presented in ways that make them accessible. My corpus, therefore, should be of use to others, first in workshops to be organized about the data and later through an official release.

Once released, the corpus should be useful for the wider research community. The features that enable this include:

- Inspection of the original audio data is possible
- The corpus has a hierarchical organization, making use of metadata software
- It's possible to search the database for the relevant data
- The transcription system used is a widely available one
- Translations in a major language (i.e. English) are provided
- There are morphosyntactic glosses
- Parts of the data will be annotated for various further aspects.

An example of how utterances appear in the corpus is given below.

1	NAC:	**dün televizyonda gördüm cem yılmazı.**			
2		dün	televizyon-da	gör-dü-m	cem yılmaz-ı.
3		yesterday	television-LOC	see-PAST-1sg	cem yılmaz-ACC
4		ADV	N-LOC	V-PAST-1sg	Name-ACC
5	wo:	ADV	ADV	V	DO
6	pro:	zero			
7		"I saw Cem Yılmaz on TV last night"			

The first line is the basic text of the utterance by speaker NAC; the second breaks it up into morphemes, which are glossed in English on the third line. Lines 4 and 5 provide morphological tagging and morphosyntactic parsing respectively (the latter indicated with "wo" for "word order"). The last line before the idiomatic English translation is an example of a very project-specific code: it says how the subject is encoded (as "noun," as "pronoun," or as "zero," which is the case here). This is relevant if one wants to know whether Turkish, a language that doesn't normally use subject pronouns except if they are contrastive, has increased its use of such pronouns in the Netherlands because of contact with Dutch, in which subject pronouns are always used.

These seem to be the most crucial elements any linguistic database needs to have when released to the public. Without the audio data, no further transcription can be done by others, nor is phonological analysis possible. Without some sort of hierarchical organization, a large corpus is fairly inaccessible for outsiders. Such large corpora have many different kinds of data, even if they are all conversational, and researchers must have a way to navigate this labyrinth so that they don't end up looking at the wrong data. Without the use of a transcription system that is widely available, it will be hard for users in other parts of the world to read the transcripts, let alone work with them. In addition, the system will usually come equipped with all kinds of statistical support that makes quantitative analysis much easier. Translations in English or another major language are necessary to ensure that non-Turkish speakers have access to the data, and glosses are helpful for some, and crucial for others, depending on what they want to do with the data. The annotations developed were needed for the research questions we had in mind, but many others are possible and will hopefully be added at some point in the near future by other users.

Section summary

In order to search your corpus for the passages that are relevant for answering your research questions, you will need to annotate (a portion of) the data for the relevant features. Organizing this within a framework developed for work on language corpora facilitates this task tremendously.

Further reading and resources

There are various good textbooks on corpus construction, e.g. Kennedy (1998), and references there. The corpora themselves tend to have very good and accessible websites, which you can easily find by typing in useful words in your search engine, e.g. "English spoken corpus." A discussion list on the Internet is hosted by the University of Bergen, Norway, and can be reached at corpora@uib.no. The International Corpus of English is also archived at Bergen and can be accessed at http://nora.hd.uib.no/icame.html. The organization that manages the corpus also publishes a journal (*ICAME Journal*) and organizes conferences. Information about the Ottawa-Hull corpus can be found at http://aix1.uottawa.ca/~sociolx/slxhold-e.html. This site also lists many other resources associated with the pioneering work of Shana Poplack and her associates. Access to these corpora, and most other corpora, is only possible after requesting permission. Information on the LIDES database can be found at http://talkbank.org/data/LIDES/ and www.ling.lancs.ac.uk/staff/mark/lipps/easylides.htm. The well-known CHILDES database is at http://childes.psy.cmu.edu. This is also where the CHAT transcription system can be downloaded, as well as the CLAN analysis tools. The Max Planck Institute has accumulated much expertise on corpora, which is reflected on their website: www.mpi.nl/world/corpus/index.html. The transcription system ELAN and the metadata management system IMDI can be found here. A very useful website is www-nlp.stanford.edu/links/statnlp.html, with many links to corpora of various languages and tools with which to mine them. There are many other websites like this, and as with so many things on the Web, once you have an initial page from which to start your explorations, the numerous links will guide you further and further into the world of language corpora and corpus linguistics.

14 Doing Ethnography

Monica Heller

14.1 Why Do Ethnographies of Bilingualism?

Research methods are not interchangeable; it makes more sense to use some methods than others to address certain kinds of questions, formulated in the context of different theoretical or epistemological ideas about the nature of the phenomena we are asking questions about (Mason, 1996/2002). In this chapter I will first spell out the assumptions about the nature of bilingualism that lie behind most ethnographic work on that subject. These are assumptions that are *interpretivist* rather than *positivist*: that is, they posit that "bilingualism" is a social construct, which needs to be described and interpreted as an element of the social and cultural practices of sets of speakers, rather than a fixed object existing in nature, to be discovered by an objective observer. (Interpretivism usually refers to a scientific stance which assumes that knowledge is socially constructed; positivism refers to a stance which assumes that reality exists objectively and can be empirically discovered.) I will then turn to some of the questions ethnographic work can usefully address, and which range from descriptions of language practices to critical analyses of the ways in which those practices shed light on ideologies of language and society, and on relations of social difference and social inequality.

Section 14.4, the principal part of the chapter, will discuss what doing ethnographies of bilingualism might mean in practical terms. It will treat issues of site selection and sampling, as well as the range of methods that can form part of doing ethnography (observation, interviews, tape-recording interactions or activities, discourse analysis of texts or visual documents). Along the way it will be necessary to discuss the principles used to make the series of choices which form part of any study, and which here will be understood to flow from the set of ontological and epistemological principles described in section 14.2 (*ontology* refers to the things we believe about the nature of reality; *epistemology* refers to what we believe about how we can come to know that reality). Those principles influence: how we see ourselves as researchers; how we understand our relationship to the people we work with (and hence to ethical considerations) and to the phenomena we are enquiring about (and hence to theoretical and epistemological, but also political and practical, considerations); how we decide what counts as data; what constitutes a convincing (or valid) argument; what is the extent of the claims we can make (generalizability); and how we represent both data and analysis. In section 14.5, I will provide a concrete example from my own work on bilingualism in a French-language minority school in Canada to illustrate what I mean, bearing in mind that the questions about bilingualism that interest me might not be the ones that drive the work of my readers. It will be important to keep in mind throughout this chapter that I am writing from a perspective which assumes that researchers are active participants in the construction of knowledge about bilingualism, and that we therefore have to think about research as a meaningful social activity which can have social, economic, and political consequences. Bilingualism is not a neutral concept, and researching bilingualism is not a neutral act.

Having said that, we need to start by asking what the point of doing ethnographies of bilingualism might be. Fundamentally, ethnographies allow us to get at things we would otherwise never be able to discover. They allow us to see how language practices are connected to the very real conditions of people's lives, to discover how and why language matters to people in their own terms, and to watch processes unfold over time. They allow us to see complexity and connections, to understand the history and geography of language. They allow us to tell a story; not someone else's story exactly, but our own story of some slice of experience, a story which illuminates social processes and generates explanations for why people do and think the things they do.

Section summary

- Ethnographies usually take an *interpretivist* stance: they aim to discover how people use language, what they believe about language, and why, as aspects of socially constructed reality
- They are useful means of gaining in-depth descriptions and explanations which can capture complexities, contradictions, and consequences
- They can capture how processes unfold over time and space

14.2   What Reality? Whose Reality?

The position I want to outline here (and which is certainly not the only ontological position possible) might be described as poststructural realism: a stance which assumes that reality may be socially constructed, but it is constructed on the basis of symbolic and material structural constraints that are empirically observable. The things we do and the things we believe are influenced by some of the concrete, practical conditions of our lives (how we organize ourselves to eat or get shelter, for example, and what materials we have to work with to do so), and by some of the cultural frames of meaning we have developed to make our way in the world.

Within that context, we do usually have some room to maneuver, to do things or make sense of things in new ways. Research is as much a part of this dynamic as any other social activity. Therefore, it is the process of construction of social reality which is, for me, at the heart of the activity of research. I believe that there is no objective truth that it is my job to identify and describe; rather, it is my job to provide evidence for some phenomenon by describing what I see in a systematic way and accurately predicting its recurrence, its variations, and its consequences in specific sets of circumstances.

While this means that I need to take responsibility for constructing an account which is always necessarily rooted in my historically and socially situated subjectivity (and not somehow transmitting the voices of others, or simply revealing reality as it exists outside my ability to apprehend it), at the same time, this account is not just my opinion, freely formed on the basis of my own private experience. It is an account based on systematic enquiry, conducted according to selection principles which I have to describe and justify; I can't just spend some time somewhere and claim what happens there is typical, or representative, or meaningful in some way. It is, therefore, my job to provide a rationale for what I am asking questions about and for how I want to ask them, not in terms of what I personally happen to think is interesting, but in terms which allow others to grasp the significance of my choices in a more general way.

In this respect, ethnographies are not about what is sometimes referred to as "giving voice" to participants. It is about providing an illuminating account for which the researcher is solely responsible. At the same time, since ethnography is a social activity, it does not occur in a vacuum, and it is likely that many other people, including but not limited to the direct participants, will have a stake in what comes out of the research, and in how things are represented. Doing ethnography therefore means entering into, or in some cases continuing but on a slightly different basis, an ongoing conversation with many interlocutors. It means taking on the responsibility for what one says and for the effects it might have on others. But it does not require the researcher to necessarily agree with anyone else about what is going on or why; it only requires us to be able to back up our claims.

It is also sometimes claimed that ethnography is about holism; that it is about getting the full picture, the complete range. I want to take a different perspective here, one that assumes that there is no such thing as a bounded whole, there are only processes which link together across space and time (Giddens, 1984). There are boundaries, certainly, but these boundaries are always socially constructed, and need to be described and analyzed as such. (One can think of boundaries as the practices which allow people to sort themselves into groups of various kinds, for example, to distinguish who counts as "male" versus who counts as "female," or "old" versus "young," or "Christian/Jewish/Muslim/Buddhist/Hindu/atheist . . . ," and so on.) They are, however, as a result, unlikely to be impermeable and un-changing, and certainly unlikely to contain only homogeneous material on either side of the boundary (Barth, 1969). They are therefore amenable to analysis: we can find out how they are constructed, resisted, overcome, or maintained. We can discover why people bother with them, that is, what they gain or lose from organizing their lives around them the way they do. And we can certainly use those observations as a grounded basis for making sampling choices, as long as it is clear that we have to justify the nature of the piece or thread we want to pick up in terms of empirically observable boundaries, and that we know that those boundaries are probably porous, with people and things and ideas and practices constantly traversing them and going off in all directions. And this is one of the compelling things about ethnographies of bilingualism, since bilingualism is all about boundaries: it is all about what counts as the difference between two languages, about who counts as a speaker of particular languages, and about how the categorization of languages and language practices is connected to the categorization of groups of people.

The stance I want to take is poststructural in that it assumes this kind of constructivist, interpretivist, subjectivist, and socially located approach. Furthermore, it is realist in that it nonetheless assumes that it is possible, and indeed necessary, to apprehend what counts as reality. It is also materialist, insofar as that reality is understood to be socially constructed on the basis of shared experiences which involve symbolic and material resources and conditions for producing them, distributing them, gaining access to them, and attributing value to them. Finally, it is critical, in that I want to put at the center of my questions the issue of the ways in which social differences are connected to social inequality, or, put differently, how categorization is related to power (see Heller, 2002, for a longer discussion of this stance). This brings me to the question of why it makes sense to approach bilingualism in this critical ethnographic way.

Section summary

- Ethnographies are our accounts, offered as a contribution to ongoing conversations about bilingualism with many different kinds of stakeholders.
- They always follow some threads more than others, for reasons having to do with the research questions asked and with the possibilities afforded to certain researchers under certain circumstances.
- Ethnography is about processes, such as the making and shifting of categories of language and language practices, not objects.

14.3   Bilingualism, Ideology, Difference, and Power

It is not my purpose here to provide an exhaustive account of questions about bilingualism that have been or could be approached ethnographically. Rather, I want to set out a few major lines of enquiry.

The first has to do with critical, historical examinations of the notion of "bilingualism" itself. If we accept that notions such as this one are socially and historically produced, we can fruitfully examine where they come from, and what sense they make to whom and why (see Blackledge, chapter 17 in this volume). This moves the field away from a "common-sense," but in fact highly ideologized, view of bilingualism as the coexistence of two linguistic systems, towards developing a critical perspective which allows for a better grasp on the ways in which language practices are socially and politically embedded. It opens up enquiry to the examination of the loci of production of discourses of bilingualism as it has developed in linguistics and its use in social regulation in State and civil society in the twentieth and twenty-first centuries.

This raises a second set of questions, more specific ones, about ways in which the idea and practice of bilingualism figure in major forms of social organization and regulation. Bilingualism has been centrally linked to the construction of discourses of State and nation, and is therefore tied to the regulation of citizenship (and related processes, notably colonialism, neocolonialism, and migration) and of ethnonational identity, to education and other important agencies and sites (such as language training, the media and communications technologies, government immigration bureaucracy, the workplace), to the role of the State in the organization of economic activities, and to the construction of what it means to be a competent person on an individual level (and therefore to general ideas about competence and normalcy, in ways that link the social and the moral orders). It is also tied to other central forms of social organization, notably religion, often with complicated relations to the State. Other forms of social categorization (race, gender, class, for example) are also usually involved, in complex structurations of relations of power. Under current conditions of late modernity, the discourse of bilingualism is increasingly produced by non-government organizations (NGOs) and agencies of supra-national bodies, such as the European Union, the United Nations, or UNESCO, and done so frequently in terms of human rights, ecology, and biodiversity. Throughout this history, academics have played a major role, both as producers of legitimizing expert discourses and as activists.

The perspective I want to raise here requires linking linguistic form to linguistic practice in a number of sites and in a number of ways, which can cover the terrain from agency to structure, from interaction to institution, from practice to ideology and discourse. What ethnography allows is precisely this kind of linking of analyses of the workings of discursive spaces (that is, spaces where discourses of bilingualism or discourses relevant to the construction of the idea of bilingualism are produced), to the trajectories of social actors and social resources, to the construction of social boundaries and to relations of inequality. This entails tying the communicative practices of everyday life to the processes of categorization, participation, and affiliation that construct social difference, and to the regulation of the production and circulation of resources.

The scope, the range, the depth of such examinations all fall within the set of choices any ethnographer has to make. In the next section I turn to operationalizing the principles and concerns I have discussed so far, in a consideration of what all this means for how you decide where, with whom, for how long, and how to conduct what might be called an critical ethnographic study of bilingualism.

Section summary

Ethnographies can address a broad range of questions, including questions about, for example, ideologies of language, the relationship between practices and beliefs about language, or the role of languages in the construction of relations of difference and inequality in many sites, from face-to-face interaction to institutional and State- or enterprise-level forms of social organization.

14.4   What Might an Ethnography of Bilingualism Look Like?

As Mason (1996/2002) repeatedly insists, ethnography, or any kind of interpretivist qualitative undertaking, does not come with a set of recipes. Rather, everything one does is guided by the ontological and epistemological stance of the researcher and by the questions he or she is asking (partly as a consequence of that stance). The single most important thing, then, is the identification of one's research questions. Are you interested in how speakers call upon a range of communicative resources to accomplish interaction? Or in the consequences of those practices for how boundaries get constructed, negotiated, or changed? Do you want to know what language practices are tied to people's abilities to participate in networks or activities, or to how they are judged? Are you concerned about institutional or State policies and practices around the management of bilingualism, about how they get produced or how they get implemented? About their consequences for people's life chances? Are you interested in what people's ideas about bilingualism can tell us more broadly about their ideologies of language? All these questions, whether about practices, policies, or ideologies, are amenable to ethnographic enquiry.

Ethnography asks that you identify the phenomena you are interested in, and then go about discovering where those phenomena occur and how they are linked. The first step in an ethnographic project, then, requires identifying where to look: there is no magic recipe for this; it simply requires doing the groundwork for finding out, if you don't already have an idea, where the phenomena you are interested in occur. Of course, like every other step of an ethnographic project, it also requires starting somewhere and then finding out that one hadn't got it quite right, and adjusting one's plans until one's expectations are confirmed by the data.

Beginning an ethnographic project also involves working out with the participants how to make sense of what you will be doing in ways which are both transparent and meaningful. Since the stance I take always assumes that reality is socially constructed, I start from the point of departure that there is no "true" reality somewhere that we need to try to gain access to by somehow effacing ourselves. No matter what, by virtue of the questions we ask and how we ask them we are there; we are better off trying to understand how people make sense of us and our activities than trying to pretend we can disappear. We also need to build a relationship of trust. This certainly means, in my view, telling people what we are doing. It also requires, and permits, the discovery of what the stakes are, and for whom, in the issues we are looking at. Finally, it allows us to understand the limits and possibilities related to our own social positions, which already illuminates what categories are meaningful to people and why.

While these considerations are vital points of departure, they are also part of an ongoing negotiation of relationships and understandings which will unfold throughout the ethnography and continue well beyond it. It is important, therefore, to be prepared to make mistakes and to have to repair them, and to have to make difficult choices and to understand their consequences. So, if you want to enter a conversation, you need to find out where it is happening, who can take part, and you have to learn the rules of turn-taking and politeness which operate there.

At the same time, at its heart, ethnography is most focused on what happens; hence the notion many people have that it is primarily about description. And as a first step, that is certainly true: the first ethnographic commitment is to discovering what is going on (without assuming beforehand that we know). But it is important not to stop there; the second key dimension of data collection has to do with what will help us explain why things happen the way they do, in the circumstances in which they occur. Such an explanation then allows us to make predictions (about what might happen next, or what would happen in similar circumstances), and if we feel we need to, it would also allow us to figure out where and how to intervene to change things. Explanatory data come in two varieties: the first concerns the (observable) context in which things happen, the ways in which bilingual practices are tied to particular conditions, particular resources, particular interests; the second connects practices to people's accounts of why they do what they do (recognizing that all accounts are just that: not transparent windows into the workings of intentionality, but rather narratives which help us see how actors make sense of their world). Any ethnographic project needs to include data-gathering techniques that allow for an adequate description of the phenomena of interest, in the circumstances in which they occur, and for an adequate explanation of why they occur where they do, when they do (see Lanza and Codó, chapters 5 and 9 in this volume). These techniques should also allow for the discovery of consequences: what difference does it make and to whom that things happen the way they do?

These ethnographic techniques can, and indeed should, be multiple: the more routes you have into apprehending and understanding something, the better off you are. Nonetheless, sometimes choices have to be made, and some techniques might make more sense than others under certain circumstances. For example, one research project I was involved in concerned the language practices and ideologies of francophone Canadian women married to anglophone men (cf. Heller & Lévy, 1994). The research budget was small, and it is difficult to find comfortable ways to spend time sharing the intimate lives of couples; as a result, we opted for an interview study, with questions inspired by the kinds of ethnographic concerns we might have liked to have been able to investigate more directly. The consequence, however, is that we had to treat our data as accounts, as discursive performances, with no way of verifying whether or not the practices reported bore any connection to practices we might have observed. The interest of the study ended up lying more in how such women portrayed their bilingual lives, rather than in how they may have lived them.

Further, some research techniques are more amenable to helping us interpret the data they generate than others. Questionnaires, for example, may help generate data for a large population, but it is generally difficult to be present when participants fill them out. As a result, we have little way of knowing how our participants interpret either the communicative act of filling out a questionnaire (for many people it is reminiscent of complying with State bureaucratic procedures of social control, and may be more or less welcome as a result; other people may have no frame for understanding it at all) or the questions themselves (for example, does "What language do you speak with your children?" mean what that language would be called if it were the standard version, or what I call it? Do you mean my biological children or the ones I take care of? and so on). In addition, in order to be usable, questionnaires usually have to ask questions in ways that are more context-free and more closed than bilingual practices and ideologies usually are. They may not, therefore, be the best ways of getting at the complexity of bilingualism.

Much ethnographic research on bilingualism uses a combination of observation (usually accompanied by audio- or videotape recording) and interviews, since so much of this work is devoted to spoken language. Some studies also pay attention to other forms of expression, whether in the form of written manifestations of bilingual practices or in the form of artifacts (written or otherwise) relevant to contextualizing spoken and written bilingualism.

I have made the point already that interviews (and other forms of elicitation) provide you with accounts, accounts which are situated performances in and of themselves (see also Lafont, 1977; Briggs, 1986; Cicourel, 1988). They are what a certain kind of person tells another certain kind of person, in certain ways, under certain conditions. In the mixed-marriages study to which I referred above, it was clear from a variety of traces (explicit comments, hesitations about using English, flagging of various kinds) that participants oriented to my colleague and to me as speakers of normed varieties of French, as well as to public discourses about the importance of the quality of French and about maintaining French as a minority language in Canada; we had to take all that into account in understanding what they had to say about things like the choices they made regarding languages of instruction for their children, or how they managed bilingualism at family gatherings. In a study I did in a high school in the early 1990s, it was clear from the use of polite address forms ("Madame"), and of fully formed but rather short and hard-to-elicit sentences, that adolescent boys did not feel fully comfortable with me; interviews with them would produce impoverished accounts intended for the eyes of authority (a male graduate student did them instead).

These are not arguments against using interviews; they are simply arguments that interviews need to be understood for what they are and analyzed accordingly, and that they will generate the most useful data when it is possible to understand what they mean to participants. This can mean that it makes more sense to do them once relationships have been established, and once the researcher has a sense of what things mean to participants. This is particularly important in research on bilingualism, since it is so often the case that people are oriented towards norms which value monolingual over bilingual performances, and certain kinds of bilingualism over others; people may not want to display their bilingualism, or even own up to it, in what they perceive to be a communicative situation governed by dominant discourses on language which favor monolingual standard-variety performances. Alternatively, they may be inclined to claim greater bilingualism than their practices might actually warrant. My point is that bilingualism is a particularly charged topic, traversed by all kinds of ideologies and values, and these will emerge in any communicative situation one way or another, whether connected explicitly to research or not. Having said that, interviews are indeed one very useful way to elicit people's accounts in two major areas. They are important for getting a sense of participants' life trajectories and social positioning, data which can help explain the interests they have in doing things certain ways (such as code-switching or not), or trying to get certain things to happen or opposing them (such as bilingual education). They are also important sources of accounts, which allow glimpses into the beliefs and values and ideologies which inform what people do and why they do it. These can also then be juxtaposed to data about practices, or to other kinds of accounts, as ways of discovering coherences and contradictions and how people strategize around them.

Practices and accounts are usually approached through observation, the hallmark technique of ethnographic research. As I mentioned earlier, many people spend a lot of time worrying about how to be a fly on the wall, so as not to unduly influence people's behavior. My own view is that this is impossible, and not even desirable; we are present by virtue of the questions we ask and what we attend to, and we are best off taking our participation fully into account, and constructing our ethnographies as the stories we tell about things we want to argue are interesting and important. And we *can* take our participation into account: the data are always full of traces of how we are taken up, oriented to and understood, information which in and of itself provides indices of the norms, frames of reference, ideologies, positionings, and interests which are such important dimensions of research on bilingualism.

Observation then is centrally a question of discovering where it is that things relevant to our concerns occur, and under what circumstances. It is about mapping out the landscape of bilingualism, and then investigating the interesting bits in greater detail. Some things can be recorded manually, in writing, by memory; some things require recording and more careful transcription, bearing in mind that like any other research technique, recording can be more or less familiar or more or less comfortable for different kinds of participants, and is therefore probably best begun once participants know you and have a sense of what you are doing. Many participants, school-age children in particular, like to satisfy their curiosity about how the research process, and the machine, works; they need to appropriate it for themselves in order to be at ease.

There is some debate as to whether to ask participants to record themselves or whether to be present, and as to whether to audio- or video-record. I doubt there is a hard and fast rule to follow; rather, as usual, it will be a question of trade-offs and feasibility. Recorders do tend to get taken up as mechanical incarnations of the researcher; participants send you little messages whether or not you are there, some of which can be extremely interesting (Rampton, 1995; Heller, 2006). But sometimes the recorder will be invited into situations that your body may be excluded from. Not being there, though, does deprive you of contextual information which can be so crucial to understanding language practices.

There are also trade-offs to ponder regarding audio- and video-recording. Both now can be done with relatively small and mobile machines. Video recordings provide information about non-verbal communication, a dimension of interaction to which bilingualism research could surely usefully attend to better than it has in the past. At the same time, they do frame observation in rather constricted ways (see Clemente, chapter 10 in this volume).

In either case, recordings should not be relied on alone. Fieldnotes help contextualize them, providing the information needed to make sense of interactions, and to build up the basis for comparison or developmental analysis that allows us to link interactions to institutional and social processes and structures (Heller, 2001). They can also tie what is recorded to other kinds of material which may be physically co-present or linked in looser ways to the interactions being recorded (for example, texts used in the classroom, posters on the wall, flyers lying around the office, the policy document being discussed at a meeting). And of course, much written material deserves analysis as a source of information on bilingualism in its own right; one can learn a great deal, for example, about the Canadian federal government's ideology of bilingualism simply by inspecting the ways it displays that bilingualism in the documents it produces.

Because ethnographic analysis relies heavily on the discovery of patterns of co-occurrences across time and space, it matters greatly what happens where and when, and with whose involvement. The different kinds of data generated by the techniques I have discussed are best used by linking them together, by discovering not only the various dimensions of what is happening, but also how these phenomena are produced and unfold over time, how they are linked across space, and, perhaps most importantly, what difference they make to whom. We can compare what people do (practices), to what they say (accounts), explain them in terms of the resources different kinds of people are able to mobilize, look at their consequences, and see what difference it makes to whom that things go the way they go.

Another dimension of ethnography that requires discussion is representation: how we tell the story we think the analysis of the data warrants. This is an issue discussed elsewhere in this volume as concerns transcription; here I want to attend to questions of ideology of language and discourse, and to questions of voice. Clearly, as in transcription, how we represent the linguistic resources and practices we wish to discuss says a lot about how we think of them: Do we consider them to be elements of distinct and separate linguistic systems? Are we most concerned with how speakers orient to them? Do we want to portray them as varied elements of speakers' repertoires? Are we most concerned with form, or do we want to attach our representation to what we understand to be the discursive position adopted by speakers? What about how we represent written or non-verbal material? How do we represent the elements of context (spatial or temporal organization, for example) that we consider important to the analysis? Finally, how do we make clear that, while we do want to make claims about how we understand speakers to orient themselves and to construct accounts, this is, in the end, a story we tell, one for which we must find our own voice, and for which we must take our own responsibility? Our own accounts, our representations, are major turns at talk in an extended conversation. We have to think about them in terms of what we want to say and to whom, in terms of how what we say is likely to be understood, and in terms of what the potential consequences may be of the claims we want to make.

For all these concerns are connected to ethical issues. Bilingualism is always somewhere about power, if we understand power to be the control over the production and distribution of resources, and the ability to attribute value to them, whether those resources are material or symbolic, including linguistic or other communicative resources. It is always, as I said earlier, about categorization, about the construction or contestation of boundaries which serve to regulate relations of power. Doing research on bilingualism cannot avoid that dynamic; it is necessarily part of it, not only because as researchers we enter and engage with that social world (differently if we are already part of it), but also because we produce knowledge about bilingualism which has its own value in the discursive space we participate in. We therefore need to think about how to manage those relations of power and how we fit into them, so as to protect our participants, and, sometimes, ourselves.

In the next section I provide a concrete example from my own research, as a way of illustrating some of the above outline. I do not provide this account as typical or exemplary, since ethnography is by definition context-sensitive and grounded. What works for me in my context, now, may not work for me in five years, or for you ever. But it is important to recognize that the choices we make need to be both principled and pragmatic, and so I offer my own story as a potential starting point for your own explorations. The story will be simplified and truncated in many ways, but will nonetheless offer some grounding for the more abstract discussion we have just finished (and the full version is available: Heller, 2006).

Section summary

- The most important thing to start with is your research question: what do you want to know?
- You need data that is both descriptive (what is going on?) and explanatory (why is it happening that way?); you can also look for data about consequences (what difference does it make to whom?).
- You can combine observation, interviews, recording and document analysis for different kinds of data or different perspectives on the same data; these can focus on practices or on accounts (for example, of life trajectories, institutional histories, ideas about bilingualism, and so on) and the conditions of their production.

14.5   Bilingualism and School

The story I want to tell concerns an ethnography of a French-language minority high school in a part of Canada which is mainly English-speaking. It is not a bilingual high school *per se*, insofar as it was explicitly set up as a monolingual institution for the preservation of a minority language, namely French (except that it did teach the majority language, English, both as a second language to those students unfamiliar with it, and as a regular native-speaker subject for the vast majority of students who were fluently bilingual). The ethnography focused on bilingualism in the space of this school, as a window onto the construction of minority identities and ideologies at a particular time (the early 1990s, a period of social and economic transition into the globalizing new economy of services and information) and a particular place (an urban area of Canada, a country long wrestling with the politics and economics of bilingualism, and at the same time long attractive to immigrants). There was a reason for looking at a school: schools have been the focus of battles over minority language rights in English Canada from the late nineteenth century until the present day. And there was a reason for looking at *this* school: its place and time, and its historical importance as the first State-funded French-language high school opened in this part of the province. I do want to note, in addition, that institutional ethnographies are in some ways also the easiest to accomplish, since their boundaries tend to be relatively clear and their explicit forms of regulation allow for linking interactional processes to broader social structural ones in ways more evident than might be the case in more loosely organized spaces or activities.

I understood my job to comprise both understanding the history of the school and the system it was situated in (available through some published texts, interviews with key actors, or a variety of primary sources: school board minutes, newspaper articles, government-commissioned reports on French-language minority education, court judgments, legislation, etc.), and its contemporary speech economy, as connected to its double role as agency of social and cultural reproduction (Bourdieu & Passeron, 1977). It is the latter aspect that I discuss in some detail here, although I do not want to minimize the importance of the historical work involved.

We did want to get a sense of the school population, and indeed of the population of French-language schools in the area. Census data were of some help in getting an idea of the population, but only approximately, since it is far from clear what the relationship is between how people respond to Canadian census language questions and how they orient to ethnolinguistic boundaries in daily life (thus there tend to be far more people who claim some affiliation to the francophone group in daily life than who claim on the census to have French as their "first language learned and still understood"). We attempted a questionnaire, but I remain unsatisfied with the results. School board regulations required us to send the questionnaire in French only, thereby reducing the likelihood of response from people more comfortable in other languages, and to send it home with and have it returned by students, a route notorious for producing lonely documents lying around houses or scrunched in backpacks. The return rate was low, and answers not always easy to interpret.

We charted the school's institutional position (its official discourse about itself and the institutional constraints under which it operates) by collecting relevant documents (the yearbook, policy documents, ministry regulations, teaching materials), interviewing key actors (school board and school administrators, teachers, elected school board members), and by spending time in the staff room.

Mapping language practices at school required getting a handle on the organization of space and time, which meant in practical terms spending a lot of time at school, exploring its different spaces and activities. It quickly became apparent that language practices varied tremendously according to whether interactions occurred in circumstances that could be said to be under fairly direct school control (classes, assemblies, the main office, and during the official school day) or elsewhere or other times when students had greater control over their own activities (corridors, the parking lot, the smoking area, the cafeteria, dances, and before or after school or on weekends). They also varied by type of class (humanities and social sciences had a stronger normative orientation to French monolingualism in class than did other subjects), and by category of student (university-preparatory-stream students tended to comply more with school regulations, including language norms, than did the others). Spending time at school, and getting to know students and teachers, did allow us to get an idea of personal trajectories, and, perhaps more importantly, what it was about those trajectories that was important to the participants.

Building that map required a lengthy process of establishing the patterns, identifying the participants and the activities, and discovering what the actors and activities that grouped together had in common (and further, what about those common characteristics could help explain why they acted similarly or had similar effects). Once we had a sense of that map, we could decide which threads to follow. We focused on some classrooms, which we observed, and eventually recorded, basing our selections on the dimensions of variability we had earlier discovered. The recordings, always accompanied by fieldnotes, were designed to help us discover the relationship between bilingualism and the interactional order of the classroom, as a way of getting at how bilingualism was linked to the definition of what counted as good or competent linguistic performances and who counted as good or competent speakers (or what counted as legitimate language and who counted as legitimate speakers in the sense of Bourdieu, 1977a), within the constraints of prevailing ideologies of teaching and learning of different kinds of subjects, and of the distribution of communicative and other relevant kinds of resources. They were designed to help us answer the questions of what counts as bilingualism in a school like this, who gets to count as bilingual, and how that does or does not tie into academic or social success.

We also focused on some specific students, as a way of getting at how individual students occupying different social positions navigated the sociolinguistic space of the school. We spent days with them, including time outside school, as a way of understanding where school fit into the rest of their lives, what they were trying to achieve by going there (especially since they had choices about where to go) and of getting a handle on the kinds of resources they had access to outside school. As a way of deepening the data on those issues, we tried to reconstruct their life trajectories through informal conversation and more formal interviews with the students and, sometimes, the adults responsible for them.

Finally, we paid close attention to key events, that is, to performances in which ideologies of language and identity would be on display. The school stage and the foyer were two spaces where performances were held, ranging from cultural events meant to construct a certain idea of what Franco-Ontarian culture might be, to general assemblies, and from student council rallies to celebrations of the 25th anniversary of the school's founding.

Overall, three graduate students and I spent one or two days a week doing fieldwork of various kinds, over the course of about two and a half years. Ethnographic work can of course be done in less time, with accompanying restrictions in scope. The main issue has to do with what kinds of data you need in order to answer the question you are asking; or conversely, what questions it is reasonable to ask given the human, financial, and temporal resources available. In any case, an ethnography will not only always provide some answers, but in the best of cases it will also generate more questions, to be pursued as resources permit.

14.6   Following Up

Probably the best way to get a feel for doing ethnographies of bilingualism is to just spend time listening, reading, and generally watching for bilingual practices, or reports of bilingual practices, in the world around you. Newspapers and magazines often do carry reports on bilingualism, and in many parts of the world bilingualism is all around us in a variety of spaces. I have found examples in graffiti on walls and in bathroom stalls, in conversations with waiters in restaurants and with bus drivers, in conversations overheard waiting in line to buy tickets to a movie. Experiment with fieldnotes, with trying to write down from memory what you saw and heard. Explore the array of different kinds of information about bilingualism that may be available to you: ask questions, pick up leaflets, look at what is written on walls, check out websites.

It also is helpful to read ethnographies of bilingualism; some examples are Urciuoli, 1996; Zentella, 1997; Jaffe, 1999; Pujolar, 2001; Kanno, 2003; and Heller, 2006. These will not only acquaint you with some of the historical, social, economic, and political issues linked to bilingualism in various parts of the world, and some of the ways individuals navigate those contexts, they will also give you a sense of how to tell your own story once you are ready to tell it.

Acknowledgments

I thank the editors of this volume as well as Emanuel da Silva for useful comments on an earlier version of this article. The research I refer to was supported by the Social Sciences and Humanities Research Council of Canada.

15 Social Network Analysis

Xu Daming, Wang Xiaomei, and Li Wei

What effect do our relationships with others have on our own social practices, including language practices? What role does language play in our developing social relations? How do changes in group membership affect individual members' behavior? Are our attitudes towards others related to our relationships with them and our social group memberships? These are just some of the questions that applied social network analysts ask. This chapter outlines how Social Network Analysis (SNA) has been applied to language research, especially to studies of bilingualism and multilingualism.

15.1 Approaches to Social Networks

A social network is defined as the web-like pattern of relationships among individuals (Gelles & Levine, 1999: 207). SNA as a major analytical approach has two different but related origins – one in the Chicago and later Harvard schools of structural sociology and social psychology, particularly sociometry (as exemplified in the work of Harrison White, Barry Wellman, S. D. Berkowitz, and Mark Granovetter) and the other in the Manchester school of cultural anthropology (associated with the work of J. A. Barnes, Clyde Mitchell, and Elizabeth Bott) (see further Scott, 2000). Two broad approaches to the description and analysis of the relationship patterns can be distinguished: the whole-network (or sociological) approach and the egocentric (personal) network (or anthropological) approach. Both approaches focus on the quantitative measurement of relationships between people, the former focusing on the overall structure of the network and the latter on the profile (size and content) of the ties. For example, the Harvard group's main contribution was the development of mathematical models of network analysis, in which concepts such as equivalence and centrality were the most important, whereas the Manchester group was more interested in the effect of integration into a group on individuals' behaviors and attitudes. SNA is now applied to a wide range of research fields, including psychology, political science, ecological and environmental

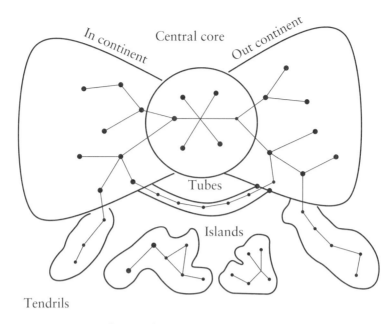

Figure 15.1: Society as social networks.

sciences, public health, business management, information sciences, education, and linguistics.

It is important to note that social network analysts have a specific conceptualization of society. In their view, there is no independent entity of "social structure"; society is constituted of a series of social relationships (see figure 15.1). These relationships have a number of dimensions – time, space, and power. We can therefore talk about, for example, historical networks, geographical networks, and hierarchical networks. Social change is also a change of social relationships and networks.

Moreover, social networks not only connect us with each other, but also provide an individual's social locale. An individual's social locale is very important because it plays a part in determining the specific information that the individual is exposed to. Individuals in different social locations may receive different information and participate in different social events; so they may come to construct knowledge differently. For instance, people whose networks are separated from others', sometimes called "islanders," exchange information amongst themselves but not with other groups. Because the locale social networks provide is closely related to patterns of social interaction, it also influences individuals' social expectations and may lead to certain types of socio-cognitive bias. Social networks are therefore an important part of social cognition, because cognitive processes may directly involve the individual's perceptions of his or her social locale. Those at the center of social activities and social relationships receive and perceive information quite differently from people who are at the periphery.

> **Section summary**
>
> • Social network analysts argue that there is no independent entity of social structure, but a series of social relationships.
> • Social networks provide the social locale of individuals and determine the information they receive.
> • Social networks can be analyzed in different ways: in terms of structural patterns of whole networks or in terms of contents of ego-centered ties.

15.2 Applications of SNA in Language Research

The concept of social networks is now well integrated into sociolinguistics. It has been used both as a methodological approach to data collection and as a theoretical framework for data analysis. Milroy and Gordon (2003), for example, describe the advantages of using a "friend-of-a-friend" approach to access speakers, speech communities, and speech events which might have otherwise been difficult to make contact with. There are a number of advantages to such a network approach. First, it may help the researcher to gain access to aspects of social life that may not be usually open to outsiders. For instance, it enabled Lesley Milroy to go into neighborhoods of different religious affiliations in Belfast, Northern Ireland, in the 1970s. Second, it offers the researcher a specific perspective that is embedded in human social relations. Suzanne Moffatt (1990), an English-speaking white woman, was able to study the bilingual behavior of Pakistani children and their parents through the social networks she developed in her role as a teaching assistant in a Pakistani-majority school in the west end of Newcastle upon Tyne, England. This perspective helped her to observe and understand the children's and parents' attitudes towards bilingualism. Third, it may help the researcher to contact a large number of people in a relatively short period of time.

In data analysis, social networks were initially used as a metaphor to describe speech communities which were either "close-knit" or "open". In his studies of language variation in India, Gumperz (1971) found that informal friendship contacts were one of the key social factors accounting for the phonetic variations of the dialects in Khalapur, a village in north India. The phonetic features of the speech of members of close-knit networks were more "focused", whereas those of open networks were "diffused" (see also Gumperz, 1982b). But it was the variationist sociolinguists who first used social network as an analytic concept and specifically collected network data which were used in their explanation of linguistic variation and change.

Labov's (1972b) study of black teenagers in Harlem, New York City, investigated the linguistic behaviors of members of street gangs known as the Thunderbirds and the Aces, as well as those of outsiders of the same age group, known as Lames.

Adolescents worldwide are notorious for their tendency to form dense networks and place great value on being "part of the gang." These dense networks exert peer pressure on their members' behavior including the use of language. Labov discovered that the gang members used much higher frequencies of non-standard vernacular variants. The Lames, on the other hand, used fewer vernacular features. Similarly, Eckert (1988), in her study of teenagers in Detroit, identified two networks, called Jocks and Burnouts, that differed essentially in the role of the high school culture in their everyday activities – the Jocks were into sports, school politics, and other social and academic activities, whereas the Burnouts were outsiders, hanging out in restaurants and malls and getting themselves into trouble from time to time. Eckert found significant linguistic correlations depending upon network affiliations: the Jocks displayed more middle-class variants while the Burnouts used more typically working-class variants.

Both Labov's and Eckert's studies adopted the whole-network approach and used social networks to define social differentiation of language. As figure 15.2 illustrates, different social networks have different structural patterns. Some are highly centralized with clear internal hierarchical structures, while others may be more distributed. Memberships of differently structured networks will display different social behaviors, and individuals with different roles inside specific networks will have their distinctive social behaviors. To carry out a whole-network analysis, one needs to observe all the members of the network in question and find out what their roles are in the overall network. There are computer programs for plotting the structural patterns of whole networks as well as individuals' positions within them.

Perhaps the best-known sociolinguistic application of SNA is Milroy's (1987) study of phonological variation and change in three working-class communities in Belfast. Instead of looking at whole-network structures, Milroy focused on individuals' network ties and their relationships with the differences that had been observed in their use of phonological variables. This is a different approach to social network analysis from the whole-network approach. It focuses on the

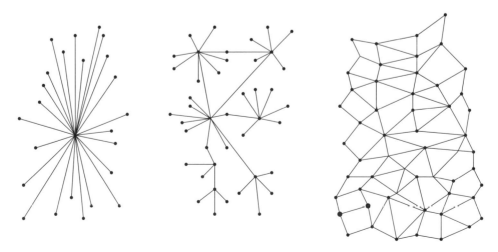

Figure 15.2: Structural patterns of different kinds of social networks

individual, uses him or her as the anchor person, and observes the network contacts he or she has for different social purposes. Milroy developed a Network Strength Scale, with a maximum score of 5, which assessed speakers' network characteristics with reference to various relationships within the neighborhood of kin, work, and friendship that had emerged in the course of the fieldwork as significant to participants. Speakers scored one point for each of the following conditions they satisfied:

- They were members of a high-density, territorially based group (e.g. a bingo- or card-playing group, a gang or a football team, or a football supporters' club);
- They had kinship ties with more than two households in the neighborhood;
- They worked at the same place as at least two others from the neighborhood;
- They worked in the same place as at least two others of the same sex from the neighborhood;
- They associated voluntarily with workmates in leisure hours.

A series of statistical analyses revealed that the strongest vernacular speakers were generally those whose neighborhood network ties were the strongest.

As Milroy and Gordon (2003: 120) point out, a social network approach is attractive to variationist sociolinguists for a number of reasons. First, it provides a set of procedures for studying small groups where speakers are not discriminable in terms of any kind of social class index. This is, however, not to say that social networks are not linked with social class. In fact, there is a lot of evidence that social network patterns interact with socioeconomic class and gender. A second advantage is that since the social network is intrinsically a concept that relates to local practices, it has the potential to elucidate the social dynamics driving language variation and change. Social networks are often associated with a range of social and psychological factors, and they develop and change over time. Finally, network analysis of the ego-centered kind, as exemplified in Milroy's (1987) study, offers a procedure for dealing with variation between individual speakers, rather than between groups constructed with reference to predetermined social categories.

Section summary

- Social networks can be used as an effective way to access speakers and data.
- As an analytic tool, social network analysis compares individual differences in the degree of integration in relationships that exert normative pressures on their members' behaviors.
- The information used to construct network index is locally relevant and must be retrievable from data.

15.3   SNA in Bilingualism and Multilingualism Research

The capacity of SNA to allow comparison of individual differences in the degree of integration in relationships that exerts normative pressures on social behaviors is particularly attractive to those who study immigrant and transnational communities. Such communities typically have to deal with issues of social integration during the course of migration and settlement, and the success of their integration efforts has long-term consequences for their development in terms of their identity, internal structure, and relationships with other groups. Amongst the earliest studies of social network structures, integration and language use in bilingual communities was Gumperz's account of the Slovenian-German community in a remote part of Austria's Gail Valley (e.g. Gumperz, 1982b). He found that members of the poor and socially stigmatized farming community had traditionally been embedded in close-knit networks of mutual support. However, such behaviors changed as the economy shifted from a dependence on subsistence farming to a service economy. Improved transport and communication systems also meant that a host of other changes affected network structures and everyday social practices, including language practices. As interactions with urban outsiders increased, reliance on the local support network diminished. The use of German also increased significantly over time and the use of Slovenian only was confined to specific traditional networks.

Gal's (1979) study of language shift in Oberwart, a village on the Austrian-Hungarian border, found similar patterns. German/Hungarian bilingualism had existed in Oberwart since before the sixteenth century. However, the two languages were functionally quite different: German was a language to be used with outsiders and Hungarian was the linguistic symbol of group identity for the Oberwart peasants. This state of affairs began to change after the Second World War, when local industrial and commercial economy developed so significantly that non-agricultural employment was an increasingly attractive option. Gal found a parallel language shift from Hungarian-dominant bilingualism to German-dominant bilingualism. She ranked individual speakers according to their degree of "urbanization" or "Austrianness" and observed a strong correlation between their language-choice patterns and social network contacts.

In his study of language choice and language shift in three-generation Chinese families in the UK, Li Wei (1994) specifically collected social network data and analyzed them in terms of ethnic and peer-group content in three different types of contacts: exchange networks, interactive networks, and passive networks. Exchange networks are collectives of people with whom the probability of rewarding exchanges (and unrewarding exchanges in cases of conflict-habituated relationships) is high (Milardo, 1988). In other words, these are the people with whom the ego not only interacts routinely, but also exchanges direct aid, advice, criticism, support, and intervention. Although in principle an individual's social networks can be boundless, empirical evidence suggests that for practical reasons exchange networks are effectively limited to first-order contacts, which are normally between 20 and 30 people (Mitchell, 1986). Interactive networks, on the other hand, consist of people with whom the ego interacts frequently and perhaps over prolonged periods of time, but crucially, the probability of rewarding exchange is low, that is, the ego does not rely on these contacts for personal favors and other material or symbolic resources. An example of interactive ties is a shop-owner and his or her customers. The identification of "passive networks" was particularly useful for studying migrant communities. Passive ties are marked by an absence of regular contact, but are equally considered important by the ego who depends on such relationships for emotional and moral support or influence. Many migrants, for example, would have relatives and friends who for various reasons are physically distant from them, but who are still regarded as important relations. Migrants often cling psychologically to their traditional ties, despite the passing of time. Passive ties can be "activated" by home visits and other interactions.

Adopting an ego-network approach, Li Wei collected information on the social contacts of 58 individuals in the Chinese community. For the exchange networks, participant observation elicited an initial list of around 30 contacts. The list was then presented to the speaker for verification and amended accordingly. A resulting 20 non-kin contacts were used as the basis for analyzing the individual speaker's exchange networks. In order to examine individuals' degree of social integration, two network indices were constructed: an ethnic index, which was calculated in terms of the number of Chinese versus non-Chinese ties out of the 20 exchange contacts for each speaker, and a peer index, reflecting the number of people belonging to the same generation as the speaker as opposed to those of other generations, either older or younger. The indices were used to test two basic hypotheses (see further Li Wei, 1994: 121–2):

- Speakers whose exchange networks consist of a relatively large number of ethnic (Chinese) ties would display more traditional social behaviors such as using the Chinese-dominant language choice patterns, while those with fewer ethnic ties within their exchange networks would have moved away from such traditions and adopted an English-oriented behavior.
- Speakers whose exchange networks consist of a relatively large number of peer ties would display behaviors which conform to the overall pattern of the generation to which they belong.

Notice here that the indicators used in measuring personal networks are different from those used in Gal or Milroy. Milroy (1987: 141) comments on the principles followed in selecting the appropriate network indicators and designing network measures. They must first of all reflect the conditions which have been found important in a wide range of network studies in predicting the extent to which normative pressures are applied by the local community, and they must be recoverable from data collected in the field and easily verifiable.

In a similar vein, "ethnic" and "peer" indices were constructed for interactive and passive ties. However, whereas the numbers for the exchange networks indicated specific individuals, those for interactive networks represented proportions. Each speaker was observed in terms of how many people he or she interacted with routinely but without exchange of material or moral support. The total numbers of interactive ties obviously varied. Percentages of ethnic and peer contacts were then calculated. Ten passive ties were analyzed for each speaker in the sample.

Using Analysis of Variance (ANOVA), Li Wei found that the ethnic index of the exchange networks was the best predictor for an individual's language choice patterns – the more Chinese contacts a speaker has in the exchange network, the more likely it is that the speaker speaks Chinese all the time. The ethnic index also worked to a lesser extent in interactive networks. However, peer contacts worked in very complex ways: peer content of exchange networks contributed to language maintenance *within* generations on the one hand, and to language shift, from Chinese to English, *across* generations on the other. This was even more true of interactive networks: The more peer-group contacts (members of the same generation) a grandparent had, the more Chinese was used; the more contacts a parent had with members of the grandparent generation, the more Chinese he or she used, while the more contacts a parent had with members of the child generation, the more bilingual he or she may be; and the more peer-group contacts a child had the more English was used.

This kind of social network analysis also allowed Li Wei to compare individual differences in language-choice patterns. Figure 15.3 illustrates two hypothetical individuals, whose social networks are rather different in terms of content and size. The hypothesis here is that there are significant behavioral differences between these two individuals which are conditioned by the networks they operate in.

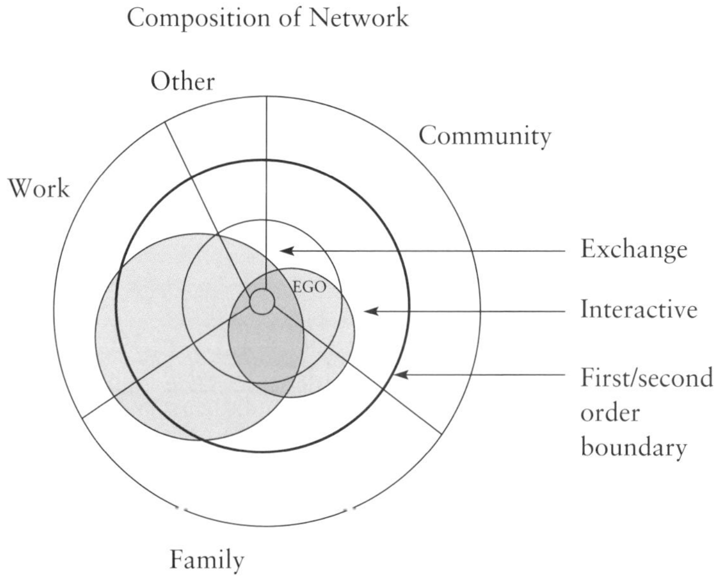

Figure 15.3: Comparison of two individuals' networks

Li Wei's study revealed that two of the male grandparents, for example, used a lot more English than other members of their own generation. In fact, their language-choice patterns were more typical of the parent generation. When social network contacts were examined, it was revealed that these two individuals had significantly more non-ethnic (Chinese) contacts in both their exchange and interactive networks than their peers.

Other studies of language choice, language maintenance and language shift in migrant communities that used the SNA include: Bortoni-Ricardo's (1985) work on rural dialect speakers in Brazil who migrated to a satellite city of the capital Brasilia, where she found that the social network ties of the migrant workers, especially whether or not they were kinsfolk, or whether the ties had been contracted in the pre-migration period, were closely correlated with their use of standard language versus dialect features; Schooling's work on language maintenance in Melanesia in which he developed a typology of social networks that corresponded to the observed patterns of language choice; Stoessel's (2002) study on immigrant women in the US, where the "maintainers" and "shifters" were differentiated on both their language-choice patterns and their social-network contacts; Wang's work (2006) on 13 Chinese families in the State of Johore, West Malaysia, where the shift from various Chinese dialects to Mandarin was linked to generational differences in social-network types.

Section summary

- Individuals develop different social networks for different purposes, which they can activate or deactivate at different times to achieve specific communicative and social goals.
- The contents of network ties are particularly significant to individuals from bilingual and migrant communities.

15.4 SNA and Bilingual Acquisition

Although sociolinguists who use the social network concept in their work take a particular interest in changes over time, the approach they use tends to be cross-sectional rather than longitudinal, i.e. they focus on different groups of speakers at a specific time rather than following one group of speakers over time. Yet, social networks are developed over time and are subject to constant changes. Applications of social network analysis in other fields often focus on the time dimension of network development and change and their impact on the individual's behavior.

Li Wei (2005b) specifically addresses the issue of change in social network ties in a longitudinal study of four British-born Chinese children – two boys and two girls – who are growing up as Chinese-English bilinguals. Two of the children – one boy and one girl – have older siblings, and one girl has a monolingual grandparent living with the family. Using a combination of research instruments and data sources, including parental checklist (British English version of MacArthur-Bates Communication Development Inventories (CDI) and CDI-style Chinese vocabulary checklist), weekly family recording of joint activities, parental diary (language choice, social activities, developmental features, and milestones), monthly home observation with recording, and interviews with parents, Li Wei was able to track the changes in quantity and quality of input the children received and their effects on lexical development, measured in terms of lexical diversity, and development of code-switching over time. As in his earlier work on language maintenance and language shift in the Chinese community in the UK, Li Wei focuses on the contents of social networks (e.g. peer vs. non-peer, Chinese vs. non-Chinese, bilingual vs. monolingual), adding this time the size of the network, particularly its growth over time. The following is a list of the highlights of his findings vis-à-vis social network effect:

1 Sibling effect
A sibling forms an important part of a child's social network. Both second-born subjects reached the two-word stage earlier than singletons by between 3 and 5 months.

2 Interlocutor effect

(a) There is a strong correlation between the primary caregiver's (person who spends most time in joint activities with the child) first language and the child's language dominance (measured in terms of language-choice preference and lexical diversity).
(b) Code-switching is restricted to specific interlocutors (bilingual parents).

3 Changes over time
Language development over time is strongly correlated with (changes in) primary carer's language dominance/preference.

(a) Lexical diversity in two languages combined grows according to the number of contacts the child has *outside* the family.
(b) Attendance of English-speaking nursery leads to reduced amount of code-switching (reduced amount of time in joint activities with parents).
(c) As the child grows older, the two languages develop in very separate contexts. The type of joint activities in which children engage differs in different contexts. Code-switching patterns change – there is more inter-sentential codeswitching; intra-sentential code-switching is restricted to English content words.

Li Wei's study demonstrates the potential of social network analysis as a practical, quantitative method of measuring variation and change in language input and their effect on the language development of young children. It also helps to break the artificial boundaries between sociolinguistics and developmental psycholinguistics.

Section summary

- Social networks develop and change over time.
- Social network analysis offers a practical, quantitative method of measuring variation and change in language input and their effect on the language development of bilingual children.

15.5   Conclusion

Social networking is a pervasive human condition. Social networks are as indispensable as language is for members of any society. The connections among individuals, linguistic and otherwise, make life possible, efficient, and enjoyable. Social networks provide an important social locale for their members. An individual's social locale plays a critical part in determining the specific information that individual is exposed to. People in different social locales receive information in different ways and participate in different social events; so they may come to construct knowledge differently. Social networks therefore influence individuals' social expectations, which may lead to certain types of socio-cognitive bias, which in turn affect their construction of knowledge.

Social network analysis is now well integrated into the study of language, as well as in a number of other disciplines. It has prospered in recent years in the study of bilingualism and multilingualism by providing findings and theories specifically accounting for phenomena such as language choice, language maintenance and language shift, and language development. It has been proven to be one of the most promising avenues to the understanding of linguistic dimensions of human life.

Further reading and resources

Brandes, Ulrik and Thomas Erlebach (eds.) (2005) *Network Analysis: Methodological Foundations*. Berlin and Heidelberg: Springer-Verlag.

Carrington, Peter J., John Scott, and Stanley Wasserman (eds.) (2005) *Models and Methods in Social Network Analysis*. New York: Cambridge University Press.

Cochran, Moncrieff, Mary Larner, David D. Riley, and Lars Gunnarsson (1990) *Extending Families: The Social Networks of Parents and Their Children*. Cambridge: Cambridge University Press.

Scott, John (2000) *Social Network Analysis: A Handbook*. 2nd edn. London: Sage.

The International Network for Social Network Analysis is the professional association for social network analysis.

Netwiki is a scientific wiki devoted to network theory, which uses tools from subjects such as graph theory, statistical mechanics, and dynamic systems to study real-world networks in the social sciences, technology, biology, etc.

Many social network tools for scholarly work are available on-line, such as the longtime standard *UCINet*, *Pajek*, or the "network" package in "R." They are relatively easy to use to present graphical images of networks. An open-source package for Linux is Social Networks Visualizer or *SocNetV*; a related package installer of *SocNetV* for Mac OS X is available.

Up-to-date research can be found in the journals *Social Networks*, *Connections*, and the *Journal of Social Structure*.

16 Conversation and Interactional Analysis

Holly R. Cashman

16.1 Introduction: Researching Bilingual Conversation

To the monolingual, bilingual conversation, especially the rapid switching between two languages, may seem chaotic and even exotic. To the bilingual, however, such code-switching may be seen as perfectly ordinary, or as incorrect, a corruption of the rules of two languages. To the advanced student of linguistics, the field of bilingual conversation may initially appear overwhelming, full of confusing terminology and rife with conflicting approaches. What can the study of bilingual conversation tell linguists about the structure of language? About social structure? About conversation? The answers to these questions depend on the analyst's approach to bilingual conversation, that is his or her data and method of analysis. A researcher's theoretical approach informs his or her decisions at every juncture, from identification of participants and research questions to data collection to analysis. As in many fields, there is incredible diversity in the body of research on bilingual conversation, from theoretical approaches to methodological choices to types of analysis (e.g. qualitative vs. quantitative).

Despite this diversity, linguists who research bilingual conversation agree on several key points. First, code-switching is not a dysfunctional language practice. Whatever meaning they attach to code-switching and language choices in bilingual conversation, analysts agree that code-switching is a normal, functional communicative practice found in virtually every bilingual context around the world. Rather than judge bilingual language practices as "correct" or "incorrect," researchers of bilingual conversational interaction instead attempt to describe how and why bilinguals switch between language varieties. Second, bilingual conversation is not qualitatively different from monolingual conversation. While bilingual speakers' linguistic repertoires contain varieties of more than one language, all speakers have linguistic repertoires with more than one language variety (style, register, dialect, or even language) and have the ability to switch between those language varieties in conversation. Third, whether they use recordings of spontaneous conversation or institutional discourse, language of the media or even literary sources, researchers of bilingual conversation base their conclusions on the analysis of data.

Over the past three decades, researchers have examined bilingual conversation from one of two broad approaches, which will be referred to here as symbolic and sequential. Both approaches, growing out of the groundbreaking work of John Gumperz, seek to understand the social motivations for language choice and code-switching. The *symbolic* approach argues that different language varieties carry different symbolic meanings which speakers exploit to make meaning in interaction, while the *sequential* approach focuses on the sequential positioning of language choices in conversation, arguing that it is the contrast of the code-switch itself that is meaning-making. In this chapter, the background of each approach will be described briefly, examples of analyses of bilingual conversation using each approach will be discussed, and what each approach can tell us about bilingual conversation will be summarized. Section 16.2 provides an overview of the relevant work of Gumperz, and is followed by descriptions of the symbolic approach to bilingual conversation in section 16.3 and the sequential approach in section 16.4. The integration of these approaches is discussed in section 16.5. Section 16.6 summarizes a few of the issues facing the field, new developments in the field, and resources for further information. The goal of this chapter is to give a basic introduction to the methods of carrying out research on bilingual conversational interaction. The chapter should be read in conjunction with other relevant chapters in this volume, especially chapters 4, 10, 11, and 14.

16.2   Blazing the Trail

The pioneering work of John Gumperz (cf. 1982a) continues to influence both approaches to the analysis of social motivations for code-switching in bilingual conversation today. Gumperz's insights into speakers' strategies for the making of meaning in conversation led researchers to look at bilingual conversation data in innovative, productive ways. To lay the groundwork for the discussion of the symbolic and sequential approaches to bilingual conversation, the following concepts stemming from the work of Gumperz will be reviewed in turn below: *we code vs. they code*, *situational switching vs. metaphorical switching*, and *contextualization cues*.

Blom and Gumperz (1972) examined, among other things, conversational interaction in Hemnesberget, a bidialectal community in Norway. Their unstructured ethnographic investigation yielded the following observations: (1) community members switched from Ranamål to Bokmål when outsiders, such as tourists or the researchers, approached their group; (2) teachers delivered lectures in Bokmål, but they used Ranamål in order to involve students in discussion; and (3) in the local community administration office, the clerk and the townspeople carried out official interactions in Bokmål, while they used Ranamål for informal talk about family and friends. These observations led Blom and Gumperz to two main conclusions:

first, they found that language usage in Hemnesberget was not homogeneous, and that the existing variation mapped onto social network factors; second, they found that use of the two different codes surpassed mere appropriateness or conformation with norms, and conveyed "information about values, beliefs and attitudes" (Gumperz, 1982a: 27). Gumperz explains: "What was normal usage for some in some situations counted as marked for others. Marked forms, moreover, tended to be used to convey indirect inferences" (ibid.). On the basis of this analysis, they proposed the existence of an in-group code (*we code*) and an out-group code (*they code*) in the community they studied and, by extension, in bilingual communities generally. The we/they code distinction explained a great deal of code-switching that occurred due to changes in the situational factors impacting a given interaction. Blom and Gumperz termed this code-switching "situational switching." *Situational switching* is the switch from one code to another involving a clear change in the participants' definition of each other's rights and obligations (Blom & Gumperz, 1972). In other words, situational code-switching is a practice in which:

> [d]istinct varieties are employed in certain settings (such as home, school, work) that are associated with separate, bounded kinds of activities (public speaking, formal negotiations, special ceremonials, verbal games, etc.) or spoken with different categories of speakers (friends, family members, strangers, social inferiors, government officials, etc.). (Gumperz, 1982a: 60)

According to Gumperz, the situational type of code-switching is observed in situations of diglossia, or other bilingual situations with stable norms for language usage.

The situational switching described above was distinguished by Blom and Gumperz from what they termed metaphorical switching. Unlike situational switching, metaphorical switching may occur when there is no change in situational factors such as participants or topic. *Metaphorical switching*, according to Blom and Gumperz, is the use of a switch in language variety to convey social meaning or reference social categories and groups. This referencing relies on speakers' shared association of language varieties with social identities (e.g. local vs. non-local, majority vs. minority) and activities (e.g. informal vs. formal). This shared association allows speakers to index certain social identities or activities through the use of a language variety in an unexpected context or by a different speaker (e.g. the use of the local dialect in a formal setting for humorous effect or the use of the standard in a family dispute to index an authoritative identity).

Like the metaphorical/situational distinction and the we/they code distinction described above, the concept of contextualization conventions or contextualization cues also relates to the problem of how participants in conversation make meaning. Gumperz (1982a: 131) defines *contextualization cues* as "constellations of surface features of message form [that] are the means by which speakers signal and listeners interpret what the activity is, how semantic content is to be understood and *how* each sentence relates to what precedes or follows" (original emphasis). He explains that any linguistic feature may perform this signaling function, from choice of prosody, syntactic structure, or lexical item to switch of language variety, register, or style. These cues themselves do not have referential meaning, but rather their use in interaction imbues them with a specific, context-bound meaning or interpretation. Gumperz indicates that "the situated interpretation of the meaning of any one such shift in context is always a matter of social convention" (p. 132), so that speakers must share an awareness of the signaling function these cues have, which varies interculturally, in order to share "situated judgments," or interpretations of the cues' meanings in interaction. It is for this reason that Gumperz suggests the importance of understanding the functioning of contextualization cues in order to examine breakdowns in communication or misunderstandings in inter-ethnic communication (p. 152).

These three key concepts from Gumperz (we/they code, situational/metaphorical switching, and contextualization cues) find their way into the work of researchers examining bilingual conversation through the symbolic approach and the sequential approach. As analysts from both approaches attempt to uncover speakers' motivations for code choices and the processes they use to make meaning in interaction, the work of Gumperz, though critiqued and refined from a variety of perspectives, remains at the very core of the enterprise.

16.3   Symbolic Approach

The symbolic approach to bilingual conversation explains practices such as code-switching and language choice in terms of communities' sociohistorical structures and speakers' rights and obligations as members of those communities. Conversational behavior is seen as a window into social structure because speakers are seen to reflect social structure in their conversational interaction. The most influential symbolic approach in contemporary research on bilingual conversation is Myers-Scotton's (1993b) markedness model.

16.3.1   The markedness model

Building on Blom and Gumperz's concepts of marked language choice and situational vs. metaphorical switching, Myers-Scotton's (1993b) markedness model (MM) relies on an understanding of what is expected in a given interaction in light of the shared norms of a speech community. Myers-Scotton proposed that in both monolingual and bilingual communities speakers know what language choices are expected in a given interaction. This knowledge (conceptualized as a "markedness evaluator") is the result of speakers' previous interactions and accumulated experiences that become conventionalized in a set of rights and obligations (RO set) shared with other members of the speech community. Within this context, speakers' language choices are either unmarked (i.e. expected) or marked (i.e. unexpected). In other words, "in their own language use, individuals exploit the relationships that become established in a community between a linguistic variety and who uses the variety, and where and how it is used" (Myers-Scotton, 1998: 18). The MM provides a framework for describing speakers' unexpected or marked language choices, including but not limited to code-switching, by interpreting their social motivation.

The MM rests primarily on three maxims:

1   the unmarked choice maxim, which directs speakers to choose the unmarked language choice in order to affirm the existing RO set (Myers-Scotton, 1993b: 114);
2   the marked choice maxim, which directs speakers to choose a marked language variety in order to change the existing RO set for the interaction (Myers-Scotton, 1993b: 131);
3   the exploratory choice maxim, which directs speakers to switch language varieties when there is no unmarked choice in order to indicate their language preference (Myers-Scotton, 1993b: 142).

In the MM, the "negotiation principle" underlies all choices of codes in conversational interaction: the speakers' choice of code in every speech exchange references or indexes the pre-established set of rights and obligations that the speaker wants to "be in force" during the interaction.

This model is designed to account for all instances of code-switching in conversation and their social motivations in a unified typology. According to the MM, speakers may code-switch for one of the following four complementary reasons: code-switching as a sequence of unmarked choices (maxim 1); code-switching itself as an unmarked choice (also maxim 1); as a marked choice (maxim 2); and as an exploratory choice (maxim 3). *Code-switching as a sequence of unmarked choices* occurs when factors, such as conversational participants or topics, change during an interaction. This change in situational factors triggers a change in the RO set; speakers code-switch in order to maintain use of the unmarked choice. Also stemming from the unmarked choice maxim is a second type of code-switching: *code-switching as an unmarked choice*, which might occur in a conversation in which all the addressees were known by all the speakers to be bilingual. In that situation, code-switching would be expected, or at least not unexpected. *Code-switching as a marked choice* results when a speaker's code-switching is an unusual or unexpected choice, given a preestablished RO set. In fact, Myers-Scotton proposes that all occurrences of code-switching as a marked choice serve "to negotiate a change in the expected social distance holding between participants, either increasing or decreasing it" (1993b: 132) by introducing a new RO set. According to Myers-Scotton, the interactional effects of code-switching as a marked choice may vary; the specific effect might be, for example, the expression of anger or affection, aggravation or mitigation. Lastly, *code-switching as an exploratory choice* occurs when speakers "themselves are not sure of the expected or optimal communicative intent, or at least not sure which one will help achieve their social goals" (1993b: 142) due to a clash of social norms, because they are unsure which norms apply (e.g. the interlocutor is unknown to the speaker), or social norms are in a state of flux. One key assumption of the MM, later recast as a rational choice (RC) model is that, while social factors determine speakers' linguistic repertoires, rational choices explain what motivates speakers to make the language choices they make (e.g. code-switch) (Myers-Scotton & Bolonyai, 2001). Myers-Scotton and Bolonyai (2001: 6) argue that "linguistic choices – and specifically, variation in choices – are best explained by an analysis assuming that choices depend on the speaker's estimation of what choices offer him or her the greatest benefit." The recasting of the MM as an RC model includes the addition of a filter structure that narrows a limitless possibility of code choices into one rational choice. The first filter, which represents structural constraints, constrains possible choices to only those present in the speaker's linguistic repertoire; the second filter serves to bias the remaining choices according to the speaker's experience (i.e. the markedness evaluator described above); finally, the third filter is, basically, rationality – the consideration of the costs and benefits of the choice, the goals and desires of the speaker, and the social norms of the community (pp. 13–14).

16.3.2   *Examples of the symbolic approach*

The symbolic approach has been widely used to examine bilingual conversation in a variety of bilingual contexts. While much of the research using this approach uses the markedness model, a good deal of it also builds directly on Gumperz's concepts of metaphorical switching or we/they code. One example is Jørgensen's (1998) longitudinal study of strategies for constructing dominance in interaction among Turkish school children in Køge, Denmark. Jørgensen outlines the prestige of Danish vis-à-vis Turkish in the context of Turkish labor migration into Denmark. Turkish is considered unfit for scholarly pursuits and not a modern language, children's linguistic assimilation is strongly encouraged, and parents suffer high unemployment and low prestige. Danish, in contrast, is the majority language, supported by the state and spoken by the majority population (p. 240). Extensive ethnographic work also reveals distinctions among the three districts in which Turks live in Køge, and between the parent and child generations (p. 241). For the Turkish immigrant parents in Køge, Jørgensen concludes, Turkish is the "we code" of the community, and Danish is the "they code." In contrast, for the bilingual Turkish children of the community, Jørgensen proposes that code-switching may be the "we code." In peer interaction, Jørgensen finds that the association of Danish with public, institutional domains and the association of Turkish with private, community domains makes code-switching between Turkish and Danish a resource children may exploit in interaction. In one conversation, for example, a mixed-sex triad of children uses Danish to carry out school-related tasks and Turkish to talk about private, emotional matters. In fact, one child suggests turning off the recording device after a Turkish utterance (p. 247). Interactions among a group of four boys in second grade and later in fifth grade demonstrate that one boy, Erol, successfully uses switches into Danish to construct dominance in a power struggle (p. 254). Jørgensen recognizes, however, that as the children become more proficient at code-switching, and code-switching itself is less marked, there are occasions in which global factors cannot explain individual switches, presumably because code-switching is the unmarked choice. He concludes the children "developed code-switching into a tool which can be used with reference both to global power factors and to local factors" (p. 254).

Like Jørgensen, Yoon (1996) employs a symbolic approach to examine the meaning of language choice and code-switching in the conversation of Korean-English bilingual adults. Ethnographic research indicates that age, status, and rank are key social factors that are reflected in Korean interaction. Yoon (1996: 397) explains that "one is always more powerful, older, higher or lower in rank than the other . . . the respect for age, status, and rank is stressed in, and governs, social interaction in order to maintain integrity and honor for oneself and one's group." Yoon studied the language practices of Korean-born bilingual adults with other Korean-English bilinguals not known to the speaker (out-group members) and with close relatives of the same or a younger generation (in-group members). Yoon's analysis of the language choices of Korean-born bilinguals reveals that Korean is associated with out-group members and English is associated with in-group members. Tying speakers' motivations into two aspects of linguistic politeness (discernment and volition), this language choice is explained by the cultural focus on awareness of relative social position: in interaction with out-group members, speakers use Korean, which is capable of indexing fine distinctions of social position linguistically, because they are constantly managing the appropriate social relationship with their interlocutor; in contrast, interaction with in-group members does not require such close monitoring of interpersonal relationships because such relationships are fixed, allowing for the use of English, a neutral language for the Korean-English bilinguals studied (pp. 402–3). Yoon also finds a tendency to use small-size switches with out-group members and large-size switches with in-group members (p. 404).

Sebba and Wootton (1998) explore the notion of an association between language varieties and social identities in their examination of code-switching in the discourse of adolescent and adult British Caribbeans. They found that, as predicted by the we/they code framework, speakers did differentiate between the two codes they called "London Jamaican" and "London English" (p. 275); they argued, however, that the functions of the putative "we code" and "they code" should be determined through a careful analysis of the data, not assumed a priori (pp. 275–6). Finally, on the basis of a sequential analysis of the data, they conclude that the code employed by speakers may be relevant to the identity work that they are doing, although they recognize that there are instances where it may not be; that is, "[s]ocial identities are made manifest through *talk*, not just through the language or code used but also through the content and the context" (p. 284). Sebba and Tate (2002) exploit the notion of an association between language varieties and social identities in their analysis of identity construction among British Caribbeans. In an analysis of conversation, interview, and written data, they observed that British Jamaican Creole is used by speakers to index global identities associated with the African and Caribbean diaspora and a local variety of British English to index locally based identities (p. 76). Although they "do not claim that every use of British English or Creole is significant," they assert that "many are; and that the meaning of the choice of varieties within the conversations among people of Caribbean heritage is part of the taken-for-granted aspects of the interaction which are self-evident to the participants but must be 'discovered' and explained by the analyst" (p. 88).

16.3.3   *Critiques of the symbolic approach*

Four main issues are identified in critiques of the markedness model, and in some cases of symbolic approaches in general, although I would argue that they do not apply to the work of Jørgensen, Yoon, Sebba and Tate, and Sebba and Wootton, above. First, as Li Wei (1998) pointed out, it is not always possible to identify the unmarked language choice for every situation, except perhaps in the case of stable, diglossic situations (p. 173). Speakers, he claimed, are sometimes confronted with novel situations not easily comparable to previous situations, and speakers in a heterogeneous speech community may not share associations between language varieties and social identities (p. 159). Second, not all instances of code-switching carry any macro-level social meaning, as Jørgensen as well as Sebba and Wootton noted with regards to his data. Meeuwis and Blommaert (1994) explain that "codeswitching can have the function of establishing/negotiating identities, but it need not" (p. 412). It has been observed in research on bilingual conversation around the world that some, if not many (or even most, depending on the community), code-switches are neither situational nor metaphorical. Gafaranga (2005), referring to Cameron's (1990) article in which she critiques what she calls the language-reflects-society approach that dominates sociolinguistics, alleges that this approach has also dominated the symbolic approach to bilingual conversation (p. 283). Specifically, Gafaranga contends that it is damaging and counterproductive to view linguistic structure as separate from and reflective of social structure rather than *as a level of* social structure in its own right. Sebba and Tate (2002: 83) agree, explaining that social identities "are constituted by social reality but also come to constitute that reality . . . Meaning *comes into being* through interactions." While the markedness model's "code-switching as an unmarked choice" might allow for code-switching that does not convey special communicative intent, it does not provide any explanation of what function code-switching might serve in these circumstances. The focus on the social meaning leads to a neglect of the possible interactional meanings of code-switching (Li Wei, 1998: 170). Third, as Myers-Scotton herself points out, "the [markedness] model presumes that much of what 'happens' is below the surface: Speakers' intentions surface as code choices. Interpretations about intentions . . . are not held up for verification; they have no empirical basis" (Myers-Scotton & Bolonyai, 2001: 15). Without any demonstrable evidence of the relevance of aspects of the social context, speakers' identities and speakers' intentions, the analyst risks imposing her or his own meaning, however unintentionally. This lack of empirical basis is especially dangerous when analysts are out-group members with little knowledge about the sociopolitical and linguistic history of a given community, including, as Meeuwis and Blommaert signal, "language-ideological concerns" (p. 415) and an understanding of "processes of distribution and acquisition of symbolic goods" (p. 418). Finally, the markedness model focuses solely on the social meaning that is "brought along" into the interaction and ignores the social structure that might be "brought about" through the interaction (Li Wei, 1998: 170). Meeuwis and Blommaert argue that focusing solely on the "brought-along" social meaning leads to the conclusion that "interaction merely consists of the reproduction or reification of pre-existing social meaning, and itself is not creative" (1994: 159).

Additional criticism of the markedness model, as it is recast as a rational choice model, is articulated by Li Wei (2005a). Central to his critique are the assumption of rationality at the level of the individual social act and the assumption of trans-parency in the deliberation process. Rationality, he explains, is insufficient for explaining what interactants will do beyond an expectation that they will behave relatively consistently (p. 377). Li Wei suggests that rational deliberation, which is meant to weigh speakers' beliefs, values, and desires in order to arrive at the best action in a given situation, is not a transparent process that can be treated as non-problematic. While Li Wei does not necessarily disagree with the concept of RO sets and the effect of interaction-external factors, he argues that a more detailed, interaction-internal analysis is necessary to support the conclusions of an RC analysis. He concludes that "a dual-level approach . . . would help to extract factors that can deepen our understanding of the way bilingual speakers use their linguistic and interactional resources and achieve a richer, more interesting, but still relevant (to the participants) explanation" (p. 388).

16.3.4 *Researching bilingual conversation through a symbolic approach*

To sum up, symbolic approaches attempt to explain what motivates speakers to code-switch or to choose one language variety over another in a given interaction according to community norms associating certain language varieties with deter-mined social identities or activities. The main question that a symbolic approach can answer is *why* speakers code-switch as a marked choice (i.e. with intent or symbolic meaning) and *why* changes in external factors (e.g. participants, topic, setting) result in code-switching as an unmarked choice. The student interested in pursuing research on bilingual conversation from a symbolic approach must examine the community and the speakers in depth. Given that the analyst must draw conclusions about speakers' intentions and reveal relationships between lan-guage varieties and symbolic meaning, it is essential, especially for outsiders to the community, to carry out extensive research on the sociopolitical, linguistic, and language-ideological history of the community. As Yoon (1996) and Jørgensen (1998) demonstrate, one cannot assume that the majority and minority language varieties will have the same meaning for all speakers in bilingual communities. This research necessarily includes both a review of the literature (i.e. published research on the community and similar communities from a variety of disciplines over time) and ethnography (e.g. participant observation for an extended period within the com-munity). Also, the researcher cannot assume that language behavior will reflect lan-guage attitudes. For example, bilingual speakers routinely criticize code-switching even though they frequently code-switch.

Section summary

Symbolic approaches focus on speakers' macro-level identities, i.e. their membership in social categories such as sex-based, racial, or ethnic groups, and how these identities are reflected in speakers' language choices. The approach builds on the concepts of we/they code and metaphorical/situational code-switching. Since the late 1980s the markedness model, based on these earlier insights, has provided researchers of bilingual conversation with a useful framework. This model argues that for every interaction there exists an established set of speakers' rights and obligations. The speaker makes unmarked choices to affirm this RO set, makes marked choices to challenge it, or makes exploratory choices to assess their interlocutor's preferences. The markedness model is criticized for its language-reflects-society perspective, its assumption that code-switching generally conveys macro-social meaning, and its reliance on the analyst's interpretation of speakers' intentions.

16.4   Sequential Approach

The sequential approach to the examination of bilingual conversation differs from the symbolic approach in several key ways. First, it does not assume an association between language varieties and social meaning. Instead, building on Gumperz's notion of the contextualization cue, the contrast created by the juxtaposition of the two languages (i.e. the switch itself) is considered potentially significant to the management of the ongoing conversation. Also, no prior assumption about the relevance of social context or the identities speakers "bring along" to the interaction is made. Rather, the sequential context, or the context provided by the preceding turns of talk, is considered relevant to the interaction in the conversation analytic (CA) tradition and "brought-about" social structure, or that which emerges through the interaction, is examined. Social context is not ignored, but it is examined only when and where speakers make it relevant to the ongoing interaction. Finally, bilingual conversation is seen as a window into social structure because social structure is seen as a product of everyday interaction (rather than merely a reflection of it). In other words, language choice in bilingual conversation is seen as "practical social action" (Gafaranga, 2001: 1915). The application of the theory of conversation analysis (CA) constitutes the main sequential approach to the study of bilingual interaction.

16.4.1   Conversation analysis (CA)

Conversation analysis (CA) was developed through the intellectual exchange of four sociologists in California in the 1960s: Erving Goffman, Harvey Sacks, Emanuel

Schegloff, and Harold Garfinkel. Sacks and Schegloff, students of Goffman's, were simultaneously influenced by Goffman's interest in interaction (cf. Goffman, 1963, 1974, 1981) and Garfinkel's (1967) focus on theorizing commonplace, everyday practices through ethnomethodology (ten Have, 1999: 5–6). Through his study of telephone calls to a suicide prevention hotline, Sacks uncovered the orderliness of conversational interaction. Hutchby and Wooffitt (1988: 23) summarize Sacks's key insights in four propositions: (1) talk-in-interaction is ordered and organized, (2) its production is methodic, (3) spontaneous talk-in-interaction should be analyzed, and (4) theoretical assumptions should not affect analysis of talk-in-interaction. Sacks died in a car accident in 1975, but his lectures are collected in two volumes (Sacks, 1992), and his collaborator Emanuel Schegloff, with others, carried on his work.

The sequential organization underlying conversation is a key discovery of CA, arising out of Sacks's research (Psathas, 1995: 13). Sacks noticed that each speaker's turn creates a context for the turn that followed; in other words, he noticed that talk is organized sequentially (Duranti, 1997: 248). The sequential context constrains the production and interpretation of turns at talk. Sacks proposed the underlying structure of units of talk called adjacency pairs, which consist of two turns linked by a relationship of conditional relevance. The first pair part (e.g. question, invitation) conditions the production and interpretation of the second pair part (e.g. answer, acceptance) (Psathas, 1995: 16–17). Given the underlying orderliness of conversation, a key question asked by analysts – key because it is thought to be key to participants' process of meaning-making – is "why that now?" (Schegloff, 1997b). In other words, why is the speaker doing what he or she is doing at a given point in conversation? What is he or she signaling to co-participants? For example, one might ask why a speaker code-switches at a certain point, what the effect of maintaining an interlocutor's language choice is or how a speaker constructs opposition to a co-participant's ideas without ever explicitly expressing disagreement. The answer to these types of questions is found by thoroughly examining the details of the interaction, paying the utmost attention to the sequential context of the point of interest. In this way, CA is a problem-solving approach, one that attempts to arrive at participants' own mechanisms for making sense of and managing interaction through a close analysis of interaction itself.

A second key proposal of CA is that this organization is co-constructed by participants locally. In other words, as Psathas (1995: 2) explains, CA's "basic position is that social actions are meaningful for those who produce them and that they have a natural organization that can be discovered and analyzed by close examination." Schegloff (1999: 427) identifies three "generic organizations" of conversation that must be resolved by co-participants in order to sustain stable interaction; these include the sequence organization described above, turn-taking organization, and repair organization (427). In addition, Shin and Milroy (2000: 370) add preference organization to this list of main tasks facing participants in conversation. Speakers use a wide range of verbal and non-verbal resources to manage these four generic organizations of conversation.

Preference organization is the term given to the notion that when the conversational sequence has established a context in which more than one action is possible, it is likely that one action is preferred, meaning that it is the expected action and the one chosen most often (ten Have, 1999: 120). The "shape" of the turn is affected by the preferred-ness of the response: preferred turns tend to be structurally simple and delivered without hesitation; dispreferred turns tend to be more complex and delayed (Pomerantz, 1984: 64). Boyle (2000: 601) describes preference organization as a very simple mechanism: preferred actions go unnoticed, but dispreferred actions are noticeable and, possibly, sanctionable. Turn-taking organization involves split-second timing in order to limit gaps and overlaps between turns, although the preference for no gaps and no overlaps in conversation likely varies cross-culturally. Also crucial to the local management of turn-taking is the allocation of turns, speaker change, or addressee selection (Sacks, Schegloff, & Jefferson, 1974). Repair organization describes speakers' methods for "resolving what is being perceived and/or defined as a 'problem' or 'trouble' in the course of an interaction" (Duranti, 1997: 261). CA examines who initiates the repair of a trouble source (speaker or interlocutor) and who performs the repair, as well as what the consequences are for the ongoing interaction (Schegloff, Jefferson, & Sacks, 1977). Self- and other-initiated repair differ not only in terms of who is carrying out the initiation, but also in how the repair initiation is carried out (Schegloff, Jefferson, & Sacks, 1977: 365–9).

The object of CA research is *talk-in-interaction*, an umbrella term that comprises a virtually infinite number of speech-exchange systems, from ordinary conversation to religious rituals (Schegloff, 1999: 407). Despite the diversity of speech-exchange systems, for CA, so-called ordinary conversation (i.e. spontaneous, peer conversation) is the fundamental speech-exchange system. Given that CA does not assume in advance the relevance of social structure and does not impose any classificatory frameworks, the ideal CA approach to examining data is "unmotivated looking." This stipulates that: "the variety of interactional phenomena available for study are not selected on the basis of some preformulated theorizing" (Psathas, 1995: 45). Schegloff describes the process of unmotivated looking thus: "it may begin . . . with the noticing of some feature of the talk and be pursued by asking what – if anything – such a practice of talking has as its outcome" (1996: 172).

16.4.2 Examining bilingual conversation

While the early research in CA examined monolingual (American) English data almost exclusively, Auer (1984) proposed that a sequential, interactional approach to the examination of code-switching had the potential to answer a question he considered to be of primary importance: "If the number of types of language alternation isn't finite, then *how* do participants agree on one interpretation or the other *in loco*?" (p. 3). To answer this question, Auer built on Gumperz's (1982a) concept of "contextualization," and suggested that code-switching might be used by bilinguals as a *contextualization cue*, or a signal to orient co-participants to changes in the ongoing interaction. Code-switching and language choice, Auer proposed, may act alone or in concert with other contextualization cues, including prosody (rhythm, tone, pitch, accent) and gesture (eye contact, posture) as a powerful resource for managing bilingual conversation, including sequence organization, turn-taking, preference, and repair (p. 18). Auer identified two types of code-switching: *discourse-related code-switching* is the juxtaposition of material from two different language systems in the same interactional episode in order to organize the ongoing conversation (1984: 12); *participant-related code-switching* is the use of such a juxtaposition to communicate to co-participants something about the language preference of the speaker (1984: 46–7). Auer clarified that this language preference may be of a stable, general nature (for example, when it relates to a speaker's competence or language proficiency) or it may be more episode-bound (relating to the identities of the co-participants, the institutional context or the nature of the interaction) (1984: 22). Importantly, the types of code-switching are not mutually exclusive; although Auer presented prototypical cases of each type, he explains that in conversation individual instances of code-switching may have polyvalent meanings. The two types of code-switching, Auer argued, reflect the participants' procedure for arriving at local meaning of instances of code-switching.

According to Li Wei (2002: 164), the CA approach has two main advantages for researchers interested in examining the meaning of code-switching in conversation. First, he points out, CA focuses on sequential rather than macro-social context, which means that speakers' language choices are examined in light of the context of preceding and following turns at talk rather than in reference to external social structure. While the relevance of social structure is not denied, it is not assumed a priori (Li Wei, 2005a: 380). Second, CA privileges speakers' interpretation of talk as evidenced through their behavior rather than analysts' interpretation of speakers' intentions. This limits the analyst's "interpretational leeway" (Auer, 1984: 6) to what is demonstrably relevant to the participants in interaction (Li Wei, 2002: 164). As Li Wei explains, "the CA approach dispenses with motivational speculation in favor of an interpretative approach based on detailed, turn-by-turn analysis of language choices . . . it is about HOW the meaning of code-switching is constructed in interaction" (2002: 167). In this way, the analyses are empirically based and eminently verifiable.

16.4.3   *Examples of the CA approach to bilingual conversation*

As has been noted often, CA has been used overwhelmingly to examine monolingual conversation, especially in English. While this is true, it has also been used to study conversations in languages other than English and bilingual conversations. Valdés and Pino (1981) were perhaps the first to apply CA to the examination of bilingual conversation in a study of compliment responses among Mexican-American bilinguals in the southwestern United States. Auer (1984) is a comprehensive study of the conversational code-switching of Italian immigrant children in Konstanz, Germany from which he drew the theoretical approach described above.

Building on the CA approach to bilingual conversation proposed by Auer, Li Wei's (1994) study of code-switching in the Newcastle upon Tyne Chinese community in northeast England is an example of the sequential approach. Li Wei examines language practices in three-generational families using long-term participant observation in addition to recordings of naturally occurring conversation. He finds that the Chinese/English bilinguals he studied use code-switching in order to manage talk-in-interaction. According to Li Wei, the use of code-switching to provide contrast between previous turns and following turns is crucial to the organization of bilingual conversation. He concludes that "code-switching contextualizes turn transition by building up a contrast, much as do changes in pitch or tempo or as . . . phonetic variations" (p. 159). Regarding preference, Li Wei finds that divergent code choice may be used to mark dispreferred second pair parts, which "are usually accompanied by various kinds of structural complexity" (p. 155), just as pauses, hedges, and other contextualization cues are used to mark dispreference in mono-lingual conversation. The pauses and hedges found in monolingual conversation are, of course, also found in bilingual conversation, but the salience of code-switching as a contextualization cue is such that the language contrast alone is often used (p. 165). Code-switching is also used to contextualize repair in Li Wei's data; he finds that speakers organize repair through the use of a contrasting language to mark repair initiators. Finally, Li Wei finds that speakers in his data use code-switching to manage sequence organization in bilingual conversation. This includes marking the shift from pre-sequences to main sequences, bracketing off side sequences, and shifting from one sequence to the next.

Another, more recent example of the CA approach to bilingual conversation is Bani-Shoraka's (2005) investigation of Persian-Azerbaijani code-switching in the Azerbaijani community of Tehran. For her qualitative analysis of bilingual talk, Bani-Shoraka uses recordings of spontaneous conversations in four multi-generational families in the minority language community. She finds that code-switching serves both to organize the talk and to communicate information about the participants' language preferences, often at the same time. In her analysis of an inter-generational argument about money-lending practices, a mother and her sister-in-law use code-switching as a resource to sustain opposition with the daughter, whose trans-interactional preferred language is Persian. Bani-Shoraka details how a variety of resources, including pauses and overlaps, laughter, and insertion of a stylized Persian variety, and code-switching, are used to challenge the "brought-along" social order by "bringing about" a different social order – through the construction of a "sociable argument" – in which the lowest-status member of the interaction, the youngest, may challenge her aunt and even her mother, as well as discuss a taboo topic. Reported speech is also examined by Bani-Shoraka, including what she terms "hypothetical future dialogue," or reported speech that has not happened and likely never will, in which speakers use contrasting codes, changes in verb tense, and variation in voice quality to construct lively narratives and "switch selves" (p. 206) in interaction.

A final example of the CA approach demonstrates that the study of bilingual conversation goes beyond the investigation of code-switching. Rieger (2003) exam-ines repetition (that is, self-initiated, same-turn self-repair) in the conversation of English German bilinguals. She finds that English German bilinguals use repetitions differently depending on which language they are speaking. In English, preposi-tions, pronoun–verb pairs and personal pronouns were repeated most often; in

German demonstrative pronouns and fillers were "recycled" most often (p. 67). Rieger finds that repetition as a self-repair strategy is an orderly phenomenon that might be affected by the structure of the language varieties involved. Rieger concludes that differences in the structure of English and German explain some aspects of this variation and differences in speakers' language proficiency explain others: the number of prepositions, for example, is greater in English than in German because of the loss of the dative and genitive cases in the former (the same *proportion* of repeated prepositions was found in both languages); fillers, in contrast, are repeated more in German because of speakers' proficiency (more of the bilingual speakers were native speakers of English). In both German and in English, Rieger observes, repetitions tended to occur at the beginning of units.

16.4.4   Critiques of the CA approach to bilingual conversation

Critiques of the CA approach come from within sociology, linguistic anthropology, and discourse analysis. The chief criticism levied by critics of the CA approach to bilingual conversation is that the approach focuses on trivial details of inter-action, ignoring social context (Li Wei, 2002: 170). According to Myers-Scotton and Bolonyai (2001: 5), CA ignores "who participants 'are' – in demographic, social network, and even ethnographic terms." Wetherell (1998) and Billig (1999), both responding to a programmatic article by Schegloff (1997b), articulate the main critiques of CA made by practitioners of critical discourse analysis (CDA). Wetherell claims that CA lacks a social theory and hence a bridge to larger social and political context; CA, therefore, is merely a technical analysis of spoken dis-course (p. 394). Billig argues that Schegloff's claim that CA is non-ideological is untrue; rather, he contends, CA has an unexamined ideological stance that accepts historical background uncritically, assumes participants have equal rights to talk, and takes for granted that speakers share the same organization principles of talk.

Similarly, Blommaert (2001) takes issue with CA's claim to transparency of method. He asserts that CA "fails to recognize even the existence of the entextualizing practices it applies to text" (p. 18), referring to the process of turning "talk" into "data" (recording, transcription, analysis), which necessarily involves ideologically motivated decisions. In addition, Blommaert argues that CA, because it views talk as single units of interaction, is not able to account for the later entextualization of that talk by others. While Schegloff (1997b) lays out that social context is relevant to CA only when it is demonstrably relevant to participants, Blommaert comments that "one of the key critical issues . . . [is] the fact that talk may *not* have certain implications to the ('direct') participants, that certain matters are not 'demonstrably relevant,' but that they *are made* relevant by later re-entextualizations of that talk by others" (p. 19). Additional critique from the field of linguistic anthropology is summarized by Duranti (1997), who articulates three central critiques (in addition to the aforementioned issue of social context): ignoring the non-verbal aspects of communication, having an impoverished notion of what constitutes speech, and a lack of interest in participants' own interpretations of their interactional behavior (p. 266).

Finally, critics specifically of CA's approach to bilingual conversation allege that CA neglects the social meaning of code-switching and ignores speakers' motivations (Myers-Scotton & Bolonyai, 2001). Myers-Scotton (1998: 36) adds further that CA does not allow for, or provide the researcher with any way of analyzing, marked choices. Myers-Scotton (1999: 1260) claims that the CA approach to bilingual conversation focuses on how structural features of discourse determine speakers' choices in selecting their next turn, or how constraints on speakers' repertoire operate. In other words, Myers-Scotton believes that CA sees the speakers' repertoire (opportunity set) as directly determining linguistic choices, leaving speakers' motivations and the dynamics of the situation as constant and unchanging (p. 1260).

16.4.5 *Researching bilingual conversation from a conversation analytic approach*

The sequential analysis of bilingual conversation attempts to explain how bilingual speakers collaboratively manage conversational interaction. The main questions that researchers in the CA approach ask relate to the use of linguistic resources, including code-switching and language choice, to achieve the ordered activity of conversational interaction and interactional goals, such as agreeing or disagreeing, inviting and responding to invitations, and complimenting and insulting. Although the CA approach traditionally examines spontaneous, peer conversation, the method has recently been used to analyze talk in a wide variety of contexts, including institutional and media contexts. Research of bilingual conversation from a CA approach requires repeated examination of detailed transcripts of audio and, when available, video, recordings. The data collection and transcription process can be very time-consuming, depending on many factors, including the level of detail of the transcript (e.g. Are changes in gaze and body position noted? Are overlapping talk, latching, breathing, pauses, laughter, etc. noted?), the number of participants involved (which often results in overlapping talk), and the linguistic repertoire of the researcher (e.g. whether or not he or she is a native speaker of the varieties being transcribed and analyzed). While not quantitative in nature, a CA study benefits from as much data as is available, since discovery of the underlying orderliness of conversation may require comparison of as many instances as possible of similar phenomena (such as repairs or closings).

Section summary

Conversation analysis (CA) is a problem-solving approach that views conversation as ordered and sequentially organized. Researchers using this approach to study bilingual conversation attempt to uncover through detailed analysis the meanings that speakers themselves attribute to code-switching in interaction.

Interpretations of speakers' utterances are based on the local, interactional context rather than on the macro-level social context. Code-switching is observed to function as a contextualization cue, a signaling device used to highlight turns at talk in order to manage the basic organizations: turn-taking, sequence organization, preference organization, and repair. The CA approach is mainly criticized for ignoring social context in favor of sequential context.

16.5   Identity-in-Interaction: Integrating the Two Approaches

Aronsson (1998) suggests the term "identity-in-interaction" to describe the co-construction of identity in conversation. Aronsson recognizes that social order/organization is the background for identity-in-interaction, but claims that as social organization shapes talk it is also shaped by talk (p. 76). Bucholtz and Hall (2004: 371) agree with this point; they argue that social groupings (nationality, ethnicity, social class, etc.) and social identities (native or non-native speaker; male or female; heterosexual, homosexual, or bisexual, etc.) are the result of "identity work" in interaction, are negotiations of sameness and difference, and involve power and agency of the participants in interaction. Bucholtz and Hall draw on recent work on identity in linguistic anthropology to describe four semiotic processes that account for how social identities are created through language: practice, indexicality, ideology, and performance (p. 370). The concept of *practice*, or praxis, grows out of the work of Bourdieu (1977a, 1977b); it is described by Bucholtz and Hall as the formation of language through "sedimentation of habitual action" (p. 378). *Indexicality* is the "semiotic operation of juxtaposition, whereby one entity or event points to another" (ibid.). *Ideology* in contemporary linguistic anthropology, Bucholtz and Hall explain, is what "organizes and enables all cultural practices as well as the power relations that result from these" (p. 379). Finally, *performance* is "highly deliberate and self-aware social display" (p. 380), which "occurs not only on stages and under spotlights but in frequent and fleeting interactional moments throughout daily life, often involving stylization (p. 381). Bucholtz and Hall's essay provides a framework for research in bilingual conversation that attempts to integrate the concerns of symbolic and sequential approaches to data analysis. Chiefly, their view of identity as "an outcome of cultural semiotics that is accomplished through the production of contextually relevant sociopolitical relations of similarity and difference, authenticity and inauthenticity, and legitimacy and illegitimacy" (p. 382) is consistent both with CA's view of accomplishing identity (i.e. analyzing the construction of identity when it is demonstrably relevant to participants) and also the MM's notions of markedness, indexicality and speaker agency.

16.5.1   *Examining bilingual identity-in-interaction*

Researchers who examine identity-in-interaction do not assume that social context in the form of social categories such as speakers' gender, race, religion, or ethnicity, or even profession, social role, or institutional identity, is relevant to individual instances of conversational interaction and they do not assume a relationship between certain codes in the speakers' linguistic repertoires and pre-established, static social identities. Rather, researchers of bilingual conversation using an identity-in-interaction approach examine how identities are co-constructed and negotiated by co-participants in talk. They find that code-switching, in addition to other verbal and non-verbal acts, serves both to transgress and to mark group boundaries, to challenge and to reinforce concepts of ethnicity and race. Gafaranga (2001) explains that identity in an interactional analysis is not about what speakers bring along into interaction, but rather about what identities speakers co-construct or bring about in conversation through language choice in addition to other resources. Gafaranga (2005: 283) calls for what he terms a "demythologised perspective on language alternation" in which conversational structure and social structure are not considered separate entities. Rather, he argues, "language itself must be seen as a social structure, as structuring society" (ibid.).

16.5.2   *Examples of identity-in-interaction*

Williams's (2005) study of the local construction of social roles in a Chinese-American bilingual family dispute is an example of the investigation of identity-in-interaction in a bilingual conversation. She examines the negotiation of authority in a dispute between a mother and a daughter. The daughter, she finds, uses code-switching, repetition, and loud volume to construct authority, challenge her own role as daughter, and deconstruct her mother's parental authority; the mother uses code-switching to reject her daughter's challenges and reinforce her parental authority. Through her analysis, Williams demonstrates that a traditional, static view of a speaker's identity or social role (as mother, for example) cannot constrain the speaker's behavior to the point where the analyst can predict or explain the speaker's behavior in terms of his or her social role. Williams concludes that "while social roles and expectations are indeed significant in the interpretation of many instances of code-switching in this family argument, they are not relevant in every case" (p. 326). She argues that "in order to determine if there is a relationship between language alternation and social context or social structure at a given point in the conversation, the analyst must employ a method that does not assume this relevance, but rather allows for it to be discovered in the conversational context" (p. 327).

Cashman (2002, 2005) also examines the emergence of identities in interaction from an integrated approach. Cashman (2002), for example, investigates the construction and negotiation of bilingual identities in a talk-show interview using the detailed, sequential analysis of the conversation analytic approach. She demonstrates that, although observers might label both speakers as bilingual US Latinos, they use interactional resources (e.g. turn-taking, repair, code-switching) to construct and deconstruct this identity, both in concert with and in contrast to their roles as "talk-show host" and "talk-show guest." Cashman (2005) addresses more specifically the relationship between social structure and conversational structure, analyzing a bilingual interaction at a senior citizens' day program. The sequential analysis reveals how speakers of varied ethnolinguistic backgrounds talked into being social structure (e.g. "superiority of English"), institutional identities (e.g. "facilitator"), ethnic identities (e.g. "Anglo," "Chicana"), and linguistic identities (e.g. "competent bilingual") through language alternation, sequence organization, and repair organization (p. 313). She concludes that in the detailed studies of talk "we can observe how the social categories that play such an important part in people's lives are constructed, ascribed, accepted, and rejected. In this way language alternation may be seen as constituting and changing, not merely reflecting, social structure" (ibid.).

Finally, Greer (2003a, 2005) examines the intersubjective nature of identities of multi-ethnic teenagers in an international school in Japan through the analysis of focus-group discussions. Greer (2003a) demonstrates how multi-ethnic teenagers ascribe, resist and interrogate problematic terms of ethnic identity including 'haafu' (half), 'gaiijin' (foreigner), and 'konketsuji' (half-breed), among others. Greer (2005) finds that participants describe different experiences of ethnification in different contexts (i.e. Japan vs. Western countries) and with different interlocutors (i.e. Japanese, non-Japanese, other multi-ethnic Japanese). While not denying the background of the Japanese/non-Japanese dichotomy, he concludes that the 'haafu' (half) identity, which is often ascribed to them by others, is not static; rather, it is a complex, complicated identity situated and accomplished by multi-ethnic Japanese speakers in interaction (Greer, 2005).

Section summary

Identity-in-interaction is an approach that attempts to integrate concerns of the symbolic approach and the sequential approach in order to examine bilingual conversation, including the meaning of code-switching. This approach takes into consideration the "brought-along" aspects of identity (that is, global social identity categories such as racial or ethnic group, institutional identity, social role, or occupation, and sex, gender, or sexuality) as well as the intersubjective and emergent aspects of identities (that is, locally relevant and interactionally accomplished identities). Therefore identity is seen as both who people are and what they do in interaction, and code-switching and language choice in interaction are seen as resources for both indexing social identities and constructing them.

16.6   Concluding Remarks

Regardless of your theoretical approach, research on bilingual conversation presents many challenges. Access to good-quality recordings of spontaneous interaction is not always easy to get, given that in almost every bilingual context around the world, the mixing of language varieties in conversation is disparaged. Transcription of bilingual conversation is difficult and wrought with technical and ideological challenges, even more so if the two languages in conversation are typologically very different or if any of the language varieties does not have an established writing system. Researchers' access to the language varieties of the community and in-group knowledge can also be a challenge. If the researcher is not a native speaker of all of the language varieties being studied or an in-group member of the community, additional research and consultation with native speakers is necessary in order to handle the data honestly and responsibly. If the researcher is an in-group member and a native speaker of the language varieties being studied, insider knowledge must be questioned and language attitudes examined. When the community you are studying is a minority language community, additional challenges and opportunities might await you. Whether or not you are a member of the community, you may be called upon to provide information, assistance, and advocacy for the community, even on language issues that do not fall in your area of expertise. Many sociolinguists feel that it is the responsibility of the researcher to repay the community by services such as error correction and advocacy for the community (Labov, 1982a), by empowerment of research participants through involving community members in every aspect of the research (Cameron, Frazer, Harvey, Rampton, & Richardson, 1993), and by providing linguistic gratuity to the community in the form of services, educational information, and products (Wolfram, 1993, 1998, 2000). For those who research bilingual conversation, especially in language minority communities in states or countries where anti-bilingual ideologies prevail, special challenges, responsibilities, and opportunities await (Cashman, 2006).

Despite the challenges, bilingual conversation is a fascinating field that offers the advanced student of linguistics nearly limitless possibilities for research and contribution to its growth. While the description of the two main approaches to the study of the motivations for code-switching in bilingual conversation above is necessarily brief and superficial, the field is remarkably diverse. The study of bilingual conversation is not limited to the analysis of code-switching. Instead, researchers of bilingual conversation examine a variety of subjects, from laughter to silence, from talk at work to talk at play, and including topics in linguistic politeness (requests, compliments, disagreement, or mitigation). The growing field of interactional linguistics, which combines linguistics, anthropology, and conversation analysis, includes the study of emergent, conversational syntax and prosody (Couper-Kuhlen & Selting, 1996; Ochs, Schegloff, & Thompson, 1996; Selting & Couper-Kuhlen, 2001). Goodwin, Goodwin, and Yaeger-Dror (2002), for example, use this approach profitably to examine data including bilingual children's disputes arising at play.

Further reading and resources

For more information on the markedness model, consult Myers-Scotton (1993b) and subsequent articles by Myers-Scotton, especially Myers-Scotton (1999) and Myers-Scotton and
Bolonyai (2001). To read in more depth about conversation analysis, begin with Sacks
(1992) and Prevignano and Thibault (2003). For practical information about doing conversation analysis, consult Schegloff (forthcoming), ten Have (1999), Hutchby and Wooffitt
(1998), or Psathas (1995). Further information on the application of CA to bilingual conversation can be found in Auer (1984) and Li Wei (1994), as well as Auer (1998) and Li Wei
(2002, 2005a). For additional examples of work that integrates the symbolic and sequential
approaches, see "Accomplishing Identity in Bilingual Interaction," a special issue of the
journal *Multilingua* (Cashman & Williams, 2008).

17 Critical Discourse Analysis

Adrian Blackledge

17.1 Introduction

This chapter focuses on critical discourse analysis (CDA) as theory and method in researching bilingualism. Researchers who are interested in the relationship between language and society use CDA to describe, explain, and interpret such relationships (Rogers, 2003a). CDA enables researchers to make links between the structural and the interactional in studying bilingualism, connecting language ideologies and linguistic practices. CDA is of particular value to social scientists engaging in bilingualism research, because in many Western democracies bilingualism is a political issue. CDA sets out to investigate the linguistic in the political, and the political in the linguistic. In doing so it is able to engage with bilingualism as a political issue in several ways.

First, in viewing language as social practice, CDA sees discursive practices as both structured and structuring, and is therefore able to engage with both social structure and social action. This is important because both structures and practices of bilingualism inform, produce, and potentially shift relations of power in multilingual societies. Second, in focusing on language and power CDA is able to investigate interactions in which multilingual identities are negotiated, or are found to be non-negotiable (Pavlenko & Blackledge, 2004b). Many bilingual people in societies where one language dominates others attempt to negotiate identities in contexts of asymmetrical relations of power. CDA makes visible negotiations at the interactional level and connects them to structures of power. Third, multilingual identities are negotiated, or found to be non-negotiable, in relation to other texts and interactions which preceded them (indeed, they inevitably also connect to other texts and interactions which succeed them). That is, CDA is able to identify the connections and recontextualizations between texts and interactions that provide the context for the inequalities which are frequently produced and reproduced in multilingual settings. Fourth, in its focus on the detail of discourse strategies and linguistic means, rather than merely content, CDA makes evident discourse which discriminates against speakers of minority languages, even where it purports to be egalitarian discourse. Fifth, the transdisciplinary or "postdisciplinary" orientation of CDA makes connections between language and broader social theory. CDA is more interested in the social world than simply in the linguistic, and sets out to remove traditional disciplinary boundaries.

CDA allows researchers to understand how linguistic practices are connected to asymmetrical relations of power in societies. CDA has a political orientation, and in its theory and method is equipped to investigate how multilingual societies continue to reproduce (but in some instances resist) deep-rooted discriminatory ideologies relating to minority languages. This chapter sets out theoretical and methodological principles which unite the critical orientation to language in action which has become known as CDA. The first half of the chapter establishes the theoretical features of CDA. In the second half, methodological issues of discourse, context, genre, and voice are summarized with reference to practical questions about bilingualism in society. CDA is not an exclusive research method. It can, and should, be used in conjunction with other methods, such as those discussed in chapters 14, 18, and 19 of this volume.

17.2   Discourse

One of the criticisms leveled at CDA has been that the term "discourse" has been used so loosely and frequently in recent times that it has lost all meaning (Widdowson, 1995: 169). As the significance of language in social research has increasingly been recognized, "discourse" (or, sometimes, "Discourse") has come to refer to just about any use of language. Chilton (2004) concisely distinguishes between "language" and "discourse" by proposing that discourse may be conceptualized as the use of a language, or "language-in-use." Blommaert (2005: 2) proposes the term "language-in-action", as investigation of social worlds requires attention to both action and language. Blommaert suggests that discourse comprises "all forms of meaningful semiotic human activity seen in connection with social, cultural, and historical patterns and developments of use" (2005: 3). In this definition, "discourse" refers to spoken and written texts, but also to texts which are visual and non-verbal. In relation to bilingualism research, "texts" and "discourses" include not only the things people say in and about languages, but also the verbal and non-verbal representation and reproduction of attitudes, beliefs, and values relating to languages. Wodak similarly offers a definition of "discourse" as a complex bundle of inter-related linguistic acts, which manifest themselves as interrelated semiotic, oral, and written tokens, very often as "texts," that belong to specific genres (Wodak, 2001: 66). This definition highlights the complexity of discourse. Texts relate to other texts across fields of action, and across temporal, generic, and thematic dimensions. In social research, "discourse" often refers broadly to language used in relation to a particular topic. In CDA, discourse analysis is taken to involve a far more detailed analysis of texts than is commonly undertaken in other areas of social research.

17.3   CDA as Theory

Blommaert (2005) points out that power, and especially institutionally reproduced power, is central to CDA. CDA aims to make visible and transparent the ways in which discourse acts as an instrument of power in contemporary societies. In relation to bilingualism, CDA demonstrates how discriminatory ideologies about minority languages are produced and reproduced in discourse, and how such ideologies play out in discursive interactions. A key feature of CDA is the position it takes in relation to social theory, a position which is characterized by attention to power and ideology, and by an attempt to overcome structuralist determinism (Blommaert, 2005). CDA views discourse as both socially constitutive and socially conditioned. At the same time, a relation between agency and structure is characterized by a dynamic equilibrium which proposes that linguistic practices can be formative of larger social processes and products.

There is no *single* theory or method which is uniform and consistent throughout CDA (Fairclough, 2001, 2003a; Meyer, 2001; Weiss & Wodak, 2003). While pointing to the positive features of a theory and methodology which is characterized by plurality and dynamism, Weiss and Wodak (2003: 6) suggest that "the whole theoretical framework of CDA seems eclectic and unsystematic." Martin and Wodak (2003) point out that CDA has never been and has never attempted to be one single specific theory or methodology. Titscher and colleagues suggest that this plurality is born of the concern of CDA with the social rather than the purely linguistic: "CDA is concerned with social problems. It is not concerned with language or language use per se, but with the linguistic character of social and cultural processes and structures (Titscher, Meyer, Wodak, & Vetter, 2000: 146). It is this concern with social life, and with the role of discourse in social life, that is most characteristic of CDA. Fairclough (2003b) points out that CDA developed as a response to the traditional divide between linguistics and areas of social science such as sociology. Whereas linguistics traditionally focused on the microanalysis of texts and interactions, social science was traditionally concerned with social practice and social change. That is, linguistics was concerned with the interactional dimension of analysis, and social science with the structural dimension. In CDA the analysis of social life requires investigation of a combination of the interactional and the structural (Fairclough, 1995). Van Dijk (2001: 96) presents a harder edge to the claim that CDA is concerned with social problems, representing it as "discourse analysis with an attitude." In van Dijk's view CDA emphatically opposes those who abuse text and talk in order to establish, confirm or legitimate their abuse of power: "CDA does not deny, but explicitly defines and defends its own socio-political position. That is, CDA is biased – and proud of it." CDA is fundamentally political in its orientation, interdisciplinary in its scholarship, and diverse in its focus. Chilton (2004) concludes that while a primarily critical standpoint *per se* will not necessarily offer new insights into language and the human mind (after all, it is possible to be critical without being analytical), the political standpoint of the analyst should never be entirely absent, as it may be impossible to analyze political language behavior unless one exercises one's political intuitions. Of course, as Chilton fully acknowledges, nor is it sufficient to base analysis on intuition. The salient characteristic of CDA is that it pays very close attention to the detail of textual features, which may serve to either confirm or contradict one's initial hunches about a discourse.

Since CDA is not a specific direction of research, it does not have a unitary theoretical framework (van Dijk, 2003a, 2003b). Van Dijk points out that critical analysis of newspaper reports is different from analysis of television debates, just as critical analysis of magazine advertisements is different from analysis of political speeches or interactions in the school classroom, and so on. However, it is not sufficient to say that CDA is eclectic and diverse. If we are to make any claim that CDA is more than a method, a toolbox to service a plurality of theoretical frameworks, it is necessary to say what unites CDA as well as what divides it.

Theory formation is not a process which aims to produce a representation of an immutable truth, but rather "a continued development of tools and resources designed to help us understand the world" (Weiss & Wodak, 2003: 9). Weiss and Wodak cite Bourdieu's statement that theory formation involves "the ability to actively reproduce the best products of the thinkers of the past by applying the production of instruments they left behind" (Bourdieu, 1997: 65). That is, the adoption of instruments and tools from linguistic and social theories can be incorporated and integrated in the research process in the production of innovative theory. It is precisely in the adoption of methods from a range of theories that CDA makes explicit the links between theory and practice in bilingualism research. CDA does not construct theory for its own sake, but works in a transdisciplinary way in the mutually informing development of theory and method (Chouliaraki & Fairclough, 1999: 17). CDA brings a range of social and linguistic theories into dialogue, allowing analysis of the linguistic practices of bilingual speakers to be situated in their social, cultural, and historical contexts.

Section summary: CDA as theory

- A key feature of CDA is the position it takes in relation to social theory, a position which is characterized by attention to power and ideology.
- CDA is not concerned with language or language use *per se*, but with the linguistic character of social and cultural processes and structures.
- CDA pays very close attention to the detail of textual features.
- CDA operates across disciplines, allowing analysis of the linguistic practices of bilingual speakers to be situated in their social, cultural, and historical contexts.

17.4   CDA as Method

17.4.1   *Context*

As briefly suggested above, a key feature of CDA is analysis of the relation of a text to its social, discursive, and historical context. Rogers (2003b) argues that CDA offers a theoretical model that accounts for and explains the relationship between ways of interacting, ways of representing, and ways of being. Further, CDA provides a fine-grained analysis of the intersection of the individual and the larger context of texts, institutions, and subjectivities. CDA does not read political and social ideologies into texts, but rather the task of CDA is to work out all the possibilities between texts, ways of representing, and ways of being, and to look for and discover the relationships between texts and ways of being and why certain people take up certain positions vis-à-vis situated uses of languages (Rogers, 2003b). CDA goes beyond describing discourse practices to explaining the relationship between language and social structure, and attends to contexts at the local, institutional, and societal levels of analysis (Fairclough, 1995).

In an examination of reading policy in California, for example, Woodside-Jiron (2003) analyzed local practices of classroom interactions, the institutional context of specific school reading policy, and the policy-making and political context of public discourse; they argued that to understand the way in which political and policy-making changes are embedded in practice, it is necessary for the analyst to look over time and across contexts. She concludes that the critical analysis of educational policy using CDA offers an exciting way to analyze how power is used in producing and distributing ideologies, discourse practices and texts in societies and schools. Woodside-Jiron's analysis provides a good example of the way in which CDA situates discourse in local, institutional, and societal contexts. Rogers (2003a) argues that it is in the interaction between ethnography and CDA that analysts can understand the relationship of discourse to its local, institutional, and societal contexts. Bloor and Bloor (2007) suggest that CDA shares interests and methods with disciplines that study social groups and social structures. These methods include context analysis, observational methods, including recording and transcribing natural language, participant observation, and the use of informants to explain or interpret what is happening in a particular setting with respect to discourse practices. Bloor and Bloor propose that while CDA is an ideal means of analyzing discourses such as the language of the media, political speeches, and cross-examination in court, critical discourse analysts may need to work collaboratively with experts in other fields to investigate some social problems. For example, investigations of classroom talk would benefit from a critical analysis of discourse, in collaboration with an ethnographic orientation to the field. There is great scope for the development of CDA in team research (Bloor & Bloor, 2007: 3). Gee (2003) proposes that context refers to an ever-widening set of factors that accompany language in use, including the material setting, the people present, the language that comes before and after an utterance, the social relationships of the people involved, and cultural, historical, and institutional factors. Critical approaches to discourse differ from non-critical approaches in that they view social practices not just in terms of social relationships, but also in terms of their implications for status, solidarity, distribution of social goods, and power. CDA argues that language in use is always constitutive of specific social practices, and that social practices always have implications for status, solidarity, distribution of social goods, and power. Therefore discourse is inherently political. Discourses are always defined in relation to other discourses. For this reason CDA needs to attend to as many contexts as possible, situating texts socially, culturally, and historically, as well as locating them in their local, institutional, and societal contexts. Context is potentially everything, and contextualization is potentially infinite (Blommaert, 2005). Rogers (2003a) rightly points out that of course CDA (or any other theoretical framework) cannot attend to all contexts at the same time. Rather, analysis pays attention to the ways in which contexts construct and are constructed by discourses and how these contexts change over time. Practical analysis of texts should always take account of the context of the text, rather than attempting to "read off" ideologies from an individual text in a decontextualized way. Theoretically, research should attend to all other texts, both synchronic and diachronic, which bear textual traces of the text currently subject to analysis. However, in some cases this will have practical difficulties: for example, whereas British political discourse relating to, say, English-language testing legislation for British citizenship may be sufficiently finite to enable the researcher to examine all of it, other political issues may have generated an unwieldy corpus of data. In such instances selection may be necessary, according to appropriate criteria, in order to analyze a cross-section of data. For example, some researchers (e.g. Blommaert & Verschueren, 1998) have restricted both the medium (e.g. liberal broadsheet newspapers) and the timescale (e.g. a single day, a week, a month) of their dataset. The extent and scope of contextual analysis will depend on the research questions, but also on the resources available to the researcher.

The context of a text is further established through examination of the processes of "intertextuality," "interdiscursivity," and "recontextualization." The notion of *intertextuality*, based on the theories of dialogism developed by Mikhail Bakhtin and Valentin Nikolaevich Voloshinov and adapted by Kristeva (1986), has been widely adopted as a cornerstone of CDA. In this model it is assumed that every text is embedded in a context and is synchronically and diachronically related to many other texts. For any particular text or type of text, there is a set of other texts and a set of voices which are potentially relevant, and potentially incorporated into the text (Fairclough, 2003a). In some cases it may be possible to identify the source of these voices and texts, but often it is difficult to be precise about the specific source, and analysis then may attend to genre or to typical argumentation strategies. In fact, the texts and voices incorporated in a text may be multiple and complex. For example, if a political speech on immigration in Britain includes the word "swamped" in relation to numbers of new arrivals, this will be understood as a specific reference to an infamous television interview given by Margaret Thatcher in 1978, when she was lagging behind in the opinion polls. In the interview for the *World in Action* program, Margaret Thatcher said that immigration was excessively high, and that the British people were "rather afraid that this country might be rather swamped by people with a different culture . . . We do have to hold out the prospect of an end of immigration, except, of course, for compassionate cases" (Hansen, 2000: 210). Margaret Thatcher went on to suggest that she would like to see supporters of the (ultra-right-wing) National Front return to the Conservatives. Her interview provoked an outcry, and some commentators believe that it was influential in the Conservatives' subsequent election victory. Similarly, the phrase "rivers of blood" is irrevocably associated with a speech given by Conservative MP Enoch Powell in Birmingham, England, in April 1968, in which he warned of the dangers to social cohesion posed by mass immigration (in fact, Chilton, 2004, notes that although this infamous speech is widely referred to as the "rivers of blood" speech, this phrase was not included in the speech itself). On the other hand, if a political speech on immigration uses the phrase "floods of immigrants," this similarly powerful metaphor has a less specific source. While it may be possible to track down other uses of the phrase in discriminatory political discourse, it is less likely to have a specific origin. These two types of intertextuality, specific and non-specific, perform similar roles in reproducing previous texts within new texts.

Interdiscursivity refers to the intertextual relation of genres and discourses within a text. That is, while a text may refer to, and incorporate, a specific text, it also refers to, and incorporates, a type of text, or genre. Interdiscursive analysis links the text to what Fairclough (1995: 12) terms the order of discourse, the "ordered set of discursive practices associated with a particular social domain or institution." Orders of discourse are the particular conventionalized practices which are available to text producers in particular circumstances. There are types of discourse practices associated with different social domains, for example the school classroom, the doctor's surgery, the political debate, the newspaper editorial, and so on. Features of these orders of discourse are genres. While orders of discourse are usually associated with relatively localized and specific practices (e.g. the school classroom), they can also be thought of at a broader, societal level. For example, in debates about immigration there may be similarities in the discursive strategies used, which transcend apparent institutional and social boundaries.

Particularly useful in understanding ideologies of bilingualism in discourse is the notion of *recontextualization*, which can be used to chart shifts of meanings across semiotic dimensions (Wodak, 2000). Caldas-Coulthard (2003: 276) points out that "as soon as one writes or speaks about any social practice, one is already recontextualizing. The moment we are recontextualizing, we are transforming and creating other practices." The recontextualization of discourse does not refer merely to the repetition of the same argument in a new context. Rather, recontextualization involves the transformation of discourse. The repetition, verbatim, of the same argument in a new context involves a transformation, as discourse almost always attracts new meanings in new settings. But argument is rarely repeated verbatim. Instead it is often summarized, with new parts added, and others deleted or substituted, so that while it bears many features of the original, it is transformed in ways which comment on, legitimate, or otherwise evaluate it.

A key question in CDA is that of how communicative events are transformed as they move along a chain of discourse. One text may recontextualize others, even across genres and semiotic dimensions. For example, an argument made in a newspaper editorial that British Asians ought to speak English at home for their own good and for the good of their families, may be transformed as new parts of the argument are added, some parts are deleted, some terms are substituted for others (which may be more or less liberal in their sense), and the main points may be rearranged so that particular features of arguments are foregrounded (Blackledge, 2005). The transformation of discourse through changes to the discursive strategies and linguistic means and realizations used is not the whole story in the process of recontextualization, however. Another feature of the transformation of discourse is in the repetition of argument in a new, perhaps more authoritative, context. That is, each recontextualization may move the argument into an increasingly non-negotiable materiality. As a meaning is repeated in a more authoritative voice, and in a more legitimate context, it gains power and status. To return to the above example, if an argument is made in the queue in the local post office that British Asian people ought to speak English at home, the argument may have some influence and authority. If the same argument is made in an editorial piece in the local newspaper, it gains in status. When repeated in the debating chamber of the Town Council, the argument continues to move "up" the chain of discourse. When this same argument is repeated by an elected Member of Parliament in a Westminster debate, the argument moves further along the chain of discourse – all this time transforming itself as some features are deleted, substituted, added, and rearranged. The argument is then repeated and contested in the national newspapers, and perhaps on national radio and television. It continues to gain status and authority as the argument is picked up by Government ministers, even members of the Cabinet, and it enters official discourse as part of a Government policy paper. After a period of further debate, the argument may become part of draft legislation, and finally become law, entering into the least negotiable materiality (see Blackledge, 2005, for a more fully developed example). This is not to suggest that this is a linear process in all or even most cases, nor that the origin of Government legislation is to be found in the conversation of the post office queue. In fact "chains" of discourse are neither straightforward nor unidirectional, but are likely to be circular, reflexive, tangential, and fractured. Also, it is important to recognize that the everyday linguistic practices of multilingual people in Britain may contribute to contestation of the monolingual ideology which is reproduced in political, media, and other public discourses (Blackledge & Creese, 2005). Nevertheless, the dimension of the increased authority and power of discourse as it gains legitimacy in new semiotic domains is crucial for understanding how existing representations of differentiated groups in society come to constitute dominant ideologies. This process of the transformation of discourse through the movement of meanings along a chain of discourse towards a more legitimate and authoritative context is a key, and often neglected, aspect of recontextualization (although see Wodak, 2000).

Blommaert (2005) argues that, in some versions of CDA, analysis may merely confirm a priori perspectives on relations of power in discourse. That is, CDA only tells us what we already know, and context provides the background to the text. Blommaert offers an alternative to such a partial analysis, in which he proposes merging discourse and social structure, so that contexts are not features of single texts but of larger economies of communication and contextualization. He further argues that discourse shifts across contexts, and that precisely this shifting of texts between contexts involves crucial questions of power. Every act of discourse production, reproduction, and circulation involves such shifts in contexts.

17.4.2   *Voice*

The notion of intertextuality does not suggest that just any voice has equal opportunity to inform authoritative and powerful discourse. Relations of power in society are influential in determining which voices gain authority as they are transformed along chains of discourse, and which voices diminish either partly or entirely. To develop an understanding of how the voices of social actors are shaped in the process of their transformation, it is helpful to turn to the work of Mikhail Bakhtin. Bakhtin emphasized the dialogicality of language, in the sense that a text is always aware of, responding to, and anticipating other texts, and also in the sense that discourse is at times "double-voiced." The process of the transformation of discourse, outlined above, is recognizable here:

> The speech of another, once enclosed in a context, is – no matter how accurately transmitted – always subject to certain semantic changes. The context embracing another's word is responsible for its dialogising background, whose influence can be very great. (Bakhtin, 1984: 78)

In Bakhtin's theory of language as responsive to the social world, discourse is dialogic, shaped and influenced by the discourse of others. An utterance is a link in a complex chain of other utterances, and is informed and shaped by other utterances in the chain. For Bakhtin dialogical relationships are possible not only between entire utterances: the dialogical approach can be applied to any meaningful part of an utterance, even to an individual word, "if we hear in that word another person's voice" (1973: 152).

In dialogic discourse, more than one voice is evident in a single utterance, shaping and reshaping the word, so that the author's thought no longer completely dominates, and it responds to the voice of the other. It is important to recognize that this is a *social* model of language – that is, the relation between the various voices within an utterance is subject to the relations of power within society. The authority of the authorial voice is likely to be maintained where it belongs to those in powerful positions in society. Its discourse may nevertheless be double-voiced, where it dismisses or deletes voices which contradict its perspective. In public (especially media and political) discourse about bilingualism, illiberal argument often masquerades as egalitarian liberalism.

Section summary: CDA as method

- CDA engages with the relation of a text to its social, discursive, and historical context.
- The context of a text is established through examination of the processes of "intertextuality," "interdiscursivity," and "recontextualization."
- Relations of power in society are influential in determining which voices gain authority.
- In Bakhtin's notion of "dialogic discourse" more than one voice may be evident in a single utterance.

17.5   Critical Analysis and Discourse of Multilingualism

The following example engages with context and voice in its analysis. This reports a small section of analysis of the multiple discourses included in a language-ideological debate about the extension of language testing for citizenship in Britain. The texts analyzed in the extended project included the speeches of Members of Parliament, ministers and Secretaries of State, local newspaper reports of language debates over a five-year period, broadsheet news reports of political statements, reports of local and national government inquiries, a Government White Paper and Act of Parliament, Home Office notes for the implementation of new legislation, and interviews and articles authored by politicians (Blackledge, 2004, 2005). In the present chapter, however, I engage with just one of the myriad texts representing the language testing debate.

In October 2002 the (then) United Kingdom Home Secretary, David Blunkett, wrote an article which set out the Home Secretary's vision of democracy, citizenship, and civil society (Blunkett, 2002). The context of the Home Secretary's article was informed by political discourse relating to violent disturbances in the streets of towns and cities in the north of England in the summer of 2001. These disturbances, popularly described in the British media as "race riots," principally involved young British Asian men, young British white men, and the police. In November 2002, the Nationality, Immigration and Asylum Act was granted royal assent, and passed into British law. Included in this legislation was a change to the existing law: whereas previously spouses of British citizens had not been required to demonstrate their proficiency in English when applying for British citizenship, now the legislation was extended to include this group. In addition, the Home Secretary's powers to test the English proficiency of all applicants for citizenship were extended. The disturbances on the streets and the new legislation were connected through complex chains of discourse. In these chains of discourse political actors argued that the violence was caused at least partly because some Asian residents of the northern towns and cities either

were unable, or refused, to speak English. Absurd as this causal association may
seem, it was an argument made not merely by ultra-right-wing activists, but by
mainstream politicians whose discourse was reiterated, recontextualized, and transformed in increasingly legitimate contexts, gaining authority as it traveled, until it
was enshrined in the least negotiable domain of all – the law.

The Home Secretary's article included the following words:

> An active concept of citizenship can articulate shared ground between diverse commun-
> ities. It offers a shared identity based on membership of a political community, rather
> than forced assimilation into a monoculture, or an unbridled multiculturalism which
> privileges difference over community cohesion.

The repetition of "shared" in the first two sentences of this section of the article
frames the Home Secretary's discourse in a liberal context. "Shared ground" and
"shared identity" promise a solution to the apparent problems of diverse communities. The Home Secretary claims that "an active concept of citizenship" provides
a desirable alternative to the equally negative options of "forced assimilation" and
"unbridled multiculturalism." In the phrase "forced assimilation" David Blunkett's
discourse senses its opponents, and attempts to deal with them by distancing itself
from any accusation that his proposals force minority groups to leave behind their
own culture as they are required to assimilate to the host society. The discourse
here implies that, of course, the Home Secretary would never *force* anyone to
assimilate to British society.

While "assimilation" is here held to belong to illiberalism, "integration" is characterized as desirable and legitimate. The phrase "unbridled multiculturalism" carries
with it a world of history. Although the sense of "multiculturalism" has usually been
positive in British political and educational discourse, denoting an affirmative
orientation to diversity in societies, here the pejorative adjective insists that "multiculturalism" is negative. Now "multiculturalism," associated with liberal education
in Britain in the 1970s and 1980s, either threatens to go, or has gone, too far, and
should be stopped. The adjective "unbridled," with its animalistic, untameable
associations, implies that if it is allowed to do so, multiculturalism will create a
turbulent, uncontrolled world. In this oppositional discourse, the positive interpretation of diversity is held to privilege difference over community cohesion, as if
this were a simple, mutually exclusive dichotomy. In the Home Secretary's view, you
can't have *both* an acceptance and understanding of people from different cultural
groups, *and* community cohesion. In the chain of discourses examined here, "community cohesion" means an end to violence on the streets. That is, in a topos
of threat, "unbridled multiculturalism" should be stopped because it will lead
inevitably to social disorder.

The Home Secretary's article continues:

> I have never said, or implied, that lack of fluency in English was in any way directly
> responsible for the disturbances in Bradford, Burnley and Oldham in the summer of
> 2001. However, speaking English enables parents to converse with their children in Eng-
> lish as well as their historic mother tongue at home, and to participate in wider modern
> culture. It helps overcome the schizophrenia which bedevils generational relationships.

The first sentence of this paragraph either responds to, or anticipates, its opposition. This is what Bakhtin (1973: 163) termed "hidden dialogicality," a single utterance which has the character of the dialogue of two people in which the speeches of the second are omitted. The utterance has the character of a conversation, since "every word that is present answers and reacts with its every fibre to the invisible interlocutor, it points outside itself, beyond its own borders to the other person's unspoken word." David Blunkett is arguing robustly against an invisible opposition. Of significance here is the word "directly." If lack of fluency in English was not *directly* responsible for the rioting, the possibility, and even the implication, remains that it was therefore *indirectly* responsible. Here "speaking English" seems to mean the ability to speak English as well as actual use of English. In this sentence "historic" is oppositional to "modern," creating a tension between Asian languages and "wider modern culture," which is presumably British. That is, Asian languages are linked to that which is narrow, and perhaps narrow-minded, archaic and out of date. Speaking English at home, and the *ability* to speak English, can prevent "the schizophrenia which bedevils generational relationships." The definite article lends authority here: there is a presupposition that "schizophrenia" is a recognized and agreed phenomenon for people who speak minority languages at home. The verb "bedevils" adds a sinister note, implying evil. The implication appears to be that a failure to speak English, and to learn English, is somehow linked to mental health difficulties, family disharmony, and social disorder, and the ability, or inability, of new migrants to speak English is associated with segregation, ignorance, and hostility.

In the chain of political discourse linking the civil disorder in northern England in 2001 with legislative change in 2002, an ideology becomes visible which clearly privileges the English language above the other languages of England. This ideology is most strongly evident as argument moves closer to the center of Government. The official discourse of a parliamentary speech, an interview with a Home Office minister, a Home Office statement, a Government-commissioned report, a Government White Paper, an article by the Secretary of State, and a new Act of Parliament, all contribute to an ideology which places English above the other languages spoken and written in multilingual England. Not only is English consistently positioned as the language of communication and democracy, but languages other than English are consistently linked with a range of negative features, including civil disorder, school underachievement, social segregation, threats to citizenship, nationhood, and democracy. The languages of Pakistan, Bangladesh, and India in particular are accorded negative associations which can only be described as discriminatory.

In some examples from the political discourse, the use of Asian languages is tolerated, as long as this is in private domains. There is no support in any of these texts for policy which encourages the use of languages other than English in public settings. Instead, the drive behind the political texts is one that associates a range of problems with the use of Asian languages, and sets out to devise policy and legislation to insist that all residents of England speak English. The means towards this end is the extension of the requirements for applicants for naturalization as British citizens to demonstrate that they have sufficient English proficiency to undertake their duties and obligations as citizens. However, this policy is flawed on a number of counts. The associations between languages other than English and civil disorder, school underachievement, social segregation, societal burden, and threats to democracy, nationhood, citizenship, and community are fallacious arguments. First, the civil disorder in the north of England was at least partly fomented by the presence in the area of the racist British National Party, which recognized and capitalized on the conditions for tension created by oppositional discourse in the local media. Second, school underachievement of linguistic-minority children is not *caused* by children coming to school able to speak a language other than English. Rather, in a multilingual classroom environment, minority languages can potentially become a resource for learning. There are many British schools in which children successfully learn through their home language alongside English in the early days of their school career. In fact recent statistics confirm that the two groups achieving the best grades in public examinations in secondary schools are currently the "Chinese" and "Indian" groups – both of which generalized categories comprise linguistic-minority groups (Department for Education and Skills, 2004). These findings add to the already robust research which indicates that speaking languages other than English is by no means necessarily a barrier to high educational attainment in English schools. Third, social segregation is undoubtedly a characteristic of many British cities. However, it is not necessarily a result of people speaking languages other than English. Factors such as discriminatory housing policy, racist employment practices, and the economic status of linguistic-minority people play a major role in the demographic distribution of linguistic groups. Fourth, minority Asian languages are not inevitably a burden on society, but have the potential to be a considerable resource (languages such as French, German, and Japanese are viewed in this way). Fifth, speakers of languages other than English can only be said to be a threat to participation in the democratic process when all political discourse, election campaigns, and institutional texts are presented solely in English. Where this is the case, some people who mainly use Asian languages may be disenfranchised. However, the responsibility to present political argument in accessible forms lies with political institutions, not with the individual. Sixth, participation as a citizen is not essentially determined by proficiency in English, providing that opportunities for participation are available in languages other than English. In fact many monolingual English citizens do not "participate" in the political process, suggesting that language may not be the most important factor in determining the extent of participation. Seventh, languages other than English are not a threat to the communities in which they are spoken unless the dominant institutions in society determine that this should be so. Where English is the sole language of powerful institutions such as schools and colleges, the legal system, and the welfare system, some speakers of languages other than English may not be able to activate their cultural and linguistic capital within these institutions. Where these institutions present themselves as multilingual environments, however, it is more likely that linguistic-minority speakers will be able to gain access to them, and to activate their symbolic resources in these settings.

There is a difference between coercing someone to learn a language and giving them access to an environment where learning can take place. There are questions of how speakers of languages other than English activate their social and linguistic capital to gain entry to a place of learning which may be perceived as "white," middle-class, and academic. Learning English will not remove other barriers to participation for linguistic-minority groups whose language is racialized in the ideological debate. If linguistic discrimination is a form of symbolic racism, other symbolic features will replace it, even where discrimination based on accent and non-nativelike usage is not activated. Finally, the coercive nature of a policy that requires applicants to learn "sufficient" English or be refused access to the community of citizens strengthens the existing gate-keeping mechanism so that it is more socially exclusive than before. In almost all of the discourse surrounding this policy development there is a tension between political argument that the policy and legislation is liberal and egalitarian, and the practice, which is illiberal and discriminatory.

Section summary: Critical analysis and discourse of multilingualism

- In some public discourse, minority languages, and their speakers, are associated with problems such as social segregation, family breakdown, and school underachievement.
- Discriminatory discourses about multilingualism and minority languages in political and other public discourse can be revealed through CDA.
- Discriminatory discourses about multilingualism and minority languages often masquerade as egalitarian argument.
- Language-ideological debates are often about attitudes to the speakers of minority languages, rather than about language alone.

17.6 Researching Multilingual Britain

The political discourse encountered in charting the story of legislative change relating to English-language testing for citizenship is less than encouraging. However, the monolingual ideology constructed in official discourse is at odds with the linguistic practices which characterize British society, which are diverse, changing, and complex. Political discourse is often out of touch with the way people use their languages and think about their languages, and with the values and beliefs they attach to their languages. Bilingual and multilingual people in Britain, and monolingual minority-language speakers, whether they are British citizens or not, engage in a broad range of multilingual linguistic practices in their homes, in their schools, in their communities, in their places of worship, in the course of their business, in social settings, and in their leisure activities. Well over 300 languages are spoken in London alone. These languages are used for pragmatic purposes, for symbolic purposes, and for religious purposes. They are used in the negotiation of identities, and in claiming national, regional and religious belonging. They are used in mixed forms, in hybrid forms, and in entirely separate forms. These bilingual and multi-lingual practices do not cause problems or difficulties to the speakers of these languages. On the contrary, they are for many people a crucial part of their sense of themselves. The dominant monolingual ideology produced and reproduced in official and political discourse, as well as in local discourses at the micro-level, constructs a society in which the many languages of England largely remain within particular groups, as a process of symbolic domination persuades multilingual speakers that their languages are not welcome in the wider public domain. The effect of this is that in a multilingual society a monolingual arena is constructed and constantly reinforced, and the use of languages other than English remains hidden. The insistence that languages other than English have negative associations clearly reinforces the dominant ideology of monolingualism, which continues to be at odds with actual linguistic practices in society, and reproduces social stratification and inequality. However, this process is not inevitable. Whilst those who engage in multilingual practices may not have the power to change the social arena, senior political actors do have this power. The legislative machine has the authority and legitimacy to make changes which can break the cycle of reproduction of discrim-inatory language ideology, and better reflect the multilingualism of the people of England. Critical Discourse Analysis is methodologically and theoretically equipped to investigate discourses which constitute ideologies which are monolingual, dis-criminatory, and illiberal. Of course we cannot finally know where hegemonic ideologies have their origin, or all the contexts in which they are reproduced. We need further studies which investigate the production and reproduction of such ideologies in interactional as well as political and media discourses.

Further reading

Useful texts in the field of Critical Discourse Analysis include the following: Meriel Bloor and Thomas Bloor (2007) *The Practice of Critical Discourse Analysis: An Introduction* provides an excellent introduction to CDA as theory and practice. The work of Norman Fairclough (1989, 1995, 2003a) has been key to the development of the field, as has the research of Jim Martin and Ruth Wodak (2003), Ruth Wodak and Paul Chilton (2005), and Martin Reisigl and Ruth Wodak (2001). The work of Teun van Dijk (2001, 2003a, 2003b) has also been significant in shaping the field. For a more critical summary, see Jan Blommaert, *Discourse* (2005).

18   Narrative Analysis

Aneta Pavlenko

18.1   Introduction

Narratives have several advantages over other means of linguistic data collection. They approximate language use in context and thus allow researchers to study language properties that emerge only in connected speech, such as temporal reference or cohesiveness. At the same time, elicited narratives can be controlled for topic and, to a degree, for items and structures to be elicited. As a result, narratives are among the most popular means of data collection in the study of bilingualism. Narrative analysis, however, is among the least understood and theorized means of data analysis in the field. The purpose of this chapter is to show what research questions can be answered with the help of narratives in the study of bi- and multilingualism and to familiarize the readers with multiple approaches to narrative collection and analysis (due to space limitations, I will not discuss methods of text analysis).

The term *narrative*, as used here, refers to "all types of discourse in which event structured material is shared with readers or listeners, including fictional stories, personal narratives, accounts and recounts of events (real or imagined)" (Mistry, 1993: 208). Two types of narratives are commonly used in the field of bilingualism, fictional and personal. In what follows, I discuss first how fictional narratives can be collected and analyzed, and then collection and analysis of personal narratives. Throughout, I will focus mainly on bilinguals' narratives, because the study of multilinguals' narratives is at present in its inception.

18.2   Fictional narratives

18.2.1   *Data collection*

Fictional narratives are stories about fictional events, elicited with non-verbal prompts, such as pictures or videos. Researchers working with bilingual children and adults commonly use these narratives to answer questions about cross-linguistic influence, language attrition, and the development of vocabulary, temporality, and narrative competence. While personal narratives can also be used for these purposes, they exhibit a significant amount of variation across participants and contexts and are less amenable to analysis of intra- and inter-group similarities and differences. To obtain comparable language samples, researchers elicit fictional narratives using non-verbal stimuli, such as cartoons, picture books, and short films, that allow them to hold the semantic referent constant. Below, I consider three issues in the collection of fictional narratives: the types of prompts used with different age groups, the elicitation procedure, and baseline data.

Researchers working with bilingual children commonly favor cartoons, pictures, and picture books, because storytelling elicited by means of these prompts does not require children to imagine events and thus reduces the cognitive load imposed by the task (Berman, 1995). A particularly common prompt is a picture book *Frog, Where Are You?* (Mayer, 1969), popularized by Berman and Slobin's (1994) cross-linguistic study and used in several studies with bi- and trilingual children (Reetz-Kurashige, 1999; Yoshitomi, 1999; Cenoz, 2001; Kellerman, 2001; Verhoeven & Strömqvist, 2001; Pearson, 2002; Álvarez, 2003; Ordóñez, 2004). The advantages of using Mayer's (1969) book for elicitation purposes include established elicitation procedures, analytical frameworks, and availability of monolingual corpora in a variety of languages (Bamberg, 1987; Berman & Slobin, 1994; CHILDES: Child Language Data Exchange System).

Researchers working with bilingual adults also use cartoons (Nistov, 2001), picture series (Strömqvist & Day, 1993; Berman, 1999) or picture books, such as *Frog, Where Are You?* (Olshtain & Barzilay, 1991; Kellerman, 2001; Bennett-Castor, 2002; McKinnie & Priestly, 2004; Polinsky, 2007). Often, however, they favor short films and videos, either silent or with musical soundtrack. These stimuli also allow the semantic referent to be held constant, but in addition they make the storytelling task more "adult-like," less artificial, and more similar to spontaneous narratives. The two films most frequently used in the field are the *Pear film*, a six-minute film created for research purposes by Wallace Chafe and his team (Chafe, 1980), and Chaplin's *Modern Times*, of which usually only a segment is used. Bilinguals' Pear Stories are examined in Nistov (2001), and stories elicited by *Modern Times* in Jarvis (1998, 2000, 2002), Bardovi-Harlig (2000), and Noyau and Paprocka (2000), among others. Bardovi-Harlig (2000: 199–201) offers a useful overview of studies that employ *Modern Times* and other films as elicitation prompts with second and foreign language learners. The advantage of using these stimuli is once again in the availability of analytical frameworks and monolingual corpora collected in a variety of languages (Chafe, 1980; Tannen, 1982, 1993; Erbaugh, 2001; Aske, 2002).

Despite the multiple advantages and conveniences of using already established prompts, researchers who are looking to elicit particular lexical items or linguistic structures may want to think about adopting different stimuli, or even creating their own stimuli, as existing prompts may be unsuccessful in serving their specific needs. In my research, I have opted for creating my own prompts, engaging students (director, cameraman, and actors) in two film schools, one in the US and one in

Kiev, Ukraine, to create videos based on specific scripts. This approach has two major advantages. First, I could directly address my research questions by creating films that elicited lexical items I was interested in: the notions of privacy and personal space (Pavlenko, 2003a) and emotion vocabulary (Pavlenko, 2002a). Second, I could control for context effects by filming the same scripts in two different environments and examining the influence of context on linguistic framing and directionality and on the amount of language transfer (Pavlenko & Jarvis, 2002).

To collect rich narrative data and comparable language samples it is important to follow appropriate elicitation procedures. The standard protocol for story elicitation through *Frog, Where Are You?* is offered in Berman and Slobin (1994: 22–3), it requires the use of the actual book and thus eliminates memory demands from the task. This protocol is often modified in the studies with bi- and multilinguals, some of which examine narratives elicited by the actual book (Kupersmitt & Berman, 2001; Severing & Verhoeven, 2001; Stavans, 2001), and others co-construction of the story with the caretakers (Boyd & Nauclér, 2001) or retellings of the previously heard story (Lanza, 2001). The standard protocol for Pear Story elicitation is described in Chafe (1980: xiv–xv), while Jarvis (1998) and Bardovi-Harlig (2000: 200–1) offer detailed discussions of narrative elicitation through *Modern Times* and other films.

What makes elicitation of bilinguals' narratives particularly challenging is the fact that "the same" narratives have to be elicited twice, once in each of the bilingual's languages. As a result, these narratives may be subject to order effects, with the second telling less detailed than the first one. Alternatively, they may be subject to practice effects. For instance, when a story is elicited by an unfamiliar series of pictures, the second telling may be more elaborate, since, having seen the ending during the first telling, the narrator can now attribute significance to previously unnoticed elements of the plot (Bennett-Castor, 2002). These effects are easily overcome if more than one prompt is used. In this case, half of the participants, randomly selected, are asked to tell or write stories elicited by the first prompt in language A and stories elicited by the second prompt in language B, while the other half are asked to do the reverse. In cases where only one prompt is used, narratives in different languages are commonly elicited during different sessions, typically two weeks apart, preferably with the help of different interviewers. If the languages of the speakers are fairly balanced, language order is randomized; in some cases, narratives in a non-dominant language are elicited first (Lanza, 2001). Another possibility is to ask the storytellers to switch languages in the middle of the story, so that half of the participants tell the first half of the story in language A and the second in language B, and the other half do the opposite (Kupersmitt & Berman, 2001).

Another issue to consider is the form in which narratives are elicited, as oral and written narratives elicited by the same prompt may differ in meaningful ways (Tannen, 1982). Both oral and written elicitation modes have advantages and disadvantages. Written narratives are time-efficient in terms of data collection, and allow the inclusion of more participants, yet the language used is not necessarily representative of speech. Furthermore, the ability to write down stories is constrained by participants' ages, and levels of literacy and proficiency in the languages in question. On the other hand, oral narratives are more representative of spontaneous speech, yet their transcription is extremely time-consuming. An additional choice to be made in oral narratives is between narratives elicited after the participants saw the entire film or set of pictures and narratives that offer a running commentary on what is going on in the pictures or in the film. One's final choice will depend on the research questions – some can be resolved through the written narratives, others require oral elicitation, and others are best addressed through analysis of both oral and written discourse.

Finally, we also need to consider the issue of baseline data from monolingual speakers. In the case of established prompts, monolingual corpora may already exist in the required language and age group. If one is using a prompt for which no monolingual corpus has yet been collected, it is very important to collect narratives from monolingual speakers of similar age and socioeconomic background. Such a corpus will provide invaluable information about age norms and regional variation; in the absence of such data, regionalisms, colloquialisms, and structures specific to particular developmental stages may be mistakenly qualified as errors or instances of cross-linguistic influence. The existence of monolingual and bilingual corpora collected with the same prompts also facilitates cross-linguistic comparisons (cf. Bennett-Castor, 2002) and comparisons in terms of bilinguals' ages and levels of acculturation and proficiency.

18.2.2 *Data analysis*

The first step taken in analysis of elicited oral narratives is the choice of transcription conventions. There is no standard way to transcribe oral narratives – transcription conventions are usually chosen with the research questions and the theoretical framework in mind (Ochs, 1979). Regardless of the actual conventions, two types of errors need to be avoided – additions and omissions. Inexperienced transcribers tend, for instance, to organize spoken discourse into written prose, i.e. a series of sentences. Note that while punctuation makes transcripts easier to read, it is not a faithful representation of the data – this addition may negatively affect subsequent analysis. Inexperienced transcribers may also decide to omit repetitions and false starts. This can also create problems for analysis – self-corrections, repetitions, slips of the tongue, false starts and restarts, code-switches, and requests for help are crucial cues in analysis of lexical retrieval problems. To increase transcript reliability you need to go over the tape and the transcript many times. If possible, use two or more independent transcribers. To facilitate your own task and that of the reader, try to use standard transcription conventions and include whatever conventions you used in the appendix of your study. Conventions for transcription of Frog Stories are discussed in Berman and Slobin (1994: 657–9) and Pearson (2002: 141); Chafe (1980: xv) makes suggestions for transcription of Pear Stories (additional sources of transcription conventions are listed in the "Further reading and resources" section at the end of the chapter).

The second commonly undertaken step is to use descriptive statistics to characterize the corpus in terms of narrative word length, number of clauses per narrative, and mean length of utterance (MLU). You may want to include this information in a table that provides mean values, ranges, and standard deviations for all groups in question. Unless lexical diversity and narrative structure are the foci of your extended analysis, you may also want to include information on average lexical diversity in your narratives and on their basic structure. Then you can use inferential statistics to see if there are significant differences between your groups or participants, between narratives elicited by different prompts or in different languages, and between first and second tellings. If you have adopted a commonly used prompt, you may also consider comparing the characteristics of your corpus with those of other corpora collected with the same stimuli. After you have familiarized yourself and your readers with the general characteristics of your corpus, you are ready to begin answering your questions. Your analytical framework will depend on the questions posited in your study. Below I review the most common frameworks used for analysis of fictional narratives in studies of bilinguals' linguistic development, narrative development, cross-linguistic influence, and language attrition.

The first set of questions about language development and attrition answered with the use of elicited fictional narratives involves the lexicon, and more specifically lexical choice and lexical diversity. What factors affect lexical choice in bilingual speakers? How do bilinguals' choices compare with those made by monolingual speakers? Are speakers experiencing any difficulties in lexical retrieval and, if so, why? How rich are the L1 and L2 lexicons of the study participants? How do these lexicons compare with those of monolingual speakers within the parameters of a retell task? What factors affect lexical diversity in bilinguals' lexicons?

Your first interest may be in the use of specific words, because you suspect their choice might be affected by cross-linguistic influence, language attrition, or other factors of interest to you. In this case, you identify all references to specific target denotata in your narratives (e.g., deer, stag, antelope, elk), including circumlocutions (e.g., little animal), arrange them in a convenient format (typically a table), and analyze lexical choice tendencies quantitatively and qualitatively in terms of inter-group similarities and differences. In your qualitative analysis you may want to pay particular attention to instances of lexical borrowing, semantic extension and narrowing, and conceptual transfer (Pavlenko, 2002a, 2003a, 2003b; Pavlenko & Jarvis, 2002). Detailed recommendations on quantification and statistical analysis of lexical references in elicited narratives are offered in Jarvis (1998, 2000). Qualitative analyses of bilinguals' choices in Frog Stories can be found in Kaufman (2001) and Olshtain and Barzilay (1991).

Your research questions may also require you to consider the use of a particular type of vocabulary in your narratives, for instance, emotion vocabulary. In this case, you will identify all instances of the use of what you consider to be "emotion words," and consider the richness and use of this vocabulary across the groups in your study through a series of analyses of variance (ANOVA) (cf. Dewaele & Pavlenko, 2002). You may also be interested in lexical diversity in general. Definitions of lexical diversity, also known as lexical richness or variation, vary across studies. Most commonly it is measured through a type–token ratio (TTR), which compares the number of different words (types) with the number of total words (tokens). This approach is not without problems. For detailed discussions of problems with TTR and for suggestions of alternative measures of lexical diversity in elicited narratives, see Jarvis (2002) and Dewaele and Pavlenko (2003: 123–6).

The second set of questions about language development and attrition answered with the use of elicited fictional narratives involves morphosyntactic accuracy and complexity, most frequently temporal reference: How do bilingual speakers use particular forms (e.g., tense and aspect) in their stories in comparison with monolingual speakers of respective languages? What factors affect their morphosyntactic choices? Is there any evidence of cross-linguistic influence or language attrition? To answer these questions, you will identify all instances of the morphosyntactic forms of interest to you and analyze these instances quantitatively and qualitatively. If your focus is on temporal relations you also need to code all clauses for anchoring tense, in order to identify instances of tense shift.

Quantitative analyses of morphosyntactic forms typically examine similarities and differences in the proportion of particular forms across languages and groups or individuals (Bos, 2001; Lanza, 2001; Stavans, 2001; Viberg, 2001; Bennett-Castor, 2002), as well as the overall morphosyntactic accuracy and syntactic complexity (Berman, 1999; Kupersmitt & Berman, 2001; Severing & Verhoeven, 2001; Pearson, 2002; Polinsky, 2007). Qualitative analyses examine morphosyntactic choices, including tense shifts, in the context of various narrative structures and functions. Bardovi-Harlig (2000: 279–337) offers an excellent discussion of distribution of tense and aspect across different narrative structures, types, and functions, and an overview of the studies of temporality in narratives told in a second or foreign language. Studies of temporality in both languages of bilingual individuals include Aarssen (2001), Bos (2001), Kupersmitt and Berman (2001), Lanza (2001), Stavans (2001), Viberg (2001), Bennett-Castor (2002), and Polinsky (2007). Morphosyntactic analyses may also consider other form–function relationships, e.g., the framing of emotions (Pavlenko, 2002a).

The third set of questions involves narrative development. These studies examine narrative structure in order to assess children's narrative competence and language and literacy development or adults' levels of proficiency in particular languages (for a discussion of specific approaches to analysis of narrative structure, see the section on personal experience narratives below). Pearson (2002) offers a detailed and well-exemplified discussion of coding, analysis, and evaluation of linguistic and narrative competence in bilingual children's Frog Stories in terms of age levels. Other studies examine bilinguals' narratives in terms of overall structure and amount of evaluation and detail (Shrubshall, 1997; Berman, 1999; Akinci, Jisa, & Kern, 2001; Kupersmitt & Berman, 2001; Lanza, 2001; Stavans, 2001; Viberg, 2001; Bennett-Castor, 2002; Ordóñez, 2004), character introduction and reference continuation (Strömqvist & Day, 1993; Nistov, 2001; Severing & Verhoeven, 2001; Álvarez, 2003), subject ellipsis (Kupersmitt & Berman, 2001; Stavans, 2001), and the use of connectors (Berman, 1999; Stavans, 2001; Viberg, 2001).

Some studies also use additional approaches to determine speakers' language dominance and to examine proficiency, cross-linguistic influence, or attrition. These studies analyze the degree and directionality of transfer, code-mixing, and lexical borrowing (Cenoz, 2001; Lanza, 2001; Pavlenko & Jarvis, 2002; Pavlenko, 2003a, 2003b), speaking rates and fluency (Tomiyama, 1999; Yoshitomi, 1999; Polinsky,

2007), and the use of monitoring devices (Severing & Verhoeven, 2001) in each of the speaker's languages. Studies of language attrition and cross-linguistic influence pay particularly close attention to deviation from lexical choices made by monolingual speakers, and to the use of compensatory strategies, such as circumlocution, pausing, code-switching, omission, attempts at word retrieval, and explicit requests for help (Olshtain & Barzilay, 1991; Tomiyama, 1999; Cenoz, 2001; Kaufman, 2001; Polinsky, 2007).

Section summary

In sum, if you are planning to use fictional narratives in your research, you need to:

- decide on your initial research questions and/or hypotheses and make sure that they are indeed best answered through the means of elicited fictional narratives;
- select the prompts that fit the age of your participants and allow you to collect the data that will answer your questions; don't be tempted by the most popular prompts if they do not elicit the types of language you need; if in doubt, pilot a few different prompts;
- decide on the baseline data (existing corpora or monolingual participants);
- think through the elicitation procedure, considering both the format (oral or written) and instructions (when and who will the story be told to?); unless you study repetition effects, do not use the same prompt to elicit stories in both languages within one session;
- use standard transcription conventions but modify them if necessary for your purposes;
- create an overall description of your narrative corpus;
- proceed to coding and analysis that allow you to answer your research questions.

18.3   Personal Narratives

18.3.1   *Data collection*

While fictional narratives have an established place in the repertoire of bilingualism researchers, personal narratives are just beginning to gain recognition. *Personal narratives* are stories based on speakers' personal knowledge and experiences. They can be either spontaneous or elicited with verbal prompts, such as interview questions or key words. These narratives cannot be controlled in the same way as narratives elicited by non-verbal prompts; nevertheless, they can be used for the same purposes, namely, to answer questions about linguistic and narrative development, cross-linguistic influence or attrition. In some cases they may in fact be a better source of data. For instance, Noyau (1984) argues that because they are less rigidly structured than fictional narratives elicited by non-verbal prompts, personal narratives offer researers a better opportunity to examine how learners manage temporal reference. Shiro (2003) shows that there is a larger gap between children of different social classes in retelling of fictional stories than in narratives of personal experience. She argues that in some social classes and subcultures children are not required to retell what they read or saw on TV and thus personal experience narratives constitute a better tool for evaluation of their narrative competence. The autobiographic content of these narratives also makes them excellent instruments for the study of language socialization, for inquiries into emotional expression and narrative construction of bilinguals' selves, for investigations of sociolinguistic determinants of language learning, attrition, and shift, and for historical and dia-chronic research in contexts where other sources are scarce.

Two types of personal narratives are commonly used in the study of bilingualism: personal experience narratives and linguistic autobiographies. Both types can be oral or written, elicited or spontaneous. *Personal experience narratives* are stories about real, imagined, or possible events that draw on speakers' experiences. They can be elicited in experimental settings through key words, interview questions, or requests to tell particular types of stories, such as earliest memories, stories about holidays or car accidents, or stories about times when the speakers felt a particular emotion. McCabe and Bliss (2003: 6–10) provide detailed guidelines for elicitation of personal experience narratives and recommend specific prompts for use with children and adults. To maximize representativeness, they recommend collecting several narratives from each individual. Researchers interested in spontaneous narratives tape-record narratives co-constructed in conversations among friends or family members (Pfaff, 2001), or in interviews and informal conversations between researchers and participants (Wenzell, 1989; Teutsch-Dwyer, 2001; Vitanova, 2004, 2005). Schlyter (1996) tape-recorded narratives produced by children in interaction with parents over the span of two years, and Dart (1992) tape-recorded narratives spontaneously produced by a four-year-old bilingual girl playing by herself.

Depending on the research questions, stories may be collected in the two languages of bilingual individuals (Dart, 1992; Javier, Barroso, & Muñoz, 1993; Maeno, 1995; Schlyter, 1996; Koven, 1998, 2001, 2002; Pfaff, 2001; Marian & Kaushanskaya, 2004), in the first language (Schmid, 2002), or in the second language (Wenzell, 1989; Rintell, 1990; Teutsch-Dwyer, 2001; van Hell, Bosman, Wiggers, & Stoit, 2003). Koven (1998) offers excellent recommendations for elicitation of stories on the same topic in two languages, including the use of different interviewers.

Three issues need to be considered by bilingualism researchers in elicitation of personal experience narratives in two languages. The first one involves order and practice effects that may affect the consecutive tellings of the same story. In order to minimize these effects, second tellings are usually collected after a two-week interval. The second issue to be aware of is the fact that the amount of detail and emotional intensity may be higher in narratives told in the language in which the original experience took place (Javier, Barroso, & Muñoz, 1993; Marian & Kaushanskaya, 2004). The third issue to consider is the source of speaking dysfluency – it may be caused by the lower proficiency itself, or by anxieties stemming either from the topic of the conversation, or from insecurities about one's level of proficiency. Attrition researchers are particularly concerned about speakers "brushing up" on the language before the interviews. In some cases, this problem can be overcome through the use of previously collected narrative corpora, in particular corpora collected for non-linguistic purposes. An excellent example of such use is offered in Schmid's (2002) study of language attrition, where the researcher analyzed autobiographical interviews collected from German Jews in anglophone countries by historians as part of an oral history project conducted by the Düsseldorf Holocaust Memorial Center.

Linguistic autobiographies or *Sprachbiographien* are a subtype of personal experience narratives; they focus on the languages of the speaker and discuss how and why these languages were acquired, used, or abandoned. Linguistic autobiographies are elicited through interviews or questionnaires (Nekvapil, 2000, 2003; Meng, 2001; Meng & Protassova, 2002; Cmejrková, 2003; Franceschini, 2003; Protassova, 2004) or as classroom assignments (Hinton, 2001; Tse, 2000a; Pavlenko, 2003c). To avoid influencing speakers' responses, researchers have also analyzed spontaneously created linguistic autobiographies, such as learners' diaries and journals, and published autobiographies, otherwise known as language memoirs (Schumann, 1997; Pavlenko, 1998, 2001, 2004; Norton, 2000; Tse, 2000b; Granger, 2004).

When life histories and linguistic autobiographies are used for analysis of sociolinguistic situations, researchers tend to collect them only in one language, the one most convenient for analysis. There are several problems with this choice. Elicitation in the participant's weaker language involves a possibility that some information may get misrepresented or left out. Elicitation in the participant's dominant language may necessitate the use of a translator, which might also compromise the integrity of the narrative. More importantly, the tendency to collect linguistic autobiographies in one language positions them as "facts" rather than as discursive constructions. To get a comprehensive picture and to enable analysis of linguistic autobiographies as narratives, Nekvapil (2003) recommends collecting several autobiographies from the same informant, at significant intervals, and in both of the informant's languages. When possible, these narratives should be collected by different interviewers, because informants may choose to foreground different ethnic identities with different interlocutors.

18.3.2 Data analysis

18.3.2.1 Personal experience narratives

Just as it is with fictional narratives, the initial step in analysis of orally elicited personal experience narratives involves decisions about transcription: how much of the material should be transcribed and what conventions should be used. Subsequent analysis should be based on the transcripts as well as on the original tapes, because some characteristics of speech, in particular affect, are hard to capture on paper. Several approaches can be taken toward analysis of personal experience narratives and the final choice will depend on the researcher's interests (linguistic or narrative development) and on specific questions.

In the study of language development and attrition, personal experience narratives could be subject to the same linguistic analyses as fictional narratives, including inter-group comparisons between monolingual and bilingual corpora (Schmid, 2002; van Hell, Bosman, Wiggers, & Stoit, 2003). Narratives can be analyzed quantitatively in terms of length, lexical diversity, morphosyntactic accuracy and complexity, and degree of cross-linguistic influence (Dart, 1992; Schlyter, 1996; Schmid, 2002; van Hell, Bosman, Wiggers, & Stoit, 2003). They can also be analyzed qualitatively to examine, for instance, the use of parts of speech, relative clauses, or tense and aspect in terms of narrative functions (Dart, 1992; Wenzell, 1989) or the development of temporal reference over time (Schlyter, 1996; Teutsch-Dwyer, 2001). From a uniqely bilingual perspective, narratives in the two languages may also be compared in emotional intensity and amount of detail (Javier et al., 1993; Marian & Kaushanskaya, 2004).

Considering that narrative structures and conventions differ across languages and cultures (Mistry, 1993; Blum-Kulka, 1997; McCabe & Bliss, 2003; Klapproth, 2004), personal experience narratives can also be analyzed as narratives to compare speakers' narrative competencies and performances of self in respective languages. Five approaches are commonly used in traditional narrative analysis: high point, story grammar, stanza analysis, narrative assessment profile, and form–function analysis (Berman, 1995; McCabe & Bliss, 2003).

High point analysis examines narrative functions of particular utterances and episodes in terms of the structure outlined by Labov (1972a; Labov & Waletzky, 1967) and consisting of an abstract, orientation, complicating action, evaluation, resolution, and a coda. *Story grammar analysis*, developed by Stein and Glenn (1979) and Mandler (1982), based on Propp's (1968) analysis of Russian folk tales, examines the degree to which the story is structured around the explicit goals of the protagonist (setting, initiating event, character's internal response and plan, character's attempts to solve the problem, consequences). These approaches, which focus on the episodic structure and the degree and richness of evaluation, have been successfully used in the study of narrative competence of bilingual children and adults in both fictional (Shrubshall, 1997; Ordóñez, 2004) and personal experience narratives (Rintell, 1990; Maeno, 1995).

Critics argue however that high point and story grammar analyses may be biased toward Western narratives, and, more specifically, toward the European tradition (cf. Mistry, 1993; McCabe & Bliss, 2003). This concern is addressed in the third approach, stanza analysis, advanced by Hymes (1982) and Gee (1991). *Stanza analysis* breaks the narrative into lines and then groups the lines into hierarchical levels, such as stanzas (a group of lines about a single topic), scenes, and acts, presenting the narrative as if it were a prose poem. Stanza analysis was successfully used by Maeno (1995) to examine narratives of English-Japanese bilinguals. At the same time, even though this approach is helpful in illuminating the structure of Japanese or Zuni narratives, it does not apply well to all cultures (McCabe & Bliss, 2003).

The fourth approach, *narrative assessment profile*, advocated by McCabe and Bliss (2003) on the basis of many years of work with children from a variety of cultural and linguistic backgrounds, addresses the cultural concerns through its multidimensionality. This approach involves evaluation of topic maintenance, event sequencing, informativeness, referencing, conjunctive cohesion, and fluency (McCabe & Bliss, 2003: 15–20) and has been successfully used by the authors in analysis of bilingual children's narratives. Finally, *form–function analysis* (Bamberg, 1987; Berman & Slobin, 1994; Berman, 1995) considers how linguistic forms are deployed to express narrative functions, i.e. encode temporal and causal relations, or create textual cohesiveness. The multiple applications of this approach to bilinguals' stories have been discussed earlier with regard to fictional narratives.

Over the years, these narrative approaches have faced a number of critiques, in particular from conversation analysts, who argue that narratives have to be examined as a fundamentally interactional activity (cf. Edwards, 1997; Schegloff, 1997a). These critiques have been heeded by bilingualism researchers who began to examine conversational narratives and their interactional functions (cf. Pfaff, 2001). To date, the most elaborate framework for interactional analysis of bilinguals' narratives of personal experience has been advanced by Koven (1998, 2001, 2002). Her studies of French-Portuguese bilinguals' stories examine the following discursive forms, both quantitatively and qualitatively: (1) speaker roles, i.e. ways in which speakers position themselves as interlocutors, narrators, or characters; (2) denotational characterizations, i.e. speakers' references to various characters and entities (e.g., woman vs. chick); (3) metapragmatic descriptors, i.e. speakers' descriptions of the verbal actions of others (e.g., he said vs. he groaned); (4) quotation, also known as voicing (Bakhtin, 1981), i.e. speakers' renderings of the speech of others (e.g., direct vs. indirect); (5) epistemic modalization, i.e. the status speakers give to the events described relative to the event of speaking, oftentimes indexed through manipulation of tenses (e.g., present vs. past).

What is particularly intriguing about Koven's approach is that she does not stop at using this elaborate schema but appeals to two additional analytical sources to shed light on how the selves are situated within the local order of meanings: self- and other-evaluations (Koven, 1998). Thus, immediately after the story elicitation the participants were asked how they felt telling the stories in each language and how they thought they came across. Then, the researcher played the recordings to other French-Portuguese bilinguals and elicited their opinions on the similarities and differences between speakers' personae in each language.

18.3.2.2 *Linguistic autobiographies*

Linguistic autobiographies and life histories are rapidly gaining popularity in the field of bilingualism as a unique means of gaining first person insights into the processes of language learning, attrition, and shift. Sociolinguistic analyses of linguistic autobiographies commonly appeal to some form of thematic or content analysis, in which narratives are coded according to emerging themes and conceptual categories (cf. Strauss & Corbin, 1990). The advantage of this approach is its sensitivity to

recurrent motifs salient in participants' stories. Unfortunately, in many cases content analysis amounts to nothing more than a generous use of quotes in support of
researchers' observations. This approach treats narratives "as observation notes
and transcripts" (Tse, 2000b: 191) and displays uncritical reliance on what is said
in the narratives, neglect of what is omitted, and lack of insight as to why certain
things are said in certain ways at particular times and others are excluded. In its
worst realizations content analysis is characterized by complete insensitivity to
linguistic, interactional, and discursive properties of narratives, and to particularit-
ies of storytelling in a second language.

Several scholars have argued that linguistic autobiographies cannot and should not
be treated as observation notes, transcripts, or collections of facts (Kramsch & Lam,
1999; Nekvapil, 2000, 2003; Pavlenko, 2002b). Rather, they should be treated as
discursive constructions, similar to other personal experience narratives, and as
such be subject to analysis that considers their linguistic, rhetorical, and interactional
properties, as well as the sociolinguistic and sociohistoric contexts in which they were
produced. The innovative uses of linguistic autobiographies by European researchers
also show that these narratives function best if they supplement, not supplant, other
means of data collection (Meng, 2001; Meng & Protassova, 2002; Nekvapil, 2000,
2003; Protassova, 2004).

From this perspective, the first step in analysis of linguistic autobiographies should
consider the sociohistoric circumstances of their production. For instance, a comparison of language memoirs written in different time periods shows that historic
and political events significantly affect the ways in which individuals position
themselves with regard to their languages (Pavlenko, 2004). This means that
researchers working with linguistic autobiographies need to take into account
the speakers' social, historic, political, and economic circumstances, and language
ideologies and discourses that have currency in the speakers' communities and
with regard to which they position themselves. Čmejrková (2003) provides a great
example of such sociohistorically sensitive analysis of Ukrainian Czechs' narratives
of repatriation.

The second step is to consider the circumstances surrounding the interview process,
power relations between the interview participants, roles taken by the participants
at different points in the interview, and ways in which various formulations, and
more generally societal attitudes, might have affected speakers' decisions about
the tellability of particular events. In research with bi- and multilingual speakers
this sensitivity is particularly important, as some participants may be refugees or
immigrants, and thus occupy inherently powerless positions not only vis-à-vis the
researcher but vis-à-vis the society in general. This means that they may produce a
version of their institutionally oriented narratives, i.e. narratives they have already
produced for a variety of governmental representatives. An example of such awareness can be found in Simon-Maeda's (2004) discussion of why lesbian educators either
refused to participate in her study or chose to downplay their sexual identities.

The third analytical step involves a decision with regard to the focus of the study
and the relative importance of the three types of information that can be gathered
from life history narratives: life reality (i.e. findings on how "things" are or were),
subject reality (i.e. findings on how "things" or events were experienced by the

respondents), and text reality (i.e. ways in which "things" or events are narrated by the respondents) (Nekvapil, 2003: 69). Some researchers are primarily interested in how their subjects narrate themselves and, hence, in text reality. They focus on rhetorical properties of texts and appeal to positioning theory (Pavlenko, 2001, 2004), Bakhtinian analysis (Vitanova, 2004, 2005), or rhetorical analysis (Kramsch & Lam, 1999) to examine how non-native speakers create textual homes and selves in a second language and how they position themselves with regard to societal discourses on language and identity.

Others are interested in subject reality. These studies appeal to content analysis to examine bilinguals' attitudes toward their respective languages (Pavlenko, 1998, 2003c; Pavlenko & Lantolf, 2000; Tse, 2000a; Heinz, 2001; Yelenevskaya & Fialkova, 2003) and heritage-language speakers' ethnic identification and attitudes toward language maintenance (Tse, 2000b; Hinton, 2001). The weakest applications of content analysis usually appear as summaries of themes, interspersed with quotes. Other studies supplement content analysis with discourse analysis (Pavlenko, 2003c; Yelenevskaya & Fialkova, 2003) or membership categorization analysis (Nekvapil, 2000) and apply poststructuralist (Norton, 2000), sociocultural (Pavlenko & Lantolf, 2000) or psychoanalytic (Granger, 2004) theory to move beyond a summary approach and understand internal and external influences on the authors' positioning.

And yet others are interested in life reality, be it linguistic trajectories of individual speakers or sociolinguistic circumstances of particular communities. The strongest analyses in this area use autobiographies in conjunction with linguistic, historic, and ethnographic data to examine the situation of Ukrainian Czechs (Čmejrková, 2003), Czech Germans (Nekvapil, 2000, 2003), Turkish and Russian immigrants in Germany (Meng, 2001; Meng & Protassova, 2002; Franceschini, 2003) and the Russian diaspora in Finland (Protassova, 2004). The weakest analyses, on the other hand, confuse textual and experiential reality and analyze narrated episodes as real-life events. Kramsch and Lam (1999) criticize this approach, using specific examples to show that the act of narration inalterably transforms its subject and any further interpretation interprets the telling and not the event in question. Furthermore, regardless of what type of reality one is interested in, it is quite likely that the realities of life, subject, and text are not easily separable and those interested in one aspect still need to be fully cognizant of the other two (Nekvapil, 2003).

Section summary

In sum, if you are planning to use personal narratives in your research, you need to:

- decide on your initial research questions and/or hypotheses and make sure that they are indeed best answered through the means of personal narratives;
- determine what type of personal narratives will be most helpful for your purposes: (1) personal experience narratives or linguistic autobiographies; (2) spontaneous or elicited narratives; (3) oral or written narratives, and in the latter case, elicited or previously published ones;

- estimate the size of the corpus you need to answer your questions and then decide on the collection procedure: (1) if you decide on published narratives, what are the criteria by which you will select them; (2) if you decide on spontaneous narratives, how and where you will collect them and for how long; (3) if you decide on elicited narratives, what type of prompts, cues, interview questions, or instructions you will use, how many narratives will be collected from each individual, and over what span of time;
- decide on the language or languages of narrative elicitation, and consider both pros and cons of collecting narratives in all of the participants' languages for your own research purposes;
- choose appropriate transcription conventions;
- consider the advantages and disadvantages of several approaches to narrative analysis and settle on a combination of approaches that best addresses your own research needs; remember to consider the circumstances surrounding the production of the narratives and their possible influence on the narrative structure and content.

18.4 Conclusion

I hope that this chapter highlighted the multiple possibilities narrative analysis has to offer to bi- and multilingualism researchers interested in various aspects of linguistic and narrative development, and sociolinguistic determinants of language learning, attrition, and shift. I end it with words of caution. Several studies demonstrate that speakers' performance on narrative tasks depends on numerous factors, including the nature of the prompt, participants' social and cultural background, elicitation mode, and context (Tannen, 1980, 1982, 1993; Berman, 1995; Shiro, 2003; van Hell, Bosman, Wiggers, & Stoit, 2003; McKinnie & Priestly, 2004). This means that conclusions about the narrative competence of specific speakers cannot be reached on the basis of just one type of narrative; rather, narratives of different kinds need to be collected across different contexts, over time, and in all of the languages of the speakers. Similarly, the seductive ease with which linguistic autobiographies can be obtained should not obscure the fact that participants' stories are interpretations, and not representations, of reality, and are best used in conjunction with other means of data collection. Moreover, precisely because these narratives offer ready-made interpretations, researchers should resist the appeal of a summary and instead attempt to offer analyses that incorporate participants' views but go beyond them.

Further reading and resources

Films

Professor Chafe has generously agreed to free distribution of the *Pear film*. The film can be downloaded from his website at www.linguistics.ucsb.edu/faculty/chafe/ pearfilm.htm or from the website created by Mary Erbaugh at www.pearstories.org/. Both *Modern Times* and the *Pear film* can also be downloaded from Jon Aske's website at www.lrc.salemstate.edu/aske/ basquecorpus/movies/index.htm.

Narrative corpora

The CHILDES website at http://childes.psy.cmu.edu/ offers several monolingual and bilingual Frog Stories corpora. Transcripts of Pear Stories and stories elicited by *Modern Times* in Basque are found at Aske's website at www.lrc.salemstate.edu/aske/basquecorpus/movies/ index.htm. Pear Stories elicited in seven Chinese dialects can be found on Erbaugh's website at www.pearstories.org/.

Transcription conventions

Several websites offer useful information on transcription conventions, including www. linguistlist.org and www.celt.stir.ac.uk/resources/ML51/transcription_symbols.html. The website at www.speech.psychol.ucl.ac.uk/transcription/transcript.html offers an on-line training course for phonological descriptions of stuttering and fluent speech, and includes transcription conventions, exercises, and links to the International Phonetic Association (IPA) charts. The website at www.ldc.upenn.edu/Projects/Transcription offers project-specific transcription conventions for Korean, Russian, Mandarin, and Spanish.

Narrative elicitation, coding, and analysis

Newcomers to research will benefit from the discussion of narrative elicitation, as well as from a more general overview of second language research, offered in Mackey and Gass (2005), a text that also offers samples of consent forms, institutional review board applications, and transcription conventions. McCabe and Bliss (2003) offer useful recommendations on narrative elicitation and analysis and specific coding schemas. Pearson (2002) provides a coding sheet and instructions for Frog Story coding. Studies in Berman and Slobin (1994) and Chafe (1980) constitute an excellent primer in all aspects of elicitation and analysis of fictional narratives. Denzin (1989a) and Riessman (1993) offer useful introduction to analysis of personal narratives. Nekvapil (2003) provides informative discussion of elicitation and analysis of linguistic autobiographies. Verhoeven and Strömqvist's (2001) volume is a unique collection of studies of bi- and multilinguals' narratives.

19   Media Analysis

Tony Purvis

In Taiwan I was different because I couldn't speak Chinese; in the West I was different because I looked Chinese.

Ien Ang, On Not Speaking Chinese:
Living Between Asia and the West

19.1   Introduction

These observations of Ang suggest that how a subject is culturally encoded and subsequently decoded depends on the contexts and situations of specific regimes of mediation and representation. In Taiwan, Ang's linguistic and cultural subjectivity is problematical because she does not fit into specific interpretive frameworks. She is different because she cannot speak Chinese. Alternatively phrased, her linguistic subjectivity is mediated on the basis of a speech act which is, paradoxically, a silence. In the West, however, Ang is subjected to another decoding. She *looks* Chinese, though this is yet another form of silence: looking is not speaking. Here, cultural recognition is conferred not on the basis of a speech act but on the basis of what Western subjects imagine Chinese people to look like. But what does it mean to speak Chinese? And what does it mean to "look" Chinese? Does the Chinese subject ever recognize him- or herself? Or are all forms of linguistic and cultural recognition tied to systems of representation and mediation? How does any subject perform an act of self-recognition? How do we imagine the multilingual subject?

Ang's observations on one level highlight the extent to which language and subjectivity are socially constructed. However, we can supplement Ang's points by suggesting that linguistic and cultural recognition are also tied to the specific ways in which the mass media construct subjects as linguistically or culturally identifiable in the first instance. Michel Foucault's theorization of "subjectivity" contends that all subjects emerge in relation to the enabling and constraining contexts of *discourse* so that, for instance, the discourses of whiteness or gender construct subjects one way and not another. In contemporary cultures, it is the discursive strategies of the mass media which have often been pivotal in the construction of bilingual and multilingual subjects.

In popular Western media representations, a bilingual speaker is someone whose second language is English. However, in the same popular media output, the bilingual subject is not so much a bilingual speaker as someone whose command of the dominant (English) language code is not considered proficient or fluent. This is a deficit model. But it is also a model which positions media constructions of Englishness (nationhood) in relation to an ideologically dominant model of language (in this case Standard English and Received Pronunciation). What kinds of issues, then, can media studies and media analysis bring to the study of bilingualism and multilingualism? How do contemporary mass media construct bilingual and multilingual subjectivities? How might the trajectories of media analysis assist research in bilingualism and multilingualism? This chapter introduces some of the principal frameworks of media analysis and in so doing addresses some of the issues raised by these opening questions. The discussion is organized as follows: section 19.2, "Frameworks of Media Analysis," suggests in broad terms what the mass media are, "who" the media are, and why analysis of the media is useful in cross-cultural and multilingual research contexts. The first case study looks at how to analyze news media, using Endemol/Channel 4's (UK) *Celebrity Big Brother* by way of practical illustration. Section 19.3, "Media Analysis and the Contexts of 'Global' Multilingual Subjects," considers issues of linguistic-cultural inclusivity, participation, and representation. Section 19.4, "Media Analysis and the Discourses of the Bilingual 'Other,'" attends to the operation of the signifiers of linguistic identities in media analysis. Section 19.5 offers some conclusions and suggests that multilingual subjects are not simply represented in the media but are actually constructed in relation to the media's management of the discourses of language, culture, and identity.

19.2　Frameworks of Media Analysis

Increasingly and unceasingly, locally and globally, cultures and societies are dominated by images and representations (see Hall, 1997: 13–74). It is the mass media (television, cinema, newspapers, radio, popular music, the Internet, mobile phones) which mediate, represent, and construct the world to subjects: audiences, spectators, readers, listeners, speakers, consumers, and producers. In appearing to *represent* the world, as Herman and Chomsky (2002) suggest, the mass media are also in a position to *construct* the world, to make some parts of the world seem more or less alien than others, more or less distant than the world of the local and the familiar. It is today's media which make the global, international, and multilingual seem local, regional, and familiar. Events which from one point of view might seem distant are, because of television, radio, the Internet, and mobile technologies, immediate and instantaneous. Consider, for example, how the reporting of war and conflict, religious spectacle, Olympic sporting moment, or natural disaster can become media events. The experience of television's liveness, its sense of now-ness, means that the media are able to exercise and command considerable power (see McCullagh, 2002). Because of the media's power to represent the world, it is important to understand what the mass media are, what they do, and what frameworks can be used in media analysis.

The analytic frameworks that follow are listed here in order to promote the value of media analysis, to encourage analysis of media texts from the outset of media study in the research contexts of multilingualism, and to consider the importance of structure in all media analysis. There is no one way to do media analysis, though useful outlines, summaries, and details of media analysis are found in Jostein Gripsrud's *Understanding Media Culture* (2000) and Eoin Devereux's *Understanding the Media* (2003). Both these texts variously commend media analyses which (1) attend to the identity and influence of the audience, (2) refer to the usefulness of semiotics and interpretation in relation to content analysis, (3) stress the importance of industrial and production contexts in understanding the media; and (4) underline approaches to media analysis which examine the global power of the media. How, then, might an introductory analytic framework look?

19.2.1   *Analytic frameworks*

At this initial stage, the mass media can be imagined as media producers, media institutions and organizations, media audiences/users, and media output. Media analysis, then, will be concerned with the discussion, examination, and assessment of *all* the components above which constitute the media. One way of beginning to understand and undertake media analysis is to think of the media's output. Advertising, films, television, newspapers, and magazines are familiar, everyday examples of media texts. Media output can be thought in terms of the texts, the written and spoken narratives and stories, and the audiovisual sounds and images which are used to construct and represent a specific reality at a particular point in time and space. To analyze such output is to undertake media analysis, and so anyone who comments – critically or otherwise – on media output might be said to be engaging at an analytical level. More specifically, critical and analytic work can be framed as follows:

19.2.1.1   *Media and textual relations*

Using text-based models of analysis, media output can be analyzed in terms of its (seemingly) self-contained textual status (e.g. film as film text, and similarly with TV drama, popular music lyrics, or advertisements). Models of media analysis that stress the "text" in terms of its textual qualities (style, form, language features, use of color, etc.) will view it as the key object of analysis. In the case of an advertisement, for example, the key object of analysis will be the advertisement itself. What is also clear in advertising is the degree to which the text is also intertextual – constructed around combinations of other cultural texts and references which contribute to the advertisement's appeal. In the case of television output, the genre becomes a useful term in the analysis of texts. Genre means "classification" or "type" and the term is used in media analysis to designate fictional, dramatic, filmic, or visual-artistic text. Using genre labels, texts can be categorized (e.g. soap opera, sitcom, romance), and texts can be bundled into subgroups. For example, documentary alone has subcategories such as drama-doc, docu-drama, and docu-soap. But genre also serves a critical and defining purpose, operating as a way of *classifying* the text in question. One way of undertaking this kind of media analysis has been proposed by Nick Lacey. He suggests (2000: 136) that a useful starting point "is to list the following: types of character, setting, iconography, narrative and style of the text and then consider whether it fits into any genre." Similar listings and definitional outlines are proposed by Holland (1997: 153–9), Watson (1998: 137–42), and Burton (2000: 86–94).

19.2.1.2 *Media and cultural relations*

Working with this framework, mass media (e.g. the popular romance novel or the advertisement) will be analyzed in relation to wider aspects of social and cultural dynamics. If we take the example of popular fiction, then this will not be analyzed solely in terms of its content but assessed on the basis of its relationships to cultural identities, social and political formations, and contexts of audience or user interaction. The work of Janice Radway (1987) and Ien Ang (1985) has done much to situate the analysis of popular media texts in relation to the users of the text and the subsequent "communities" of viewers and readers that emerge around the mediated product. Ang's work has additionally analyzed how North American television output is culturally consumed in multilingual contexts. The advertising of the Sony Walkman, moreover, became a key element in the analysis by du Gay, Hall, Janes, Mackay, and Negus (1997) in *Doing Cultural Studies: The Story of the Sony Walkman*. This research attends to the cross-cultural and international dimensions of cultural identities against the back-drop of the mass media, marketing, and global capitalism.

19.2.1.3 *Media and political-economic relations*

This model situates the film or product in relation to the political economy of the mass media and industrial production. Media texts in this framework will be analyzed as commodities, constructed in spheres where the financial and the economic dynamics are made intelligible in the spheres of the social, the ideological, and the cultural. The media text, whether this be films, advertisements, or newspapers, is part of an industry, has emerged in relation to the development of mass communications systems, and takes much of its meaning from the wider political economy in which the text circulates. To ignore the economic and ideological dimensions of any media text is to disregard discussion of media power in the financial economy. *Doing Cultural Studies: The Story of the Sony Walkman* makes links with the cultural economy of media output, whereas studies influenced by political economy will approach the media in terms of the economic structures which underpin, and to a large extent determine, the tripartite links between media institutions, media output, and ideology (for discussion of political economy, see Garnham, 1979; Mosco, 1996).

19.2.1.4   Media's relation to contexts of use

Here, the mass media and their products (film is a good example, but so is popular music) are understood in relation to practices of cinema-going and not simply film analysis. In the case of popular and "indie" music, then it is the subcultures that emerge around music or club-going which become important in terms of media analysis. Audience relations, ethnographic research, and the industries on the apparent periphery of the media industry become important in the understanding of media output, media industries, and wider social formations. Insights into conducting media and cultural analyses along these lines can be seen in Howard Jenkins's *Textual Poachers* (1992) and Joke Hermes's *Reading Women's Magazines* (1995).

19.2.2   Usefulness of frameworks for media analysis: Contexts of language and identity in the news

Having absorbed some of the key terms and debates, how might someone fairly new to the subject commence a media analysis? We can consider one way of undertaking such an analysis in relation to news reports surrounding the now internationally renowned *Celebrity Big Brother* (Endemol/Channel 4, UK: January, 2007).

We have seen in the opening points made in this chapter that the media are principally concerned with representations of social relations. A media analysis is also an analysis of the media representations used in the *construction* of social life and social relations. However, another dimension of media analysis is concerned with the *form* in which the representation is mediated. Representations are produced in forms and genres which reflect visual, linguistic, spoken, and written structures. Moreover, if representations are not "representative," or if output can determine social behavior (e.g. the media's impact on perceptions of ethnicity, gender, sexuality, and age), then it will be necessary to analyze this output in terms of its impact on *audiences*. How might these different elements be brought together in an analysis of media output?

At some point, society's organizations, institutions, and social researchers need to have an indication of how the media are representing and constructing a particular issue or topic. For instance, the recent UK series of *Celebrity Big Brother* received lots of complaints from national and international audiences because of claims that contestants' behavior and language was racist. What is particularly interesting in the case of this current volume of essays is not so much the fact that Shilpa Shetty, an Indian actress and the eventual winner of the show, is bilingual but that the accusations about racism focus on Shetty's linguistic competence in a number of languages other than her mother tongue.

The accusations have been discussed in web chatrooms, newspapers, television talk-shows, and the British House of Commons, with public demonstrations on the streets of a number of Indian cities and beyond. Using *Celebrity Big Brother*

(*CBB*) as our illustration, it can be seen that analysis of this particular output will be concerned with the interrelations between audiences, institutions, and media representation (texts, programs, news articles, and so on). Any media analysis will foreground the ways in which these areas interoperate in the construction of "news." But these interrelations are specifically concerned with one of the most important areas covered in any media analysis: the construction of social identity in language. The dynamics and conflicts surrounding these interrelations are particularly evident in the *Celebrity Big Brother* incident. Media analysis, then, is carried out in order to gain some understanding of claims, such as the ones alluded to, that output and organizations impact on how social life is lived "outside" of the media text.

Analysis of the representation of the *CBB* story in news media can be undertaken in two stages.

The first stage comprises the following:

1 Identify articles and reports about the *CBB* story or series and select a manageable sample to analyze; if, for example, 400 articles are identified that deal with Shetty, they will be reduced to a representative sample with fewer articles. If the team of analysts is big enough, then all the articles may be examined.
2 Begin to examine how messages are framed and pay attention to the sorts of messages being conveyed.

    The *CBB* stories – the representation of the events surrounding Shetty in the *Big Brother* house – are subsequently reported in national and international news media (e.g. television and newspapers). Thus, analysis of the story is not so much about the house itself but about how the news reports reconstruct the story/house as it is unfolding in the "real time" of the contestants' lives. We can think about how to proceed with a more detailed media analysis by looking at how the news media report the story surrounding the housemates and the topic of racism.

The second stage has the following components:

1 Consider how the news media frame public discussion of the *CBB* story. For example, which elements are repeated? Are common language devices being used in the reports? How many times are actual soundbites or quotes used? Who is being quoted?
2 Take account of the principal sources used as "evidence." It will be important to ask who the main spokespeople are, how they are quoted or referred to, and how many times.
3 Examine the specific ways in which sources are used. Sources can be used to advocate, to negate, to affirm, to provide expertise, or to provide a sense of authenticity.
4 Investigate the specific topics which are being covered, and what is being discounted. Here, it will be useful to compare and contrast the reporting of the same event or incident using two or more examples. For instance, BBC news reports can be compared with commercial or non-British sources.

5 Consider why the event is or is not a major news item or front-page story.
6 Ask why the institution has used the reporters it has to "front" or write the story or event.

   In order to add dimension and depth to the media analysis outlined above, it will be necessary to establish *methodologies*.

1 Construct a list of key search terms or items for analysis.
2 Construct a list of terms used in similar or ancillary ways.
3 Identify which reports will be used.
4 Identify whether or not the story reported in the news is constructed on the basis of *opinion*, *news*, or *feature*. Opinion stories are based on what people say via letters or interviews with the "general public." News stories are reports that list the events with some degree of objectivity. Feature reports are in-depth and provide greater coverage of the story.
5 Ask where in the running order or newspaper the story is positioned, and consider why it is positioned as it is.
6 Compare the running order (in the case of a news broadcast) with programs on the same day or subsequent days.
7 Consider when the story was broadcast or published if this is relevant to the analysis (e.g. weekdays as opposed to weekends).

   All of the above outline strategies are important in any media analysis. By way of illustration, we can see that "where" a story ran in a newspaper or on television news can make a significant contribution to how the media messages are interpreted by audiences. Consider:

1 whether the story ran on the front page, and the headlines associated with the story;
2 how far the news is viewed as "national" or "international" and whether or not it was reported in the arts, lifestyles, or other sections;
3 any evidence for editorial control over the placing of the story. Editors make significant judgments regarding where to place each story;
4 the potential audience range for the story. A report on America's CBS *Evening News* might be classified as national news; a story on *BBC News 24* might be itemized as international news.

Structure your media analysis:

1 Begin with an *abstract* or *executive summary*.
2 Follow this with an *introduction*.
3 Continue with a section that outlines the *aims and objectives* of your analysis.
4 Present *major findings*.
5 Offer an *evaluation* which highlights any ambivalence and how such ambivalence might be addressed.
6 Draw *conclusions*.

> **Section summary: Doing media analysis**
>
> • All media analysis will involve some investigation of the relations between producers of texts and output, and users of texts and output.
> • Media analysis will situate production and consumption in relation to local and global contexts and histories.
> • Media analysis will be interested in the multilingual and multicultural discourses of media readers, listeners, viewers, and spectators.

19.3   Media Analysis and the Contexts of "Global" Multilingual Subjects

19.3.1   *Global circuits and media analysis*

Consider when or how you last made use of the mass media. Typically, watching television, going to the cinema, reading a local or national newspaper, using the Internet or email, listening to radio, or simply being inundated by advertisements on public transport or in public spaces are activities associated with the mass media. On the one hand, the mass media are in a position to make local happenings into global events. The mass media create a mass audience. On the other hand, the media are in a position to determine what audiences see, hear, read about, and understand as "news." Not all events are accorded the same status in terms of how they are reported: some locations are ignored, and some languages are never broadcast or heard. And how far are the mass media "multilingual" in their globalizing of local cultures? Is one language more dominant than others in the representation and construction of culture?

One way of imagining media analysis is via what has become known as the "circuit of culture." This model – outlined in the work of Stuart Hall and others (Hall: 1997) – allows the links between media and culture to be understood in relation to five terms: representation, identity, production, consumption, and regulation. Much media output and activity can be analyzed using the circuit, though three strategies emerge in relation to the understanding of the media against the wider backdrop of multilingualism. Firstly, all media is at some point concerned with language and representation. Hall stresses that language is central in all representations and meanings of cultures. But a key question for any media analysis which is interested in bilingual/multilingual representation is the extent to which the mass media do or do not represent or construct a world which exceeds the monolingual or homogeneous culture of Western or hegemonic media representation. Secondly, all media are concerned with the linguistic construction, production, and consumption of identities. Media analysis on the one hand will want to examine the linguistic and cultural identities of the audiences that consume the images and representations, and on the other hand will be concerned with the production processes that construct the meanings in the first instance. Thirdly, how far do mass media representations, particularly in terms of advertising and marketing, construct subjects who on one level appear multicultural (and thus multilingual?) but who, in fact, are simply the constructions of the Western media's fantasy of the "third world"? (see Franklin, Lury, and Stacey, 2000: 1–16, 97–187).

This last point – the media's construction of the third world in the Western imaginary – is of particular concern for media analysis in the context of the discourses of multilingualism and multiculturalism. Globalization is thought to be transforming how the world is understood. The mass media, central to the processes of globalization, can appear to make the "globe" seem smaller, and quicker and easier to traverse, where multicultural subjects are thought to inhabit a world without linguistic, cultural, or national boundaries. Anthony Giddens describes how there is an "intensification of worldwide social relations which link distant localities in such a way that local happenings are shaped by events occurring many miles away and vice versa" (1990: 64).

Section summary: Global language and media?

The mass media are central to this sense of intensification, but as media analysts we need to ask:

- How far is the media's globalizing reach necessarily dismantling linguistic and national barriers?
- Is there a language of international communications which crosses cultures and languages? If so, how far is this a "language" in the traditional sense?
- In what ways do the media represent the global in multilingual terms, and is the multilingual subject someone whose social construction is tied to the Western media's appropriation of the discourses of liberalism and pluralism?

19.3.2   *Media analysis and/in cross-cultural contexts*

In the case of media analysis which attends to language difference and culture, and which draws attention to the media's homogenizing strategies, Valerie Alia (2004: 52) argues for a practice and mode of analysis whose ethics is marked by "accuracy and inclusion" and which respects "diversity." Noting that the principle of inclusivity is an "essential requirement of any ethical media practice" (p. 52), she highlights the two essential aspects of any inclusivity: "media participation" and "media representation" (p. 52). Alia makes some important points for analysis of any text or representation: "Ideally, an ethical media practice would include . . . participation roughly proportional to their numbers in the general population of members of all minority groups" (p. 53). She goes on to suggest that such groups be represented "in appropriate proportions, with appropriate respect and treatment equivalent to that of the majority population" (p. 53).

Before outlining some of the important details of Alia's analysis, we may note her approaches to and assumptions about analysis. Canadian government guidelines for media practitioners allow Alia to establish how media analysis of mainstream and alternative representations must reflect an ethics of inclusivity.

> Words, images and situations are the tools of journalists. In our coverage . . . it is very important that we do not reinforce erroneous preconceptions or suggest that all or most members of a racial/ethnic group or nation state are the same.
>
> . . . Avoid words which could cloud the fact that all attributes may be found in all groups and individuals. Avoid qualifiers that reinforce racial and ethnic stereotypes.
> . . . Be aware of the self-identification preferences of racial groups and cultural groups, e.g. "Inuit" is preferable to "Eskimo." (Alia, 2004: 62)

Alia provides a useful illustration of media analysis and the representation of multilingualism in the context of a visit to Canada by the British Queen Elizabeth. A national and international news broadcast described how the Queen, visiting Baffin Island, was "'greeted by some of the local Inuit Indians'" (p. 55). Alia perceptively discusses how there is no such "thing" as "Inuit Indians." Her analysis is grounded in an understanding of language, colonialism, and multilingualism in Canada and the Americas more generally, and she develops her argument in relation to discourses of "Inuit." "Inuit" used to be called Eskimos by outsiders, suggests Alia. "In Canada and the US," she writes, "some non-Inuit indigenous people are called 'Indians' – an error dating back to Columbus's arrival in 1492, when he thought he had found India" (pp. 55–6). Describing the various linguistic mechanisms through which Inuit are variously constructed but misrepresented, she illustrates what happens when bilingual speakers are represented in terms of the majoritarian (in this case English) language.

Having listed numerous inaccuracies, she unpicks the confusions and complexities of media representations of Inuit. The main thrust of her analysis is to expose how mainstream media representations are grounded in representational strategies which homogenize language groups and speakers. Her observations are worth citing in detail, offering as they do important insights into media analysis of mono- and multilingual speakers against the backdrop of cultural (mis)representation.

> Most Inupiaq-speakers live in Alaska and Siberia. "Inuit" cannot refer to "an" anybody because it is plural. "Native American" refers to indigenous people of the United States, sometimes including people from Canada. Inuit live mainly in Arctic and subarctic Canada, Alaska, Greenland and Siberia. Inupiat constitute only one of the Inuit subcultures; Yup'ik are also Inuit and have their own language. Inuvialuit are Inuit who live in the western Canadian Arctic. The generic term for the language is Inuktitut, though there are several related languages. I have heard Inuit jokingly or ironically call themselves "Inuks," when speaking in English to *Qallunaat* (non-Inuit people), anglicizing the plural. . . . But there is no such thing as this plural in the Inuktitut language. And no Inuit, even jokingly, call themselves "Inuits." This is an invention of the British "scholars" who misinformed Oxford's publications – and consequently much of the media public. (Alia, 2004: 56–7).

Section summary: Media analysis and/in cross-cultural contexts

What might be summarized about strategies of media analysis in relation to the ethics of practice, representation, and multilingual cultures and communities?

- All representations involve, at some point, the analysis of language and texts. However, language and texts have ethical dimensions – for the media analyst and the producer of the text.
- Media analysis of intercultural identities will always to some extent be an analysis of the monolingual *and* the multilingual dimensions in any culture or community. Language here is understood in terms of its cultural situatedness more than its abstract formal features.
- Media analysis will always require an analyst to confront issues of linguistic inclusivity, participation, and representation.
- Media analysis will always seek to examine how mainstream media representations and constructions do or do not reflect in balanced ways minority- and majority-community concerns.
- In attending to the previous point, the media analyst will consider the historical and cultural dimensions in which language communities are constructed as majoritarian or minoritarian in the first instance. Often this means deconstructing the text to expose how ideology and history impact on that which is presented as "natural" or transparent.

19.4 Media Analysis and the Discourses of the Bilingual "Other"

"How do we represent people and places which are significantly different from *us*? Why is 'difference' so compelling a theme, so contested an area of representation?" (Hall, 1997: 225; italics mine). These questions posed by media and cultural theorist Stuart Hall usefully frame some of the key questions which beset contemporary media analysis in the context of debates surrounding the discourses of bilingualism and multiculturalism. If culture or "way of life" is about how a particular way of life is lived in terms of people, places, and difference, then which language will be used in the representation of this way of life? Terms such as "us" and "them" assume an inside and an outside in language and culture, dominant and subordinate formations, native speakers and an "other," often imagined in terms of a first-language or mother-tongue speaker, and a second-language speaker who in acquiring a linguistic voice is also required to assume something of the cultural repertoires associated with the language. But to the extent that *all* languages and texts are marked by the traces of other languages, is not all linguistic and visual representation always already marked, if not flawed, at least to some extent, by the imprint of cultural hybridity?

19.4.1 *Monolingual* and *multicultural? Visual-media analysis*

In the work of Roland Barthes (1973), media output is not solely concerned with texts, signs, and content but with the construction, flow, structuring, and interpretation of meanings, identities, and audiovisual images within and across cultures. In a sense, media analysis for Barthes involves all the factors that shape the production and consumption of a media text. The stress here on production and consumption, terms often found in the analysis of political economy, also indicates the degree to which media analysis involves taking into account the dialogic and dialectical (or conflictual) nature of media output. For instance, when the news media use shots of the White House to represent the United States, or transmit pictures of the Union Flag flying over Buckingham Palace in order to signify the United Kingdom, these image concentrations can often paper over the political and cultural dissensus at the center of the state's apparent coherence. Barthes's famous analysis of a popular French magazine highlights how images of the nation in the media are always precariously balanced between conditions of concord and conflict, cohesion and collapse, linguistic colonization and linguistic fragmentation.

Barthes's analysis of the media is one that focuses on the placing and structure of signs in cultural life and media output. Because Barthes uses examples from the field of visual media, especially advertising, his work is particularly useful for anyone working in bilingual and multilingual contexts. Drawing on and expanding work in the field of language, popular media, and semiotics, he shows how a sign operates at the level of denotation (primary signification) and connotation (secondary signification). For instance, the signifier "donkey," operating at the level of denotation, signifies a four-legged animal. However, this sign, now working at the level of connotation, produces a secondary signification "donkey": a "person who is both stupid and stubborn." Terms which are used to describe national and ethnic identities expose the positive and pejorative dimensions attached to these labels of self-nomination. Terms such as "black" and "white" can never fully eradicate the ideological terrain from which the terms take some of their meanings. This is also true of gender, sexual, and social identities.

In terms of media analysis, Barthes's work is very useful indeed. Firstly, all signs work at the level of denotation and connotation. Secondly, all media output relies on sign systems which are culturally and linguistically polysemic or which contain far more than one meaning. Thirdly, media output, because it draws on and exploits this plurality of meaning, is necessarily involved in activities which are never far from a society's myths and ideologies. For Barthes, media analysis is always engaged in laying bare or opening up that body of ideas and beliefs which seem to operate in the interests of the dominant cultural or linguistic group. Here is an extract from one of his most-cited discussions of the popular French magazine *Paris Match*.

I am at the barber's, and a copy of Paris Match is offered to me. On the cover, a young Negro in a French uniform is saluting, with his eyes uplifted, probably fixed on the . . . tricolour [French flag]. But . . . I see very well what it signifies to me: that France is a great Empire, that all her sons, without colour discrimination, faithfully serve under her flag, and that there is no better answer to the detractors of an alleged colonialism than the zeal shown by this Negro in serving his so-called oppressors. I am therefore faced with a greater semiological system: there is a signifier . . . (a black soldier giving the French salute); [and] there is a signified (it is a purposeful mixture of Frenchness and militariness). (Barthes, 1973: 125–6)

Barthes's work enables us to see that media analysis, undertaken in whatever language, entails watching, looking at, listening to, and reading, media output in terms of its signs, words, images, etc. In a sense, anyone who makes comments about the media can be said very generally to be a media analyst. But note how Barthes draws attention to the naturalization of one language and one speech community over another. For Barthes, media analysis is an analysis of language and image in relation to ideology. His analysis suggests that the critical examination and textual analysis of the media will be concerned on one level with its representations (what we see or hear), and its *ways* of representing (how the sound or image is put together for consumption). Barthes's work analyzes facial expression, the significance of skin color, the subject's way of looking and gazing, and the context in which the subject is situated. Yet these are media images which make assumptions about the speech and language of the audience.

Section summary: Roland Barthes

- Barthes draws attention to media sign systems and common-sense discussions about cultural meaning (what does "soldier" mean in the context of France and its history at this point?).
- He shows how the black soldier who fronts the magazine does not speak: France speaks for him.
- For Barthes, media analysis aims to uncover the relations between political ideology, language, and power (French colonialism), and the monolingual nation (the media construction of Frenchness).

19.4.2   Bilingualism and the silence of the "other"

More recently, the political implications of multilingualism and representation are usefully highlighted in research undertaken by Ien Ang. "In Taiwan," she writes, "I was different because I couldn't speak Chinese; in the West I was different because I looked Chinese" (Ang, 2001: vii). In *On Not Speaking Chinese: Living Between Asia and the West*, Ang describes what it means to be (mis)represented as "Chinese." Ang, an Indonesian-Chinese academic living and working in Australia, makes these comments in the context of a journey to a conference in Taiwan in 1992. It is during her travels that her experience of "representation" is, complexly, a moment of cultural reconstruction as well as a moment of misrepresentation. Why can she not speak Chinese? Is her monolingualism also a monoculturalism?

The visible markers of Ang's ethnicity seem to suggest that she should and must speak a language which in fact she can't and doesn't. Her performance of language (her speech act) is, in effect, a speech act of silence which is also a cultural resistance. Her example highlights a key problem for media analysis in the context of ethnicity, language, and, in the case of Ang, a presumed bilingualism. If all subjects speak languages which are marked by the traces of other languages, then how are multilingual concerns addressed in research issues and questions of media analysis? What language would or should Ang speak in order to communicate? What is communicated: language then identity, identity then language, or a complex interoperation of both? How can the media represent or construct such complexity? Alternatively phrased, what constitutes a bilingual or multilingual subject in the sphere of media texts, media representations, and media visualization? Is the bilingual subject always constructed at the point of a dominant and a marginal conjunction, someone who is precariously speaking the language of the majoritarian community but whose "identity" is always defined linguistically and culturally in opposition to such alignments?

Ang's own response to these issues is to argue for a perspective which acknowledges cultural and linguistic hybridity, producing a subject who, when represented, is always both one thing and another thing, a "neither/nor" subjectivity. Ang's "not speaking Chinese" is also a way of addressing issues of language and culture which go beyond the specificities of an arbitrary personal history (pp. 30ff). Ang's experiences are in part tied to her Indonesian-Chinese family who spent formative years in the Netherlands. But her experiences usefully underline how the identities which media and cultural analysis are thought also to construct are never simply transparent representations of authentic subjects whose linguistic and cultural situations are pure. Rather, Ang's work stages linguistic and cultural identity as a performance and as something which is performative. "If I am inescapably Chinese by descent, I am only sometimes Chinese by consent. When and how is a matter of politics" (p. 36). Here, multilingualism and multiculturalism are not seen as natural states of affairs so much as they are figured as performances in cultures which require a homogenized media representation. While one language is marked always by traces of a language which would undo the prior language's claims to purity (e.g. Standard English by British Black English, dominant code by Creole, and so on), so Ang shows how all cultural constructions of identities are similarly marked by the indelible trace of other cultures.

Ang's work privileges what she calls "complicated entanglement." Identity and language are not natural givens so much as they are ways of being interpellated by cultures as difference. The language of diaspora is "fundamentally nationalist," but, unlike majoritarian nationalism, is "deterritorialized," yet "symbolically bounded nevertheless" (p. 83). Ang questions the normative ethnocentrism of the Chinese diaspora. She seeks to rupture organic conceptions of culture and instead situates arguments to do with monolingualism, bilingualism, and identity in terms of complex cultural spaces and representations. Ang's languages and identities, her Chineseness, are not simple instances of multiculturalism or multilingualism. Rather, she proposes constructions which are "diluted, hybridized, and creolized" (p. 56). In Ang's account, multiculturalism represents the state's attempt to enclose ethnic diversity within the fixed zones of the nation-state. Multiculturalism constrains the complex entanglements of "living hybridities." Ang's discussion underlines her indebtedness to media and cultural analysis that draws on the intersections which structure a broadly post-colonialist trajectory. Her work in the field of culture and hybridity highlights a theoretical and analytic space which combines theories of language and discourse in understanding the social construction of a multilingual identity. For Ang, identity formation, whether this be mono- or multilingual, is also a media and cultural construction, not something which emanates from a prediscursive capacity to be mono- or multilingual.

Section summary: Media analysis and the "others" of language

- A postcolonial media analysis of representations of multilingual subjects will attend to the subject's linguistically hybrid status.
- The monolingual subject is only such on the basis of the media's attempts to homogenize subjects. But the multilingual subject is a subject who is not immune from media construction.
- Ang's analysis is influenced by the work of theorists such as Mikhail Bakhtin, Jacques Derrida, Michel Foucault, Edward Said, and Gayatri Chakravorty Spivak. It is work that constitutes an important development in the fields of media and cultural analysis of multilingualism, to the degree that it is transdisciplinary and not wholly reliant on linguistic formalism.
- Ang's postcolonial critique of identity, diaspora, ethnicity, and gender exposes the limitations of inside/outside, center–margins models of multilingualism and multiculturalism.

19.5 Conclusions

Stuart Hall, in *Formations of Modernity* (Hall & Gieben, 1992: 277), discusses how "the West" is "a historical, not a geographical concept." The concept of the "West" emerges in relation to the European Renaissance and the discourses of both modernity and enlightenment. The West's linguistic and cultural hegemony is confirmed via industrialization and economic expansion. But the West, because it is a historical and linguistic concept tied to colonization and empire, takes some of its meaning from a series of binary oppositions. The "West," understood partly in relation to the hegemony of the languages of England, France, Germany, and the Latin-speaking countries, is formed in opposition to the negatively encoded "East" (which can mean "non-Western," "eastern Europe," "the Far East," or "the Middle East"). These oppositions have regulated and classified how knowledge of these linguistic "others" have been constructed.

Drawing on the work of Michel Foucault, Hall illustrates how "discursive strategies" of media and culture have constructed the West in terms of a linguistic privilege. His account contends that "the discourse of 'the West and the Rest' is alive and well in the modern world" (Hall & Gieben: 318), active in constructing "knowledge" about the West's internal as well as its external "others." In terms of media constructions of bilingualism, then, it is possible to observe a number of representation strategies which underpinned the construction of the bilingual speaker in Western media.

Often, a bilingual speaker is someone who is constructed – at least in the "anglophone" imaginary (Australia, United Kingdom, United States) – as a subject whose second language is English. In popular British and American television, the bilingual subject is not so much a bilingual speaker as someone who does not have fluent command of the dominant (English) language. This is a deficit model. But it is also a model which positions Englishness (nationhood) in relation to an ideologically dominant model of language (in this case Standard English and Received Pronunciation). In terms of media analysis, however, and to incorporate some of Hall's early work on media analysis (Hall, Hobson, Lowe, & Willis, 1992), we can note how any investigation of the media in relation to the contexts of multilingualism will also confront the degrees to which all media production and consumption operates according to dominant-hegemonic, negotiated, and resistant analyses. Thus, media analysis in the context of the discourses of multilingualism will not simply attend to "language" but will consider how multilingual audiences interoperate with media products in the ongoing construction of subjects whose agencies are positioned in relation to media, culture, and language.

Further reading and resources

General books

The following five books are useful in the study of media and culture. They variously provide general outlines of the field, offer systematic coverage of key themes, concepts, and theorists, stimulate further discussion, and supply details of further reading.

Barthes, R. (1973) *Mythologies*. London: Jonathan Cape.
Du Gay, P., S. Hall, L. Janes, H. Mackay, and K. Negus (1997) *Doing Cultural Studies: The Story of the Sony Walkman*. London: Sage.
Gripsrud, J. (2000) *Understanding Media Culture*: London: Hodder Arnold.
Hall, S. (ed.) (1997) *Representation: Cultural Representations and Signifying Practices*. London: Sage.
Purvis, T. (2006) *Media and Cultural Studies*. Edinburgh: Edinburgh University Press.

Books dealing with cultural consumption and media analysis

P. du Gay, S. Hall, L. Janes, H. Mackay, and K. Negus (1997) *Doing Cultural Studies: The Story of the Sony Walkman*, London: Sage. The work of the Open University (UK) is particularly useful in the analysis of cultural consumption and everyday life. However, for important critiques of this work, especially in the field of minority ethnic studies in the United States, see Rosemary Hennessy, *Profit and Pleasure: Sexual Identities in Late Capitalism*, New York and London: Routledge, 2000. Hennessy's work is an important contribution to the study of identity, marginalization, and cultural analysis.

Works dealing with media analysis and political economy

Edward S. Herman and Noam Chomsky (2002) *Manufacturing Consent: The Political Economy of the Mass Media*. London: Pantheon.
web.mit.edu/linguistics/www/chomsky.home.html.
www.synaptic.bc.ca/ejournal/chomsky.htm.
Chomsky's work is important in the analysis of mass media, the news, and conflict. Chomsky has written and taught widely on theories of language, language acquisition, politics and philosophy, history of ideas, the mass media and globalization, international affairs, and US foreign policy.

Specific authors

Professor Ien Ang is a key international figure in the field of media and cultural studies. Her work is interdisciplinary and focuses in particular on media consumption and audiences studies. However, she also writes on identity politics, nationalism and globalization, and ethnicity. Her recent work has focused on the dynamics of social formations in contemporary Asia, including Australia–Asia relations. She is also interested in theory, methodology, and cultural critique.

Stuart Hall has long been an important figure in cultural and media studies. His important early essay "Encoding/Decoding" (1980) marks the beginnings of his critical analysis of media and cultural output in the West. He is also a leading intellectual of the British left and has incorporated into his work important insights surrounding ethnicity and race. He made invaluable contributions to cultural studies at the Centre for Contemporary Cultural Studies at Birmingham University.

Useful Internet resources for media analysis

www.aber.ac.uk/media/
www.cultsock.ndirect.co.uk/MUHome/cshtml/
www.scils.rutgers.edu/~favretto/media.html
www.theory.org.uk/
www.michaelmoore.com/
www.theory.org.uk/
www.mediawatch.com/
www.lboro.ac.uk/research/mmethods/resources/index.html

Part III Project Ideas, Dissemination, and Resources

20 Project Ideas

Li Wei and Melissa G. Moyer

20.1 Introduction

A fact of academic life today is that we not only need to have interesting research topics but also to seek financial support from various agencies in order to carry out our plans. Unfortunately, funding agencies often have their own ideas and plans which are not always compatible with ours. Many of us have felt frustrated that funding bodies never call for proposals "in the right area" for us. Nevertheless, there are ample funding opportunities for researchers working on bilingualism and multilingualism. After all, bilingualism and multilingualism are an essential part of today's world. This section sets out some of the project ideas that might be used in responding to broad-based calls for research proposals such as Change, Migration, Conflict, and Children. The aim of the section is to help students and new researchers to think more creatively and to make links between their personal research interests and broad themes and topics of wider concern. The lists of topics and ideas are intended to be illustrative and by no means exclusive or exhaustive.

As Parts I and II of this volume show, bilingualism and multilingualism research is a multidisciplinary enterprise, attracting the attention and interest of a wide range of researchers. One of the first issues any researcher intending to respond to broad theme calls on topics such as Change, Migration, Conflict, and Children has to deal with is cross-disciplinary links and synergies. A multidisciplinary or interdisciplinary approach would make the project richer, more exciting, and more rewarding. We have therefore provided illustrative research questions under four disciplinary perspectives – linguistics, psycholinguistics, sociolinguistics, and education – as well as an interdisciplinary perspective where examples are given as to how researchers from different disciplinary backgrounds could work together on a common theme or topic.

20.2 Change

Change is understood as a sociocultural process that involves communities and their members. Sociocultural changes inevitably have an impact on individuals' behavior and their psychological state. The questions listed below are typically asked by linguists, psycholinguists, sociolinguists, and educational specialists working on bilingualism and multilingualism with respect to change.

Linguistics

Research questions:

1 What kinds of structural innovations can language contact induce?
2 To what extent is structural convergence affected by typological difference?
3 Does a dominant language affect the structural organization of bilingual speech?
4 How does the structure of bilingual speech change over time with shifts in dominant language? And why?

These questions can be investigated by using quantitative and longitudinal methods with recorded speech. It may also be appropriate to obtain grammaticality or acceptability judgments from informants.

Psycholinguistics

Research questions:

1 Are different lexical categories subject to different patterns of attrition and loss? What is the role of age of acquisition on pathological/non-pathological language loss and recovery?
2 What prompts changes in the level of brain activation in bilingual processing?
3 How do changes in bilingual proficiency affect language processing?
4 How does the process of second language acquisition/socialization affect first language competence and performance?

Most of these questions will require psycholinguistic experiments in laboratory conditions, but the last question could also be answered through a case study of a single individual or a group of individuals. Imaging technologies are useful for establishing levels of brain activation. Statistical analysis of the result is usually warranted.

Sociolinguistics

Research questions:

1 How do changes in language and social practices reflect shifts in attitudes towards different languages and language groups?
2 How do language choice and language shift reflect the process of wider social and cultural change?

3 How do political and economic policies at local, national, and supranational levels lead to new multilingual practices?

Data to answer the above questions are typically obtained through ethnographic observation, interviews and questionnaires. The data can be examined through conversational analysis, critical discourse, networks, narrative, and media analysis.

Education

Research questions:

1 How do policy changes affect bilingual educational provision?
2 How do different classroom interactions produce changes in practices and attitudes towards bilingualism?
3 How do new information and communication technologies (ICT) affect changes in classroom practices in multilingual education?
4 How can Action Research help to bring about change, and critically examine and advance curriculum building and the accommodation of students with multilingual and multicultural backgrounds?

Observation, interviews, and questionnaires are useful methods for collecting data on classroom interactions. Analysis of the data can be carried out through critical discourse and critical cultural perspectives that take into account relations of power, inclusion and exclusion.

Interdisciplinary

The study of attrition and language loss is interdisciplinary and requires examination from different perspectives. For example, linguistic evidence is needed to determine the particular structural features that are in the process of being lost. A psychological perspective contributes an understanding of the cognitive processes of individuals undergoing processes of language shift. Language loss is embedded in a particular sociopolitical context where attitudes and actual practices are enacted and need to be understood. The applications of studies on attrition have important educational implications that should be informed by work from the perspectives mentioned previously.

20.3 Migration

Migration, the movement of people on a world scale, has social and cultural consequences. It can be voluntary, for economic reasons, or forced. The term migration also refers to post-migration settlement. The impact of such movement on the linguistic practices of migrant populations, their memories of past places and people, and the formation of new identities and social contacts are all relevant to the topic.

Linguistics

Research questions:

1 What new linguistic features of English as a global language are developing in migrant contexts?
2 What are the conversational strategies whereby speakers who do not share proficiency in a common language negotiate meaning in context?
3 What are the processes sustaining or modifying pre-migration dialects and languages in new linguistic contexts?
4 What happens to the migrant language after a period of interrupted contact?
5 Which groups of speakers are most likely to maintain their language and which groups spearhead language shift to the majority language?

The data needed to answer such questions can come from observation, recording of spontaneous speech, interviews, and questionnaires. Corpus-based analysis will be useful. Some quantitative analysis may be necessary.

Psycholinguistics

Research questions:

1 What are the effects of age and of the amount and form of exposure on second language learning by migrants?
2 What is the role of migrant language in bilingual episodic memory?
3 What emotional links do migrants develop to their various languages?

Case or group studies, either cross-sectional or longitudinal, will be useful. Laboratory experiments could be designed. Narrative analysis is a useful tool.

Sociolinguistics

Research questions:

1 To what extent are variations in language used by migrant groups as a means of social and cultural differentiation or empowerment?
2 How is cultural hybridity reflected in the linguistic practices (e.g., hip-hop, salsa, text-messaging) of migrant groups, and of other social groups?
3 What role does language play in the conceptualization of citizenship?

4   To what extent are languages and language issues used by migrants as critical and subversive tools?
5   To what extent are languages and language issues used by governmental institutions as tools to exert power?

There are multiple sources of data for questions like these. Narrative analysis, critical discourse analysis, and media analysis are all useful tools.

Education

Research questions:

1   How far are the linguistic conceptions of citizenship reflected in policy making and education?
2   What is the role of multilingualism in learning, access to knowledge, and processes of social inclusion and exclusion?
3   What is the role of complementary education through ethnic, heritage, or community language schools in fostering culture, social identity, attitudes, and linguistic proficiency?
4   What role does literacy, in its bi- and multilingual forms, play in the regulation of access to resources and in the drawing of social boundaries?

Observations of educational practices, combined with critical analysis of policy documents can help to address these questions.

Interdisciplinary

The topic of intercultural communication involves people from different linguistic, cultural, and social backgrounds. It is important to understand the way migrants use the resources in their linguistic repertoire to communicate in intercultural encounters that are socially embedded and part of inherent power structures. Related to this is how competing cultural and cognitive schemata are reflected in these strategies. It is also necessary to explore the sociolinguistic context, the role of ideology, and power relations in intercultural encounters.

20.4   Conflict

Conflict arises when groups in contact compete for social, political, linguistic, or cognitive space. The study of conflict assumes opposition, variation, and difference. In each case, there is a principled outcome that needs to be understood through the appropriate theoretical framework and research tools.

Linguistics

Research questions:

1 How is structural (i.e., syntactic, phonological, morphological) divergence in typologically different languages resolved in bilingual speech?
2 How do the lexicon, grammar, phonology, and prosody interact in bilingual speech?
3 What are the linguistic features of processes of individual or community language loss?

Familiarity with data collection, transcription, or managing a corpus is needed. Knowledge of statistics is useful for identifying patterns and quantifying the importance of occurrence of salient structures.

Psycholinguistics

Research questions:

1 What factors affect selective activation in bilingual processing?
2 What is the role of the weaker language in bilingual processing?
3 What role does affect or emotion play in bilingual processing?
4 What factors lead to differential loss and recovery in pathological cases of bilingual/multilingual aphasics?

Familiarity with experimental paradigms is essential, as is knowledge of statistics. Study design (e.g., single case vs. group, longitudinal vs. cross-sectional studies) needs to be carefully considered.

Sociolinguistics

Research questions:

1 What leads to the adoption of a shared language in bilingual conversation?
2 How is convergence or divergence constructed in various sorts of encounters?
3 What practices of linguistic struggle and contestation are used by minority-language speakers or marginalized groups of the linguistic majority in a particular bilingual institutional context?
4 What conflicts might arise over former lingua francas in postcolonial and post-communist contexts, and how might these conflicts be resolved through language policy and planning?
5 How does the analysis of life story narratives shed light on the way bi/multilingual individuals reconcile their diverse linguistic and cultural backgrounds?

Data to answer the above questions are typically obtained through ethnographic observation, interviews, and questionnaires. Analysis of the data can be carried out through conversational analysis, critical discourse, network analysis, and narrative analysis.

Education

Research questions:

1 How do schools promote the incorporation of minority students through teaching practices and pedagogic materials? What is the role of mainstream ideology in determining these practices?
2 What is the role of new technologies in fostering multilingualism in schools?
3 What standards of proficiency and measurement are established for minority or second languages? Do these standards bear in mind level of development, age, and cultural and linguistic background? Whose standard is it? Who legitimates such standards?
4 How can multimodality in teaching bilingual literacy be effectively used in the classroom?

These questions can be examined by means of classroom observation and documentary information on school policies and on state and local legislation relating to schools. Ethnographic observation of all participants may also be used. Familiarity with statistics is of high importance in undertaking the study of proficiency and its measurement.

Interdisciplinary

The study of the competing role of languages can be studied from various perspectives within a given educational context. The collection of linguistic data is needed to determine precise levels of language proficiency of either minority speakers or speakers of a second language. From a psycholinguistic perspective, it is relevant to examine the role of the dominant language in relation to levels of proficiency and language processing. A sociocultural perspective sheds light on the way wider societal ideology is implemented in local teaching and learning practices. An interdisciplinary approach is necessary in order to improve inclusion of minority students, and to change attitudes towards multilingualism.

20.5 Children

More and more children across the world are growing up to be bilingual and multilingual. Yet, bilingual and multilingual children are still often being compared to monolingual children in research. A recognition that childhood bilingualism is the norm of modern life entails a set of new research questions, such as the following:

Linguistics

Research questions:

1   How do typological differences in language affect bilingual acquisition?
2   How does learning two languages, either simultaneously or consecutively, differ from learning different registers and styles?
3   Are there structural constraints on code-switching in a developing bilingual grammar? If so, are they the same as or different from those of adult code-switching?

These questions need be addressed with longitudinal data, through either a single case study or a group study. Quantitative, variationist analyses may be needed to reveal any patterns.

Psycholinguistics

Research questions:

1   What are the cognitive processes involved in bi-scriptal reading?
2   What are the diagnostic features of speech and language disorders in bilingual children?
3   What is the role in language processing of the "weaker" or "dormant" language in a bilingual child's linguistic repertoire?

These questions are typically addressed using laboratory experiments. The data are usually analyzed quantitatively using statistics.

Sociolinguistics

Research questions:

1   To what extent are bilingual children's linguistic practices influenced by their parents, peers, and immediate social networks?
2   Is there any evidence that bilingual children use their bilinguality as a means of social resistance or subversion?
3   How do bilingual children resolve and/or manage competing cultural values?

Questions such as these can be addressed by ethnographic observations, questionnaires, and interviews, and by recordings of social interaction.

Education

Research questions:

1 What is the role of heritage language/complementary schools in the identity development of bilingual children?
2 What are the effects of different kinds of bilingual education programs on the language and social development of bilingual children?
3 How can bilingual children be used as an educational resource in mainstream schools?
4 How do textbook materials and the norms they assume include or exclude bilingual, minority children?

Data to address these questions can come from observation, interviews, and question-naires, from recordings of interaction, and from standard assessment and experiments.

Interdisciplinary

Bilingual children's linguistic and metalinguistic awareness has been an issue of interest to researchers from a variety of disciplines. To understand it fully, one needs to examine how bilingual children perform on language-awareness tasks (e.g., phonology, lexis, grammar), the cognitive demands and processes of metalinguistic tasks, the effects of language-learning history and exposure, attitudes towards bilingualism and towards certain languages, and the effects of schooling. Explana-tions of any apparent advantages and disadvantages bilingual children have in linguistic and metalinguistic awareness have to be multidimensional, taking into account the linguistic, psycholinguistic, sociolinguistic, and educational factors.

21 Disseminating Research: A Guide to Conference Presentation and Journal Publication

Melissa G. Moyer and Li Wei

21.1 Disseminating Research

Disseminating research to a wider audience is a duty. We owe it to our colleagues, sponsors, friends, families, and society at large. It can also be a joy, if we get it right. We can take pride in our work and get the recognition we deserve. In this chapter, we offer some practical advice on two main venues of research dissemination – conference presentation and journal publication.

21.2 A Guide to Conference Presentation

21.2.1 Attending conferences

It is not necessary to be a well-known academic in order to present your research results at specialized conferences. As long as your research is scientifically rigorous and makes a contribution to knowledge in the field, it is usually welcome at professional meetings. Conferences are excellent forums for making valuable contacts with colleagues working in a similar area to you and who can give you constructive feedback on your work. Meetings provide a venue for learning about the research going on in your field and the contacts you make there often become part of your academic network.

A first step is to find out about the upcoming conferences related to your area of research. Some conferences are specifically organized by and for students while others, especially those organized by professional groups, are aimed at more experienced researchers. Many associations provide information on upcoming conferences that can be consulted on-line. Some well-known conferences on multilingualism, language contact, and acquisition that are held on a periodic basis are the International

Symposium on Bilingualism (ISB), the Association Internationale de Linguistique Appliquée (AILA), the European Association of Second Language Acquisition (EUROSLA), and the Sociolinguistics Symposium (SS). For additional information on professional meetings see chapter 22 in this volume. You should also consider meetings relating to specific languages or to subfields of linguistics that are organized by various professional associations, such as the British Association of Applied Linguistics (BAAL), the Linguistic Society of America (LSA), and Generative Approaches to Language Acquisition (GALA). It is helpful to consult the organization's abstract booklets from previous conferences in order to take a look at a successful abstract and to get a feeling for the type of research that is reported at the forum you have chosen.

21.2.2   Writing an abstract

Presentations at conferences are selected on the basis of the abstracts researchers submit. There are several presentation formats you can choose for reporting on your research at a conference: paper, poster, or as part of a planned colloquium or panel on a given theme. No matter which format you choose, it is important to bear in mind that abstracts must be written in a clear and precise manner, because you have a limited number of words in which to get across the content of your presentation. Calls for papers usually specify the theme, the various formats and their requirements, as well as the deadline for submission. It is good academic practice to follow these instructions strictly.

An abstract should have a title that indicates the content of the research being reported; it should not be too long. As for the content of an abstract, you need to make sure that your research question or the main idea of your talk is stated clearly. It is also necessary to show how this point is connected to prior relevant work on the topic. Familiarity with the related literature is also important. References in the text of the abstract to relevant authors help reviewers to situate your proposal. The typical format is to include the author's name followed by the date of the publication to which you make reference in parenthesis and, if there is room at the end of the abstract, you may include the full format of the citation. Explain the arguments you wish to make and the sort of data you use and how they support your main point or research question. An abstract should also point out the originality or the contribution that is made from your analysis and the data collected.

A scientific committee named by the organizers of the conference usually carries out the evaluation of abstracts. Evaluators consider a number of abstracts and they do not have a lot of time to spend on proposals that are poorly written or unclear as to what the research is about. Examples of the sort of criteria used by a scientific committee to select abstracts are: (1) the appropriateness and significance of the topic, (2) the presentation of original research and whether it represents a contribution to knowledge in the field, (3) the writing, and the clarity with which the research question or topic, data and collection procedures, and the analytic approaches are stated, and (4) the manner of presentation – the abstract should be indicative of a clear and well-organized presentation that can be presented in the allotted time. If your abstract is rejected it may be because it does not fit the theme of the conference, because it is poorly written, or because it does not contain enough information for the evaluators to decide whether it is appropriate to the conference theme. Whatever the case, it is best to take a rejection with a constructive spirit and as an experience from which you can learn. Do not feel shy about asking the organizers for feedback about your abstract. Doing research is a learning process and it is the responsibility of good academics to help teach newcomers to the field.

20.2.3 *Preparing a talk*

Preparation for an oral presentation must include consideration of the time allotted for the talk and how much of it to allow for questions; the audience and their background; the use of visual aids such as PowerPoint, transparencies, or a handout; and, finally, the sort of questions that may be asked and what answers you can give. Fraser and Pullum (August 2006: http://lsadc.org/info/lsa-res-guide.cfm) suggest that 25 percent of a presentation be dedicated to the introduction and framing of the question, 50 percent to presentation of the data and findings or arguments, and 25 percent to the summary and significant points. It is not easy to condense all of one's research into 15 or 20 minutes, but the key to a successful presentation is to select a few main ideas you wish to get across and then explain the data and arguments that support them. Questions at the end of a talk are a good indication of the interest raised by your talk. You, better than anyone, know your research and the questions it raises, so you should be able to anticipate some of the questions beforehand. Remember, though, that you are speaking to an intelligent crowd and be prepared to be surprised by someone's question. The style people have of asking questions varies but you should not be intimidated by the tone. If you do not understand a question ask the person to repeat it. All questions should be answered as long as they are pertinent to the content of your talk. Avoid saying "I don't know." When you have not thought about the point being raised by the questioner you can try to say how you think the question raised is or is not relevant to the claims you are making. Comments from colleagues are a unique opportunity to get feedback and ideas on your work, so do take advantage of it.

Another consideration is pitching the content of a presentation at the right level for the audience. It is realistic to assume that the audience will include experts in an area, as well as well-informed colleagues. You may decide, for example, to address your talk to experts, but in that case you need to make sure that the rest of your audience can get something out of your presentation even if they are not entirely familiar with the field. This is why clarity and conciseness are important.

Whether to use a visual aid, and if so which type (PowerPoint, transparencies, or a handout), needs to be decided at the planning stage. Handouts can be used jointly with transparencies or PowerPoint, but usually they are a substitute. The information presented in PowerPoint or transparencies should be very specific and center on the ideas or points being made in the talk. A handout can include more information, even if you only choose a part of the material to talk about. Some crucial considerations about visual aids such as transparencies and PowerPoint are font and font size. Arial or Helvetica font in sizes that range from 28 to 32 points will make your text clear and readable from the back of a large room. Font colors need to be in the range of white to yellow for dark backgrounds and black to dark blue for light backgrounds for the audience to be able to read your slides. It is advisable to include no more than six words per line and no more than six lines per slide. This gives the audience enough time to quickly read the slide and simultaneously follow what you are saying. For a 20-minute presentation, about 12 slides is appropriate. Nowadays, you can usually have your PowerPoint presentation placed on the computer hard disk in the room where you will be giving your talk. Close to the delivery of your talk, check with the conference organizers that the audio-video equipment you will need is in working order.

21.2.4 *Delivering a presentation*

Remember that the purpose of giving a presentation is to get across your ideas and make a favorable impression on your audience. Listeners have only one chance to hear your talk, and they cannot rewind or reread something you have said in a confusing way. A presentation should not replace your written paper, but rather create an interest in reading it. Make sure that your voice is loud enough, and that the microphone (if there is one) is attached and working properly. The first time a person gives a presentation they may feel a bit nervous and as a result speak very quickly or get their ideas or notes confused. It helps to make a point of speaking slowly and articulating your words carefully. If you lose the connection with the point or idea you are trying to make or you get confused or misplace your notes, do not panic. It is best to stop for a moment and calmly take a deep breath and retrace your line of argument or find the outline or notes of your talk. Avoid reading your presentation. Written papers should be prepared to be presented in a natural speaking style. While you talk, eye contact with the audience helps to make a connection with them, and gives you a sense of whether you are being understood. Control your time and try not to go over the period allotted for your talk and questions. It is inconsiderate to others who follow you and also for members of the audience who may wish to attend a talk in another room. It helps to practice beforehand in front of people who can give you feedback on the clarity of your delivery.

21.2.5 *Conference follow-up*

There are various follow-up tasks to take care of once you have returned from a conference. One of the first things you need to deal with is the suggestions and ideas that you received and which you find helpful. They should be incorporated as soon as possible and while they are still fresh in your mind. Once you have revised your paper in light of the feedback you received you can send it to the people who expressed an interest in reading your work. Some conference organizers circulate the email addresses of the conference participants in case you did not have a chance to obtain the addresses of your contacts on the spot. Another matter you need to consider is whether there will be conference proceedings and whether your presentation can be included. If information about proceedings was not announced at the meeting it is appropriate to contact the organizers about their intentions and find out the details such as the submission date and format requirements you will need to follow. Another option is to submit your paper to a specialized journal for publication.

21.3   A Guide to Journal Publication

Publication of journal articles is often regarded as the ultimate dissemination of research results. Some peer-reviewed academic journals have very high prestige in the academic community. Publishing articles in such journals can lead to immediate international recognition and major career advances. Other journals may be aimed at practitioners in specific fields. They have a much wider impact on policy and practice.

Getting one's research published is a major, complex task. It presupposes a number of things. In particular, it assumes that one has carried out a significant piece of research, which is well thought out and executed and has obtained interesting findings. Most researchers do not get their work published until they have reached the postdoctoral level. Some research postgraduates work as part of a larger team with their advisors and other colleagues. They may get their work published by the team. The following advice is aimed at those who have had substantial research experience and are considering getting their work published for the first time. Postgraduate students should take advice from their supervisors and other more experienced colleagues before deciding if their work is suitable for publication.

The first step in the process of preparing for a journal publication is to decide which journal is the most appropriate for the piece of research you wish to disseminate. Amongst the factors that need to be considered are: Is the journal academic or professional? Is it refereed or non-refereed? Is it international or local? Is it "open" or "invited"?

Academic journals are aimed at academic peers and publish research that advances theory or method. The articles usually contain original findings. Professional journals, on the other hand, are aimed at informing the practitioner community of the latest research or ideas that have a direct relevance to policy and practice. They tend to focus on issues of wider, practical concern. Academic journals are usually refereed, i.e. read by two or three peers who provide independent views on the originality of the findings, the rigor of the argument, the appropriateness of the methods, and the coherence of the presentation. Many professional journals are also refereed, but the focus may be more on the relevance to the community and the clarity of the presentation. Many journals, academic or professional, publish articles that have an international appeal, while some have a local focus. For example, there are journals devoted to issues concerning Africa, the Arabic-speaking countries, or the Asian Pacific. However, journals with words such as *European* or *Southeast Asian* in the title may be international in content. They simply originated from specific geographical regions or are associated with regional academic or professional bodies. The majority of journals accept open submission from anyone who has a suitable paper. But there are some journals that publish specially commissioned papers only or they require that you become a member of the association with which the journal may be connected.

In deciding whether to submit a paper to a particular journal, it is important to familiarize yourself with its aims and scope. Most journals issue a statement on their aims and scope. It is useful to have a good look at articles published recently in the journal, paying special attention to recurring topics, themes, and debates. If the article you are preparing engages with questions that have been discussed by others in recent articles in the same journal, it stands a much better chance of being accepted for publication.

Once you have chosen a target journal, common-sense practice of preparing a good research paper then applies. This includes having a clear argument or thesis running through the article, setting out the context, explaining the methods, and including a "so what" section in the discussion. It is also very important to remember to follow the journal's guidelines for authors, especially on subheadings, the captioning of diagrams and figures, citation style, and referencing. Journal editors and publishers prefer manuscripts that are professionally presented; they do not like submissions that fail to meet the stylistic requirements. Again, take a good look at past articles in the target journal, examine their structures and characteristics, and attempt to model your own on them. It is also important to keep to the word limit. For mainly economic reasons, publishers set page limits for their journals, and the editors translate them into word limits on individual papers. They are usually very strict about the limit.

For the first-time journal article writer, the refereeing process is full of mystery and causes real anxiety. Yes, some referees can be very brutal in expressing their views and there are occasions when the referee takes a rather personal view because the paper may be critical of his or her own work. However, the refereeing process is a process of peer review and is aimed at ensuring the quality of the journal. Nobody wishes to waste time reading something that does not advance one's knowledge. So the refereeing process should be viewed positively, as free feedback and a way of making your article better.

Sometimes, researchers feel that their submission has "fallen into the wrong hands." One way to make sure that your article is reviewed by the most appropriate referees is to provide a clear and informative *title*, an *abstract*, and a set of *key words*. Journal editors normally use these, plus the references you have listed at the end of the article, to determine which referees the paper should be sent to. Do not try to be too clever with the title. A catchy phrase may get you some attention, but it may not be the attention you need for the refereeing process. The abstract is a very important part of a journal publication. It may appear independently of the paper in other abstracting and indexing journals or a database. It is the first thing people will read of your article.

A good abstract should clearly state what the research question is. There is no space in the abstract to justify the importance of the research. Leave that to the main paper. The key research methods, database, and sample size should be outlined. There should be a couple of sentences summarizing the main research findings, and a brief statement on "so what." Reference to other people's work is generally not necessary in the abstract. However, if your research is in direct response to someone else's work, then a reference will help to get your paper to the right referee. Remember that the journal editors normally send your abstract to potential referees first when seeking their agreement to review your manuscript.

Many academic journals still have a policy of maintaining the anonymity of contributors during the reviewing process. It is common practice to remove your name and references to your work in the manuscript. However, increasingly, journals ask authors and referees if they wish their identities to be disclosed. For medical and laboratory science journals, it is usually expected that authors and referees should declare any conflict of interest. Journal editors would normally consider it acceptable if you explain why you think some researchers may or may not be appropriate referees for your article.

Once the referees have returned their reports, the editors make a decision whether to accept a paper for publication or not. It is rare for any paper to be accepted for publication without revision. Papers that require more substantial revisions may need to be reviewed by referees again before a final acceptance is given. Other revisions, whatever amount of work they may involve, tend to be about clarification and elaboration, rather than changing the argument or method. Occasionally, some additional analyses of data may be required. It is very important in resubmitting your article after revision to include a cover letter. The cover letter should explain in detail exactly what you have done in response to the referees' comments. It is helpful to follow the order of the referees' comments in your response. If for whatever reason you decided not to change the original presentation where a revision is recommended by the referees, you should explain your reason why this is not done.

It is good practice to keep to the deadline set by the editors in revising your paper. During the revision process, you can communicate with the editors if you have any query. You must let the editor know if there is any change of contact details once you have submitted a paper.

Journal publication has become an integral part of an academic's life. Publishing a high-quality article in a reputable journal can lead to major advances in one's academic career. Conversely, a low-quality article, while filling up one's résumé or CV, can damage an author's reputation as a researcher. Publication therefore needs to be taken very seriously.

22 Resources for Research on Bilingualism and Multilingualism

Li Wei and Melissa G. Moyer

This chapter provides a non-exhaustive list of the main resources available to researchers working on bilingualism and multilingualism.

22.1 Journals

Journals contain the latest research. The following are key journals that publish bilingualism and multilingualism research.

Journal of Multilingual and Multicultural Development (Clevedon: Multilingual Matters) is a long-established international journal, focusing particularly on the sociological and sociolinguistic aspects of language contact. It is published six times a year.

International Journal of Bilingualism: Cross-disciplinary Cross-linguistic Studies of Language Behaviour (London: Kingston Press) is a quarterly journal which is devoted to the study of the language behavior of bilingual and multilingual individuals. It also covers cross-linguistic studies of language development and impairment.

Bilingualism: Language and Cognition (Cambridge: Cambridge University Press), published three times a year, focuses on bilingualism from a cognitive science perspective. It contains keynote articles with invited commentaries, research articles, and notes.

International Journal of Bilingual Education and Bilingualism (Clevedon: Multilingual Matters) focuses on bilingual education and other areas of applied bilingualism research. It is published six times a year.

International Journal of Multilingualism (Clevedon: Multilingual Matters) focuses on three or more languages in contact.

Bilingual Research Journal is the official publication of the National Association for Bilingual Education in the USA and is published (electronically) by the Center for Bilingual Education and Research of Arizona State University: http://brj.asu.edu.

Heritage Language Journal is an on-line journal dedicated to the issues underlying the teaching and learning of heritage languages, hosted by the UCLA Center for World Languages: www.heritagelanguages.org/.

A new journal, *International Multilingual Research Journal*, published by Lawrence Erlbaum from 2007, focuses on bi/multilingualism, bi/multi-literacy, and linguistic democracy.

The following journals often carry articles on aspects of bilingualism:
Applied Linguistics (Oxford University Press)
Applied Psycholinguistics (Cambridge University Press)
Brain and Language (Academic Press)
English World-Wide (John Benjamins)
International Journal of Applied Linguistics (Novus Press)
International Journal of the Sociology of Language (Mouton de Gruyter)
Journal of the Acoustical Society of America (American Institute of Physics)
Journal of Child Language (Cambridge University Press)
Journal of Experimental Psychology: Learning, Memory, and Cognition (American Psychological Association)
Journal of Language, Identity and Education (Lawrence Erlbaum)
Journal of Memory and Language (Academic Press)
Journal of Multilingual Communication Disorders (Taylor and Francis)
Journal of Neurolinguistics (Elsevier Science)
Journal of Phonetics (Seminar Press)
Journal of Psycholinguistic Research (Plenum Press)
Journal of Sociolinguistics (Blackwell)
Language and Cognitive Processes (VNU Science Press)
Language, Culture and Curriculum (Multilingual Matters)
Language and Education (Multilingual Matters)
Language in Society (Cambridge University Press)
Language and Speech (Kingston Press)
Language Learning (Blackwell)
Language Problems and Language Planning (John Benjamins)
Linguistics and Education (Elsevier)
Memory and Cognition (Psychonomic Society)
Multilingua (Mouton de Gruyter)
Studies in Second Language Acquisition (Cambridge University Press)

22.2   Book Series

Multilingual Matters, published by Multilingual Matters Ltd., is a companion series of the *Journal of Multilingual and Multicultural Development* and focuses on the sociological and sociolinguistic aspects of language contact.

Bilingual Education and Bilingualism, published by Multilingual Matters, is a companion series of the *International Journal of Bilingual Education and*

Bilingualism and focuses on bilingual education and applied areas of bilingualism research.

Studies on Bilingualism, from John Benjamins, publishes research monographs and general texts on various aspects of bilingualism.

Child Language and Child Development: Multilingual and Multicultural Perspectives, published by Multilingual Matters, focuses on the language development of bilingual children and children speaking languages other than English.

Cambridge Approaches to Language Contact, published by Cambridge University Press, publishes general texts on linguistic aspects of language contact.

22.3   Conferences

Major forums for research on bi/multilingualism organized on a regular basis include the following:

ISB, the International Symposium on Bilingualism, is the largest international conference on bilingualism and multilingualism. Other conferences are usually run by professional associations such as:

AILA   Association Internationale de Linguistique Appliquée
EUROSLA   European Second Language Association
AAAL   American Association of Applied Linguistics
BAAL   British Association of Applied Linguistics
IPrA   International Pragmatics Association
IAM   International Association of Multilingualism
SPCL   Society for Pidgin and Creole Linguistics

The Sociolinguistics Symposium usually contains presentations on bilingualism and multilingualism.

Conference announcements are most easily found on the LINGUIST List: www.linguistlist.org.

22.4   Research Tools

The LIDES Coding Manual, compiled by the LIPPS Group (Language Interaction in Plurilingual and Plurilectic Speakers) is a guide to preparing and analyzing language interaction data, published in 2000 by Kingston Press as a special issue of the *International Journal of Bilingualism*, 4(2).

The Child Language Data Exchange System (http://childes.psy.cmu.edu/) contains a database of bilingual child language acquisition and offers tools for analyzing child language data.

22.5   Websites, Electronic Mailing Lists, and Other Resources

NB. Web addresses are subject to change.

The Bilingual List (BILING@asu.edu), run by the Center for Bilingual Education and Research of Arizona State University, is the most popular electronic discussion service for bilingualism research. To view the archive and manage your subscription, see http://lists.asu.edu/archives/biling.html.

The Code-Switching Forum (code-switching@yahoogroups.com) is an e-discussion group for people with an interest in code-switching (www.groups.yahoo.com/group/code-switching).

The Linguist List is a worldwide electronic discussion forum on a variety of issues related to language and linguistics. For further information, see: http://linguistlist.org/.

The Human Languages Page contains a catalogue of language-related Internet resources (www.june29.com/HLP/).

Speech on the Web links important sites related to phonetics and speech sciences (http://fonsg3.let.uva.nl/Other_pages. html).

The National Council for Bilingual Education's homepage (www.ncbe.gwu.edu/) contains information about NCBE and links to important websites.

Clearinghouse for Multicultural/Bilingual Education has a homepage with useful links to important sites: www.weber.edu/mbe/Htmls/MBE-resource.HTML.

Bilingual Families Web Page provides practical information about raising children with two languages (www.nethelp.no/cindy/biling-fam.html).

Bilingual Education Resources on the Internet (www.edb.utexas.edu/coe/depts/ci/bilingue/resources.html) offers links to other pages which have information on bilingual education.

The American Speech-Language-Hearing Association (ASHA) produces a number of fact sheets on multilingual and multicultural issues in speech/language therapy. They can be viewed on-line at: www.asha.org/professionals/multicultural/fact_hp.html.

The Center for Applied Linguistics (USA) has a website at www.cal.org.

The Centre for Information on Language Teaching and Reseach (CILT) can be reached at www.cilt.org.uk.

Bilingual Family Newsletter (Clevedon: Multilingual Matters) is an informal publication, six issues a year, exchanging news and views from bilingual people. It contains useful advice and lists of contacts (www.multilingual-matters.com).

References

Aarsæther, F. (2004) To språk i en tekst. Kodeveksling i samtaler mellom pakistansk-norske tiåringer [Two languages in a text. Code-switching in conversations among Pakistani-Norwegian ten-year-olds]. Dr. art. dissertation, University of Oslo.

Aarssen, J. (2001) Development of temporal relations in narratives by Turkish-Dutch bilingual children. In L. Verhoeven and S. Strömqvist (eds.), *Narrative Development in a Multilingual Context*. Amsterdam: John Benjamins, pp. 209–31.

Abney, S. (1996) Statistical methods and linguistics. In J. Klavans and P. Resnick (eds.), *The Balancing Act: Combining Symbolic and Statistical Approaches to Language*. Cambridge, MA: MIT Press, pp. 1–26.

Abutalebi, J., S. F. Cappa, and D. Perani (2001) The bilingual brain as revealed by functional neuroimaging. *Bilingualism: Language and Cognition*, 4, 179–90.

Abutalebi, J., S. F. Cappa, and D. Perani (2005) What can functional neuroimaging tell us about the bilingual brain? In J. F. Kroll and A. M. B. de Groot (eds.), *Handbook of Bilingualism: Psycholinguistic Approaches*. Oxford: Oxford University Press, pp. 497–515.

Abutalebi, J. and D. W. Green (2007) Bilingual language production: The neurocognition of language representation and control. *Journal of Neurolinguistics*, 20, 242–75.

Agnihotri, R. K. (1987) *Crisis of Identity: The Sikhs in England*. New Delhi: Bahri.

Aguirre, G. K., E. Zarahn, and M. D'Esposito (1998). The variability of human BOLD hemodynamic responses. *NeuroImage*, 8, 302–6.

Aitchison, J. (1994) *Words in the Mind: An Introduction to the Mental Lexicon*. Oxford: Blackwell.

Akinci, M., H. Jisa, and S. Kern (2001) Influence of L1 Turkish on L2 French narratives. In L. Verhoeven and S. Strömqvist (eds.), *Narrative Development in a Multilingual Context*. Amsterdam: John Benjamins, pp. 189–208.

Albert, M. L. and L. K. Obler (1978) *The Bilingual Brain*. New York: Academic Press.

Alia, V. (2004) *Media Ethics and Social Change*. Edinburgh: Edinburgh University Press.

Allopenna, P. D., J. S. Magnuson, and M. K. Tanenhaus (1998) Tracking the time course of spoken word recognition using eye movements: Evidence for continuous mapping models. *Journal of Memory and Language*, 38, 419–39.

Álvarez, E. (2003) Character introduction in two languages: Its development in the stories of a Spanish-English bilingual child age 6;11–10;11. *Bilingualism: Language and Cognition*, 6(3), 227–43.

Alvarez-Caccamo, C. (1998) From "switching code" to "code-switching": Towards a reconceptualization of communicative codes. In P. Auer (ed.), *Code-switching in*

Conversation: Language, Interaction and Identity. London and New York: Routledge, pp. 29–50.

Androutsopoulos, I. (2003) Online-Gemeinschaften und Sprachvariation. Soziolinguistische Perspektiven auf Sprache im Internet. *Zeitschrift für Germanistische Linguistik*, 31–2, 173–97.

Ang, I. (1985) *Watching Dallas*. London: Methuen.

Ang, I. (2001) *On Not Speaking Chinese: Living Between Asia and the West*. London and New York: Routledge.

Aronsson, K. (1998) Identity-in-interaction and social choreography. *Research on Language and Social Interaction*, 31(1), 75–89.

Aske, J. (2002) www.lrc.salemstate.edu/aske/basquecorpus/movies/index.htm (accessed June 24, 2005).

Atkinson, J. M. and J. C. Heritage (eds.) (1984) *Structures of Social Action: Studies in Conversation Analysis*. Cambridge: Cambridge University Press.

Auer, P. (1984) *Bilingual Conversation*. Amsterdam: Benjamins.

Auer, P. (1995) The pragmatics of code-switching. In L. Milroy and P. Muysken (eds.), *One Speaker, Two Languages*. Cambridge: Cambridge University Press, pp. 115–35.

Auer, P. (2000) Why should we and how can we determine the base language of a bilingual conversation? *Estudios de Sociolinguistica*, 1(1), 129–44.

Auer, P. (ed.) (1998) *Code-switching in Conversation: Language, Interaction and Identity*. London: Routledge.

Baayen, R. H., R. Piepenbrock, and L. Gulikers (1995) *The Celex Lexical Database*, Release 2 (CD-ROM). Philadelphia: Linguistic Data Consortium, University of Pennsylvania. http://citeseer.ist.psu.edu/context/49127/0.

Backus, A. (1992) *Patterns of Language Mixing: A Study of Turkish-Dutch Bilingualism*. Wiesbaden: Harrassowitz.

Backus, A. (1996) *Two in One: Bilingual Speech of Turkish Immigrants in the Netherlands*. Tilburg: Tilburg University Press.

Backus, A. (2005) Codeswitching and language change: One thing leads to another? *International Journal of Bilingualism*, 9(3–4), 307–40.

Bakhtin, M. (1973) *Problems of Dostoevsky's Poetics*. Trans. R. W. Rotsel. Ann Arbor, MI: Ardis.

Bakhtin, M. (1981) *The Dialogic Imagination*. Austin: University of Texas Press.

Bakhtin, M. (1984) *Problems of Dostoevsky's Poetics*. Ed. and trans. C. Emerson. Manchester: Manchester University Press.

Balota, D. A. (1994) Visual word recognition: The journey from features to meaning. In M. Gernsbacher (ed.), *Handbook of Psycholinguistics*. New York: Academic Press, pp. 303–58.

Balota, D. A., A. Pollatsek, and K. Rayner (1985) The interaction of contextual constraints and parafoveal visual information in reading. *Cognitive Psychology*, 17, 364–90.

Bamberg, M. (1987) *The Acquisition of Narrative: Learning to Use Language*. Berlin: Mouton de Gruyter.

Bani-Shoraka, H. (2005) *Language Choice and Code-Switching in the Azerbaijani Community in Tehran: A Conversation Analytic Approach to Bilingual Practices*. Studia Iranica Upsaliensia, 9. Uppsala: Uppsala University Press.

Bardovi-Harlig, K. (2000) *Tense and Aspect in Second Language Acquisition: Form, Meaning, and Use*. Malden, MA: Blackwell.

Barnett, R., E. Codó, E. Eppler, M. Forcadell, P. Gardner-Chloros, R. van Hout, M. Moyer, M. C. Torras, M. T. Turell, M. Sebba, M. Starren, and S. Wensing (2000) *The LIDES*

Coding Manual, special issue of the *International Journal of Bilingualism*, 4(2). London: Kingston Press.

Barth, F. (ed.) (1969) *Ethnic Groups and Boundaries*. Boston: Little, Brown.

Barthes, R. (1973) *Mythologies*. London: Jonathan Cape.

Bayley, R. and S. R. Schecter (2003) *Language Socialization in Bilingual and Multilingual Societies*. Clevedon: Multilingual Matters.

Bennett-Castor, T. (2002) The "frog story" narratives of Irish-English bilinguals. *Bilingualism: Language and Cognition*, 5(2), 131–46.

Bennis, H., G. Extra, P. Muysken, and J. Nortier (eds.) (2002) *Een buurt in Beweging*. Amsterdam: Aksant.

Bentahila, A. (1983) *Language Attitudes among Arabic-French Bilinguals in Morocco*. Clevedon: Multilingual Matters.

Bentahila, A. and E. E. Davies (1998) Codeswitching: An unequal partnership? In R. Jacobson, *Codeswitching Worldwide*. Berlin: Mouton, pp. 25–51.

Bentin, S., G. McCarthy, and C. C. Wood (1985) Event-related potentials, lexical decision and semantic priming. *Electroencephalography and Clinical Neurophysiology*, 60, 343–55.

Berk-Seligson, S. (1986) Linguistic constraints on intrasentential code-switching: A study of Spanish/Hebrew bilingualism. *Language in Society*, 15, 313–48.

Berman, R. (1995) Narrative competence and storytelling performance: How children tell stories in different contexts. *Journal of Narrative and Life History*, 5(4), 285–313.

Berman, R. (1999) Bilingual proficiency/proficient bilingualism: Insights from narrative texts. In G. Extra and L. Verhoeven (eds.), *Bilingualism and Migration*. Berlin: Mouton de Gruyter, pp. 187–208.

Berman, R. and D. Slobin (1994) *Relating Events in Narrative: A Crosslinguistic Developmental Study*. Hillsdale, NJ: Lawrence Erlbaum.

Berns, G. (1999) Minireview: Functional neuroimaging. *Life Sciences*, 65(24), 2531–40.

Besson, M., M. Kutas, and C. Van Petten (1992) An event-related potential (ERP) analysis of semantic congruity and repetition effects in sentences. *Journal of Cognitive Neuroscience*, 4, 132–49.

Best, C. T. (1995) A direct realist perspective on cross-language speech perception. In W. Strange (ed.), *Speech Perception and Linguistic Experience: Theoretical and Methodological Issues in Cross-Language Speech Research*. Timonium, MD: York Press, pp. 167–200.

Bhatia, T. and W. Ritchie (eds.) (2004) *Handbook of Bilingualism*. Cambridge, MA: Blackwell.

Bialystok, E. (2005) Consequences of bilingualism for cognitive development. In J. F. Kroll and A. M. B. De Groot (eds.), *Handbook of Bilingualism: Psycholinguistic Approaches*. New York: Oxford University Press, pp. 417–32.

Billig, M. (1999) Whose terms? Whose ordinariness? Rhetoric and ideology in Conversation Analysis. *Discourse and Society*, 10(4), 543–58.

Bird, H., S. Franklin, and D. Howard (2001) Age acquisition and image ability ratings from a large set of words, including verbs and function words. *Behavior Research Methods, Instruments, and Computers*, 33, 73–9.

Birdsong, D. (1999a) Introduction: Whys and why nots of the Critical Period Hypothesis. In D. Birdsong (ed.), *Second Language Acquisition and the Critical Period Hypothesis*. Mahwah, NJ: Lawrence Erlbaum Associates, pp. 1–22.

Birdsong, D. (1999b) *Second Language Acquisition and the Critical Period Hypothesis*. Mahwah, NJ: Lawrence Erlbaum Associates.

Bissonnette, V., W. Ickes, I. Bernstein, and E. Knowles (1990a) Item variances and median splits: Some discouraging and disquieting findings. *Journal of Personality*, 58, 595–601.

Bissonnette, V., W. Ickes, I. Bernstein, and E. Knowles (1990b) Personality moderating variables: A warning about statistical artifact and a comparison of analytic techniques. *Journal of Personality*, 58, 567–87.

Black, A. W. and N. Campbell (1995) Optimising Selection of Units from Speech Databases for Concatenative Synthesis. http://citeseer.ist.psu.edu/black95optimising.html.

Blackledge, A. (2004) Constructions of identity in political discourse in multilingual Britain. In A. Pavlenko and A. Blackledge (eds.), *Negotiation of Identities in Multilingual Contexts*. Clevedon: Multilingual Matters, pp. 68–92.

Blackledge, A. (2005) *Discourse and Power in a Multilingual World*. Amsterdam: John Benjamins.

Blackledge, A. and A. Creese (2005) Integrating the structural and agentic in researching multilingualism. Paper presented at the International Symposium on Bilingualism, Barcelona, March 2005.

Blackledge, A. and A. Pavlenko (2001) Negotiation of Identities in Multilingual Contexts. Special issue of *International Journal of Bilingualism*, 5(3).

Blair, R. C. and W. Karniski (1993) An alternative method for significance testing of waveform difference potentials. *Psychophysiology*, 30, 518–24.

Blaxter, L., C. Hughes, and M. Tight (1996) *How to Research*. Buckingham, UK: Open University Press.

Blom, J.-P. and J. Gumperz (1972) Social meaning in linguistic structure: Code-switching in Norway. In J. Gumperz and D. Hymes (eds.), *Directions in Sociolinguistics*. New York: Holt, Rinehart and Winston, pp. 407–34.

Blommaert, J. (2001) Context is/as critique. *Critique of Anthropology*, 21(1), 13–32.

Blommaert, J. (2005) *Discourse*. Cambridge: Cambridge University Press.

Blommaert, J. and J. Verschueren (1998) *Debating Diversity: Analysing the Discourse of Tolerance*. London/New York: Routledge.

Bloor, M. and T. Bloor (2007) *The Practice of Critical Discourse Analysis: An Introduction*. London: Hodder Arnold.

Blum-Kulka, S. (1997) *Dinner Talk: Cultural Patterns of Sociability and Socialization in Family Discourse*. Mahwah, NJ: Lawrence Erlbaum.

Blunkett, D. (2002) *Integration with Diversity: Globalisation and the Renewal of Democracy and Civil Society*. London: Foreign Policy Centre.

Bod, R., J. Hay, and S. Jannedy (eds.) (2003) *Probabilistic Linguistics*. Cambridge, MA: MIT Press.

Boersma, P. and D. Weenik (2001) Praat: A System for Doing Phonetics by Computer. www.praat.org.

Boeschoten, H. (1998) Codeswitching, codemixing, and code alternation: What a difference. In R. Jacobson (ed.), *Codeswitching Worldwide*. Berlin: Mouton de Gruyter, pp. 253–64.

Boix, E. (1993) *Triar no és trair. Identitat i llengua en els joves de Barcelona*. Barcelona: Edicions 62.

Bortoni-Ricardo, S. M. (1985) *The Urbanization of Rural Dialect Speakers: A Socio-linguistic Study in Brazil*. Cambridge: Cambridge University Press.

Bos, P. (2001) Temporality issues in Moroccan Arabic and Dutch. In L. Verhoeven and S. Strömqvist (eds.), *Narrative Development in a Multilingual Context*. Amsterdam: John Benjamins, pp. 233–54.

Bosch, L., A. Costa, and N. Sebastián-Gallés (2000) First and second language vowel perception in early bilinguals. *European Journal of Cognitive Psychology*, 12, 189–222.

Bossevain, J. (1974) *Friends of Friends: Networks, Manipulators and Coalitions*. Oxford: Blackwell.

Bourdieu, P. (1977a) The economics of linguistic exchanges. *Social Science Information*, 16(6), 645–68.

Bourdieu, P. (1977b) *Outline of a Theory of Practice*. Trans. R. Nice. Cambridge: Cambridge University Press. (Original work published 1972.)

Bourdieu, P. (1997) *Der Tote packt den Lebenden: Schriften zu Politik und Kultur 2.* Hamburg: VSA.

Bourdieu, P. and J.-C. Passeron (1977) *Reproduction in Education, Society and Culture.* London: Sage.

Boyd, S. and K. Nauclér (2001) Sociocultural aspects of bilingual narrative development in Sweden. In L. Verhoeven and S. Strömqvist (eds.), *Narrative Development in a Multilingual Context.* Amsterdam: John Benjamins, pp. 129–51.

Boyle, R. (2000) Whatever happened to preference organization? *Journal of Pragmatics*, 32, 583–604.

Bradlow, A. R. (1995) A comparative acoustic study of English and Spanish vowels. *Journal of the Acoustical Society of America*, 97, 1916–24.

Brasileiro Reis Pereira, I. (2004) Stageverslag: Een onderzoek naar codewisseling in een experimentele setting. MS, Utrecht University.

Briggs, C. L. (1986) *Learning How to Ask: A Sociolinguistic Appraisal of the Role of the Interview in Social Science Research.* Cambridge: Cambridge University Press.

Broca, P. (1861) Perte de la parole, ramollissement chronique et destruction partielle du lobe antérieur gauche du cerveau. *Bulletin de la Société d'Anthropologie*, 11, 235–7.

Bucholtz, M. (2000) The politics of transcription. *Journal of Pragmatics*, 32(10), 1439–65.

Bucholtz, M. and K. Hall (2004) Language and identity. In A. Duranti (ed.), *A Companion to Linguistic Anthropology.* Cambridge: Cambridge University Press, pp. 369–94.

Burton, G. (2000) *Talking Television: An Introduction to the Study of Television.* London: Arnold.

Caldas-Coulthard, Carmen R. (2003) Cross-cultural representation of "Otherness" in media discourse. In G. Weiss and R. Wodak (eds.), *Critical Discourse Analysis: Theory and Interdisciplinarity.* Basingstoke: Palgrave Macmillan, 272–96.

Callahan, L. (2002) The matrix language frame model and Spanish/English codeswitching in fiction. *Language and Communication*, 22, 1–16.

Cameron, D. (1990) Demythologizing sociolinguistics: Why language does not reflect society. In J. E. Joseph and T. J. Taylor (eds.), *Ideologies of Language.* London: Routledge, pp. 79–93.

Cameron, D., E. Frazer, P. Harvey, B. Rampton, and K. Richardson (1992) *Researching Language: Issues of Power and Method.* London: Routledge.

Cameron, D., E. Frazer, P. Harvey, B. Rampton, and K. Richardson (1993) Ethics, advocacy and empowerment: Issues of method in researching language. *Language and Communication*, 13(2), 81–94.

Carreiras, M. and C. Clifton, Jr. (2004) On the on-line study of language comprehension. In M. Carreiras and C. Clifton, Jr. (eds.), *The On-line Study of Sentence Comprehension: Eye-tracking and Beyond.* New York: Psychology Press, pp. 1–14.

Cashman, H. (2002) Constructing a bilingual identity: Conversation analysis of Spanish/English language use in a television interview. *Texas Linguistic Forum*, 44 (Proceedings of the Symposium About Language and Society – Austin: Salsa VIII), 33–47.

Cashman, H. (2005) Identities at play: Language preference and group membership in bilingual talk-in-interaction. *Journal of Pragmatics*, 37, 301–15.

Cashman, H. (2006) Who wins in research on bilingualism in an anti-bilingual state? *Journal of Multilingual and Multicultural Development* (thematic issue, ed. C. Raschka,

P. Sercombe, and M. Garner: Sociolinguistic Research: Issues of Power and Method Revisited), 27(1), 42–60.

Cashman, H. and A. Williams (eds.) (2008) Accomplishing Identity in Bilingual Interaction. Special issue of *Multilingua*, 27.

Cattell, J. M. (1887) The time taken up by cerebral operations. *Mind*, 11, 524–38.

Cenoz, J. (2001) The effect of linguistic distance, L2 status and age on cross-linguistic influence in third language acquisition. In J. Cenoz, B. Hufeisen, and U. Jessner (eds.), *Cross-linguistic Influence in Third Language Acquisition: Psycholinguistic Perspectives*. Clevedon, UK: Multilingual Matters, pp. 8–20.

Chafe, W. (ed.) (1980) *The Pear Stories: Cognitive, Cultural, and Linguistic Aspects of Narrative Production*. Norwood, NJ: Ablex.

Chan, B. (1999) Aspects of the syntax, production and pragmatics of code-switching with special reference to Cantonese-English. PhD dissertation, University College London.

Chen, H.-C. and M.-L. Ng (1989) Semantic facilitation and translation priming effects in Chinese-English bilinguals. *Memory and Cognition*, 17, 454–62.

Cheshire, J. and P. Gardner-Chloros (1998) Code-switching and the sociolinguistic gender pattern. *International Journal of the Sociology of Language*, 129, special edition on Women's Languages in Various Parts of the World, ed. S. Ide and B. Hill, 5–34.

CHILDES: Child Language Data Exchange System, http://childes.psycmu.edv (accessed June 25, 2005).

Chilton, P. (2004) *Analysing Political Discourse: Theory and Practice*. London: Routledge.

Chomsky, N. (1986) *Knowledge of Language: Its Nature, Origin and Use*. New York: Praeger.

Chouliaraki, L. and N. Fairclough (1999) *Discourse in Late Modernity: Rethinking Critical Discourse Analysis*. Edinburgh: Edinburgh University Press.

Cicourel, A. (1988) Elicitation as a problem of discourse. In U. Ammon, N. Dittmar, and K. Matthier (eds.), *Sociolinguistics: An International Handbook of the Science of Language and Society*. Berlin: Walter de Gruyter, pp. 903–10.

Clahsen, H. (1999) Lexical entries and rules of language: A multidisciplinary study of German inflection. *Behavioural and Brain Sciences*, 22, 991–1060.

Clark, H. H. (1973) The language-fixed-effect fallacy: A critique of language statistics in psychological research. *Journal of Verbal Learning and Verbal Behavior*, 12, 335–59.

Clemente, I. (2005) Negotiating the limits of uncertainty and non-disclosure: Communication and culture in the management of pediatric cancer treatment in Barcelona. Unpublished doctoral dissertation, University of California, Los Angeles.

Clyne, M. (1967) *Transference and Triggering: Observations on the Language Assimilation of Postwar German-Speaking Migrants in Australia*. The Hague: Martinus Nijhoff.

Clyne, M. (2003) Dynamics of Language Contact: English and Immigrant Languages. Cambridge: Cambridge University Press.

Čmejrková, S. (2003) The categories of "our own" and "foreign" in the language and culture of Czech repatriates from the Ukraine. *International Journal of the Sociology of Language*, 162, 103–23.

Codó, E. (2003) The struggle for meaning: Immigration and multilingual talk in an institutional setting. Unpublished PhD dissertation, Universitat Autònoma de Barcelona, Bellaterra.

Cohen, J. (1983) The cost of dichotomization. *Applied Psychological Measurement*, 7, 249–53.

Cohen, J. (1988) *Statistical Power Analysis for the Behavioral Sciences*. Hillsdale, NJ: Erlbaum.

Cohen, J. and P. Cohen (1988) *Applied Multiple Regression/Correlation Analysis for the Behavioral Sciences*. 2nd edn. Hillsdale, NJ: Lawrence Erlbaum.

Colomé, À. (2001) Lexical activation in bilinguals' speech production: Language-specific or language-independent? *Journal of Memory and Language*, 45, 721–36.

Connolly, J. F., S. H. Stewart, and N. A. Phillips (1990) The effects of processing requirements on neurophysiological responses to spoken sentences. *Brain and Language*, 39, 302–18.

Cook, V. (1993) *Linguistics and Second Language Acquisition*. London: Macmillan.

Costa, A. (2005) Lexical access in bilingual production. In J. F. Kroll and A. M. B. De Groot (eds.), *Handbook of Bilingualism: Psycholinguistic Approaches*. New York: Oxford University Press, pp. 308–25.

Costa, A., M. Miozzo, and A. Caramazza (1999) Lexical selection in bilinguals: Do words in the bilingual's two lexicons compete for selection? *Journal of Memory and Language*, 41, 365–97.

Cots, J. M. and L. Nussbaum (2003) Consciència lingüística i identitat. In J. Perera, L. Nussbaum, and M. Milian (eds.), *L'educació lingüística en situacions multiculturals i multilingües*. Barcelona: Institut de Ciències de l'Educació de la Universitat de Barcelona, pp. 71–89.

Coulmas, F. (1997) *Handbook of Sociolinguistics*. Oxford: Blackwell.

Couper-Kuhlen, E. and M. Selting (eds.) (1996) *Prosody in Conversation*. Cambridge: Cambridge University Press.

Crago, M. B., B. Annahatak, and L. Ningiuruvik (1993) Changing patterns of language socialisation in Inuit homes. *Anthropology and Education Quarterly*, 24, 205–23.

Crama, R. and H. van Gelderen (1984) Structural constraints on code-mixing. MA thesis, University of Amsterdam.

Dale, A. M. and R. L. Buckner (1997) Selective averaging of rapidly presented individual trials using fMRI. *Human Brain Mapping*, 5, 329–40.

Damasio, A. R. (1992) Aphasia. *New England Journal of Medicine*, 326, 531–9.

Danet, B. and S. Herring (eds.) (2003) The Multilingual Internet. Special issue of *Journal of Computer-Mediated Communications*, 9(1).

Dart, S. (1992) Narrative style in the two languages of a bilingual child. *Journal of Child Language*, 19, 367–87.

David, A. (2004) The developing bilingual lexicon. Unpublished PhD thesis, Newcastle University, UK.

Davies, B. and R. Harré (1990) Positioning: the discursive production of selves. *Journal for the Theory of Social Behaviour*, 20, 43–63.

De Houwer, A. (1990) *The Acquisition of Two Languages from Birth: A Case Study*. Cambridge: Cambridge University Press.

De Houwer, A. (1995) Bilingual language acquisition. In P. Fletcher and B. MacWhinney (eds.), *The Handbook of Child Language*. Oxford: Blackwell, pp. 219–51.

De Houwer, A. (2004) Trilingual input and children's language use in trilingual families in Flanders. In C. Hoffmann and J. Ytsma (eds.), *Trilingualism in Family, School and Community*. Clevedon: Multilingual Matters, pp. 118–35.

DeKeyser, R. (1991) The semester overseas: What difference does it make? *ADFL Bulletin*, 22, 42–8.

DeKeyser, R. (2000) The robustness of critical period effects in second language acquisition. *Studies in Second Language Acquisition*, 22, 499–534.

Dell, G. S. and P. G. O'Seaghdha (1991) Mediated and convergent lexical priming in language production: A comment on Levelt et al. (1991). *Psychological Review*, 98, 604–14.

Denzin, N. K. (1989a) *Interpretive Biography*. Newbury Park, CA: Sage.

Denzin, N. K. (1989b) *Interpretive Interactionism*. Newbury Park, CA: Sage.

Department for Education and Skills (2004) All ethnic groups improve at GCSE/GNVQ. Press release. London: DfES.

Deprez, C. (1999) *Les Enfants bilingues: langues et familles*. Paris: Didier.

Deuchar, M. and S. Quay (2000) *Bilingual Acquisition: Theoretical Implications of a Case Study*. Oxford and New York: Oxford University Press.

Devereux, E. (2003) *Understanding the Media*. London: Sage.

Dewaele, J. M. (2007a) Becoming bi- or multilingual later in life. In P. Auer and Li Wei (eds.), *The Handbook of Multilingualism and Multilingual Communication*. Berlin: Mouton de Gruyter, pp. 89–118.

Dewaele, J. M. (2007b) Diachronic and/or synchronic variation? The acquisition of sociolinguistic competence in L2 French. In D. Ayrton (ed.), *The Handbook of French Applied Linguistics*. Amsterdam: Benjamins, pp. 208–36.

Dewaele, J.-M. and A. Pavlenko (2002) Emotion vocabulary in interlanguage. *Language Learning*, 52(2), 263–322.

Dewaele, J.-M. and A. Pavlenko (2003) Productivity and lexical diversity in native and non-native speech: A study of cross-cultural effects. In V. Cook (ed.), *Effects of the Second Language on the First*. Clevedon, UK: Multilingual Matters, pp. 120–41.

Dijk, T. A. van (2001) Multidisciplinary CDA: A plea for diversity. In R. Wodak and M. Meyer (eds.), *Methods of Critical Discourse Analysis*. London: Sage, pp. 95–120.

Dijk, T. A. van (2003a) The discourse–knowledge interface. In G. Weiss and R. Wodak (eds.), *Theory, Interdisciplinarity and Critical Discourse Analysis*. London: Palgrave, pp. 85–109.

Dijk, T. A. van (2003b) Critical discourse analysis. In B. Schiffrin, D. Tannen, and H. Hamilton (eds.), *The Handbook of Discourse Analysis*. Oxford: Blackwell, pp. 352–71.

Dijkstra, T., J. Grainger, and W. J. B. van Heuven (1999) Recognition of cognates and interlingual homographs: The neglected role of phonology. *Journal of Memory and Language*, 41, 496–518.

Dijkstra, T. and W. J. B. van Heuven (1998) The BIA-model and bilingual word recognition. In J. Grainger and A. M. Jacobs (eds.), *Localist Connectionist Approaches to Human Cognition*. Mahwah, NJ: Lawrence Erlbaum Associates, pp. 189–225.

Dijkstra, T. and W. J. B. van Heuven (2002) The architecture of the bilingual word recognition system: From identification to decision. *Bilingualism: Language and Cognition*, 5, 175–97.

Dijkstra, T., H. Van Jaarsveld, and S. Ten Brinke (1998) Interlingual homograph recognition: Effects of task demands and language intermixing. *Bilingualism: Language and Cognition*, 1, 51–66.

Di Sciullo, A. M., P. Muysken, and R. Singh (1986) Government and code-mixing. *Journal of Linguistics*, 22, 1–24.

Dodd, B., A. Holm, Zhu Hua, S. Crosbie, and J. Broomfield (2006) English phonology: Acquisition and disorder. In Zhu Hua and B. Dodd (eds.), *Phonological Development and Disorder: A Multilingual Perspective*. Clevedon: Multilingual Matters, pp. 25–55.

Doeleman, R. (1998) *Native Reactions to Nonnative Speech*. Tilburg: Tilburg University Press.

Dolitsky, M. (ed.) (2000) Special Issue on Code-switching. *Journal of Pragmatics*, 32.

Donchin, E. (1979) Event-related brain potentials: A tool in the study of human information processing. In H. Begleiter (eds.), *Evoked Potentials and Behavior*. New York: Plenum, pp. 13–75.

Donchin, E., W. Ritter, and C. McCallum (1978) Cognitive psychophysiology: The endogenous components of the ERP. In E. Callaway, P. Tueting, and S. H. Koslow (eds.), *Brain Event-related Potentials in Man*. New York: Academic Press, pp. 349–411.

Döpke, S. (1992) *One Parent One Language*. Amsterdam: Benjamins.

Döpke, S. (2000) *Cross-Linguistic Structures in Simultaneous Bilingualism*. Amsterdam: Benjamins.

Dorfman, A. (1998) *Heading South, Looking North: A Bilingual Journey*. New York: Farrar, Straus, and Giroux.

Dörnyei, Z. (2003) *Questionnaires in Second Language Research: Construction, Administration and Processing*. Mahwah, NJ: Lawrence Erlbaum.

Doughty, C. J. and M. H. Long (2003) The scope of inquiry and goals of SLA. In C. J. Doughty and M. H. Long (eds.), *The Handbook of Second Language Acquisition*. Malden, MA: Blackwell, pp. 3–16.

Du Gay, P., S. Hall, L. Janes, H. Mackay, and K. Negus (1997) *Doing Cultural Studies: The Story of the Sony Walkman*. London: Sage.

Duranti, A. (1997) *Linguistic Anthropology*. Cambridge: Cambridge University Press.

Dussias, P. E. (2003) Syntactic ambiguity resolution in L2 learners: Some effects of bilinguality on L1 and L2 processing strategies. *Studies in Second Language Acquisition*, 25, 529–57.

Eades, D. (1982) You gotta know how to talk . . . : Information seeking in south-east Queensland Aboriginal society. *Australian Journal of Linguistics*, 2, 61–82.

Eastman, C. M. (ed.) (1992) *Codeswitching*. Clevedon: Multilingual Matters.

Eckert, P. (1988) Adolescent social structure and the spread of linguistic change. *Language in Society*, 17, 183–207.

Edwards, D. (1997) *Discourse and Cognition*. London: Sage.

Edwards, J. A. and M. D. Lampert (1993) *Talking Data: Transcription and Coding in Discourse Research*. Hillsdale, NJ: Lawrence Erlbaum Associates.

Edwards, M. and P. Gardner-Chloros (2007) Compound verbs in code-switching: Making Do? *International Journal of Bilingualism*, 11(1), 73–91.

Eliasson, S. (1989) English-Maori language contact: Code-switching and the free morpheme constraint. Reports from Uppsala University Department of Linguistics (RUUL), 18, pp. 1–28.

Eppler, E. (1999) Word order in German-English mixed discourse. UCL Working Papers in Linguistics, 11, pp 285–308.

Eppler, E. (2004) "because dem computer brauchst du es nicht zeigen": Because + German main clause word order. *International Journal of Bilingualism*, 8(2), 127–43.

Erbaugh, M. (2001) www.pearstories.org/ (accessed June 25, 2005).

Erill, G., F. Marcos, and J. Farràs (1992) *L'ús del català entre els joves a Sabadell*. Barcelona: Generalitat de Catalunya.

E-Rramdani, Y. (2003) *Acquiring Tarifit-Berber by Children in the Netherlands and Morocco*. Studies in Mutlilingualism. Amsterdam: Aksant.

Escudero, P. and P. Boersma (2004) Bridging the gap between L2 speech perception research and phonological theory. *Studies in Second Language Acquisition*, 26, 551–85.

Extra, G. and D. Gorter (2001) Comparative perspectives on regional and immigrant minority languages in multicultural Europe. In G. Extra and D. Gorter (eds.), *The Other Languages of Europe*. Clevedon: Multilingual Matters, pp. 1–41.

Extra, G. and K. Yagmur (2004) *Urban Multilingualism in Europe*. Clevedon: Multilingual Matters.

Eze, E. (1998) Lending credence to borrowing analysis: Lone English-origin incorporations in Igbo discourse. *International Journal of Bilingualism*, 2(2), 183–201.

Fabbro, F. (1999) *The Neurolinguistics of Bilingualism: An Introduction*. Hove, Sussex: Psychology Press.

Fabiani, M., G. Gratton, P. M. Corballis, J. Cheng, and D. Friedman (1998) Bootstrap assessment of the reliability of maxima in surface maps of brain activity of individual subjects derived with electrophysiological and optical methods. *Behavior Research Methods, Instruments, and Computers*, 30, 78–86.

Fairclough, N. (1989) *Language and Power*. London: Longman.

Fairclough, N. (1995) *Critical Discourse Analysis: The Critical Study of Language*. London/New York: Longman.

Fairclough, N. (2001) The dialectics of discourse. *Textus*, 14(2): 231–42.

Fairclough, N. (2003a) *Analysing Discourse: Textual Analysis for Social Research*. London: Routledge.

Fairclough, N. (2003b) Semiotic aspects of social transformation and learning. In R. Rogers (ed), *An Introduction to Critical Discourse Analysis in Education*. Mahwah, NJ: Lawrence Erlbaum, pp. 225–36.

Felser, C., L. Roberts, R. Gross, and T. Marinis (2003) The processing of ambiguous sentences by first and second language learners of English. *Applied Psycholinguistics*, 24, 453–89.

Fender, D. H. (1987) Source localization of brain electrical activity. In A. S. Gevins and A. Rémond (eds.), *Methods of Analysis of Brain Electrical and Magnetic Signals*. Handbook of Electroencephalograpy and Clinical Neurophysiology. Revised series, vol. 1. Analysis of electrical and magnetic signals. Amsterdam: Elsevier, pp. 355–403.

Fender, M. (2003) English word recognition and word integration skills of native Arabic- and Japanese-speaking learners of English as a second language. *Applied Psycholinguistics*, 24, 289–315.

Ferguson, C. A. (2000 [1959]) Diglossia. In Li Wei (ed.), *The Bilingualism Reader*. London: Routledge, pp. 33–47.

Fernández, E. (2003) *Bilingual Sentence Processing: Relative Clause Attachment in English and Spanish*. Amsterdam: John Benjamins.

Fishman, J. (1980) Bilingualism and biculturalism as individual and as societal phenomena. *Journal of Multilingual and Multicultural Development*, 1, 3–15.

Fishman, J. (2000 [1965]) Who speaks what language to whom and when? In Li Wei (ed.), *The Bilingualism Reader*. London: Routledge, pp. 55–71.

Fishman, J., R. Cooper, R. Ma, et al. (1971) *Bilingualism in the Barrio*. Language Science Monographs, 7. Bloomington: Indiana University.

Flege, J. E. (1987) The production of "new" and "similar" phones in a foreign language: Evidence for the effect of equivalence classification. *Journal of Phonetics*, 15, 47–65.

Flege, J. E. (1988) The production and perception of foreign language speech sounds. In H. Winitz (ed.), *Human Communication and its Disorders: A Review*. Norwood, NJ: Ablex, pp. 224–401.

Flege, J. E. (2002) Interactions between the native and second-language phonetic systems. In P. Burmeister, T. Piske, and A. Rohde (eds.), *An Integrated View of Language Development: Papers in Honor of Henning Wode*. Trier: Wissenschaftlicher Verlag, pp. 217–44.

Flege, J. E. (2003) Assessing constraints on second-language segmental production and perception. In N. Schiller and A. Meyer (eds.), *Phonetics and Phonology in Language Comprehension and Production: Differences and Similarities*. Berlin: Mouton de Gruyter, pp. 319–55.

Flege, J. E. and W. Eefting (1987) Cross-language switching in stop consonant perception and production by Dutch speakers of English. *Speech Communication*, 6, 185–202.

Fodor, J. A. (1983) *The Modularity of Mind*. Cambridge, MA: MIT Press.

Fowler, F. J. (1984) *Survey Research Methods*. Beverly Hills, CA: Sage.

Fox, R., J. E. Flege, and M. J. Munro (1995) The perception of English and Spanish vowels by native English and Spanish listeners: A multidimensional scaling analysis. *Journal of the Acoustic Society of America*, 97, 2540–51.

Fox, P. and M. Raichle (1986) Focal physiological uncoupling of cerebral blood flow and oxidative metabolism during somatosensory stimulation in human subjects. *Proceedings of the National Academy of Sciences of the United States of America*, 83, 1140–4.

Franceschini, R. (2003) Unfocussed language acquisition? The presentation of linguistic situations in biographical narration. *Forum: Qualitative Social Research* (on-line journal), 4(3), Art. 19. Available at www.qualitative-research.net/fqs-texte/3-03/3-03franceschini-e.htm.

Franklin, S., C. Lury, and J. Stacey (2000) *Global Nature, Global Culture*. London: Sage.

Frenck-Mestre, C. and J. Pynte (1997) Syntactic ambiguity resolution while reading in second and native languages. *Quarterly Journal of Experimental Psychology*, 50A, 119–48.

Friederici, A. D., E. Pfeiffer, and A. Hahne (1993) Event-related brain potentials during natural speech processing effects of semantic, morphological, and syntactic violations. *Cognitive Brain Research*, 1, 183–92.

Friedland, D. and N. Miller (1999) Language mixing in bilingual speakers with Alzheimer's dementia: A conversation analysis approach. *Aphasiology*, 13, 427–44.

Friel, B. M. and S. M. Kennison (2001) Identifying German-English cognates, false cognates, and non-cognates: Methodological issues and descriptive norms. *Bilingualism; Language and Cognition*, 4, 249–74.

Friston, K. J., A. P. Holmes, C. J. Price, C. Buchel, and K. J. Worsley (1999) Multisubject fMRI studies and conjunction analyses. *Neuroimage*, 10, 385–96.

Gafaranga, J. (2001) Linguistic identities in talk-in-interaction: Order in bilingual conversation. *Journal of Pragmatics*, 33, 1901–25.

Gafaranga, J. (2005) Demythologising language alternation studies: Conversational structure vs. social structure in bilingual interaction. *Journal of Pragmatics*, 37, 281–300.

Gafaranga, J. and M.-C. Torras (2002) Interactional otherness: Towards a redefinition of code-switching. *International Journal of Bilingualism*, 6(1), 1–22.

Gal, S. (1979) *Language Shift: Social Determinations of Linguistic Change in Bilingual Austria*. New York: Academic Press.

Gal, S. and J. Irvine (1995) The boundaries of language and disciplines: How ideologies construct difference. *Social Research*, 62, 967–1001.

Gardner-Chloros, P. (1991) *Language Selection and Switching in Strasbourg*. Oxford: Clarendon Press.

Gardner-Chloros, P. (forthcoming 2008) *Code-switching*. Cambridge: Cambridge University Press.

Gardner-Chloros, P., R. Charles, and J. Cheshire (2000) Parallel patterns? A comparison of monolingual speech and bilingual codeswitching discourse. *Journal of Pragmatics*. Special issue on Code-switching, ed. M. Dolitsky, 32, 1305–41.

Gardner-Chloros, P. and M. Edwards (2007) Compound verbs in code-switching: Bilinguals making do? *International Journal of Bilingualism*, 11(1), 73–91.

Gardner-Chloros, P., M. Sebba, and M. Moyer (2007) The LIDES Corpus. In J. C. Beal, K. P. Corrigan and H. Moisl (eds.), *Models and Methods in the Handling of Unconventional Digital Corpora. Vol. 1: Synchronic Corpora*. London: Palgrave, pp. 91–121.

Garfinkel, H. (1967) *Studies in Ethnomethodology*. Englewood Cliffs, NJ: Prentice Hall.

Garnham, N. (1979) Contribution to a political economy of mass communication. *Media, Culture and Society*, 1(2), 123–46.

Garrett, P. B. and P. Baquedano-López (2002) Language socialization: Reproduction and continuity, transformation and change. *Annual Review of Anthropology*, 31, 339–61.

Gee, J. (1991) A linguistic approach to narrative. *Journal of Narrative and Life History*, 1(1), 15–39.

Gee, J. P. (2003) Discourse analysis: What makes it critical? In R. Rogers (ed.), *An Introduction to Critical Discourse Analysis in Education*. Mahwah, NJ: Lawrence Erlbaum, pp. 19–50.

Gelles, R. J. and A. Levine (1999) *Sociology: An Introduction*. Boston: McGraw-Hill College.

Genesee, F. (1989) Early bilingual language development: One language or two? *Journal of Child Language*, 16, 161–79.

Genesee, F. (2002) Rethinking bilingual acquisition. In J.-M. Dewaele, A. Housen, and Li Wei (eds.), *Bilingualism: Beyond Basic Principles*. Clevedon: Multilingual Matters, pp. 204–28.

Gerard, L. D. and D. L. Scarborough (1989) Language-specific lexical access of homographs by bilinguals. *Journal of Experimental Psychology: Learning, Memory, and Cognition*, 15, 305–15.

Gibbons, J. (1987) *Code-mixing and Code-choice: A Hong Kong Case Study*. Clevedon: Multilingual Matters.

Giddens, A. (1984) *The Constitution of Society*. Berkeley and Los Angeles: University of California Press.

Giddens, A. (1990) *The Consequences of Modernity*. Cambridge: Polity.

Gil, M. and M. Goral (2004) Nonparallel recovery in bilingual aphasia: Effects of language choice, language proficiency, and treatment. *International Journal of Bilingualism*, 8(2), 191–219.

Gilboy, E. and J. M. Sopena (1996) Segmentation effects in the processing of complex NPs with relative clauses. In M. Carreiras, J. E. García-Albea, and N. Sebastián-Gallés (eds.), *Language Processing in Spanish*. Mahwah, NJ: Lawrence Erlbaum Associates, pp. 191–206.

Goffman, E. (1963) *Behavior in Public Places: Notes on the Social Organization of Gatherings*. New York: Free Press.

Goffman, E. (1974) *Frame Analysis: An Essay on the Organization of Experience*. New York: Harper & Row.

Goffman, E. (1979) Footing. *Semiotica*, 25, 1–29.

Goffman, E. (1981) *Forms of Talk*. Oxford: Basil Blackwell.

Goodwin, C. (1993) Recording human interaction in natural settings. *Pragmatics*, 3(2), 181–209.

Goodwin, C. (2002) Time in action. *Current Anthropology*, 43, S19–S35.

Goodwin, M. H., C. Goodwin, and M. Yaeger-Dror (2002) Multi-modality in girls' game disputes. *Journal of Pragmatics*, 34, 1621–49.

Granger, C. (2004) *Silence in Second Language Learning: A Psychoanalytic Reading*. Clevedon, UK: Multilingual Matters.

Green, D. W. (1986) Control, activation and resource: A framework and a model for the control of speech in bilinguals. *Brain and Language*, 27, 210–23.

Green, D. W. (2003) The neural basis of the lexicon and the grammar in L2 acquisition. In R. van Hout, A. Hulk, F. Kuiken, and R. Towell (eds.), *The Interface between Syntax and the Lexicon in Second Language Acquisition*. Amsterdam: John Benjamins.

Green, D. W. and C. Price (2001) Functional imaging in the study of recovery patterns in bilingual aphasics. *Bilingualism: Language and Cognition*, 4, 191–201.

Greer, T. (2003a) Multiethnic Japanese identity: An applied conversation analysis. *Japan Journal of Multilingualism and Multiculturalism*, 9(1), 1–23.

Greer, T. (2005) The multiethnic paradox: Towards a fluid notion of being "haafu." *Japan Journal of Multilingualism and Multiculturalism*, 11(1): 1–18.

Gripsrud, J. (2000) *Understanding Media Culture*. London: Hodder Arnold.

Groot, A. M. B. de (1992) Determinants of word translation. *Journal of Experimental Psychology: Learning, Memory, and Cognition*, 18, 1001–18.

Groot, A. M. B. de, L. Dannenburg, and J. G. van Hell (1994) Forward and backward word translation by bilinguals. *Journal of Memory and Language*, 33, 600–29.

Groot, A. M. B. de and G. L. J. Nas (1991) Lexical representation of cognates and noncognates in compound bilinguals. *Journal of Memory and Language*, 30, 90–123.

Grosjean, F. (1980) Spoken word-recognition processes and the gating paradigm. *Perception and Psychophysics*, 28, 267–83.

Grosjean, F. (1988) Exploring the recognition of guest words in bilingual speech. *Language and Cognitive Processes*, 3, 233–74.

Grosjean, F. (1989) Neurolinguists, beware! The bilingual is not two monolinguals in one person. *Brain and Language*, 36, 3–15.

Grosjean, F. (1996) Gating. *Language and Cognitive Processes*, 11, 597–604.

Grosjean, F. (1998) Studying bilinguals: Methodological and conceptual issues. *Bilingualism: Language and Cognition*, 1, 131–49.

Grosjean, F. (2000) Processing mixed language: Issues, findings, and models. In Li Wei (ed.), *The Bilingualism Reader*. London: Routledge, pp. 443–70.

Grosjean, F. (2001) The bilingual's language modes. In J. L. Nicol (ed.), *One Mind, Two Languages: Bilingual Language Processing*. Cambridge, MA: Blackwell, pp. 1–22.

Grosjean, F. and U. Frauenfelder (eds.) (1997) *A Guide to Spoken Word Recognition Paradigms*. Hove, Sussex: Psychology Press.

Grosjean, F., Li P., T. F. Munte, and A. Rodriguez (2003) Imaging bilinguals: When the neurosciences meet the language sciences. *Bilingualism: Language and Cognition*, 6, 159–65.

Gubrium, J. and J. Holstein (eds.) (2002) *Handbook of Interview Research: Context and Method*. Thousand Oaks, CA: Sage.

Guion, S., T. Harada, and J. Clark (2004) Early and late Spanish–English bilinguals' acquisition of English word stress patterns. *Bilingualism: Language and Cognition*, 7(3), 207–26.

Gumperz, J. J. (1971) Dialect difference and social stratification in a north Indian village. In A. S. Dil (ed.), *Language in Social Groups: Essays by John J. Gumperz*, Stanford, CA: Stanford University Press.

Gumperz, J. J. (1982a) *Discourse Strategies*. Cambridge: Cambridge University Press.

Gumperz, J. J. (ed.) (1982b) *Language and Social Identity*. Cambridge: Cambridge University Press.

Gumperz, J. and E. Hernandez (1969) Cognitive aspects of bilingual communication. Working Paper 28, Language Behavior Research Laboratory, December, Berkeley: University of California Press.

Gumperz, J. J. and D. Hymes (eds.) (1972) *Directions in Sociolinguistics: The Ethnography of Communication*. New York: Basil Blackwell.

Hagoort, P., C. Brown, and J. Groothusen (1993) The syntactic positive shift as an ERP-measure of syntactic processing. *Language and Cognitive Processes*, 8, 439–83.

Hagoort, P., C. M. Brown and L. Osterhout (2000) The neurocognition of syntactic processing. In C. M. Brown and P. Hagoort (eds.), *The Neurocognition of Language*. Oxford: Oxford University Press, pp. 273–316.

Hagoort, P., L. Hald, M. Bastiaansen, and K. M. Petersson (2004) Integration of word meaning and world knowledge in language comprehension. *Science*, 304, 438–41.

Hahne, A. (2001) What's different in second-language processing? Evidence from event-related brain potentials. *Journal of Psycholinguistic Research*, 30, 251–66.

Hahne, A. and A. D. Friederici (2001) Processing a second language: Late learners' comprehension mechanisms as revealed by event-related brain potentials. *Bilingualism: Language and Cognition*, 4, 123–42.

Hall, S. (ed.) (1997) *Representation: Cultural Representations and Signifying Practices*. London: Sage.

Hall, S. (1980 [1973]) Encoding/Decoding. In Centre for Contemporary Cultural Studies (ed.), *Culture, Media, Language: Working Papers in Cultural Studies, 1972–79*. London: Hutchinson, pp. 128–38.

Hall, S. and B. Gieben (1992) *Formations of Modernity*. Cambridge: Polity.

Hall, S., D. Hobson, A. Lowe, and P. Willis (1992 [1980]) *Culture, Media, Language*. London: Routledge.

Halmari, H. (1997) *Government and Codeswitching: Explaining American Finnish*. Amsterdam/Philadelphia: John Benjamins.

Hamers, J. F. and M. H. A. Blanc (2000) *Bilinguality and Bilingualism*. Cambridge: Cambridge University Press.

Hammersley, M. (2003) "Analytics" are no substitute for methodology: A response to Speer and Hutchby. *Sociology: The Journal of the British Sociological Association*, 37(2), 339–51.

Hammersley, M. and P. Atkinson (1983) *Ethnography: Principles in Practice*. London: Routledge.

Handy, T. (ed.) (2004) *Event-related Potentials: A Methods Handbook*. Cambridge, MA: MIT Press.

Hansen, R. (2000) *Citizenship and Immigration in Post-war Britain*. Oxford/New York: Oxford University Press.

Harding-Esch, E. and P. Riley (2003) *The Bilingual Family: A Handbook for Parents*. 2nd edn. Cambridge: Cambridge University Press.

Hatch, E. and H. Farhady (1982) *Research Design and Statistics for Applied Linguistics*. Rowley, MA: Newbury House.

Haust, D. (1995) *Codeswitching in Gambia: eine soziolinguistische Untersuchung von Mandinka, Wolof und Englisch in Kontakt*. Cologne: Köppe Verlag.

Haust, D. and N. Ditmar (1998) Taxonomic or functional models in the description of codeswitching? Evidence from Mandinka and Wolof in African contact situations. In R. Jacobson (ed.), *Codeswitching Worldwide*, Berlin: Mouton de Gruyter, pp. 79–90.

Have, P. ten (1999) *Doing Conversation Analysis: A Practical Guide*. London: Sage.

Heath, J. (1989) *From Code-switching to Borrowing: Foreign and Diglossic Mixing in Moroccan Arabic*. London/New York: Kegan Paul International.

Heinz, B. (2001) "Fish in the river": Experiences of bicultural bilingual speakers. *Multilingua*, 20(1), 85–108.

Hell, J. van, A. Bosman, I. Wiggers, and J. Stoit (2003) Children's cultural background knowledge and story telling performance. *International Journal of Bilingualism*, 7(3), 283–303.

Hell, J. G. van and T. Dijkstra (2002) Foreign language knowledge can influence native language performance in exclusively native contexts. *Psychonomic Bulletin and Review*, 9, 780–9.

Heller, M. (1988) Strategic ambiguity: Code-switching in the management of conflict. In M. Heller (ed.), *Code-switching: Anthropological and Sociolinguistic Perspectives*. Berlin: Mouton de Gruyter, pp. 77–98.

Heller, M. (1995a) Bilingualism and multilingualism. In J. Verschueren, J.-O. Östman, and J. Blommaert (eds.), *Handbook of Pragmatics: 1995 Installment*. Amsterdam/Philadelphia: John Benjamins, pp. 1–15.

Heller, M. (1995b) Language choice, social institutions, and symbolic domination. *Language in Society*, 24, 373–405.

Heller, M. (2001) Undoing the macro-micro dichotomy: Ideology and categorisation in a linguistic minority school. In N. Coupland, S. Sarangi, and C. Candlin (eds.), *Sociolinguistics and Social Theory*. London: Longman, pp. 212–34.

Heller, M. (2002) *Éléments d'une sociolinguistique critique*. Paris: Didier.

Heller, M. (2006) (with the collaboration of Campbell, Dalley, and Patrick) *Linguistic Minorities and Modernity: A Sociolinguistic Ethnography*. 2nd edn. London: Continuum.

Heller, M. and L. Lévy (1994) Les contradictions des mariages linguistiquement mixtes: les stratégies des femmes franco-ontariennes. *Langage et société*, 67, 53–88.

Herman, E. S. and N. Chomsky (2002) *Manufacturing Consent: The Political Economy of the Mass Media*. London: Pantheon.

Hermans, D., T. Bongaerts, K. De Bot, and R. Schreuder (1998) Producing words in a foreign language: Can speakers prevent interference from their first language? *Bilingualism: Language and Cognition*, 1, 213–29.

Hermes, J. (1995) *Reading Women's Magazines*. Cambridge: Polity.

Hernandez, A. E., E. Bates, and L. X. Avila (1994). On-line sentence interpretation in Spanish-English bilinguals: What does it mean to be "in between"? *Applied Psycholinguistics*, 15, 417–46.

Hernandez, L., T. Wager, and J. Jonides (2002) Introduction to functional neuroimaging. In H. Pashler and J. Wixted (eds.), *Stevens' Handbook of Experimental Psychology*. New York: John Wiley, pp. 175–222.

Hill, J. H. and K. C. Hill (1986) *Speaking Mexicano: Dynamics of Syncretic Language in Central Mexico*. Tucson: University of Arizona Press.

Hinton, L. (2001) Involuntary language loss among immigrants: Asian American linguistic autobiographies. In J. Alatis and A. Tan (eds.), *Language in our Time: Bilingual Education and Official English, Ebonics and Standard English, Immigration and the Unz Initiative*. Georgetown University Round Table on Languages and Linguistics 1999. Washington, DC: Georgetown University Press, pp. 203–52.

Hirsh, K. W., C. M. Morrison, S. Gaset, and E. Carnicer (2003) Age of acquisition and speech production in L2. *Bilingualism: Language and Cognition*, 6, 117–28.

Hoffman, E. (1989) *Lost in Translation: A Life in a New Language*. London: Heinemann. (Reprinted London: Vintage Books, 1998.)

Hoge, R. D., J. Atkinson, B. Gill, G. R. Crelier, S. Marrett, and G. B. Pike (1999) Investigation of BOLD signal dependence on cerebral blood flow and oxygen consumption: The deoxyhemoglobin dilution model. *Magnetic Resonance in Medicine*, 42, 849–63.

Holland, P. (1997) *The Television Handbook*. London: Routledge.

Howseman, A. M. and R. W. Bowtell (1999) Functional magnetic resonance imaging: Imaging techniques and contrast mechanisms. *Philosophical Transactions: Biological Sciences*, 354(1387), 1179–94.

Hummel, K. (1986) Memory for bilingual prose. In J. Vaid (ed.), *Language Processing in Bilinguals: Psycholinguistic and Neuropsychological Perspectives*. Hillsdale, NJ: Lawrence Erlbaum, pp. 47–64.

Hutchby, I. and R. Wooffitt (1998) *Conversation Analysis: Principles, Practices and Applications*. Cambridge: Polity Press.

Hvenekilde, A. and E. Lanza (2001) Applying social network analysis to the Filipino community in Oslo. In A. Hvenekilde and J. Nortier (eds.), *Meetings at the Crossroads: Studies of Multilingualism and Multiculturalism*. Oslo: Novus Forlag, pp. 296–313.

Hymes, D. (1982) Narrative form as a "grammar" of experience: Native American and a glimpse of English. *Journal of Education*, 162, 121–42.

Iverson, P., P. K. Kuhl, R. Akahane-Yamada, E. Diesch, Y. Tohkura, A. Kettermann, and C. Siebert (2003) A perceptual interference account of acquisition difficulties for non-native phonemes. *Cognition*, 87, B47–B57.

Izura, C. and A. W. Ellis (2004) Age acquisition effects in translation judgment tasks. *Journal of Memory and Language*, 50, 165–81.

Jackendoff, R. (2002) *Foundations of Language*. Oxford: Oxford University Press.

Jackson, B. (1987) *Fieldwork*. Urbana and Chicago: University of Illinois Press.

Jacobson, R. (ed.) (1998) *Codeswitching Worldwide*. Berlin: Mouton de Gruyter.

Jacobson, R. (ed.) (2001) *Codeswitching Worldwide II*. Berlin: Mouton de Gruyter.

Jaffe, A. (1999) *Ideologies in Action: Language Politics on Corsica*. Berlin: Mouton de Gruyter.

Jake, J. L., C. Myers-Scotton, and S. Gross (2002) Making a minimalist approach to codeswitching work: Adding the Matrix Language. *Bilingualism: Language and Cognition*, 5(1), 69–91.

Jakobson, R. (1941/1968) *Child Language: Aphasia and Phonological Universals*. The Hague: Mouton.

James, W. (1890) *Principles of Psychology*. New York: Holt.

Jarvis, S. (1998) *Conceptual Transfer in the Interlingual Lexicon*. Bloomington, IN: IULC Publications.

Jarvis, S. (2000) Methodological rigor in the study of transfer: Identifying L1 influence in the interlanguage lexicon. *Language Learning*, 50(2), 245–309.

Jarvis, S. (2002) Short texts, best-fitting curves and new measures of lexical diversity. *Language Testing*, 19(1), 57–84.

Javier, R., F. Barroso, and M. Muñoz (1993) Autobiographical memory in bilinguals. *Journal of Psycholinguistic Research*, 22(3), 319–38.

Jenkins, H. (1992) *Textual Poachers*. New York: Routledge.

Johanson, L. (2002) *Structural Factors in Turkic Language Contact*. London: Curzon.

Johnson, J. and E. Newport (1989) Critical period effects in second language learning: The influence of maturational state on the acquisition of English as a second language. *Cognitive Psychology*, 21, 60–99.

Johnstone, B. (1996) *The Linguistic Individual: Self-Expression in Language and Linguistics*. New York: Oxford University Press.

Johnstone, B. (2000) *Qualitative Methods in Sociolinguistics*. Oxford: Oxford University Press.

Joos, M. (1967) *The Five Clocks*. New York: Harcourt Brace Jovanovich.

Jørgensen, J. N. (1998) Children's acquisition of code-switching for power-wielding. In P. Auer (ed.), *Code-Switching in Conversation: Language, Interaction and Identity*. London: Routledge, pp. 237–58.

Joshi, A. K. (1985) Processing of sentences with intrasentential code-switching. In D. R. Dowty, L. Karttunen, and A. M. Zwicky (eds.), *Natural Language Processing: Psychological, Computational and Theoretical Perspectives*. Cambridge: Cambridge University Press, pp. 190–205.

Ju, M. and P. A. Luce (2004) Falling on sensitive ears: Constraints on bilingual lexical activation. *Psychological Science*, 15, 314–18.

Juffs, A. and M. Harrington (1996) Garden path sentences and error data in second language sentence processing research. *Language Learning*, 46, 286–324.

Just, M. A. and P. A. Carpenter (1980) A theory of reading: From eye-fixations to comprehension. *Psychological Review*, 87, 329–54.

Just, M. A., P. A. Carpenter, and J. D. Woolley (1982) Paradigms and processes in reading comprehension. *Journal of Experimental Psychology – General*, 111, 228–38.

Kallmeyer, W. and I. Keim (2003) Linguistic variation and the construction of social identity in a German–Turkish setting: A case study of an immigrant youth group in Mannheim, Germany. In J. K. Androutsopoulos and A. Georgakopoulou (eds.), *Discourse Constructions of Youth Identities*. Amsterdam and Philadelphia: John Benjamins, pp. 27–46.

Kanno, Y. (2003) *Negotiating Bilingual and Bicultural Identities: Japanese Returnees Betwixt Two Worlds*. Mahwah, NJ: Lawrence Erlbaum.

Kaufman, D. (2001) Narrative development in Hebrew and English. In L. Verhoeven and S. Strömqvist (eds.), *Narrative Development in a Multilingual Context*. Amsterdam: John Benjamins, pp. 319–40.

Kellerman, E. (2001) New uses for old language: Cross-linguistic and cross-gestural influence in the narratives of non-native speakers. In J. Cenoz, B. Hufeisen, and U. Jessner (eds.), *Cross-linguistic Influence in Third Language Acquisition: Psycholinguistic Perspectives*. Clevedon, UK: Multilingual Matters, pp. 170–91.

Kennedy, Graeme (1998) *An Introduction to Corpus Linguistics*. (Studies in Languages and Linguistics.) London: Longman.

Kerekes, J. A. (2006) Winning an interviewer's trust in a gatekeeping encounter. *Language in Society*, 35, 27–57.

Kesharvarz, M. H. and D. Ingram (2002) The early phonological development of a Farsi-English bilingual child. *International Journal of Bilingualism*, 6(3), 255–69.

Klapproth, D. (2004) *Narrative as Social Practice: Anglo-Western and Australian Aboriginal Oral Traditions*. Berlin: Mouton de Gruyter.

Klavans, J. (1985) The syntax of code-switching: Spanish and English. In *Proceedings of the Linguistic Symposium on Romance Languages*. Amsterdam: Benjamins, pp. 213–31.

Klavans, J. and P. Resnick (1996) *The Balancing Act: Combining Symbolic and Statistical Approaches to Language*. Cambridge, MA: MIT Press.

Kohler, K. J. (ed.) (1994) *Lexica of the Kiel PHONDAT Corpus, Read Speech*, volume I, no. 27/28, Institut für Phonetik und digitale Sprachverarbeitung, Universität Kiel. http://citeseer.ist.psu.edu/context/832541/0.

Kohler, K. J. (ed.) (1995) *The Kiel Corpus of Read Speech* (CD-ROM). Institut für Phonetik und digitale Sprachverarbeitung, Christian-Albrechts-Universität zu Kiel. http://citeseer.ist.psu.edu/context/832542/0.

Kohnert, K. (2002) Picture naming in early sequential bilinguals: A 1-year follow up. *Journal of Speech, Language, and Hearing Research*, 45(4), 759–71.

Kohnert, K., E. Bates, and A. E. Hernandez (1999) Balancing bilinguals: Lexical-semantic production and cognitive processing in children learning Spanish and English. *Journal of Speech, Language, and Hearing Research*, 42(6), 1400–13.

Kolers, P. and E. Gonzalez (1980) Memory for words, synonyms, and translation. *Journal of Experimental Psychology, Human Learning and Memory*, 6, 53–65.

Koppe, R. and J. Meisel (1995) Codeswitching in bilingual first language acquisition. In L. Milroy and P. Muysken (eds.), *One Speaker, Two Languages*. Cambridge: Cambridge University Press, pp. 276–301.

Koven, M. (1998) Two languages in the self/the self in two languages: French-Portuguese bilinguals' verbal enactments and experiences of self in narrative discourse. *Ethos*, 26(4), 410–55.

Koven, M. (2001) Comparing bilinguals' quoted performances of self and others in tellings of the same experience in two languages. *Language in Society*, 30, 513–58.

Koven, M. (2002) An analysis of speaker role inhabitance in narratives of personal experience. *Journal of Pragmatics*, 34, 167–217.

Kramsch, C. and W. E. Lam (1999) Textual identities: The importance of being non-native. In G. Braine (ed.), *Non-native Educators in English Language Teaching*. Mahwah, NJ: Lawrence Erlbaum, pp. 57–72.

Kristeva, J. (1986) *The Kristeva Reader*. Ed. Toril Moi. Oxford: Basil Blackwell.

Kroll, J. F. and P. Dussias (2004) The comprehension of words and sentences in two languages. In T. Bhatia and W. Ritchie (eds.), *Handbook of Bilingualism*. Cambridge, MA: Blackwell, pp. 169–200.

Kroll, J. and E. Stewart (1994) Category interference in translation and picture naming: Evidence for asymmetric connections between bilingual memory representations. *Journal of Memory and Language*, 33, 149–74.

Kuhl, P. (2000) A new view of language acquisition. *Proceedings of the National Academy of Science*, 97, 11850–8.

Kulick, D. (1992) *Language Shift and Cultural Reproduction: Socialization, Self, and Syncretism in a Papua New Guinean Village*. Cambridge: Cambridge University Press.

Kumar, R. (1999) *Research Methodology: A Step-by-Step Guide for Beginners*. London: Sage.

Kupersmitt, J. and R. Berman (2001) Linguistic features of Spanish-Hebrew children's narratives. In L. Verhoeven and S. Strömqvist (eds.), *Narrative Development in a Multilingual Context*. Amsterdam: John Benjamins, pp. 277–317.

Kutas, M. (1997) Views on how the electrical activity that the brain generates reflects the functions of different language structures. *Psychophysiology*, 34, 383–98.

Kutas, M. and S. A. Hillyard (1980) Reading senseless sentences: Brain potentials reflect semantic incongruity. *Science*, 207, 203–5.

Kutas, M. and S. A. Hillyard (1984) Brain potentials during reading reflect word expectancy and semantic association. *Nature*, 307, 161–3.

Kutas, M. and R. Kluender (1991) What is who violating? A reconsideration of linguistic violations in light of event-related brain potentials. In H.-J. Heinze, T. F. Münte, and G. R. Mangun (eds.), *Cognitive Electrophysiology*, pp. 183–210.

Kutas, M. and C. Van Petten (1994) Psycholinguistics electrified: Event-related brain potential investigations. In M. A. Gernsbacher (ed.), *Handbook of Psycholinguistics*, San Diego: Academic Press, pp. 83–143.

Kvale, K. (1993) Segmentation and labelling of speech. PhD dissertation, Norwegian Institute of Technology. http://citeseer.ist.psu.edu/context/832543/0.

Labov, W. (1972a) *Language in the Inner City: Studies in the Black English Vernacular*. Philadelphia: University of Pennsylvania Press.

Labov, W. (1972b) *Sociolinguistic Patterns*. Philadelphia: Pennsylvania University Press.

Labov, W. (1972c) The study of language in its social context. In *Sociolinguistic Patterns*. Philadelphia: University of Pennsylvania Press, pp. 183–259.

Labov, W. (1982a) Objectivity and commitment in linguistic science: The case of the Black English trial in Ann Arbor. *Language in Society*, 11, 165–201.

Labov, W. (1982b) *The Social Stratification of English in New York City*. Washington, DC: Center for Applied Linguistics.

Labov, W. (1984) Field methods of the project of linguistic change and variation. In J. Baugh and J. Sherzer (eds.), *Language in Use: Readings in Sociolinguistics*. Englewood Cliffs, NJ: Prentice Hall, pp. 28–54.

Labov, W. and J. Waletzky (1967) Narrative analysis: Oral versions of personal experience. In J. Helm (ed.), *Essays on the Verbal and Visual Arts*. Seattle: University of Washington Press, pp. 12–44.

Lacey, N. (2000) *Narrative and Genre: Key Concepts in Media Studies*. Basingstoke and London: Macmillan.

Lafont, R. (1977) À propos de l'enquête sur la diglossie: l'intercesseur de la norme. *Lengas*, 1, 31–9.

Lambert, W. (1967) A social psychology of bilingualism. *Journal of Social Issues*, 23, 91–109.

Lane, P. (1999) Language contact in Buyøynes–Pykeä: Norwegian verbs in a Finnish morpho-syntactic frame. Cand.Philol. thesis, University of Oslo.

Lane, P. (2006) A tale of two towns: A comparative study of language and culture contact. Dr. art. dissertation, University of Oslo.

Lanza, E. (1997) *Language Mixing in Infant Bilingualism: A Sociolinguistic Perspective*. Oxford: Oxford University Press.

Lanza, E. (2001) Temporality and language contact in narratives by children bilingual in Norwegian and English. In L. Verhoeven and S. Strömqvist (eds.), *Narrative Development in a Multilingual Context*. Amsterdam: John Benjamins, pp. 15–50.

Lanza, E. (2004a) *Language Mixing in Infant Bilingualism: A Sociolinguistic Perspective*. 2nd edn. Oxford: Oxford University Press.

Lanza, E. (2004b) Language socialization of infant bilingual children in the family: Quo vadis? In X. P. Rodriguez-Yanez, A. M. Suarez, and F. Ramallo (eds.), *Bilingualism and Education: From the Family to the School*. Munich: Lincom Europa, pp. 21–39.

Lanza, E. and B. A. Svendsen (2007) Tell me who your friends are and I *might* be able to tell you what language(s) you speak: Social network analysis, multilingualism, and identity. *International Journal of Bilingualism*, 11(3), 275–300.

Lawson, S. and I. Sachdev (2000) Codeswitching in Tunisia: Attitudinal and behavioural dimensions. *Journal of Pragmatics*, 32, 1343–61.

Leech, G., G. Myers, and J. Thomas (eds.) (1995) *Spoken English on Computer: Transcription, Mark-up and Application*. London: Longman.

Lehmann, C. (2004) Data in linguistics. *Linguistic Review*, 21, 175–210.

Lenneberg, E. H. (1967) *Biological Foundations of Language*. New York: Wiley.

Leopold, W. (1970) *Speech Development of a Bilingual Child: A Linguist's Record*. New York: AMS Press.

Le Page, R. and A. Tabouret-Keller (1985) *Acts of Identity: Creole-based Approaches to Language and Ethnicity*. Cambridge: Cambridge University Press.

Levelt, W. J. M. (1989) *Speaking: From Intention to Articulation*. Cambridge, MA: MIT Press.

Levelt, W. J. M., A. Roelofs, and A. S. Meyer (1999) A theory of lexical access in speech production. *Behavioral and Brain Sciences*, 22, 1–75.

Li P., S. Sepanski, and X. Zhao (2006) Language history questionnaire: A web-based inter-face for bilingual research. *Behavior Research Methods*, 38, 202–10.

Li Wei (1994) *Three Generations, Two Languages, One Family: Language Choice and Language Shift in a Chinese Community in Britain*. Clevedon, Avon: Multilingual Matters.

Li Wei (1998) The "why" and "how" questions in the analysis of conversational code-switching. In P. Auer (ed.), *Codeswitching in Conversation: Language, Interaction and Identity*. London: Routledge, pp. 156–76.

Li Wei (ed.) (2000) Methodological questions in the study of bilingualism. In Li Wei (ed.), *The Bilingualism Reader*. London: Routledge, pp. 475–86.

Li Wei, L. Milroy, and S-C. Pong (2000) A two-step sociolinguistic analysis of code-switching and language choice: The example of a bilingual Chinese community in Britain. In Li Wei (ed.), *The Bilingualism Reader*. London: Routledge, pp. 188–209.

Li Wei (2002) "What do you want me to say?" On the conversation analysis approach to bilingual interaction. *Language in Society*, 31, 159–80.

Li Wei (2005a) "How can you tell?" Towards a common sense explanation of conversational code-switching. *Journal of Pragmatics*, 37, 375–89.

Li Wei (2005b) Social network analysis in bilingualism research: Applications and evaluations. Keynote speech at the Fifth International Symposium on Bilingualism, Barcelona.

Li Wei (ed.) (2005c) Special issue on conversational code-switching. *Journal of Pragmatics*, 37.

Lijmbach, L. (1995) "Telkens als de kinderen comer, fala papa telkens": Mudança de código nas crianças bilingues português-neerlandês. MA thesis, Utrecht University.

Linde, C. (1993) *Life Stories: The Creation of Coherence*. New York: Oxford University Press.

LIPPS Group (2000) The LIDES coding manual. *International Journal of Bilingualism*, 4(2), 131–270.

Lipski, J. M. (1978) Code-switching and the problem of bilingual competence. In M. Paradis (ed.), *Aspects of Bilingualism*. Columbia, SC: Hornbeam Press.

Lo, A. (1999) Codeswitching, speech community membership, and the construction of ethnic identity. *Journal of Sociolinguistics*, 3, 461–79.

Macdonald, C. and G. Pesigan (eds.) (2000) *Old Ties and New Solidarities: Studies on Philippine Communities*. Manila: Ateneo de Manila University Press.

Mackey, A. and S. Gass (2005) *Second Language Research: Methodology and Design*. Mahwah, NJ: Lawrence Erlbaum.

MacNamara, J. (1967) The linguistic independence of bilinguals. *Journal of Verbal Learning and Verbal Behaviour*, 6, 729–36.

MacNamara, J. and S. Kushnir (1971) Linguistic independence of bilinguals: The input switch. *Journal of Verbal Learning and Verbal Behaviour*, 10, 480–7.

MacSwan, J. (2004) Code-switching and grammatical theory. In T. K. Bhatia and W. C. Ritchie (eds.), *The Handbook of Bilingualism*. Oxford: Blackwell, pp. 283–311.

MacWhinney, B. (1995) *The CHILDES Project: Tools for Analyzing Talk*. 2nd edn. Hillsdale, NJ: Erlbaum.

MacWhinney, B. (1997) Second language acquisition and the competition model. In A. M. B. De Groot and J. F. Kroll (eds.), *Tutorials in Bilingualism: Psycholinguistic Perspectives*. Mahwah, NJ: Lawrence Erlbaum Publishers, pp. 113–42.

MacWhinney, B. (2000) *The CHILDES Project: Tools for Analyzing Talk. Volume 2: The Database*. 3rd edn. Mahwah, NJ: Lawrence Erlbaum Associates.

MacWhinney, B. and C. E. Snow (1990) The Child Language Data Exchange System: An update. *Journal of Child Language*, 17, 457–72.

Maeno, Y. (1995) Acquisition of oral narrative skills by foreign language learners of Japanese. In D. MacLaughlin and S. McEwen (eds.), *Proceedings of the Boston University Conference on Language Development (BUCLD) 19*. Boston, MA: Cascadilla Press, pp. 359–66.

Mahootian, S. (1993) A null theory of codeswitching. PhD dissertation, Northwestern University, Chicago.

Mandler, J. (1982) Some uses and abuses of a story grammar. *Discourse Processes*, 5, 305–18.

Marian, V. and M. J. Spivey (2003) Competing activation in bilingual language processing: Within- and between-language competition. *Bilingualism: Language and Cognition*, 6, 97–115.

Marian, V. and M. Kaushanskaya (2004) Self-construal and emotion in bicultural bilinguals. *Journal of Memory and Language*, 51, 190–201.

Markham, D. (1997) *Phonetic Imitation, Accent, and the Learner*. Lund: Lund University Press.

Martin, J. and R. Wodak (2003) Introduction. In J. Martin and R. Wodak (eds), *Re/reading the Past: Critical and Functional Perspectives on Time and Value*. Amsterdam: John Benjamins, pp. 1–18.

Martin-Jones, M. (1995) Code-switching in the classroom: Two decades of research. In L. Milroy and P. Muysken (eds), *One Speaker, Two Languages: Cross-disciplinary Perspectives on Code-switching*. Cambridge: Cambridge University Press, pp. 177–98.

Martin-Jones, M. (2000) Bilingual classroom interaction: A review of recent research. *Language Teaching*, 33, 1–9.

Mason, J. (1996/2002) *Qualitative Researching*. London: Sage Publications.

Maxwell, S. E. and H. D. Delaney (1993) Bivariate median splits and spurious statistical significance. *Psychological Bulletin*, 113, 181–90.

Mayer, M. (1969) *Frog, Where Are You?* New York: Dial.

McCabe, A. and L. Bliss (2003) *Patterns of Narrative Discourse: A Multicultural, Life Span Approach*. Boston, MA: Allyn and Bacon.

McConkie, G. W. and K. Rayner (1975) The span of the effective stimulus during a fixation in reading. *Perception and Psychophysics*, 17, 578–86.

McCormick, K. (2002) *Language in Cape Town's District Six*. Oxford: Oxford University Press.

McCullagh, C. (2002) *Media Power: A Sociological Introduction*. Basingstoke: Palgrave Macmillan.

McKinnie, M. and T. Priestly (2004) Telling tales out of school: Assessing linguistic competence in minority language fieldwork. *Journal of Multilingual and Multicultural Development*, 25(1), 24–40.

McLaughlin, B. (1984) *Second Language Acquisition in Childhood*. Hillsdale, NJ: Lawrence Erlbaum Associates.

Mechelli, A., J. T. Crinion, U. Noppeney, J. O'Doherty, J. Ashburner, R. S. Frackowiak, and C. J. Price (2004) Neurolinguistics: Structural plasticity in the bilingual brain. *Nature*, 431, 757.

Meeuwis, M. and J. Blommaert (1994) The "markedness model" and the absence of society: Remarks on codeswitching. *Multilingua*, 13(4), 387–423.

Meisel, J. M. (1989) Early differentiation of languages in bilingual children. In K. Hyltenstam and L. Obler (eds.), *Bilingualism across the Lifespan: Aspects of Acquisition, Maturity and Loss*. Cambridge: Cambridge University Press, pp. 13–40.

Meisel, J. (ed.) (1994) *Bilingual First Language Acquisition*. Amsterdam: Benjamins.

Meng, K. (2001) *Russlanddeutsche Sprachbiografien: Untersuchungen zur sprachlichen Integration von Aussiedlerfamilien*. Tübingen: Gunter Narr Verlag.

Meng, K. and E. Protassova (2002) Jazykovaja integratsija rossijskih nemtsev v Germanii [Linguistic integration of Russian Germans in Germany]. *Izvestija AN. Serija literatury i jazyka*, 2002, 61(6), 29–40.

Mereu, L. (2004) Linguistic data as complex items. *The Linguistic Review* 21, 211–33.

Mesulam, M. (1990) Large-scale neurocognitive networks and distributed processing for attention, language, and memory. *Annals of Neurology*, 28, 597–613.

Meyer, M. (2001) Between theory, method, and politics: Positioning of the approaches to CDA. In R. Wodak and M. Meyer (eds.), *Methods of Critical Discourse Analysis*. London: Sage, pp. 14–31.

Michael, E. (1998) The consequences of individual differences in cognitive abilities for bilingual language processing. Unpublished dissertation, Pennsylvania State University.

Michael, E. and T. H. Gollan (2005) Being and becoming bilingual: Individual differences and consequences for language production. In J. F. Kroll and A. M. B. De Groot (eds.),

Handbook of Bilingualism: Psycholinguistics Approaches. New York: Oxford University Press, pp. 389–407.

Milardo, R. M. (ed.) (1988) *Families and Social Networks*. Newbury Park, CA: Sage.

Mills, J. (2004) Mothers and mother tongue: Perspectives on self-construction by mothers of Pakistani heritage. In A. Pavlenko and A. Blackledge (eds.), *Negotiation of Identities in Multilingual Contexts*. Clevedon: Multilingual Matters, pp. 161–91.

Milroy, L. (1987) *Language and Social Networks*. 2nd edn. Oxford: Basil Blackwell.

Milroy, L. and M. Gordon (2003) *Sociolinguistics: Method and Interpretation*. Oxford: Blackwell.

Milroy, L. and Li Wei (1995) A social network approach to codeswitching: The example of a bilingual community in Britain. In L. Milroy and P. Muysken (eds.), *One Speaker, Two Languages: Cross-Disciplinary Perspectives on Code-Switching*. Cambridge: Cambridge University Press, pp. 136–57.

Milroy, L. and P. Muysken (eds.) (1995) *One Speaker, Two Languages: Cross-Disciplinary Perspectives on Code-Switching*. Cambridge: Cambridge University Press, pp. 177–98.

Mistry, J. (1993) Cultural context in the development of children's narratives. In J. Altarriba (ed.), *Cognition and Culture: A Cross-cultural Approach to Psychology*. Amsterdam: Elsevier Science Publishers, pp. 207–28.

Mitchell, C. (1986) Network procedures. In D. Frick (ed.), *The Quality of Urban Life*. Berlin: Mouton de Gruyter, pp. 73–92.

Mitchell, D. C. (2004) On-line methods in language processing: Introduction and historical overview. In M. Carreiras and C. Clifton, Jr. (eds.), *The On-Line Study of Sentence Comprehension: Eye-tracking and Beyond*. New York: Psychology Press, pp. 15–32.

Mitchell, R. and F. Miles (2004) *Second Language Learning Theories*. 2nd edn. London: Arnold.

Moffatt, S. (1990) Becoming bilingual: A sociolinguistic study of the communication of young mother-tongue Panjabi-speaking children. Unpublished PhD thesis, University of Newcastle upon Tyne.

Morita, E. (2003) Children's use of address and reference terms: Language socialization in a Japanese-English family. *Multilingua*, 22(4), 367–95.

Mosco, V. (1996) *The Political Economy of Communication*. London: Sage.

Mosso, A. (1881) *Ueber den Kreislauf des Blutes in menschlichen Gehirn*. Leipzig: Verlag von View.

Moyer, A. (1999) Ultimate attainment in L2 phonology: The critical factors of age, motivation and instruction. *Studies in Second Language Acquisition*, 21, 81–108.

Moyer, M. G. (1992) Analysis of codeswitching in Gibraltar. Unpublished PhD thesis, Universitat Autònoma de Barcelona.

Moyer, M. G. (1998) Bilingual conversation strategies in Gibraltar. In P. Auer (ed.), *Code-Switching in Conversation: Language, Interaction and Identity*. London: Routledge, pp. 215–34.

Moyer, M. (2000) Negotiating agreement and disagreement in Spanish-English bilingual conversations with *no*. *International Journal of Bilingualism*, 4(4), 485–504.

Muysken, P. (2000) *Bilingual Speech: A Typology of Code-Mixing*. Cambridge: Cambridge University Press.

Myers-Scotton, C. (1983) The negotiation of identities in conversation: A theory of markedness and code choice. *International Journal of the Sociology of Language*, 44, 115–36.

Myers-Scotton, C. (1986) Diglossia and code-switching. In J. A. Fishman, A. Tabouret-Keller, M. Clyne, B. Krishnamurti, and M. Abdulaziz (eds.), *The Fergusonian Impact*, 2 vols. Berlin: Mouton de Gruyter.

Myers-Scotton, C. (1992) Comparing codeswitching and borrowing. *Journal of Multilingual and Multicultural Development*, 13(1–2), 19–39.

Myers-Scotton, C. (1993b) *Social Motivations for Codeswitching: Evidence from Africa.* Oxford: Clarendon Press.

Myers-Scotton, C. (1997) *Duelling Languages: Grammatical Structure in Codeswitching.* 2nd edn. Oxford: Clarendon Press.

Myers-Scotton, C. (1998) A theoretical introduction to the markedness model. In C. Myers-Scotton (ed.), *Codes and Consequences: Choosing Linguistic Varieties.* New York and Oxford: Oxford University Press, pp. 18–38.

Myers-Scotton, C. (1999) Explaining the role of norms and rationality in codeswitching. *Journal of Pragmatics*, 32, 1259–71.

Myers-Scotton, C. (2002) *Contact Linguistics: Bilingual Encounters and Grammatical Outcomes.* Oxford: Oxford University Press.

Myers-Scotton, C. (2005) Supporting a differential access hypothesis: Code-switching and other contact data. In J. Kroll and A. M. B. De Groot (eds.), *Handbook of Bilingualism: Psycholinguistic Approaches.* Oxford: Oxford University Press, pp. 326–48.

Myers-Scotton, C. (2006) Natural codeswitching knocks on the laboratory door. *Bilingualism: Language and Cognition*, 9(2), 203–12.

Myers-Scotton, C. and A. Bolonyai (2001) Calculating speakers: Codeswitching in a rational choice model. *Language in Society*, 30, 1–28.

Myers-Scotton, C. and J. L. Jake (2000) Matching lemmas in a bilingual competence and production model. In Li Wei (ed.), *The Bilingualism Reader.* London: Routledge, pp. 281–320.

Näätänen, R. (2001) The perception of speech sounds by the human brain as reflected by the mismatch negativity (MMN) and its magnetic equivalent (MMNm). *Psychophysiology*, 38, 1–21.

Nekvapil, J. (2000) On non-self-evident relationships between language and ethnicity: How Germans do not speak German, and Czechs do not speak Czech. *Multilingua*, 2000, 37–53.

Nekvapil, J. (2003) Language biographies and the analysis of language situations: On the life of the German community in the Czech Republic. *International Journal of the Sociology of Language*, 162, 63–83.

Neuman, W. L. (2003) *Social Research Methods: Qualitative and Quantitative Approaches.* 5th edn. Boston: Allyn and Bacon.

Ngom, F. (2003) The social status of Arabic, French, and English in the Senegalese speech community. *Language Variation and Change*, 15, 351–68.

Nistov, I. (2001) Reference continuation in L2 narratives of Turkish adolescents in Norway. In L. Verhoeven and S. Strömqvist (eds.), *Narrative Development in a Multilingual Context.* Amsterdam: John Benjamins, pp. 51–85.

Nivens, R. J. (2002) Borrowing versus Code-switching in West Tarangan (Indonesia). Dallas, TX: SIL International.

Nortier, J. (1990) *Dutch-Moroccan Arabic Code Switching among Moroccans in the Netherlands.* Dordrecht: Foris.

Nortier, J. (1995) De relatie tussen codewisselingstypen en karakteristieken van de tweetalige gemeenschap. In E. Huls and J. Klatter-Folmer (eds.), *Artikelen van de tweede socio-linguïstische conferentie.* Delft: Eburon, pp. 451–62.

Norton, B. (2000) *Identity and Language Learning: Gender, Ethnicity, and Educational Change.* London: Pearson.

Noyau, C. (1984) The development of means for temporality in French by adult Spanish-speakers: Linguistic devices and communicative capacities. In G. Extra and M. Mittner (eds.), *Studies in Second Language Acquisition by Adult Immigrants: Proceedings of the ESF/AILA Symposium held on the 9th of August 1984 in Brussels*. Tilburg: Tilburg University, pp. 113–37.

Noyau, C. and U. Paprocka (2000) La représentation de structures événementielles par les apprenants: granularité et condensation. *Roczniki Humanistyczne*, 48(5), 87–122.

Ochs, E. (1979) Transcription as theory. In E. Ochs and B. B. Schieffelin (eds.), *Developmental Pragmatics*. New York: Academic Press, pp. 43–72.

Ochs, E., E. Schegloff, and S. Thompson (eds.) (1996) *Interaction and Grammar*. Cambridge: Cambridge University Press.

Ogawa, S., T. M. Lee, A. R. Kay, and D. W. Tank (1990) Brain magnetic resonance imaging with contrast dependent on blood oxygenation. *Proceedings of the National Academy of Sciences of the United States of America*, 87, 9868–72.

Oliver, P. (2003) *The Student's Guide to Research Ethics*. Philadelphia: The Open University.

Oller, D. K. and R. E. Eilers (eds.) (2002) *Language and Literacy in Bilingual Children*. Clevedon: Multilingual Matters.

Olshtain, E. and M. Barzilay (1991) Lexical retrieval difficulties in adult language attrition. In H. Seliger and R. Vago (eds.), *First Language Attrition*. Cambridge: Cambridge University Press, pp. 139–50.

Ordóñez, C. (2004) EFL and native Spanish in elite bilingual schools in Colombia: A first look at bilingual adolescent Frog Stories. *International Journal of Bilingual Education and Bilingualism*, 7(5), 449–74.

Osterhout, L. and P. J. Holcomb (1990) Syntactic anomalies elicit brain potentials during sentence comprehension. *Psychophysiology*, 27, S5.

Osterhout, L. and P. J. Holcomb (1992) Event-related potentials elicited by syntactic anomaly. *Journal of Memory and Language*, 31, 1–22.

Osterhout, L. and P. J. Holcomb (1993) Event-related potentials and syntactic anomaly: Evidence of anomaly detection during the perception of continuous speech. *Language and Cognitive Processes*, 8, 413–37.

Osterhout, L., P. J. Holcomb, and D. A. Swinney (1994) Brain potentials elicited by garden-path sentences: Evidence of the application of verb information during parsing. *Journal of Experimental Psychology: Learning, Memory and Cognition*, 20, 786–803.

Osterhout, L. and D. A. Swinney (1989) On the role of the simplicity heuristic in language processing: Evidence from structural and inferential processing. *Journal of Psycholinguistic Research*, 18, 553–62.

Otheguy, R. (1992) A reconsideration of the notion of loan translation in the analysis of U.S. Spanish. In A. Roca and J. Lipski (eds.), *Spanish in the United States: Linguistic Contact and Diversity*. Berlin: Mouton de Gruyter, pp. 21–45.

Paller, K. A., M. Kutas, A. P. Shimamura, and L. R. Squire (1987) Brain responses to concrete and abstract words reflect processes that correlate with later performance on test recall and stem-hyphen completion priming. *Electroencephalography and Clinical Neurophysiology*, 40, 360–5.

Pallier, C., À. Colomé, and N. Sebastián-Gallés (2001) The influence of native-language phonology on lexical access: Exemplar-based vs. abstract lexical entries. *Psychological Science*, 12, 445–9.

Papadopoulou, D. and H. Clahsen (2003) Parsing strategies in L1 and L2 sentence processing: A study of relative clause attachment in Greek. *Studies in Second Language Acquisition*, 25, 501–28.

Paradis, J. (2001) Do bilingual two-year-olds have separate phonological systems? *International Journal of Bilingualism*, 5(1), 19–38.

Paradis, J. and F. Genesee (1996) Syntactic acquisition in bilingual children. *Studies in Second Language Acquisition*, 18, 1–25.

Paradis, M. (1983) *Readings on Aphasia in Bilinguals and Polyglots*. Quebec: Marcel Didier.

Paradis, M. (1987) *The Assessment of Bilingual Aphasia*. Hillsdale, NJ: Erlbaum.

Paradis, M. (ed.) (1995) *Aspects of Bilingual Aphasia*. Oxford: Pergamon.

Paradis, M. (1998) Language and communication in multilinguals. In B. Stemmer and H. Whitaker (eds.), *Handbook of Neurolinguistics*. San Diego, CA: Academic Press, pp. 417–30.

Paradis, M. (2004) *A Neurolinguistic Theory of Bilingualism*. Amsterdam and Philadelphia: John Benjamins.

Paradis, M. and S. Navarro (2003) Subject realization and crosslinguistic interference in the bilingual acquisition of Spanish and English: What is the role of the input? *Journal of Child Language*, 30, 371–93.

Pavlenko, A. (1998) Second language learning by adults: Testimonies of bilingual writers. *Issues in Applied Linguistics*, 9(1), 3–19.

Pavlenko, A. (2001) "In the world of the tradition I was unimagined": Negotiation of identities in cross-cultural autobiographies. *International Journal of Bilingualism*, 5(3), 317–44.

Pavlenko, A. (2002a) Bilingualism and emotions. *Multilingua*, 21(1), 45–78.

Pavlenko, A. (2002b) Narrative study: Whose story is it anyway? *TESOL Quarterly*, 36(2), 213–18.

Pavlenko, A. (2003a) Eyewitness memory in late bilinguals: Evidence for discursive relativity. *International Journal of Bilingualism*, 7(3), 257–81.

Pavlenko, A. (2003b) "I feel clumsy speaking Russian": L2 influence on L1 in narratives of Russian L2 users of English. In V. Cook (ed.), *Effects of the Second Language on the First*. Clevedon, UK: Multilingual Matters, pp. 32–61.

Pavlenko, A. (2003c) "I never knew I was a bilingual": Reimagining teacher identities in TESOL. *Journal of Language, Identity, and Education*, 2(4), 251–68.

Pavlenko, A. (2004) "The making of an American": Negotiation of identities at the turn of the twentieth century. In A. Pavlenko and A. Blackledge (eds.), *Negotiation of Identities in Multilingual Contexts*. Clevedon, Avon: Multilingual Matters, pp. 34–67.

Pavlenko, A. and A. Blackledge (eds.) (2004a) *Negotiation of Identities in Multilingual Contexts*. Clevedon, Avon: Multilingual Matters.

Pavlenko, A. and A. Blackledge (2004b) New theoretical approaches to the study of negotiation of identities in multilingual contexts. In Pavlenko and Blackledge (2004a), pp. 1–33.

Pavlenko, A. and S. Jarvis (2002) Bidirectional transfer. *Applied Linguistics*, 23(2), 190–214.

Pavlenko, A. and J. Lantolf (2000) Second language learning as participation and the (re)construction of selves. In J. Lantolf (ed.), *Sociocultural Theory and Second Language Learning*. Oxford: Oxford University Press, pp. 155–77.

Payrató, L. (2002) Non-verbal communication. In J. Verschueren, J.-O. Ötsman, J. Blommaert, and C. Bulcaen (eds.), *Handbook of Pragmatics 2002*. Amsterdam/Philadelphia: John Benjamins, pp. 1–35.

Pearson, B. (2002) Narrative competence among monolingual and bilingual school children in Miami. In D. Kimbrough Oller and R. Eilers (eds.), *Language and Literacy in Bilingual Children*. Clevedon, UK: Multilingual Matters, pp. 135–74.

Penfield, W. (1965) Conditioning the uncommitted cortex for language learning. *Brain*, 88, 787–98.

Perani, D. and J. Abutalebi (2005) Neural basis of first and second language processing. *Current Opinion in Neurobiology*, 15, 202–6.

Perani, D., J. Abutalebi, E. Paulesu, S. Brambati, P. Scifo, S. F. Cappa, and F. Fazio (2003) The role of age of acquisition and language usage in early, high-proficient bilinguals: An fMRI study during verbal fluency. *Human Brain Mapping*, 19, 179–82.

Petten, C. Van and M. Kutas (1990) Interactions between sentence context and word frequency in event-related brain potentials. *Memory and Cognition*, 18, 380–93.

Pfaff, C. (1979) Constraints on language-mixing: Intrasentential code-switching and borrowing in Spanish-English. *Language*, 55, 291–318.

Pfaff, C. (2001) The development of co-constructed narratives by Turkish children in Germany. In L. Verhoeven and S. Strömqvist (eds.), *Narrative Development in a Multilingual Context*. Amsterdam: John Benjamins, pp. 154–88.

Pierce, B. (1852) Criterion for the rejection of doubtful observations. *Astronomical Journal*, 2, 161–3.

Pinker, S. (1999) *Words and Rules: The Ingredients of Language*. New York: Basic Books.

Piske, T., I. R. A. MacKay, and J. E. Flege (2001) Factors affecting the degree of foreign accent in an L2: A review. *Journal of Phonetics*, 29, 191–215.

Pitres, A. (1895) Étude sur l'aphasie chez les polyglottes. *Revue de médecine*, 15, 873–99.

Polinsky, M. (2007) Heritage language narratives. In D. Brinton, O. Kagan and S. Bauckus (eds.), *Heritage Language: A New Field Emerging*. Mahwah, NJ: Lawrence Erlbaum.

Pollatsek, A. and K. Rayner (1990) Eye movements and lexical access in reading. In D. A. Balota, G. B. Flores d'Arcais, and K. Rayner (eds.), *Comprehension Processes in Reading*. Hillsdale, NJ: Lawrence Erlbaum Associates, pp. 143–63.

Pomerantz, A. (1984) Agreeing and disagreeing with assessments: Some features of preferred/dispreferred turn shapes. In J. M. Atkinson and J. Heritage (eds.), *Structures of Social Action: Studies in Conversational Interaction*. Cambridge: Cambridge University Press, pp. 57–101.

Poplack, S. (1980) "Sometimes I'll start a sentence in English Y TERMINO EN ESPAÑOL": Toward a typology of code-switching. *Linguistics*, 18, 581–618.

Poplack, S. (1988) Contrasting patterns of code-switching in two communities. In M. Heller (ed.), *Code-switching: Anthropological and Sociolinguistic Perspectives*. Berlin: Mouton de Gruyter, pp. 215–45.

Poplack, S. (1993) Variation theory and language contact: Variation theory and language contact. In D. R. Preston (ed.), *American Dialect Research*. Amsterdam and Philadelphia: John Benjamins, pp. 251–86.

Poplack, S. (2000) Preface to the reprint of "Sometimes I'll start a sentence in English Y TERMINO EN ESPAÑOL": Toward a typology of code-switching. In Li Wei (ed.), *The Bilingualism Reader*. London: Routledge, pp. 221–3.

Poplack, S. and M. Meechan (1995) Patterns of language mixture: Nominal structure in Wolof-French and Fongbe-French bilingual discourse. In L. Milroy and P. Muysken (eds.), *One Speaker, Two Languages: Cross-disciplinary Perspectives on Codeswitching*. Cambridge: Cambridge University Press, pp. 199–232.

Poplack, S. and M. Meechan (eds.) (1998) Instant Loans, Easy Conditions: The Productivity of Bilingual Borrowing. Special issue of *International Journal of Bilingualism*, 2(2).

Poplack, S., D. Sankoff, and C. Miller (1988) The social correlates and linguistic processes of lexical borrowing and assimilation. *Linguistics*, 26, 47–104.

Potter, M. C., K.-F. So, B. Von Echardt, and L. B. Feldman (1984) Lexical and conceptual representation in beginning and more proficient bilinguals. *Journal of Verbal Learning and Verbal Behaviour*, 23, 23–38.

Poulisse, N. (1999) *Slips of the Tongue: Speech Errors in First and Second Language Production*. Amsterdam/Philadelphia: John Benjamins.

Poulisse, N. and T. Bongaerts (1994) First language use in second language production. *Applied Linguistics*, 15, 36–57.

Poyatos, F. (2002) *Nonverbal Communication across Disciplines*. 3 vols. Amsterdam/Philadelphia: John Benjamins.

Press, G., D. Amaral, and L. Squire (1989) Hippocampal abnormalities in amnesic patients revealed by high-resolution magnetic resonance imaging. *Nature*, 341, 54–7.

Prevignano, C. and P. J. Thibault (eds.) (2003) *Discussing Conversation Analysis: The Work of Emanuel A. Schegloff*. Amsterdam/Philadelphia: John Benjamins.

Propp, V. (1968 [1928]) *The Morphology of the Folktale*. Austin: University of Texas Press.

Protassova, E. (2004) *Fennorossy: Zhizn' i upotreblenie jazyka* [Finno-Russians: Life and language use]. St. Petersburg: Zlatoust.

Psathas, G. (1995) *Conversation Analysis: The Study of Talk-in-Interaction*. Thousand Oaks, CA: Sage.

Pujadas, J. J., M. Pujol Berché, and M. T. Turell (1988–92) *Catalan-Spanish Database*.

Pujolar, J. (2001) *Gender, Heteroglossia and Power: A Sociolinguistic Study of Youth Culture*. Berlin/New York: Mouton de Gruyter.

Quay, S. (2001) Managing linguistic boundaries in early trilingual development. In J. Cenoz and F. Genesee (eds.), *Trends in Bilingual Acquisition*. Amsterdam and Philadelphia: John Benjamins, pp. 149–99.

Raaijmakers, J. G. W. (2003) A further look at the "language-as-fixed-effect fallacy." *Canadian Journal of Experimental Psychology*, 57, 141–51.

Raaijmakers, J. G. W., J. M. C. Schrijnemakers, and F. Gremmen (1999) How to deal with the "language-as-fixed-effect fallacy": Common misconceptions and alternative solutions. *Journal of Memory and Language*, 41, 416–26.

Radway, J. (1987) *Reading the Romance: Women, Patriarchy, and Popular Literature*. London: Verso.

Ramat, A. G. (1995) Codeswitching in the context of dialect/standard relations. In L. Milroy and P. Muysken (eds.), *One Speaker, Two Languages: Cross-disciplinary Perspectives on Codeswitching*. Cambridge: Cambridge University Press, pp. 45–67.

Rampton, B. (1995) *Crossing: Language and Ethnicity among Adolescents*. London: Longman.

Rampton, B. (1999) *Styling the Other*. Thematic issue of *Journal of Sociolinguistics*, 3(4).

Rapp, S. (1995) Automatic phonemic transcription and linguistic annotation from known text with Hidden Markov Models. An aligner for German. http://citeseer.ist.psu.edu/rapp95automatic.html.

Ratcliff, R. (1993) Methods for dealing with reaction time outliers. *Psychological Bulletin*, 114, 510–32.

Rayner, K. and S. A. Duffy (1986) Lexical complexity and fixation times in reading: Effects of word frequency, verb complexity and lexical ambiguity. *Memory and Cognition*, 14, 191–201.

Redmond, M. V. (2000) *Communication: Theories and Applications*. Boston/New York: Houghton Mifflin.

Reetz-Kurashige, A. (1999) Japanese returnees' retention of English-speaking skills: Changes in verb usage over time. In L. Hansen (ed.), *Second Language Attrition in Japanese Contexts*. New York: Oxford University Press, pp. 21–58.

Reisigl, M. and R. Wodak (2001) *Discourse and Discrimination: Rhetorics of Racism and Antisemitism*. London: Routledge.

Rindler-Schjerve, R. (1998) Codeswitching as an indicator for language shift? Evidence from Sardinian-Italian bilingualism. In R. Jacobson (ed.), *Codeswitching Worldwide*, Berlin: Mouton de Gruyter, pp. 221–48.

Rieger, C. (2003) Repetitions as self-repair strategies in English and German conversations. *Journal of Pragmatics*, 35, 47–69.

Riessman, C. (1993) *Narrative Analysis*. Newbury Park, CA: Sage.

Rietveld, T. and R. van Hout (1993) *Statistical Techniques for the Study of Language and Language Behaviour*. London: Mouton de Gruyter.

Rintell, E. (1990) That's incredible: Stories of emotion told by second language learners and native speakers. In R. Scarcella, E. Andersen, and S. Krashen (eds.), *Developing Communicative Competence in a Second Language*. Boston, MA: Heinle & Heinle, pp. 75–94.

Roberts, C. (1997) The politics of transcription. *Tesol Quarterly*, 31(1), 167–71.

Roberts, C. and P. Sayers (1987). Keeping the gate: How judgements are made in interethnic interviews. In K. Knapp, W. Enninger, and A. Knapp-Potthoff (eds.), *Analyzing Intercultural Communication*. Studies in anthropological linguistics, 1: Berlin: Mouton de Gruyter, pp. 111–36.

Rogers, R. (2003a) An introduction to critical discourse analysis in education. In R. Rogers (ed.), *An Introduction to Critical Discourse Analysis in Education*. Mahwah, NJ: Lawrence Erlbaum, pp. 1–18.

Rogers, R. (2003b) *A Critical Discourse Analysis of Family Literacy Practices: Power In and Out of Print*. Mahwah, NJ: Lawrence Erlbaum.

Romaine, S. (1983) Collecting and interpreting self-reported data on the language use of linguistic minorities by means of "language diaries." *MALS Journal*, 9, 3–30.

Romaine, S. (1986) The syntax and semantics of the code-mixed compound verb in Panjabi-English Bilingual Discourse. In D. Tannen, and J. Alatis (eds.), *Language and Linguistics: The Interdependence of Theory, Data and Application*. Washington, DC: Georgetown University Press, pp. 35–49.

Romaine, S. (1995) *Bilingualism*. 2nd edn. Oxford: Blackwell.

Rugg, M. D. (1990) Event-related brain potentials dissociate repetition effects of high- and low-frequency words. *Memory and Cognition*, 18, 367–79.

Rugg, M. D. and S. E. Barrett (1987) Event-related potentials and the interaction between orthographic and phonological information in a rhyme-judgement task. *Brain and Language*, 32, 336–61.

Ryan, E. (1979) Why do low-prestige varieties persist? In H. Giles and R. St Clair (eds.), *Language and Social Psychology*. Oxford: Blackwell.

Sachdev, I. and R. Y. Bourhis (2001) Multilingual communication. In W. P. Robinson and H. Giles (eds.), *The New Handbook of Language and Social Psychology*. Chichester, NY, Weinheim, Brisbane, Singapore, Toronto: John Wiley & Sons, pp. 407–29.

Sachdev, I. and H. Giles (2004) Bilingual accommodation. In T. K. Bhatia and W. C. Ritchie (eds.), *The Handbook of Bilingualism*. Oxford: Blackwell, pp. 353–78.

Sacks, H. (1992) *Lectures on Conversation*, ed. G. Jefferson. 2 vols. Oxford: Blackwell.

Sacks, H., E. Schegloff, and G. Jefferson (1974) A simplest systematics for the organization of turn-taking for conversation. *Language*, 50(4), 696–735.

Sarangi, S. (1987) Is there no alternative? A further look at data acquisition and data treatment within human communication research. In A. Littlejohn and M. Melouk (eds.), *Research Methods and Processes*, pp. 43–54. Lancaster: Lancaster University, Department of Linguistics and Modern English Language.

Sarangi, S. (1996). Conflation of institutional and cultural stereotyping in Asian migrants' discourse. *Discourse and Society*, 7(3), 359–87.

Sarangi, S. (2001) A comparative perspective on social theoretical accounts of the language-action interrelationship. In N. Coupland, S. Sarangi, and C. Candlin (eds.), *Sociolinguistics and Social Theory*, pp. 29–60. London: Longman.

Sarangi, S. and C. Candlin (2001) Motivational relevancies: Some methodological reflections on social theoretical and sociolinguistic practice. In N. Coupland, S. Sarangi, and C. Candlin (eds.), *Sociolinguistics and Social Theory*, pp. 350–88. London: Longman.

Schecter, S. R. and R. Bayley (2002) *Language as Cultural Practice*. Mahwah, NJ: Lawrence Erlbaum.

Schegloff, E. (1996) Turn organization: One intersection of grammar and interaction. In E. Ochs, E. Schegloff, and S. Thompson (eds.), *Interaction and Grammar*, Cambridge: Cambridge University Press, pp. 52–133.

Schegloff, E. (1997a) "Narrative analysis" thirty years later. *Journal of Narrative and Life History*, 7(1–4), 97–106.

Schegloff, E. (1997b) Whose text? whose context? *Discourse and Society*, 8(2), 165–87.

Schegloff, E. (1999) Discourse, pragmatics, conversation, analysis. *Discourse Studies*, 1(4), 405–35.

Schegloff, E. (forthcoming) *A Primer in Conversation Analysis: Sequence Organization*. Cambridge: Cambridge University Press.

Schegloff, E., G. Jefferson, and H. Sacks (1977) The preferences for self-correction in the organization of repair in conversation. *Language*, 53, 361–82.

Schieffelin, B. B., K. A. Woolard, and P. V. Kroskrity (1998) *Language Ideologies: Theory and Practice*. New York and Oxford: Oxford University Press.

Schlyter, S. (1996) Bilingual children's stories: French *passé composé/imparfait* and their correspondences in Swedish. *Linguistics*, 34, 1059–85.

Schmid, H. (1995) Improvements in Part-of-Speech Tagging with an Application to German. http://citeseer.ist.psu.edu/schmid95improvement.html.

Schmid, M. (2002) *First Language Attrition, Use and Maintenance: The Case of German Jews in Anglophone Countries*. Amsterdam: John Benjamins.

Schneider, E. (2004) How to trace structural nativization: Particle verbs in world Englishes. *World Englishes*, 23(2), 227–49.

Schooling, Stephen J. (1992) Language maintenance in Melanesia. Dallas, TX: Summer Institute of Linguistics.

Schumann, J. (1997) *The Neurobiology of Affect in Language*. Malden, MA, and Oxford: Blackwell.

Schütze, C. T. (1996) *The Empirical Base of Linguistics: Grammaticality Judgments and Linguistic Methodology*. Chicago: University of Chicago Press.

Scoresby-Jackson, R. (1867) Case of aphasia with right hemiplegia. *Edinburgh Medical Journal*, 12, 696–706.

Scott, J. (2000) *Social Network Analysis: A Handbook*. 2nd edn. London: Sage.

Sebastián-Gallés, N. and S. Soto-Faraco (1999) On-line processing of native and non-native phonemic contrasts in early bilinguals. *Cognition*, 72, 112–23.

Sebba, M. (1993) *Focussing on Language*. Lancaster: Definite Article Publications.

Sebba, M. and S. Tate (2002) "Global" and "local" identities in the discourses of British-born Caribbeans. *International Journal of Bilingualism*, 6(1), 75–89.

Sebba, M. and T. Wootton (1998) We, they and identity: Sequential vs. identity-related explanations in code-switching. In P. Auer (ed.), *Code-Switching in Conversation: Language, Interaction and Identity*. London: Routledge, pp. 262–86.

Segalowitz, S. J. (1983) *Two Sides of the Brain*. Englewood Cliffs, NJ: Prentice Hall.

Selting, M. and E. Couper-Kuhlen (eds.) (2001) *Studies in Interactional Linguistics*. Amsterdam/Philadelphia: John Benjamins.

Selting, M. et al. (1998) Gesprächsanalytisches Transkriptionssystem (GAT). *Linguistische Berichte*, 173, 91–122.

Severing, R. and L. Verhoeven (2001) Bilingual narrative development in Papiamento and Dutch. In L. Verhoeven and S. Strömqvist (eds.), *Narrative Development in a Multilingual Context*. Amsterdam: John Benjamins, pp. 255–75.

Shin, S. and L. Milroy (2000) Conversational codeswitching among Korean-English bilingual children. *International Journal of Bilingualism*, 4(3), 351–83.

Shiro, M. (2003) Genre and evaluation in narrative development. *Journal of Child Language*, 30(1), 165–95.

Shrubshall, P. (1997) Narrative argument and literacy: A comparative study of the narrative discourse development of monolingual and bilingual 5–10 year old learners. *Journal of Multilingual and Multicultural Development*, 18, 402–21.

Silva-Corvalán, C. (1986) Bilingualism and language change: The extension of estar in Los Angeles Spanish. *Language*, 62, 587–608.

Silva-Corvalán, C. (1994) *Language Contact and Change: Spanish in Los Angeles*. Oxford: Oxford University Press.

Silverman, D. (1993) *Interpreting Qualitative Data: Methods for Analysing Talk, Text and Interaction*. London: Sage.

Simon-Maeda, A. (2004) The complex construction of professional identities: Female EFL educators in Japan speak out. *TESOL Quarterly*, 38(3), 405–36.

Slobin, D. I., J. Gerhardt, A. Kyratzis, and J. Guo (eds.) (1996) *Social Interaction, Social Context, and Language: Essays in Honor of Susan Ervin-Tripp*. Mahwah, NJ: Lawrence Erlbaum Associates.

Snodgrass, J. G. (1984) Concepts and their surface representation. *Journal of Verbal Learning and Verbal Behavior*, 23, 3–22.

Sokoloff, L. (1975) Influence of functional activity on local cerebral glucose utilization. In D. H. Ingvar and N. A. Lassen (eds.), *Brain Work: The Coupling of Function Metabolism and Blood Flow in the Brain*. Copenhagen: Munksgaard, pp. 385–88.

Sokolov, J. and B. MacWhinney (1990) The CHIP framework: Automatic coding and analysis of parent–child conversational interaction. *Behavior Research Methods, Instruments, and Computers*, 22, 151–61.

Speer, S. A. and I. Hutchby (2003a) From ethics to analytics: Aspects of participants' orientations to the presence and relevance of recording devices. *Sociology: The Journal of the British Sociological Association*, 37(2), 315–37.

Speer, S. A. and I. Hutchby (2003b) Methodology needs analytics: A rejoinder to Martyn Hammersley. *Sociology: The Journal of the British Sociological Association*, 37(2), 353–9.

Stake, R. E. (1995) *The Art of Case Study Research*. Thousand Oaks, CA: Sage.

Stavans, A. (2001) Trilingual children narrating in Hebrew, English and Spanish. In L. Verhoeven and S. Strömqvist (eds.), *Narrative Development in a Multilingual Context*. Amsterdam: John Benjamins, pp. 341–71.

Stein, N. and G. Glenn (1979) An analysis of story comprehension in elementary school-children. In R. Freedle (ed.), *New Directions in Discourse Processes*. Norwood, NJ: Ablex, pp. 53–120.

Stoessel, S. (2002) Investigating the role of social networks in language maintenance and shift. *International Journal of the Sociology of Language*, 153, 93–132.

Strauss, A. and J. Corbin (1990) *Basics of Qualitative Research: Grounded Theory Procedures and Techniques*. Newbury Park, CA: Sage.

Strömqvist, S. and D. Day (1993) On the development of narrative structure in child L1 and adult L2 acquisition. *Applied Psycholinguistics*, 14, 135–58.

Stroop, J. R. (1935) Studies of interference in serial verbal reactions. *Journal of Experimental Psychology*, 18, 643–62.

Svendsen, B. A. (2004) Så lenge vi forstår hverandre. Språkvalg, flerspråklige ferdigheter og språklig sosialisering hos norsk-filippinske barn i Oslo [As long as we understand each other: Language choice, multilingual competence and language socialization among Norwegian-Filipino children in Oslo]. Dr. art. dissertation, University of Oslo.

Svennevig, J. (2003) Echo answers in native/non-native interaction. *Pragmatics*, 13(2), 285–309.

Tabouret-Keller, A. (1997) Language and identity. In F. Coulmas (ed.), *The Handbook of Sociolinguistics*. Oxford: Blackwell, pp. 315–26.

Taeschner, T. (1983) *The Sun is Feminine: A Study of Language Acquisition in Bilingual Children*. Berlin: Springer.

Tajfel, H. (1974) Social identity and intergroup behaviour. *Social Science Information*, 13, 65–93.

Tajfel, H. (1981) *Human Groups and Social Categories*. Cambridge: Cambridge University Press.

Tannen, D. (1980) A comparative analysis of oral narrative strategies: Athenian Greek and American English. In W. Chafe (ed.), *The Pear Stories: Cognitive, Cultural, and Linguistic Aspects of Narrative Production*. Norwood, NJ: Ablex, pp. 51–87.

Tannen, D. (1982) Spoken and written narrative in English and Greek. In D. Tannen (ed.), *Coherence in Spoken and Written Discourse*. Norwood, NJ: Ablex, pp. 21–41.

Tannen, D. (1993) What's in a frame? Surface evidence for underlying expectations. In D. Tannen (ed.), *Framing in Discourse*. New York: Oxford University Press, pp. 14–56.

Teutsch-Dwyer, M. (2001) (Re)constructing masculinity in a new linguistic reality. In A. Pavlenko, A. Blackledge, I. Piller, and M. Teutsch-Dwyer (eds.), *Multilingualism, Second Language Learning, and Gender*. Berlin: Mouton de Gruyter, pp. 175–98.

Thomason, S. G. (1997) Introduction. In S. G. Thomason (ed.), *Contact Languages: A Wider Perspective*. Amsterdam/Philadelphia: Benjamins, pp. 1–9.

Thomason, S. G. (2001) *Language Contact: An Introduction*. Washington, DC: Georgetown University Press.

Thomason, S. G. and T. Kaufman (1988) *Language Contact, Creolization and Genetic Linguistics*. Berkeley: University of California Press.

Timm, L. (1978) Code-switching in *War and Peace*. In M. Paradis (ed.), *Aspects of Bilingualism*. Columbia, SC: Hornbaum, pp. 302–15.

Ting-Toomey, S. (1999) *Communicating across Cultures*. New York: Guilford Press.

Titscher, S., M. Meyer, R. Wodak, and E. Vetter (2000) *Methods of Text and Discourse Analysis*. London: Sage.

Tokowicz, N. (1997) Reevaluating Concreteness Effects in Bilingual Translation. Master's thesis, Pennsylvania State University.

Tokowicz, N. and J. F. Kroll (2007) Number of meanings and concreteness: Consequences of ambiguity within and across languages. *Language and Cognitive Processes*, 22, 727–79.

Tokowicz, N., J. F. Kroll, A. M. B. De Groot, and J. G. Van Hell (2002) Number-of-translation norms for Dutch-English translation pairs: A new tool for examining language production. *Behavior Research Methods, Instruments, and Computers*, 34, 435–51.

Tokowicz, N. and B. MacWhinney (2005) Implicit and explicit measures of sensitivity to violations in second language grammar. *Studies in Second Language Acquisition*, 27, 173–204.

Tokowicz, N., E. B. Michael, and J. F. Kroll (2004) The roles of study-abroad experience and working-memory capacity in the types of errors made during transition. *Bilingualism: Language and Cognition*, 7, 255–72.

Tomiyama, M. (1999) The first stage of second language attrition: A case study of a Japanese returnee. In L. Hansen (ed.), *Second Language Attrition in Japanese Contexts*. New York: Oxford University Press, pp. 59–79.

Treffers-Daller, J. (1991) French-Dutch language mixture in Brussels. PhD thesis, Universiteit van Amsterdam.

Treffers-Daller, J. (1994). *Mixing Two Languages: French-Dutch Contact in a Comparative Perspective*. Berlin/New York: Mouton de Gruyter.

Trochim, W. (2000) *The Research Methods Knowledge Base*. 2nd edn. Cincinnati, OH: Atomic Dog Publishing.

Tse, L. (2000a) Student perceptions of foreign language study: A qualitative analysis of foreign language autobiographies. *Modern Language Journal*, 84(1), 69–84.

Tse, L. (2000b) The effects of ethnic identity formation on bilingual maintenance and development: An analysis of Asian American narratives. *International Journal of Bilingual Education and Bilingualism*, 3(3), 185–200.

Tukey, J. W. (1978) Measurement of event-related potentials. Commentary: A data analyst's comments on a variety of points and issues. In E. Callaway, P. Tueting, and S. H. Koslow (eds.), *Event-related Brain Potentials in Man*. New York: Academic Press, pp. 139–51.

Turell, M. T. and M. Forcadell (1992) Catalan/Spanish/English Corpus. Unpublished database. For further information contact the authors at teresa.turell@upf.edu.

Türker, E. (2000) Turkish–Norwegian codeswitching: Evidence from intermediate and second generation Turkish immigrants in Norway. Dr. art. dissertation, University of Oslo.

Ulrich, R. and J. Miller (1994) Effects of truncation on reaction time analysis. *Journal of Experimental Psychology: General*, 123, 34–80.

Urciuoli, B. (1996) *Exposing Prejudice: Puerto Rican Experiences of Language, Race and Class*. Boulder, CO: Westview Press.

Vaid, J. and R. Hull (2002) Re-envisioning the bilingual brain using functional neuroimaging: Methodological and interpretive issues. In F. Fabbro (ed.), *Advances in Neurolingusitics of Bilingualism*. Udine, Italy: Forum, pp. 315–55.

Valdés, G. and C. Pino (1981) Muy a tus órdenes: Compliment responses among Mexican-American bilinguals. *Language in Society*, 10(1), 53–72.

Valdes-Fallis, G. (1977) Code-switching among bilingual Mexican-American women: Towards an understanding of sex-related language alternation. *International Journal of the Sociology of Language*, 74, 71–89.

Verhoeven, L. and S. Strömqvist (eds.) (2001) *Narrative Development in a Multilingual Context*. Amsterdam: John Benjamins.

Viberg, A. (2001) Age-related and L2-related features in bilingual narrative development in Sweden. In L. Verhoeven and S. Strömqvist (eds.), *Narrative Development in a Multilingual Context*. Amsterdam: John Benjamins, pp. 87–128.

Vilardell, E. (1998) Canvi i manteniment de la llengua en parelles lingüísticament mixtes a Sabadell. Unpublished MA thesis, Universitat Autònoma de Barcelona, Bellaterra.

Vitanova, G. (2004) Gender enactments in immigrants' discursive practices: Bringing Bakhtin to the dialogue. *Journal of Language, Identity, and Education*, 3(4), 261–77.

Vitanova, G. (2005) Authoring the self in a non-native language: A dialogic approach to agency and subjectivity. In J. K. Hall, G. Vitanova, and L. Marchenkova (eds.), *Dialogue with Bakhtin on Second and Foreign Language Learning: New Perspectives*. Mahwah, NJ: Lawrence Erlbaum, pp. 149–69.

Volterra, V. and T. Taeschner (1978) The acquisition and development of language by bilingual children. *Journal of Child Language*, 5, 311–26.

Von Studnitz, R. E. and D. W. Green D. W. (2002) Interlingual homograph interference in German-English bilinguals: Its modulation and locus of control. *Bilingualism: Language and Cognition*, 5, 1–23.

Wang, X. (2006) Language shift in three-generation Chinese families in the State of Johor, Malaysia. Paper presented at the First Malaysian International Conference on Chinese Linguistics: Exploring Diversity, Variation and Standardization of Language, University of Malaya, Kuala Lumpur, March 4–5.

Warren, C. A. B. and T. X. Karner (2005) *Discovering Qualitative Methods: Field Research, Interviews and Analysis*. Los Angeles: Roxbury.

Wartenburger, I., H. R. Heekeren, J. Abutalebi, S. F. Cappa, A. Villringer, and D. Perani (2003) Early setting of grammatical processing in the bilingual brain. *Neuron*, 37, 159–70.

Wasserman, S. and U. Bockenholt (1989) Bootstrapping: Applications to psychophysiology. *Psychophysiology*, 26, 208–21.

Watson, J. (1998) *Media Communication: An Introduction to Theory and Process*. Basingstoke and London: Macmillan.

Weber-Fox, C. M. and H. J. Neville (1996) Maturational constraints on functional specialization for language processing: ERP and behavioral evidence in bilingual speakers. *Journal of Cognitive Neuroscience*, 8, 231–56.

Weinreich, U. (1953) *Languages in Contact: Findings and Problems*. New York: The Linguistic Circle of New York.

Weiss, G. and R. Wodak (2003) Introduction. In G. Weiss and R. Wodak (eds.), *Theory, Interdisciplinarity and Critical Discourse Analysis*. London: Palgrave.

Wenzell, V. (1989) Transfer of aspect in the English oral narratives of native Russian speakers. In H. Dechert and M. Raupach (eds.), *Transfer in Language Production*. Norwood, NJ: Ablex, pp. 71–97.

Wernicke, C. (1874) *Der aphasische Symptomenkomplex. Eine psychologische Studie auf anatomischer Basis*. Breslau: Cohn and Weigert.

Wetherell, M. (1998) Positioning and interpretative repertoires: Conversation analysis and post-structuralism in dialogue. *Discourse and Society*, 9(3), 387–412.

Whitney, W. D. (1881) On mixing in language. *Transactions of the American Philological Association*, 12, 5–26.

Widdicombe, S. (1998) "But you don't class yourself": The interactional management of category membership and non-membership. In C. Antaki and S. Widdicombe (eds.), *Identities in Talk*. London: Sage, pp. 52–70.

Widdowson, H. (1995) Discourse analysis: A critical view. *Language and Literature*, 4(3): 157–72.

Williams, A. (2005) Fighting words and challenging expectations: Language alternation and social roles in a family dispute. *Journal of Pragmatics*, 37, 317–28.

Williams, G. (1992) *Sociolinguistics: A Sociological Critique*. London: Routledge.

Winford, D. (2003) *An Introduction to Contact Linguistics*. Oxford: Blackwell.

Winkler, I., T. Kujala, H. Tiitinen, P. Sivonen, P. Alku, A. Lehtokoski, I. Czigler, V. Csépe, and R. Näätänen (1999) Brain responses reveal the learning of foreign language phonemes. *Psychophysiology*, 26, 638–42.

Wodak, R. (2000) Recontextualisation and the transformation of meanings: A critical discourse analysis of decision making in EU meetings about employment policies. In S. Sarangi and M. Coulthard (eds.), *Discourse and Social Life*. London: Longman, 185–206.

Wodak, R. (2001) The discourse-historical approach. In R. Wodak and M. Meyer (eds.), *Methods of Critical Discourse Analysis*. London: Sage, pp. 63–94.

Wodak, R. and P. Chilton (eds.) (2005) *A New Agenda in (Critical) Discourse Analysis: Theory, Methodology and Interdisciplinarity*. Amsterdam, John Benjamins.

Wodak, R. and M. Meyer (eds.) (2001) *Methods of Critical Discourse Analysis*. London: Sage.

Wolfram, W. (1993) Ethical considerations in language awareness programs. *Issues in Applied Linguistics*, 4(2), 225–55.

Wolfram, W. (1998) Scrutinizing linguistic gratuity: Issues from the field. *Journal of Socio-linguistics*, 2(2), 271–9.

Wolfram, W. (2000) Endangered dialects and social commitment. In J. Kreeft Peyton, P. Griffin, W. Wolfram, and R. Fasold (eds.), *Language in Action: New Studies of Language in Society*. Cresskill, NY: Hampton Press, pp. 19–39.

Wolfram, W. and R. W. Fasold (1974) *Field Methods in the Study of Social Dialects*. Englewood Cliffs, NJ: Prentice Hall.

Wolfson, N. (1976) Speech events and natural speech: Some implications for sociolinguistic methodology. *Language in Society*, 5(2), 189–209.

Woodside-Jiron, H. (2003) Language, power, and participation: Using Critical Discourse Analysis to make sense of public policy. In R. Rogers (ed.), *An Introduction to Critical Discourse Analysis in Education*. Mahwah, NJ: Lawrence Erlbaum, pp. 173–206.

Woolard, K. (1989) *Doubletalk: Bilingualism and the Politics of Ethnicity in Catalonia*. Stanford, CA: Stanford University Press.

Woolford, E. (1983) Bilingual code-switching and syntactic theory. *Linguistic Inquiry*, 14, 520–36.

Wray, A., K. Trott, and A. Bloomer (1998) *Projects in Linguistics*. London: Arnold.

Yelenevskaya, M. and L. Fialkova (2003) From "muteness" to eloquence: Immigrants' narratives about language. *Language Awareness*, 12(1), 30–48.

Yin, R. K. (2003a) *Applications of Case Study Research*. Thousand Oaks, CA: Sage.

Yin, R. K. (2003b) *Case Study Research: Design and Methods*. Thousand Oaks, CA: Sage.

Yoon, K. K. (1996) A case study of fluent Korean-English bilingual speakers: Group membership and code choices. *Journal of Pragmatics*, 25, 395–407.

Yoshitomi, A. (1999) On the loss of English as a second language by Japanese returnee children. In L. Hansen (ed.), *Second Language Attrition in Japanese Contexts*. New York: Oxford University Press, pp. 80–111.

Zekhnini, A. (2001) Second language learners' L2-contacts and acquisition away-from-classroom. In A. Hvenekilde and J. Nortier (eds.), *Meetings at the Crossroads: Studies of Multilingualism and Multiculturalism in Oslo and Utrecht*. Oslo: Novus Forlag, pp. 232–48.

Zentella, A. C. (1997) *Growing up Bilingual: Puerto Rican Children in New York*. Oxford and Malden, MA: Blackwell.

Zhu Hua and B. Dodd (2006) *Phonological Development and Disorders: A Multilingual Perspective*. Clevedon: Multilingual Matters.

Index